Digital Performance

Leonardo

Roger F. Malina, series editor
Sean Cubitt, Editor-in-Chief

Digital Performance

A History of New Media in Theater, Dance,
Performance Art, and Installation

Steve Dixon
with contributions by Barry Smith

The MIT Press
Cambridge, Massachusetts
London, England

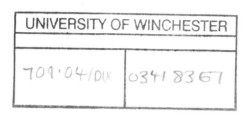
MIT Press books may be purchased at special quantity discounts for business or sales promotional use. For information, please email special_sales@mitpress.mit.edu or write to Special Sales Department, The MIT Press, 55 Hayward Street, Cambridge, MA 02142.

This book was set in Bell Gothic and Garamond 3 by SNP Best-set Typesetter Ltd., Hong Kong and was printed and bound in Spain.

Library of Congress Cataloging-in-Publication Data

Dixon, Steve.
Digital performance : a history of new mdia in theater, dance, performance art, and installation / Steve Dixon.
    p.   cm.—(Leonardo)
ISBN-13: 978-0-262-04235-2 (alk. paper)
1. Technology and the arts. 2. Digital media. 3. Arts, Modern—20th century. 4. Performing arts—History—20th century. I. Title.

NX180.T4D538   2007
700'.285—dc22

2006049426

10 9 8 7 6 5 4 3 2 1

Contents

Series Foreword

The arts, science, and technology are experiencing a period of profound change. Explosive challenges to the institutions and practices of engineering, art making, and scientific research raise urgent questions of ethics, craft, and care for the planet and its inhabitants. Unforeseen forms of beauty and understanding are possible, but so too are unexpected risks and threats. A newly global connectivity creates new arenas for interaction between science, art, and technology but also creates the preconditions for global crises. The Leonardo Book series, published by the MIT Press, aims to consider these opportunities, changes, and challenges in books that are both timely and of enduring value.

Leonardo books provide a public forum for research and debate; they contribute to the archive of art-science-technology interactions; they contribute to understandings of emergent historical processes; and they point toward future practices in creativity, research, scholarship, and enterprise.

To find more information about Leonardo/ISAST and to order our publications, go to Leonardo Online at <http://lbs.mit.edu/> or e-mail <leonardobooks@mitpress.mit.edu>.

Sean Cubitt
Editor-in-Chief, Leonardo Book series

Leonardo Book Series Advisory Committee: Sean Cubitt, Chair; Michael Punt; Eugene Thacker; Anna Munster; Laura Marks; Sundar Sarrukai; Annick Bureaud

Doug Sery, Acquiring Editor
Joel Slayton, Editorial Consultant

Leonardo/International Society for the Arts, Sciences, and Technology (ISAST)

Leonardo, the International Society for the Arts, Sciences, and Technology, and the affiliated French organization Association Leonardo have two very simple goals:

1. to document and make known the work of artists, researchers, and scholars interested in the ways that the contemporary arts interact with science and technology and
2. to create a forum and meeting places where artists, scientists, and engineers can meet, exchange ideas, and, where appropriate, collaborate.

When the journal *Leonardo* was started some forty years ago, these creative disciplines existed in segregated institutional and social networks, a situation dramatized at that time by the "Two Cultures" debates initiated by C. P. Snow. Today we live in a different time of cross-disciplinary ferment, collaboration, and intellectual confrontation enabled by new hybrid organizations, new funding sponsors, and the shared tools of computers and the Internet. Above all, new generations of artist-researchers and researcher-artists are now at work individually and in collaborative teams bridging the art, science, and technology disciplines. Perhaps in our lifetime we will see the emergence of "new Leonardos," creative individuals or teams that will not only develop a meaningful art for our times but also drive new agendas in science and stimulate technological innovation that addresses today's human needs.

For more information on the activities of the Leonardo organizations and networks, please visit our Web sites at <http://www.leonardo.info/> and <http://www.olats.org>.

Roger F. Malina
Chair, Leonardo/ISAST

ISAST Governing Board of Directors: Martin Anderson, Michael Joaquin Grey, Larry Larson, Roger Malina, Sonya Rapoport, Beverly Reiser, Christian Simm, Joel Slayton, Tami Spector, Darlene Tong, Stephen Wilson

Preface

This book developed out of a major research project undertaken by Steve Dixon and Barry Smith from 1999 to 2001, funded by the Arts and Humanities Research Council (UK).[1] *The Digital Performance Archive* (*DPA*) was established to record and analyze an extraordinary and unprecedented period of activity and experimentation within performance practice where computer technologies and techniques were increasingly integrated into live productions, and new forms of interactive performance emerged in participatory installations, on CD-ROM, and on the Web. An initial announcement sent to relevant arts and new media culture lists in 1999 summarized the project's scope:

The Digital Performance Archive (*DPA*)—http://ntu.ac.uk/dpa/—is a research project documenting developments in the creative use of computer technologies in performance, from live theater and dance productions that incorporate digital media to cyberspace interactive dramas and webcasts. DPA also collates examples of the use of computer technologies to document, discuss, or analyze performance, including specialist websites, e-zines and academic CD-ROMs.

While the level of such activity was high at that time, its recording and documentation was uncoordinated and sporadic, and the *DPA* sought to retain for posterity some traces of this work. During the years 1999 and 2000, the Archive recorded all activity it could find within the field, and provided an extensive online database of individual works, with data fields including date, venue, credits, types of technologies employed, summaries of the works, photographs, artists' statements, biographies, and website links (many artists' websites were also cloned by the Archive to ensure their longevity). In parallel, Dixon video recorded twenty-five live performances in the United States and Europe (some with a single camera, others with a four camera crew), including works by Blast Theory, Amorphic Robot Works, Random Dance Company, Guillermo Gómez-Peña, and ieVR.

Artists and companies were also contacted and asked to preserve some of their own documentation with the Archive, and textual materials (production flyers, programs, reviews, articles), photographs, CD-ROMs, DVDs, and videotapes were received. These can still be viewed by appointment at the reference libraries of the *DPA*'s two UK host institutions, Nottingham Trent University and Salford University.

The Archive's two years of intensive research into the field, 1999 and 2000, constituted a historic period for digital performance where its zenith was unarguably reached—in terms of both the amount of activity and the originality, quality, and significance of many seminal productions—prior to a general downturn of activity and interest. Inevitably, this book pays particular attention to those years, but as a "history" it has also involved extensive research into the pioneering work of the 1980s and 1990s, and of subsequent work in the early 2000s. We also trace digital performance's historical lineage back to earlier conjunctions of performance and technology, particularly since the early twentieth century.

The scope of the book is therefore wide, as it subtitle suggests—"a history of new media in theater, dance, performance art, and installation"—but is also quite specific. Digital Performance, in the terms that we define it, concerns the conjunction of computer technologies with the live performance arts, as well as gallery installations and computer platform-based net.art, CD-ROMs, and digital games where performance constitutes a central aspect of either its content (for example, through a focus on a moving, speaking or otherwise "performing" human figure) or form (for example, interactive installations that prompt visitors to "perform" actions rather than simply watch a screen and "point and click"). Apart from occasional references, our study excludes the use of digital technologies in "non-live" and "non-interactive" performance forms such as film, television, and video art.

The one major area of the live performance arts the book omits is music, for two primary reasons: we do not have sufficient specialist knowledge and expertise to approach a worthy analysis; and our focus is in any case already wide enough. We would nonetheless note that music was one of the first artistic fields to experiment significantly with and embrace computer technologies, and in terms of both creative production and commercial (as well as illegal) distribution, music has arguably been more radically revolutionized by the "digital revolution" than the other performance arts we explore.

We readily acknowledge that our term *digital performance* is somewhat problematic. "Digital" has become a loose and generic term applied to any and all applications that incorporate a silicon chip; and the term "performance" has acquired wide-ranging applications and different nuances both within and outside the performance arts. Indeed, over the past forty years understandings of the word "performance" have been so stretched and reconfigured that it has become a paleonymic term: one that has retained its name but has transformed its fundamental signification and terms of reference. In academia, the emergence of the interdisciplinary field of "performance studies" in the 1990s stretched the term widely to embrace varied facets of philosophy, linguistics, history, cultural and social sciences, and the general field of human activity in "everyday life," just as Joseph Beuys had urged the visual arts to do many years earlier: "enlarge the old concept of Art, making it as broad and large as possible . . . to include every human activity."[2] The related term "performative" has similarly been adopted, used, and often abused across many academic disciplines to denote and encompass seemingly anything and everything. As J. L. Austin put it in 1961, "You are more than entitled not to know what the word 'performative' means. It is a new word and an ugly word, and perhaps it does not mean anything very much . . . it is not a profound word."[3]

Elsewhere, "performance" is related to the qualitative measurement of the capabilities of cars, aircraft, and other machinery under test conditions. The word retains a specific meaning within the computing industry itself, being applied to the speed and accuracy of processing, and the "architecture" of particular models of computer. A Web search for "digital performance" therefore prompts not only examples of the types of performance arts we discuss, but also sites related to, for example, testing and improving the processing speeds and operations of home PCs. But at the time of writing we are heartened that such a Web search still places our Digital Performance Archive at the top of most search engines' lists.

Since 2000, the use of the term "digital performance" (in the sense that we intend it) has become more frequent within performance studies as well as in university education where, for example, a master's degree in Digital Performance was launched in 2004 at Doncaster College, UK, led by Robert Wechsler (artistic director of the German dance and technology company Palindrome) and David Collins (editor of the *International Journal of Performance Arts and Digital Media*). In 2002, a new e-journal titled *Digital Performance: The Online Magazine for Artists Embracing Technology* was created by The Gertrude Stein Repertory Theatre (New York), which began by noting the "tricky task" of defining digital performance and invited dialogue from readers as well as "individual artists and observers of the field . . . as a way of clarifying the terms and finding out how much we all have in common."[4] Although this approach to definitions indicated the danger that the term could be all-inclusive, the journal was more precise in locating a working definition for the term "digital" within this broad context, seeing it primarily as a "tool" to be exploited, but one with far-reaching performative consequences:

"Digital" is a more purely technical concept, narrow in origin but extremely broad in its applications. It is a particular way of describing the real world, a specific technique of encoding sensory data (sound, music, movement, sets, costumes, etc.) that allows that information to be communicated, altered, manipulated, and ultimately interpreted in a complex and potentially intelligent manner. It is an enabling concept. It includes multimedia and interactivity as you have a huge and constantly expanding toolbox of theatrical effects that each has their own intelligence, sensitivity and subjectivity, that in a sense become characters on stage.

And we would argue that it is potentially a new paradigm in theater and performance.[5]

We share many of the ideas expressed here, and throughout this volume have sought not only to provide a history of the fascinating development of digital performance, but also to identify and evaluate the degree to which the use of new media in the performance arts has brought about new paradigms, genres, aesthetics, and interactive experiences.

Acknowledgments

Steve Dixon is the primary writer of this volume, but Barry Smith has contributed substantial sections; hence the use of, "we" throughout. The book's research and writing has been a collaborative endeavor between the two writers that developed directly out of their joint project, the *Digital Performance Archive* (1999–2001, see: http://art.ntu.ac.uk/dpa). The project was established with funding from the UK Arts and Humanities Research Council, and we gratefully acknowledge the Council's support, without which this book would not have been possible.

Colleagues who worked on the *Digital Performance Archive* were research fellow Rachael Beach; research assistants Marcel Thomson and Tim White; video technician Fraser Dury; and video editor Marcus Daley. Video technicians involved in shooting and postproduction of the Archive's documentation of live performances were Sarah Atkinson, Robin Ellis, Laurence Murphy, Paul Murphy, and Lloyd Peters, and technicians from the International Media Centre at the University of Salford.

Administrative staff at the Archive's host universities, Salford and Nottingham Trent (and latterly Brunel University), also provided invaluable support, including Paula Barrett, Mary Byrne, Liz Lines, Sally Phillips, Amy McNulty, John Miley, Rachel Russell, Stuart Simpson, Rebecca Turnock, Anna Vowles, Liz White, and Diane Woodhead. We are also indebted to many academic colleagues at our universities for their help, support, and facilitation of the project, particularly Ron Cook, Walt Denning, Rachel Cooper, Stan Challis, Richard Joyner, Simon Lewis, Brian Longhurst, Roland Metcalf, Colin Muir, Carole O'Reilly, Gareth Palmer, Lloyd Peters, Derek Scott, Jackie Smart, and John Sweeney.

We would like to thank the many artists and performance groups who submitted documentation to the Archive, and who discussed their work with us in correspondence or in person through interviews and at performances, symposia, and conferences. We also gratefully acknowledge many theorists and art and performance commentators whose own research we have drawn upon and quoted, most notably Philip Auslander, Jean Baudrillard, Johannes Birringer, Jay Bolter, Matthew Causey, Mark Dery, Gabriella Giannachi, RoseLee Goldberg, Guillermo Gómez-Peña, Diane Gromala, Katherine Hayles, Eduardo Kac, Susan Kozel, Michael Kirby, Arthur and Marilouise Kroker, Brenda Laurel, Lev Manovich, Janet Murray, Christiane Paul, Marie-Laure Ryan, Theodore Shank, Stephen Wilson, and Andrea Zapp.

We would like to thank MIT Press for all their work in bringing the book to fruition, in particular Doug Sery, Katherine Almeida, Gregory McNamee, and Valerie Geary.

Thanks also go to Anthony Lister, who acted as editor and compiler of bibliographic and historical references; and to Florence Dixon, Samuel Kennedy, Daniel Wilkinson, Tim Nott, and Peggy Kirby, who assisted in the preparation of the final draft. Special thanks go to Sarah Rubidge, who has provided invaluable advice about digital dance performance, and who has also kindly contributed to some of the writing.

Steve Dixon would like to sincerely thank his wife Prue and his daughters Sophie, Amelia, and Florence for their endless support, good humor, love, and patience over the many years of the book's research and preparation; and also his brother Jonathan, whose apartment was a regular retreat for periods of sustained writing, and whose company was perennially humorous, upbeat, and uplifting.

Finally, we would like to thank all our colleagues and friends who have influenced our discourse and thoughts and have assisted in a multitude of ways, in particular Frank Abbott, Matt Adams, Josie Akers, David Applebaum, Roy Ascott, Paula Atwell, Sara Ayers, Christopher Bannerman, Mark Batty, Christopher Baugh, Colin Beardon, Johannes Birringer, Ghislaine Boddington, Susan Broadhurst, Reggie Brown, Lou Burnard, Patrick Campbell, Rebecca "Bex" Carrington, Christie Carson, Gavin Carver, David Collins, Susan Collins, Mark Coniglio, Richard Coyne, Tracy Crossley, Scott deLahunta, Liam Doona, Tamsin Drury, Barry Edwards, Tim Etchells and Forced Entertainment, Anna Fenemore, Bronac Ferran, Michael Fraser, Mathias Fuchs, Lance Gharavi, Ruth Gibson, Sallie Goetsch, Lizbeth Goodman, Geraldine Harris, Adrian Heathfield, Leslie Hill, Mark Jones, Michael Joyce, Sue Keen, Petra Kuppers, Martina Leeker, Robert Lepage, Sophia Lycouris, Wayne McGregor, Chico McMurtrie, Susan Melrose, Thomas Mulready, Robin Nelson, Helen Paris, Julian Petley, Peggy Phelan, Fran Pietri, Mark Reaney, Wendy Reed, Jennifer Ringley, Sita Popat, David Saltz, Richard Schechner, Paul Sermon, Yacov Sharir, Stephan Silver, Joel Slayton, Paul Smith, Jennifer Starbuck, Stelarc, Denise Vernon, Susanne Vill, Ian Watson, Robert Weschler, Martin White, Ron Willis, Niki Woods, Andrea Zapp, and all our colleagues and friends in SCUDD (Standing Conference of University Drama Departments, UK) and Performance Studies International.

Sections of the book have previously appeared in different forms within the following journal articles and book chapters, and we gratefully acknowledge the permissions granted from the publishers for their inclusion here.

Steve Dixon

2005a. "Metal Performance: Humanizing Robots, Returning to Nature, and Camping About." *TDR: The Drama Review*, 48, no. 4 (Winter 2004): 15–46.

2005b. "Theatre, Technology, and Time." *International Journal of Performance Arts and Digital Media* 1, no. 1: 11–29.

2004. "Metal Gender." In *Life in the Wires: The CTHEORY Reader*, ed. Arthur and Marilouise Kroker, 207–214. Victoria, BC: New World Perspectives/CTheory Books. [First published in *CTHEORY* 26, nos. 1–2 (Article 128). http://www.ctheory.net/text_file.asp?pick=384.]

2004. "Adventures in Cyber-theatre (or, The Actor's Fear of the Disembodied Audience)." In *Networked Narrative Environments as Imaginary Spaces of Being*, ed. Andrea Zapp, 99–121. Manchester: MIRIAD/FACT.

2004. "The Digital Double." In *New Visions in Performance: The Impact of New Technologies*, ed. Colin Beardon and Gavin Carver, 13–30. Lisse, The Netherlands: Swets & Zeitlinger.

2003. "Futurism e-Visited." *Body, Space and Technology* 3, no. 2. http://www.brunel.ac.uk/depts/pfa/bstjournal.

2003. "Absent Fiends: Internet Theatre, Posthuman Bodies and the Interactive Void." *Performance Arts International*, "Presence" online issue, http://www.mdx.ac.uk/www/epai/presencesite/index.html.

2002. "Remediating Theatre in a Digital Proscenium." In *Digital Creativity: A Reader*, ed. Colin Beardon, 199–205. Lisse, The Netherlands: Swets & Zeitlinger. [First published in *Digital Creativity* 10, no. 3 (December 1999): 135–142.

2001. "Virtual Theatrics: When Computers Step into the Limelight." In *Theatre: The Reflective Template*, ed. Loren Ruff, 21–48. Dubuque, IA: Kendall/Hunt Publications.

2000. "Hypermedia Theatre." In *Ville en Visite Virtuelle*, ed. Marie-Madeleine Martinet, 121–144, Paris: University of Paris-Sorbonne Press.

1999. "Digits, Discourse and Documentation: Performance Research and Hypermedia." *TDR: The Drama Review* 43, no. 1 (Spring 1999): 152–175.

1998. "Autonomy and Automatism: Devising Multi-Media Theatre with Multiple Protagonists." *Studies in Theatre Production* 18 (December 1998): 60–79.

Barry Smith

2005. "Jennicam, or the Virtual Theatre of a Real Life." *International Journal of Performance Arts and Digital Media* 1, no. 2: 91–100.

1998. "Changing Shades: Review of *Metabody* and *Chameleons 2*." *Computers & Texts* 16/17. Also available at: <http://info.ox.ac.uk/ctitext/publish/comtxt/ct16-17/smith.html>.

Digital Performance

1

Introduction

There is not enough RAM
In the known universe to complete
The task you have requested.

Accept?   Rejoice?

—ERROR MESSAGE IN PERRY HOBERMAN'S INTERACTIVE INSTALLATION *CATHARTIC USER INTERFACE* (1995)

Overview

During the last decade of the twentieth century, computer technologies played a dynamic and increasingly important role in live theater, dance, and performance; and new dramatic forms and performance genres emerged in interactive installations and on the Internet. Theater practitioners such as Robert Lepage, The Builders Association, and George Coates Performance Works surrounded their actors with screens projecting digitally manipulated images. The Gertrude Stein Repertory Theatre and Kunstwerk-Blend incorporated video-conferencing software to bring performers from remote locations together, live on stage. Webcams, webcasts, and the virtual environments of MUDs and MOOs provided new forms of live and interactive performance via the Internet. Laurie Anderson and William Forsythe created pioneering interactive performance CD-ROMs, and the computer games industry adopted ever more performative paradigms while its own influence looped back significantly into digital performance practice.

Yacov Sharir choreographed entire dance works in the computer using *Life Forms* and *Poser* software. Merce Cunningham projected images of virtual dancers on stage, created by combining motion-capture techniques and advanced animation software (figure 1.1). Troika Ranch, Company in Space, and Marcel.lí Anthúnez Roca used custom-made motion sensing software to manipulate images, avatars, sound, and lighting live on stage;

Figure 1.1 An image from veteran choreographer Merce Cunningham's pioneering collaboration with Paul Kaiser and Shelley Eshkar, *BIPED* (1999). Photo: Stephanie Berger.

and Toni Dove and Sarah Rubidge turned over those technologies to the audience, to experience them firsthand in advanced media-performance installations. Blast Theory fused paradigms from theater, Virtual Reality (VR), computer games, and "real life" to create complex audience improvisations; and David Saltz fed stage directions from the plays of Samuel Beckett direct into the computer, which re-presented them as algorithmic light-shows. Richard Beacham re-created ancient theaters using Virtual Reality, and ieVR harnessed the technology to create computer-generated, three-dimensional sets inhabited by live actors.

Performance artist Stelarc wired his body up to the Internet and was thrown around like a rag doll by audience members in other countries who manipulated him using touch-screen computers, and donned advanced robot prosthetics to enter a "cyborg reality." Guillermo Gómez-Peña viciously satirized cyborgic visions, while Eduardo Kac implanted his own body with computer chips and created art and performance at the frontiers of science and organic life. Survival Research Laboratories staged apocalyptic robot wars, while Amorphic Robot Works presented gentler, ecological fables in inflatable environments filled with robot humanoids and animals. The interactive potentials of computers were vividly dramatized and "performed" by users through myriad installations, CD-

ROMs, and video games. This book examines these practices and practitioners, and analyzes the artistic, theoretical, and technological trends that emerged in digital performance during the 1990s and have continued (though with considerably less impact and fervor) into the new millennium.

We define the term "digital performance" broadly to include all performance works where computer technologies play a *key* role rather than a subsidiary one in content, techniques, aesthetics, or delivery forms. This includes live theater, dance, and performance art that incorporates projections that have been digitally created or manipulated; robotic and virtual reality performances; installations and theatrical works that use computer sensing/activating equipment or telematic techniques; and performative works and activities that are accessed through the computer screen, including cybertheater events, MUDs, MOOs, and virtual worlds, computer games, CD-ROMs, and performative net.art works. As already noted in the preface, space as well as our lack of expert subject knowledge does not allow the study to extend to "non-interactive" digital artworks, nor to the extensive and inventive use of digital technologies in the fields of music, cinema, television, and video.

The application of new media to performance arts is extremely diverse, and the Internet has proved particularly significant in its development, not only as an immense interactive database, but also as a performance collaboration and distribution medium. The interactive capabilities opened up by computer networks allow for shared creativity, from textual or telematic real-time improvisations to globally constituted group projects, with distance no barrier to collaboration. New technologies thus call received ideas about the nature of theater and performance into question. The computer has become a significant tool and agent of performative action and creation, which has led to a distinct blurring of what we formerly termed, for example, communication, scriptwriting, acting, visual art, science, design, theater, video, and performance art. Finite distinctions apply less and less or, as John Reaves contests, they collapse altogether:

> In the digital world you cannot distinguish different disciplines by the physical nature of the media or by which work is created. . . . Theater has always been an integrative, collaborative art which potentially (and sometimes actually) includes all art: music, dance, painting, sculpture, etc. Why not be aggressive in the tumultuous context of the Digital Revolution? Why not claim all interactive art in the name of theater?[1]

Internet communication has been theorized as a type of virtual performance of the self, and thus "digital performance" is rationalized by many as being already ubiquitous, embracing multiple communicational and presentational aspects of electronic everyday life. Theater is thus created not only by those who consciously use computer networks for theatrical events, but also by millions of "ordinary" individuals who develop e-friendships, use MOOs, IRC, and chatrooms, or create home pages and "blogs" on the World Wide Web. Many home pages and blogs constitute digital palimpsests of Erving Goffman's

Figure 1.2 Online visual chat environments include highly theatricalized settings for user's role-plays such as Desktop Theater's *Waitingforgodot.com* (1997) site, which is examined in chapter 20.

notions of performative presentations of the self, with the subject being progressively erased, redefined, and reinscribed as a persona/performer within the proscenium arch of the computer monitor. Personas are honed like characters for the new theatrical confessional box, where, like postmodern performance artists, individuals explore their autobiographies and enact intimate dialogues with their inner selves. Seduced by the apparent intimacy and privacy of this most public of spaces, they confess all online and reveal secrets to strangers that they have never told their closest friends.[2] The World Wide Web is a site of therapeutic catharsis-overload, and it constitutes the largest theater in the world, offering everyone fifteen megabytes of fame (figure 1.2).

What's "New" about New Media?

The question of how "new" or "old" digital technologies are in relation to former media, and how they might offer progressive as opposed to merely repackaged or "remediated" paradigms in performance, is a recurrent and insistent thread that weaves throughout this volume. The "Histories" section contextualizes recent digital performance in relation to the artistic philosophies of modernism and the experiments of the early-twentieth-century avant-garde; and a large majority of the chapters dealing with different manifestations of digital performance link these developments unequivocally to artistic or theatrical precedents from a pre-digital age. But we are equally unequivocal that the conjunction of performance and new media *has* and *does* bring about genuinely new stylistic and aesthetic modes, and unique and unprecedented performance experiences, genres, and ontologies.

While postmodern perspectives tend to emphasize how artistic ideas are simply being endlessly recycled in different ways, we argue that certain practices and technological systems *are* genuinely new, distinct and avant-garde, and we endeavor to identify and define how and why. We are also interested in cutting through both the hyperbole and the critical "fuzzy logic" that has surrounded the field. One of our foremost digital culture commentators, Lev Manovich, suggests that the greatest artists of today are computer scientists and the greatest artworks are new technologies themselves. Manovich argues that the Web represents the greatest hypertext work, "more complex, unpredictable and dynamic" than James Joyce could create; "the greatest avant-garde film is software such as *Final Cut Pro* or *After Effects*" since they offer endless possibilities and combinations; and "the greatest interactive work is the interactive human-computer interface itself."[3] We would dispute each of these specific ideas, and, more important, suggest that Manovich's formulation encapsulates an indiscriminate techno-postmodern aesthetic theory of infinite (yet always-already recycled) possibilities and "technology for technology's sake" that has tended to mar rather than advance critical understandings of the relationships between technology and art. A core problem with this now widely held perspective is that it fetishizes the technology without regard for artistic vision and content. The concern of this book is to take a generally reverse stance to much of the writing around cyberculture, digital arts, and performance, which has tended to discuss technological aspects first and foremost and content/aesthetics second (if indeed at all). Rather, our focus and concern is to assess and analyze the particularities of *performance* and *performances* in relation to how they have adopted and utilized technological developments in varied ways in order to create different types of content, drama, meanings, aesthetic impacts, physiological and psychological effects, audience-performer relationships, and so on.

The tension behind the "technology versus content" issue was tellingly underlined in an exchange on the "Dance-tech" user group mail list in August 2001. Company in Space, a pioneering digital dance group from Australia, sent an announcement advertising their new telematic work *CO3* (2001) which they described as "a landmark performance . . . the next startling stage in cybernetic performance art."[4] The e-mail described in some detail the coming Internet-linked performance between two dancers, one in Florida and one in Melbourne, who wear state-of-the-art motion-capture suits to animate two avatars that perform in real time within a shared virtual reality environment. A curt reply was posted by digital performance artist Nick Rothwell: "I'd rather hear about the artistic content and motivation for using the technology, not just the technology itself. What is the content, exactly?"[5] The same issue was emphasized during a 1999 UK conference focusing on the use of computers in art and design, where a succession of speakers stressed that style and medium should never subsume content and message, and computer technology should be seen merely a means to an end, not an end in itself. The British film producer Lord David Puttnam dubbed new technology as "more of a bridge than a destination,"[6] and the late, great British multimedia designer Roy Stringer stressed how "authorship has nothing to do with technology." He observed that although artists, authors, and directors love to work in new forms and experiment with new digital techniques, "the killer application in new technologies is *content*."[7]

Therefore, to say, as Manovich does, that the Web is the greatest hypertext work is to propose the theater building as the greatest piece of theater, since that is where the finest performances *can*—or may, at some time, perhaps—be staged. We do not doubt that Web surfing can produce "great" artistic experiences, but like performances in theaters, quality is highly variable, and true greatness is rare. Similarly, the video-editing software programs he cites only produce what he terms "the greatest avant-garde film" when high quality footage is input, and its manipulation is undertaken with artistic sensibility and mastery. Manovich's claim for the artistic and interactive greatness of the computer screen interface is by far the strangest and most hyperbolic of all. The modern PC he deifies remains a dreadful and pathetic interface design: an anachronistic dinosaur of a machine that places file-cabinet icons borrowed from nineteenth-century offices onto a TV screen monitor design originated in the 1930s, above a QWERTY keyboard that, even when it was launched as a typewriter in 1878, was shown to have the worst possible letter pattern configuration.

Perhaps we are being too harsh on Manovich, who is more often one of the more astute academic commentators on digital technology. But his discourse here is indicative of a tendency in cyberculture criticism to romanticize (or else demonize) technology, to generalize its ontology and to forge links between computer technologies and other cultural and theoretical discourses too readily and indiscriminately. His primary point is more general and pertinent, and it concerns the emancipation of the everyday user of the Web, of editing programs and computer interfaces to manipulate and become the creator of artistic experiences. This is a fundamental area of what can be considered genuine "newness" within new technologies—the ability of lay users to become sophisticated artists. But this newness is most often a recycling of the old, and primarily relies on the computer as an accessor and manipulator of preexisting materials. The user, for example, can kangaroo jump around sites on the Web to map a unique but not in the true sense "new" terrain, or can transform, amend, and append others' work through a cut-paste-alter computational artistic model.

Resisting Postmodernist Perspectives

Alongside our running themes of relating contemporary practices to historical precedents and attempting to discern evidence of genuine newness in digital performance, there runs a parallel and in many ways complementary discourse that challenges and attempts to undermine dominant postmodern and deconstructive critical positions on cyberculture in general, and digital performance in particular. Our mistrust of postmodern critical perspectives (which is developed in detail in Chapter 7) derives partly from the fact that postmodern theory since the 1970s has largely perceived the ubiquity of media and the mediatized "image" as a cynical spiral of social domination and cultural degeneration. For many commentators, the coming of the digital age simply extends the paradigm. But by contrast for others, including what we believe to be a majority of the digital artists and performers we discuss, it has borne a new optimism about the potentials of media that is at complete odds with the knowing cynicism and cool distantiation of postmodern art and discourse. The positivity and excitement of scientists, technologists, and artists using computer technologies presents a discord between contemporary theory and practice. Progressive ideals and practices clash with postmodern theory's intransigent and homogenizing worldview, that is to say, with its now inherent conservatism (whereas once upon a time—specifically, the late 1970s and early 1980s—it was radical). Postmodern theory, once nemesis and destroyer of the author, the sign and the metanarrative, has itself become an authorial patriarch of conformist cultural commentary; a burning yet myopic critical sign; an oppressive metanarrative beyond compare within the history of critical theory.

Christopher Norris suggests that postmodernism and deconstruction have become "a prison-house of discourse"[8] and leading digital arts commentator Stephen Wilson wonders whether the technologists and cultural analysts occupy the same world.[9] Faced with arts practices that today are inextricably bound to ideas of research and academic enquiry, Wilson maintains that artists are forced to choose between three theoretical stances open to them:

(1) continue a modernist practice of art linked with adjustments for the contemporary era; (2) develop a unique postmodernist art built around deconstruction at its core; (3) develop a practice focused on elaborating the possibilities of new technology.[10]

He concludes that artists now interweave all three approaches—an equivocal but generally accurate summation. However, while digital performance combines the old and the new in "classic" postmodern terms, we consider it as an emergent avant-garde, rather than merely a manifestation of a wider, all-consuming postmodernism. Indeed, we challenge many of the repetitious and often wearisome postmodern and poststructuralist discourses applied to digital performance, which cast it within a vast and undifferentiated artistic, cultural, and philosophical soup of fragmentation, appropriation, and deferred meaning.

Rather, pioneers of digital performance equate fully with the "avant-garde" in its original military sense of individual soldiers going ahead of the main batallion, to penetrate and explore unknown and hostile territories.

Such work is avant-garde in relation to key definitions, such as Russell's understanding of "a *vanguard* art"[11] and Peter Bürger's definition as "the attempt to organize a new life praxis from a basis in art."[12] As we argue in the Histories section, clear parallels can be drawn between the early twentieth century avant-garde movements such as futurism, which emerged at a time of comparable technological "revolution" to the digital one of the 1990s, when "an engineering or machine 'aesthetic' would come to define avant-garde architecture and art."[13] For Andreas Huyssen, "no other single factor has influenced the emergence of the new avant-garde as much as technology, which has not only fuelled the artists' imagination (dynamism, machine cult, beauty of technics, constructivist and productivist attitudes), but penetrated to the core of the work itself."[14]

Digital performance is an *emergent* avant-garde in that it has begun, but has not yet fully encapsulated the historical avant-garde's concern to cause and advance major social change and to transform "the way art functions in society."[15] But popular Internet collectivism, as well as the cyberactivism of groups such as Critical Art Ensemble and the Electronic Disturbance Theatre accords with Bürger's notion of "the avant-gardiste's demand that art become practical once again,"[16] and the proliferation of Web-based "virtual" communities with Russell's definition of the avant-garde as "in advance of, and the cause of, significant social change."[17] Russell's notion of social change and Bürger's "new life praxis from a basis in art" is nowhere more evident than within cyborgic performance praxis, which celebrates the conjunction of humans with machines and heralds the (contested) emergence of a posthuman society.

For many performance artists, digital technologies remain tools of enhancement and experimentation, rather than a means to reconfigure fundamentally artistic or social ontologies. Yet digital performance's impulse toward the creation of new avant-garde forms and a more radical engagement with the nature of virtual realities places it outside the confines of dominant postmodern paradigms. As it traces this trajectory, performance is undertaking a shift in the conception of technology, which relates to R. L. Rutsky's analysis of early twentieth century avant-garde film and architecture. Rutsky defines a turning point where:

A notion of technology as instrumental, as the functional application of science, begins to give way to a conception that sees technology as a matter of form, of representation. And just as representation, for the avant-gardes, becomes increasingly allegorical, arbitrary, simulacral, so too does the technology. Indeed, this new conception of technology can be designated as *simulacral* or *techno-allegorical*.[18]

Structure, Content, and Arguments

This is a long book, covering numerous theories and practices within a wide and diverse field of activity. It is broadly divided into two sections, the first examining the histories, theories, and contexts of digital performance, the second dealing with specific practices and practitioners. There is nonetheless considerable overlap and interrelationship between them so that, for example, the histories/theories/contexts section includes case studies of recent digital performances that illustrate and encapsulate key arguments and ideas, while theoretical perspectives and historical precedents are continually brought to bear on the close analyses of works examined in the performance practices section.

The histories of digital performance span four chapters, beginning with chapter 2's analysis of "The Genealogy of Digital Performance," which is traced from the Greek *Deus ex machina* to Wagner's concept of the total artwork (*Gesamtkunstwerk*) to early dance and technology experiments by Loïe Fuller in the late nineteenth century and by the Bauhaus artist Oskar Schlemmer in the 1920s. Chapter 3 examines in detail the legacy of the early-twentieth-century avant-garde, closely linking today's digital performance with the theories and practices of futurism, constructivism, Dada, surrealism, and expressionism. In doing so, we argue the absolute centrality of futurist aesthetics and philosophies to current performance work utilizing computer technologies, and suggest that futurism's legacy to new media art in general and to digital performance in particular has been greatly underestimated. To pick on Manovich as an example yet again (a writer so good he can take it), his "Avant-Garde as Software" (1999) paper argues that the modernist avant-garde period between 1915 and 1928 represents the most important historical period relevant to new media, and his discourse concentrates on "the techniques invented by the 1920s Left artists," leaving the right-wing futurists out of the equation. While futurist art and performance was at its peak during this very period, Manovich instead focuses on Bauhaus design, constructivist typography, Dadaist photomontage, and surrealist cinema as the key artistic and methodological precursors to computer operations and paradigms. We argue that futurism, which emerged prior to all of these avant-garde movements and exerted significant influence upon them (particularly constructivism), deserves a much higher place in the history of digital arts and performance. We devote considerable attention to a close analysis of futurist theater manifestos, which reveal clear relationships between performance plans and practices separated by almost a century. These include fundamental principles of futurist art and performance such as alogicality, parallel action, photodynamism, luminous scenography, virtual actors, "synthetic theater," and the cult of the machine (figure 1.3). We contest that Italian futurist performance theory and practice between 1909 and 1920 laid the foundations for fundamental philosophies and aesthetic strategies found within digital performance.

As cinema and, later, television and video have exerted a significant influence on the development of performance over the last hundred years, so too have they been brought together since the turn of the twentieth century, as we examine in chapter 4,

Figure 1.3 The early twentieth-century futurist cult of the machine is updated for the digital age by performance artist David Therrien in *BODYDRUM* (2005). Photo: Gregory Cowley.

"Multimedia Theater 1911–1959." It includes analysis of early "film-theater" experiments; the theories of Robert Edmund Jones; and seminal productions including Erwin Piscator's *Hoppla, Wir Leben!* (*Hurrah, We're Living!* 1927) and Frederick Kiesler's *R.U.R.* (*Rossum's Universal Robots*, 1922), which we relate to recent digital performances by Blast Theory, Paul Sermon, and Andrea Zapp. Throughout the twentieth century, not only did live performance integrate film into productions, but both mainstream and experimental theater also competed with cinema in terms of its own sense of spectacle, and theater became more cinematic in conception, particularly in the latter half of the century. Playwriting saw increasing use of short scenes, cross-cut parallel action, and the use of flashbacks and dramatic time shifts, while theater staging drew inspiration from the cinema, increasingly employing neocinematic devices such as the introduction of incidental music and the use of lighting to create sharp montage or gentle dissolve effects. This aimed to intensify the theatrical experience, and to approximate cinema's absolute control of space and time, and the flow and location of the audience's attention.

Chapter 5's review of "Performance and Technology Since 1960" analyzes two landmark art and technology events from the 1960s: the New York *Nine Evenings: Theater and*

Engineering (1966) performances and the *Cybernetic Serendipity—The Computer and the Arts* (1968) exhibition at the ICA in London. It goes on to highlight key practitioners such as Nam June Paik and Billy Klüver, who brought about pioneering changes in the design and development of technologies for performance, and artists such as The Wooster Group and Laurie Anderson, whose radical approaches to the incorporation of technologies in their live work over many years have exerted a significant influence on a whole generation of practitioners.

The section on "Theories and Contexts" begins with chapter 6's analysis of the slippery and problematic concept of "Liveness." Philip Auslander's *Liveness: Performance in a Mediatized Culture* (1999) provided an important, if controversial, discourse on how cinema and ubiquitous television media have affected live performance practice and its reception by audiences. He argues that traditional ideas of theatrical "liveness" have been eroded to such a point that there now seems precious little difference between live and recorded forms. We contrast his position with Peggy Phelan's assertion of live performance's unique ontology and its resistance to media reproductions, and trace complementary critical oppositions between Walter Benjamin and Roland Barthes in relation to the "aura" of the photograph. We adopt a phenomenological perspective to interrogate and undermine some of Auslander's ideas, while also arguing that Phelan's position is equally untenable in relation to fundamental understandings of artistic "presence" and psychologies of audience reception.

Chapter 7, "Postmodernism and Posthumanism," begins with a discussion of Jay Bolter and Richard Grusin's theory of "remediation" and goes on to analyze how postmodern and deconstructive theories have dominated critical approaches to digital performance. But a close deconstruction of the antimedia and antitheater prejudices of (respectively) Jean Baudrillard and Jacques Derrida provides a basis for our argument that postmodernism and deconstruction can at best offer only outdated, and theoretically generalized and partial, discourses on the marriage of performance and technology. There follows a discussion of cybernetics and the related, more recent concept of posthumanism, which are seen to offer alternative and perhaps more fitting theoretical positions from which to approach the critical analysis of digital performance.

The tensions and dualities surrounding "The Digital Revolution" are explored in chapter 8. While Hans-Peter Schwarz has declared that we are living in "an epoch of media-morphosis,"[19] and Nan C. Shu has discussed how we now use computers without deliberately thinking about it, "in a manner akin to driving a car,"[20] we stress the equally potent forces of the "digital divide" that separate industrialized nations from the so-called third world. Further divisions are traced, from the dominance of the English language (which marginalizes digital performance works using other languages) to the border and frontier metaphors of cyberspace, and the battles between "proprietary" and "free" computer code. Brenda Laurel's influential thesis on the links between computers and theater

Figure 1.4   Mark Coniglio's *Isadora* software is used to control dazzling projection effects in Troika Ranch's *16 [R]evolutions* (2006).

is explored, and the chapter concludes by contrasting the hyperbole surrounding the "digital revolution" expounded by journals from *Wired* to *Scientific American* with the skepticism of writers such as Richard Coyne and Arthur Kroker, and artists including Guillermo Gómez-Peña and the Critical Art Ensemble.

Chapter 9's examination of "Digital Dancing and Software Systems" analyzes a range of software systems which have been developed by or for artists, particularly in dance, from desktop applications such as *Life Forms* and *Character Studio* to motion sensing systems such as *Isadora* and *EyeCon* that activate real time sonic and media effects during live performance (figure 1.4). The influential collaborations between Paul Kaiser and Shelley Eshkar's Riverbed company and choreographers Merce Cunningham and Bill T. Jones are shown to have taken the form and aesthetics of the virtual body to new heights through the conjunction of motion tracking systems with computer anima-tion in works such as Cunningham's *BIPED* (1999) and Jones' *Ghostcatching* (1999). Short case studies of performances by Barriedale Operahouse, Palindrome, Half/Angel, and Paulo Henrique illustrate the way in which particular interactive features and performance aesthetics have emerged through the design and utilization of different custom-built programs.

Digital Performance Practice

The second part of the book deals with digital performance practice. It is structured in three major sections that engage with ancient and perennial fundamentals of theater and performance: The Body, Space, and Time. These core concepts are demonstrated to have undergone significant changes in numerous areas of performance arts practice where there has been engagement with and adoption of computer techniques and technologies. The book's final section investigates interactivity, with separate chapters devoted to performative installations, CD-ROMs, and computer games.

The section on the body begins with chapter 10's discourse on the concept of "Virtual Bodies," where the general fetishization of "the body" in recent social and performance theory is shown to have intensified in relation to its digital counterpart. We argue that cultural theories of the virtual body commonly misread and misconstrue its basic ontology, while also unconsciously confirming Cartesian notions of a mind-body divide. Analysis of a seminal article by Susan Kozel is used to contrast the positions of theorists and practitioners in relation to the virtual body, and to show how the performer's phenomenological experience reveals a part-split, part-organic relationship between their corporeal and virtual selves. The notion of a split body is further developed through analyses of artworks and performances inspired by the multimillion-dollar U.S. National Library of Medicine's *Visible Human Project* (1994), and the chapter concludes by dissecting the different ways in which Random Dance Company, Dumb Type, and the Corpos Informáticos Research Group employ virtual bodies in performance works.

Chapter 11 narrows the focus to examine the ways in which artists and performers conceive, manipulate, and interact with their "Digital Doubles." Ideas from anthropological research to Artaud's *The Theatre and Its Double* and Freud's notion of the uncanny (*unheimlich*) contextualize the discussion of works by Blast Theory, Igloo, Troika Ranch, Company in Space, and Stelarc. We offer a series of new categories to provide distinct theorizations of different types of "digital double" in the forms of a reflection, an alter-ego, a spiritual emanation, and a manipulable mannequin. The reflection double announces the emergence of the self-reflexive, technologized self, conceived as becoming increasingly indistinguishable from its human counterpart. The alter-ego double is the dark doppelgänger representing the Id, split consciousness, and the schizophrenic self (figure 1.5). The double as a spiritual emanation symbolizes a mystical conception of the virtual body, performing a projection of the transcendent self or the soul. The manipulable mannequin, the most common of all computer doubles, plays myriad dramatic roles: as a conceptual template, as a replacement body, and as the body of a synthetic being.

Robot and cyborg performances are examined in separate chapters (12 and 13), although a central argument runs through both that performative depictions of the robot and cyborg are commonly characterized by a camp aesthetic sensibility. We also argue that robot and cyborg representations belie deep-seated fears and fascinations associated with mechanical embodiments, and that these are explored by artists in relation to two

Figure 1.5 Hamlet encounters his digital doppelgänger in Robert Lepage's one-man show *Elsinore* (1995). Photo: Richard Max Tremblay.

distinct themes: the humanization of machines and the dehumanization (or "machinization") of humans. We go on to demonstrate how such performances frequently dramatize a return to nature and the animal, and to representations of *theranthropes*[21] (human-animal hybrids) that recall the gods and demons of folk legends and Greek mythology. Chapter 12 considers the history of robot performance from its roots in the automata of antiquity to the recent work of Norman White and Laura Kikauka, Simon Penny, Istvan Kantor, Momoyo Torimitsu, Survival Research Laboratories, and Amorphic Robot Works (figure 1.6). Chapter 13 delves into cyborg theory and considers the "real world" computer chip-implantation experiments of scientist Kevin Warwick and artist Eduardo Kac, before presenting detailed analyses of the futuristic techniques of quintessential cyborgic artists Stelarc and Marcel.lí Antúnez Roca (figure 1.7).

The next section, on Space, begins with "Digital Theater and Scenic Spectacle" (chapter 14) and examines ways that computer technologies have been combined with giant projection screens in theater events to transform and extend spatial perceptions and to create

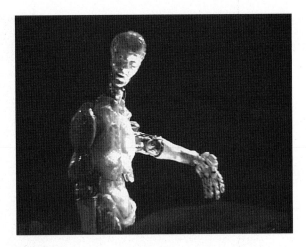

Figure 1.6 One of sixty robot "performers" appearing in Amorphic Robot Works' *The Ancestral Path through the Amorphic Landscape* (2000).

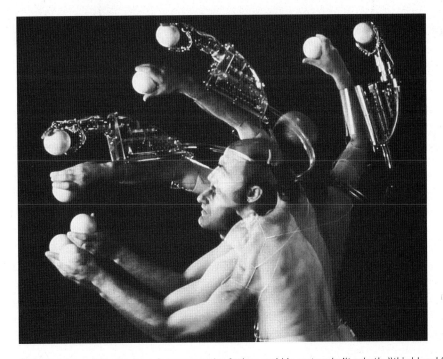

Figure 1.7 Quintessential cyborg performance artist Stelarc and his custom-built robotic "third hand."

Figure 1.8 Exquisite multimedia theater using post-Brechtian aesthetics: The Builders Association's *Jump Cut (Faust)* (1997).

immersive and kinetic theater scenography. Three companies are highlighted to demonstrate different technical and artistic approaches: the deep-perspective, illusory effects of
George Coates Performance Works; the inventive visual eclecticism of Robert Lepage's
Ex Machina company; and the post-Brechtian aesthetics of The Builders Association
(figure 1.8).

Chapter 15 provides a detailed discussion of a field of computer technology that would
seem to offer theater and performance unique and compelling possibilities, but where surprisingly few, though notable experiments have so far materialized: "Virtual Reality." Two
of the earliest performative works using VR, Brenda Laurel and Rachel Strickland's *Placeholder* (1993) and Char Davies's *Osmose* (1994–95), use the futuristic technologies to return
to prehistoric landscapes and times, while Yacov Sharir and Diane Gromala's *Dancing with
the Virtual Dervish* (1994) also returns to nature, exploring the interior of the human body;
all three of these pioneering works are also united by an anti-Cartesian concern to excite
an "embodied" experience. VR's employment as a three-dimensional scenographic
medium is examined through analyses of custom-built desktop theater design programs,
Mark Reaney's immersive live theater designs for the Institute for the Exploration of
Virtual Realities (ieVR), and Richard Beacham's extraordinary navigable VR reconstruc-

Figure 1.9 Richard Beacham's VR reconstruction of the ancient Theatre of Pompey. Courtesy of Kings Visualisation Lab, Centre for Computing in the Humanities, Kings College London.

tions of ancient theaters, which use the medium to bring archaeological ruins back to life (figure 1.9).

"Liquid Architectures and Site-Specific Fractures" (chapter 16) shifts the focus to artists' explorations of the relationships between physical and virtual space. It begins by discussing Marcos Novak's computational concept of "liquid architecture"—a fluidly responsive and abstracted, yet still physical form of space—and Slavoj Žižek's topological notion of virtual space as a "hole in reality," a type of supernatural fracture in the fabric of space which is always just out of view, "a floating anamorphotic shimmer, only accessible with a glance over the corner of one's eye."[22] These concepts are applied to analyses of theater works by Uninvited Guests and Bud Blumenthal, and to site-specific digital performances by a number of artists, including Susan Collins and Joel Slayton.

"Telematics: Conjoining Remote Performance Spaces" (chapter 17) considers the history of networked performance from early 1970s satellite and telex experiments and Kit Galloway and Sherrie Rabinovitz's *Hole-in-Space* (1980) to the pioneering telematic performances of the Gertrude Stein Repertory Theatre in the 1990s. The real-time linking of performers working in remote locations has been one of the most popular uses of the Internet for live performance, and we analyze a range of exemplars including works by Lisa Naugle, Fakeshop, Company In Space, Floating Point Unit, Guy Hilton, and Kunstwerk-Blend.

A fundamental piece of telematic hardware—the "webcam"—is afforded a complete chapter (18), where it is conceptualized in terms of an instrument for the performative subversion of surveillance society. Works by artists such as Mongrel and Natalie Jeremijenko/The Bureau of Inverse Technology (BIT) challenge and take issue with the ethics of CCTV and surveillance culture; others by artists including Elizabeth Diller and Ricardo Scofidio parody and undermine notions of webcam authenticity and "liveness," while artists such as Andrea Zapp invert the negative power politics of Bentham and Foucault's *panopticon* to present positive multi-webcam environments highlighting notions of community and social anthropology. The chapter considers the relationship between the live act of striptease and the interactive behavior of pornographic webcam models and concludes with a detailed historical analysis of the most famous and longest-running webcam performance of all, *Jennicam*, which we relate to post-Beckettian theatre, soap opera, and durational performance art. Watching empty rooms with no characters within the *Jennicam* set—previously "occupied" but now "empty," previously "empty" but now suddenly "occupied"—presents an ever-shifting kaleidoscope of patterns and banal yet dramatically loaded activity where, like a Beckett play, like an Eliot stanza, people "come and go."

Other forms of Internet drama and performance appear in chapter 19's discussion of "Online Performance," which begins with a discussion of cyberspace as "place"; a brief history of the Internet since the 1969 military ARPANET; and an acknowledgment that tensions continue to exist in cyberspace between social libertarianism and centralist governmental and military instincts to police and control. In the mid-1990s, online drama communities such as ATHEMOO, the Virtual Drama Society, and the WWW Virtual Library of Theatre and Drama Resources emerged, while ambitious, globally constituted collaborative projects such as *Oudeis* (1995) were conceived. The chapter considers what Michael Heim has characterized as "The Erotic Ontology of Cyberspace" (1991) and its relationship to performative online spaces such as MUDs and MOOs, including analysis of stage plays featuring online sexual encounters and the infamous Mr. Bungle cyber-rape in LambdaMoo in 1993. The focus shifts to exploration of online identity in MOOs, chatrooms and virtual worlds, where users carefully and consciously create quasi-Stanislavskian character biographies, establishing themselves as fictional beings and engaging in improvisational performances. Online "worlds" are traced through early environments such as *Habitat* (1985, using home Commodore 64 computers) through to the graphical worlds of *The Palace*, to the anarchic work of the Austrian company Bilderwerfer, who steal and assume other people's (real) identities to comment mischievously on notions of self in the electronic age and to pour scorn on the shallowness and falsity of Internet identity and chatroom relationships.

The final chapter dealing with space centers on notions of "'Theater' in Cyberspace" (chapter 20), beginning with a survey of hypertext literature and drama from Michael Joyce to the Hamnet Players and Desktop Theater, which we relate to earlier artistic movements and groups such as Fluxus and Oulipo. "Chatterbots"—autonomous, artificially intelligent "robot" characters that reside and converse in cyberspace—from *Eliza* (1966) to *Julia* (1990) are considered in relation to Alan Turing's theories and "tests" and to

Philip Auslander's argument that the chatterbot phenomenon: "undermines the idea that live performance is a specifically human activity; it subverts the centrality of the live, organic presence of human beings to the experience of live performance; and it casts into doubt the existential significance attributed to live performance."[23] The chapter goes on to pose the question "Is There Such a Thing as Online Theater?" drawing on a range of critical perspectives that argue, on the one hand, that the absence of flesh denies the presence of theater, and on the other, as Alice Rayner puts it, that while theater may be "particularly susceptible to a kind of annihilation under the pressure of digitalization. That annihilation, however, opens the way to the credibility of 'denatured' space and time. . . . The digital production of time and space dematerializes one kind of presence but institutes another."[24] The chapter concludes with detailed case studies analyzing the interactive online theater experiments of artists including Guillermo Gómez-Peña and the Chameleons Group.

"Time" (chapter 21) has been an emergent artistic and philosophical theme in digital performance practice, and the conjunction of live performance and recorded/computer rendered imagery has been used in innovative ways to elicit particular temporal distortions and effects. In theater works by the Builders Association, Robert Lepage, Richard Foreman, Curious.com, and Uninvited Guests, these effects can be seen not only to disorient an audience's understanding and experience of theatrical time, but also to challenge and go beyond established postmodern notions such as "atemporality" or temporal montage. Rather, we theorize such works as operating in ways that situate them within more ancient and mythical understandings of the *extratemporal*. The live and the virtual combine to dramatize the experience of existing and functioning outside of time.

Chapter 22's examination of digital artists' and performers' articulations of the theme of "Memory" begins by analyzing the importance of memory and personal autobiography to recent performance practice; and the postmodern theories surrounding memory, which clash between notions of contemporary society's total amnesia and its absolute obsession with memory and mnemonics. These ideas, together with Marcel Proust's literary meditations on the theme, interweave through analyses of performances from Andrea Polli's *Fetish* (1996), which develops her abiding central theme of "the fluid nature of the experience of a memory,"[25] to Curious.com's *Random Acts of Memory* (1998), which highlights the way in which our faith in computational RAM as a memory repository may be gradually eroding human memory. Remediations of the visionary "Memory Palace" (aka "Memory Theatre") project of Italian Guilio Camillo (1480–1544) by artists such as Emil Hrvatin and Stephen Wilson are considered; as are a range of performative treatments centring on themes from traumatic memory (Dumb Type's *Memorandum*, 1999–2000) to time travel, *deja-vu*, and short-term memory loss (Blast Theory's *10 Backwards*, 1999).

The book's final section investigates interactivity, spanning interactive installation and performance works, performance CD-ROMs, and computer/video games. Chapter 23 begins an exploration of "'Performing' Interactivity" by defining four hierarchical categories of interactive art and performance ranked in ascending order in relation to the openness of the system and the consequent level/depth of user interaction—Navigation, Participation, Conversation, and Collaboration—with separate subsections analyzing each paradigm. Navigational works range from simple web photo-dramas to complex flexi-narrative installations by Lynn Hershman, Grahame Weinbren, and Jill Scott, and commercial interactive movies by Bob Bejan and David Wheeler. The live audience participatory stimuli that trigger Paul Vanouse's interactive films mark a transition to the Participation paradigm, where the user or audience's active complicity is seen as central to a number of installations and performances (figure 1.10). Analysis of the work of Perry Hoberman affords a further transition into the Conversation category, where works by Paul Sermon, Toni Dove, Luc Courchesne, and the Centre for Metahuman Exploration are discussed; and the final category, Collaboration, examines ways in which audiences/users' own creativities guide and define works initiated by artists including Stephen Wilson, Webbed Feats, and Satorimedia.

Chapter 24's examination of "Videogames" begins with a survey of theoretical perspectives that emphasizes the critical oppositions between the "ludologists" who focus upon the game itself (its practice, gameplay, visuals, manipulation, the experience of

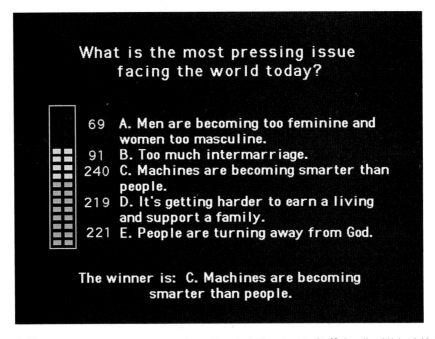

Figure 1.10 In the interactive cinema experience *Terminal Time* (1999, Steffi Domike, Michael Mateas, Paul Vanouse) the audience is posed questions and the volume of applause to each answer triggers a computer program to intelligently compile a film montage customized to their tastes and sensibilities.

playing it) and the "narratologists" who are concerned with cultural significations, meanings, and the philosophies underlying the progression of events. We go on to undertake a Brenda Laurel–style discourse on "video games as theater" by analyzing unifying principles and characteristics common to both, including narrative, simulation, terminology, and the fact that by the end characters will be left either dead or alive—a parameter that is as true of *Hamlet* as of *Final Fantasy.* Parallels are further drawn between violent video games and theatrical models from Greek tragedy and mythology to the *Grand Guignol,* while nonviolent, socially based games such as *The Sims* are related to the kitchen-sink dramas of the 1950s and '60s and to soap opera. The final part of the chapter investigates the increasing use (and creative abuse) of computer game engines/programs for artistic and performative ends by practitioners including Feng Mengbo, Tom Betts, and Mathias Fuchs and Sylvia Eckermann (figure 1.11). The chapter ends with a detailed analysis of Blast Theory's extraordinary VR war-game experience *Desert Rain* (1999), and our conclusion that rather than representing simplistic, inconsequential, or "plebeian" experiences, video games should now be viewed academically as the most prolific and dramatically effective form of "popular theater" of the contemporary age.

The rise and demise of performance "CD-ROMs" (chapter 25) offers a microcosm of the general development and adoption of digital technologies and techniques—how they

Figure 1.11 Abusing videogames to create art and theatre: Mathias Fuchs and Sylvia Eckermann's exploration of the liquid nature of identity, *fluID: Arenas of Identities* (2003).

commenced, developed, became fashionable, were absorbed, were replaced by a more advanced alternative, and then faded into relative obscurity. Three broad categories are defined and analyzed in relation to a number of case studies—educational; documentary/analytical; and performative. Educationally oriented performance CD-ROMs include works on Shakespeare by academics such as Christie Carson and Lizbeth Goodman, and by commercial companies such as Voyager and the BBC; performance documentation and analysis CD-ROMs include William Forsythe's acclaimed *Improvisation Technologies* (1994 and 1999) and works by the Bedford Interactive Institute, La Compagnie Les Essentiels, and Desperate Optimists. Our examination of performative CD-ROMs considers the different ways CD-ROMs have been designed to bring a sense of live theatricality to the "canned" format, from Laurie Anderson's labyrinthine *Puppet Motel* (1995 and 1998, with Hsin-Chien Huang) and Forced Entertainment and Hugo Glendinning's enigmatic *Frozen Palaces* (1996) and *Nightwalks* (1998) to Ruth Gibson and Bruno Martelli's upbeat interactive soap opera meets dance-theater work *Windowsninetyeight* (1998).

Our conclusion (chapter 26) does not seek to resummarize all our themes and arguments, but rather draws together and consolidates some central discourses. It begins by discussing the way that computers became firmly embedded into the social, business, and artistic fabrics of industrialized societies during the 1990s; yet by the turn of the millennium a severe backlash was underway marked by apathy, suspicion, and cynicism following the unfulfilled hyperboles of digital nirvanas, the whimper of the "millennium bug," and the dot.com collapse. The digital bubble, if not exactly bursting overnight, lost pressure remorselessly and has continued so to do with significant consequences for digital applications across the full span of associated activities, including the arts. The decline in investment, interest, and development became endemic; and academic, commercial, and artistic reevaluations were underway. In performance studies, academics such as Patrice Pavis pleaded a passionate humanist case for the humble live body and for theatrical text in the face of digital spectacle and robotic performance forms,[26] while numerous previously enthusiastic digital performance artists appeared to heed the call (or else to have become bored or frustrated with the technological palette) by turning their backs on technology and returning to the live. We revisit the rise and fall of what we identify as digital performance's true historical ancestor—futurism—to discern a parallel story of youthful optimism for a new and glorious future which ultimately fell short of the promised tomorrow. Both futurism and digital technologies initially presented themselves as *philosophies* of life only for it to be realized a little later that they were technical developments that would rapidly become dated and demand further enhancement to avoid becoming entrenched in their own technical difficulties, limitations, and clichés. But at the same time, at least the hyperbolic wishful thinking of a Marinetti manifesto from 1921 had actually become a reality by the year 2000:

If today a young . . . theatre exists with . . . unreal persons in real environments, simultaneity and interpenetration of time and space, it owes itself to our *synthetic theatre*.[27]

Our location of digital performance within traditions of avant-garde modernist practice rather than as part of an all-consuming postmodernism is concluded with a polemical analysis evidencing digital performance's "newness" and resistance to the self-consuming snake of postmodern theory and its state of blind denial of the new. Digital artists and performers around the turn of the millennium created something that has not been seen before, something still highly experimental, not fully formed, but nonetheless *new*. Blast Theory's *Uncle Roy All Around You* (2004) provides a final case study to emphasize the point—a one-person journey experience through city streets with a networked palm computer that mixes paradigms from computer games, performance art, virtual reality, online communities, architecture, and interactive art, and culminates in an unforgettable climax involving the arrival of a *deus ex machina*.

Theater "versus" Technology

We will conclude our introduction by focusing on a fundamental issue that surrounds and frequently clouds both the theory and practice of digital performance—the inherent tensions at play between the live ontology of performance arts and the mediatized, non-live, and simulacral nature of virtual technologies. Marie-Laure Ryan traces the word "virtual" back to the Latin *virtualis*, meaning "the potential, 'what is in the power (virtus) of the force,'"[28] and relates it to Aristotle's distinction between the actual and the potential, noting that in these terms an acorn is a potential (or virtual) oak. Thus "the virtual is not what is deprived of existence, but that which possesses the potential, or force of developing into actual existence."[29]

In ancient scholastic philosophy, the relationship between virtual and actual was dialectical, but in the eighteenth century this changed to one of binary opposition, with the virtual denoting the non-actual, the fictive, or the fake. Ryan suggests, "If the virtual is fake, cyberspace is a virtual space because it creates a sense of place, even though it does not exist physically; and the Internet provides the experience of virtuality because it transports the user into the non-existing territory of cyberspace."[30] She concludes that the pre- and post-eighteenth-century lexical definitions of "virtual" encapsulate the at once positive (the potential to actuality) and negative (the illusory or fake) aspects of computational virtuality. These dual notions operate clearly in advanced computer simulations such as Virtual Reality, where the environment projection is "fake" but the physical interactivity with it is direct and "actual." She goes on to note that postmodernism's obsession with the virtual and the fake has now rendered the negative aspect of virtuality a positive: "the late twentieth century regards the fakeness of the fake as an inherent source of gratification."[31]

Against the background of activity in the application of digital technologies within performance practice, the idea of computational "fakeness" has ensured an equal and opposite reaction against it. Whatever its potentials for artistic creation and theatrical effect, many resist or reject its inherent artificiality. The perception of digital images' lack of authenticity has progressively intensified in recent years as more and more people use sophisticated software packages, including image applications such as Adobe Photoshop, which were once the sole preserve of artists and designers. The realization of the speed and ease with which the ubiquitous digital airbrush can enhance, adjust, montage, and falsify representations has rocked to its very foundations whatever vague notion of "truth" may have clung to the already shaky status of the old analog photograph or the electronic video image. For many performance artists inclined toward notions of "artistic truth," virtual images and systems have thus been viewed with some suspicion, while electronic image media in general have long been eschewed by many because of their relationship to television: the most dulling, manipulative, hegemonic and aesthetically lowbrow of all art forms and art "spaces."

The artificiality or falsehood of the digital image has therefore limited appeal to many live artists on aesthetic, ideological, and political grounds. This is particularly the case in fields such as physical theater and body art, where the primary aim is the enactment of "embodied" authenticity, realized through the "no smoke and mirrors" and "no-strings-attached" material tangibility of the visceral, physical body. There is therefore a tension, even conflict, between those within performance practice and criticism at either side of the digital divide, which should not be underestimated. This has been exacerbated by the paradoxical rhetoric of disembodiment and virtual bodies, which have turned ideas of corporeal reality full circle by the claim that the digital body has equal status and authenticity to the biological one. The paradox that projected databodies and alternate identities enacted in cyberspace can be viewed as being just as, or even more vital and authentic than their quotidian referents, is now a source of belief and wonder to some and a totally unpalatable conception to others.

In the 2001 Performance Studies conference in Mainz, Germany, amid a performance program dominated by the conjunction of performance and high technology, Nigel Charnock's one-man show *Fever* (2001)[32] reveled in the resolutely nontechnological and the distinctly live (including live musicians on stage) (figure 1.12). Then at one point, an operator with a video camera enters the stage, and Charnock opens a curtain at the back to reveal a projection of the live video feed, ironically small and a little off-center, onto the cyclorama. "Look, it's the future!" he cries in comic mock-wonder, rushing around the stage in melodramatic paroxysms of joy. He then begins to undulate his torso and stretch out his limbs, clearly expecting a sonic response from a computer-sensory interactive system. When nothing happens and all is silence, his face turns to disappointment. "Where are the computer sounds?" he asks, to guffaws of laughter from the audience.

Figure 1.12 Nigel Charnock expresses the joys of the "solely live" in *Fever* (2001). Photo: Thomas Ammerpohl.

Charnock succeeds here in ridiculing performances that rely on technology as an add-on or novelty, and points out that digital dance is already tired and riddled by cliché. Just as significantly, Charnock demonstrates the exhilaration and unique quality of the live body in a magnificent and comic display of joyful dance, chat, and free improvisatory movement on a bare stage with a plain, white lighting "wash" (figure 1.13). The performance is also punctuated with more genuine "interactivity" than an onstage sensor system would achieve, as he runs around and through the audience, embracing them, flirting, talking face-to-face with individuals, and jumping like a naughty child over the rows of theater seats to steal their handbags, jackets, and coats, enacting the playfulness, freedom, and joyful intimacy of the *solely live*.

Monsters of Grace

One of the most publicized digital performances of all time, director/designer Robert Wilson and composer Philip Glass's *Monsters of Grace* (1998) provides an even more interesting example of the frictions between performance and new media, as well as providing an illustration of how the history of digital performance has been continually distorted and rewritten. In 1998, audiences in packed theaters around the world eagerly donned 3D glasses for the much-hyped *Monsters of Grace*, a performance Wilson and Glass described as "a digital opera." Their only previous collaboration, *Einstein on the Beach*

Figure 1.13 Nigel Charnock in *Fever*. Photo: WDR/Anneck.

(1976), was acclaimed as a landmark in the development of American (and world) theater, and the new project's exploration of virtual technologies aroused enormous anticipation and pre-publicity. The production featured thirteen lavish computer-animated 3D films, created by Jeffrey Kleiser and Diana Walczac, which were projected onto a screen suspended above the musicians and singers. Some films were figurative, others abstract, some seemed closely synchronized with the music, while others appeared to have little or no correlation.

The production and the largely (though not universally) negative reaction it provoked from audiences and critics, bring into sharp focus a number of fundamental issues and debates confronting virtual theater and performance. Firstly, expectations were too high, spurred on by overly optimistic and (at least currently) unrealistic rhetoric about the emergence of a totally new, immersive theatrical art form. Secondly, there is still fierce debate about the actual virtue of integrating digital imagery within live theater. Opponents fiercely contest that there is a mismatch of media and a corruption of theater's purity as a live form, a discourse (as we examine in more detail in chapters 4 and 6) that first emerged during the "film-theater" experiments of the early twentieth century and that was given even greater credence following the publication of Jerzy Grotowski's seminal *Towards a Poor Theatre* in 1968.

Grotowski emphasized the elimination of the superfluous, including makeup and "autonomic costume and scenography"[33] so that theater became reduced to its essence: "the actor-spectator relationship of perceptual, direct, 'live' communion."[34] Noting that this corresponds to an "ancient theoretical truth," Grotowski nonetheless acknowledges that it challenges the notion of theater as a *synthesis* of different arts. But, punning on the word, he characterizes contemporary theater as the "synthetic theatre," one dependent upon artistic kleptomania "constructing hybrid spectacles, conglomerates without backbone or integrity", a "'Rich Theatre'—rich in flaws."[35] He sees the Rich Theater as futilely emulating film and television with a "blatantly compensatory call for 'total theatre,'" which includes the use of moving scenery and "movie screens onstage." "This is nonsense," he declares. "No matter how much theatre expands and exploits its mechanical resources, it will remain technically inferior to film and television. Consequently I propose poverty in the theatre."[36] He warns that theater must recognize its limitations, and since it cannot compete with recorded media in richness, lavish spectacle, and "technical attraction, let it renounce all outward technique. Thus we are left with a 'holy' actor in a poor theatre."[37]

Grotowski's praxis at the Polish Theatre Laboratory was an ascetic *via negativa* (negative way) of pruning and elimination. For both actor and spectator, "the struggle with one's own truth, this effort to peel off the life-mask" involves a consequent peeling away of theater's illusory devices and the trappings of spectacle. "If we strip ourselves and touch an extraordinarily intimate layer, exposing it, the life-mask cracks and falls away."[38] Although these words were first published (in article form) in 1965, their influence remains profound. Grotowski is widely considered the seminal theatrical theorist and practitioner of the late twentieth century, a guru who has in turn greatly influenced other theatrical high priests of theory and practice such as Peter Brook and Eugenio Barba.[39] As Richard H. Palmer observes, Grotowski was "an outspoken antagonist to the incorporation of increased technology in the theatre . . . [and] provides theoretical legitimacy to late twentieth-century resistance to theatre's developing technology."[40] For Grotowski's actors, the *via negativa* also involved a rigorous stripping away of bodily conditioning and psychological resistances in order to approach pure, animal bodily impulses, and good old-fashioned "spiritual truth." In the same year Grotowski published his theory, Peter Brook waxed lyrical about the purity of *The Empty Space* (1968), where the simple act of a person walking across a stage ignited some magical electrical charge called "theater."[41] One is prompted to reflect just how much times, theories and aesthetic sensibilities have changed. Meanwhile, minimalism and conceptualism brought the *via negativa* to bear on art theory and practice, where white canvases, and lines of bricks took aesthetic distillation to new heights, and the tabloid press into apoplexy.

Via Positiva

Digital performance is by and large the polar opposite: *via positiva*. Rather than stripping away to reveal essences, like the classical image of Michelangelo hammering and sculpting stone to reveal and bring into being something already there but hidden underneath, digital performance is by definition an additive process. New technology is *added* to performance, a new ingredient that is delicious for some but unpalatable for others. In digital performance, extra technologies are added, extra effects, extra interactions, extra prostheses, and extra bodies.

In many ways, criticism leveled at *Monsters of Grace* and other digital performance productions continue precisely the same arguments expounded by the antagonistic critics of 1920s film-theater experiments, and by Grotowski: media projections do not enhance the intellectual power or visual spectacle of theater, rather their technological intrusion is alien; the two forms are aesthetic enemies. The wider tension between theater and technology in fact goes back even further. In *The Poetics*, Aristotle placed spectacle firmly at the bottom of his list of constitutive elements of dramatic tragedy, and Jacobean playwright Ben Jonson fought famously and furiously against the spectacular designs of Inigo Jones that threatened to upstage his text. The same argument still prevails today about commercial (and particularly musical) theater which is accused of succumbing "to a taste for expensive high-tech gadgetry in lieu of substantive writing."[42]

Jean Baudrillard echoes the sentiments (though not in relation to theater), and takes it further by insisting that people "prefer to renounce their creative powers in order to exercise and enjoy them through the mediation of machines first. For what such machines offer is, above all, the spectacle of thought and, in their dealings with machines, people opt for the spectacle of thought rather than thought itself."[43] Arnold Aronson attacks technology's wider impact on theater and dramatic writing, arguing that surface artifice rather than substance has become paramount: "In the midst of a modern era of spectacle, there is scant evidence that it is contributing in any tangible way to the development of drama . . . what is the point of trying to recreate 'virtual' imagery on a real, three-dimensional stage?"[44]

These ideas and resistances also relate to long-standing debates within modernist art whereby, for example, Malraux defined the modern in painting "as that which refuses—effaces—all values foreign to painting."[45] But equally, we would note that there were frequent assaults on this notion from artists within the modernist avant-garde itself. In 1921, Varvara Stepanova declared in a catalogue for an exhibition of the radical Soviet Institute for Artistic Culture (Inkhuk) that "the 'sanctity' of a work of art as a single entity is destroyed."[46] Susan Sontag summarized the debate in relation to multimedia theater in 1966:

The big question is whether there is an unbridgeable division, even opposition, between the two arts. Is there something genuinely "theatrical," different in kind from what is genuinely "cinematic"? Almost all opinion holds that there is. A commonplace of discussion has it that film and theatre are distinct and even antithetical arts, each giving rise to its own standards of judgement and canons of form.[47]

The criticism leveled at *Monsters of Grace* centered on precisely this perceived mismatch and lack of integration between two distinct art forms, and its consequent diminution of the production's sense of "theatricality." Whereas the heightened, formalist theatricality of the collaborators' earlier *Einstein on the Beach* was critically considered to have broken new ground, *Monsters of Grace* received condemnation for its distinct lack of theatricality and liveness. Critics noted that the live performance element was closer to a chamber concert than a dramatic opera and moreover, due to the distinct separation between the musicians and the screen above them, there was a division, rather than unification between the live and the virtual. Although this was a deliberate artistic strategy by Wilson and Glass who stated publicly (perhaps mindful of the reviews) that later versions of the production were conceived strictly as a 3D movie with live musical accompaniment, it appears to have largely disengaged audiences. This is not to say, of course, that other practitioners have not successfully engaged their live audiences and enhanced a sense of theatricality through the integration of digital projections, as we make clear in due course.

Rewriting History

It is equally important to note that the extremely high pre-publicity profile of *Monsters of Grace* aroused fears from the large, well-networked community of pioneering digital performance practitioners. Their concerns were compounded by amazement at the scale of the budget invested in assuring its high production values. The digital animators, for example, were hired from their own high-end commercial film company specializing in advanced computer graphics and the creation of "synthesbians" (synthetic actors) for Hollywood movies and theme parks, and their 3D animations were rendered in extremely high-resolution 70 mm film (most Hollywood movies are on 35 mm).

Following many patient and difficult years of experimentation by numerous "unsung" artists and innovators working in metaphorical or actual garrets, there seemed the distinct possibility that Wilson and Glass, two of America's highest-status artists, would suddenly step in to steal the digital performance limelight, and that history would credit them with "inventing it." This was doubly ironic and distressing since despite Wilson's deserved reputation as a magisterial designer of visual spectacles, he was a relative novice in terms of his experience of combining theater and media projections, having rarely used them since including film footage in his early *Deafman Glance* (1971). As its title suggests, *Cyberstage* editor Mark Jones's article, "Monsters of Mediocrity" gives the production a distinctly lukewarm response, and goes on to suggest that Wilson and Glass were naïve in implying that their work was heralding a new form of art:

This showed a lack of awareness or acknowledgement of the other work which has being going on for a long time. . . . Not to consider the work done by such groups as The George Coates Performance Works, The Gertrude Stein Repertory Theatre, or The Institute for the Exploration of Virtual Realities at the University of Kansas is to deny them their fair place in the history of art and their valuable contribution to it. The problem, of course, is that when someone as famous as Philip Glass continues to say that he and Robert Wilson are the first ones to do this, some people are eventually bound to believe him, and that becomes that—the books are written. . . . Years from now, when authors write books on the history of electronic art, they will site Robert Wilson and Philip Glass as the pioneers of a new artform. And this makes me very, very nervous.[48]

This book is one such history, and Jones will be relieved to hear that the pioneers he highlights figure far more prominently than Wilson and Glass. It is *a* history of digital performance, but like all histories it is partial and incomplete. The degree of attention we pay to literally hundreds of artists and performance makers is dependent on numerous factors, from our particular interests and tastes to the pure, blind chance of whose work we have happened to see, sometimes live, and sometimes "secondhand" through documentation such as videotapes, CD-ROMs, and DVDs sent to our *Digital Performance Archive*. We are also highly conscious that there are numerous digital performance artists that, for reasons of space or final editing, the flow of narrative or our sheer ignorance should be included but are not, and to them we sincerely apologize. These are the sad drawbacks of historicizing, though future editions may provide the opportunity to reevaluate and remedy any drastic imbalances or glaring omissions.

Mark Jones's concerns about an unformed history of digital performance where big-budget, high-status established artists walk in, take over, take the headlines and take the credit is a serious issue and one we hope to redress in some way. The type of fear Jones has in relation to a selective historiography of live digital performance similarly applies to other areas, such as the academic genealogy of the performance CD-ROM. Here, another well-known and established figure, the choreographer William Forsythe, came in relatively late on the scene, but is now popularly considered to be the first real innovator, if not originator of dance CD-ROMs. His beautifully conceived and executed *Improvisation Technologies* CD-ROM (1994 and 1999), designed by Christian Ziegler and Volker Kuchelmeister, is rightly considered the most aesthetically and pedagogically advanced example of the "genre," but most of its acclaimed technical "innovations" had in fact been developed and honed years earlier by lesser known artists and educationalists.

Jacqueline Smith-Autard and Jim Schofield at the Bedford Interactive Institute (UK), for example, have been creating disc-based dance applications for schools and colleges since the late 1980s, struggling through a plethora of here-today gone-tomorrow hardware systems that have rendered years of painstaking research and digital dance-analysis

Figure 1.14 Bedford Interactive's award winning *The Dance Disc* (1989) is an early example of an interactive dance analysis disc. In this section, it allows the user to study video footage in conjunction with synchronized dance notation.

materials largely obsolete (figure 1.14). The use of split-screen simultaneous camera angles, and the superimposition of computer-graphical lines over video footage to trace and analyze arcs of movement (the most critically praised technical "innovation" of Forsythe's CD-ROM), were actually pioneered by the Bedford Interactive Institute years earlier in laser discs such as their analysis of Siobhan Davies's *Pilot Study* (1994) (figure 1.15). Their more recent and advanced CDi and CD-ROM package, *The Wild Child* (1999, with Ludus Dance Company), continues to overlay computer graphics onto video footage so as to dissect dance processes and aesthetics. More than once we have winced to hear dance academics discussing how the Bedford Institute has copied Forsythe's technique (figure 1.16).

One of our key objectives, therefore, has been to trace back the roots of and early experiments in digital performance, and to highlight the often unsung pioneers in the field who might otherwise slip into history without recognition. This means an inevitable concentration on the decade of the 1990s, its "golden era" and the key focus of our study, over more recent practice (although we nonetheless discuss many works from 2000 to

Figure 1.15 From 1994 Bedford Interactive used overlaid graphics to trace lines and arcs of movement, predating William Forsythe and ZKM's more celebrated use of the technique in 1999.

Figure 1.16 A screen shot of William Forsythe demonstrating a rotation movement in ZKM's beautifully designed *Improvisation Technologies: A Tool for the Analytical Dance Eye* CD-ROM (1999). Courtesy of ZKM, Center for Art and Media Karlsruhe.

2005). As Sarah Sloane has joked, books on computer technologies generally have the shelf life of a carton of milk, and we have not attempted to write a cutting-edge book about the "latest" developments in the field that would be likely to be here today and gone tomorrow. Rather, this volume attempts to provide a comprehensive survey, analysis, and history of digital performance's emergence in myriad aesthetic forms and on varied platforms; and the fascinating people—artists, technologists, theorists, and commentators—who influenced, shaped, and defined its development.

Histories

The Genealogy of Digital Performance

Those who forget the past are doomed to reboot it. . . . To know where we're going, we need only look in the rear-view mirror.
—MARK DERY[1]

Introduction

Throughout our research, we have attempted to question and discern what is genuinely new in the ontology of new media technologies and their application within the performance arts. As we argue later, the computer does give rise to unique artistic modes of expression and new generic forms of networked and interactive performance, and we dispute the contentions of writers such as Matthew Causey, who declares, "There is nothing in cyberspace and the screened technologies of the virtual that has not been already performed on the stage."[2] But equally, it is acknowledged that in digital performance the computer is commonly employed as an agent for the remediation of old and established artistic forms and strategies rather than as a means of originating authentically new performance processes and phenomena.

New media commentators have frequently taken polar positions, pronouncing computer technologies either as revolutionary and heralding radical new paradigms or as the emperor's new clothes dressing the same old techniques and models. This critical divide is dependent upon differing attitudes and perspectives that are both culturally and ideologically formulated. The sense of the "newness" of computer technologies is clearest when they are considered and contextualized as media of significant social, cultural, and artistic change. In this sense they can be seen to generate a genuine reevaluation of models and a rethinking of artistic and communicational techniques and paradigms. But when computer technologies are considered more dispassionately in relation to older communications media and artistic forms, it is relatively easy to draw close parallels and thereby argue the contrary.

Both critical positions are thus equally logical and sustainable, a point that Sandy Stone has touched upon in her discussions on cyberspace where she poses two possible answers to the question, "What's new about networking?" The first is "Nothing," since the tools differ little from technologies such as the telephone, but the second is "Everything," since networking has transformed ideas of cultural and performative space. "Computers are arenas for social experience and dramatic interaction, a type of media more like public theater, and their output is used for qualitative interaction, dialogue and conversation. Inside the little box are *other people*."[3]

In examining the complex history of multimedia performance and its antecedents, it is not our intention to adopt a dispassionate or cynical "it's all been done before" position. Susan Greenfield warns of an inflexible and conservative "crystalline intelligence" that can only relate new technologies to old ones,[4] and Theodore W. Adorno reminds us "nothing is more damaging to theoretical knowledge of modern art than its reduction to what it has in common with older periods."[5] But looking back, particularly at the early-twentieth-century avant-garde, brings into sharp focus an historical landscape littered with a surprising amount of complementary work, albeit within different contexts, and using pre-digital technologies.

Echoes of Bauhaus

This fact was highlighted during a highly charged and, for the artists, uncomfortable discussion following a performance demonstration by brothers Noah and Seth Riskin during the *Performative Sites* conference at Penn State University in 2000. The brothers had discussed their work at great length before the performance, and suggested that it broke new ground. Seth Riskin's solo performance demonstration used geometrically shaped light projections, which beamed out from a number of lamp sources attached to his futuristic bodysuit. A kinetic "light sculpture" was created by manipulating the lighting shapes and sources; by altering their visual scales with Riskin's movements towards and away from an upstage screen; and by projecting the light beams out onto the walls and ceiling of the auditorium. In the post-demonstration discussion, the artists were critically attacked both for their earlier intimations that they could communicate telepathically and for their claims that their work constituted innovative use of technology to create a unique and spiritualized experience. One delegate, a leading performance studies academic, stopped not far short of accusing them of charlatanism, suggesting that their claim to technological originality was disingenuous since the performance derived directly from the work of German Bauhaus artist and choreographer Oskar Schlemmer.[6]

Schlemmer's work, including his 1923 "light plays" (with Ludwig Hirschfeld-Mack and Kurt Schwerdtfeger), which the Riskin brothers' performance echoed, presents an important precursor to many current explorations in digital performance. Experimenting with Adolph Appia's ideas on light, Gordon Craig's notion of the *Übermarionette*, and his own conceptions of space, line, and plane, Schlemmer took narrative, spatial, and choreographic abstraction to new heights during the 1920s. He designed robotic costumes for the Futurist dance *The Triadic Ballet* (1922); utilized mechanical devices to move flat, metallic figures rapidly around the stage on wires; and enclosed a female performer's head and hands in science-fiction-style silver spheres for *Metal Dance* (1929), staged within a corrugated tin-plate set. Schlemmer also prefigured ideas of avatars and artificially intelligent robots in his plans to create an artificial figure (*Kunstfigur*) without wires. This would be remote controlled, or even self-propelled: "almost free of human intervention" and permitting "any kind of movement and any kind of position for as long a time as desired."[7]

In his *Stäbentanz* (*The Pole Dance*, 1927), Manda von Kreibig danced holding two poles around two meters long, with another eight poles attached to the costume, emphasizing a geometric choreography where the human body was "literally reduced to being the carrier of the line."[8] Schlemmer's radical reorientation of the topography of the body in space, and its reduction to two-dimensional planes equates with the reconfiguration of the dancing body within digital environments and cyberspace. M. L. Palumbo's study of *New Wombs: Electronic Bodies and Architectural Disorders* (2000) relates Schlemmer's work to current virtual body paradigms, describing Schlemmer as a performer whose body is "*extended through space*" using technologies that merge and unite scenic elements into single spatial and geometric forms, while Sue-Ellen Case links what she calls his "cyborgic" pole extensions to the quasi-prosthesis of the computer mouse.[9]

Johannes Birringer suggests that Schlemmer's *Kunstfigur* ballets effected a deformation of familiar movement and physiology and a fissured "double abstraction . . . between inner and outer realities."[10] He also links Schlemmer's theoretical sketches for his *Tänzermensch* to the cyborgic body designs on Stelarc's website that accompany his statement "The Hollow Body would be a better host for technological components."[11] For Pelle Ehn, the optimistic vision of social and artistic progress promoted by the Bauhaus movement offers a model for a contemporary equivalent of the unification of art and modern technology, which he articulates in his "Manifesto for a Digital Bauhaus" (1998).

The Historical Lineage of Digital Performance

Theater, dance, and performance art have always been interdisciplinary, or "multimedia," forms. For centuries, dance has been an intimate marriage with music and has included the visual elements of sets, props, costume, and lighting to enhance the body in space. Theater, from its ritual roots through classical manifestations to contemporary experimental forms, has similarly incorporated all of the above, while additionally foregrounding the human voice and spoken text. Throughout the centuries, theater has been quick to recognize and utilize the dramatic and aesthetic potentials of new technologies:

Theatre has always used the cutting edge technology of the time to enhance the "spectacle" of productions. From the early Deus ex machina, to the guild-produced Medieval pageant wagons, to the innovation of perspective painting and mechanical devices on Italian 16th Century stage sets, to the introduction of gas, and later electric, lighting effects, to the modern use of computer to control lighting, sound and set changes, technology has been used in ways that have created incredible visual and auditory effects.[12]

The roots of digital performance practices can therefore be traced back through decades, even centuries of performance history. The same is true of computer arts, as Oliver Grau demonstrates persuasively in *Virtual Art* (2003), undertaking a near-archaeological analysis of the lineage of Virtual Reality and immersive environments through two millennia, from the friezes of ancient Pompeii in ca. 60 BCE to late-twentieth-century panoramic wallpaper vistas. Along the way, Grau visits fourteenth-century French frescoes, sixteenth-century Italian ceiling painting, post-Renaissance *trompe l'oeil*, and the panoramas of great artists, ancient and modern. Immersive and sensorial cinematic experiments and innovations are also traced, from the *Cinéorama* of the 1900 World Exhibition in Paris through *Futurama* at the 1939 World's Fair in New York and *Cinemascope* and 3-D films in the 1950s to the IMAX (Image Maximization) cinemas of the 1990s. Art and performance's relationship to technological change in distant history has also been mapped by Norman Klein, whose *From Vatican to Special Effects* compares the treatment of space in Baroque times to our understandings of cyberspace.[13] A number of valuable anthologies and readers were published just after the turn of the millennium, which bring together historically important texts that foresaw or influenced new media theory and practice. These include Randall Packer and Ken Jordan's *Multimedia: From Wagner to Virtual Reality* (2001); Dan Harries's *New Media Book* (2002); Darren Tofts, Annemarie Jonson, and Alessio Cavallaro's *Prefiguring Cyberculture: An Intellectual History* (2002); and Noah Wardrip-Fruin and Nick Montfort's excellent (and epic) edited collection *The New Media Reader* (2003). The latter juxtaposes seminal texts by computer pioneers and media theorists against artists' writings, tracing historical parallels between their thoughts and works since World War II.

Digital performance is an extension of a continuing history of the adoption and adaptation of technologies to increase performance and visual art's aesthetic effect and sense of spectacle, its emotional and sensorial impact, its play of meanings and symbolic associations, and its intellectual power. Dance, ostensibly that most nakedly corporeal of all performance forms, has similarly been conceptualized as a continually evolving technological praxis, as the title of an article by Arnd Wesemann makes clear: "Mirror Games with New Media: The Story of Dance has Always Been the Story of Technology" (1997).

The dancer Loïe Fuller provides an interesting example, undertaking some extraordinary experiments from 1889 with the then "new technology" of electricity. Fuller, a contemporary of Isadora Duncan, performed wearing huge, diaphanous, semitransparent gauze robes and held long batons in her hands to extend the length of her arms (prefiguring Schlemmer's 1927 *The Pole Dance* and Stelarc's 2000 *Extended Arm*, which updates the image for the robotics age). As she danced, the billowing robes became a kind of "screen" on which were projected multidirectional, multicolored lights, including those emanating from a glass panel in the floor that lit her from below. The complex plays of light on the vast folds of material that extended far into space beyond the strict limits of her body transformed (or, in computer parlance, "morphed") the dancer's body shape and visual form as Fuller danced and span in circles. The then "high" technology of electric light combined with the "low" technology of hidden wooden extension poles to transform the flow of energy of the human body into an image of pure energy and light, which conjured metaphors of clouds, butterflies, and dancing fire.

Like today's digital dance artists, Fuller diminished the fleshiness of the body in order to transform its materiality (or to make it immaterial) and render it like a metamorphosing, liminal trace. The first modern dance choreographer to use new technologies in her work, she continued her experiments until 1923 (she died in 1928), incorporating film projections and shadow effects as a means of transforming her body shape in live performance, and even created a piece where she tried to get her costumes to glow like radium. Fuller's work can be seen as a kind of harbinger of the way Wayne McGregor uses stage lights in his solo *Cyborg* (1995) where lighting gobos fragment his dancing body, making it appear to morph from one shape to another, throwing sections of his body into shadow and illuminating others. Here McGregor, one of the leading lights of British digital dance, uses old technology to generate the effects of new ones, and to conjure visual echoes of one of dance technology's earliest pioneers.

Wagner and the Total Artwork

Artistic Man can only fully content himself by uniting every branch of Art into the *common* Artwork.
—RICHARD WAGNER, 1849[14]

While writers such as Grau have traced precedents to digital arts stretching back through antiquity, we will begin our own analysis of the ancestry of digital performance in the nineteenth century, with Richard Wagner and his notion of the *Gesamtkunstwerk* (Total Artwork). Wagner's vision, expressed in writings such as *The Artwork of the Future* (1849), was the creative unification of multiple artforms: theater, music, singing, dance, dramatic poetry, design, lighting, and visual art. Wagner's conception is central to the lineage of digital performance both in its advocacy for grand theatrical spectacle and in the paradigm of "convergence" that unites the *Gesamtkunstwerk* with contemporary understandings of the modern computer as a "meta-medium" that unifies all media (text, image, sound, video, and so on) within a single interface.[15]

Wagner's own version of the *Gesamtkunstwerk*, as expressed in his epic "music-dramas" (he disdained those who described his work as "opera") sought not only a synthesis of artforms but also the Holy Grail of many multimedia endeavors: user immersion. Wagner attempted to engineer a wholly immersive audience experience through a variety of technical and artistic strategies, from hiding the orchestra out of view to negate any "alienation effect" to his use of hypnotically repetitive musical leitmotifs and sonorous, elongated chords. Wagner's immersive ambitions extended to the construction of his own theater, the Bayreuth Festspielhaus (opened in 1876), which was designed with a fan-shaped auditorium to ensure perfect sightlines from every seat, and which eliminated the visual distractions of traditional nineteenth-century theaters (pillars, balconies, boxes, gilding, and so on) to focus all attention on the stage action. The acoustically sophisticated theatre also utilized the latest innovations in stage machinery to intensify the illusion of Wagner's mythic images, such as mermaids swimming in the Rhine and the destruction of Valhalla. The hidden orchestra pit was (and still is) terraced in steep steps underneath the stage to separate the different instruments, and a huge curved cowl funnels the sound directly on to stage. Unlike in conventional theater orchestra pits, the music is directed first onto the stage itself in order to merge with the singers' voices, before the composite sound resonates back out into the auditorium. Wagner was thus the first theater producer to design and construct a sophisticated (and today still unique and powerful) audio "mixing" system.

Theater historians such as J. L. Styan consider Wagner to be the seminal influence on experimental theater,[16] and the totalizing artistic vision of the *Gesamtkunstwerk* had a lasting and profound impression on subsequent theories and practices in twentieth-century performance. In 1919, the pioneering Dadaist montage artist Kurt Schwitters wrote, "I demand the complete mobilization of all artistic forces to create the *Gesamtkunstwerk*. . . . I demand inclusion of all materials. . . . I demand the revision of all the world's theatres."[17] In 1930, Meyerhold wrote in *The Reconstruction of the Theatre* (*Rekonstruktsia Theatra*) that Wagner's ideas were once regarded as "purely utopian" but that he could now see that his ideas about the fusion of artforms and "all the magic of the plastic parts . . . is exactly what a production should be."[18] Just as Wagner had custom-built his Bayreuth stage and amphitheater-shaped auditorium, Meyerhold called for a destruction of the box-stage in order to achieve a dynamic spectacle "where there is no division of the audience into separate classes."[19]

In recent digital performance practice, Wagner's spiritual music-drama *Parsifal* (1882) was staged by Anja Diefenbach and Christoph Rodatz as *Cyberstaging Parsifal* (2000) in a highly distinctive interpretation that combines split projection screens and digital effects, numerous television monitors, and live and recorded singers (figures 2.1 and 2.2). Commentators in darkened booths, lit only by angle-poise lamps, interject, using microphones to complicate the action. Sandy Stone, a leading feminist cyberculture commentator, paid ironic homage to Wagner's *Götterdämmerung* (1876) in her *Cyberdämmerung* (1997), a performance ritual presented as part of the "Apocalypso" residency on apocalyptic narratives held at the Banff Centre for the Arts. The climactic suicidal leap of Brünhilde into the

Figure 2.1 Anja Diefenbach and Christoph Rodatz's *Cyberstaging Parsifal* (2000), a high-tech remediation of Wagner's *Parsifal* (1882).

funeral pyre of her lover, Siegfried, is parodied in Stone's rock-and-roll stage dive into the audience.

The idea of the total artwork articulated by Wagner would find many different advocates and forms in the early twentieth century, from Hugo Ball's "Cabaret Voltaire" to the theories of Antonin Artaud, to the designs for immersive multimedia theaters and performances conceived by the German Bauhaus artists.[20] The complete reorientation of the conventional proscenium arch theater space through use of light and film projections was central to the theories of László Moholy-Nagy, and to the conception of Andreas Weininger's "Spherical Theatre," Farkas Molnár's "U-Theatre," and Walter Gropius's "Total Theatre." In his plan for his "Total Theatre," Gropius wrote:

An audience will shake off its inertia when it experiences the surprise effect of space transformed. By shifting the scene of action during the performance from one stage position to another and by

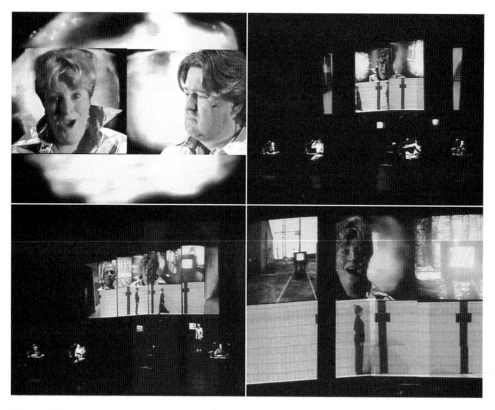

Figure 2.2 Split-screen video art, digital effects, and live opera combine in *Cyberstaging Parsifal* (2000).

using a system of spotlights and film projectors, the whole house would be animated by three-dimensional means instead of the "flat" picture effect of the customary stage. This would also greatly reduce the cumbersome paraphernalia of properties and painted backdrops.

The playhouse itself, made to dissolve into the shifting, illusory space of the imagination, would become the scene of action itself. Such a theatre would stimulate the conception and fantasy of playwright and stage director alike; for if it is true that the mind can transform the body, it is equally true that structure can transform the mind.[21]

The Bauhaus artists, whose first public exhibition was entitled *Art and Technology—A New Unity* (1923), were influential in questioning notions of space and space/time to enhance and reconfigure artistic and dramatic forms. Oskar Schlemmer worked, as he put it, to "break the narrow confines of the stage and extend the drama to include the building itself, not only the interior but the building as an architectural whole . . . we might demonstrate to a hitherto unknown extent the validity of the space-stage as spectacle."[22] Gropius conceived a composite amalgam of art forms to create new "entities" imbued with what he termed an "architectonic spirit." In architecture itself, there would be a perfect unification of sculpture, painting, and architectural form leading to fantastical buildings of the future, "which will rise one day toward heaven from the hands of a million workers like the symbol of a new faith."[23] "Technology," a word derived from the Greek work *techne*, meaning craft (also translated as skill or art) demanded that these Babel-like structures could not be built by unskilled laborers; but rather Gropius's million workers would be *"a new guild of craftsmen."*[24] Although the subsequent seventy-year history of architecture bears testimony to the relative failure of his visionary project, a new guild of craftsmen and women far more than a million strong are now creatively engaged in the architectonic "new faith" of digital multimedia.

Futurism and the Early-Twentieth-Century Avant-Garde

The work of art is valuable only in so far as it is vibrated by the reflexes of the future.
—ANDRÉ BRETON[1]

Futurism E-visited

Critics tracing back digital performance practices to experiments undertaken in the modernist avant-garde movements of the early twentieth century have described and analyzed a vast range of influences and precursors spanning all of the avant-garde movements, from Schlemmer and Gropius's Bauhaus experiments to futurism, constructivism, expressionism, Dada, and surrealism. Futurism, the first twentieth-century avant-garde movement, has thus been placed as merely "one on a long list" of historical predecessors. This has marginalized its central position in the lineage of performance and technology, and we will argue that digital performance's ancestry is precisely and inextricably linked to the philosophies, aesthetics, and practices of the futurist movement.

In the early twentieth century, the Italian futurists worked toward a new synthesizing and technological performance form, just as performance practitioners using computer technologies are attempting today. Exalting "the machine" and the new technologies of their day, the futurists sought a multimedia convergence of artforms and the marriage of art with technology.[2] In 1916, this *Gesamtkunstwerk* was afforded a mathematical formula, like a piece of computer code designed to activate a virtual event, what they termed *synthetic theater*:

Painting + sculpture + plastic dynamism + words-in-freedom + composed noise [*intonarumori*] + architecture = synthetic theatre.[3]

Although we will relate futurism closely to the PC (personal computer), futurism is certainly not PC in the other sense of the acronym (politically correct), and early futurist rhetoric is particularly offensive to liberal sensibilities. In places, the first futurist manifesto (1909) reads like the posturing taunts of drunken men spoiling for a fight, full of youthful machismo: "the oldest of us is thirty," it brags, not once, but twice.[4] Probably conscious of the negative impact it might have on his readers, in the first comprehensive study of futurist performance in English, Michael Kirby (1971) chose not to include the first and historically most important manifesto while including sixteen later, less offensive ones in his appendix.[5] In its rebellion against Italy's stagnant and *passéist* cultural malaise, the first manifesto preached art as violence. It concluded that "Art, in fact, can be nothing more but violence, cruelty, and injustice"[6] in much the same way that Antonin Artaud would react in the face of *passéist* French literary theater some twenty years later. The message and tone of the first futurist manifesto was destructive and reactionary, and denigrated women:

We intend to exalt aggressive action, a feverish insomnia, the racer's stride, the mortal leap, the punch and the slap. . . . Except in struggle, there is no more beauty. No work without an aggressive character can be a masterpiece. Poetry must be conceived as a violent attack on unknown forces, to reduce and prostrate them before man. . . . We will glorify war—the world's only hygiene—militarism, patriotism, the destructive gesture of freedom-bringers, beautiful ideas worth dying for, and scorn for woman. We will destroy the museums, libraries, academies of every kind, will fight moralism, feminism, every opportunistic and utilitarian cowardice.[7]

The futurists' bullish aggression and marginalization of women led to the disillusionment of many of its initial female followers, including Mina Loy. After writing a feminist futurist manifesto and a number of important futurist plays between 1913 and 1915, Loy left the movement and attacked its misogyny in her satirical play *The Pamperers* (1916).[8] The messianic phallocentrism of the early days of the movement is summed up, perhaps unconsciously, in the ejaculatory final words of the first manifesto: "Erect on the summit of the world, once again we hurl defiance to the stars!"[9] However, the abhorrent first manifesto was also something of an aberration, as none of the subsequent manifestos included such overt misogyny, nor did they approach the levels of aggression and right-wing political rhetoric of the first. Kirby is quick to point out that very few futurist plays and performances "were political in any way and none was explicitly Fascist."[10]

Futurist visual art still retains an important place in art history, but futurist performance has been largely neglected within theater history, despite the fact that many of the most important futurist manifestos specifically addressed theater rather than visual art. The 1915 manifesto *The Futuristic Synthetic Theatre* screamed in capitals that "EVERYTHING OF ANY VALUE IS THEATRICAL," and futurism's key founding figures devoted much of their energies to performance practice, including its leader Filippo Tommaso Marinetti, who was first and foremost a playwright. The relative academic neglect of futurist performance derives both from a distaste for the movement's associations with fascism, and from a widely held but largely inaccurate belief that it was "more manifesto than practice, more propaganda than actual production."[11]

Future Tense

But the first manifesto also included important and subsequently highly influential artistic philosophies, including the declaration that "Time and Space died yesterday,"[12] a theoretical perspective that has experienced a significant revival in recent discussions of cyberspace. Nicholas de Oliveira interprets the slogan as meaning an end to the concept of rational, ordered space within arts practice, and suggests that "the Futurists' image of a dynamic, fragmented, alogical world was essentially a theatrical one."[13] Futurism's perennial concern to dynamically explore aspects of time and space, as well as its evangelical faith in high technology, places it in a precise relationship with developments in digital performance. There are uncanny artistic parallels and synchronicities between the two artistic "movements" that appear to operate in precise harmony, yet some eighty years apart. Art historian Giovanni Lista's description of futurism, for example, involves direct associations with contemporary understandings of the computer as a convergence-machine, and cyberspace as a site for new personal and cultural evolutions:

an anthropological project: a new vision of man faced with the world of machines, speed and technology . . . a permanent cultural revolution . . . introducing art in the everyday media, and . . . exalting the mythology of the new over the conformism inherent to traditions. . . . Another task of Futurism was to bring art closer to life. The Futurists wanted to reformulate the myth of the total work of art, attuned with urban civilization and its vital, sensorial experience: words-in-freedom, music of noises, kinetic sculptures, mobile, sonorous and abstract plastic compositions, glass, iron and concrete architecture, art of motion, plastic dancing, abstract theater, tactilism, simultaneous games. . . . Futurism is above all a philosophy of becoming, that is expressed by an activism exalting history as progress and celebrating life as the constant evolution of being . . . a Futurist of today would be a fan of computer-generated images.[14]

Central philosophical and stylistic elements of futurist performance, such as plastic dynamism, "compression, simultaneity and the involvement of the audience,"[15] accord with core notions within digital performance practice. The concept of the *alogical*, which Kirby asserts to be the single most important aspect of futurist performance, has clear correspondences with nonlinear computer paradigms and hypermedia structures. Futurist innovations in the use of simultaneous, parallel action on stage (which borrowed cinematic techniques) can equally be related to interactive theater forms and performance CD-ROMs which present the user with options on what to choose to focus on and follow. Marinetti's *Simultaneity* (*Simultaneià*, 1915) featured two separate narratives being played out in parallel, and for *The Communicating Vases* (*I Vasi Communicanti*, 1916) partitions separated different action taking place in three unrelated locations. In both plays, the barriers between these distinct "worlds" are eventually shattered as characters cross the marked boundaries and invade the other spaces. Other performances played with notions of (nihilistic) existential "menu" choices between alternatives, as in Corra and Settimelli's *Faced with the Infinite* (*Davanti all'Infinito*, 1915), in which the philosopher protagonist dispassionately weighs up whether to read the newspaper or to shoot himself, and finally opts for the latter.

Futurist performance's juxtaposition of divergent artistic elements, and the playing of oppositional narratives simultaneously continued in the anarchic, "anti-art" alogicality of Dadaist and surrealist performance in the 1920s. Futurist thought also lay many of the foundations of what today we understand as a postmodern aesthetic, melding high and low art to become what Kozintsov called "art without a pedestal or a fig leaf . . . art that is hyperbolically-vulgar . . . [and] mechanically—exact."[16] Marinetti's manifesto *The Variety Theatre* (1913) describes an artistic philosophy closely akin to the contemporary postmodern sensibility, proposing a theater that acts as a synthesizing crucible. This crucible is fiercely deconstructive:

an ironic decomposition of all the worn-out prototypes . . . [revealing] the necessity of complication . . . the fatality of the lie and the contradiction. . . . It whimsically mechanizes sentiment, disparages and tramples down . . . every unhealthy idealism. Instead, the Variety Theatre gives a feeling and a taste for easy, light and ironic loves. . . . The Variety Theatre destroys the Solemn, the Sacred, the Serious and the Sublime in Art with a capital A. It cooperates in the Futurist destruction of immortal masterworks, plagiarizing them, parodying them, making them look commonplace by stripping them of their solemn apparatus as if they were mere *attractions*.[17]

Time to Dynamically Divide

The futurist principle of "divisionism" and its corollary in painting "the divided brushstroke" reflects the binary and multitasking paradigms of computer technologies. Techniques applied in futurist painting and photography to the depiction of motion in relation to time have exact parallels with digital motion effects and multiple-imaging techniques that are commonly employed, for example, in digital dance works. In many futurist paintings, different stages through the progress of movement are combined to create a blurred and dynamic expression of motion. The walking dog in Giacomo Balla's painting *Dynamism of a Dog on a Leash* (1912), for example, is depicted in a flurry of movement. Its wagging tail is painted in nine separate positions of motion, its hind legs comprise seven discernible leg shapes amidst a blur of other brushstrokes, and its front legs are completely indistinct, a swirling, barely decipherable form.

Futurist photography (known as "chronophotography" or "photographic dynamism") similarly sought to reveal and capture the "force lines" of movement as they occur through time. Italian brothers Anton Giulio and Arturo Bragaglia created numerous startling photographs by exposing the negative for a number of seconds to capture in sharp focus the stationary start and end positions of a complete human movement, but to blur the motion in between. The temporal movement is thus captured and tracked across the space of the photograph, and human faces and bodies appear to liquefy, like ghostly phantoms.

Today, the stroboscopic movement effects and the visual dissolving of bodily forms associated with futurist aesthetics are commonplace in the moving media images of digital performance, with startling examples including the prismatic effects of a dividing and shattering body in Bud Blumenthal's dance-theater production *Les Entrailles de Narcisse* (2001). A screen projection of a male dancer splits and doubles, with ghostly traces and afterimages fizzing around the figure as though electrically charged, in a mesmeric sequence highly redolent of chronophotographs such as the Bragaglia brothers' portrait of Umberto Bocciono (1913) and *Change of Position* (1919) (figure 3.1). But significantly, these divisionist effects (which were also evident in cubism, which predated futurism) are

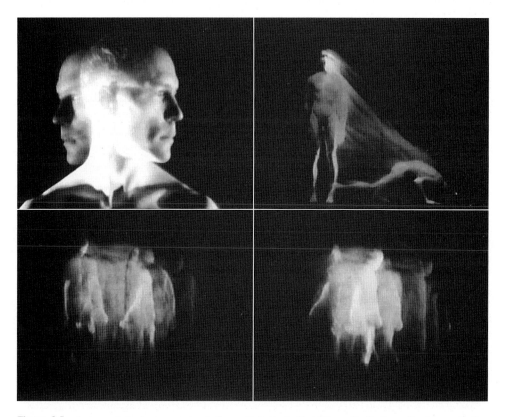

Figure 3.1 A dancer's body appears to shatter and divide in Bud Blumenthal's dance-theater production *Les Entrailles de Narcisse* (2001).

Figure 3.2 Movement phrases by dancer Reyna Perdomo are digitized and manipulated in real time in Christian Ziegler's *Scanned III,* performed during the Performance Studies International Conference 2000 in Mainz.

now brought onto stage in dynamic temporal form, rather than as still chronophotographs or paintings. For *Scanned* (2000), Christian Ziegler combines and interrelates live action with still digital-chronophotographic forms, using a video camera to record intermittently short movement phrases performed by dancer Monica Gomis. He uses custom-built software linked to a digital video scanner to create extraordinary still images tracing the movement, which appear and gradually mutate as they render on an onstage projection screen. The results are painterly (despite their technical reliance on pixelation), and while echoing the movement blurs and spatial divisions of the subject in chronophotography, they have their own unique aesthetic, mixing the geometric, the photographic and the amorphous. Hard-edged, clinical blocks of color and "realistic" photographic fragments of body parts merge with wholly abstracted, color-saturated forms, and blurred, quivering limb trajectories composed of tightly meshed dots and lines (figure 3.2).

The futurists used the mechanical eye of the camera to suggest a new view of the world, a mechanical one, able to observe and preserve time and space in a way beyond normal human capabilities. In the computer age, the same philosophy is at play, but the new digital eye enables the visions and predictions of the futurist theater to be realized fully and with relative ease. Thus, the once idealistic and grandiose plans of stage designer Fortunato Depero in *ca.* 1916 have become commonplace reality through ubiquitous software applications such as Adobe's *Photoshop* and *AfterEffects*:

A single figure, too, can become the protagonist of plastic-magic phenomena: enlargement of the eyes and various illuminations of them. Decompositions of the figure and the deformation of it, even until its absolute transformation; e.g., a dancing ballerina who continually accelerates, transforming herself into a floral vortex. . . . Everything turns-disappears-reappears, multiplies and breaks, pulverizes and overturns, trembles and transforms into a cosmic machine that is life.[18]

Depero's image of the violently accelerating, spinning ballerina recalls Tony Brown's installation *Two Machines for Feeling* (1986), which juxtaposes a *Metropolis*-style cyborg robot with a projection of a porcelain ballerina in a Plexiglas box. The contrast between the heavy mechanical movements of the robot and the delicacy of the small, rotating, virtual ballerina is marked. The ballerina is mounted on a cyclotron, and it whirls in increasingly blurring and mutating circles as the speed is accelerated. Despite the brittle fragility of the porcelain dancer in comparison to the metal robot, its centrifugal movement is far more frenetic and violent. As Brown puts it "narrative continuity in information society can only be assured by a violent speeding up of the dynamo."[19]

Arthur Kroker undertakes a lively analysis of the piece in relation to what he considers to be the "cold" cybernetic theories of Paul Virilio, who places the technologized, "disappeared" body in "a twilight zone between inertia and a violent psychosis of speed."[20] Kroker interprets the sculptural installation as exposing the interior world of virtual technologies, and its fundamental mirror-reversals and space shifts. *Two Machines for Feeling* constitutes a Virilio-like discourse on technology, since it is "a perfect simulacra of a culture modelled on pure speed"[21] and presents a postmodern semiology of the body as "war machine." The parallels with futurism's obsessions with speed and war encapsulated in the first manifesto echo clearly again. For Kroker, "everything here plays at the edge of the ecstasy of speed and the detritus of inertia; a psychoanalysis of war machines where fascination turns into psychosis . . . and we are ideologically positioned as inert observers of the spectacle of velocity in ruins."[22]

Manifesto Time

There have been no major manifestos for digital performance, but the scores of futurist theater manifestos between 1909 and 1920 could stand in for them, almost without revision except for simple word substitutions such as "digital" replacing "electric." Tracing the lineage of digital performance through the canon of futurist theater manifestos has been a strange and sometimes spine-tingling experience for us, akin to one of those supernatural movie scenes where a dusty, mysterious, and improbably prophetic antique book is discovered in the attic. In Italy, *The Futurist Synthetic Theatre* manifesto of 1915 announces an "entirely new," mechanical theater, and in Russia, the 1921 *Eccentrism* (aka *Eccentric Theatre*) manifesto opens with a plea to the actor to "forget about emotions and celebrate the machine."[23] It goes on to propose a "mechanically exact" theater where the author becomes "inventor-improvisor" and the actor is "mechanized movement."[24] Yuri Annenkov's manifestos describe a technological theater embodying "mechanic elasticity, vibrations of the human body that you do not recognize, lines of multicolored luminous rays."[25] His 1921 manifesto *The Theatre to the End* perfectly encapsulates late-twentieth-century understandings of the role of the director and programmer within digital performance practice:

The master of the new theatre will have a conception of the theatre completely different from that of the contemporary playwright, director, stage designer. Only the mechanical and the electric will be the creative ones in the new liberated theatre. Chronometer and metronome are going to be on the directorial table of the master of the theatre.[26]

Eighty-two years later, in 2003, Patrice Pavis would both confirm and lament that Annenkov's prediction had come true: "When certain directors escape into new technology . . . from the inside to the outside of theatrical performance, they no longer consider themselves as the central subject, artist or aesthetic subject, but simply as an organiser of functioning, a functionary of meaning. . . . But it is necessary to pick out, amongst the machines, videos, technology and other computers, some fragments of body and some scraps of text."[27] The same sentiments were expressed during the period of futurism, where dynamic scenography pushed to the foreground what had been placed traditionally in the background, often overwhelming the human figures on stage. As Julie Schmid notes, in futurist plays such as Mina Loy's *Collision* (1915), "dwarfed by scenography made up of colliding planes, light, mountains and city scapes, the sole character, Man, becomes incidental."[28]

Enrico Prampolini's 1915 manifesto, *Futurist Scenography* conjures another precise and accurate premonition, describing luminous stages and virtual bodies in exactly the forms that we now see them, almost a century later:

The stage will no longer be a colored backdrop but a *colorless electromechanical architecture, powerfully vitalized by chromatic emanations from a luminous source.* . . . From these will arise vacant abandonments, exultant, luminous corporealities. . . . Instead of the illuminated stage, let's create the *illuminating stage: luminous expression that will irradiate the colors demanded by the theatrical action with all its emotional power.* . . . In the totally realizable epoch of Futurism we shall see the luminous dynamic architectures of the stage emanate from chromatic incandescences that, climbing tragically or showing themselves voluptuously, will inevitably arouse new sensations and emotional values in the spectator. Vibrations, luminous forms (produced by electric currents and colored gases) will wriggle and writhe dynamically, and these authentic actor-gases of an unknown theatre will have to replace living actors.[29]

Prampolini's vision encapsulates the digital performance project. The idea of a luminous stage is inherent in the phosphor computer screen itself—the "stage" interface for online performance—and is manifest in the bright projection screens surrounding actors and dancers in digital theater settings, in immersive performance installations, and in the miniature dual screens of 3D head-mounted display systems used in Virtual Reality experiences. Prampolini's stage designs developed and implemented many of the ideas of Edward Gordon Craig and Adolphe Appia towards kinetic set design. These have now been reconceptualized and synthetically fashioned within the computer, as seen in Mark Reaney's kinetic 3D Virtual Reality scenography for ieVR theater productions such as *The Adding Machine* (1995) and *Machinal* (1999).

Time for Virtual Actors

Prampolini's description of the replacement of living actors by luminous forms is a commonplace in digital performance, through digitally manipulated human forms, as well as computer-generated figures and avatars. One of the most interesting "synthetic performers" to appear on a recent theater stage is Jeremiah, an Artificial Intelligence avatar designed by Richard Bowden for Susan Broadhurst's *Blue Bloodshot Flowers* (2001) (figure 3.3). Jeremiah, a luminous, computer-generated animated head based upon Geoface technology, appears on a rear screen and interacts autonomously and in real time with a live performer, Elodie Berland. Jeremiah's vision and motion tracking system enables "him" to

Figure 3.3 Jeremiah, an advanced AI avatar "performer" shares the stage with Elodie Berland in Susan Broadhurst's *Blue Bloodshot Flowers* (2001).

see Berland, and his intense eyes follow her every movement across the stage. As she dances, argues and flirts with him, his lifelike expressions change from happiness to sadness, anger, and fear, while "a simple Newtonian model of motion" with random elements of movement, blinking, and ambient motion enhances his uncanny resemblance to a human form.[30] Jeremiah's vision system, AI, and emotion engine software enable him to be a wholly spontaneous and independent "actor," a true "futurist" creation, whose actions and reactions are not controlled by offstage technicians (he is essentially turned on and let loose), and neither can they be predicted from performance to performance as Jeremiah progressively learns and evolves. Broadhurst relates *Blue Bloodshot Flowers* to the "making perceptible the imperceptible forces" and the "becomings and intensities" of Deleuze and Guattari, and also makes clear that she considers such work to constitute "the new":

The hybridization of the performance and the diversity of media employed . . . these imperceptible intensities, together with their ontological status give rise to new modes of perception and consciousness. Although much interest is directed toward new technologies such as Jeremiah, technology's most important contribution to art may well be the enhancement and reconfiguration of an aesthetic creative potential which consists of interacting with and reacting to a physical body, not an abandonment of that body. For, it is within these tension filled (liminal) spaces of physical and virtual interface that opportunities arise for new experimental forms and practices.[31]

In the futurists' day, it was animated, life-size marionettes that replaced human performers, as in Gilbert Clavel and Fortunato Depero's *Plastic Dances* (1918) and Casavola and Prampolini's *The Merchant of Hearts* (1927). Prampolini's *Futurist Scenography* manifesto (1915) declares that "in the final synthesis, human actors will no longer be tolerated,"[32] echoing the famous opening of Gordon Craig's 1908 "The Actor and the Übermarionette," where he pronounces that the actor "as *material* for the Theatre . . . is useless." It is a prophesy to which many may be skeptical, given the unique qualities of the live performer within a "real" space and performance's history of change to compete and survive against the non-live dramatic forms of cinema and television. But cinema in particular has already demonstrated its ability to create digitally artificial human performers or *synthesbians* that are rendered so realistically that they are now visually indistinguishable from human ones.

Mauro Montalti's 1920 futurist scenario for the adaptation of Leonid Andreyev's *The Life of Man*[33] replaces actors with representative shapes composed of points and rows of colored lights, which rhythmically darken and light up, rotate, form nebulas, and disintegrate. Precisely the same concept has been undertaken (almost certainly without knowledge of Montalti's little-known scenario) by artists such as David Saltz, whose interpretation of Samuel Beckett's *Quad* (1996) replaces the four actors with a computer-programmed grid of colored LED lights,[34] and by Australian group Company in Space.

In their dance-theater performance *Incarnate* (2001) a projected graphical form composed of colored, luminous points of lights materializes, rotates, and transforms into the shape of a female body. The small, circular lights move busily and rotate to expand and contract the size of the figure, to change its body positions and to disintegrate and rematerialize the luminous body like exploding and imploding nebulae.

It is a precise articulation of Montalti's unrealized conception for what he termed "The Electric-Vibrating-Luminous Theater." This is to suggest neither homage nor plagiarism, but rather the significance of the quintessential parallels between the futurists' ideas and those of the digital performance avant-garde. Comparing Montalti's scenario with *Incarnate* reveals closely interlinked aesthetic concepts concerning the representation of the human body as a site for dynamic metamorphosis through technological intervention. In both examples, the body's cycle of materialization, dematerialization, and rematerialization is articulated by way of a dynamic transformation of starlike colored lights. These animate and define shimmering human life forms against a surrounding darkness to evoke a spiritualized and ethereal vision of the technologically mutating body. This is a recurrent image within digital performance, and it links to Depero's notion of the disappearing-reappearing body as a "cosmic machine."[35] In *Winter¹Space²* (2001), innovative British digital dance group Igloo digitally manipulate live video footage of two dancers to transform their bodies into beautiful, star-filled forms. The dancing figures are entirely black apart from the flickering stars that fill their shapes. No visible traces of their real-life flesh remain; their referent humanity is only evident in their outlines and physical movements. The figures, composed only of tiny, pulsating stars, sometimes dance their celestial duet against a dense blackness, and at others amidst a star-filled outer space, with only the fluid movements of their star-bodies distinguishing them from the light-speckled cosmic galaxy that surrounds them, and of which they are a part (figures 3.4 and 3.5).

In digital arts, such starburst imagery extends beyond bodies to virtual objects and spaces. In Knowbotic Research's *Dialogue with Knowbotic South* (1994), one of the most advanced interactive installations of its time, real-time data from scientific research stations in Antarctica (monitoring everything from climatic conditions to the movements of icebergs) is processed by software and "knowbots." These activate currents of cold air within the darkened installation space and project abstracted representations of the natural phenomena being monitored. Wearing headsets and using a "touchwand," users navigate through and interact with changing visualizations of Antarctica in the form of constellations and metamorphosing star formations "pulled together, as if attracted by a magnet, and then burst apart again, like supernovas."[36] Such symbolic transformations from the physical plane to the celestial sphere mark a particular artistic concern to employ the computer to conjure forms and spaces corresponding to the unknown of outer space. Like Igloo's *Winter¹Space²*, the input data originates from the natural and the "known" of Earth, but this is transformed and output in the form of distant and "unknown" cosmological representations.

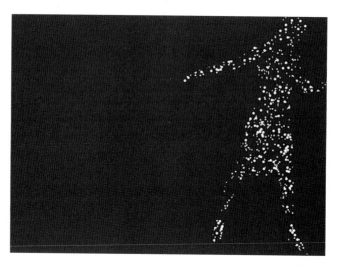

Figure 3.4 Igloo's starry *Winter¹ Space²* (2001) recalls Fortunato Depero's futurist notion of the performing body as a "cosmic machine."

Prampolini's 1915 manifesto also addresses the futurist theater's concern with what has since become a central tenet of digital culture, interactivity. He suggests that "the audience will perhaps become the actor as well," a point echoed in Marinetti's *The Variety Theatre* manifesto (1913): "[Futurist Theatre] is alone in seeking the audience's collaboration. It doesn't remain static like a stupid *voyeur*, but joins noisily in the action . . . communicating with the actors."[37] Futurist performance's position in the history of interactivity is little recognized, and a revision of this is long overdue. The Futurists produced a succession of interactive plays and performance events called *serate* and *sintesi*, which called on the physical involvement of the audience. In Bruno Cora and Emilio Settimelli's *Gray + Red + Violet + Orange* (1921) an actor turned on an audience member to accuse him of murder, and in Cangiullo's *Lights! (Luce!)* (1919) performers were "plants" in the auditorium who provoked the audience to demand that the lights be put on in the completely darkened theater. Only after the audience responded and their shouting reached an appropriately loud, consensual climax did the lights illuminate the stage, at which point the curtain immediately fell to signify the end.[38] In his study *Environments and Happenings* (1974), Adrian Henri discusses a performance that he considers one of the earliest examples of an interactive happening. A Futurist he describes only as "a friend of Bragaglia" constructed a special tent in which he chased the audience on a motorcycle through a labyrinth of hanging objects and pieces of material.[39]

The aggressive futurist stance of the early manifestos and the direct threatening or abuse of audiences in many *serate* and *sintesi* performances, marks a difference between the

Figure 3.5 The Igloo performers in costume for *Winter*[1]*Space*[2] (2001).

"politics" of futurist performance and of digital performance today, where such direct aggression is rare, particularly in theatrical performance. But there are numerous performative net.art sites whose orientation is focused on "offending the audience," including work by the anonymous Italian hacktivists and self-styled "cultural terrorists" 0100101110101101.ORG and the Dutch-Belgian artist duo Jodi (Joan Heemskerk and Dirk Paesmans). Browsing their work, such as Jodi's CD-ROM *OSS/***** (1998), can be a digitally traumatic experience as the desktop starts to flicker and splutter, and to develop earthquake-like shudders as if about to crash fatally or explode:

If you click the mouse hoping to get rid of the computer virus or whatever it is, windows open up everywhere, your cursor starts leaving a trial, your pull-down menus become either empty or unintelligible, thick horizontal stripes start running across your screen, suddenly changing into vertical ones. There is no escape. . . . This is the end of pretty pictures. Your operating system has started to attack you.[40]

Some interactive installations have also been notable for their levels of audience abuse. Norman White's *Helpless Robot, or HLR* (1988) is a dual-computer-controlled talking robot that has been exhibited in numerous venues including shopping malls.[41] Infrared motion sensors detect people nearby, and *HLR* begins to speak to them, asking them to physically help to turn and move it on its metal axis base. As the person engages with the robot and begins to manipulate it, *HLR* becomes increasingly annoyed, accusing the person of putting it in the wrong position, and telling them to move it further left, then right, then left, then right. Whatever the spectator does, its abuse continues and worsens, until it is soon yelling and berating them for hurting it. The more the helpful visitor attempts to correct *HLR*'s position, the louder the abuse and the fiercer the accusations. When the spectator finally gives up and moves away, *HLR*'s tone changes into a pathetic whine. "I'm sorry. Please come back. I'll behave," it says, and the cycle begins again.

Machine Time

Most fundamentally of all, the centrality of the *machine* links futurism to digital performance. In the *Manifesto of Futurist Playwrights* (1911) the twenty signatories including Marinetti declared that it was "necessary to introduce into theatre the feeling of the domination of the machine."[42] This sensibility is finding increasing expression in digital performance, from the monumental, kinetic machine set of Robert Lepage's *Zulu Time* (1999) to the work of Japanese company Dumb Type. Their early large-scale theater performance *pH* (1990–93) was staged in traverse with a long, narrow, white linoleum stage banked by the audience in raked seating either side. Above the performers, a horizontal bar with integral projectors fitted underneath moved back and forth along the length of the space. On its relentless journeys, its beam of projected images illuminated the performers below, suggesting the passage of a huge medical or computer scanner, or a monstrous photocopier (figure 3.6). In its wake, as the group put it: "performers (human beings) acted and danced under the mercy of and/or against the machine (society)."[43] Johannes Birringer reflects how the company juxtapose the performers' ferocious physical movements against "dense, quivering and pulsing image projections, taken to the limits of maximum acceleration." Meanwhile,

the computerized "image system" appears like an automatic machine moving outside of anyone's control. The dancers appear as mapping modules of the image machine: they are completely permeated by its effects, by the video-light and the intensely loud sound, and their physical presence is no longer autonomous but integrated into the machine.[44]

In David Therrien's *Machines for a New Inquisition* (1995) a robotic arm with a three-fingered hand relentlessly beats the metal breastplate of a naked and hooded crucified man, who is painted white. Haloed by a circular neon light, and lit by pulsating flashes from

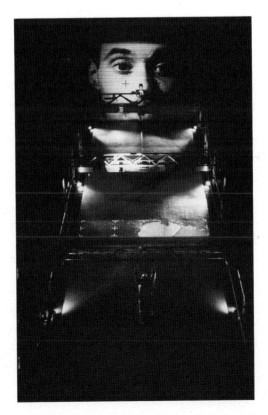

Figure 3.6 The 1911 call in the *Manifesto of Futurist Playwrights* "to introduce into theatre the feeling of the domination of the machine" is firmly answered in Dumb Type's *pH* (1990). Photo: Shiro Takatani.

eight strip-lights above his head, the insistent, crashing sounds reverberate as the robot flagellation ignites electrical sparks from the man's body armor. Performers drum ferociously on the huge, torture-chamber machine set, while naked and abject souls in spherical metal cages ascend and descend, and other dehumanized figures are suspended in metal harnesses that recall medieval instruments of torture. TV monitors relay gruesome close-ups of this deafening and apocalyptic vision of human sacrifice and martyrdom at the hands of an insatiably sadistic bondage machine (figure 3.7).

The futurists' call for the machine's dominance within theater reaches a zenith in such events, as well as in robot performances where the mechanical "soundtrack" of reverberating metal upon metal corresponds to the futurist conception of a new musical form of machine noise, most famously pronounced in Luigi Russolo's manifesto *The Art of Noise* (1913). The manifesto retained a major influence on music theory and practice throughout the twentieth century, and is cited as a seminal work by, among others, John Cage. Futurist performance manifestos such as *Dynamic and Synoptic Declamation* (1914) called for mechanized, declamatory vocal techniques, staccato movement and geometric gesticulation; theater performances such as Balla's *Printing Press (Macchina Tipografica)* (1914) depicted human personifications of machines; and mechanical ballets designed by Depero

Figure 3.7 The futurists' machine aesthetic becomes a sadistic and apocalyptic vision in David Therrien's performances such *Bodydrum*. This performance was staged in San Francisco in 2003 as a benefit for his late partner, Timothy North. Photo: Gregory Cowley.

(including Franco Casavola's *Machine of 3000* (*Machina del 3000*, 1924)) and Ivo Pannaggi featured dancers in some fearsome robotic costumes. Early conceptions of cyborgism appear within a number of futurist manifestos, including the *Manifesto of Futurist Mechanical Art* (1922):

Today it is the MACHINE which distinguishes our epoch . . . mechanical sense which determines the atmosphere of our sensibility. . . . We feel mechanically and we feel made of steel; we too are machines, we too are mechanized by the atmosphere that we breathe. . . . This is the new necessity and the basis of the new aesthetic.[45]

This aesthetic reached unprecedented heights in 1918, when Fedele Azari took to the air for his "Futurist Aerial Theatre" performances—looping, somersaulting, and diving in an aircraft with a customized hood and exhaust that increased the sonority of its artful noise, or what Azari calls its "voice." In his manifesto, Azari compares flight to a grandiose form of dance, and predates McLuhan by discussing the airplane as an "extension of man." Flight performance, he says, precisely expresses the aviator's mind and "rhythm of desire . . . given the absolute identification between the pilot and his airplane, which becomes like an extension of his body: his bones, tendons, muscles, and nerves extend into longerons and metallic wire."[46]

Fillia's theater performance *Mechanical Sensuality* (*Sensualità Meccanica*, 1927) epitomizes the futurist obsession with the machine and the mystical status in which it was held. There is no visible human presence, and five planes of vibrating metallic sheets, placed in perspective, dominate the stage. Other elements within the set are "personified" by three voices representing Spirit (a red spiral), Matter (a white cube), and Action (three colored geometric figures representing a machine), who describe how

men have been engrossed by mechanical expansion. Necessity constructed from sensual spirit, the enrichment of the environment. . . . Everything is geometrical—lucid—indispensable: splendour of the artificial sex that has speed in place of beauty. . . . The world drinks the oxygen of machines for its insatiable lungs and sings more strongly! . . . It is necessary to liberate ourselves from TIME, ascend, ascend, ascend, ASCEND![47]

Future-Perfect

Our Futurist Theatre will be:
Synthetic. That is, very brief."
—MARINETTI, SETTIMELLI, AND CORRA, "THE FUTURIST SYNTHETIC THEATRE"[48]

The type of liberatory ascension Fillia evokes was never fully realized in the futurist theater of his time, but the computer has offered the potential to enable it in ours. Central concepts and practices within contemporary digital performance constitute not merely a lineage that can be traced back to futurism, but fundamentally *encapsulate and extend* the futurist project. The futurist movement emerged at a directly comparable period of technological change and contingent cultural and sociological transformation as the so-called digital revolution. Futurism was born out of a faith in and fascination with significant, life-changing "new technologies" that all emerged and converged around the same time: film, automobiles, airplanes, and, perhaps most important of all, electricity. One might imagine that these technological transformations were even more seismic in their effects on people than those associated with computers. The effect must also have been different. Mechanical innovations were all "out there." Walking in the street was a new experience: there were suddenly electric streetlights, loud, speeding automobiles, and airplanes in the sky. Human excitement at these innovations was projected outward. By contrast, the digital transformation is all "*in* there," visibly changing little in the outside world and taking people's attention away from it, into a small screen, and further into themselves. The projection of human excitement and creativity takes an opposite trajectory: inward.

The introversion of the computer paradigm may offer a clue as to why there are no manifestos for digital performance, in contrast to the scores there were for Futurist performance. Digital performance artists generally lack the aggressive, extrovert bravado of the futurists, their fiery rhetoric and grandiose claims. But they are on an uncannily parallel path. And unlike their aesthetic ancestors, they may have ultimately realized the futurist vision for performance laid down, and largely forgotten, almost a century ago.

Constructivism

The great Russian theater director Vsevolod Meyerhold was allied to the Russian futurist movement before embracing constructivism in the early 1920s, and he produced futurist performances including Mayakovsky's *Mystery Bouffe* (1918) and Verhhaeren's *The Dawn* (1920).[49] Meyerhold developed his training system, "biomechanics" (the term itself suggestive of the cyborgic futurist impulse) following his appointment as Director of the State Higher Theater Workshop in Moscow in 1921, and first publicly demonstrated the techniques in June 1922.[50] His biomechanical system was directly influenced by the American industrial time-and-motion studies of Frederick Winslow Taylor (1857–1915), which were transforming Soviet approaches to industrial production. Taylor pioneered "scientific management" and studied the movement of production-line workers to advance ideas of "motion economy" and a system of "work cycles" in order to maximize output. Meyerhold mirrored the system in his physical performance training,[51] embracing the ideology and aesthetics of the new mechanized age, and rejecting the "unscientific and anachronistic" approaches of Stanislavski and Tairov.[52]

Meyerhold's paper "The Actor of the Future and Biomechanics" (1922) argues that the actor's art has always conformed to the social context and that in the future, the actor "must go even further in relating his technique to the industrial situation."[53] The "actor of the future" is compared not to a machine, but to a skilled industrial worker who demonstrates rhythm, balance, stability, and an absence of movement superfluous to productivity. For Meyerhold, these characteristics equate skilled workers to dancers, and to observe them at work is an equally aesthetically pleasurable activity, since their physical precision "borders on art."[54] He goes on to present a quasi-mathematical formula for acting (as the futurists had done for "synthetic theater") comparable to the computer's combinatory use of creative software and infrastructural hardware:

N = A1 + A2 (where N = the actor; A1 = the artist who conceives the idea and issues the instructions necessary for its execution; A2 = the executant who executes the conception of A1).[55]

Meyerhold's calls to "cinematify" the theater and his ideas on the aesthetic mechanization of the performer were echoed by another important Russian constructivist, Nikolai Foregger. Foregger developed his own mechanically inspired physical training system, *tafiatrenage*, which highlighted "the dancer's body as a machine and the volitional muscles as the machinist."[56] His *Mastfor Studio* presented performances that fused techniques and influences from classical dance, commedia dell'arte, music-hall, and circus (which he called theater's "Siamese twin"), most famously his *Mechanical Dances* (1923) which included neo-futurist "art of noise" music such as shattering glass and metal-on-metal percussion. He employed pioneering filmmakers, including Eisenstein and Yutkevich, to design productions, and his experiments in attempting a "cinefication" of the theater included the projection and dispersion of light via revolving discs for *The Kidnapping of the Children* (1922) and *Be Kind to Horses* (1922), where Yutkevich "devised a fully mobile environment with moving steps and treadmill, trampolines, flashing electric signs and cinema posters, rotating décor and flying lights."[57]

However, it is the influence and legacy of cinema's radical engagement with image editing processes that most intimately relates constructivism to digital performance practice. In the 1920s, Sergei Eisenstein, who had worked as a designer with both Foregger and Meyerhold, revolutionized the art of cinema through his theories of shot construction and editing as a "montage of attractions," which juxtaposes images for politically dialectic ends.[58] The pounding rhythms and increasing tempos of his montage editing technique intensified the sensory and dramatic impact of his films, while the dialectical shot juxtapositions operated simultaneously on the audience's intellectual understanding and interpretation of the films' ideological substrata. Eisenstein's montage technique thus effected shocks to both sensory and intellectual reception, in a praxis he compared to the rapid and cumulative explosions that activate the internal combustion engine. His artistic philosophy is akin to Meyerhold's in relating art to industrial labor, and just as Meyerhold had offered a Taylorization of theater, Eisenstein announced a Taylorization of cinema:

What we need is science, not art. The word *creation* is useless. It should be replaced by *labor*. One does not create a work, one constructs it with finished parts, like a machine. *Montage* is a beautiful word: it describes the process of constructing with prepared ingredients.[59]

Dziga Vertov

Although considered a "lesser" figure in the history of constructivist cinema, and a challenger to the theories of both Eisenstein and Pudovkin, the iconoclastic Russian filmmaker Dziga Vertov deserves particular consideration. Vertov's thought and works links futurism, surrealism, and constructivism, and Eisenstein dubbed him "a visual hooligan" following his surrealistic and hallucinatory *Man With A Movie Camera* (1929). In the film, the movie camera is the central protagonist, and it comes to life: its tripod legs walking and its camera head rotating as a giant, ominous robotic figure observing antlike swarms of people below. In extreme wide shots of crowded city streets, the screen splits in the center and the two sides part and veer, creating a vertiginous effect. The camera is mounted in unusual and often extreme high angles and on moving automobiles. The film is slowed down and sped up; there are numerous frenetically edited sequences; and frequent superimpositions such as close-ups of workers visually fused with fast-moving factory machines.

Vertov's controversial Kinoki (or "Kino-Eye") theory rested on a belief that "the eye obeys the will of the camera." Kinoki propounds the techno-positivist stance of the futurists, the sense of dream-reality of the surrealists, and the formal geometric systems of the constructivists. It also encapsulates a messianic vision of the transformational potentials of new technologies:

I am eye. I have created a man more perfect than Adam; I create thousands of different people in accordance with previously prepared plans and charts.

I take the most agile hands of one, the fastest and most graceful legs of another, from a third person I take the handsomest and most expressive head, and by editing I create an entirely new perfect man.

I am eye. I am mechanical eye.[60]

It is striking how closely Vertov's understanding of Kinoki cinema's montaging "eye" parallels the visual compositing functions of computer systems. The fragmentation, reordering, and reanimation of bodies and body parts is a common theme within digital arts and performance, although it is more likely to result in a strange, fantastical, or dysfunctional new figure than Vertov's biblically referenced "perfect man." Meanwhile, the Frankensteinian subtext to Vertov's creationist concept reemerges in the work of current robotic, biotech, and artificial-life artists. Vertov's legacy to digital performance is reflected in frequent references and citations: Douglas Rosenberg pays homage in the very title of his dance and technology company, Dziga Vertov Performance Group (established in

1991), and performance group Talking Birds paid their respects in *Girl with a Movie Camera* (1999), which combined archive film and digital video to trace six decades of the English city of Coventry.

In his thought-provoking study *The Language of New Media* (2001), Lev Manovich uses Vertov's *Man with a Movie Camera* as a starting point and "guide" to understanding the language and paradigms of new media.[61] Using illustrations of fifty-four different frames from the film, Manovich analyzes how "the computer fulfils the promise of cinema as a visual Esperanto."[62] He links Vertov's film to computational notions of editing, "cut-and-paste" montage, superimposition, and seamless compositing; the mobile "virtual camera"; angles of "superhuman vision"; dynamic database access; and the use of visual trick effects to create "a meaningful artistic language."

Constructivism's adoption of geometric, scientific, and formal systems as part of the artistic process links closely to the way that the computer's formal systems of mathematical logic are creatively employed in digital performance. Patricia Railing describes Russian constructivist artist Malevich's innovative methods as being a significant early example of artists' use of mathematical and scientific laws to bring a formal system to their work. In his essay "On New Systems in Art" (1919), Malevich rejected traditional art derived from and reflecting the natural world in favor of a more abstracted art that makes use of formal scientific systems: "a law for the constructional inter-relationships of forms."[63] For Linda Candy and Ernest Edmonds, Malevich's writings and experiments provide an early "starting point for the history of art and computers."[64] They note that nowadays many artists involved in computer programming may not consciously conceive their work as adopting a "system" or ever use the term; but inevitably they are using a rigorously scientific, formal system in practice.[65]

Dada, Surrealism, and Expressionism

If futurism forms a fundamental philosophical and conceptual basis for contemporary digital performance, and constructivism provides its mathematical model and formalist methodology, then the other movements of the early European avant-garde (Dada, surrealism, expressionism, and Bauhaus) provide fountains of inspiration for much of its content and styles of artistic expression. We have already discussed the importance of Bauhaus artists such as Schlemmer and Gropius to digital performance's lineage, and an equal claim can be made for the dadaists and surrealists. Digital performance commonly explores representations of the subconscious, dreams, and fantasy worlds, as well as other central themes of early twentieth century surrealist art, film, and theater. The collages and cut-ups of French Dada and surrealism move into a virtual realm, with the computer becoming the image manipulator par excellence whose cut-and-paste montages are de rigueur. Dada's cut-up legacy to hypermedia and interactive fiction has been noted by many, including Jay Bolter, Sarah Sloane, and Benjamin Wooley, who also observes how Tristan Tzara inspired William Burrough's experiments into "narrative disintegration."[66]

Figure 3.8 The spirit of Dada and the Cabaret Voltaire is evoked by the Hungarian group Vakuum TV.

Dadaist performance structures, such as Hugo Ball's Cabaret Voltaire events in Zurich from 1916, which mixed "bits" of performance, music, manifestos, theory, and art images, have been reinvented to foreground digital bytes. A fascinating example is the Budapest-based group Vakuum TV, which presented fifty-three eclectic live cabaret events between 1994 and 1997 combining performance, short films, "multimedia choreography," and interactive elements between the audience and performers. The group conceive these interactions and interventions to mirror "the context of the relation between computer and its user" and different types of games are a common feature, designed to complement "the associative system of VakuumNet which simulates net surfing"[67] (figure 3.8). Vakuum TV performances are typically staged within a large TV-style frame, and the eclectic and fast-changing performance elements enhance the sense of channel-hopping and web-surfing. Members of the company discuss their work in terms of an intimate relationship between art and play, and emphasize their close affinity to the early café theater performances of Cabaret Voltaire. Their performances have become increasingly technological over the years, incorporating advanced digital projections and animations in events such as *The Parallel of Human Being* (2000), an idiosyncratic quasi-Dada exploration of the evolution of robotics and the emergence of the cyborg, what the company call "a weird montage of low-tech futurology"[68] (figure 3.9).

The destabilization of time and space and, equally significantly, the visual fragmenta-tion of the human body, unite the artistic thrusts of many surrealist and digital perfor-

Figure 3.9 Vakuum TV's photomontage of their cabaret performance images reflects their idiosyncratic style and their theatricalization of web surfing and channel hopping paradigms.

mance experiments. The sinister inner life and animation of inanimate objects observed in surrealist art, and particularly film,[69] are expressed once more in computer animations incorporated within performances, and attain "live" embodiments in mechanized robot artworks and performances. In his eloquent study of surrealism, *Compulsive Beauty* (2000), Hal Foster promotes the figure of the Minotaur in the labyrinth as a quintessential symbol of surrealism's condensation of desire/death, the maternal/paternal and pre-Oedipal/Oedipal, and its psychic allegiance to the mythological.[70] As we discuss later, mythological *theranthrope* (animal-human) images and Freudian conceptions of "the uncanny" resonate loudly within dramatic depictions of digital doubles, robots, and cyborgs.

In his examination of critical and philosophical perspectives on technology *Technoromanticism* (1999), Richard Coyne relates in detail how the tenets of surrealism "resonate with those who expound the IT world as vertiginous, full of strange juxtapositions, complexities, layerings of meaning, and contradiction."[71] He expands this to a consideration of one of surrealism's artistic progeny, the theater of the absurd of the 1950s and '60s where "the unities of time and place were violated, and the workings of dreams, hallucinations and paradoxes prevailed . . . a mingling of realism with highly fantastic and magical elements."[72] In her study of *Digital Art* (2003), Christiane Paul similarly makes reference to the influential legacy of Dada and surrealism, and in particular to Marcel Duchamp's Dadaist ready-made works. Duchamp's (as well as others') cubist paintings have also been considered important precursors to the multilayered and split-image aesthetics of digital arts, while his abiding cubist masterpiece *Nude Descending a Staircase* (1912) has been remediated by Shigeko Kubota. The video installation, *Duchampiana: Nude Descending a Staircase* (1976) centers on a treated, distressed video image of a naked woman who walks downward, from one video screen to another, on separate monitors configured in a series of descending steps.[73]

In 1925, the Director of Surrealist Investigations was the French theater theorist and visionary Antonin Artaud, a figure whose influence has been central to much experimental performance practice since the 1960s, and continues undiminished in the digital performance arena.[74] Numerous artists and commentators have observed the correspondences between Artaudian thought and digital performance, including Stephen A. Schrum, who suggests that Artaud's writings deserve a new reading in the light of new technologies.[75] Greg Little points out that Artaud discussed a "body without organs" half a century before Deleuze and Guattari's famous philosophical formulation, which has been widely used as a metaphorical critical construct within discourses on virtual bodies. In "A Manifesto for Avatars" (1998), Little suggests that Artaudian thought should be the inspiration for the creation of new types of avatars "that speak of hyperembodiment, of extremes of physicality, like the visceral, the abject, the defiled, and the horrific." In "Artaud Unleashed: Cyberspace Meets the Theatre of Cruelty," George Popovich suggests that Virtual Reality technology and techniques such as black-effect "Clean Video" projections offer possibilities for the realization of Artaudian ideals of "an 'immense space' from which images and actors materialize as if emanating from the psychic space of pure archetype."[76] Stephen Metcalf and Sadie Plant both emphasize his importance within cybertheory in their contributions to the edited collection *Virtual Futures* (1998);[77] and Artaud will later emerge as a significant and recurring leitmotif within our own discourses on digital performance practice.

To complete the consideration of early-twentieth-century avant-garde movements, expressionism's lineage to digital performance is the least distinct, and primarily relates to the use of distortion and exaggeration in visual forms, from the human face and body to scenic vistas and virtual worlds. Brecht dismissed expressionism as "a purely inflationary phenomenon"[78] and expressionist set designs particularly amplified and emphasized the macabre and the fearful, using design elements as symbolic visual representations of the psychological and the hallucinatory. Expressionist theater design was closely related to lens-based media, mirroring the cinematographic effects of extreme wide-angle and distorting lenses. The use of exaggerated lines in makeup and expressionism's emotional, "ecstatic" acting style placed the actor as an integrated part of this darkly grand conceptual design.[79]

Expressionistic styles and particular techniques of exaggeration have been adopted by a number of artists and companies, and expressionist plays from the 1920s have been reconceived for digital theater productions, notably Elmer Rice's *The Adding Machine* and Sophie Treadwell's *Machinal* by The Institute for the Exploration of Virtual Realities (ieVR). Many performance artists have also used the ludic and hallucinatory design capabilities of new technologies to explore expressionist theater's primary thrust "to express something in outward form which is essentially interior, to project a soul-state."[80] As we explore in detail later, metaphysical realms, astral bodies, alchemy, altered states of consciousness, the depiction of souls, and related spiritual narratives all emerge as significant themes and fascinations within digital performance.

Multimedia Theater, 1911–1959

The theatre is not concerned with reality; it is only concerned with truth.
—JEAN-PAUL SARTRE[1]

Bringing Film into the Theater Space: Experiments 1911–1927

Theater-based performances that incorporate digital media and computer generated projections have a long historical lineage stretching back around a hundred years to Loïe Fuller's experiments with projected film on her diaphanous robes, and the first integration of film within theater performance, during a lighthearted Berlin revue in 1911.[2] In 1913, Valentine de Saint-Point, the futurist dancer and author of the *Manifesto of Lust* (1913), created an idiosyncratic multimedia dance performance at the Comédie des Champs-Elysées in Paris. In this elaborate choreographic exploration of love and war, performed to music by Satie and Debussy, poems, lighting effects, and mathematical equations were projected onto multiple cloth screens and walls.[3]

In 1914, Winsor McCay toured the United States with *Gertie the Dinosaur*. Standing onstage in a spotlight, holding a whip and costumed with a pith helmet and long boots, McCay issued gestural and verbal commands to Gertie, a silent animated film character projected onto a movie screen at the back of the stage. Through McCay's precision timing, the female dinosaur animation appeared to respond instantly to his instructions by nodding or shaking her head, sitting up, rolling over, and performing tricks like a circus animal. The film element of the performance is still extant, and includes images of Gertie getting angry and snapping in McCay's direction, and crying following a scolding. Gertie also catches an apple in her mouth; onstage, McCay used a cardboard prop apple, and gestured throwing it to the screen in synch with onscreen Gertie's catch, but actually "palmed" it rather than letting go. The performance's climax involved the live McCay walking behind one side of the screen, whereupon he instantly reappeared in the same position and in scale on the film, continuing the walk as an animated stick figure. The "virtual" McCay then stepped onto Gertie's open lower jaw, and the dinosaur lifted her head to allow him to step onto her back, whereupon they rode off into the distance, in classic cowboy-movie style.[4] One of the very earliest examples of the integration of film in theater was thus also the first to use ideas of close timing to "cheat" a sense of "liveness" and dialogic interactivity between the live performer and the media imagery, prefiguring numerous digital theater performances that utilize essentially the same technique. Equally, McCay's "walk into the screen" to transform him into a virtual counterpart is a much-used technique (and a much-loved effect) in current digital theater.

The pioneering experiments conjoining film and theater between 1900 and 1915 provide the starting point and inspiration for *Opera* (2000) by one of the leading digital theater companies in the United States, the Builders Association. The company describe the performance as reinterpreting the early-twentieth-century experiments "using the current explosion of club-oriented ambient and 'drum and bass' music and video. *Opera* combines these two elements 'sampling' fragments of theatrical history through the language of contemporary DJ and VJ culture."[5] The performance uses a system of MIDI triggers that are activated by the onstage performers and offstage technicians to prompt video samples and sound loops in real time. In drawing parallels between the film-theater experiments of the early 1900s and recent techno and club culture events, the Builders Association explicitly links past and present technologically driven enhancements of performance spectacle. In doing so, it also implicitly places contemporary digital performance developments in relation to an equivalent stage of highly embryonic experimentation; both periods of performance history share the same opportunities and struggles inherent in adopting and adapting "new" technologies to reconfigure and advance established theatrical forms.

In the 1920s, film projection was incorporated into many cabaret and music hall performances, and performers continued to experiment with and refine illusory conjunction effects. These included the French magician Horace Goldin who juggled with a combination of actual and filmed objects; and Robert Quinault, who created dances that synchronized live movement with slowed-down film versions of the same actions.[6] In Russia, particularly after the 1917 revolution, Italian futurism became highly influential, and it spawned Russian futurist performance companies such as *The Factory of the Eccentric Actor (FEKS)*. Their controversial theater production of Gogol's *The Wedding* (1922) integrated film projections in what the publicity poster pronounced an "electrification of Gogol," and what one of the actors described as "putting a plug and electric wire into his [Gogol's] posterior."[7] Eisenstein incorporated his film *Glumov's Diary* (1922) with theater, circus acts, sketches, agitprop, and song in *A Wise Man* (1922);[8] and from 1923 the Russian "Blue Blouse Group" followed his example in numerous popular club-theater performances. RoseLee Goldberg estimates that at its height, the Group involved more than

100,000 people across clubs throughout Russia, and in many ways marked "the ultimate realisation, on a grand scale, of Marinetti's variety theatre."[9]

Frederick Kiesler

Frederick Kiesler's 1922 multimedia design for the Berlin production of Karel Capek's *R.U.R.* (*Rossum's Universal Robots*, written in 1921) was one of the most extraordinary and high-tech of the early 1920s.[10] Using kinetic elements including moving side screens and an eight-foot iris that opened and closed to blind the audience with spotlights, Kiesler believed the mise-en-scène ensured that "from beginning to end, the entire play was in motion. . . . It was a theatrical concept to create tension in space."[11] The monumental stage backdrop was an impressive and elaborate mix of visual elements drawing on graphic design, cubism, constructivism, and the geometric abstract paintings of Kandinsky. It incorporated flashing neon lights, a circular film screen, and a rectangular screen that represented a type of closed-circuit television monitor for the factory director to observe and vet visitors approaching the factory. For this, a backstage mirror arrangement reflected and "projected" the live image of (offstage) visitors who walked in accurate perspective, as if towards the factory's spy "camera." When their admittance to the secret factory was authorized, the factory director used a remote control device to shut the screen window, and the visitors walked onto the stage from the wings.

The circular film screen was used to back-project prerecorded film sequences of the robot factory workers. The use of a moving camera to film these sequences created an engaging illusion whereby "since the camera was walking into the interior of the factory . . . the audience had the impression that the actors on the stage walked into the perspective of the moving picture too."[12] After the first few performances, Berlin police raised concerns over the potential fire hazard posed by the film projection system, and Kiesler constructed a trough of water above the screen. Thereafter, the film sequences were projected onto a waterfall, creating a "beautiful, translucent effect,"[13] and securing the production's place in history as the first to marry media projection and flowing water.

Among recent performances and installations following Kiesler's lead are Blast Theory's Virtual Reality performance *Desert Rain* (1999), whose title evokes its central metaphors of a desert terrain (a computer game–style representation of the battleground landscape of the first Gulf War) that is projected onto sprayed, running water, like a sheet of rain. The water-projection technique is "doubled" to evocative effect in Paul Sermon and Andrea Zapp's *A Body of Water* (1999) where high-pressure showerheads create a water curtain in the middle of a large shower room in a disused coal mine in Herten, Germany, which is projected onto from both front and rear (figure 4.1). From one side, visitors see a color projection of life-size, live images of some audience members in the colliery, who are visually composited (using chromakey techniques) with visitors interacting with them as they watch from the Lehmbruck Museum in Duisberg. The telematic link and blue screen effects between the two sites enables a visitor in one location to appear on the water

Figure 4.1 Paul Sermon and Andrea Zapp's *A Body of Water* (1999) uses fine water spray as a projection surface, a technique first employed in 1922 for *R.U.R.*

curtain projection together with a visitor in the other location, and to virtually scrub one another's back, as though together in the shower itself. Moving round the space to the other side of the water screen reveals another projection, old black-and-white archive footage of the shower room when it was operative and was used by over a thousand men each day. The "life-size documentary images of naked coalminers showering just as they once did in the very same place"[14] and their complementary action of *bukeln* (the local term for scrubbing each other's backs) is a powerful "realist" contrast to the colorful and cheerful virtual playacting of the telematic conjunctions on the other side. The two images do not overlap, although only a thin sheet of water separates them. Sermon notes the correspondences between the installation and Eisentein's use of the Moscow Gas Factory as a determining social narrative:

The visuals, together with the site-specific smells and sounds of coal dust and running water, as well as the location of the installation in the old mining complex, underline Eisenstein's concept of a metaphor that is reinforced by the reality and the given evocative aspects of a space. In *A Body of Water*, the simple yet complex act of "telepresent showering performance" turns into a collaborative re-experience and reflection of the former authentic social and working space.[15]

His collaborator and partner Zapp draws attention to the metaphoric aspects of the water screen, and the way it acts as a meeting point connecting past, present and future:

The flowing medium forms the heart of the installation and metaphor; it transports the public interaction and at the same time it reflects the area, the Ruhrgebiet, as a pulsating web of rivers and waterways. All the visual and conceptual layers meet here. On the one hand, the viewers are confronted by the new era, the interactive platform of networked communication, as a possible future. Yet on the other, they discover the ghost-like shadows of the past miners showering in the water—a flashback to the abandoned space and its former working culture.[16]

Erwin Piscator

In the 1920s, documentary footage was also employed with marked effect when Erwin Piscator brought edited newsreel film into the theater space to emphasize the political dialectics of his devised documentary production *In Spite of Everything* (1925). According to Hugh Rorrison, Piscator thereby contrived for the first time in theater's history "a dialectical interplay of factual material, for example setting off political intent (patriotic speeches in the War Credits debates in the Reichstag) against its military consequences (atrocity footage of the slaughter on the Western front)."[17] Piscator himself wrote how his combination of theater and film transformed the dramatic framework so that a didactic play (*Lehrstück*) could be developed from what might appear on the surface to be a spectacle-play (*Schaustück*).[18]

Piscator provoked anger from the management of the Berlin Volksbühne theater when he controversially inserted film of Lenin in his staging of Ehm Welk's play *Storm over Gotland* (1927), set in medieval times, as well as specially shot footage of five of the actors marching toward camera. As they march, their period costumes transform in a series of cinematic dissolves, placing them as characters within four historical left-wing revolutions—the Peasants' War, 1789, 1848, and 1918. The sequence epitomized Piscator's conception of the play as itself "an episode in the march towards communism,"[19] and its ultimate censorship by the Volksbühne led to Picator's resignation after three years at the theater.[20]

The year 1927 was a historic one in which the use of an onstage screen to project photographs and moving film images reached new artistic heights. In France, Paul Claudel's *Le Livre de Christophe Colomb* (1927) experimented with using the screen as a "magic mirror" to enhance the atmosphere and intensity of the text and, according to Frederick Lumley, to "open a road to dreams, remembrances and imagination."[21] Claudel wrote of the immense visual power, but equally the subtlety and sophistication of the stage projection screen in its ability to suggest, entice, and capriciously transform meanings. Where Piscator's film-theater was intellectual and politically didactic, Claudel's was sensory and psychological, disrupting notions of time and affecting audience "sensation"; and conceiving the projected body in relation to "shadows" and "ghosts" of the past and the future:

Why, when a flood of music, action and poetry entrances the minds of the audience, reply with a false heaven as crude and trivial as a café mural? Why not utilise the screen as a magic mirror where all sorts of shades and suggestions more or less vague and designs may pass, follow, and eliminate each other. Why not open the door of this troubled world where the idea gives birth to sensation and where the ghost of the future unites with the shadow of the past?[22]

But in the same year it was Piscator who provided the definitive early-twentieth-century multimedia theater production with his film-theater treatment of Ernst Toller's expressionist "Stationendrama" *Hoppla, Wir Leben!* (*Hurrah, We're Living!* 1927). Statio-nendramas progress through discrete self-contained episodes, in much the same way that hypermedia fictions and other online experiences including web-surfing do; and it seems apt and pertinent that this episodic structure served Piscator so well in creating one of the most historic precursors to digital theater. As in hypermedia dramas (and the medieval passion plays from which the dramatic term derives), the individual sequences in Stationendramas bear *some* connection to one another, but are distinct and do not progress through a conventionally logical, accumulative, or fluid dramatic structure. Nor do they conform to Aristotelian ideas of a unity of action, time and place. The "stations" through which the expressionist protagonist progresses (Karl Thomas in the case of *Hoppla!*) act as fateful signposts and crossroads where the forces of fate, choice, chance, and human will converge. They are points of revelation, reflection, and decision, and their paradigmatic equivalence to the hyperlinks, portals, and navigational nodes of today's computer-mediated experiences is clear. In *Hoppla!* Karl Thomas is released after eight years in a lunatic asylum, and becomes increasingly disillusioned when he discovers all his former revolutionary friends have conformed to bourgeois values, including Kilman, who has become a government minister. He plots to murder him, only for a right-wing assassin to succeed in the task before him. But Thomas is mistakenly arrested for the crime and is again declared insane. He hangs himself inside his cell minutes before his innocence is discovered.

For Piscator's production, Traugott Müller's complex set design comprised six rooms housed in two vertical scaffolding structures at either side of a central projection screen. The rooms' decor dispensed with painted backdrops in favor of mobile, transparent screens onto which film and slides of alternate locations—prison cells, living rooms, hotel rooms, and offices—were back-projected. This technique of using projection in place of traditional scenographic materials (wood, fabric) has been used to place performers within changing locations throughout the history of multimedia theater ever since, and has now reached new technological heights in three-dimensional digital designs by companies such as George Coates Performance Works.

On the central screen, film narratives and images of war, boxing matches, monetary crises, dancing, and newsreel montages, were sometimes projected during the stage action, and at others constituted a discreet interlude during blackouts between scenes. Two specially produced films opened the production. The first was an edited sequence of news-reels juxtaposing the First World War with the German Revolution, and incorporated specially filmed footage of the actor playing Thomas, locating him as a participant in both events. For the second,

The film screen in front of the set went up, the gauzes came down for the projected décor, and the scene in the condemned cell started. This was followed by the most effective part of the production. A huge clock on the screen intermittently ticked away the years from 1919 to 3 November 1927—that is, right up to the opening night, another bid for topicality—while news-flashes from Karl Thomas's lost years flashed on the screen. Political events like the communist risings in the Ruhr, Lenin addressing a mass audience, the rise of Mussolini, Sacco and Vanzetti, and the election of Hindenburg as German President in 1925, were punctuated with shots of dancing legs, boxing matches, and the frivolity of the 1920s. Loud jazz underscored the excitement of the eight-minute film, and at the end of it Karl Thomas's attempt to rehabilitate himself started.[23]

Piscator used a range of technical effects including loudly amplified radio broadcasts, and the theater's first use of ultraviolet light, which illuminated (only) the white skeleton-bone markings on the black costumes of performers for a macabre dance of death following the assassination, choreographed by the celebrated dancer Mary Wigman, a protégé of Rudolf Laban. Film footage ran for approximately half of *Hoppla!*'s overall production time, and was particularly important for its opening and climactic sections. Following Thomas's arrest, as Toller remarked at the time, "by the aid of the film he [Piscator] could show dozens of prison cells and soldiers silently marching up and down outside so that they were as oppressive to the audience as to the prisoners themselves."[24] In the final scene, prisoners in different cells within the three-tier set tap on the ventilation pipes to pass messages to one another as Thomas prepares his noose. Written transcripts of their communications are projected in motion onto the front gauze. A visually stunning climax is reached with the inclusion of a film projection of the Milky Way in the twenty-five-foot high center section of the set, a dense, exploding cloudburst of stars.

Nicholas Hern argues that Piscator's use of film was "partly for the sake of documentary precision and partly to render the composite impact of eight years' technological advance on the bewildered mind of Karl Thomas."[25] Lumley presents an alternative perspective: that Piscator felt Toller's social satire was not radical enough, and employed film primarily to provide the political and dramatic punch the play lacked.[26] While acknowledging the innovation and impact of Piscator's methods, Lumley goes on to warn of what he perceives to be the dangers of theater's incorporation of film, adopting a theater purist tone typical of many critics past and present: "The effect can be used in moderation to great effect (Piscator's methods were a sensation), but beyond a certain point the method becomes a trick as precious as a toylike Cinerama. It is no substitute for good drama, and the temptations it offers for crude sensationalism are only too apparent."[27] Toller was equally skeptical about the effect of the use of film in the production of his play, and later described Piscator's attempt to unify theater and film as "a mistake," since he considered that "the two arts followed different laws."[28]

Critical references to multimedia performance work in the following thirty years are rare, and it appears that after a few years of experimentation with film at the end of the 1920s, theater returned to its traditional live roots, with only occasional and normally relatively incidental inclusion of film. The political climate of the 1930s dampened or explicitly repressed avant-garde activity, with economic depression in the United States and elsewhere, the rise of fascism in Spain, Italy, and Germany, and the 1934 dictat by arts minister Zhdanov that Russian art should solely dedicate itself to socialist realism. From 1939, the trauma of the Second World War, and its long aftermath of political remappings and socioeconomic reconstruction, marked a twenty-year hiatus in multimedia performance, and indeed, avant-garde performance in general. RoseLee Goldberg's history of performance art is indicative of this, devoting over one hundred pages to the period 1909–1932, but less than four pages to cover the period 1933–1951.[29]

Robert Edmond Jones and the Multimedia "Theater of the Future"

Although little multimedia theater actually took place during the 1940s and early 1950s, throughout that period Robert Edmond Jones toured the United States to preach its gospel with what Frederick C. Packard Jr. describes as a "missionary zeal."[30] Jones, one of America's leading theater designers, toured the country between 1941 and 1952 delivering lectures with such titles as "The Theatre of the Future" (1941). Jones's vision, which he first discussed in a contribution to the *Encyclopaedia Britannica* in 1929 entitled "Theory of Modern Production," was the fusion of theater and cinema. "In the simultaneous use of the living actor and the talking picture," he wrote, "there lies a wholly new theatrical art, an art whose possibilities are as infinite as those of speech itself."[31] He argued that film offered a resolution of the theater dramatists' problem of how to express effectively the inward reality and subconscious of their characters, since film offered "a direct expression of thought before thought becomes articulate . . . the moving picture is thought made visible." In his "theater of the future," the live actor would thus represent the character's outer self and the screen imagery the inner world of imagination, subconscious, and dream: "the two worlds that together make up the world we live in."[32]

The synthesis of film and theater was an obsessive theme that Jones developed in his book *The Dramatic Imagination* (1941), the leading textbook for American theater students at the time,[33] and later reworked and distilled as great orations during years of lecture tours. The lectures, finally transcribed by Delbert Unruh and published in 1992 as *Towards a New Theatre*, essentially elaborate the ideas expressed in the 1929 *Encyclopaedia Britannica* article. However, perhaps out of frustration that such experimentation was not taking place in the United States, they emphasize the universality and beautiful simplicity of the model. "At the root of all living" he says in "Curious and Profitable" (1941) "is a consciousness of our essential duality . . . and now there is a way to say all this in the theatre—simply, easily, straight and plain."[34] He explains in quasi-Freudian terms how film images can be used to reveal a character's inner thoughts and feelings, concluding in typically direct and economical fashion:

On the stage: their outer life; on the screen: their inner life. The stage used objectively, the screen used subjectively, in a kind of dramatic counterpoint. Not motive as it is revealed in action, but action *and motive* simultaneously revealed to us. The simultaneous expression of the two sides of our nature is an exact parallel to our life process. We are living in two worlds at the same time—an outer world of actuality and an inner world of vision.[35]

We would note that Jones's characterization of the synthesis of film and theater as a straightforward, uncomplicated process—"It's as simple as that" he declares at one point[36]—fails to acknowledge the significant demands the form makes on both theater-makers and audiences. Jones provides no sample scenarios, and the few examples of the types of subconscious screen images he envisions are fairly trite. Nor does he engage with the problematics of spectatorship within the "new theater," but rather assumes that audiences will intuitively and readily understand and embrace this realization of the split duality of humanity made existentially whole before their eyes in film-theater. Rather, as Grotowski once said of Artaud, he "left no concrete techniques behind him, indicated no method. He left visions, metaphors."[37]

Jones's extraordinary lectures are largely unread, despite the fact that they have an arguably equivalent power and originality of theatrical vision as the canonical works of Artaud, Grotowski, Barba, and Brook, and similarly evoke a transformational, magical theater. The allegorical "Curious and Profitable" begins with Jones describing his creation of a spell to conjure a wise, godlike figure to Earth. This virtual visitor, a man "from Utopia," is taken around theaters of all kinds: popular and variety, classical and literary. The visitor, who has never seen theater or film, analyzes these sagely and acutely, describing the "unforgivable" dreary mediocrity of a theater that should be teeming with life but has lost its wonder, predating Peter Brook's notion of "Deadly Theatre";[38] a tepid, jaded, stunted theater of uncertainty that can only reflect life's uncertainty, not its vibrant magic; a theater corresponding not to consciousness, but to an inner life that is "pitifully meager."

The visitor is then taken to the cinema, where he describes film as a medium of pure thought: "This screen drama we are watching is not a drama at all—it is a dream about a drama, a memory of a drama, the thought of a drama. . . . For the past hour we have been dreaming. . . . This medium is a dream medium."[39] But he explains how the film-makers are misguided in making pathetic efforts to try to pass off the images as real when they cannot be so, when they are "apparitions, emanations, part of the self sent forth at will." The film he witnesses is a substitute, ersatz, "poor man's" theater, when it should be pure imagery, "pure thought stream," pure dream.[40] The visitor then rushes out of the cinema and into a theater for a few minutes to compare the two. He describes the contrasting ontologies of spectatorship in the two spaces: the shared, communal experience of theater, its audience awake and aware; the somnambulant cinema audience "an agglomeration, not an entity,"[41] each person solitary and dreaming separately, even though they dream the same dream.

Finally, Jones and the visitor attend a theater where a vaudeville comedian sings a song while behind him a film image of him is projected, which sings along in a duet, whereupon the visitor gravely declares: "I know now why I came."[42] This fragment from a musical comedy is "the germ of a new theater" of limitless possibilities. "A man sings to us and his inner self sings with him. Such a thing has never happened before in the history of theatre. . . . [It] is tiny, it is tentative, but it is alive. And it is pivotal."[43] In its relationship to the live performer, the film image becomes "visible thought" and "visible emotion," creating a new expressive form conjoining the subjective, dream quality of film with the power of actuality, where the "unembodied part" of the performer meets the embodied part.[44]

Jones's largely forgotten discourses constitute the first major theories of multimedia theater, and they remain important to our understandings of many digital performance works. He defines fundamental principles and divisions between theater and moving-image media, including their contrasting modes of spectatorship that affect the sensory and psychological experiences of audiences. These ideas are now being endlessly re-rehearsed and recycled by numerous writers grappling with ontological definitions in current discussions of "liveness," normally without any reference to him—although this is not the case with Philip Auslander, in many ways the central protagonist/antagonist in the debate. Jones is one of the first theorists to analyze and define precisely why our mental energies and physical metabolisms appear to alter when watching a live or recorded body in performance. Jones's understanding of the filmed and projected body as "unembodied . . . part of the self sent forth at will" also predates parallel theories of the virtual body within cyberculture, which were considered radical ideas in the early 1990s, fifty years after Jones had already theorized them.

But where Jones's argument differs from some fields of virtual theory is in his call to reunite the virtual and physical bodies; since the virtual body on its own (as in the cinema image) is an apparition, a memory, a reverie. Jones stresses that it must be brought into conjunction with the live body to ignite a total theater based on a quasi-spiritual paradigm of making the split subject whole. By contrast, cybertheory's prevalent reading of the virtual body invokes the Cartesian division between mind and body: in effect, the mind and body swap roles, with the mind projected outward to become a virtual body operating in cyberspace. Jones's theater concerns their symbolic unification in space and time—real and virtual, mind (film) and body (stage).

The metaphorical framing of the "Curious and Profitable" paper, where Jones speaks to his own double, encapsulates the central metaphor for the theater he envisions: a doubled theater, as we are seeing today, where actors and dancers perform with their projected doubles and alter-egos. The importance of "Curious and Profitable" extends to media reception-theory, including an early example of a critical exploration of the psychologically coercive and propaganda effects of media products. On viewing a newsreel, the visitor questions why the audience accept the images as reality: "These are not events. They are mental pictures of the events occurring after the events have taken place. . . . They are canalizing our thought processes. They are telling us what our desires and motivations should be."[45]

Laterna Magika and 1950s "Happenings"

It was not until 1958, with the founding of the Laterna Magika in Czechoslovakia by Joseph Svoboda and Alfred Radok, that multimedia theater practice began to develop significantly once again. Inspired by fellow Czechoslovak Emil Burian's use of slide and film projections in his "theatregraph" productions, including Wedekind's *Spring's Awakening* (1936), the company used film in conjunction with multiple screens and trick effects to create illusions and fantasy spectacles. Complex "polyscreen" systems were developed in conjunction with moving conveyor belts and diffused and directional lighting effects to attain a "theatrical synthesis of projected images and synchronised acting and staging."[46] On their 1958 European tour, they carried stage and projection technology weighing over 15,000 pounds, including ten different sizes of mobile projection screens and two moving belts, which slid them into place during performance. For Svoboda, conjoining film and theater offered a unique cross-disciplinary art form that would expand dramaturgic possibilities, and create new meanings and artistic dimensions. An equanimity and balance between the aesthetic and dramatic functions of the two forms was fundamental to his conception: "The play of the actors cannot exist without the film, and vice-versa—they become one thing. One is not the background for the other; instead you have a simultaneity, a synthesis and fusion of actors and projection. . . . The film has a dramatic function."[47]

In its detailed attention to scale and precision timing between stage action and film image, Laterna Magika was highly influential in demonstrating the potential for visual syntheses of the live and the recorded, and for its narrative possibilities. The company holds a unique place in the history of multimedia theater, undertaking some of the most advanced and pioneering experiments aimed at visually melding film and live performers; and creating "a sense of life that came from the ability to see reality from several angles, on several time levels, connecting images which cannot be joined in our limited 'real' world."[48] The company continues today in their own theater in central Prague, and our visit to their production of *Odysseus* in 2004 confirmed their continuing visual invention in the creation of a complex narrative "theater without words" combining dance, drama, film projection, and mechanical stage effects (figure 4.2).

While Laterna Magika developed techniques to intensify dramatic narratives, more abstract projection experiments and happenings were beginning to take place, most

Figure 4.2 Laterna Magika's historic work since 1958 fusing live theater with film and video imagery continues today with productions such as *Odysseus* (2004).

notably in the United States. Milton Cohen's *Space Theatre*, in conjunction with the ONCE Group was established in 1958, and developed a neo-Bauhaus environmental space where rotating mirrors and prisms cast multiple projections onto triangular screens and a ceiling dome above spectators who sat or lay down on cushions. Similar spaces would be developed later in the early 1970s, such as Alan Finneran's elaborate Theater Machine, which used kinetic sculptures and rotating film and slide projection screens.[49]

Film and slides were projected around the walls and ceilings in some of the first "Happenings" during the 1950s, including Allan Kaprow's ground-breaking *18 Happenings in 6 Parts* (1959), and the seminal, untitled 1952 Black Mountain College performance by artists including John Cage, Robert Rauschenberg, and Merce Cunningham. Rauschenberg "flashed 'abstract' slides (created by coloured gelatine sandwiched between the glass), and film clips projected onto the ceiling showed first the school cook, and then, as it gradually moved from the ceiling down the wall, the setting sun."[50] Rauschenberg's later art gallery piece, *Broadcast* (1959) brought together a painting and three radios, which the viewer could retune to create different auditory effects, in what Hans-Peter Schwarz considers "possibly the first direct predecessor to interactive media art."[51]

In 1958, the German Fluxus artist Wolf Vostell placed an arrangement of television sets in the window of a Parisian department store for *TV De-coll/ages* (1958). In part a commentary on the intrusion of television media into daily life, the monitors played highly distorted images and set the scene for the explosion in video art experimentation that was to come in the 1960s.[52] Its aesthetic would be developed by Nam June Paik into breathtaking, monumental sculptural works using hundreds of TV sets playing treated found footage and abstracted color images—"TV has attacked us all of our life" said Paik, "now we're hitting back!"[53] Other artists would go on to emulate Vostell's conscious and explicit conceptual aim to follow the lead of the futurists and surrealists to attempt to revolutionize life itself by infusing art into daily life, and to create new, mediatized forms of the *Gesamtkunstwerk*:

Marcel Duchamp has declared readymade objects as art, and the Futurists declared noises as art—it is an important characteristic of my efforts and those of my colleagues to declare as art the total event, comprising noise/ object/ color/ & psychology—a merging of elements, so that life (man) can be art.[54]

Performance and Technology Since 1960

Art is produced by a succession of individuals expressing themselves; it is not a question of progress.
—MARCEL DUCHAMP[1]

Duchamp was in error; nothing comes of nothing in the history of art.
—BRIAN SEWELL[2]

The 1960s: A New Poetics of Media Performance

Like political and social history, the history of performance has involved gradual and incremental evolutions punctuated by intense periods of more sudden or revolutionary change.
We would characterize three such periods in the history of multimedia performance, each
roughly corresponding to a decade: Futurism during the 1910s, mixed-media performance
in the 1960s, and experiments linking performance and the computer during the 1990s,
which constitutes the main focus of this book. The first and last of these were most directly
inspired by the development of "new technologies," and we have already discussed futurism in relation to the impacts and influence of wider technological breakthroughs of its
time. In the 1990s, although the computer was by no means new and digital arts had
been developing since the 1960s, computer technologies became much more accessible to
artists and led to widespread digital performance activity. This was particularly linked to
what is popularly termed the "digital revolution" following the introduction of more
affordable hardware and "user-friendly" software; digital cameras; the home PC; and the
establishment of the World Wide Web.

Computer-generated imagery began to emerge as a distinct art form in the early 1960s.
John Whitney's *Catalog* (1961) was one of the first films to use computer transformations
(created on military analogue computer equipment), and was followed by important
computer films such as Stan Vanderbeek's *Poem Fields* (1964), and by artists such as Vera
Molnar and Charles Csuri. The 1965 *Computer Generated Pictures* exhibition at New York's

Howard Wise Gallery included work by pioneering computer artists such as Michael A. Noll and Bela Julesz, and computer arts continued to develop steadily throughout the '60s. But the catalysts for "revolutionary" developments involving analog and electronic media within theater, dance, and performance during the 1960s, particularly in the later half of the decade, were more inspired by cultural and ideological change than technological leaps or the emergence of computer art. At the same time, the 1960s did see a period of technological optimism and innovation, crowned by the 1969 American moon landing. Equally, just as the impetus for artistic innovation in the 1990s relied on the accessibility of computer technologies, there was a comparable sense of accessibility and democratization of video technology following the introduction of portable camera systems, most notably the Sony Portapak in 1965. However, the proliferation of multimedia performances during the late '60s actually relied far more on the much older technology of film, and video would find its place in live performance later, during the 1970s and '80s. This was primarily because video shooting became portable and accessible in the mid-'60s, but video-editing equipment remained expensive and in the hands of professional companies, and it was not until the 1970s that more affordable, semi-professional three-quarter-inch tape-editing systems emerged.

The late 1960s marked a period of intense political and cultural changes that converged from many sides. The women's liberation and gay rights movements blossomed, and the politics of the anti-establishment left reached a peak in Europe with the Paris student revolts of May 1968 and in the civil rights and anti–Vietnam War movements in the United States. Around the same time, a counter cultural youth movement took up Timothy Leary's call to "turn on, tune in, and drop out" so as to undergo profound changes of consciousness inspired by psychedelic drugs, political activism, new age spirituality, and a new politics of the body conceived through sexual revolution. Mark Dery would later reconfigure Leary's mantra for the computer age, suggesting (following Philip Proctor) that "the '90s are just the '60s upside down"[3] and a new "cyberdelia" is emerging where "turn on, boot up, jack in" becomes the chant of cyber-hippies and techno-transcendentalists.[4]

The performance of the sixties reflected, embodied, and arguably provided some direct impetus for these movements, leading by example. The Living Theatre combined revolutionary politics and Eastern mysticism to demand *Paradise Now* (1968), and ecstatic body rituals were conceived by Carolee Schneeman to celebrate *Meat Joy* (1964), and by The Performance Group to relocate *Dionysus in 69* (1969). In 1968, Peter Brook's *The Empty Space* and Jerzy Grotowski's *Towards a Poor Theatre* set fresh and demanding theatrical agendas concerned with communion and spirituality, making the invisible visible, and Artaudian notions of cruelty and physical rigor. Performance art blossomed as a significant and influential form, and political theatre found its radical, agitprop voice. The Fluxus group of artists, performers, and musicians began creating quasi-algorithmic work reliant on the execution of tasks based on predetermined models and instructions, and made audience participation a key theme. Theater loosened its ties from dramatic text and reinvented itself in happenings and myriad vibrant forms of interdisciplinary, visual, and environmental performance. At the same time, dance was breaking free from its own rule-bound roots, whether classical or modern, in the work of choreographers including Merce Cunningham, Ann Halprin, Trisha Brown, Lucinda Childs, Steve Paxton, Yvonne Rainer, and Twyla Tharp. The Judson Dance Theatre in New York became a center for experiments reevaluating the nature of dance and choreography and offering potent alternatives to dominant dance aesthetics using simple walking and everyday movement, personal gestures, chance structures, geometric patterns, ritual actions, and repetitions.

Just as the futurists in 1913 had spoken of an age of new beginnings, with "no tradition, no masters, no dogma,"[5] many '60s artists had a similar sense of shaking off the past and wiping cultural and artistic slates clean: an equivalent feeling of liberation from *passéist* tradition. Geoff Moore, director of the Welsh multimedia theater group Moving Being recalls that "at the time both inner and outer space were seemingly innocent unpolluted frontiers. It was as if we had the privilege of starting a new journey."[6] He goes on to observe that the excitement of audiences equaled that of artists, and that there was a shared unspoken agreement about mutual discoveries: "If you didn't come out of a performance challenged, potentially changed, with a feeling that you had been taken further, you had been cheated."[7] It is interesting to note that in 1999, at the height of the digital performance movement, Forced Entertainment director Tim Etchells echoed the sentiments: "Ask this of each performance: will I carry this event with me tomorrow? Will it haunt me? Will it change you, change me, will it change things? If not it was a waste of time."[8]

Intermedia Performance

Multimedia performances began to proliferate. In 1960, *The Ray Gun Spex* performances at Judson Church included a piece by Al Hansen where performers moved around the space at different speeds with handheld film projectors, directing projections of airplanes and parachutists around all the walls and ceiling.[9] His *Requiem for W. C. Fields Who Died of Acute Alcoholism* (1960) featured clips of Fields's movies projected onto Hansen's white shirt. In 1964, in a movie theater near the Pratt School of Art and Design in New York, one of Robert Wilson's earliest performances combined film and live choreographed dance movements.[10] Jeffrey Shaw, nowadays one of digital arts' leading innovators, experimented with projecting film onto inflatable structures, and choreographers such as Alex Hay incorporated film in performances such as *Grass Field* (1966).

From 1961, Roberts Blossom developed what he called "Filmstage," expertly combining live and filmed dance pieces, sometimes in counterpoint to one another, at others in perfect synchronisation, with film close-up details of feet and body parts moving in precise time to the live dancers' routines. The same essential techniques are now still being applied in numerous digital dance theater performances, whether using prerecorded footage or networked (telematic) links to other live dancers performing in synchronization elsewhere. Blossom also utilized laboratory film processing effects, such as sudden switches to negative, or from black and white to color, which were timed to coincide with live stage transitions such as changes of costume, music, or choreographic tempo-rhythms.

While most artists and groups at that time primarily created their own media projections, others used found footage, including one of the first performances to incorporate video (rather than film), Wolf Vostell's *You* (1964). Three television sets on three hospital beds were placed by the side of an outdoor swimming pool, each running a separate distorted image of a different basketball game. The mise-en-scène included a supine woman on a trampoline between a pair of inflatable cow lungs, and another naked woman on a table clutching a vacuum cleaner. Whereas before the 1960s film had generally been employed in live performance for its positive aesthetic impact or dramatically synthesizing effects, *You* typifies the use of video by artists during the 1960s and '70s to politically critique television culture as a negative and hegemonic force. Video commonly became employed to portray television and mass media as a tool of consciousness numbing, social coercion and disintegration, and political propaganda and oppression. In *You*, although the audience is offered a symbolic liberation through the actual destruction of the televisions, the message is deeply ironic, with a patronizing "big brother" voice issuing the instructions through loudspeakers. "Allow yourself to be tied to the beds where the TVs are playing", the voice commands, "Free yourself. . . . Put on a gas mask when the TV burns and try to be as friendly as possible to everyone."[11]

The ONCE Group's large-scale open-air performance *Unmarked Interchange* (1965) had the feel of a drive-in movie, with a giant screen playing the Fred Astaire and Ginger Rogers movie musical *Top Hat* (1935). Within the screen were numerous sliding doors and panels at different levels, which opened and closed to reveal live performers engaged in various narratives and activities. These open sections of the screen ruptured the visual totality of the film projection to highlight the live actions: a candlelit meal for two; a man playing a piano; a man reading the pornographic novel *The Story of O* through a microphone and having custard pies thrown in his face; women putting drawings of human figures onto a moveable washline.[12] Found footage was also central to John Cage and Ronald Nameth's *HPSCHD* (1969), a five-hour "immersive" event surrounding the audience with projections of one hundred films and eight thousand slides.[13]

Robert Whitman became a leading figure in the development of multimedia happenings in the 1960s, creating what Sally Banes describes as events with "a magical, mythic aura . . . fairy tales for Americans."[14] He was adept at conjoining the real and the projected in surprising and highly theatrical ways, and in *Shower* (1965) he projected film footage of a life-size woman taking a shower onto the water-sprayed, billowing curtain of a working shower (figure 5.1). By synchronizing the scale and action of both the film and live performance, in much the same way that the Laterna Magika and other "Black

Figure 5.1 Robert Whitman's *Shower* (1965). Photo: Museu d'Art Contemporani de Barcelona.

Light" Prague theater companies conceive performances, Whitman created memorable effects to simultaneously confound and delight audiences. In *Prune Flat* (1965), a double image of one of the performers was achieved by projecting a film of her onto her live figure, in exact scale. The live performer wore a long white dress and synchronized her physical movements exactly with her superimposed film projection. As her celluloid image took off her coat and other clothing, throwing them aside, the live performer mimed and mirrored the same actions precisely, but without undressing, until finally both the live and film figures stood still, her projected body naked on the live performer's dress (figure 5.2).

This idea has been repeated in a number of recent digital performances, including the Gertrude Stein Repertory Theatre's interpretation of Alfred Jarry's *King Ubu* (2000). The company specialize in conjoining live actors with actors from different locations projected into the theater space using video-conferencing software. In *King Ubu*, digital figures are projected and mapped onto the bodies of live performers wearing neutral costumes to create what they call "digital puppets" or "distance puppets." A similar technique is used to powerful effect in Tony Oursler's video installations of the 1990s, where mini-projectors beam video faces onto the blank cloth heads of small rag dolls. Set on stands or lying in open suitcases like forgotten ventriloquist dummies, the tiny bodies of these

Figure 5.2 Live performers, their shadows and their filmed counterparts converge in Robert Whitman's 1965 production *Prune Flat*. Photos: Babette Mangoldt.

mannequins remain inert while the faces and heads are eerily animated. Bemused eyes stare out and flick nervously from side to side; one doll cries softly; another talks briefly and then is silent; another moans and erupts into a scream, and its straining face of pain appears to be trying to break itself away from its spherical head of rags and out of its nightmare.

Michael Kirby's 1966 structuralist happening *Room 706* used a triangular concept in both its setting and performance structure, repeating the same discussion by three men three times: first on audiotape, then on film, and finally as live performance. In his reflections on the incorporation of film into what he called the "New Theatre" of the 1960s, Kirby emphasizes how ideas of meaning and information structures are redefined to become dependent on the relationship between elements, rather than the character of the images themselves. He makes distinctions between images and actions that work to communicate meaning, and more conceptual and abstract forms, which are often juxtaposed within multimedia theater. Information and images pass back and forth between stage and screen and the composite effect increases the "intellectual density" of each, but there is often no attempt to form a cumulative meaning through the addition of film. Rather, it is employed to form a continuum of meaning and abstraction: "Meaning and significance are not synonymous," he points out, before suggesting, "the limits of this new theatre are only the limits of science and the imagination."[15]

Kirby's article appeared with a number of other important viewpoints from theorists and practitioners including Susan Sontag, Alain Virmaux, Joseph Svoboda, and Roberts Blossom in the Fall 1966 edition of *TDR: The Drama Review*, which has become one of the most cited journal issues in the history of multimedia performance. It is notable how the enthusiastic optimism for film-theater conjunctions following only a relatively few years of significant activity in the US from around 1960 parallels a similar wave of critical euphoria in relation to digital performance in the mid 1990s following the advanced experiments taking place from around 1990.

Nam June Paik

The year 1966 saw the emergence of a brief artistic manifesto relating cybernetics to new art processes, "Cybernated Art" by Korean-American video and performance artist Nam June Paik, which included the following:

Cybernetics, the science of pure relations, or relationship itself, has its origin in karma. Marshall McLuhan's famous phrase "Media is message" was formulated by Norbert Wiener in 1948 as "The signal, where the message is sent, plays equally important role as the signal, where message is not sent". . . . As the Happening is the fusion of various arts, so cybernetics is the exploitation of boundary regions between and across various existing sciences. . . .
The Buddhists also say

    Karma is a samsara

      Relationship is metempsychosis

  We are in open circuits[16]

Paik's prolific and remarkable work in video art and performance was influential throughout the 1960s (and well beyond), and he famously manipulated video images of McLuhan's head in *Demagnetizer (Life Ring)* (1965). Displaying television footage and videotape he had shot as one of the first proud owners of the newly introduced Sony Portapak camera, Paik held a powerful magnet in the shape of an eighteen-inch diameter ring and moved it toward, away from, and against the TV screen. The electrostatic onscreen faces of McLuhan and others distorted and swirled in dramatic spiral-like (and interestingly, computer artlike) patterns in response.[17] He continued to rework the electronic video image throughout the '60s, using a range of powerful magnets in conjunction with televisions whose internal circuitry and controls he had adjusted, and developing other idiosyncratic imaging devices including the "Paik-Abe Video Synthesizer" (from 1964) in collaboration with Japanese engineer Shuya Abe. Paik also created a number of interactive systems to allow gallery visitors to affect screen images, such as *Participation TV* (1963), where visitors spoke into a microphone to visually mutate abstract electronic images on a video monitor.

Paik's McLuhan-meets-cybernetics message became even clearer when he began to sculpt television sets that thrust out physical ganglions and extensions; and his images and signals bled into both artificial and natural forms. Paik's aesthetic developed to reconfigure televisions not simply as sculptures, but as clothing, gardens, forests, buildings, and robots. As Margaret Morse puts it: "our image-surround no longer represents a world apart: it is our world. The computer processing of images, in which Paik played a pioneering role is another indication that images were now themselves raw material, the natural world upon which we exercise our influence as subjects."[18] By the 1980s Paik was constructing literally awesome creations such as *The More the Better* (1988), a three-channel, circular video installation tower sixty feet (18 m) high, housing 1,003 television monitors. Randall Packer and Ken Jordan suggest that Paik "presents himself as a techno-shaman, synthesizing art and technology in an effort to exorcise the demons of a mass-consumer, technology-obsessed society," and describe his art of the period as "poignantly cynical pieces that comment on American techno-culture dominated by starry-eyed optimists."[19] But Paik's cynicism is extremely mischievous, highly aesthetic, and sagely Zen, as demonstrated in his essay for the catalogue of the New York Museum of Modern Art's *The Machine: As Seen at the End of the Mechanical Age* exhibition in 1968:

Plato through the word, or the conceptual, expresses the deepest thing.
St. Augustine thought the sound, or the audible, expresses the deepest thing.
Spinoza through the vision, or visible, expresses the deepest thing.
TV commercials have all three.[20]

As John Cage had famously "composed" the ultimate minimalist piece of music without any notes (4′33′, 1952), Paik created a film without images or sound in 1964, *Zen for Film*, where he projected clear film leader. Just as the four and a half minutes of Cage's silence had highlighted the ambient and random sounds in the auditorium, the audience's attention was drawn to the chance tiny scratches and subtle changes in the "dance" of dust particles in the projector gate on the blank white screen. The film predated Owen Land's[21] similar but more famous *Film in Which There Appear Sprocket-Holes, Edge Lettering, Dirt particles, etc.* (1965–66)—a busy film by comparison with its visual revelation of the holes and lettered edges of a clear piece of celluloid. The *Zen for Film* screening became a "performance" when Paik appeared and stood with his back to the screen to become part of the frame, illuminated in the projected light.

This ultra-minimalist mise-en-scène of the film-plus-performer has been remediated in the digital age by British artist Anita Ponton, whose work features in Franklin Furnace's extensive web archive of performance art conceived for streaming video. In *Seen. Unsaid* (1998), wearing a peroxide blonde wig and a man's suit, she stands in front of a Super 8 projection of clear film, which is treated with intermittent large scratches and hand-drawn marks. Closely edited lines and fragments of dialogue from old Hollywood movies (predominantly from the '30s and '40s) provide a soundtrack to which Ponton's mouth mimes, her head jerking anxiously from side to side as she schizophrenically "plays" the dozens of characters. As she puts it, her startled figure lip-syncs "as if speaking in tongues, as if unable to help herself. . . . She is a trapped, ephemeral figure, perhaps a figment of celluloid imagination. Yet she is also live, breathing and moving. . . . The female body is here a machine."[22] To the background sound of an insistent heartbeat, the fragmented film voices begin to dramatically argue and disagree, and the live figure, trapped in the white cinema frame, becomes increasingly frantic and agitated, like a medium who has contacted and is now possessed by malevolent, warring spirits.

In *Dies Irae* (1998), Ponton is similarly subject to technological possession, hanging in a long black dress, suspended by her hair with just the tips of her toes in contact with the floor, as if floating. As a soundtrack plays the voices in her head, she gently sways, never blinking, "an automaton, a dolly, mutely isolated in her own melodrama. . . . She presents herself as a spectacle of the unpenitent sinner, condemned for being herself by the voices that engulf her."[23] These Beckettian echoes (redolent of *Not I*, 1972) also suffuse the opening to her *Say Something* (1996), where she rocks herself forward and backward with the precision of a metronome in a large, Gothic wooden throne. The movements are punctuated by moments of absolute, intense stillness, recalling the figure of the woman in her rocking chair in Beckett's *Rockaby* (1981). Later, the ever-present ghostly spirit of media that characterizes her work suddenly appears to intrude upon and entrap Ponton's figure: a film projection of a laughing, talking face projected and mapped directly and eerily onto Ponton's own.

Sexy Technology

In the 1960s and '70s, Paik's numerous performance collaborations with avant-garde cellist and performance artist Charlotte Moorman included her submerged in a tank of water,[24] and playing a "TV Cello," where she bowed three different sized television screens between her legs.[25] Media scandal followed both of their arrests following the premiere of *Opera Sextronique* (1967) that the police interrupted and stopped after she performed a striptease while simultaneously playing the cello. The police were perhaps forewarned by Paik's characteristically caustic publicity poster showing a picture of Moorman in black bra and pants, cello in hand, and the words:

After three emancipations in 20th century music (serial, indeterministic, actional) . . . I have found that there is still one chain to lose . . . that is. . .

PRE-FREUDIAN HYPOCRISY

Why is sex a predominant theme in art and literature prohibited ONLY in music?

How long can New Music afford to be sixty years behind the times and still claim to be serious art?

The purge of sex under the excuse of being "serious" exactly undermines the so-called "seriousness" of music as a classical art, ranking with literature and painting.

Music history needs its D. H. Lawrence, its Sigmund Freud.[26]

Later, in a wonderfully sardonic response to the incident, Moorman's modesty and public decency were preserved when two miniature television screens playing Paik's treated videos were fitted inside two Plexiglas cases and taped to her breasts when she played the cello topless for *TV Bra for Living Sculpture* (1969). During the 1970s, Paik's giant video installations and colorful, highly treated and quickly edited tapes such as *Global Groove* (1973) continued to echo the ideas of both McLuhan and cybernetics to emphasize the medium of TV, the raw signal itself as its own self-defining content.[27] *Global Groove* opens with a prophetic statement read by Russell Connor: "This is a glimpse of the video landscape of tomorrow, when you will be able to switch on to any TV station on the earth, and the *TV Guide* will be as fat as the Manhattan phone book."

Paik's other pioneering achievements include one of the first important experimental "dance for screen" videos, a kaleidoscopic collaboration with Merce Cunningham, *Merce by Merce by Paik* (1975, with Charles Atlas and Shigeko Kubota). Using video synthesizers, Paik created dazzling (though by today's standards crude) color-saturated multi-layered effects, and chromakeyed Cunningham against a range of landscapes, dance studios, and abstracted environments where he interacted with other dancers, outline figures, and doppelgängers. He would later offer a unique take on one of America's most inventive theater companies in his half-hour video art "documentary" *Living with the Living Theatre* (1989, with Paul Garrin and Betsy Connors).

Billy Klüver and U.S. Partnerships Between Artists and Scientists

During the 1960s, Swedish electronic engineer Billy Klüver became in many ways the central figure in the art and technology movement, collaborating with many seminal artists and performance makers, including Paik. In 1960 he worked with Jean Tinguely on *Homage to New York* to create a large and elaborate junkyard machine that destroyed itself through the self-activation of electrical triggers in a ground-breaking twenty-seven-minute performance at New York's Museum of Modern Art.[28] During the early 1960s, Klüver worked for four years with Robert Rauschenberg on *Oracle* (1965), the most advanced interactive art project of its time. It was conceived as an environment where light, sound, temperature, and smell would change as a person walked through it; and Rauschenberg insisted that no wires should connect its different sculptural elements. Klüver used wireless Sennheiser microphones and built his own wireless transmitters, but struggled for years trying to eliminate interference and technical gremlins, later reflecting that he just "couldn't do it with the technology available in the 1960s."[29]

Over the same period, he worked on a neon painting with Jasper Johns and on a performance collaboration, *Variations V* (1965) with, among others, Merce Cunningham and John Cage, which included the projection of a film by Stan Vanderbeek and a video by Paik. Klüver built an elaborate system whereby photoelectric cells registered movements within the space and an array of microphones detected sounds, and these phenomena were processed to create soundscapes that acted as the audio score for the dancers. The performance was an important precursor of computer-controlled interactive artwork, as critics including Michael Rush and Söke Dinkla have noted.[30]

By far the most historic event conjoining performance and technology during the 1960s involved Klüver's collaboration with a wide range of artists, theater and dance makers, and thirty of his engineering colleagues from Bell Laboratories for the seminal *Nine Evenings: Theater and Engineering* (1966). Ten performances took place in New York's Sixty-Ninth Regiment Armory building over nine evenings in October 1966, which were attended by more than ten thousand people. They included dance and technology works by choreographers Lucinda Childs and Deborah Hay and involved huge numbers of performers. Yvonne Rainer's *Carriage Discreteness* featured many future luminaries, including Carl Andre, Ed and Kathy Iverson, Meredith Monk, Michael Kirby, and Steve Paxton. Rainer spontaneously chose actions and placements from a remote plotting table and relayed the choreographic instructions live to the performers via walkie-talkie. In parallel, as the program notes put it:

Event continuity to be controlled by TEEM (theatre electronic environment modular system) in its memory capacity. This part will consist of sequential events that will include movie fragments, slide projections, light changes, TV-monitored close-ups of details of the dance-proper, tape recorded monologues and dialogues, and various photo-chemical phenomena including ultra-violet light.[31]

For John Cage's *Variations VII*, David Tudor modulated live sounds picked up via telephone lines, microphones, and communications bands to create an "indeterminate" musical composition, also featuring frequency generators and household appliances.[32] Rauschenberg's performance *Open Score (Bong)* took place in near darkness and involved five hundred volunteers who made gestures that were monitored by infrared cameras and projected onto three screens within the vast performance space, part of which was laid out as a full-size tennis court. During the performance, visual artist Frank Stella played a tennis match with professional tennis star Mimi Kanarek, using wired, sound-emitting rackets designed by Klüver. The sounds of the rackets also controlled the lighting, and video images of the match were relayed onto the video screens. Rauschenberg reflects how "the unlikely use of the game to control the lights and to perform as an orchestra interests me. The conflict of not being able to see an event that is taking place right in front of one except through a reproduction is a sort of double exposure of action. A screen of darkness and a screen of light."[33]

The success of *Nine Evenings* prompted discussions between Klüver, Rauschenberg, Robert Whitman, and Fred Waldhauer to establish an organization to further collaborations between artists and engineers, and led to the formation of Experiments in Art and Technology (E.A.T.) in 1967, which continued with Klüver as President until his death in 2004. Klüver publicized E.A.T. vigorously to recruit engineers willing to volunteer their expertise to arts projects, publishing advertisements in the *New York Times*, articles in technical journals such as *IEEE Spectrum*, and establishing a competition with a prize for the best artwork. By the following year, he had established a network of some three thousand engineers, and E.A.T. matched these to artists and brokered and supported their relationships. The organization's mission to unite artists with technologists has since been mirrored in recent large-scale organizations such as ZKM[34] in Germany (established 1989) where guest artists are invited to collaborate with technologists and software designers.

Klüver's pioneering work in the 1960s has led Garnet Hertz to dub him "the God-father of Art and Technology,"[35] and Klüver offers interesting perspectives on the rapid development of arts practice incorporating technologies in the United States during the 1960s and '70s. He maintains that in Europe, artists were conditioned to follow artistic agendas set by intellectuals who were not part of the practice of art, but nonetheless exerted massive influence on the arts world, like "little dictators." He describes how European artists would agonize over their directions and which manifesto to sign, despite the fact that they had been drawn up "by intellectuals who had nothing to do with art."[36] By contrast, Klüver suggests that in the United States there was not the same concern with "intellectual overlay," and this resulted in far greater artistic freedom and experimentation.

Whether or not one accepts Klüver's reasoning, it is beyond dispute that during the 1960s and '70s the most important developments in the conjunction of technology with theater, dance, and performance art took place in the United States. That is not to say that some multimedia performances did not go on in Europe and elsewhere, but they had neither the adventurous thrust nor the lasting impact of work in the States. During the same period in the United Kingdom, for example, there was an equivalent and highly significant golden age of experimental theater and performance, but in the form of a sociopolitical and aesthetic avant-garde firmly rooted in the live, which rarely incorporated media technology. Sandy Craig's overview of the period, *Dreams and Deconstructions: Alternative Theatre in Britain* (1980) surveys significant developments in new writing, performance art, actor-based ensembles, and political, feminist, community, ethnic, physical, and visual theater. But her book makes only one reference to a British company incorporating media into their live events: Moving Being. If we contrast this with an equivalent overview of the same period in the United States, Theodore Shank's *American Alternative Theatre* (1982),[37] we find a veritable plethora of references to artists and companies incorporating media and technology into their performances.

It is interesting to note that Craig's edited book on British alternative theater includes a page of analysis by Steve Grant of Nicholas Wright's production of Heathcote William's play *AC/DC* (1969) at London's Royal Court Theatre. In his lengthy description and analysis, Grant makes no reference whatsoever to the production's use of a bank of video monitors playing news bulletins, which perhaps reflects the temperature of British interest in the use of media in live performance at that time. While omitting any reference to the media onslaught directed at the audience through the video monitors, Grant nonetheless emphasizes the play's attack on the dangers of the effects of "the constant barrages of undifferentiated media information . . . [an] assault of 'psychic capitalism' . . . [and] the enveloping horrors of 'media rash'."[38] *AC/DC* aroused equal excitement and controversy through its exploration of the erosion of individuality within the contemporary media and drug culture, and was described in a review in *The Sunday Times* newspaper as "an electronic nightmare."[39] In line with more recent debates on mediatized consciousness and cloning, one of the play's characters declares: "They're altering my neural rhythms . . . they're coding my cells . . . the whole atmosphere needs cloning."[40]

Moving Being

Geoff Moore, director of Moving Being, the only multimedia theater company referenced in Craig's book, reflects that in the United Kingdom in the 1960s a false polarity was set up between companies beginning to experiment with mixed media, and defenders of traditional theater and the "well-made play." While hybrid theater forms were developing in America and other parts of Europe, "establishment" conservatism in theater criticism compounded by the rigid artistic categories defined by the Arts Council for funding, inhibited interdisciplinary, cross-media creative freedom.[41] In an illuminating self-published monograph reviewing Moving Being's huge body of work from 1968 to 1988, Moore reflects on the peculiar myopia and "visual illiteracy" of British theater critics, and their staunch resistance to more abstract, nontextual forms. He also recalls a conversation he had with Robert Wilson in 1976, who vented his frustration that his internationally acclaimed production of *Einstein on the Beach* (1976, with Philip Glass) was not invited to London:

There is no viewpoint in the English for people doing anything outside your country. You don't want it. It's a backward country with no understanding of contemporary art. They tell me to do Shakespeare. I do what I do, someone else can do Shakespeare. Centuries after everyone else you take Martha Graham. She's an old lady dying and you bring her to London and go crazy.[42]

Moving Being created visually compelling large-scale theater performances with a "Wilson-esque" sense of pageant and grand, operatic design, which skillfully incorporated 16mm film and video projection. *Dreamplay* (1974) melded August Strindberg's play with sublime pieces of dance and allusions to Sigmund Freud and Edvard Munch. Thought unstageable when it was written in 1901, Strindberg had originally conceived it as a multimedia performance which would incorporate projections using the recently developed magic lantern to enhance "the inconsequent yet transparently logical shape of a dream."[43] We recall a memorable integrative sequence between stage and screen, where the live performers mirrored their movements on film, synchronously entering the stage space and camera frame, and walking forward carrying large pieces of wood. These were assembled as a tower in the center of the stage, and onscreen in the center of the field, where it was set alight and burned as a bright bonfire.

Film was used to intensify the heady, erotic atmosphere of the company's exploration of *The Journals of Anaïs Nin* (1975) with dramatis personae including Antonin Artaud, Kenneth Anger, Henry Miller, and Luis Buñuel. The company traveled to Paris to find the house Nin lived in when she wrote her journals. They found it boarded up and deserted, and used a ladder to gain entry to the garden where she had entertained the likes of Artaud, Miller, and André Breton, and filmed it as one of the back-projections for the piece. On their return to their base in Wales, they discovered that by a strange twist of fate there had been a problem with the gate mechanism on the film camera, which rendered a juddering effect to the footage, but which nonetheless gave "the exact shimmer of French Impressionism that the production required."[44]

Moving Being was the foremost British multimedia theater group of the '60s and '70s, bringing together actors, dancers, musicians, film, and video to create intensely dramatic, complex, and at times sublimely beautiful stage works. In 1975, *The Guardian* newspaper described them as "a company of eight performers in partnership with twentieth century technology [who] create a rich theater tapestry," adding that director Geoff Moore was "a master" of a new language of multimedia theater.[45] The following year, *The Irish Times* enthused at the spectacles they achieved which "make use of just about every means to which a theater may give house room. . . . The result is utterly joyous, enchanting, life-enhancing, a spring breeze blowing through the stage door to disturb the fixed assumptions of a less flexible theater . . . [that] may spur imagination and beget progeny."[46]

Cybernetic Serendipity

Although British developments in multimedia performance in the 1960s lagged behind what took place in the United States, initiatives in the conjunction of computer technologies with the wider visual and musical arts did not. The *Cybernetic Serendipity—The Computer and the Arts* exhibition at London's Institute of Contemporary Arts in 1968 involved 325 artists and engineers, and was seen by more than 60,000 people.[47] Exhibits included computer graphics and film animations, computer texts, music composed and played by computers and, according to exhibition director Jasia Reichardt, "the first computer sculpture."[48]

The exhibition marked an important celebration of the history of cybernetics—whose genealogy was highlighted on the exhibition walls and on IBM computer displays—and the creative potentials of computers as quasi-autonomous art-makers. Computer art pioneers who used algorithms as direct prompts and sources for machinic "inspiration" displayed works, including Charles Csuri, Kenneth Knowlton, and Herbert W. Franke. Robots and "cybernetic machines" took center stage, including Gordon Pask's *Colloquy of Mobiles* (1968); machines that created their own drawings; and a computer linked to television sets that transferred sound into visual patterns displayed on the monitors. Visitors whistled tunes into a computer programmed by Peter Zinovieff, which then improvised around the captured musical themes; and there were environmental installations by artists including James Seawright, Gustav Metzger, and Wen Ying Tsai, some of which responded to changes in light and sound.

Margaret Masterman's *Computerized Haiku* (1968) was a particularly popular interactive exhibit, and emphasized the creative partnership and cybernetic feedback relationship between human and machine. The computer was equipped with a thesaurus, and programmed with semantic directives and an algorithm using a haiku-frame corresponding to the pattern of the Japanese poem: three lines of 5, 7, and 5 syllables. Users chose a number of single words from different menus corresponding to different frames, and the computer filled in the gaps using its thesaurus to produce a completed haiku. Masterman provides examples in her article about the piece:

ALL BLACK IN THE MIST,
I TRACE THIN BIRDS IN THE DAWN.
WHIRR! THE CRANE HAS PASSED.
ALL GREEN IN THE BUDS,
I FLASH SNOW PEAKS IN THE SPRING.
BANG! THE SUN HAS FOGGED.[49]

Masterman notes the quality of haikus produced and how visitors, including scientists of international repute, "carefully treasured" and took home the poems they had created. She reflects how computer algorithms empower the non-poet, since they provide a framing structure and a series of formulaic "tricks" in the same way that traditional poetry applies the tricks of alliteration, rhythm, rhyme, and so on. These "allow words to combine more freely (because more mechanistically), that is, with fewer socially and psychologically motivated constraints."[50]

Mitchell Whitelaw divides the *Cybernetic Serendipity* artworks on display into two types, the first generative, like Masterman's haiku machine, "exploring the aesthetics of permutation" to bring forth objects such as paintings, patterns, and poems, the second "non-object" or "post-object" oriented, concerned instead with dynamic and interactive processes. The first type he relates to "plastic explorations of the machine aesthetic," the second to transparent "translations across sensory-kinetic modes (sound into light, light into motion)" where the viewer's attention is drawn to the dynamic processes under way.[51]

As with Klüver's collaborations and the establishment of E.A.T. in the United States, *Cybernetic Serendipity* involved close collaborations between artists, engineers, and computer systems designers. Jasia Reichardt's book *Cybernetics, Art and Ideas* (1971) reflects on the three years of collaborations leading up to the exhibition, and its seventeen essays by artists and scientists reveal enthusiastic optimism about the aesthetic capabilities of computers in late 1960s art. Gordon Pask discusses "the cybernetic psychology of pleasure,"[52] Iannis Xenakis provides scientistic theories "towards a metamusic,"[53] and Dennis Gabor muses on "the mechanization of genius."[54] Reichardt's own essay argues that although throughout history new technologies have always resulted in changes to artistic forms, the development of the computer has brought about a unique and unprecedented change. This involves the sudden, unanticipated participation in art-making of large numbers of non-artists. This is the result of the new technologies enabling a different approach to the creation of art, rather than, as in the past, simply being refinements of older media (such as the invention of oil paint) or offering new forms of image-making (such as screen printing). They have thus inspired engineers and others, who in the past would never have thought of creating artworks, "to make images for the sheer pleasure of seeing them materialize."[55] For Reichardt, the computer collapses previous assumptions by engineers, scientists and, mathematicians (that "art is magic") and by artists, composers and poets (that "technology is a mystery"), defining a turning point whereby ingrained classifications and labels such as "artist" and "scientist" are shrugged off. The computer's role as an accessible "art for all" machine would be confirmed later, when Apple released its very first home computer in 1984, which was sold with integral painting and drawing programs.[56]

The *Cybernetic Serendipity* exhibition later toured the United States, and highlighted not only an unprecedented crossover of interests between artists and scientists in the potentials of the computer as an art-machine, but also the popular interests of lay individuals of all ages and backgrounds. Its monumental popular (as well as critical) success is reflected in the numerous enthusiastic British press reviews highlighting its universal appeal; Reiner Usselman notes that the press were in unanimous agreement that the exhibition was "guaranteed to fascinate anyone from toddling age to the grave."[57] *The Guardian* described the huge numbers of delighted people who would previously "never have dreamed" of attending a contemporary art exhibition, while the London *Evening Standard* posed the rhetorical question: "Where in London could you take a hippy, a computer programmer, and a ten-year-old schoolboy and guarantee that each would be perfectly happy for an hour without you having to lift a finger to entertain them?" Even that bastion of old-fashioned British conservatism, *The Lady* magazine waxed lyrical to its upper-middle class (or aspiring upper-middle class) readership. "One must go," it began in perennially regal tone, "to the present exhibition at the Institute of Contemporary Arts, not to understand in the least what is going on but to experience that particular tingle which is inherent in an act of threshold-crossing."[58]

Crossing Thresholds

The idea that a threshold was being crossed was an inherent part of the political, social, and sexual mores of 1968. Following the huge success of the 1966 *Nine Evenings: Theater and Engineering* performances in the United States, the crossover between art and science became a popularly celebrated marriage in the United Kingdom through the 1968 *Cyber-*

netic Serendipity exhibition. In the same year, Jack Burnham published his influential article on systems approaches within art, "Systems Esthetics" (1968), and in the following year "Real Time Systems" (1969), which explored early ideas of artistic conjunctions between organic and nonorganic systems, and of man-machine symbioses. He discusses the cybernetic organism as an artwork, and the articles still retain a vital currency, proposing art as a system that embraces "realtime information processing", interactive dynamics, and the notion of the "post-object," predating our current understanding of the "virtual object."[59] A number of writers have taken up the theme of the "post-object" in relation to work of the late 1960s, including Paul Brown, who notes the profound effect the *Cybernetic Serendipity* exhibition had on him: "Previously . . . I had seen artworks as objects. Now they became processes."[60]

The following year heralded the earliest example we have been able to find of the conjunction of live actors and digital computers (in this case, a primitive mainframe), Malcolm Le Grice's *Typo Drama* (1969), presented at the Event One computer art exhibition at London's Royal College of Art in April 1969.[61] Le Grice and Alan Sutcliffe's custom-designed software generated pieces of text and instructions, which the actors then spoke and executed. In the same year, spurred on by the computer film experiments of Stan Vanderbeek and John and James Whitney, Le Grice gained access to the largest computer in Britain (and the only one with a direct visual output), taught himself Fortran 4 programming, and spent nine arduous months creating the abstract computer-generated film *Your Lips* (1970).

The year 1969 also saw video art celebrating an artistic high point with the New York *TV as a Creative Medium* exhibition, and the founding of Frank Oppenheimer's Exploratorium in San Francisco, a "hands-on museum of science and art dedicated to the concept of museum as a learning center."[62] In 1970 the Jewish Museum in New York hosted *Software—Information Technology: Its New Meaning for Art*, an exhibition featuring a time-shared central computer, and exhibits including a "guerilla radio system" by John Giorno, and solar-powered broadcasts from the windows of the museum by Theodosius Victoria. MIT's Architecture Machine Group exhibited *Seek* (1970), a computer-controlled environment populated by live gerbils, where electromagnets continually rearranged lines and towers of small, high-tech cubes, in what Adrian Henri describes as "a metaphor for the planners' constant problem of human demands versus planned programme."[63] In 1971 the Los Angeles County Museum held an *Art and Technology* exhibition at Los Angeles County Museum, and many such sci-art festivals, events, and exhibitions were to follow.

Multimedia Performance Since 1970

From 1970 to the end of the twentieth century there was a proliferation of the use of media projections in theater, dance, and performance art, using both screens and video monitors. The relative inexpensiveness, immediacy, and ease of use of video technology led many artists and groups to explore possibilities for the integration of visual media within their live work, as well as to create video art pieces in their own right. The three decades from 1970 was a period of theatrical experimentation that elevated the visual over the verbal, and for Bruce King, "the use of media technology (film, video, sophisticated sound equipment) has become a hallmark of experimental theater."[64] The vast majority of the period's most celebrated performance artists, theater groups, and directors created work incorporating film or video. An indicative but by no means comprehensive list includes Richard Foreman, Robert Wilson, Peter Brook, The Wooster Group, Jan Fabre, IOU, Robert Lepage, Forced Entertainment, Tim Miller, Mabou Mines, Station House Opera, Laurie Anderson, Meredith Monk, Ping Chong, Peter Sellars, Linda Montano, Squat Theater, Lee Breuer, John Jesurun, George Coates, Blast Theory, Joan Jonas, Moving Being, Gob Squad, Forkbeard Fantasy, Desperate Optimists, Meredith Monk, Yvonne Rainer, Trisha Brown, Lucinda Childs, La Fura Dels Baus, Guillermo Gómez-Peña, and Rachel Rosenthal.

Space here does not allow a comprehensive review of the vast range of the work combining live performance and recorded media since the 1970s, and many examples will emerge in later chapters as precedents to particular digital performances. But we will look briefly at a few theatrical examples that are either indicative of the types of experiments taking place during the period, or that have since proved influential. Phaedre Bell has discussed how film or video may be used as a primary or secondary medium within theater—whether the event is primarily a film that also uses performance, or a theater performance that also uses film. She coins a third category *dialogic media productions*, where there is an equal balance between the live and the recorded, and where the film/video has real agency and interactive impact on the performance through "inter-media exchange".[65] This emphasis on the media's real agency upon and dialogic exchange with the live action on stage emerged strongly within multimedia theatrical performance during the 1970s and '80s, and would become a central and defining feature of digital theater production in the 1990s.

Bell's own analysis centers on Laura Farabough's solo performance *Bodily Concessions* (1987) as an "exemplary" dialogic media production, in which the live Farabough on stage represents her sleepwalking self, video monitor footage represents her conscious self, and a video projection screen represents her dreams. The subtle interactions between the three elements—live performer, video monitor, and screen—is at the core of the piece, where "the currencies of exchange can include gaze, movement, language and light . . . [and] constructions of time, space, presence and absence."[66]

Literal "dialogic" exchange between stage and screen in the form of spoken dialogue exchanged between live and recorded performers has been commonly used, as in John Jesurun's *Deep Sleep* (1985). Characters onstage and onscreen argue about who is more real, and the live performers are gradually drawn into the screen spaces, leaving a sole figure on stage at the end. The scripted discourses and the free movements between stage and screen of Jesurun's performers emphasize his stated belief in the complementarities of the live and the mediatized rather than their opposition. A similar dialogue about the nature of live and mediatized reality takes place in his *White Water* (1986) between live actors and twenty-four recorded ones, each shown in close-up on monitors surrounding the audience.[67]

The Wooster Group

The Wooster Group's controversial *Route 1 & 9 (The Last Act)* (1981), a deconstruction of Thornton Wilder's play *Our Town*, utilized video in all the three forms that Bell defines: as primary, secondary, and dialogic media. The first part of the performance dispenses with live performers, and consists of a video lecture on the meaning of *Our Town* delivered by Ron Vawter on four suspended TV monitors in a gallery space within the Performance Garage (New York), before the audience move into the main theater space. There, four monitors are suspended over the stage, and as the performance progresses, scenes from Wilder's plays are performed in naturalistic, soap-opera style close-ups, in stark contrast to the rowdy, pantomimic acting of the live performers, who all wear blackface makeup (figure 5.3). This use of blackface and the group's deliberately provocative stereotyping of

Figure 5.3 Willem Dafoe plays a naturalistic scene from Thornton Wilder's play *Our Town* on video monitors above a pantomimic, blackface Ron Vawter in The Wooster Group's *Route 1 & 9 (The Last Act)* (1981). Photo: Nancy Campbell.

black characters aroused considerable controversy and accusations of racism, leading to a 40 percent cut in their funding from the New York State Council for the Arts.[68]

As an onstage party progresses, the monitors are lowered and the video narrative becomes the primary action and the live performers become quieter and less animated on stage, "giving focus" to the screens. As the actors on video finally reach a tearful dramatic climax, the live performers pull focus once more and burst into an exuberant song and dance routine. In the final section, the live actors sit quietly on stage, and the focus shifts again to the monitors, with color footage (previous video was all black and white) of a van traveling out of New York and onto the open highway. As this progresses, another, very old black and white television is wheeled onto the stage, showing video of a copulating couple.[69]

Three years later, the use of separate video sequences running on numerous onstage monitors in one of The Wooster Group's most celebrated productions, *LSD . . . Just The High Points* (1984) marked what Marianne Weems describes as "a watershed for cross-media work."[70] Its cool and detached use of close-up performers, guns, point-of-view walking, and numerous other low-key, nuanced images on multiple monitors within the set provided a distinctive, ultra-hip, Brecht-meets-postmodernism gestalt to one of the bravest and most truly innovative performances of the late twentieth century. Since it is one of the most academically discussed productions in performance history, we will decline to describe it in detail here, but rather leave it to Weems to summarize some key points and the underlying pragmatics of its multimedia features:

The actual media in the performance was pretty low-tech, but the aesthetic was built on a sophisticated electronic sensibility, for example "rewinding" and "fast-forwarding" through enormous sections of text, or staging some performers on monitors, and some live. The thing that distinguished this work from performance art's mandatory television-on-stage aesthetic was that the inclusion of the technology was pragmatic, content-driven. For instance, it was necessary to put Michael Kirby on stage because he couldn't be at the show that night, and it was necessary to rewrite, speed through, and "blur" the text because the Group had been threatened by a lawsuit from Arthur Miller (for their adaptation of his 1953 play *The Crucible*).[71] (figure 5.4).

Laurie Anderson

We have not structured this volume in a series of practitioner profiles, but rather examine particular works by artists and performance companies in relation to our thematic divisions of chapters around notions such as the body, space, and time. Practitioners whose bodies of work seem to us primarily to relate to a single and particular terrain are discussed only there, while others reoccur throughout the volume. But we will break with our own tradition here to look in detail at Laurie Anderson, whose longevity and iconic status within the field through decades of innovation seems to warrant a more holistic analysis to trace her work and influence through time.

Figure 5.4 The Wooster Group's *LSD . . . Just The High Points* (1984). Left to right: Jeff Webster, Michael Kirby (on video), Peyton Smith, and Willem Dafoe. Photo: Bob Van Dantzig.

Anderson is justifiably considered the doyenne of digital performance, one of its most senior and prominent exponents, with a worldwide reputation for technological invention and early adoption of digital techniques in music, narration, elaborate multimedia theater events, and visual and electronic art works. Anderson's work speaks quietly in measured tones, carefully explicating her position and view, and she remains at heart an old-fashioned storyteller who has perfected her craft with finesse but with remarkably little mystery or camouflage. The stories frequently use poetic forms and complex interdisciplinary techniques but are invariably extremely direct, inasmuch as her stated aim is first and foremost to communicate: "One of my jobs as an artist is to make contact with the audience."[72] This primacy of purpose is not always evident in digital performance practice, where many works have left audiences bemused, but despite Anderson's voracious experimentation with technologies, the *issue* of her artistic vision has remained at center stage.

Her concern to utilize high technology yet retain simplicity of form and directness of narrative was evident in some of her earliest work, including *For Instants* (1976/77) which represents an interesting early example of the technique of live "motion sensing." At the conclusion of the performance she lay down on the stage and delivered a monologue toward a candle flame in front of her face that moved and danced in response to her speech and breath. As it flickered away from her, it crossed the track of a photocell beam linked to the lighting board, causing a spotlight to activate and intermittently illuminate her. The intimate candlelit monologue thus progressed through bursts of bright light alternating with near darkness, in direct response to the kinetic effects affected by her voice and breath on the flame.

Anderson's use of digital technologies, and particularly her creation of new instruments, effects, and sounds, bears testimony more to her drive to find the most appropriate means of communicating what she wants to say, than to any formalist approach to technology, or desire to experiment with it for its own sake. Indeed, her performances and lyrics frequently reveal a concern that technology is becoming a substitute for humanity; and her love/hate relationship with it is clear in the hit song *O Superman* (1981), which first brought her to international prominence. It is critical of distance, of absence, and of American military applications of new technologies.

Anderson experiments and creates with digital technologies in exactly the same fashion as she experiments and creates with everything else to maximize the effectiveness of her statement, using myriad available tools—digital, nondigital, analog, nonanalog, organic, inorganic. With hindsight it seems that Anderson is an artist who *happens to be* a digital artist: if one could deny her access to any computers, to digital manipulation, to electricity even, she would still be an important experimental artist telling stories. As a storyteller, Anderson maintains a fascination for and undertakes constant experimentation with, above all, words. For her first major performance, *As: If* (1974), a series of words was projected on to a large screen to emphasize thematic and narrative elements of her narration. On the left, words were associated with language, on the right, words referred to ideas and concepts connected with water, for example, "SOUND: DROWN."[73] The relationship between "liquid" and "language" and the combined sense of the "liquid nature of language"[74] have been an abiding point of exploration throughout her work. Early performances such as *Engli-SH* (1976) centered on ideas of the translation and transformation of language, as well as the creative exploration of the patterns and sounds of spoken language. In *United States Part II* (1980), Anderson again made use of projected onscreen words, which appeared following an announcement that "language is a virus from Outer Space." Against a musical sequence—with her band incanting the refrain "letter words"—a series of projected words ran in alphabetical order, concluding with "V Sign; WWII; X Ray; Y Me; Zzzzzzzz."[75] Figures from one of the first videogames, *Space Invaders,* then swarmed onto the screen before the words "Game Over" flashed on and off, in one of the earliest examples of a performer appropriating imagery from the world of digital games. The game paradigm, invariably also including the "Game Over" coda, has since been used in numerous digital performance works including Blast Theory's

Desert Rain (1999) and ieVR's *A Midsummer Night's Dream* (2000, with the University of Kent).

Anderson's notebooks demonstrate constant invention with turning objects into media devices: performers become screens (1975); speakers are put *into* the mouth (1978); audio glasses (1979); headlight glasses (1983, built by her longtime electronics engineer Bob Bielecki and destined to become one of the emblematic images of Anderson's working persona); light in mouth (1985); "hand-lights" (1985); and video glasses (1992). *Drum Dance* (1985), part of *Home of the Brave* (video 1986, audio CD 1990) explored an early form of wearable computing in the form of a dissembled electronic drum kit that could be activated by "playing" or dancing in the suit in which it was embedded, much in the manner being explored simultaneously by Benoit Maubray in various streetwise electro-costumed audio-manifestations in Germany during the mid and late 1980s. The same inventiveness in converting ordinary objects into media transmitters is still apparent much later, most noticeably in the development of the "Talking Stick" for *Moby Dick* (1999). A digital instrument and control center in the form of a six-foot stick (also built by Bielecki with Interval Research Corporation) in wireless contact with a six-foot bank of computers, Anderson employs it variously as a lance, harpoon, gun, violin, and jackhammer.[76] The Talking Stick produces richly textured sounds as well as controlling (via the computers) lighting, sound, and visual projections; mixing live instrumentation and voices; and adding digitally processed loops and samples.

The violin, which Anderson learned to play as a very young child and which she has frequently transformed and adapted with electronic appendages, is her most familiar trademark and regular companion. The fluid relationship between music, technology, and language is epitomized in her designs for various violins, commencing with one she adapted in the late 1970s. Recalling Nam June Paik's *Random Access* (1963), in which strips of audiotape were hung on a wall for spectators to play by running them over the playback head of a magnetic tape player, the violin strings were replaced by an analog audio head, and the horsehair of the bow by strips of audiotape: "This 'tape-bow-violin' can create a sound-speech that never existed before. As the bow is passed across the audio bridge, a totally reversible music-language is heard: 'no' on the up-bow becomes 'one' on the down-bow, 'yes' becomes 'say'."[77]

Themes and techniques frequently recur to be further developed or perfected in subsequent performances. *At the Shrinks* (1975) explored the relationship between patient and psychologist using a simple technology she described as "a fake hologram," where projections were cast onto a 3D modeled figure. This permitted, in her words, "a way of doing a performance without being there,"[78] and this capacity for performance at distance realized its full digital and emotional potential nearly a quarter of a century later in her major gallery event *Dal Vivo (Life)* (1998) at the Prada Gallery in Milan. On the ground floor were multiple "fake holograms" with projected images of ambiguous or mistaken identities, while the upstairs gallery displayed a full-size statue of a seated prisoner on which was cast, via a live video feed, the live image of a prisoner in a cell five miles away. Anderson recounted that the prisoner offered to participate because for him it was a "virtual escape," whereas gallery visitors were confronted with being party to one-way surveillance and a living being in their midst whom they could not affect and who acted as if they were not present—an arresting creation of simultaneous presence and absence.[79]

The same continuity in progressively developing the creative potentials of technology is evident if one compares *United States* (1983), the first occasion Anderson used an ortho-dox large-scale (2,000-seat) theater space, with her later multimedia spectacle *Moby Dick* (1999). The former was an "opera" of giant proportions that contained thousands of film and slide images, projected using equipment specially adapted by Bielecki and artist Perry Hoberman; sixteen years later, "absolutely everything is run through a computer," but *Moby Dick* (1999) is likewise "visually . . . a transparent, ever shifting sea of images [and] technically it is a model of electronic engineering."[80] Acclaim followed both productions, although Anderson has not been without her critics. Sally Banes, for example, acknowl-edges the technological invention of *United States* but seriously questions its content:

Like its subject, Anderson's *United States* is monumental (eight hours, heavy technology) and fre-quently dull. . . . Must a performance about trivial culture—or the trivial aspects of a very complex culture—be as shallow and pretentious as the life it describes? . . . The references to popular culture are eerie and empty, rather than vibrant. They desiccate, rather than vitalize, the world they describe. . . . In the end she says nothing, but in such a seductive package.[81]

In large-scale theater performances, Anderson's "seductive package" includes multi-faceted multimedia staging configurations that emphasize the three-dimensionality of the stage. In *Halcion Days: Stories from the Nerve Bible* (1992), four large projection screens span the lower part of the cyclorama, with one vast screen above them, while separate projec-tions are beamed onto a huge three-dimensional cube and a sphere suspended about five meters in the air. For a 1994–95 tour of a later incarnation of the project, *Stories from the Nerve Bible*, Anderson published a book and created an interactive website, "The Green Room," enabling an exchange of ideas and information between herself and her audience, attempting to find "an underground"—a methodology—whereby people could them-selves be expressive artists rather than just "fans," a condition that Anderson considers too supportive of the aesthetics of corporate America. This was also the period of another digital "first," with her release of her highly original CD-ROM *Puppet Motel* (1995 and 1998, with Hsin-Chien Huang), which we discuss in detail in a later chapter.

Amid a wealth of achievements, Anderson is still chiefly thought of as a musician/com-poser, who is ranked by critics such as William Duckworth alongside some of the great twentieth-century contributors such as John Cage and Philip Glass.[82] Her recording career is extensive and includes narration and poetry as well as experimental music recordings including *New Music of Electronic and Recorded Media* (1977), *O Superman* (1981), *Big Science* (1982), *You're the Guy I Want to Share My Money With* (1993, with John Giorno and William Burroughs), *Bright Red* (1994), and *Live at Town Hall* (2002). The latter is an extraordinarily charged album recorded in New York just eight days after the September 11 terrorist attacks on the World Trade Center in 2001. One can only tremble at the import of lines from *O Superman* (1981) on that occasion, that repetitively refer, with awe and trepidation, to the coming of American planes.

Laurie Anderson is a prolific multimedia artist in the spirit of the word's original meaning, as a *multiple*-media artist who utilizes different media forms to realize alternative creative processes, structures, and "products." The *United States* (1984) theater performance spawned a paperback that included stories, anecdotes, poems, songs, images, and commentary; the move from one medium to another is a regular feature of her output. Videos have been reinterpreted and reissued as audio CDs, as with *Home of the Brave* (video 1986, audio CD 1990); books have become performance tours and websites, as with *Stories from the Nerve Bible* (1993–95); *Dal Vivo* was both exhibition and photographic document (1998 and 1999 respectively). In addition, she has created numerous videos and films, and contributed music to films by Wim Wenders and Jonathan Demme; dance pieces by Bill T. Jones, Trisha Brown, and Melissa Fenley; radio pieces for National Public Radio, Expo 92 in Seville, and the BBC. She has exhibited artworks at major galleries including the Guggenheim Museum in New York and the Center Georges Pompidou, Paris, and in 2003 she became the first artist in residence at NASA, an experience she recounts vividly and with great comic panache in *The End of the Moon* (2004–5). It is her restless energy and multi-skilled expertise as a storyteller, performer, composer, violinist, keyboard player, digital artist, author, poet, and inventor—the compleat late-twentieth-century artist— that ensures Anderson a place in several "halls of fame," not least for being an architect of new digital forms in her ceaseless examination and sharing of observations about the human condition.

II

Theories and Contexts

Liveness

Clyde: And so finally, Miss Karma, the theatre is superior to cinema because whereas in cinema everything is misplaced, in theatre the four corners of the stage are the four corners of the earth.

Karma: But that still doesn't explain why people still walk out in the middle of a play.[1]

The Liveness Problem

The notion of liveness has been a perennial theoretical problem since it divided critics and theatergoers almost a century ago following the incorporation of film footage into live theater, and it remains a conundrum that is continually wrestled with both in performance studies and in wider cultural and cyber theory. It is an agonizing problem, which by turns clouds and obfuscates, then clarifies and illuminates understandings of digital performance. Theories of liveness take a difficult, even treacherous path. They twist and turn through wider technological theory, from Heidegger's phenomenology of "chained slaves" and Benjamin's notion of disintegrating auras, to McLuhan's "media as message" and Baudrillard's simulations and simulacra. Discourses on liveness meander, diverge and frequently hit brick walls in the contrasting positions taken by performance theorists such as Susan Sontag, Michael Kirby, Patrice Pavis, Matthew Causey, Johannes Birringer, Peggy Phelan, and Philip Auslander. We will not attempt to analyze and summarize the total picture, but we will concentrate on drawing out some key concepts from what has become a torridly dialectical debate.

We will begin by going directly to a principal and originary core of the "problem": the medium of photography. Most screen-based visual images used in digital performance are not computer generated, but derive initially from a lens-based camera system, which is then digitized for manipulation within the computer. Photography therefore provides an essential starting point for discussion of digital media imagery and its relationship to liveness. Performers use a range of media in their work from photographic stills to film, video, and digital media, and the significant aesthetic and technological differences between them are marked. But their common link is a lens-based optical recording technology, that is to say, a photographic system.

In Venice in 1845, the British art critic John Ruskin bought an early photographic daguerreotype[2] of a historic building and wrote excitedly to his father: "It is very nearly the same thing as carrying off the palace itself; every chip of stone and stain is there."[3] It is the "very nearly" of the photographic or mediatized image, its precise degree of closeness and its exact relationship to its referent and the "real," that lies at the heart of the problem of the still fiercely contested debate. We highlight the word "problem" and could equally use the term "paradox," because meditation on the different theoretical viewpoints surrounding visual recordings and reproductions can bring sudden "eureka" affirmations that are followed immediately by doubts: a nagging sense that the argument is very nearly proven, but not quite. Ruskin himself would struggle with the notion of the liveness of the photograph and revise his view. His early thoughts, so close to Barthes's, as we will see, would in 1875 become more allied to Benjamin's thesis: "A photograph," wrote Ruskin, "necessarily loses the most subtle beauty of all things . . . all glowing and warm shadows become too dark."[4]

Benjamin Versus Barthes

Even the most perfect reproduction . . . is lacking in one element: its presence in time and space.
—WALTER BENJAMIN[5]

Every Photograph is a certificate of presence.
—ROLAND BARTHES[6]

Walter Benjamin's "The Work of Art in the Age of Mechanical Reproduction" (1936) has become one of the most cited texts in theoretical discussions of digital arts and culture, perhaps only eclipsed in the citation league table by William Gibson's definition of cyberspace as a "consensual hallucination."[7] Amidst numerous discussions of the paper, its title has itself been reconfigured in digital discourses by a number of writers, including Bill Nichols's "The Work of Culture in the Age of Cybernetic Systems" (1988) and Brett Terry's "The Work of Art in the Age of Digital Historiography" (1999). Sandy Stone, less direct in her homage and less literal in her scansion (though no one has ever got that right), nonetheless pays tribute in her enjoyable book *The War of Desire and Technology at the Close of the Mechanical Age* (1996).

Benjamin's central argument is that "even the most perfect reproduction of a work of art is lacking in one element: its presence in time and space, its unique existence at the place where it happens to be. . . . The presence of the original is the prerequisite to the concept of authenticity."[8] Thus, he discerns in mechanical reproductions (such as films, photographs, and prints) a depreciation of the presence of the artwork and a withering of its essential aura.[9] This also extends to views of nature, where crucial auratic elements are eliminated when reproduced through film and photography, which issue to them "an invitation to a far-reaching liquidation."[10] Benjamin's critique of the mechanical dilution of presence and liveness in a reproduction work of art and its comparative lack of authenticity has been seized upon by both live performance purists and techno-theory dystopians to back up their arguments warning of the insidious and destructive power of technology.

But performance scholars who repeatedly cite Benjamin as guardian of the incomparability of "liveness" tend to omit that he is also aware of the unique aura and incomparability of photographic art. He describes how a *different* aura is manifest, a permanent imprint from the ghostly representation. He sees early portrait photography, for example, as a "cult of remembrance of loved ones, absent or dead. . . . For the last time the aura emanates from the early photographs in the fleeting expression of a human face. This is what constitutes their melancholy, incomparable beauty."[11] Photographic representation is thus afforded an aura by Benjamin and, crucially for understandings of its role in art and performance, an incomparably beautiful one. The photographic reproduction is incomparable not because it is less than the live moment that it captures, but because it is, in another artistic sense (the photographic sense), the *original* that is designed for reproduction. Benjamin maintains that mechanical reproduction "emancipates the work of art from its parasitical dependence on ritual . . . the work of art reproduced becomes the work of art designed for reproducibility."[12] He goes on to observe that the function of art within an age of mechanical reproduction is no longer based on ritual, but politics.[13]

"The Work of Art" opens with a quotation from Paul Valéry's *Aesthetics*, which ends, "For the last twenty years neither matter nor space nor time has been what it was from time immemorial."[14] Benjamin elaborates on the thesis, arguing that historical circumstance and change brings about reciprocal transformations in "the mode of human sense perception . . . [and] humanity's entire mode of existence."[15] Benjamin suggests that at the same time mechanical reproduction destroys aura when it pries an art object "from its shell," changes in sense perception tending to discern a "universal equality of all things" mean that this impact is diminished.[16] More recently, writers such as Baudrillard have extended the theme to argue that sense perception has transformed to such an extent that there is now little or no distinction made between originals, simulations and simulacra.[17] Philip Auslander selects this part of Benjamin's thesis to further his own argument that the politics and aesthetics of reproduction have now robbed live performance completely of its auratic and unique quality, and has led to its inherent mediatization: "Following Benjamin, I might argue that live performance has indeed been pried from its shell and that all performance modes, live or mediatized, are now equal: none is perceived as auratic or authentic; the live performance is just one more reproduction of a given text or one more reproducible text."[18] "The Work of Art" has thus been used by critics on both sides of the liveness debate. On one hand, it stands as evidence for the unique aura and presence of live performance, which can only be damaged and robbed by technology, and on the other as proof that technological incursion does not significantly alter reception of performance, since our minds (and performance itself) are already mediatized.

Benjamin engages with notions of historical changes of sense perception and identifies unique and potent properties in technological reproductions, yet his emotional attachment to originals remains, and he describes them in romantic and nostalgic tones. But the essay was of its time, and it should be remembered that when the computer is used as a reproductive technology within postmodern culture, artists tend to like the mediatized copy as much as, if not more than the original. Since postmodern theory sounded the death knell on ideas of authenticity, authors, metanarratives, and the real, the "original" work of art has become a largely displaced and friendless entity. As Forced Entertainment director Tim Etchells notes in relation to their show about an Elvis Impersonator *Some Confusions in the Law about Love* (1989): "We didn't want anything authentic, we wanted a third-rate copy—we loved that more dearly than anything authentic."[19]

For us, Roland Barthes's stubborn and unashamedly subjective *Camera Lucida* (1980) provides a more compelling and arguably ontologically advanced critique of the reproducible photographic image than Benjamin's "Work of Art"; a more poetic exploration of its nature, its psychological effect, its presence, and its relationship to authenticity and "liveness." It has many similarities with Susan Sontag's earlier *On Photography* (1977), which emphasizes photography's symbolic possession of bodies, space, and time, and the photograph's ontology as a fetish object: "Photographs are a way of imprisoning reality, understood as recalcitrant, inaccessible; of making it stand still. . . . But . . . to possess the world in the form of images is, precisely, to reexperience the unreality and remoteness of the real."[20] Barthes shares many of Sontag's thoughts, but goes even further to attempt to define a science of the subject through a strictly subjective and individual phenomenological process; *Camera Lucida* represents a highly personal quest to define photography's essence and its relationship both to philosophy and to the physical world. The photography he considers is exclusively documentary: images that capture moments from "real life" without recourse to staged mockups, trick effects, or laboratory manipulations. Posed portraits receive particular attention: children, slaves, politicians, criminals, artists (including Robert Wilson and Philip Glass), and, most important for Barthes, a specific photograph of his mother.

Barthes proceeds through a bombardment of conjectures and aphorisms relating to what he considers the authenticity and certainty, the palpable presence of the Photograph (Barthes capitalizes the first letter of "Photograph" throughout). The Photograph is "authentication itself . . . every Photograph is a certificate of presence,"[21] since the Photograph is wholly contingent upon its real-world referent, which always stubbornly adheres like "that class of laminated objects whose two leaves cannot be separated without destroying them both."[22] The physical substance of the Photograph itself is "always invisible" because it is rather the referent we see:

Photography's Referent is not the same as the referent of other systems of representation. I call "photographic referent" not the *optionally* real thing to which an image or a sign refers but the *necessarily* real thing which has been placed before the lens, without which there would be no Photograph. Painting can feign reality without having seen it. . . . in Photography I can never deny that *the thing has been there*. There is a superimposition here: of reality and the past. And since this constraint exists only for Photography, we must consider it, by reduction, as the very essence, the *noeme* of Photography.[23] (figure 6.1).

Figure 6.1 "Every Photograph is a certificate of presence . . ." (Barthes). An evocative old photograph used as part of Eduardo Kac's performance installation *Time Capsule* (1997).

But in seeking to liberate photography from its status as mere reproduction and representation, Barthes's theory at times falters and fails. He maintains that the defining essence of photography is not art or communication, nor simple representation, but "Reference" to the real ("that-has-been"). Its imaged objects are never metaphoric, but tautological: "a pipe, here, is always and intractably a pipe."[24] Barthes refers here, of course, to Rene Magritte's surrealist painting of a pipe with the words "Ceci n'est pas une pipe" (this is not a pipe) below it (*La Trahison des Images* (*The Treachery of Images*, 1929). Magritte's painted words play both with surrealist notions of the nature of reality, and with the simple idea that the painting itself is not a pipe, but merely a pictorial representation of one. Although Barthes tries to invert Magritte's famous statement to his advantage, it is not a logical or convincing manoeuvre. Despite what Barthes says, Magritte's maxim remains as true for realist photography as for painting: a photograph of a pipe is equally not a pipe *per se*, but its representation.

His meditations on the photograph as a symbol of death run throughout the book, with photographers cast as unknowing "agents of Death" in the very act of trying to preserve life.[25] Every photograph, he maintains, contains the terrible sense of "the return of the dead,"[26] because it reproduces a moment in time that can never be repeated, and in terms of mortification. When posing for a photograph, the camera's click represents a subtle moment of the transformation of the subject into object, "a micro-version of death (or parenthesis): I am truly becoming a specter."[27] Death becomes the *eidos* of the photograph, and even a photograph of a corpse "is alive, as *corpse*: it is the living image of a dead thing"[28] (figure 6.2).

Barthes plays freely with complex notions of the Photograph as both a live phenomenon and one that marks the sense of death. His views constitute an important incursion into the liveness debate, but have received little commentary within it, and there is certainly no mention in Auslander's *Liveness* book.[29] Barthes sees the photograph's immobility as confusing the two concepts of "the Real and the Live" since "the object has been real, [and] the photograph surreptitiously induces the belief that it is alive". Barthes is insistent that, although the photograph shows a reality of the past, of something already dead in time, the referent itself appears once again live to us, "*in flesh and blood*, or again *in person*."[30] The Photograph never "calls up" the past like a Proustian memory, but attests to the "live" reality of a moment and presents it equally alive in a resurrection: "the loved body is immortalized by the mediation of a precious metal, silver . . . [which,] like all the metals of Alchemy, is alive."[31] He refutes fashionable theoretical readings of the photograph as an inauthentic, fabricated construction; or as a "copy" of reality; or as "an *analogon* of the world."[32] Rather, in the Photograph, he says, "the power of authentication exceeds the power of representation."[33]

Barthes's position here is the antithesis of Benjamin's; indeed Barthes does not even consider photography to be a form of "reproduction." The photograph does not refer to or replicate any original, nor is it inherently connected to ideas of "the work of art." The

Figure 6.2 Barthes' notion of the photograph as a *memento mori* is encapsulated here using VR technology in Toni Dove and Michael Mackenzie's VR installation *Archeology of a Mother Tongue* (1993).

Photograph is an "image without code"[34]—not a copy of reality but "an emanation of a *past reality*: a *magic*, not an art."[35] Like Gibson's definition of cyberspace as a "consensual hallucination" (coined after Barthes's words), the Photograph becomes for Barthes "a bizarre *medium*, a form of hallucination . . . a temporal hallucination, so to speak, a modest, *shared* hallucination (on the one hand "it is not there," on the other "but it has indeed been"): a mad image, chafed by reality." Finally, Barthes ties together his thematics of the Photograph's play of time, death, reality, and madness to the idea of the pangs of love, the way one can feel in love in with certain images. This particular love is broader than a lover's sentiment, going beyond the unreality of representation, to enter the spectacle of the ostensibly dead photograph "crazily," to take it in one's arms, weeping "for Pity's sake."[36]

In his final work before his death, the photograph became an existential journey for Barthes, a window into the nature of reality that finally reveals photography as "superior to everything the human mind can or can have conceived to assure us of reality—but also this reality is never anything but a contingency ("*so much, no more*").[37] If we relate his work to digital performance, the contention implies that the photographic image ultimately becomes a more telling and profound presence than the live performer, at least in a philosophical sense. It opens an explanation (or at least a perspective) as to why in digital theater it is often the media projection rather than the live performer that wields the real power, the sense of (aesthetic, semiotic) reality.

Barthes discourse supports an argument that manipulated photographic images central to the digital performance project may not constitute the popularly held manifestation of a destabilized, fragmented, and disappearing reality, but rather the opposite. They do not represent a questioning of reality, but its affirmation—its proof. For Barthes, they represent the antithesis of any dehumanization, or denial of humanity; they are deeply concerned with mortality itself, with the nature, the *neome* of humanity. It is an interesting and nowadays highly unusual perspective. Barthes attempts to define the photographic image, to simplify and clarify rather than complicate it. Whether or not we accept the totality of his vision, Barthes's confidence and decisiveness, his Nietzschean "sovereignty of the ego" is a refreshing contrast to the extensive body of recent work which tries to undermine and disprove notions of technological and corporeal difference, or to offer psychologically speculative platitudes of indeterminacy.

Phelan Versus Auslander

Look closely at this card, it's a reproduction.
I confide to
You this solemn and sententious aphorism: did not
everything between us begin with a reproduction? Yes,
and at the same time nothing is more simply false, the
tragedy is there.
—JACQUES DERRIDA[38]

Having considered Benjamin's and Barthes's contrasting positions on the notion of liveness and presence within photographic media, let us consider two of the key protagonists of the current liveness debate within performance studies, Peggy Phelan and Philip Auslander. Although their theories also clash violently, it would be wrong to ally them too closely to the earlier writers, except stylistically: Auslander takes Benjamin's more skeptical, scientific stance, whereas Phelan's writing echoes Barthes's poetic, phenomenological passion. Indeed, both writers would take issue with both Benjamin's and Barthes's analyses, offering divergent perspectives. Although we have seen already how Auslander does refer to Benjamin to support his argument, Auslander is at odds with him philosophically and spends much his book discounting the whole notion of the aura of the live and the authenticity of originals. Phelan is in fact far closer to Benjamin than Barthes, valorizing the unique aura and presence of the live body and, in contrast to Barthes, denying photographic recordings any comparable "performative" presence. In *Unmarked: The Politics of Performance* (1993) she asserts, "Performance's independence from mass reproduction, technologically, economically, and linguistically, is its greatest strength."[39] She goes on to define an ontology of performance that is every bit as essentialist as Barthes's ontology of photography, but at complete odds with his argument:

Performance's only life is in the present. Performance cannot be saved, recorded, documented, or otherwise participate in the circulation of representations of representations: once it does so, it becomes something other than performance. To the degree that performance attempts to enter the economy of reproduction, it betrays and lessens the promise of its own ontology.[40]

Auslander takes Phelan to task in his celebrated book *Liveness: Performance in a Mediatized Culture* (1999), where he persuasively and exhaustively challenges traditional notions of liveness that view the live event as "real" and mediatized events as "secondary" and "artificial reproductions of the real."[41] His arguments against "the reductive binary opposition of the live and the mediatized"[42] include exploration of how live theater and performance has become increasingly mediatized, and the proposition that there may be no "clear-cut ontological distinctions between live forms and mediatized ones."[43] Echoing Benjamin, he argues that "the relationship between live and mediatized forms and the meaning of liveness be understood as historical and contingent rather than determined by immutable differences."[44] But despite the rigor and intensity of Auslander's argument, which is built carefully and relentlessly brick by brick, there is frequent hesitation and uncertainty in his voice, as though he has returned to the discourse late and insecure to insert equivocations, finally uncertain whether the bricks are made of straw.

Auslander discusses *Pôles* (1996), a digital performance by Pps Danse of Montreal that uses what he calls "holographic projections" of the two dancer's doubles, in addition to digital projections in the background. In a chase sequence through projections of a grottolike space "the three-dimensional dancers seem to be able to enter into the two-dimensional projected space as the wraith-like holograms."[45] He ponders whether such performances are perceived by audiences as a shifting interplay between the two distinct realms of the digital and the live, concluding: "that the answer is no, that we now experience such work as a fusion, not a con-fusion, of realms, a fusion that we see as taking place within a digital environment that incorporates the live elements as part of its raw material."[46] Although much of Auslander's discourse emphasizes the reciprocity and increasingly undifferentiated ontologies of live and mediatized forms, within digital performances that attempt visual syntheses of live and digital bodies, he clearly discerns that the dominant aesthetic force is the digital, into which the live is incorporated. Thus, "rather than a conversation among distinct media, its production presents the assimilation of varied materials to the cultural dominant. In this sense, Dance + Virtual = Virtual."[47] In asserting the digital as the cultural dominant over the live, he also notes that he does not discern digitality as significantly different from the televisual.[48] For Auslander, the digital is therefore just one form of ubiquitous media which is gradually replacing the live within the cultural economy, while in its turn "the live itself incorporates the mediatized, both technologically and epistemologically."[49]

Like Baudrillard's definition of *simulation* as an implosion through the telescoping and subsequent collapse of traditional "poles," Pps Danse's *Pôles* ultimately enacts, for Auslander, not only the legitimacy of the digital body within live work, but its equally co-present and "real" status alongside (rather than against) the live. In a subsection entitled "Against ontology," Auslander concludes that "according to a simple logic . . . if the mediatized image can be recreated in a live setting, it must have been "real" to begin with."[50] But is Auslander's logic itself too simple? He rightly argues that live and mediatized forms have continually influenced and referred back to one another in a circular pattern where each form has developed and derived their authority in relation to the other. But the perceptual and epistemological shift from an oscillating back-and-forth system of referencing and validation between the two poles into what amounts to a spiralling of the forms into a free-fall of indistinguishability is radical and problematic. In this conception, digital performance becomes not a black light theater of charm and illusion, but a black hole theater where gravity is irrelevant as both corporeal flesh and data-bodies are sucked into the same synthesizing vortex.

Or to mix our metaphors, when performance combines live and recorded/virtual bodies we are posed the question of whether the feast is like a quiche or a highly blended soup. Is audience consumption of digital theater a soup experience of ingredients combined in one smooth liquid form, or the binary hard and soft of pastry and egg mix? In a sense, just to pose this question indicates we have come a long way since earlier critical arguments that asserted the total incompatibility of conjoining live performance and media images, when critics viewed the repast like a fresh fruit salad with a pickled herring on the top.

Patrice Pavis tries to determine the flux of "specificity and interference"[51] at play between theater and media, and with a nod to Benjamin, concludes that live performance "cannot escape the socio-economic-technological domination" which characterizes any "work of art in the era of technical reproduction."[52] Pavis sees media and reproductive technologies not simply as an unavoidable influence on theater but as a specific "contamination" of it.[53] Auslander considers Pavis's analysis as one of many that "take on an air of a melodrama in which virtuous live performance is threatened, encroached upon, dominated, and contaminated by its insidious Other, with which it is locked in a life-or-death struggle."[54]

Auslander cites an article by Phelan where she discusses Deveare Smith's multimedia performance *Twilight: Los Angeles, 1992* (1992) and argues that "the camera's own performativity needs to be read as theatre."[55] He mischievously offers a reverse logic to this argument to maintain that rather than the media images being seen as theater, they metaphorically transform the theater event into television. As Auslander correctly reminds us, the liveness argument pivots around oppositional ideological positions privileging the live over the mediatized or vice-versa. It is understandable that champions of live performance such as Phelan and Pavis proclaim its uniquely ephemeral ontology in the face of both its increasing marginalization as a cultural form, and what is perceived as its gradual ontological erosion through the incorporation of (or contamination by) dominant media forms and paradigms. Just as techno-theorists Baudrillard, Virilio, and Kroker discuss digital reality as a virus within society, many performance theorists have discussed media as a plague on the house of performance.

It is a highly complex and difficult debate, which has many parallels with the wider philosophical and ideological battleground of humans versus machines. Phelan's discourse is humanist, political, emotive, and uplifting, and the incisiveness and performativity of her writing inspires like a call to the barricades of here-and-now ephemerality. It has been embraced by many on that particular side of the barricade within performance studies, since it is an appealing and seductive underdog position: the pure, humble, fearless David faces the corrupt Goliath might of mass media and technological capitalism. Poor theater meets Hollywood and CNN—whose side are you on? Though the rhetoric is rarely quite as baldly reductivist as this, it has sometimes comes close. But we should also recognize that the poor theater position sets up a peculiar, dialectic dynamic that celebrates the heroic radicalism of live performance's resistance to hegemonic media, yet simultaneously retains a deep conservativism through its fierce resistance to change from its traditional theatrical, historical past.

Ontologies of Media

Equally problematic are debates about the ontological nature of different media forms: film, television/video, and computational. Auslander, for example, begins by declaring little difference between televisual and digital forms[56] but then draws distinctions between the electronic (video) and the photographic (film).[57] In his discussion of video, he draws on Sean Cubitt's descriptions of the optical illusion of television and video whereby two images of each frame are interlaced by an electron scan to form the picture. He seizes upon the fact that each part-image of each frame is incomplete and fades before its matching part completes the retinal image, arguing that "disappearance may be even more fundamental to television than it is to live performance."[58] This tenuous point, based on the invisible inner workings of technology rather than human visual perception, is stretched further when Auslander contends that since videotape degrades with each viewing, "each time I watch a videotape is the only time I can watch that tape in that state of being."[59] This may be technically correct, but seems a feeble and fatuous notch on the belt, which emphasizes Auslander's tendency to be like a "dog with a bone" in his argumentation; we can only suggest, equally fatuously, that he upgrade his brand of videotape. But Auslander uses these factors to try to disprove the uniqueness of Phelan's ontology of performance as a constant state of presence followed by disappearance, by turning her argument back on itself. Videotapes degrade and scan lines replace one another, so that the image is "always as absent as it is present . . . in a very literal, material sense, televisual and other technological reproductions, like live performance, become themselves through disappearance."[60]

Auslander draws a distinction between video/television and film in terms of their respective electronic and photographic forms. But he fails to acknowledge that film operates through the same, and in fact even more distinct cycle of presence and absence as video. Each frame is shown momentarily on screen and is then replaced with black as the shutter closes and shuts off the beam to enable the projector claw to pull the next frame down and hold it still in the projector gate before opening again, so that the blurred movement is unseen. When we watch a two-hour film, our brains do not perceive that an hour of it is actually blackness, due to the phenomenon that Roget termed "persistence of vision." In terms of both its visual flux between absence and presence and its propensity to degradation, film actually differs little from video in the terms Auslander outlines, although it does significantly in other ways: resolution, grain, vanishing perspective, and so on. He is also equivocal about whether digital reproductions are subject to the same disappearance phenomenon as video since ostensibly they do not degrade: "My present feeling is that it's too soon to tell whether or not this is true."[61]

A different perspective on ontologies of live and recorded forms in relation to ideas of absence and presence is provided in Phaedre Bell's analysis of multimedia performance. She argues that cinema's signification is always presented through "absence" (since the actors, props and so on are not physically there), whereas theater's signifiers are always fully present. Thus, she insists, there are fundamental differences in how we read and interpret filmic and theatrical signs. She maintains that even when a live video camera relays pictures of the performance as it happens onto a rear screen "no matter what, the moments recorded are not the same as the moments playing on stage with the live performers."[62]

In "Screen Test of the Double" (1999), Matthew Causey examines the liveness debate, where he characterizes Phelan's position as "non-negotiable" and Auslander's as "a sophisticated legal argument." He sides more with Auslander, and develops another line of thought by adopting Lacan's argument about sexuality being inherently phantasmic, regardless of whether it is copulatory (a visceral, communal exchange equivalent to the "live" of theater) or masturbatory (a solo pursuit and pleasure, equivalent to watching television): "Lacan's argument thus challenges the assumptions inherent in the constructed binary of the live and the virtual, and thereby disputes the claims of immediacy and presence in live performance."[63] He suggests that Phelan's position is difficult to sustain since "the ontology of performance (liveness), which exists before and after mediatization, has been altered within the space of technology."[64]

Phenomenological Perspectives on Liveness

You know exactly what I feel about photography. I would like to see it make people despise painting until something else will make photography unbearable.
—MARCEL DUCHAMP[65]

The sense of technology having transformed or destabilized notions of liveness, presence, and the "real" is at the core of a long-lasting debate within performance studies, and is equally important in broader cultural theory, where Jean Baudrillard is its most vehement preacher. In the process of technology asserting itself as both the performative and the wider cultural dominant, the virtual and the actual are seen to converge or, as Baudrillard maintains, the virtual replaces the real. Many art critics, such as Malcolm Le Grice, follow Baudrillard's line that mass media

have progressively created a cultural schism between the representation and the cultural object. Instantaneous transmission of images and sounds across space have created a cultural habit reading the electronic representation as if it were present. Our discourse with the real has become a discourse with the represented image, a presence of the image not in conflict with its lack of physical proximity.[66]

Or as Causey puts it, "theatre, performance, film and new media studies seem to share similar concerns and aesthetic gestures regarding the collapse of the real into the virtual and the construction of identity in the space of technology."[67]

Yet the key problem remains that while this *sense* of convergence or confusion is now more or less beyond dispute, so too is the palpable fact that the live and the recorded, the virtual and the actual, clearly still differ in perceptual and phenomenological terms (figure 6.3). This presents a tortuously difficult ontological issue, a classic example of an *impasse* between theory and practice, which ultimately leaves theorists making some fabulously vague and unscientific dictums. Causey, for example, finally concludes that the live and mediatized are "the same, only different,"[68] a statement that may ultimately be as about as good as it gets. Marvin Carlson, despite a wonderful scholarly analysis of postmodern theoretical perspectives on performance, nonetheless ducks finite conclusions on live and recorded forms since, he maintains, the goal of reducing arts to their essences is "incompatible in any case with postmodern relativism and dissolving of boundaries."[69]

Perhaps, then, a phenomenological examination of liveness may provide a more solid foundation for unlocking its ontolology, and more tangible perspectives on the debate. Even without recourse to raw dictionary definitions of liveness, in phenomenological terms, it must be agreed that liveness has more to do with time and "now-ness" than with the corporeality or virtuality of subjects being observed. Adopting Auslander's conclusion, but discounting much of its rhetoric, from a subjective, perceptual standpoint

Figure 6.3 In digital performances such as Troika Ranch's *Future of Memory* (2003), Auslander's argument that the dominant aesthetic force is the digital into which the live is assimilated may be persuasive, but the problem remains that there are clear phenomenological differences between the digital and the live. Photo: Richard Termine.

liveness in itself has nothing to do with the media form, but at core concerns temporality. Put simply, for the spectator, liveness is just "being there," whatever performance form (live, recorded, telematic—or their combination) is being watched.

This simplifies the problem, of course, but unfortunately radically oversimplifies it by ignoring key phenomenological perceptions about presence and plenitude, and related differences in our reception of live and mediatized performance forms. Auslander is content to play down or deny perceptual differences between corporeal live performers and their mediatized counterparts (as in his analysis of *Pôles*), but we are not. In *Where the Stress Falls* (2002) Susan Sontag, for so long one of the most direct thinkers on ontologies of media, provides a useful impetus to examine audience reception of different media forms. Her analysis excludes live performance and concentrates instead on the transformation of one "non-live" media to another—a movie to television—which she suggests completely diminishes its sense of ritual and event. "To see a great film only on television isn't to have really seen that film" she says. "It's not only the difference of dimensions. . . . To be kidnapped, you have to be in a movie theatre, seated in the dark among anonymous strangers. No amount of mourning will revive the vanished rituals—erotic, ruminative—of the darkened theatre."[70] Ritual elements of location, lighting, and communality thus become Sontag's criteria for the "live" experience of cinema.

Taking the risk of extending Sontag's implied hierarchies of forms, we would expand her idea further to argue that the sense of ritual and event is (or at least, should be) far more marked in live performance than in cinema. This idea can be demonstrated clearly in relation to live multimedia theater. Where film, video, or digital projections are used in conjunction with live performers in theatrical contexts, once the performers leave the stage, there is a marked difference in the mode of spectatorship. At this point, we discern particular changes and switches of both mental and physical attention in audiences: for example, spectators typically relax and slump back a little more in their seats. Their mode of mental reception also appears to alter as the live performers exit and recorded imagery becomes the communication medium. At first sight it may appear to be a diminution of concentration, a reduction in mental energy directed toward the stage. But we feel that this is better understood as a change in the *type* of attention and focus that is afforded to the projection within the suddenly "non-live" stage. Robert Edmond Jones accounted for this by the suggestion that theater audiences are more "awake" because they view the performance with an acute awareness not only of the performers but also of each other, whereas cinema audiences view films in a more isolated, solitary, and somnambulant mode. An interesting parallel can be drawn with Walter Benjamin's 1939 essay on epic theater, where he discusses Brecht's concerns to have an audience "that is relaxed and follows the action without strain,"[71] which he then relates to the relaxation of reading a novel. But he stresses the key difference that the epic theatre audience "always appears as a collective, and this differentiates it from the reader, who is always alone with his text."[72]

But it is difficult to assess how much the differences in modes of awareness and attention in spectatorship result from sociocultural "conditioning" and traditional protocols that expect an audience to afford live performers attention and a "certain respect." Cultural expectations of levels of attention given to live performers, and indeed courtesy to others within audience spaces, differ around the world, and in the West operate at many different levels according to the type of performance being watched. Eating popcorn, continually shifting in one's seat, holding a conversation, or falling asleep are certainly perceived and tolerated differently in a cinema and the "straight" theater. But even in live performance, audience behavior and attention differs radically according to its form: audiences at variety shows, pantomimes, and standup comedy generally relax more and behave differently to those at sophisticated plays, avant-garde performances, dance productions, or the opera. Yet even where the content is of comparable artistic depth and quality, reception modes differ for spectators of live and recorded performances. They are watched in different ways. While social protocols and cultural conditioning may offer one explanation, their different ontologies offer another. Watching film, video, and digital media is a more voyeuristic experience than watching live performance, since in the literal sense of the word, the onlooker is looking from a position without fear of being seen by the watched.

Breaking the Frame

Recorded media is firmly contained within its own frame and however shocking or affecting its imagery, can never break out of that frame and personally confront us. Most live performance never actually does this, but it always can; there is a potential for the performer to see you, or speak to you, and break out of the stage frame to confront you directly. During a matinee performance in the 1970s, an actor playing Macbeth for the Royal Shakespeare Company (RSC) at Stratford-upon-Avon stared into space and spoke the words "Is this a dagger I see before me?" Unrestrained laughter and giggles broke out from a large number of schoolchildren watching the performance, which had already been marred by disturbances and inappropriate comments from the rowdy school trip. At this point, the actor playing Macbeth decided that he had had enough, and stopped. He came out of character, walked forward, and proceeded calmly but viciously to question where on earth the schoolchildren thought they were. Among other things, he pointed out, "This is not a film." There was stunned silence. He walked back upstage, looked into space, and asked once again: "Is this a dagger I see before me?" The story goes that you could hear a pin drop, but he never worked for the RSC again.

The story is interesting on a number of levels. Children and others unused to attending theater do not always behave with the deference and formality of regular theatergoers, and being more accustomed to television, treat it in the same way. Moreover, theater's corporeal liveness is no guarantee in itself of audience interest and engagement, and all too often the "fourth wall" works like the impermeable glass screen of television, which does not "let the audience in." One is tempted to add that theater might be more popular if such "really" dramatic and unpredictable events happened more often. But while the Macbeth event was very much a "one-off," live performance always carries with it the possibility that the unexpected may happen. This is not the case in cinema or television, where even though we have not seen it before, we know it is already complete, considered, passed for public consumption, the mistakes edited out. Although normally a live performance will be well rehearsed and will run (like a film) according to plan, there is a certain reciprocity of contact between audience and performers, as well as a sense of danger. The performers may do something extraordinary that night, positive or negative. Someone may create an extraordinary live moment, or stumble and fall, or like the legendary British comedian Tommy Cooper (performing live on stage and simultaneously broadcast on television), suffer a heart attack and fall down dead. There is a different tension and vulnerability in live performance, a sense of danger and unpredictability that affects the adrenalin and nerves of both the performers and the spectators—at least at the outset, even if it is not always maintained. Thus, although Sontag is correct to define a ritual and communal distinction between television and cinema spectatorship, it is even more marked when comparing theater to cinema.

For centuries, theater critics and practitioners have discussed the sense of communality and unique energy that exists between live audiences and performers. Among them is Robert Lepage who during an interview discussion at London's National Theatre in 1979 defined theatre as "a gathering, a meeting point. A gathering in the sense that a group of artists get together to tell a story, and also the collective audience. The audience in a theatre room is very different from the audience to a film, because they actually change everything on the stage by their energy."[73] Geoff Moore, who like Lepage has extensive experience directing both theater and film, as well as conjoining them in his work with Moving Being, maintains,

Theatre offers something different. Another kind of attention. You have to go out. You are required to be part of a social transaction. Your humanity is called upon. You have to be "there" with others. The higher demand often leads to higher frustration. It is a price well worth paying. . . . The space theatre offers is a human space, a societal space, a political space. Theatre's job is to keep that space relevant, and to keep it always open to question. . . . Theatre is still sweaty and vulnerable, it is unedited and anything can happen. As Artaud reminds us—"We are not free, and the sky can still fall on our heads." And the theatre has been created to teach us that first of all.[74]

The Problem of Presence

To conclude these thoughts on the liveness problem, we would like to examine the closely related notion of presence, and to show how critical positions on this concept further complicate the dialectical debate. Recently, presence has become a much-discussed and at times fetishized concept that has grown out of discourses examining the increasing mediatization and virtualization of art and culture. Following Benjamin, cultural commentators have used presence to distinguish the material, auratic, proximal "real"; and in performance studies, to denote the flesh-and-blood performer, there with you in the same shared physical space. Within cybertheory, its meaning shifts to include ideas of telematic and deferred, online presence, relating it to agency rather than to direct witnessing. As Sandy Stone points out, "Presence is currently a word that means many things to many different people. . . . These include repeated transgressions of the traditional concept of the body's physical envelope and of the locus of human agency."[75]

But the problem arises here that all art is concerned with presence, or presentness, be it painting, poetry, net-art, recorded media, or live performance.[76] The Rembrandt portrait (both the original *and* its reproduction), Jane Austen's words in a battered paperback, the images on the monitor, and the live performer on stage are all equally "present" to us when we engage with artworks. Moreover, in purely semiotic terms, there is no significant difference between the image of, for example, a woman waving a revolutionary flag as described in a novel, painted on a canvas, screened in a cinema, or standing live on a stage. Therefore, at one level, to argue the sanctity and superiority of human corporeal presence, as Phelan does, could be seen to privilege one artform over another, and to fetishize ephemeral forms of expression. In this sense, one could argue that Phelan does not present a convincing ontology of performance at all, but merely asserts her preferred medium of performance—live.

Another core problem is that reduced to its essence, presence is about interest and command of attention, not space or liveness. In considering the presence of live bodies versus media images, the now common presence of televisions in bars and other public places provides a convenient example. When the company and conversation is stimulating, the presence of the TV seems distant or unnoticed, when it is not, the TV may gain attention and command the sense of presence over the live bodies in the space. What program is on will also clearly have an impact on its interest and presence to different people. To take this idea further and to try to compare some sense of "like with like" within multimedia theater, let us consider a hypothetical live performer standing next to an exactly life-size, recorded, two-dimensional projection of herself (figure 6.4). If both figures are still and neutral, one might agree that the live performer has more presence (by virtue of her solidity, her liveness). But once either of the figures engages in activity (including concentrated thought) it will pull focus to it, gain attention, and assert its presence over the other. When both become active, the one we watch more (our attention will always flit between them), the one with the most presence, is the one engaged in what we find personally the more interesting or emotive activity. In this sense, presence in relation to audience engagement and attention is dependent on the compulsion of the audiovisual activity, not on liveness or corporeal three-dimensionality.

Figure 6.4 Live performers from The Chameleons Group compete for attention against their own and others' mediatized projections in their interactive Internet performance *Chameleons 3: Net Congestion* (2000).

Finally, it must be remembered within the liveness debate that mere corporeal liveness is no guarantee of presence. We have all experienced nights of crushing, excruciating boredom at the theater, where despite the live presence of a dozen gesticulating bodies on stage, we discern no interesting presence at all and pray for the thing to end. Such theatrical occasions are painful and all too commonplace, where initial presence slides inexorably into the most aching and abject absence. Live performance can often be defined more by absence (of ideas, of excitement, of originality, of "life") than presence. The complex play of absence and presence is of course central to poststructuralist conceptions of language and art, and its relationship to performance is discussed acutely and in depth in Marvin Carlson's *Performance: A Critical Introduction* (1996).[77] Nick Kaye draws on the theme to emphasize elements of postmodern performance's ontology as "a refusal to be placed, vacillating between presence and absence, between displacement and reinstatement."[78] Henry Sayre goes further to suggest that the deconstructive influence on performance has led to work characterized more by the aesthetics of absence than the aesthetics of presence.[79]

In his study of minimalist art, Michael Fried defines presence as "the special complicity that that work extorts from the beholder. Something is said to have presence when it demands that the beholder take it into account, that he take it *seriously*—and when the fulfilment of that demand consists simply in being *aware* of it and, so to speak, in acting accordingly."[80] As Fried makes clear, real presence occurs when the artwork demands attention, whatever form the artwork might take. It is content, not container than asserts presence. It is interesting, and salutary to note how Fried concludes his discourse: "The success, even the survival of the arts has come increasingly to depend on their ability to defeat theatre."[81]

Postmodernism and Posthumanism

Theories are nets cast to catch what we call "the world," to rationalise, to explain and to master it.
— KARL POPPER[1]

Remediation

Digital performance, and indeed cyberculture in general, is overwhelmingly theorized within the critical spaces of postmodernism and deconstruction. While postmodernist and poststructuralist critical approaches can by nature be fluid, eclectic, and "open," they can equally operate doctrinally to impose specific and sometimes inappropriate ideas onto cultural and artistic works in precisely the same way previous ideological master codes such as psychoanalysis, Marxism, feminism, and structuralism did in the past. In "Post-Poststructuralism" (2000), Richard Schechner argues that the blind acceptance of poststructuralist theories and the ready mapping of cultural studies discourses onto performance and the performative has led to sterility and atrophy within performance studies. He advocates new theoretical approaches specific to performance that are unfettered by the orthodoxies and ideologies of wider theory, particularly the hegemonic deconstructive impulse. We would echo his sentiments in relation to digital performance, and in this chapter we consider the impact that postmodern theory and deconstructive analyses have had on the academic reception and understanding of digital performance. We go on to explore the concept of posthumanism, which we suggest might afford a more apposite critical and philosophical standpoint.

But first we will consider the concept of remediation, which has became a highly influential concept following Jay Bolter and Richard Grusin's 1999 book, *Remediation: Understanding New Media*. Although it is an incisive and thoughtful consideration of the ways in which digital technologies have repackaged and reinterpreted older media forms and paradigms, it is sometimes forgotten that the term itself is not Bolter and Grusin's—for example, it had been common coinage in the waste disposal and recycling industries for some years. The authors emphasize that in creating new media forms from older ones, computer technologies fit within a long historical tradition; for example, in the same way that early cinema remediated theater. Thus, they suggest: "Digital visual media can best be understood through the ways in which they honor, rival, and revise linear-perspective painting, photography, film, television, and print."[2] But importantly, they also maintain that the reconfiguration is not trivial, since it heralds unique new forms as well as impacting on the way that older media themselves become reconfigured: "What is new about new media comes from the particular ways in which they refashion older media and the ways in which older media refashion themselves to answer the challenges of new media."[3]

The book's high profile within the field is deserved, but perhaps more for its excellent clarity and ability to distil (and remediate) key concepts within digital culture than through any real conceptual originality or critical innovation. Others had raised many of Bolter and Grusin's ideas previously, and the central tenets of retrospection and reconfiguration had long since been underlined in wider postmodern theory. Nonetheless, their discourse has been influential and has brought to prominence inherent dialectical tensions at play within computer representations and simulations, particularly the ideas of transparency and opacity, and immediacy and hypermediacy. The transparency/opacity opposition contrasts digital forms that seek to immerse the user/viewer by aiming to make the medium/interface disappear (in the way that naturalistic theater or film does) against those that expose and foreground the medium and interface (in the way that Brecht's theater or Godard's films do). Both, they note, have their own distinct pleasure principles, and Bolter later extends this thesis in his detailed examination of the digital arts on display at the SIGGRAPH 2000 exhibition, using the twin metaphors of *Windows and Mirrors* (2003, with Diane Gromala).

Bolter and Grusin particularly emphasize computer culture's "contradictory impulses for immediacy and hypermediacy . . . a double logic of remediation. Our culture wants both to multiply its media and erase all traces of mediation: ideally, it wants to erase its media in the very act of multiplying them."[4] They go on to stress the mutual dependency of immediacy (such as a live Internet webcam view) and hypermediacy (characterized, for example, by the other textual information, windows and hyperlinks that surround it) (figure 7.1). The hypermediacy of webpages and other computer displays foreground and celebrate the medium and the mediation, while the aim of immediacy is to play down or eliminate the mechanics of the interface, the medium, and the act of mediation itself. But both, they say, are opposite manifestations of the same desire to pass through the limits of representation to evoke authentic and emotional user experience. To do so, transparent computer applications disguise and deny the fact of mediation whilst the hypermedia paradigm multiplies the mediation to promote a "satiety of experience . . . the excess of media becomes an authentic experience."[5]

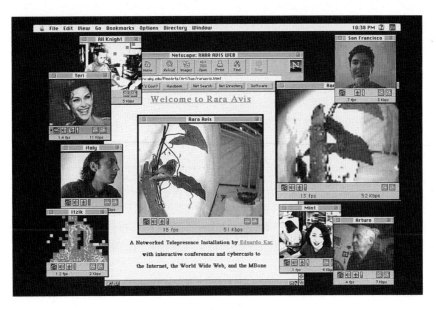

Figure 7.1 An example of what Jay David Bolter and Richard Grusin term "hypermediacy," where multiple screen elements foreground and celebrate the medium and the mediation: the website for Eduardo Kac's telerobotic installation *Rara Avis* (1996). Photo: Courtesy of the Julia Friedman Gallery.

Postmodernism and Computers

In the early 1990s there was extensive discussion around the inherent links between multimedia technologies and postmodernity. Jay Bolter's *Writing Space: The Computer in the History of Literacy* (1990) and Mark Poster's *The Mode of Information: Poststructuralism and the Electronic Context* (1990) drew analogies between hypertext and recent literary and critical theory, particularly Derridean deconstruction. George Landow followed, describing hypertextuality as "the embodiment of the Derridean text,"[6] and arguing its close relationship with poststructuralist thought, which has grown out of dissatisfaction with "the related phenomena of the printed book and hierarchical thought."[7] Landow's *Hypertext: The Convergence of Contemporary Critical Theory and Technology* (1992) was an influential text in the critical thrust to marry computational paradigms with postmodern ideology. For Landow, the new medium became a new message[8] as hypertext systems were seen to reconfigure and undermine past notions of the authority and solidity of text and the authorial voice. Landow does not merely point out how hypertext models challenge traditional literary modes, but with an evangelical zeal typical of writers at the time, he declares that the shift is so revolutionary that now "we must abandon conceptual systems founded upon ideas of center, margin, hierarchy, and linearity and replace them with ones of multilinearity, nodes, links, and networks."[9] In the same year, Edward Barrett presented a quasi-mathematical formula emphasizing the contingent relationships between hyper-textuality and contemporary deconstructive and postmodern theory:

The equation: power of the computer to dish out information in many different combinations + "traditional" approaches to textual scholarship + academic enthusiasm for the French school of thought which de-centres, deconstructs, and interleaves the text with other texts and readings = deep involvement with the concept of hypertext.[10]

In the mid-1990s Diane Gromala mapped new technologies to Lyotard's notion of tech-nology as a language game in which myths and metanarratives are reconfigured, and went on to describe Virtual Reality as embodying notions of the reconstruction of the schizo-phrenic subject described by Deleuze and Guattari, as well as the "Lacanian mirror of mis-recognition."[11] Gregory Ulmer related hypertextuality to the work of Derrida, Lacan, and Wittgenstein; and Landow returned with a later book that at one point widened the net to take in no less than seven leading critical theorists in the space of two sentences:

Like much recent work by poststructuralists, such as Roland Barthes and Jacques Derrida, hyper-text reconceives conventional, long-held assumptions about authors and the texts they write and read. Electronic linking, which provides one of the defining features of hypertext, also embodies Julia Kristeva's notions of intertextuality, Mikhail Bakhtin's emphasis upon multivocality, Michel Foucault's conception of networks of power, and Gilles Deleuze and Felix Guattari's ideas of rhizomatic, "nomad thought."[12]

However, a number of writers have since probed and questioned the veracity of such analyses. Robert Markley is skeptical of what he perceives as the "uncritical" and "unprob-lematical" theory propounded by the developers and advocates of new technologies. His own analysis is in stark contrast to the romantic and progressivist idealism of its propo-nents: "a radically constructivist technology that celebrates an undisguised essentialism."[13] Richard Grusin (prior to his collaboration with Bolter on *Remediation*) argued that writers such as Bolter and Poster too easily related poststructuralist/postmodern/deconstructive theories to electronic writing without recognizing that:

the force of the Derridean critique is to demonstrate the way in which thought and speech are always already forms of writing. Deconstruction does not need to be instantiated or embodied in new technologies; for Derrida, writing is always a technology and already electronic.[14]

Grusin observes a similar misreading in relation to Barthes's poststructuralist distinc-tions between "work" and "text," or between the "readerly" and "writerly" texts, both of which distinctions have been cited as theoretical anticipations of hypertextuality. He notes that for Barthes, as for Derrida, the "writerly" text is always "already immaterial, allusive, and intertextual—even in print. . . . The force of the deconstructive and poststructuralist critiques is to illustrate the way in which this destabilization is true of all writing."[15] He also takes issue with the uncritical generality of William Paulson's contention that the translation of texts into digital code to enable them to appear on screen in the same format, means that electronic technologies are inevitably decontextualizing technologies:[16]

In so arguing, however, he reproduces the technological fallacy by ascribing agency to the technology itself. To imagine that digitally reproducing texts from two different historical contexts would decontextualize them is to fetishize technology by making an idol of the "form" in which writing is commodified, and to fetishize the particular historical context in which those texts were reproduced. Electronic information technologies do not decontextualize the texts of Western culture, they recontextualize them.[17]

The critical squabbles reflect the yes-no, on-off, 0–1, love-hate relationship one establishes when working closely with a dualistic medium that is in itself conceived and programmed as binary. The distinct polarization of critical thought in relation to new technologies and cybernetics has been inevitable faced with a medium which is at once art and science, rational (as mathematical, computational) and irrational "(mystical, performative, and cognitively dissonant)."[18] Computer technologies are also revolutionary (synergetic, globally rhizomatic), yet conventional (essentially reliant on previous media: text, video, telecommunications). Since the mid-1990s, critical readings of the intimate interrelationship between postmodernism/poststructuralism and new technologies have grown rather than abated. Ironically, these critiques commonly celebrate the properties and potentials of these technologies enthusiastically, seemingly unaware of the dark skepticism and even nihilism with which technology is viewed by the very writers they cite.

In *The Possessed Individual*, Arthur Kroker presents a searing analysis of technological theory in French postmodern thought. He maintains that recent French theories encapsulate the essence of the contemporary American "hologram":

To reflect upon the French, is to finally understand America flipped inside out, with its ideological software (the rhetoric of technology) on the outside and its dynamic hardware (the *actual* forces of technology) on the inside. Read Baudrillard as a clinical diagnosis of the disappearance of America into digital reality; Barthes as a theorist of the empire of the (American) sign; Deleuze and Guattari as a description of the rhizomatic flows and decodings involved in becoming-America; Foucault as a historian of the genealogy of (liberal) nihilism that finds its *apogée* in American bourgeois subjectivity; and Lyotard as the most eloquent of all American pragmatists. No longer, therefore, French theory as a mirror of technology, but a reflection from beyond its dynamic horizon of the *virus* of technology in the empire of the American postmodern. . . . The French mind is a theoretical autobiography . . . of the rhetoric of the American (technical) way.[19]

Kroker concludes that writers such as Baudrillard, Barthes, Virilio, Foucault, Lyotard, Deleuze, and Guattari characterize technology in terms of a cynical power that oppresses and possesses the individual. Continental postmodern thought views technology as a predatory seducer and a terminal virus that comes alive to "eat" space, time, and culture and to confirm "the death of politics, the death of aesthetics, the death of the self, the death of the social, the death of sex."[20] It is a "catastrophe theorem" of technological nihilism replete with the "cold abstractions" of simulacra (Baudrillard), driftworks (Lyotard), and chrono-politics (Virilio).[21]

This leads us to a simple question. When postmodern and poststructuralist thought conceptualizes technology in such negative terms, are the pioneers of virtual performance who adopt these technologies really in accord with this dark fatalism, masochistically engaging in the destructive power and "terminal" ontology of technology? Do performance artists consider the technological tools they work with to have a negative and destructive force? We seriously doubt it, and hence our misgivings over the prevalent theorization of digital performance in relation to continental philosophy. Admittedly, some artists do indeed "critique" technology, articulating its dehumanizing potentials, its panoptic power relations, its darker subtexts and implications. But equally as many, and we believe, far more, celebrate and embrace technologies as positive developments, not least for their artistic and performative possibilities.

Jean Baudrillard and the "Real"

I am a nihilist.
—JEAN BAUDRILLARD[22]

Jean Baudrillard is the high priest of technological nihilism, a soothsayer of the apocalypse, and genuinely one of our favorite writers. But that does not mean to say we believe everything he writes. He is a brilliant aphorist, a seductive and compelling writer of high "drama," and a consummate critical "performer" who mesmerically barnstorms the contemporary media-theory stage delivering explosive monologues on some of the most important issues in art and culture. But like many virtuoso theater performers, he unfortunately has a slight tendency to "go over the top." Heidegger noted in 1953 that "everywhere we remain unfree and chained to technology, whether we passionately affirm or deny it,"[23] and reading (and believing) Baudrillard certainly ensures that any self-denial of this "fact" is no longer an option.

Simulacra and Simulation (1981) brought the ancient word *simulacrum* back from the past and related it to media's "evil spirit of simulation."[24] Baudrillard demonstrated how in our postmodern world, "it is the simulation that is effective, never the real."[25] Then, like a stage magician, he turned reality upside down: "The very definition of the real is *that of which it is possible to give an equivalent reproduction*."[26] He capped it all off, to tumultuous applause, with a thrilling and gymnastic piece of philosophical pyrotechnics: "in short, there is no real."[27] "Simulacra" and "the real" have become sacred critical mantras ever since, although many learned professors still remain unsure precisely what they mean. Later, Baudrillard directed his attention to digital technologies, with a similarly devastating dramatic flourish: "The coming of the virtual is itself our apocalypse, and it deprives us of the real event of the apocalypse. Such is our paradoxical situation, but we have to push the paradox to the limit."[28]

In *Disneyworld Company* (1996), Baudrillard uses the replication of Disney "worlds" as a metaphor for the commodification and virtualization of society. He suggests the Disney Corporation would like to cryogenize the planet, just as Walt Disney himself is allegedly cryogenized in liquid nitrogen, waiting for resurrection. As he continues to colonize the world from his suspended animation ("the virtual reality of death"), the irony is that if he is ever reanimated, he will find "there is no real world anymore." Instead, humans have become *figurants* (extras) in the spectral space of virtual reality, and the New World Order operates like a Disney world where "everything is possible, and everything is recyclable in the polymorphous universe of virtuality." Just as Benetton appropriated documentary news images of the intense human dramas of AIDS, Bosnia, and apartheid, reality has been transfused into a "New Mediatic Figuration (a place where suffering and commiseration end in a mode of interactive resonance). The virtual takes over the real as it appears, and then replicates it without any modification [*le recrache tel quel*], in a *prêt-à-porter* (ready-to-wear) fashion."[29]

Disneyland has come in for more than its fair share of critical bludgeoning, and its insidious appropriation and virtualization of the real has been similarly evoked in Umberto Eco's *Travels in Hyperreality* (1986), where he calls it "an immense robot . . . [where] visitors must agree to behave like robots."[30] He also laments how automata of crocodiles and pirates hold more allure for visitors than real exotic animals or corporeal actors. Mark Dery calls Disneyland "a sexless, microbe free monument to a normative future where the sole interface between the technocratic elite and the technologically illiterate masses is the point of purchase."[31] He notes the unremitting surveillance in Disneyland and the consequent unthinking, passive obedience of its visitors, who curiously applaud machines at the end of robot performances. He continues caustically, "on the other hand, such behaviour makes a strange kind of sense: The image of the happy shoppers mechanically applauding technology freezes the essence of the Disney theme parks in a single snapshot."[32]

But how sinister actually *is* Baudrillard's simulation and virtuality, as encapsulated in the metaphoric specter of Disneyland? Marie-Laure Ryan is a rare and brave voice to take issue with cultural critics who use the Disneyland tourist as a "beloved scapegoat" and easy target for ridicule. She argues that, rather than confirming some dangerous new human attraction to simulations at the expense of a loss of desire for the original, there is a much older and Aristotelian paradigm at play. In the *Poetics*, Aristotle describes a "universal pleasure in imitation . . . we take delight in viewing the most accurate possible images of objects,"[33] and Ryan links this to the whole notion of simulation, fakes, doubles, and the nature of fictionality itself. She suggests that

we enjoy images precisely because they are not "the real thing," we enjoy them for the skill with which they are crafted. This pleasure presupposes that the readers or spectators of artistic texts do not fall victim to a mimetic illusion; it is because they know in the back of their minds that the text is a mere double that they appreciate the illusionistic effect of the image, the fakeness of the fake.[34]

Fictional representations take many forms, and Ryan makes clear that she sees little significant distinction between a high-tech Disney fake and the simulations of literary fiction. It is an optimistic and reassuring position, in contrast to Baudrillard's. However, the assumption that consumers of cultural products distinguish between the virtual and the real is a—if not *the*—crucial point of contention within cultural and technological theory, and a fundamental issue in understanding many of the critical positions that have been taken on digital performance. Ryan suggests that a visitor to Disneyland and its cultural outposts does not fall under some sort of wicked spell like a character in one of its own fictions, but Baudrillard and his many followers insist with rabid, relentless fury to the contrary. Indeed, Baudrillard's position is considered so extreme that writers such as Hakim Bey contends that he has gone beyond his own critique of "Too Late Capitalism" to become a symptom of it himself.[35] In a lighter tone, in July 2003 one Amazon.co.uk customer's themed inventory of recommended books entitled "List of Nihilism" highlighted *Simulacra and Simulation*. The list's compiler, who adopted the pseudonym pil00 and the slogan "I sound out false idols," offered an acidly down-to-earth, two-sentence review of Baudrillard's most famous work: "Sorry, Jean, it's all in your head. Turn off the telly and go for a long walk, son."

What we find problematic about the uncritical adoption of Baudrillardian and related postmodern philosophy into the theorization of digital performance is its totalizing position in announcing not a gradual and attritional breakdown, but a total erasure of previous historical understandings of notions of technology, society, the self, the body, consciousness, and the "real." In its urgency to adopt a definitive and frequently apocalyptic position, it wipes the historical and phenomenological slate clean. We dispute the theorization of a totally irreal world where signification has collapsed, where simulacra have replaced entities, and where technologically possessed zombies without will or purpose have replaced humans.

The cynical power of technology is nothing compared to the cynical power of human instinct, intellect, and reason. The media image may have exerted an increasing influence or power on human consciousness, but that consciousness has not undergone total metamorphosis and collapsed into helpless zombiedom. Humans continue to value other humans above images, nature over media. In her consumption of media, the human being continually discerns, critiques, makes rational judgments, filters, and selects. She is cynical of and enraged by stupid media, she revolts against manipulation and propaganda. She is not fooled by the seductive melodrama of soaps, "reality" television, or Springer-style freakshows, but consumes them for simple diversion and amusement. Media's afterimages need not insidiously corrupt, nor be indelibly inscribed on the subject's mind and body.

Arthur Kroker shares this perspective in his critique of Baudrillard, maintaining that Baudrillard has forgotten the twin star of astrophysics, whereby every star has its invisible double exerting magnetic energy upon it, but undetected by optical scanners. Thus Baudrillard's philosophy of the fatal attraction of technological seduction has a missing twin star of repulsion, "a silence of dissent"[36] whereby human subjectivity and the power of reason counters and rejects the cynical power and seduction of technology. Kroker acknowledges that the "hot glimmer" of seduction may be the ruling paradigm of a cold technological age, but equally, he argues: "the dark cold possibility of repulsion is the forgotten term for that implacable stubborn presence which we call a human being."[37]

Simulacra and Synthetics

In postmodern philosophy, following Baudrillard and others, the word *simulacrum* used to denote a very specific, idiosyncratic product of the technologized age, a unique new form of object or representation created without a real-world referent—a copy without an original. But it has since lost its meaning in wider cultural criticism, now applied increasingly to encompass any and all images, media products, and reproduced forms: graphic, photographic, filmic, televisual, and digital. The term simulacrum thus becomes applied to anything and everything mediatized or not "real" (in the good old-fashioned sense of the word). Although its use has become indiscriminate, it still retains an intellectual cache and mystique, an aura (a beautiful irony given Walter Benjamin's thesis on reproductions) imbuing its invocation with a phantom philosophical seal of approval, whether applied to trivia or propaganda, the latest virtual reality simulation or a bad soap opera. Teeming crowds of postmodern theorists, who first railed against the corrupt, invasive ontology of late capitalism, then themselves stood defeated and in queue to buy—cheap, and wholesale—the latest product: their own shaky proposition that simulacra had taken over, and all mediatized images proved the loss of the real.

We use the past tense, not because postmodern and poststructuralist theories are no longer with us, far from it, but because their grip has loosened. The "Discontents" have emerged to question many of these theories' credentials and fundamentals. Taking the lead from Freud's *Civilization and Its Discontents* (1930), book titles announced *Postmodernism and Its Discontents* (ed. E. Anne Caplan, 1988), *Postmodernity and Its Discontents* (Zygmunt Bauman, 1997), and, most germane to digital discourses, Robert Markley's excellent edited collection *Virtual Realities and Their Discontents* (1996). As Freud had mused on the inherent tensions between conformity to civilized society and individual expression, sexuality and happiness, so the new-wave Discontents used the paradigm to attack what they considered the stifling stranglehold of postmodern doctrines, which had hijacked and repressed free, clear-sighted thought. The Discontents' core message is that most postmodern and virtual discourse is hyperbolic, and the theoretical and metaphorical is being mistakenly confused and conflated with the actual. Thus, the real is as real as it ever was, and has not disappeared in a swirling vortex of media images and simulacra. It is time for the apocalypsists and hysterics to calm down and see the forest for the trees.

As is doubtless clear, we generally (though not entirely) concur with the discontents' position. In particular, we are genuinely surprised and not a little perplexed at the obsession with "the real" that pervades and mars writing on digital performance. Gabriella Giannachi's *Virtual Theatres: An Introduction* (2004), for example, a historic work as one of the first sole-authored books in the field, is a well-researched and useful text, but it suffers from a compulsion to continually remind the reader how performances reconfigure, challenge or otherwise "explore" notions of the "real." The simple point so many critics seem to miss or not wish to acknowledge is that *the real has changed*, as it has always done. The real, and our consciousness of what is real, is subject to *time*, and for several hundred years it has had a conjoined twin: technological "progress." In the 1950s and '60s, people were at first amazed to see little people in their homes on a thing called television, and the real changed then. But we have since got over how "spooky" television is, just as we have quickly become used to and have assimilated the capabilities of the computer and the Web—it is just part and parcel of what today is *real*.

Jacques Derrida

A labyrinthine man never seeks the truth, but only his Ariadne.
— FRIEDRICH NIETZSCHE[38]

Jacques Derrida, the "god" of deconstruction and poststructuralism, holds an equal if not greater hold on the theoreticians of digital performance, and is another "extremist," though in a quite different way to Baudrillard. Though he is one of the greatest writers and thinkers of our age, we are equally suspicious of too ready mapping of Derrida's linguistic philosophy to performative practices. Amid the anxiety and panic of postmodernism, Derrida's deconstruction emerged to provide further fuel to the fire, and to add intellectual self-doubt and self-flagellation into the bargain. Everything was unstable, epistemology most of all. Derrida, a leading commentator on Artaud's theater, took Artaud's ideas to brain rather than heart and set in train a new epistemology and grammatology of cruelty. Criticism became a cerebral "affective athleticism," and theory, for many, became a theater of pain.

Derrida's poststructuralist thought is descended from Nietzsche and extends his notions of the world as a constant flux, where all beings and entities are unstable and in a state of becoming. Theater and performance's process (writing, preparation, rehearsal) adheres to this philosophy. But in its manifestation—that is to say, in its essential ontology—it seeks just the opposite: to create and stabilize a world, to unite time and space, to *become*. The liveness of theater, and its mnemonic, allegorical form, conspires to *fix* time and space, and this is seen most clearly in the idea of the coup de theatre.

The coup de theatre defines the moment when audience and performers reach, not flux, not difference, but an expression of unification, an absolute. Admittedly, this absolute is metaphoric—a point of oneness marked by complicit disbelief, illusion, and virtuality—but at that fixed point of theatrical time it *is* an absolute, an end point, a revelation. The true theatrical moment is not liquid, it is solid: its impact is a cut with a sharp knife, a hammer hitting a nail—not a slow, liquid drip. In its allegorical, metaphorical limen, the coup de theatre constitutes a place to square the poststructural circle, a locus where the fluid, deferring sign *can* become self-identical with its end, with its "meaning." As Artaud writes and Derrida cites,[39] "the highest possible idea of the theater is one that reconciles us philosophically with Becoming";[40] and as Derrida himself understands and articulates in his critique of Artaud, "theater summons the totality of existence and no longer tolerates either the incidence of interpretation or the distinction between actor and author."[41]

But Derrida's defining critical belief that "one must be separated from oneself in order to be reunited with the blind origin of the work in its darkness"[42] conjures a tempestuos play of theatrical and Cartesian dialectics. On one hand, it perfectly defines the divisional mental processes at play in acting and theatrical spectatorship; but on the other, it epitomizes their very antithesis. Theater ultimately contends the contrary: that to "be separated from oneself" is fatal both for the actor and for the experience of the spectator; and that the Cartesian division of mind and body implicit in Derrida's discourse is anathema to the central tenet of theatrical embodiment.

Although this antinomy of theatrical separation would certainly not be lost on Derrida, his is an atheistic stance: the work of art originates in blindness and out of darkness. His position is legitimate, and even defers to theatrical icons such as Beckett, Artaud, and Brecht. But it does not tread the theatrical boards; it does not play by its rules. Even Derrida's championing of the theater of cruelty is predicated upon a belief in Artaud's drive to destroy theatrical language and metaphor—on its de(con)struction rather than its creation.[43] But his position on conventional theater paradigms is antagonistic, and is precisely the same as Baudrillard's toward media. In fact, in his deconstruction of Rousseau, Derrida sounds remarkably like Baudrillard: "The theater itself is shaped and undermined by the profound evil of representation. It is that corruption itself. Theatrical representation . . . is contaminated by supplementary re-presentation."[44] Derrida's distaste for the theatrical continues in his analysis of the actor:

Vice is his natural bent. It is normal that he who has taken up representation as a profession should have a taste for external and artificial signifiers, and for the perverse use of signs. Luxury, fine clothes, and dissipation are not signifiers incidentally coming about here and there, they are the crimes of the signifier and the representer itself.[45]

We question, indeed we wonder why on earth academics of media, digital arts, and performance continually and apparently compulsively cite and pay homage to Derrida and Baudrillard, these self-confessed haters of media and performance.[46] Derrida's deconstruction of language parallels Artaud's celebration of theater as a plague. The plague analogy highlights a subversion of morality and society, where barriers become fluid, order disappears and anarchy prevails.[47] Derrida celebrates the same collapse of boundaries, the same scourge and breakdown of order and signification, as language itself becomes a plague, a cellular virus, splitting and infecting its very self. But whereas Derrida's linguistic plague darkens, divides, and undermines notions of meaning and truth, Artaud's plague is bright and blinding in its revelations, seeking transcendent, unifying meanings and nowadays highly unfashionable universal "truths":

If fundamental theatre is like the plague, this is not because it is contagious, but because like a plague it is a revelation, urging forward the exteriorisation of a latent undercurrent of cruelty through which all the perversity of which the mind is capable, whether in a person or a nation, becomes localised.[48]

Of course, performance theory has always necessitated some lifting up from the realm of the "material" (both the dramatic "content" and the physical/atomic "substance" of bodies, sets, props, and spaces) into more conceptual and abstract territories of philosophical thought, epistemology, and the dance of critical language. Performances are therefore not simply considered on their own terms, but in relation to other modes of thought and belief. While every piece of criticism is unavoidably embroiled and entangled within the tastes, prejudices, and thought systems of both author and reader, its role nonetheless is—or should be—to disentangle and thereby shed light on the object of criticism. The poststructuralist project sheds light, and sometimes brilliant, blinding rays, but primarily away from rather than toward the artwork. The rays spill and refract around 360 degrees within an infinite and fractal theater of *differance*. But the subtlety and sophistication of the interplays of differentiation and deferentiation become too often circular and philosophically self-fulfilling, and rather than acknowledging ontological difference and artistic originality, can cast all works of art as *the same*. Performances and artistic artifacts become plastic toys: of no real significance in themselves, but objects existing primarily for the pleasure of philosophical play and intellectual interaction. Since the death of the author and the birth of the deconstructive critic, artworks and performances have too often been cast as undifferentiated, homogenous lumps of putty.

Cybernetics and Posthumanism

I was born human, but this was an accident of fate—a condition merely of time and place. I believe it's something we have the power to change.

—KEVIN WARWICK[49]

Before looking in detail at current theories and debates around posthumanism, it is interesting to reflect on the influence and development of cybernetics, a forefather of posthumanism and an integral element of many digital performance works. In particular, the use of interactive and feedback-activated systems in digital performance directly relates to the cybernetic model of "communication and control." Cybernetics was a new approach to scientific theory and practice developed during and following World War II by scientists including Claude Shannon and Norbert Wiener, who coined the word from the Greek *kybernein*, "meaning to govern, as essentially the art of the steersman."[50] The system of cybernetics (the origin of the *cyber-* prefix) emphasized a move away from purely mechanical modes of technology and engineering toward communication and control systems that could "overflow the boundaries of any physical object . . . [and] spread across multiple entities."[51]

Cybernetics branched out to explore many disciplines such as biology and psychology, but the digital computer remained its prime focus of interest and experimental development, and terms such as "input," "output," and "feedback," which were adopted in Wiener's writings, have since become common terms within computer parlance. Even the simplest computer-activated art installations use a cybernetic system, and performance artists such as Stelarc use advanced cybernetics, supplanting their bodies with robotic prostheses to engage in a scientific approach to cybernetic human-machine systems where: "sensory feedback loops . . . [bring about] a collapse of the psychological distance between the operator and the robot; in other words, if the robot does what the human commands and the human perceives what the robot perceives, the human-machine system collapses into one operational unit."[52]

In numerous motion-activating systems developed by or for performers, the body affects a clear cybernetic feedback loop: an arm gesture provides a computational input that is deciphered and reconfigured to trigger an output in another form, such as a music sample or video image. Ostensibly, the body of the performer and the piece of music or video are distinct entities or "objects," but within cybernetic understandings they are no longer separated; they are intimately connected within a communication and control system. The boundary between the performer's body and the output it triggers collapses as media literally becomes, to use the phrase Marshall McLuhan adopted for the subtitle to his 1964 book *Understanding Media: "The Extensions of Man."* Although many critics remain skeptical of the extent to which the two elements of body and media are in actuality combined, it is beyond doubt that for performers and users of such systems, at least the "feeling" of cybernetic connection to the digital media they activate is extremely strong. The concept of interconnection between different physical entities propounded within cybernetics has led it to be linked with ideas within poststructuralist theory and Zen Buddhism, and to related conceptions about the human body whereby "our skins are not boundaries but permeable membranes."[53]

Katherine Hayles notes how cybernetics reconfigures the body as an information system, and intimates that body boundaries "are up for grabs."[54] Hayles's *How We Became Posthuman: Virtual Bodies in Cybernetics, Literature and Informatics* (1999) explores in detail how these ideas challenge values central to liberal humanism: "a coherent self, the right of that self to autonomy and freedom, and a sense of agency linked with a belief in enlightened self-interest."[55] She notes the irony that although Wiener himself held strong ethical and humanist beliefs, at the same time he used cybernetics to create more effective military killing machines for Vannevar Bush. But soon after World War II Wiener renounced military funding and interference, and in his open letter "A Scientist Rebels" (1947) he declared that science must have a political and social conscience, and scientists should engage with the consequences of their actions.[56] But the anxious tensions between conceptions of cybernetically extended bodies, liberal humanism, and militarism remained with Wiener throughout his life, and were articulated in fascinating papers such as "Men, Machines and the World About" (1954).

He begins by enthusiastically drawing similarities between the workings of the human nervous system and the connected binary switching operations of the computer, since the individual fibers of the nervous system follow an "all or nothing" pattern: "they fire or do not fire; they do not fire halfway."[57] Furthermore, since synapses and inhibitory fibers regulate the firing of the fibers in appropriate combinations "the nervous system is not only a computing machine but a control machine. . . . Feedback mechanisms are not only well known to occur in the voluntary actions of the human body, but . . . they are necessary for its very life."[58] He then discusses the "new industrial revolution" where computers will enable increasing automation of industrial processes, and also develop learning and artificial intelligence capabilities. Where the first industrial revolution was a simple paradigm of energy replacement where the machine took over physical tasks from humans or animals, the new industrial revolution replaces human judgment with machine judgment. The machine becomes a source of control, intelligence, and communication rather than simple muscle power. But at this point Wiener's tone changes dramatically, and he invokes a religious metaphor:

There is a very real danger in this country in bowing down before the brass calf, the idol, which is the gadget. . . . We cannot worship the gadget and sacrifice the human being to it, but a situation is easily possible in which we may incur a disaster. . . . Gentleman, there is no Santa Claus! If we want to live with the machine, we must understand the machine.[59]

His fire-and-brimstone rhetoric continues when he announces that the medieval burning of witches may have been justified where "sorcery was not the use of the supernatural, but the use of human power for other purposes than the greater glory of God,"[60] although his liberal humanism comes to the surface when he quickly stresses that he does not use the word God theistically, but rather in terms of "human value." He concludes with two well-known folk stories which serve as warnings to the analogous threats of magic and computational machines. The first is the tale of a couple who are granted three wishes. Their first, for two hundred dollars, is greeted by the news that their son had been killed in a factory accident, but the company will pay the said sum as compensation. Their second wish is that their son should return, but when he appears as a ghost their final wish is that he departs, and the couple are left penniless and mourning. Wiener's concluding tale is of the fisherman who unleashes a vengeful, malevolent genie from a bottle, but finally manages to talk him back into it. The paper ends dramatically: "Gentlemen, when we get into trouble with the machine, we cannot talk the machine back into the bottle."[61]

Despite Wiener's work as a pioneer of high technology and cybernetics, his perspective here is akin to the dystopic science fiction writer. Or more accurately, he sermonizes like an evangelist: Machines are false gods and the stuff of black magic. Like the allusions to Pandora's box in Ihab Hassan's depiction of the posthuman Prometheus we discuss later, the intelligent machine may become the evil genie that we unwittingly release from its lamp, creating irreversible mayhem. For Wiener, the moral lessons of religion, magic, and the machine are all the same. His cybernetics acts to open all boundaries and connections between machines, nature, and humans, but the boundaries of morality and liberal humanism are sacrosanct and must never be crossed. The sermon is at heart very simple, and fifty years later sounds somewhat clichéd: we must use machines for good, not for evil. But it is finally a sentimental message, like the image of the weeping couple who lost their son through their greed. Neither does it fit with his earlier discourse, which demonstrates how the human nervous system already deems us as binary machines. Like Haraway's discourse on the cyborg, the message urges us to recognize our kinship with machines, and to extend ourselves into their realm, but then some malfunction reminds us that our religious ecstasy must be pure, not sinful.

The Posthuman Body and Mind

Living beings do not belong to a uniquely organic domain anymore. Our bodies are now made of machines, images and information: We are becoming cultural bodies.
—OLLIVIER DYENS[62]

Cyberneticist Gregory Bateson took up Alan Turing's question of whether a blind man's stick is part of the man.[63] In epidermal biological terms it is not, but as far as cybernetic systems are concerned it is, as is a hearing aid or Steven Hawking's voice synthesizer, since it constitutes part of a single information flow and feedback system. If we accept this premise, then the digital manifestations of performers working telematically (video-conferenced/digitally transmitted) are also part of the performer's bodies. But to embrace fully such radical theory may also involve accepting the proposition that one has become "posthuman." Posthuman theory places "emphasis on cognition rather than embodiment"[64] toward the amalgam of human consciousness and intelligent machine, with the body becoming a manipulable evolutionary prosthesis, as exemplified in the work of Stelarc (figure 7.2).

In *The Order of Things: An Archeology of the Human Sciences* (1973), Michel Foucault suggests that "man" is "a historical construction whose era is about to end."[65] Three years later, Ihab Hassan, a thinker perennially ahead of his time, coined the term "posthumanism" in a keynote speech at the 1976 *International Symposium on Post-Modern Performance* at the Center for Twentieth Century Studies at the University of Wisconsin-Milwaukee. While others were still grappling with the new epistemologies of postmodernism and deconstruction, Hassan introduced the posthumanist concept, which would then lie mostly dormant for two decades before more recent, and predominantly women writers such as Judith Halberstam and Ira Livingston, Sandy Stone, and Katherine Hayles revived it.[66] Hassan debates whether posthumanism constitutes a "sudden mutation of the times" or the continuation of a process begun in the prehistoric firelight of the caves of Lascaux.

Years before the home computer, the Web, and modern techno-theory, Hassan also skillfully dissected the key dialectical tensions and themes that today characterize debates within digital performance, as well as cyberculture in general. Marshall McLuhan's and Buckminster Fuller's 1960s technological conceptions of (respectively) a "global village" and of "spaceship earth," and Norman O. Brown's idea of "the mystic body of mankind,"[67] clash with equally germane notions of a splintering planet, of notions of fracture and the Derridean "metaphysics of fragments."[68] Powerful conjunctions thus vie with equally potent disjunctions. Yet for Hassan "convergence and divergence are but two aspects of the same reality. Totalitarianism and anarchy summon each the other,"[69] and imagination and science are the driving agents of this change in culture and consciousness, and the ultimate will to posthumanism. The arts and sciences converge through new approaches to theory and practice that borrow from and feed each other, an osmosis where scientific models increasingly enrich the arts; and creative, imaginative processes influence the sciences. Hassan defines four areas of contemporary culture characterizing the convergence:

a. The creative process in science and art.
b. The new twilight zone of experimental science.
c. The incorporation of technology into the arts, both as theme and form.
d. The existential search for a unified sensibility.[70]

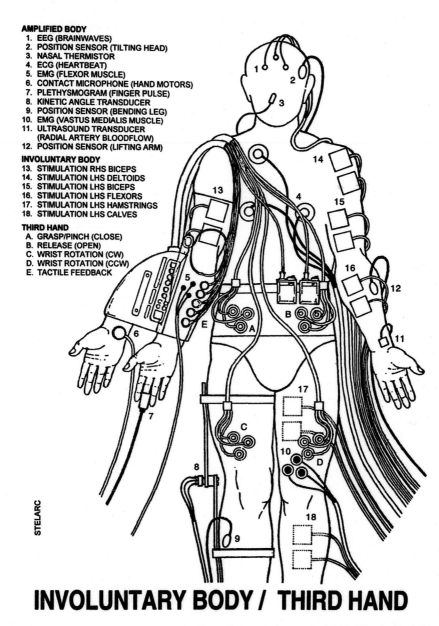

AMPLIFIED BODY
1. EEG (BRAINWAVES)
2. POSITION SENSOR (TILTING HEAD)
3. NASAL THERMISTOR
4. ECG (HEARTBEAT)
5. EMG (FLEXOR MUSCLE)
6. CONTACT MICROPHONE (HAND MOTORS)
7. PLETHYSMOGRAM (FINGER PULSE)
8. KINETIC ANGLE TRANSDUCER
9. POSITION SENSOR (BENDING LEG)
10. EMG (VASTUS MEDIALIS MUSCLE)
11. ULTRASOUND TRANSDUCER
    (RADIAL ARTERY BLOODFLOW)
12. POSITION SENSOR (LIFTING ARM)

INVOLUNTARY BODY
13. STIMULATION RHS BICEPS
14. STIMULATION LHS DELTOIDS
15. STIMULATION LHS BICEPS
16. STIMULATION LHS FLEXORS
17. STIMULATION LHS HAMSTRINGS
18. STIMULATION LHS CALVES

THIRD HAND
A. GRASP/PINCH (CLOSE)
B. RELEASE (OPEN)
C. WRIST ROTATION (CW)
D. WRIST ROTATION (CCW)
E. TACTILE FEEDBACK

STELARC

INVOLUNTARY BODY / THIRD HAND

Figure 7.2 Stelarc's posthuman man-machine design for his *Involuntary Body/Third Hand* project. Diagram: Stelarc.

The keynote speech, published the following year as "Prometheus as Performer: Towards a Posthumanist Culture?" (1977) encapsulates key concerns that now divide theoretical thought on virtual culture and digital performance. The speech itself is structured as a theatrical conflict: a five-scene dramatic masque where eight characters muse and argue over Prometheus's significance as a mirror of contemporary art, theory, and society.[71] Prometheus becomes a metaphor for "a mind struggling with the One and the Many . . . where Imagination and Science, Myth and Technology, Language and Number sometimes meet."[72] Some of Hassan's characters exalt Prometheus as a hero who defied Zeus in a quest to unite the divided mind and Heaven and Earth; others describe a darker specter of error, terror, and madness. Rather than a benevolent high priest presiding over a happy consummation between Earth and Sky, they warn of Prometheus's role as a trickster and thief who begets mutants and monsters; a representation of the "future shock" of cloning, parthenogenesis, androids, cyborgs, and chimeras. His relationship to the wider story of Epimetheus is not forgotten. Epimetheus, husband of Pandora, ignored his brother's advice and opened Pandora's box, whereupon "all the ills of mankind ensue."[73] But above all, Hassan casts Prometheus as a symbol of posthumanism, and concludes in the final words of his dramatic epilogue:

Is it not finally plain? Prometheus, prophet, Titan transgressor and trickster, giver of fire, maker of culture—Prometheus is our performer. He performs Space and Time; he performs Desire. He suffers. We ourselves are that performance; we perform and are performed every moment. We are the pain and play of the Human, which will not remain human. We are both Earth and Sky, Water and Fire. We are the changing form of Desire. Everything changes, and nothing, not even Death, can tire.[74]

Hassan's achievement was not only to coin the term and to initiate discourse on posthumanism, but also to be one of the first writers to encapsulate quintessential ideas and debates within cyberculture and digital performance. In his 1976 keynote speech, he became the first person to specifically *dramatize* and *perform* the fundamental theoretical tensions and contradictions of technological performance. But it was more than twenty years later that the posthuman theme came to widespread attention following the publication of Katherine Hayles's *How We Became Posthuman: Virtual Bodies in Cybernetics, Literature and Informatics* (1999). Hayles stresses that becoming posthuman is not contingent upon technological components or implants in the body as in the literal cyborg, but on the construction of subjectivity and informational processes. "People become posthuman when they think they are posthuman" she says.[75] If we accept this premise, we may need to acknowledge that digital performance is predominantly created *by* people who are (or believe themselves to be) posthuman *for* people who are posthuman. Within the cybernetic model, the problem of the body and embodiment is short-circuited if not erased, since it is considered that information has lost its body . . . to be conceptualized as an entity separate from the material forms in which it is thought to be embedded. . . . In the posthuman, there are no essential differences or absolute demarcations between bodily existence and computer simulation, cybernetic mechanism and biological organism, robot teleology and human goals.[76]

In cybernetic information and communication theory, embodiment is therefore immaterial, and according to Hayles is defined by pattern rather than presence.[77] If this is the case, and if questions of absence and presence are not relevant to information and communication within cybernetic discourse, should they be any more relevant to digital manifestations of performance? In a postmodern age when Foucault and others have already conceptualized the body as a primarily linguistic discourse system, does the intervention of mediating technologies alter the chain of bodily information and communication production in performance?

Not if one accepts that theater has always been the will to virtuality, and where the transformation of the human body has always been quintessential: by external (costume, makeup, lighting, physical actions) and internal means (mental focus and psychological characterization). Moreover, the notion of the "real" has never sat happily within theater and performance, notwithstanding realist theater's concern for verisimilitude. Theater is always-already a simulation; it stands for something outside of itself. Theater is the inauthentic masquerading as the authentic; the unreal posited as the real. This basic paradigm is the same as in virtual systems, as Brenda Laurel demonstrates, and Mark Poster maintains that "virtual reality systems continue the Western trend of duplicating the real by means of technology. They provide the participant with a second-order reality."[78] This second-order reality corresponds to exactly what goes on in theater production, which similarly makes use of technology to simulate an alternate reality. What binds theater in both live and virtual forms is the presence whether live or electronic of the empathetic human body and the exploration of the symbolic and the unreal. As Matthew Causey argues, "The sublimity of performance and art within the theater lies in their capacity, as Lyotard theorized it, 'to put forward the unpresentable in presentation itself.'"[79] Herbert Blau also reminds us that "There is nothing more illusory in performance than the illusion of the unmediated . . . the truth of illusion . . . haunts all performance whether or not it occurs in the theater."[80] Such perspectives and truisms, whilst not explicitly casting digital performance as a posthuman practice, nonetheless implicitly confirm that the corporeality or virtualization of a body matters little to the acts it performs, nor the theater or dance it creates.

For us, postmodernism is the explanation of how society has become consumed by mass media; how we are *becoming* the media. The posthuman notion extends this until we *are* media itself. That we can now conceive that live and mediatized bodies are the same is because we have (or will have) succeeded in "taking away" the technology, since we no longer give it a thought. Since it is part of us. Posthuman theories, extending McLuhan's concept of mediatized consciousness and Baudrillard's ideas of simulacra and simulation, suggest that there is no reason why we should recognize breathing living bodies to have greater solidity and authenticity than electronic humans similarly engaged in performative actions. Yet phenomenologically, there is a human context that is unique in proximal real space and is (at least partly) absent in recordings and virtual representations. Real and virtual bodies are not the same, and Merleau-Ponty makes clear distinctions between monocular images, which are "phantoms" and "pre-things," and binocular ones, which are "real" and "the thing."[81] Electronic or monocular images of the body "are too far from having its density to enter into competition with it . . . we cannot compare the two."[82] But cybernetic and posthuman instincts offer a contrary thesis: that this proximally live uniqueness lacks real value and significance, it merely asserts a different (albeit arguably privileged) presence. Most digital performers utilizing virtual body manifestations are likely to agree with this thesis, and, equally significantly, to assert the intimate and inextricable cybernetic/posthuman connection between their live and virtual selves. This is at odds with yet another overarching theme from postmodern theory that is frequently (and for us often inaccurately or indiscriminately) applied to digital performance practice, the notion of "split subjectivity."

Conclusion: Splitting Subjectivity

The question of the drama is not one of representation, of the thing and its reflection, but of the splitting of subjectivity.
—MATTHEW CAUSEY[83]

Coming from authoritative sources such as Lacan, and more recently Derrida and the poststructuralists, the notion of split subjectivity has become a widely accepted theoretical "given" that is liberally invoked in academic commentaries on cyberculture, digital arts, and performance studies. Lacan uses the split subject as a metaphor for the fundamental human existential problem: "there is something that establishes a fracture, a bi-partition, a splitting of being," he says[84] (figure 7.3). But to relate this ancient, perennial "truth" too readily to technological performance proves and means little, and mystifies rather than clarifies the role and ontology of the virtual double. The split subject suggests the wholly divided self, like the medical schizophrenic who lacks control over warring personas with opposing motivations. This is not the case for the posthuman performer, who is typically a control freak, with acute awareness of the double as both an embodied representation and performed index of the self, not a separate, differentiated subject, nor far less some uncontrollable chimera. We therefore dispute Matthew Causey's formulation quoted earlier. The question *is* "one of representation, of the thing and its reflection" *not* "the splitting of subjectivity."

In digital performance, one cannot but determine theory and practice frequently moving in opposite and contrary directions. Instilled postmodern belief systems stress

Figure 7.3 The notion of the split subject is encapsulated in this digitally manipulated screen projection used in Random Dance Company's live dance-theater performance *Nemesis* (2002). Photo: Ravi Deepres.

fragmentation, split subjectivity, and the rejection of meta-narratives and meanings, whereas in actuality what is *practiced* by digital/posthuman performers is commonly the search for the opposite: for cohesion, for meaning, for unity, for intimate cybernetic connections between the organic and the technological. To relate postmodern theories of fragmentation and split subjectivity to virtual bodies or digitally distributed selves is actually too literal, trite, and easy, and ultimately misses the point. Digital performance is more commonly a quest for unified subjectivity (though doubled, not split, but the many facets of self exposed in order to converge as one), a *structuralist* rather than poststructuralist project, a search to express universal myths and metaphors about the human condition.

Causey reflects that "performance studies fails postorganic performance,"[85] and Schechner pleads for performance studies to free itself from orthodox positions to create new theories specific to performance itself. That need is doubly urgent within digital performance where the actual specificities of the changing ontology of performance and the performer within virtual space are rarely addressed except in old terms. But the task is difficult and the field is already saturated with re-rehearsals and revivals of postmodern philosophy and deconstructive analysis. Some are brilliant and incisive (though others are dull and tired), but they are not the last word, and are the beginning rather than the end. There is a real danger of theoretical imperialism, of certain analytical modes and philosophical worldviews colonizing, civilizing, and trivializing digital performance in the same way that Rustom Bharucha saw Western intercultural performance theory and practice doing in relation to Eastern performance: misunderstanding it but claiming it for its own.[86] Posthuman and cybernetic perspectives in some ways merely extend postmodern critiques of mediatization, simulation and the loss of the real, but they certainly offer a fresher, even more scientific approach toward a more specific and rationally considered analysis of the field.

The Digital Revolution

In the beginning was the code, and the code was hanging out with god; soon enough some came to the conclusion that the code was god.
—MARK PESCE[1]

A Global Revolution?

In the last years of the twentieth century, digital computer technologies became increasingly ubiquitous, bringing the abstract relations of numeration—"number crunching"—to more and more aspects of life in industrialized societies. The first sparks of the so-called Digital Revolution were in defense and weaponry systems following World War II and later spread to science, engineering and clinical practices, electronics, nanotechnology, and robotics. By the 1990s, new technologies became a constituent part of information and communication processes, business practices, manufacturing, commercial retailing, and everyday life in the industrialized world. Their influence on the arts, aesthetics, creativity, and culture has been no less revolutionary, significantly affecting processes and products from film and television production to creative writing and the visual and performance arts.

Charles Ess offers the perspective that, depending upon one's viewpoint, new technology appears to offer everything "from the realization of Enlightenment democracy to the demise of print, literacy, and civilization as we know it."[2] The notion of a "third culture" emerged, particularly following John Brockman's 1995 book of that name, to denote variously the magical offspring of the art and science marriage, the negative impact of technological globalization, and what Pelle Ehn calls the "emerging third culture of nerds and digerati."[3] That a new age had dawned was a common rhetorical stance in the 1990s, and the major dispute revolved not around whether it had, but rather whether it constituted a third or second age/culture, as Mark Poster declared *The Second Media Age* (1995), and Sven Birkerts announced that technologies have created a "secondary world."[4]

Sandy Stone, despite being highly conscious of the dangers of periodizing ages, closes, and dawns, gave way to temptation and proclaimed that we had entered "the virtual age."[5] This was by nature of the human trends toward interiority and textuality in the face of virtual technologies, characterized by increased self-awareness, physical isolation, spatial displacement, and use of "prosthetic" communication.

In the United States in the 1990s, new technologies were assimilated much more rapidly than in Europe and elsewhere, where there was more skepticism and costs were higher: domestic Internet connection was charged by the minute rather than the low monthly fees of the United States. But the comparatively minimal level of government support for the arts in the United States meant that there was quicker and more wide-spread development of experimental new media arts elsewhere, particularly in Europe, Australia, and Japan. While America led many commercially driven new media developments within popular entertainment areas such as film special effects and theme park experiences, non-mainstream digital arts flourished in Europe. This was supported through the establishment of major publicly funded institutions such as Germany's ZKM (Zentrum Für Kunst und Medientechnologie/Center for Art and Media) in Karlsruhe (1989), the New Media Institute in Frankfurt (1990), and the Netherlands' Inter-Society for the Electronic Arts (ISEA, 1990).

But for most countries outside the United States, Europe, Australia, and Japan, the digital revolution did not take place. When Kim Dae-jung, the president of South Korea, opened the FIFA World Cup Football Competition in May 2002, he began his address with the words: "Citizens of the global village." His words underlined and promoted South Korea's status as a leading IT developer in the world (especially mobile phones, Internet connections, and digital television), and the invocation of McLuhan's famous phrase reflected the general belief that the Internet and digital technologies are global. In reality, of course, they are not remotely global or omnipresent. Even the huge audience of 500 million for this mammoth televised event comprised only 12 percent of the total world population, and the television set is markedly more widespread than the computer console, which is currently estimated to reach no more than 5 percent of the world's population.

The digital revolution, and in particular the Internet, is always assumed to be global because its signals instantly travel around the world. But that does not mean those signals can necessarily start or stop anywhere without vast investment in infrastructure, which is out of the reach and finances of many nations. The Internet also happens to be considerably *more* global if you speak, and spell, American English. The inequalities of "the digital divide" between the industrialized nations and the "third world" are even more startling when the essential skill of literacy becomes part of the equation. Africa for example, which has the highest illiteracy rates worldwide, is also consistently the lowest Internet user, so low in fact that some Internet traffic-flow charts simply choose not to list Africa. The ability to purchase essential facilities is equally disparate: of the world's six billion people, three billion are estimated as living on less than the equivalent of two U.S. dollars a day, and half of those on less than the equivalent of one U.S. dollar per day. Another frequently cited statistic is that 70 percent of the world's population has never used a telephone. To describe computing as a global facility thus lies somewhere between gross exaggeration and wishful thinking, and a perhaps more accurate description might be highly exclusive, disuniting and partisan. Statistically, the computer remains a luxury device for a small percentage of devotees within the most advanced industrialized nations.

Artist activists such as Guillermo Gómez-Peña have given effective and valuable voice to issues around the digital divide. Gómez-Peña effectively crossed the artistic border from being highly suspicious of digital technologies to using them extensively, yet his message retains a familiar solidarity with "border groups" and outsiders:

Like the pre-multicultural art world of the early 80s, the new high-tech art world assumed an unquestionable "center," and drew a dramatic digital border. And on the other side of the tracks, there lived all the techno-illiterate artists, along with most women, Chicanos, Afro-Americans and Native Americans in the US and Canada, not to mention the artists living in "Third World" countries. Given the nature of this hegemonic cartography, those of us living South of the digital border were forced to assume once again the unpleasant but necessary roles of webbacks, undocumented cyber-immigrants, digital viruses, techno-pirates, and virtual coyotes (smugglers). We were also shocked by the benign or quiet (not naive) ethnocentrism permeating the debates around art and digital technology, especially in California.[6]

The Borders of Cyberspace

Within theater and performance, the "border" metaphor has long symbolized fundamental concerns, not least between the audience and stage; and between different worlds and realities.[7] The digital divide presents a more concrete border for the third world, while Western digital theory tells its own border tales and presents potent new border terrains, most popularly discussed in relation to thresholds between the material and immaterial, the absent and present, the virtual and the "real." "Digital borderlands," to use Johan Fornäs's term, are frequently conceptualized in such distinct binaries, or in relation to what Peter Lunenfeld calls *The Digital Dialectic* (2000). But border consciousness in digital theory relates not only to lines of division and demarcation but also to new forms of space and territory, particularly what Ryan calls the "new frontier" of cyberspace.[8] In a report summarizing the 1995 Aspen Institute Roundtable on Information Technology, David Bollier notes:

In many ways, cyberspace represents a new frontier that should be understood in terms of the famous "frontier thesis" put forward by historian Frederick Jackson Turner in 1893. . . . Turner proposed that the American character has been indelibly influenced by the existence of a frontier—a place where anyone could stake their own claim to a free land, revel in a loosening of civilized standards and institutional authority and celebrate an extreme individualism. The tension of "taming" the

Western frontier and incorporating it into "civilized society" resemble the challenges now facing us in cyberspace.[9]

The Wild West frontier metaphor was taken up by many writers, and digital pioneers were equated with settlers and cowboys—Paul Saffo, for example discusses VR luminary Howard Rheingold as "one of those trappers in the Old West who helped open up the territory."[10] But the idea of cyberspace (or at least, the World Wide Web) being a virgin, open landscape akin to the Wild West actually lasted only a very short time after its emergence in the early 1990s. It was quickly colonized and overpopulated. The first, pioneering "cowboy" settlers were soon crowded in by swarms of sightseers, small businesses, multinational conglomerates, pornographers, rip-off artists, and what seemed like the world and his wife eagerly marking out their territories with rickety, hastily erected homesteads (called "home pages").[11]

Economist Harry Cleaver's essay "The 'Space' of Cyberspace" examines the politics of cyberspace's frontier metaphor, arguing their inextricable link to ideas of territorial resistance and non-surrender. This is because the initial free spirit of pioneering cyberspace colonists has been inexorably threatened by corporate capital, which "tries either to enclose their spaces by commercializing them if they look profitable, or crushing them if they look dangerous."[12] But according to British writer Oliver August, the Wild West analogy is a specifically American conception, and cyberspace itself offers an ultimately hollow return to the lost nineteenth-century adventure:

Britons still think of computers as a tool. Partly out of contempt for soulless machines, partly out of Luddite fear, computers have not taken centre stage in our consciousness. But in America "cyberspace" has filled the spiritual void created when the Wild West was conquered and irrigated. Cyberspace is the new frontier . . . the chance to follow their forefathers, to trek into uncharted territory, taking destiny into their own hands . . . from the comfort of their living rooms.[13]

Gómez-Peña adopts a comparably cynical view, dubbing cyberspace "a sanitized version of the pioneer and cowboy mentalities of the Old West ('Guillermo, you can be the first Mexican ever to do this and that on the Net')."[14] As we discuss in chapter 20, he brilliantly satirizes the supposed "politically neutral/raceless/genderless/classless 'territory' "[15] through his Internet bulletin board projects, which expose online bigotry and racism, as well as through his droll, self-parodic performance persona El Mexterminator, an "unwilling . . . techno-artist and an information superhighway bandido."[16] But for other performance artists, such as Phil Morle, the digital borderland offers a deep and resonant metaphor that is at once performative and metaphysical:

In between the spirit world and the living, human beings are always within and between; between a state of embodied materiality toward which we act and a state of disembodied transcendence toward which we extend ourselves. We never reach either point—cast into the limen forever, ecstatic, emergent and alive. This paper introduces my position within the limen—a personal experience generated in the virtual spaces that I am within—through my actions as a performance worker; as a cyberspace cowboy and; as an experience-maker.[17]

Lingua Excluda

As already noted, language provides another major border that extends the digital divide. Moreover, English is not only the lingua franca of the web, but also of much artistic and academic networking, communication and publication. Native English speakers (not least the British) have a generally poor reputation for acquiring the languages of other nations and thus, for example, work wholly undertaken in French may remain largely unknown in the United Kingdom, even though France is physically only twenty-two miles from the United Kingdom at its nearest point. Algerian Louis Bec creates impressive digital life-forms, but his work remains relatively unknown in the United Kingdom and the United States primarily because he lives and works in France and, more significantly, publishes mostly in French. Outside of a German-speaking public, the same problems affect the robotic work of Munich-based Nicolas Anatol Baginsky; the net.art and associated events of Austrian artist Konrad Becker; and the Internet sci-art of Richard Kriesche who exhibited at the 1995 Venice Biennale.

Digital arts and performance have nonetheless flourished in numerous and unexpected non-English-speaking countries, and Slovenia provides an interesting case in point. Marko Peljhan's work with the Slovenian Space Agency brought the nation some international artistic attention at the 2003 Venice Biennale, but for many years Slovenia had been a dynamic center for digital arts experimentation. Its Digital Media Lab had run an open-access new media laboratory and supported numerous initiatives in net.art and robotics, including operating a guest program presenting international and local artists.[18] During the 1990s, the journal *Maska* (founded 1920) undertook a significant body of interviews with key digital performance practitioners including Merce Cunningham, William Forsythe, Philip Glass, Bill T. Jones, Stelarc, Survival Research Laboratories, and Robert Wilson. Some extraordinary digital performances were developed at the Media Art Lab, including Darij Kreuth and Davide Grassi's brain and eye-scanning activated performance *Brainscore* (2000), which we discuss in detail later. Slovenian venues and galleries such as the Galerie Kapelica sponsor and promote installations, presentations and extreme body performance events including the development of Stelarc's *Extra Ear* project in 2004 (figure 8.1). The Multimedia Center Kibla in Maribor, run by Peter Dobrila and Aleksandra Kostic, organizes International Festivals of Computer Arts and has promoted and supported highly innovative work. This includes Eduardo Kac's *Teleporting an Unknown State* (1998), where light was "teleported" via webcams and the Internet from Chicago, Vancouver, Mexico City, Paris, Antarctica, Moscow, Tokyo, and Sydney to permit a seed to grow in a darkened gallery over a period of two weeks (figure 8.2). Slovenian net

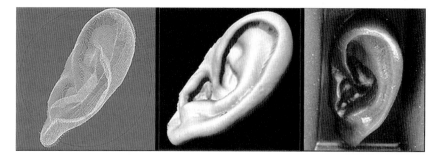

Figure 8.1   Stelarc's designs for implanting an *Extra Ear* (2004) with integrated technologies to access computer networks. Developed at the Galerie Kapelica in Slovenia. Photo: Ionat Zurr.

Figure 8.2   Eduardo Kac's *Teleporting an Unknown State*, developed at the Multimedia Center Kibla in Maribor, Slovenia in 1998.

artist/activist Vuc Cosic has also brought the country to attention by controversially laying a wreath of flowers at the German ZKM media museum to mark the death of net.art (the very genre he famously named) because it was becoming increasingly a museum exhibit. Later as part of his *Net.art per me* (2001) at the Venice Biennale, he issued a statement warning "historians of net.art not to fall into unjustified glorification of Slovenia or Eastern Europe as a natural basin for net.art" As Cosic suggests, digital artists from Eastern Europe have made a significant impact, and several artist networks have emerged such as the "Syndicalists," involving more than five hundred artists who live and work in Eastern Europe.

Japan holds a particularly interesting and unique position in the global picture of digital applications; a highly industrialized nation that is arguably the world's major developer and manufacturer of computer hardware, software, robotics, and computer games. Every month, some of the world's leading companies, including Sony, Sharp, Samsung, JVC, Fujitsu, Panasonic, Toshiba, and Nintendo, sell electronic goods worth $18 billion.[19] Yet because it preserves its own cultural traditions, as well as its own alphabet and language (websites, for example do not "travel well"), Japan can appear to remain curiously private, and relatively few of its artists have received significant critical attention from western nations. Japanese artists have therefore had to rely upon travel to exhibit their work more widely, for example to major international conferences and festivals such as Ars Electronica and SIGGRAPH, and to European new media venues such as ZKM, where Japanese performance artist Ikue Mori's elaborate drum machine sculptures were used in live performance during his stay as artist in residence in 1998–99. At the Ars Electronica Festival in Linz in 1996, there were exhibits from Virtual Reality installation artist Kazuhiko Hachiya and pioneering interactive artist Masaki Fujihata, who received a Golden NICA prize for his networked art piece using global positioning systems, *Global Interior Project* (1996).

One of Japan's leading multimedia artists, Naoko Tosa, has exhibited her fascinating work extensively, including *Talking to Neuro Baby* at the 1993 Ars Electronica, which posed the question: "Is Neuro Baby a toy, a pet, a new form of intelligence or a strange life form?"[20] For her *Interactive Poem* (1996), a computer was programmed to recognize emotions and mood in speech and to instigate a type of "dialogue" by generating images and sounds according to the speech inflections it heard. In *Unconscious Flow*, shown at SIGGRAPH 1999, a computer mapped the heartbeats of two participants who are instructed to touch hands, with the resulting signals generating images of two mermaids dancing onscreen, who interpolate the signals received.

Code

The code is necessary but unavailable except as a symptom; alien to life in three dimensions, but present; the medium of community that has no place and exists only each time it is iterated: it has no potential. The iterations of code are performances without theatre.

—ALICE RAYNER[21]

The advent of computing necessitated a new vocabulary, and during its rise in popularity during the 1980s and 1990s, much of the new terminology it brought in its wake remained a mystery to a majority of the population suddenly confronted by a strange new language and orthodoxy. Initially for many, even the distinction between hardware and software was not self-evident, and there were literally thousands of specialist terms and acronyms. Some were new such as bytes, DOS, and RAM, while others sounded familiar but had specific meanings in this new language: attachment, card, crash, directory, drag, floppy, menu, virus, and code.

The word "code," in the context of information technologies, is particularly intriguing. As well as meaning information written succinctly in an appropriate language, it also carries strong associations of secrecy: from Morse Code and the coded messages of spy thrillers to the World War II German Enigma code, whose "cracking" by Alan Turing and others necessitated the construction of one of the first computer systems. The computer has more recently been used to decipher scripts from early civilizations to reveal the intricacies of their culture and social systems.[22] Simon Singh's *The Code Book: The Science of Secrecy from Ancient Egypt to Quantum Cryptography* (2000) explains in great detail how codes have been both constructed and cracked throughout history, from the hieroglyphics of Egyptian tombs (a sign system that has only become seen as a secret code because our ability to interpret them has been lost over time) to the betrayal of Mary Queen of Scots, whose plots were suddenly revealed. An indication of the West's overriding obsession with embedded code at the turn of the millennium was the so-called Bible Code (or "Torah Code"), which claimed that predictions of future events are codified in the Christian *Holy Bible,* and on publication *The Bible Code* (1997) book topped the best-selling lists. A few years earlier, a photograph that circulated widely on the Web, presumed to be genuine, showed an unkempt youth on the sidewalk proffering a piece of torn cardboard to camera on which were scrawled the words "Hungry!—can code HTML for food".

Notions of "protocol," another word redefined for the digital age, were also invoked through code's associations with rules of etiquette and conduct: dress code, professional code, code of practice, and so on. The particular notion of code as a digest of rules by which a community lives stems from Roman law as well as the *codex,* effectively the first books with pages bound down one side, which superseded the more labor-intensive scrolls that had to be wound through to find the appropriate section. "Code" in its etymological sense thus suggests an arrangement of information into recognizable and easily accessible pieces, a paradigm that is eminently transferable to the operation of computer code.

Codes that invite interpretation are nothing new to theater and performance studies, and semiotics has been a cornerstone of performance criticism for at least the past quarter of a century. Keir Elam's seminal study *The Semiotics of Theatre and Drama* (1980) traced a history of semiotic approaches from Sausurre's linguistic analyses of the early twentieth century to the Prague Structuralists' examinations of the theatrical sign in the 1930s, to late-twentieth-century theories of theater, language, and the sign. Thereafter, works of theater criticism that adopted a semiotic code-breaking stance became legion, including Patrice Pavis on the language of the stage;[23] Jean Alter on text, actors, production and reception;[24] Marvin Carlson on deconstructing theatre architecture;[25] Elaine Aston and George Savona's student guide to the theatre as sign system;[26] Erika Fischer-Lichte's *The Semiotics of Theatre* and Marco de Marinis's *The Semiotics of Performance*;[27] a renewed approach by Susan Melrose;[28] and Jack Goody's wider survey of images, theater, and fiction across Western, Eastern, and African cultures.[29] Reinforced by deconstructivist theory ranging across the full panoply of human understanding in philosophy, the social sciences, the arts, and the humanities, the general development for performance studies was ever widening, more generalized and more interdisciplinary, mirroring the way in which the traditional boundaries between theater and performance became ever more blurred and interdisciplinary.

The interpretation of codes and the deconstruction of texts to reveal both the obvious and what lies behind the obvious became the overriding critical concern of the late twentieth century, led by linguists such as Charles Sanders Peirce, Roland Barthes, and Roman Jakobsen, and later elaborated and extended by philosophers such as Jean Baudrillard and Jacques Derrida who each, in various ways, brings to bear the subtle art and science of cryptanalysis. For Derrida, the key is "the economy of language, the codes and the channels of what is the most receivable" set alongside alternative voices and views which may be "reduced to silence, everything that does not conform to very determinate and very powerful frames or codes . . . a counter-culture that is almost inaudible in the codes."[30]

Most recently, the code metaphor has been employed by geneticists to explain in popular science terms the intricacies of DNA (deoxyribonucleic acid, a constituent of chromosomes credited with carrying genetic information) as "genetic code." This is an interesting use of the word that only comes about because of the familiarity of "code" as a mysterious constituent of computing which carries both the "agreed guidelines" *and* the mystery of a secret code. Most people feel they understand the notion of "codified information" and are satisfied with that as an explanation, despite the fact that it is a code that they cannot interpret or make any sense of.[31]

Such was the emphasis upon codes and deconstruction in all disciplines in the early 1990s that the metaphor of computer binary code, greatly assisted by the developing notion of the genetic code as the basic foundation of life itself, began to be conceived by many as the basis of all reality—everything was (or would be) reducible to a stream of bits, as Donna Haraway's influential "A Cyborg Manifesto" (1985) emphasized. For Haraway, humanity must become at one with the integrated circuit: "The cyborg is a kind of disassembled and reassembled, postmodern collective and personal self. This is the self feminists must code."[32] Haraway's capitulation to this notion is total (in her defense, she does introduce it as an ironic dream), and she includes "modern biologies" as well as communication sciences and military operations: "the translation of the world into a problem of coding, a search for a common language in which all resistance to instrumental control

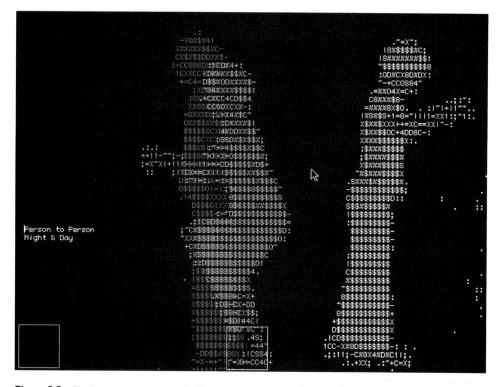

Figure 8.3 The "genetic makeup" of the three female characters is converted to ASCII code in Ruth Gibson and Bruno Martelli's *Windowsninetyeight* CD-ROM (1998).

disappears and all heterogeneity can be submitted to disassembly, reassembly, investment and exchange."[33]

Haraway's "A Cyborg Manifesto" is a powerful statement that microelectronics will affect the way we live and who we are, but it is equally a capitulation to the hyperbolic fantasy that everything is reducible to binary code. Binary code has the seductive lure of simplicity, consisting solely of 0's and 1's, and a quasi-alchemical philosophy has built up around it that believes, like the mythological story of the demented monkey flailing at the typewriter to accidentally produce the complete works of Shakespeare, that the greatest mysteries and perhaps the secret of life itself can be revealed if only the 0's and 1's can be placed in the right order (figure 8.3).

Computer Code

For many inexperienced observers of code, a computer program is a set of mathematical instructions laid out with precision. But what may not be immediately recognizable is that code is quite personal and idiosyncratic for a programmer, and lines of code can be analyzed (just as a literary critic might analyze a text) to discern approximately when it was written, and to critique idiosyncrasies of style and content and the way it was expressed and put together. Early programmers were generally united in their intention to create the very best code they could devise, and would openly share instructions, shortcuts, and completed software.

Richard Stallman was one such, a programming staff member of the MIT Artificial Intelligence Lab in the 1970s, where the standard practice was for programmers to return their day's work to a server where it could be accessed by their colleagues and, if useful to them, could be used, modified, and embedded in their work. In a now legendary story, Stallman responded to a problem when a Xerox networked printer had jammed and several people's work was in the queue. Stallman tried to embed and program a message to everyone in the queue that the printer needed attention, but found that the printer's program was not accessible: no source code was available, the printer was just running on a stream of binary 0's and 1's. He tried to obtain the source code, but his request was refused because the programmer had signed a nondisclosure agreement—in other words, the source code had been copyrighted and hidden, thus creating what is now known as "proprietary code." Proprietary code is inaccessible, and although one might buy and "own" a printer, or indeed a computer, one is only licensed to use it as decreed by the company and is not privy to the coded inner workings of its software. Stallman has since devoted much his life to finding ways to restrict this tendency as much as possible, and to make software free to access.

In attempting this, of course, he has found himself in conflict with the major commercial interests, which see their ability to maintain secrecy and retain ownership of the software as paramount to their profits. It is the very epitome of a *restricted* Information Age, not one where all information is accessible but where information becomes a secret and coded commodity that the owner can sell separately each and every time it is required. Buying a computer is thus not dissimilar to buying a train ticket, but then having to separately purchase a secret timetable so as to find and board a train that will take you to the desired destination. Both governments and software companies reserve particular venom for code-breakers and distributors whose actions make secrets available to many, and decrease the power and control of the elite code-holders. But Stallman is unlikely to suffer the penury and punishment of one of the greatest code-breakers of history, the Oxford professor John Wycliffe, born c. 1330, who was critical of the abuses and false teachings of the church, and had the audacity to translate the Latin Bible into Middle English to make it more widely available, an act decreed as heresy. Although he was sufficiently well connected with court and king to avoid punishment during his life time, half a century after his death the church wreaked its revenge by banning the English version by law, attempting (unsuccessfully) to recall and burn all (handwritten) circulating copies, deconsecrating Wycliffe's grave, exhuming the body, cremating it, crushing the bones, and scattering the ashes in a river.

In the late twentieth century, court action by commercial businesses and the movie industry mirrored the same restraining attitudes. One was against Eric Corley, who advertised (and even had printed on T-shirts) the decoding source code for overcoming regionalized DVD restrictive practices, and another challenged Norwegian teenager Jon Johanson, who wrote the decoding programme DeCSS (CSS being the encryption code) that enabled encrypted DVD films to be copied onto hard drives. In America, the latter case became a battle between the Digital Millennium Copyright Act and the freedoms embodied in the First Amendment of the Constitution (copyright finance holding sway), and the case was then taken up by the Hollywood movie industry in Norway, where a final decision decreed that Johansen had nothing to answer for. But despite such examples of David versus Goliath victories, the practice of decoding software and making it freely available continues to be a dangerous if not always criminal occupation, and has been set further obstacles through legislation to preserve the legal and commercial supremacy of copyright, such as the European Union's "E-Commerce Directive" (2002).

The "free software" movement was and is not without its own internal altercations, although its general aims remain united. In the early 1990s a Finnish student, Linus Torvalds, an excellent programmer and longtime friend of Stallman, put a message out on a programmer's list stating that "just for fun" he was attempting to create an operating system that would crash less frequently than the commercial ones (primarily Microsoft and UNIX). He offered the start that he had made as open source code, and it rapidly became the kernel of a shared Operating System program contributed to by expert programmers the world over and called, in his honor, LINUX. Within the free software movement, Torvalds was propelled to the status of a world folk hero fighting the evil monolithic software giants. The full story has been recounted in a number of readable accounts and biographies.[34]

Another individual who followed the free code ethic was the English physicist Tim Berners-Lee, the primary architect of the World Wide Web and inventor of its essential protocols, including HTTP, URLs, HTML, and WWW. All this code and all the perseverance necessary to establish and implement it was given away free by Berners-Lee rather than wrapped and restricted by intellectual property rights legislation.[35] This constant clash between giveaway and restriction, between cracking the code and keeping the faith is an unvarying feature of the years of computing development and underlines the ambiguity of the word "code" itself—secrets known by the few set against the notion of a set of rules and protocols for the many. Vying between the two forces are the characters known as "hackers," an ambiguous term in itself with overtones of both specialist and criminal, although it was originally coined to mean a computer programmer who could "hack it" (work effectively) at an advanced level. Appropriately, it was Hollywood, ever mindful of its own assets, that turned the phrase negatively and demonized the activity into one associated with illicit prying, theft, and criminal penetration of secret government and business files. Soon there was widespread fear by users of Internet commerce that marauding hackers were out to obtain their credit card numbers, and the hacker community responded in true Hollywood style by differentiating between (good) "white hat hackers" and (bad) "black hat hackers."[36]

Alan Cooper is a leading industry programmer who has written extensively on the failings of the computer industry. Cooper is credited as the "father of Visual Basic" who was awarded the coveted Microsoft "Windows Pioneer Award" in 1994 and has made fundamental contributions to the development of software, winning in 1998 a "software Visionary Award." When such a seminal insider figure publishes a book brazenly entitled *The Inmates Are Running the Asylum* (1999), it is an indication that something is amiss. A dedicated designer, Cooper constantly notes that software is there for users and should meet their requirements (and limitations) rather than the prejudices of individual programmers. He cites instance after instance where programmers have invented software without checking how people might want to use it, and others where the programmer hides a problem with an unintelligible message such as "Error 5494xK3," which could only mean something to an experienced programmer, although equally it may not, since programmers are not beyond hostile jokes. He stresses, "Many newcomers in the world of computing imagine that software behaves the way it does for some good reason. On the contrary, its behavior is often the result of some whim or accident that is thoughtlessly propagated for years."[37]

Cooper's treatise, as his title suggests, is witty as well as sharply critical: some amusing psychological profiling is drawn up distinguishing *Homo logicus* (programmers) from the normal *Homo sapiens* by such defining characteristics as "be generous in selfishness," "blindness improves vision," "keep fixing what's not broken until it's broken," and "I didn't answer incorrectly, you just asked the wrong question."[38] It is sarcasm with more than a grain of truth that any newcomer, having struggled to install software or locate instructions in any one of the fifteen languages in which they are supplied but all of which seem equally incomprehensible, will instantly recognize. This level of mystification and sometimes even despair generates a climate of magical "spirituality" where, if something suddenly appears to work as originally anticipated, it generates a sense that something miraculous has occurred, that you have been witness to a holy statue crying real tears.

A major London conference on the topic of code, open source, and the restrictions of copyright took place in April 2002 and subsequently led to the publication of *CODE: Collaboration and Ownership in the Digital Economy* (2002), with viewpoints from experts including Richard Stallman, Glyn Moody, and Roger Malina. It considers six issues and conundrums surrounding intellectual property rights and open source projects: Recovering Collectivity; Copyright vs. Community; Private Interests: Freedom and Control; Distributing Knowledge; Reward and Responsibility; Cultural Practitioners; and The Future of Knowledge.[39] At the Banff Centre for the Arts in 2000, Sara Diamond gathered together a group of software developers, media artists, and programmers to model "Code Zebra," software that would allow and encourage online chat and video streams particularly between artists and scientists: "Code Zebra is a volatile, interactive performance, software and social system where art meets science . . . CZ induces dialogues and debates between science (with an interest in computer and biological science) and arts (including visual art, design, fashion, architecture)."[40] The software was specifically designed to document and analyze many aspects of these exchanges as 2D/3D visual patterns that, Diamond claimed, "enable emotional analysis of conversations." A long-term and complex project, one of its most interesting facets was that its premise was to use drama to develop the software, rather than the usual assumption that the software will develop the drama.

Computers as Theater

As Stephen Wilson notes, the arts and sciences were culturally and philosophically united until the Renaissance, when scientific advances and different forms of specialization and codification split them apart. For centuries thereafter, the arts and sciences largely avoided or ignored each other, and developed their own languages and ideologies. In 1964, C. P. Snow announced in "The Two Cultures and the Scientific Revolution" that the values, perspectives, and languages of artists and scientists were so radically distinct that they could not understand each other.[41] While historically the arts and sciences have remained polarized and deeply suspicious of one another, new computer technologies have become an interface for their mutual coexistence: "in the realm of electronic image production the boundaries between art, science and entertainment are quite blurred."[42] Within computing, drama theory has been afforded a special place, and the importance of theater as a model for software program design has been widely discussed by critics within the computer sciences.[43]

In *Elements of Friendly Software Design* (1982), Paul Heckell maintains that dramatic art forms such as theater and film offer the most effective models for software conception and design. He goes on to suggest that there is a clear transition being effected that is transforming traditional computer science and engineering into a creative, evocative, and dramatic artform, a view echoed by Donald Norman:

The key word in finding an illuminating path through the technological maze is "interaction." These new technologies all have one thing in common: They can aid our interaction with others, with knowledge, information and experience. . . . When we look toward what is known about the nature of interaction, why not turn to those who manage it best—to those from the world of drama, of the stage, of the theatre? . . . There is much to learn from theatre.[44]

In *User Centered System Design: New Perspectives on Human-Computer Interaction* (1986), Norman emphasizes the computer interface as a place of action (rather than simple dialogue) where both the human and the computer have a role. The centrality of this notion of action within Norman's discourse, as well as in the work of Brenda Laurel, has clear parallels with the primacy with which "units of action" are afforded within the acting process in Stanislavskian theory, though neither author makes that connection explicit. Laurel nonetheless reflects that Norman's analysis "supports the view that interface design should concern itself with representing whole actions with multiple agents . . . precisely the definition of theatre."[45]

In 1991, Brenda Laurel not only equated new media technologies with theatrical modes and models, but specifically defined *Computers as Theatre* in the title of her book. A drama graduate who worked for many years in multimedia authoring, Laurel is now regarded as a seminal figure whose book foresaw and lay important theoretical foundations for the recent, rapid development of theatrical endeavours utilizing computer technologies. Fittingly, *CyberStage*, the first journal devoted to analyzing digital performance, placed her photo on the front cover of its inaugural issue in 1994. Laurel is seen smiling broadly, with head tossed back to one side like a movie star, with an accompanying caption announcing, "The Technodiva Speaks."

Laurel's influential book uses Aristotle's *Poetics* as a starting point to explore the conceptual links between theater and human-computer interfaces. She spends much of her book discussing common factors that unite theatrical performances and computer interfaces, drawing close analogies between theatrical and computational ideas of role-play, interaction, mimesis, and "make-believe." She analyzes the *Poetics* in considerable detail to demonstrate that new technology shares precisely the same concerns and contexts that Aristotle formulates: dramatic structure, empathy, engagement, and catharsis. She defines an interface as a shared context for action where both person and computer are "agents" in the Aristotelian sense of "one who initiates action." She goes on to define clear relationships between human-computer activity and the "four causes" and "six qualitative elements of structure in drama" of Aristotelian theory.

Laurel's analysis of the links between theater and computers is exhaustive (and at times exhausting), drawing numerous and varied comparisons. A computer program is analogous to a script, complete with stage directions; plays and computer programs are both "closed universes;" teams of designers and programmers have similar creative roles to personnel in theater companies (writers, directors, designers, stagehands); software and circuit boards operate like the "backstage" activity in a theater to support representations and to create "magic." She stresses that the Aristotelian notion of enactment ("the imitation of an action . . . enacted in real time, as if the events were actually unfolding") is intrinsic to multimedia because of its multisensory and interactive nature.

She argues that theatrical metaphors pervade software applications, since both are mimetic, multisensory experiences and their prime objectives of representing action with multiple agents fundamentally overlap. Both domains employ "representations of action in virtual worlds" that act as contexts for thought, and that attempt to amplify and orchestrate experience. She warns computer interface designers that:

Thinking about interfaces is thinking too small. Designing human-computer experience isn't about building a better desktop. It's about creating imaginary worlds that have a special relationship with reality—worlds in which we can extend, amplify and enrich our own capabilities to think, feel and act.[46]

Laurel thus provides a framework from dramatic theory that can be applied to designing human-computer experiences, advocating the adoption of theatrical modes and models that are "familiar, comprehensible, and evocative."[47] She suggests that the notion of theater can be applied to multimedia not simply as a metaphor, but as a way to conceptualize human-computer interaction itself. Performance academics have frequently drawn on these ideas to reflect on the complementarity between performance and computing. Thus, theater scholar Michael J. Arndt points out,

The same skills and talents used by a theatre practitioner who is an actor, director or choreographer are those most valued in the world of computers: the ability to make non-linear connections, the ability to interpret and manipulate symbols, the ability to project an end-user's reaction, the ability to effectively communicate through multiple mediums, and the ability to visualize and then execute a final product.[48]

Laurel's plea for computer interface design to adopt theatrical models has now, in effect, doubled back on itself to be reciprocated within the theater, where computational, extended "imaginary worlds" are becoming an increasingly important part of performance expression. Moreover, her arguments about the compatibility and indeed desirability of conjoining theater/performance and computing also work by default to validate the appropriateness and desirability of the use of computers in theater and performance. Laurel, Heckell, and Norman all maintain that the modality of performance is already quintessentially embodied within the technology itself: their central theses argue that it is *intrinsic*.

Laurel's ideas are interestingly applied and tested in the work of David Saltz, one of the large number of pioneering digital performance artists who balance innovative arts practice with full-time academic posts. At the State University of New York at Stony Brook in 1996, Saltz's promenade production *Beckett Space* presented technologically mediated interpretations of eight of Samuel Beckett's short plays (figure 8.4). The audience moved freely around various partitioned spaces and rooms, each ascribed to a play. These included "Godot Space," an empty area where a computer detected and tracked the movements of people passing through, outputting sound files in response which mixed segments of Beckettian drama with pieces of scholarly critical text about the playwright. In

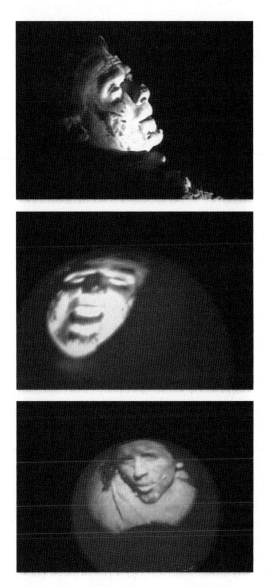

Figure 8.4 Images from David Saltz's video interpretation of Samuel Beckett's *Play* used in his promenade performance installation *Becket Space* (1996).

his article "Beckett's Cyborgs," Saltz explains that he considers Beckett's later plays to be structured like music, games such as chess, and algorithms (processes and sets of rules for mathematical calculations).

Saltz considers *Quad* to represent the quintessence of Beckett's precise and algorithmic approach to drama. *Quad* is a play without words where four characters move around a square space in a complex sequence of straight lines and diagonals. Testing his algorithmic theory (and Laurel's notions) to the limit, in Saltz's interpretation the mathematical computer completely replaces the actors, and the programmer takes the role of theater director. The sequence of the actors' movements and changing positions specified in the play were put into the computer, and four different, synchronized visual representations were created using various software and animation programs (figure 8.5). These animations, which ranged from puppetlike hooded figures (inspired by Beckett's own television production of the play) to simple colored squares, played on four monitors around the *Quad* installation space. In the center of the darkened space, surrounded by a circular hanging curtain, a grid of LED lights hung on thirty-two wires suspended above the audience. The proscribed movement sequence illuminated the appropriate LED, tracing the path of each of Beckett's "players" using different colored lights, and each movement along the grid also triggered a sampled musical sound, creating an electronic soundscape (composed by Jason Hanley). Saltz describes how "every night, a small group of spectators would settle in the *Quad* installation, lying on their backs transfixed by the repeating pattern of light and sounds over their heads."[49]

Figure 8.5 One of the four separate but synchronized representations of Samuel Beckett's play *Quad* employed in David Saltz's *Beckett Space* (1996). The animation was created using *Macromedia Director* software.

The repositioning of these plays within new computational contexts opens up a number of questions, not least how computer-mediation may extend and complement, or alternatively distort and corrupt dramatic and aesthetic elements within a playwright's works. Although Saltz is quick to point out that he does not consider the installation to be a "performance" of Beckett's play, he nonetheless considers the digital treatment he presents to be a logical and coherent extension of Beckett's algorithmic formalism. The literal metamorphosis of performers into computational bytes is seen as analogous to Beckett's own conception of the actors/characters in *Quad* (and in his later play, *Come and Go*) as functioning "as cogs in the unvarying and relentless motion of the relentless Beckettian machine."[50]

Saltz's theatrical rationale in digitizing Beckett is highly scientific and empirical. The play's essential action is reduced to computational bytes, and mathematics and computer science are relied upon to "interpret" and "create" the theatrical event. It is a genuine research experiment testing both Saltz's theories of Beckett's conceptual philosophy, and the computer's ability to effectively remediate and re-present theatrical signs and data as a new artistic form. The experiment also tests Brenda Laurel's thesis quite literally, by making a computer the prime agent and creator of theater.

Laurel's influence has also impacted where it was first targeted, on software and interface designers. Eric Dishman's work from 1993 with Colin Burns at the multidisciplinary design technology laboratory, Interval continued on from an improvisation class Laurel had led there, and involved Interval's researchers and designers in performance exercises and workshops. Dishman developed a pedagogy he terms "informance design," which uses ethnographic studies and ethnomethodological analysis to emphasize the social and personal implications of technological design, and drama games and improvisations to stress the importance of embodied action to design knowledge—replacing the idea of "brainstorming" with the corrective term "bodystorming."

Dishman discusses a rethinking of technology design "through the lens of performative theory . . . [to] move beyond the hype-or-hate technology discourse."[51] He envisions a new kind of *performer*-designer" who breaks out of the traditional paradigmatic "mire" of mimesis and realism that still inhibits both performers and computer program designers, to engage with the approaches of performance studies that explore a more critical and political relationship with performance. By understanding performativity as a synergetic cultural construction, in the way that Dwight Conquergood conceives an "interanimation" of performance modalities and discourses,[52] Dishman maintains that computer designers and programmers can use performance "to create prototypes of complex, politicized, personalized futures."[53]

Subsequent experiments, including the *Telerats* project with students at the Computer-Related Design Department at London's Royal College of Art, developed Dishman's approach, where he adapted Augusto Boal's "image theater" and "invisible theater" techniques[54] as well as ideas from Judith Butler involving bodily intimacy and touch.[55] Dishman's work and ideas typify the liberal humanist stance to computer program and interactive design taken by technologists and practitioners who emphasize the performative elements and implications of software production advocated by Laurel. He claims that his technique of "informance design"

provokes a politicization of engineering, which reveals to designers their ideo-authorial power and responsibilities to their cultures as understood through ethnographic encounters with "real users" and self-reflective reperformances. The goal is to imagine, embody, and "test drive" a technologized future that actually cares for these real people—these flesh and blood citational sources. . . . Informance evokes the politicizing, empathetic, and synergetic powers of performance in the hope that our new social machinery can be designed so that it does not come back to haunt us like some Frankensteinian monster.[56]

Hyperbole, Mysticism, and Mystifications

Because a machine, a Terminator, can learn the value of human life, maybe we can do too.
—THE FINAL LINE OF JAMES CAMERON'S *TERMINATOR 2: JUDGMENT DAY*, 1991[57]

Poetry and progress are two ambitious men who hate each other with an instinctive hatred.
—CHARLES BAUDELAIRE, 1859[58]

The digital revolution brought with it considerable digital hyperbole—what Paul Rae calls "cyperbole" (cyberculture's "bright-eyed hope in endless possibility")[59]—and this was never more evident than in popular science magazines and journals of the period, whose copyeditors realized the commercial advantage of adding to the sense of mystery and awe surrounding computers and all things digital. This was always a tendency in journals such as *Wired*, whose heyday years are wittily and irreverently recounted in Paulina Borsook's book *Cyberselfish* (2000), since their readership had a natural propensity to believe in the promised future. Titles featured on the cover each month tell their own story: "William Gibson: His latest report from the future isn't fiction" (1:4, September/October 1993), followed by "Sega's Plan for World Domination" in December of the same year; "Steve Jobs: The Next Insanely Great Thing" (4:02, February 1996), and "83 Reasons Why Bill Gates' Reign is Over" (6:12, December 1998). By April 2000 the cover title read "Why the Future Doesn't Need Us" (8:04), each headline helping to fulfil the publication's tagline, "Tomorrow Today."

Magazines such as *New Scientist, American Scientist*, and *Nature* also got caught up in the cyperbole with front-cover headlines such as "Would you agree to a head transplant?" (*New Scientist* 2207, 9 October 1999), matched in *Scientific American* by "Downloading Your Brain" (10:3, Fall 1999). An awesome "Quantum Computer" of unknowable power is promised by both journals a number of times (prompting the hope that the help programs are more comprehensible than hitherto if the newcomer has to juggle between parallel universes as well as installing the software), but all too frequently the next big breakthrough lies in a future a little beyond our understanding, always, it seems, just beyond our reach and ken. *Wired* has been promising annually since at least March 1998 that a cloned baby will be born the following year—"My name is Katy. I was born in 1999. I am a clone. My story is on page 146."[60]

If *Wired* in the late 1990s was finding difficulty locating the dividing line between Real Life and Virtual Reality, it was not alone. Popular science journalism at the end of the twentieth century seldom failed to take the opportunity to announce imminent developments in such areas as cloning and computer/brain combinations and continues to do so into our current century. In a blaze of utopia, *Scientific American Quarterly* in the fall of 1999 devoted its entire issue to promises of "Your New Body," "Your New Senses," "Your New Mind," "Your New Look," "Your New Society," and "Your New Lifestyle." By June 2000, *New Scientist* wittily suggested that the Internet will soon start demanding brain downloads to share knowledge.[61] February 2001 saw the notion of a silicon brain,[62] by February 2002 using organic brain cells as a component within computer electronics,[63] a few months later Justin Mullins's "Quantum Superbrains" reported on "the race to build a quantum computer [that will be] powerful enough to take on life, the Universe and everything."[64]

Digital Skeptics

Skeptical responses to the cyperbole of the digital revolution emerged in tandem, and perhaps the most intelligent and devastating of the cautionary taletellers was Richard Coyne, whose *Technoromanticism* (1999) tested the unending stream of digital hyperbole and found it wanting in every department: "Virtual communities are an ideal rather than an actuality, the total immersion environment is a technical impossibility now, there are no demonstrations of artificial intelligence meeting the expectations of science fiction, and there are currently no convincing digital life forms."[65] From the outset, Coyne notes that IT has a predisposition to attempt to transcend the material world:

In keeping with the romanticism of its narratives, information technology implicates itself in people's attempts to progress from one sphere of existence to another. The new sphere includes both the digital utopia promised by much IT commentary and literal transcendence through immersion in the "consensual hallucination" of the digital matrix, digital ecstasies, and participation in an ideal unity.[66]

In a period when expectancy and hope considerably outweighed any desire to establish the truth, Coyne is able to locate and examine a host of claims by the industry and its adherents that, even before he analyzes them, begin to sound more like *Private Eye's* "Pseud's Corner" or *The Jackdaw* (a scurrilous subscription newsletter of the Visual Arts) monthly feature "Artbollocks: The Usual Twaddle." Coyne's language is more measured, but the effect is much the same as he wittily recounts the development of the computer narrative through stages of "the Utopia," "the Enlightenment," "the Arts and Crafts" phase, the "Romantic Imagination," aspects of socialism; "The Romance with Systematization," and "Techno-Medievalism and Irrationalism."[67] He points out that our concept of what comprised "medieval" is itself very imprecise—even the dates—and our modern tendency to merge impressions of it with stories of King Arthur on one hand and witchcraft on the other. One aspect that seems to remain fundamental to the range is that life was generally insecure, even perilous—a state of mind and being he suggests is suitable for contemporary labyrinthine computing. Similarly, we are much given to exaggerated significances of numbers and signs and verbal nonsense ("technobabble"), which serve to mystify, "the medieval world of IT [being] a flirtation with the irrational and the other, continuing the Enlightenment and romantic tradition." Extreme cases of this, Coyne suggests, results in "cybernetic rapture" and even "the ecstatic," "romantic ecstasy," and "disembodied cyberspace."[68]

The digital revolution of the 1990s also saw the emergence of digital culture email lists and e-journals such as *CTHEORY* that critiqued the very revolution they themselves were a part of. *CTHEORY* provides an illuminating case study of how academic responses and theoretical agendas transformed throughout the 1990s in the face of the digital revolution. Edited by Arthur and Marilouise Kroker, it grew out of the all-print journal *Canadian Journal of Political and Social Theory* [CJPST], published from 1976 to 1991, where distinguished theorists such as Jean Baudrillard, Jurgen Habermas, Herbert Marcuse, Susan Sontag, Stanley Aronowitz, and Terry Eagleton probed aspects of current politics, culture, and society. *CTHEORY* embraced new media first in its online form, second by including a section featuring original new media artworks, and third by increasingly foregrounding the implications of technology in its academic articles. The site still offers downloadable versions of current and all previous volumes dating back to 1993, which reveal fascinating shifts over the decade.

Early articles address and attempt to predict the possible implications of digital developments, such as Kimberly Anne Sawchuk's questioning of David Gelertner's vision that the future would see "mirror worlds reflected in 'pint-sized' computers."[69] Eminent arts commentators advanced new theories, including Peter Weibel, who located digital arts as part of the tradition of twentieth-century anti-art: "making the technology in media art visible is not a temporary experiment, but its essence." Historical perspectives were also advanced by the Critical Art Ensemble,[70] whose "The Technology of Uselessness" (1994) essay explores utopian and dystopian tendencies through the centuries, before proposing a theory of "uselessness." New technology, they argue, will become an ironic comment on Descartes's "I think therefore I am" whereby the machine can think and therefore "be," and no more will be expected of it: "Pure technology, as opposed to pure utility, is never turned on; it just sits, existing in and of itself. Unlike the machines of the utopians and dystopians, not only is it free of humanity, it is free of its own machine function—it serves no practical purpose for anyone or anything."

The Critical Art Ensemble's antithetical view was accompanied by a collection of advertisements for bourgeois and military digital inventions that epitomized their notion of functional uselessness. "Technology so pure that its only function is to exist" ranged from the domestic Farberware Electric peeler with its built-in potato eye remover and the Shiatsu Electric Massager that "feels like real hands" to $2 million MK21 Advanced Ballistic Missile Re-entry Vehicles, which violated various treaty agreements. In the same year, 1994, Arthur Kroker and Michael Weinstein adopted the linguistic style of technological product advertisements to commence their discourse on the future human body:

Why be nostalgic? The old body type was always OK, but the wired body with its micro-flesh, multi-media channeled ports, cybernetic fingers, and bubbling neuro-brain finely interlaced to the 'standard operating system' of the Internet is infinitely better. Not really the wired body of sci-fi with its mutant designer look, or body flesh with its ghostly reminders on nineteenth-century philosophy, but the hyper-texted body as both: a wired nervous system embedded in living (dedicated) flesh.[71]

A year later, Kroker decreed cyberpunk was dead, and explained that "The lessons of the 90s have been multiple and they've been harsh: not the least of which is that data will find a way, and its way is not necessarily about becoming human."[72] But by 2002 his tone seemed altogether different: "The digital code speaks the sanitary language of culture cleansing, of photography itself at a distance, of the archive by remote control, of the deep freeze preservation of the image from the 'contamination' of time and history and memory and skin and smells and touch."[73]

In the mid-1990s, when digital performance practices began to proliferate significantly, a key debate emerged that centered on whether digital technologies were creative and life-giving or controlling and restrictive. Kroker drew attention to this ambiguity in a range of essays, drawing attention to "Net Resistance: resistance . . . emerging from different social, political and national contexts to the ideological hype of tech euphoria." Geert Lovink was emboldened to make several pithy assertions that still reverberate:

You can't have the future every day.
The computer is a utensil prior to the future.
All these machines are trash.
The inevitability of the computer should no more be allowed than letting television become a life necessity.
It's possible to be on-line without a computer—with the imagination . . .
This rap about the global village is vastly exaggerated.
To be a media consumer you have to be out of work, and maybe out of life.[74]

Simultaneously, Paul Virilio was declaring that the information superhighways were causing a fundamental loss of orientation:

To exist is to exist *in situ,* here and now, *hic et nunc.* This is precisely what is being threatened by cyberspace and instantaneous, globalised information flows.

What lies ahead is a disturbance in the perception of what reality is: it is a shock, a mental concussion. And this outcome ought to interest us. Why? Because never has any progress in a technique been achieved without addressing its specific negative aspects. The specific negative aspect of these information superhighways is precisely this loss of orientation regarding alterity (the other), this disturbance in the relationship with the other and with this world. It is obvious that this loss of orientation, this non-situation, is going to usher a deep crisis which will affect society and hence, democracy.[75]

This prevalent theme in *CTHEORY* doubtless reflected the particular dispositions of its editors, but was echoed in the wider field of cultural theory. By 1996 cyberculture pundit R. U. Sirius was declaring, "It's Better to be Inspired than Wired," and science-fiction writer Bruce Sterling was welcoming a much-needed "breathing space" as "The flash-bulb of cyber-novelty has begun to fade from the retina of the public eye." But in the same year Arthur and Marilouise Kroker were defining a field of "Code Warriors" that were causing "Bunkering In and Dumbing Down," and noting "the swift emergence of ever more grisly forms of conservative fundamentalism in response to the hegemony of the virtual class" and a "virtual elite [that] is a mixture of predatory capitalists and visionary computer specialists for whom virtualization is about our disappearance into nothingness. We are talking about a systematic assault against the human species." By 1997, even voices in Eastern Europe—not an area particularly renowned for advanced technology at the time, though some extraordinary work was to evolve in due course—were declaring "the romantic era of virtual reality and network communications is already irretrievably in the past. . . . Nowadays virtual reality is a quite mundane technology."[76]

No issues peak in quite the same way in subsequent issues of *CTHEORY* which refelcts the fact that by 1998 a period of consolidation was underway: the constant reinvention of "the new" had slowed and, as Lovink had predicted, "You can't have the future every day." Consolidation and reflection led to closer considerations of networks, the effects on the human dimension—Katherine Hayles's *How We Became Posthuman: Virtual Bodies in Cybernetics, Literature, and Informatics* was published in 1999—consideration of meaning on and of the Net, calls for a new aesthetics (possibly the clearest sign of consolidation), the effect of the new technologies upon memory and representation, and the myth of the global village. In 2001, Bruce Scott suggested that "the global village" had turned out to be more of a global gated community;[77] and by the time an article by Chris Chesher appeared beginning with the words "The digital computer is dead," (2002)[78] it seemed like rather old news.

Chesher offered a linguistic argument to question the appropriateness of words such as "digital" and "computer/computation," and one that is perhaps of greater significance to performance theory than might first appear. The argument put forward was that both words are seriously flawed for the twenty-first century, since they relate to concepts from the 1940s when they first fell into regular usage. They place an emphasis upon the mathematical "number-crunching" aspects of a process whereas their prime functions today are ones of "invocation: powers to call things up." The cultural connection between technology and magic is central to the discourse, in which Chesher recasts "digital computers" and renames them "invocation media." Although this may sound somewhat clumsy, the permission embedded in the new term (or at least the inhibitions avoided by not using the old terminology) is of greater significance. It is not until the mathematical computational aspects of the digital computer begin to subside or are taken for granted, that art and performance practitioners really begin to explore the new opportunities. The power to call things up then begins in earnest, the more so because this invocatory "magic" can involve "switching" and transformations self-evident (with hindsight) in digital arts practices from the very first computer-generated artworks to the latest Virtual Reality performances.

There can be little doubt that this notion of switching and metamorphosis has a prime significance for many practitioners: the ability to transform live movement into moving image, or gesture into music, or solo dance into group dance, or one location into another or several. In this sense, Chesher's discourse is apt in relation to digital performance practitioners, most of whom are totally disinterested in the digital computer as a mathematical calculation machine, but utterly fascinated by its rich artistic palette, its powers of invocation, and its metamorphic abilities to switch between and transform different media.

Digital Dancing and Software Developments

The real issue implied by "Art and Technology" is not to make another scientific toy, but how to humanize the technology and the electronic medium which is progressing rapidly . . . too rapidly.
—NAM JUNE PAIK, 1969[1]

The third characteristic pleasure of digital environments is the pleasure of transformation.
—JANET MURRAY[2]

Introduction

Within digital performance, creation of and access to computer code opens up two significant questions: how far does proprietary software restrict and constrain the practitioner using it, and how far does the secrecy surrounding it inhibit the development of software *by* artists and practitioners? To date the creation of original software by performance artists and groups has been limited, and almost all within the area of dance. It remains a tiny percentage of the total work in digital performance, and for one primary reason: a lack of technical expertise in code and programming skills. Although there have been a number of significant and influential applications developed by artists and performance companies, digital performance's relationship to software has been primarily through the use and creative adaptation of extant commercial programs, most notably sophisticated high-end applications such as *Max/MSP*.

The most widespread writing of software programs by artists as well as amateur enthusiasts has been in the area of desktop dance-simulation programs. These include a host of freeware titles such as *Dance*, *Compudance*, *Dance Manager*, and *In Motion*, and programs that can be downloaded for a small charge, such as *Dance Partner*, which claims to be able to create Country Western, Swing, Ballroom, Latin, Hustle, Morris, Clog, Hip Hop, Folk, Square, Ballet, Modern, Jazz, and Broadway Performance, "just to name a few." Other applications derive from academia, including Christian Griesbeck's developments at the

University of Frankfurt of computer simulations based on the codification of Laban notation.

Life Forms

The most famous, and one of the earliest software packages for dance figure simulation and animation, Credo Software Products' *Life Forms Dance Software* received attention as early as 1989 when Merce Cunningham created a new dance using its first (wireframe-only) version. Accounts of these early attempts are fascinating, including "Merce Cunningham: Cyber Dances with Life Forms" (1997) by Thecla Schiphorst, a programmer with a background in dance, who was a member of the original *Life Forms* design team and who tutored Cunningham while in parallel developing the capabilities of the software that Paul Groot would later call "the dream of a multimedia *Gesamtkunstwerk*."[3] *Life Forms* is a figure animation package that enables the choreographer both to use the computer as a drawing board to conceive movements and sequences in animated form before going into the studio with dancers; and to use the animations themselves *as* dance, either as a discreet "movie" or through projection on stage as an element of live dance performance (figure 9.1). The virtual figures are composed of hoop-shaped lines, and the visual effect of these flowing body shapes generally suit contemporary choreography well, although we have also seen examples of *Life Forms* avatars used for ballet, *en pointe* and wearing tutus, where the effect appears stilted and even comic by comparison. *Life Forms*

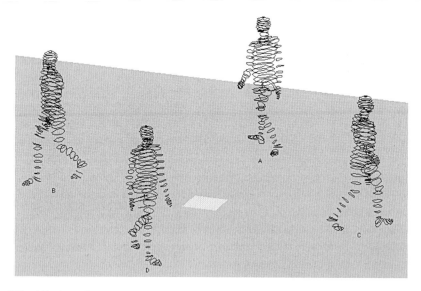

Figure 9.1 *Life Forms* figure animations used to create the four characters in David Saltz's 1996 adaptation of Beckett's *Quad*.

remains the major 3D character animation package for the Vancouver-based software company Credo Interactive, which acknowledges Cunningham's unique and early contribution to its development. Even today, the repeated patterns of Cunningham's first creation using the software, *Trackers* (1989) still have the power to intrigue with simple repeated sequences of figures drawn with hoops:[4]

Some place near the middle of *Trackers*, his first computer-assisted piece, nine or 10 performers dressed in simple T-shirts and bodysuits begin one-by-one to tread casually across the stage to a score by Emanuel Dimas de Melo Pimenta, organizing and reorganizing in what looks like randomly intersecting patterns.

Within a few minutes, the dancers have introduced a new population of shapes that are awkward and delicate, though often powerful. Most of them are completely outside the familiar universe of dance movement. A basic walk turns into a collaboration of limbs; the dancers combine primitive images and complex, independent rhythms, all overlaid onto a simple travelling motion. They pace around to one rhythm; their arms move to another rhythm. Each arc, swivel, and wave is so distinctive, it's as if fragments of the gesture were plotted and timed completely independently, then applied inside the structure of a phrase. Critics have said that some of Cunningham's work looks odd at first, but admit it all has a curious power.[5]

Sequences from *Trackers* (1989) still feature on the Credo website together with subsequent choreographic experiments by Tanuki Deku, Jessica Plescia, Yvonne Choreo/Bebe Miller, and Georgette Gorchoff, and sequences created with the company's more recent 3D animation software *PowerMoves*. In her discussion of Cunningham's early experiments with *Life Forms*, Schiphorst has discussed how closely the features of the software both complement and extend many of Cunningham's objectives and thematic principles as a choreographer, including his interest in chance elements:

Merce Cunningham, who has been using chance procedures in making dance since the early 1950s, also incorporated these procedures when creating movement with the computer. Many of Merce's movement sequences created in *Life Forms* determined how the body would move, what body parts would be used, or what physical shapes would be incorporated by the use of chance procedures. When these movement sequences appeared physically impossible, Merce worked with his dancers to discover how they could be made to work. Cunningham has said: "If a dancer tells me that something won't work, I say, 'Try it; if you fall down, you'll find out something about falling down.'"[6]

Elsewhere Schiphorst suggests, "In a sense . . . everything he learns is by mistake,"[7] and hints that the computer is the perfect tool for Cunningham's choreography because the software constantly supplies new (and sometimes humanly impossible) sequences to be tested; and computed/animated movement needs no reference to music during the compositional phase, thereby fulfilling another of Cunningham's most fundamental rules of engagement. His interests in digital methodologies were therefore rooted in their support of his own existing systems and approaches, and a succession of other dance simulations and experiments followed *Tracker* including *Loosestrife* (1991), *Enter* (1992), *CRWDSPCR* (1993), *Ocean* (1994), and a film, *Beach Birds for Camera* (1991), directed by Elliot Caplan with music by John Cage.

But both the complexity and limitations of *Life Forms* have been noted by academics and choreographers, including Scott deLahunta:

Arguably, *Life Forms* is really the "only" software of its kind for choreographers, but it is not used very much by dancemakers. Besides the matter of computer access and the time and effort it takes to learn to use the program, *Life Forms* "embodies," if one could say that, the dancing aesthetic of Cunningham . . . Perfect for Cunningham, but of limited use to choreographers whose movement vocabulary and aesthetic is directed along another line.[8]

DeLahunta's observation was made as part of his analysis of *Interference: A Performance Experiment in Internet Choreography* (1998),[9] an audacious Internet project set up via various email lists by digital artist Guy Hilton, who invited choreographers—he hoped to recruit forty worldwide—to participate in a collaborative project using *Life Forms*. It may have seemed initially unlikely to succeed because the software was not without its critics, and all forty recruits needed to own or access it and be competent in using it. But in the event it attracted *more* than forty volunteers worldwide,[10] including Cunningham, who were each asked to develop a *Life Forms* movement sequence of between thirty and sixty seconds. The format followed the surrealist game of *cadavre exquis* (exquisite corpse),[11] wherein sections of drawn bodies or written sentences are completed without seeing much of what went before, with each participant developing their choreographic section starting from a single *Life Forms* keyframe; the final frame of that sequence would then be forwarded to the next participant who would add a further sequence, and so on. The resulting choreography, which, Hilton stressed, "reflects no individual's prior artistic plan, but will be emergent and collective,"[12] was finally interpreted for real time performance by three live dancers (Ruth Gibson, Julia Griffin, and Grace Surman) during the festival, and was simultaneously webcast.

Before the performance, the three dancers may have been a little apprehensive that Hilton had offered the *Life Forms* choreographers such an extremely open brief, including the following: "You may devise any movement you see fit, and may choose not to observe gravity or the limitations of the human body if you wish."[13] This reflected the optimism of the times within digital performance: "the real" would simply have to find ways around the improbable, not least because the technological process and formalism of the experiment was paramount rather than the performance itself: "The movement themes, the structure and motifs of the piece are moulded wholly by the fractured communication process from which they emerge."[14] In the event, Cunningham choreographed the opening and closing sequences, and the other volunteers contributed sequences between five and one hundred seconds. The completed *Life Forms* choreography lasted 16 minutes and the live performance interpreted the sequence twice, firstly following the sequence as closely as was practically possible, the second time with a freer more personal interpretation (lasting thirty-three minutes). *Interference* was performed on 12 September 1998 to a sold-out audience at the Green Room in Manchester.

Cunningham's work with *Life Forms* and other software applications since the late '80s has ensured his position as one of the leading pioneers of digital performance, and in 1990, the same year that he was conferred the United States National Medal of Arts by President Bush (Senior) at the White House to honor his fifty years of dance, in London he received the *Digital Dance Premier Award* for invention in the new medium, at the age of seventy-one. Cunningham's close artistic involvement with technology stretches back much further, of course, to the Black Mountain College "happening" of 1952, and his involvement with E.A.T., including the 1966 *Nine Evenings* performances in New York. Nearly four decades later, the same experimentation is still evident, and in his recent fiftieth anniversary season he created a new dance piece, *Split Sides,* featuring music by leading British alternative rock group Radiohead, and *Fluid Canvas*, first premiered in London a year earlier, which utilized data from motion capture of choreographed hand movements personally undertaken by now octogenarian Cunningham, and computed by his long-term collaborators Paul Kaiser and Shelley Eshkar.

Riverbed and Merce Cunningham

Kaiser and Eshkar, and their Riverbed company, also hold a unique place in the development of digital dance, using a range of technologies and software applications in major collaborations with leading artists and choreographers including Cunningham and Bill T. Jones. In 1991, Kaiser won a Computer World/Smithsonian Award for computer multimedia work when working as a teacher with students with severe learning disabilities. This encouraged him to pursue a career in digital arts, which involved a move to New York in 1994, where he formed Riverbed with Eshkar, a multimedia artist and experimental animator who had developed an innovative style in three-dimensional figural drawing and animation. Riverbed's mission was to design and develop new media projects primarily for the visual and performing arts,[15] and they shared a keen interest in new advanced computer animation software being developed at the time by two graduate students, Michael Girard and Susan Amkraut at Ohio State University. Their alpha software, called *Biped*, was demonstrated at SIGGRAPH95 (1995) to considerable acclaim, and it became commercially available a year later, embedded within a larger animation package, *Character Studio.*[16] In 1997, Kaiser and Eshkar invited Cunningham to collaborate on a project using *Biped* and *3D Studio Max* that had already been broadly conceived, a virtual dance installation called *Hand-drawn Spaces*, and in 1998 Cunningham invited them to work on his full-length live dance project, appropriately entitled *BIPED* (figure 9.2). As Kaiser and Eshkar put it, "*BIPED* was as apt a term for Cunningham's choreography as

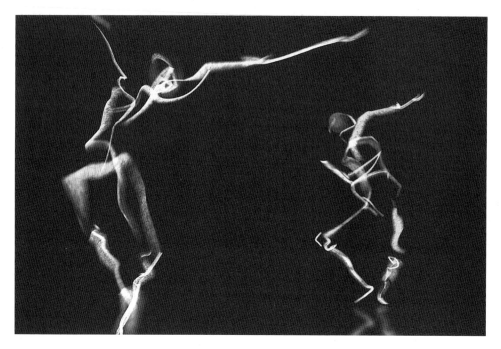

Figure 9.2 An image from Merce Cunningham's first collaboration with Riverbed, *Hand-drawn Spaces* (1997). Courtesy of Paul Kaiser and Shelley Eshkar.

it was for the software, for Merce's lifelong interest has been to figure out all that a body on two legs can do."[17]

A particular quality of the Girard and Amkraut's *Biped* software was its attention to detail which made animated figures appear "lifelike," so that, for example, a foot landing on the ground affected transformations throughout the rest of the body, which were triggered and computed within the program by code registering "the foot to ground collision response."[18] Other detailed "kinematic" effects, including skin and tendon behaviors, were also mapped in using another module called "Physique," developed by John Chadwick, and the software permitted combinations of movements to be easily interrelated, repeated, reversed or combined. For Cunningham's dance, named after the software, Riverbed used motion-capture techniques to map in three dimensions the movements of three dancers performing some twenty Cunningham movement sequences in a studio (figure 9.3). Using reflective markers on the joints and body parts of the dancers, cameras around the studio relayed the images to computers, which calculated and rendered their kinetic shapes in relation to 3D space, and this data was then manipulated in *Character Studio* to create complex and beautiful hand-drawn figure animations performing the same dances (figure 9.4).

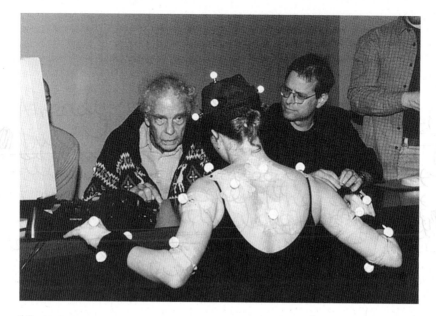

Figure 9.3   Merce Cunningham (left), Paul Kaiser (right) and dancer Jeannie Steele (center) preparing for a motion-capture session during the production of *BIPED* (1999). The balls taped to Steele's body act as reflective nodes that are detected and traced by a ring of cameras around her as she dances. A computer combines and interprets all the 360-degree data coordinates and provides a 3D rendering of the balls moving in space. These dots are joined up to create kinetically accurate dance animations using *Character Studio* software. Photo: Shelley Eshkar.

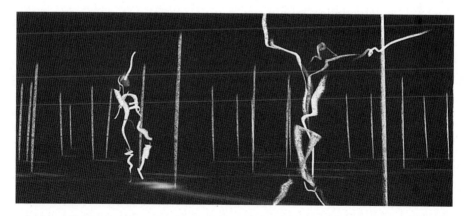

Figure 9.4   One of Riverbed's animations for *BIPED*, derived from motion-capture data. The two virtual dancers move in and out of the vertical lines that represent trees in a forest. Courtesy of Paul Kaiser and Shelley Eshkar.

These were projected during the *BIPED* live dance performance, the projections being cast onto a front scrim, allowing the live dancers to appear to interrelate with the virtual dancers in various abstractions and spatial configurations. These projected figures, hand-drawn abstractions but capable of unerringly lifelike movement, also changed in scale, from giant thirty-foot dancers to smaller, life-sized ones. *BIPED*, with music by Gavin Bryars, was premiered at Berkeley in April 1999 and received its New York debut on 21 July 1999 at the State Theater of the Lincoln Center. The projections lasted for approximately half the duration of the live performance, and Cunningham only determined their sequential order just before the first performance, selection being made on a chance basis. Kaiser has since revealed that the only guidance he had received from Cunningham was that the animations and performance could reflect the experience of television channel-hopping. Before the first performance Cunningham had not seen the virtual dancer animations, nor had Eshkar and Kaiser seen Cunningham's dancers perform the choreography. But the overall effect, when suddenly combined, appeared to many reviewers of the time as something approaching the supernatural, affording insights into the great unexplained. Critics were enthralled by the experience, and given to eulogies and superlatives, as Dee Reynolds recounts:

Comments by critics leave no doubt that a large part of the attraction of Cunningham's dance for contemporary audiences lies in its appeal to a kind of utopian imagination, rooted in the corporeal, in which the human intermingles with the natural (animal) and the technological. In fact, some critics even suggest that certain works by Cunningham transcend the human itself in a Zen-like, cosmic space, which has a meditative and reconciling effect.[19] (figure 9.5)

With hindsight, the long-term significance of the event might have been predicted since Cunningham's work already carried the highest kudos, and the software was genuinely innovative and had already received plaudits within the circles of professional graphics. The wider computer industry and its marketing arms also had a stake in the venture, having supplied the latest high-performance equipment. As the *Wired* reviewer had correctly concluded the day following the Berkeley premier three months earlier, "Its success will pry open the door between dance and technology and drive innovation in both fields."[20] It did precisely that and its wider impact was so significant, particularly following its international performances (whether people saw the piece or simply read about it), that it has been regarded as a turning point and seminal moment in the development of digital performance.

Of course, as we demonstrate throughout this volume, any suggestion that digital performance arises from *one* seminal moment is entirely false: there is a long and complex history before 1999 of hundreds of practitioners experimenting with new computer technologies, and it is interesting to note that real acclaim and public attention only greeted *BIPED* in New York; the premiere in Berkeley three months earlier had *not* produced a

Figure 9.5 The powerful aesthetics and poetic interrelationships between Cunningham's dancers and their digital counterparts in *BIPED* prompted some critics to describe the experience in metaphysical and religious terms. Photo: Stephanie Berger.

"seminal moment" response. But the first New York performance of 21 July 1999 did mark a turning point when the wider western world's arts media became more aware than ever of the potential of digital performance, and with some reason given *BIPED*'s formal, conceptual and technical originality. Reviewers recorded first-night audience gasps and were drawn into the poetry of the interactions between the live and virtual dancers, even though most were aware that the relationships they described were chance, rather than deliberate occurrences:

The audience gasped as the first virtual dancers appeared. . . . Composed of spare and colorful lines, the hand-drawn animations moved gracefully across the scrim, appearing to mingle with the real dancers. . . . Some of the movements were so subtle that the animated figures seemed almost human. . . .

In a performance where even the creators were unsure of how the combined media would fare together onstage, there were incredible moments where dance and technology seemed to speak the same language. At one point, a hand-drawn animation danced across the scrim. Before vanishing, it turned to the real dancer onstage, as if in a parting gesture. During a duet in the middle of the piece, two dancers turned and reached toward each other while the virtual dancer stepped slowly and tentatively on their outstretched arms.[21]

Such moments are of course the ephemeral and intangible essence of live performance, and images from *BIPED* have since become archetypical of digital performance, in much the same way that William Latham and Steven Todd's mutating organic spirals for IBM (1987–1994) became the archetypal visual "digital art" image[22] (figure 9.6).

Bill T. Jones and *Ghostcatching*

Ghostcatching (1999), choreographer Bill T. Jones's collaboration with Riverbed, marked another influential milestone in aesthetic manifestations of the virtual body, leaving its mark in a number of forms. These comprised a video installation, an eight-and-a-half minute digital animated film (shown at the Cannes Film Festival), and an exhibition of large prints. Somewhat ironically, it found its most lasting fame in the form of a conventional art catalogue book. *Ghostcatching*'s virtual body images were created using motion capture techniques, with computers tracking the three-dimensional movements of twenty-four reflector sensors taped to Jones's naked body as he danced within a studio surrounded by video cameras. As with *BIPED*, Kaiser and Eshkar manipulated the data so that the transformed "anatomies are intertwinings of drawn strokes, which are in fact painstakingly modelled as geometry on the computer—never drawn on paper."[23]

At this point the dancer can be conceived as expendable, because the computer now holds, in Kaiser's words, "the position and rotation of the body in motion, without preserving the performer's mass or musculature. Thus, movement [has been] extracted from the performer's body."[24] Some critical commentaries on *Ghostcatching* focused around this

Figure 9.6 *BIPED* images such as these have been so admired and reproduced that they have become archetypical of the digital dance and performance movement. Photo: Stephanie Berger.

conception of the computer's ability to extract essences from the human body and, like the older belief (which still holds in some parts of the world) that a photograph captures part of the subject's soul, reconceived a notion of some form of capturing of a human *spirit*. The conceit seemed closer to a metaphorical extraction of DNA than a simple computer-transformed recording; and like the DNA debate, here was the "spirit" being "cloned," since the data from Jones's naked, dancing body was repeated and multiplied to create several different dancers who moved in relation to one another. So not only was the dancer reproduced identically, but he also appeared to be dancing with himself and performing functions that the living dancer could not. For the viewer, such a sequence creates interesting moving images of dancing shapes that can be judged according to agreed criteria, but philosophically, ethically, and in time probably legally, it was opening up a complex debate about boundaries and ownership. Kaiser recalls that Jones struggled with this issue as his choreography was computed:

In the earlier motion-capture session, Jones saw his disembodied motions on the screen. He kept returning to the philosophic question: who is that really? At the same moment, we were thinking about the way in which Jones choreographed. He improvises his phrases, then sets them on the diverse bodies of his dancers. We imagined this could be done virtually, and pictured Jones spawning other bodies with different identities.[25]

Kaiser and Eshkar's painstaking graphical manipulations of their detailed data from Jones's body movements achieved their aims to conjure an ethereal, ghostlike figure, but one which retained the rhythm, gravity, dynamics, weight, and intent of Jones's original dance within the ring of computer-feeding cameras. The imagery at play in *Ghostcatching* (as in *BIPED*) provides an example of a genuinely new aesthetic phenomenon brought about in the intersection of dance and computer art (figure 9.7). On the surface, since the animated dancers appear like colored hand-drawings, one might conceive that a skilled human artist/animator could have created them through conventional means. But it would require a cross between a latter-day Michelangelo and an anatomy genius capable of

Figure 9.7 In *Ghostcatching* (1999), dance and computer science combine to bring about a genuinely new aesthetic phenomenon. Bill T. Jones's dancing body is motion-captured and transformed into eerie animations, some of which represent multiple and interrelated images of him, all dancing simultaneously. Courtesy of Paul Kaiser and Shelley Eshkar.

visualizing every tiny human muscle and joint movement within three-dimensional space to perfect the details of the trajectories of the virtual body form through every frame of its fluid, lifelike choreography.

Ghostcatching is genuinely "uncanny" in Freud's sense of the word (*unheimlich*), possessing a sense of reality and familiarity but at the same time a strange, unworldly quality. The virtual body *is* and *is not* Jones, but in a quite different way than by which the same could be said of traditional mediatizations such as photographs or video recordings. This is a majestic, spectral incarnation of Jones dancing which literally takes the breath away— or at least did on its release in 1999, since which time we have perhaps become accustomed to repetitions of the effect.

The computer's ability to map and render complex moving forms precisely within three-dimensional space affords a genuinely unique and original performative manifestation of Jones's body, and the piece was highly and almost unanimously acclaimed. *The Village Voice* spoke of the "incredibly accomplished feat" of replacing Jones's form with "calligraphy twisting in space"; and *Time Out* interpreted the fusion of digital and actual as "solidly pinning virtual reality to the context of art." For Anita Hamilton in *Time*, "The results are spectacular. The eight-and-a-half minute film is difficult to capture in words. But your body will understand . . . a landmark in the computerized rendering of the human form"[26] (figure 9.8).

Max/MSP

Software such as *Life Forms*, *Biped*, and *Character Studio* were each developed as proprietary code programs for commercial use particularly in the cinema, television, video games, and advertising industries. Digital performance artists have also been increasingly drawn to another high-end piece of commercial software due to its genuine flexibility of use and adaptation, *Max/MSP*. Created by a company called Cycling 74[27] and named after its initial inventor, Max Mathews, it is now one of the most widely used programs in the digital performance field. It is essentially a set of building blocks for creating programs, and, like most current software, it uses graphical display rather than mathematical code for manipulation; the user manipulates graphical symbols (called "objects"), and the embedded, hidden mathematical code moves with them. The *Max* part of the software allows the user to build programs by manipulating and building up the graphical symbols whilst the *MSP* part works on the same principle for audio objects. The user can immediately see, or with *MSP*, hear, the results of a particular congregation of objects, and accept, reject or modify as appropriate. When first released in the mid-1980s, retailing at around $12,000, it was regarded as highly specialist and very expensive, but by 2002 (with *MSP* added) its price had dropped to under $500 and a wide range of artists were buying and using it.

Other performance artists have preferred to write their own code to create specific software for their digital performance applications, particularly in dance where the principal

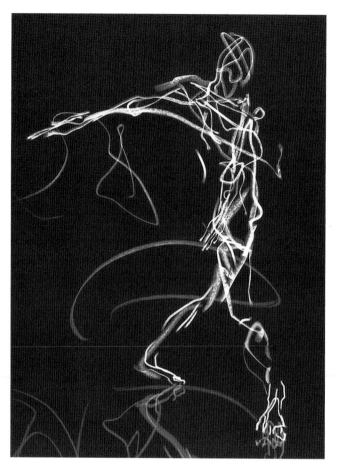

Figure 9.8 In *Ghostcatching*, Bill T. Jones and Riverbed's spectral dance animations marked what one critic described as "a landmark in the computerized rendering of the human form." Courtesy of Paul Kaiser and Shelley Eshkar.

focus has been on programs that respond to and interact with the movements of live dancers in real time. This includes the use of sensory devices worn by the performers that are linked, by cables or through wireless systems, to a computer that registers their movements or vocalizations. The computer then translates the data into digital signals to manipulate lighting, digital video, and audio material in relation to the performer's actions. This creates a "live" relationship between the performer and the visual media projections and audio samples. Members of New York dance-theater group Troika Ranch explain that they create such systems to bring to life "dead" electronic media to imbue it with the same sense of liveness as the corporeal performance elements:

We are drawn to do this because most electronic media is dead, in the sense that it is precisely the same each time it is presented—quite different from what happens when a dancer or actor performs the same material twice. We want the media elements in our performances to have the same sense of liveness as the human performers it accompanies. We impose the chaos of the human body on the media in hope of bringing it to life.[28]

Mark Coniglio, *MidiDancer*, and *Isadora*

As early as 1989, Troika Ranch's artistic director Mark Coniglio developed the group's wearable hardware movement sensing system *MidiDancer*, which sends wireless MIDI signals to the computer. It uses flex sensors attached to the dancer's joints (elbows, knees, wrists, hips, and the like), which are attached by wires to a single-chip microcomputer in a small box usually worn on the dancer's back. The computer measures the degree of "flexion" of each joint thirty times per second, assigning it a number between zero (straight) and 100 (fully bent), and transmits the information via radio waves to an off-stage receiver/microcomputer. This checks for errors and ignores any corrupted information before sending MIDI signals to a Macintosh computer running software that "intelligently interprets" the data and triggers technical cues and manipulates media from files stored on hard disk or Laser Disc, or from the input of a live video camera.

The company's first software system, *Interactor* was developed by Coniglio and Mort Subotnick, and was later superseded by Coniglio's *Isadora*. The software enables a range of media manipulations such as playing video at different speeds and in reverse, and visual distortions such as warping, keying, and spinning.[29] Troika Ranch conceptualize media-activating computer-sensing systems as something equivalent to a musical instrument. Thus, just as a violin responds to the gestures of its player and transforms them into sound, *MidiDancer* amplifies the movements of the performer and translates them into another medium. But they acknowledge that the analogy breaks down "when one considers that we look to the dancer's body for meaning, a burden we do not typically place on a violinist's fingers."[30] They identify the challenge to conceive performances that utilize sensor-activated media effectively but do not compromise the traditional role of the choreographer and dancer.

Troika Ranch and other companies also employ a range of non-wearable motion sensing systems, from camera-tracking linked systems such as *BigEye* to laser-controlled devices such as *LaserWeb*, where a series of laser beams cross the stage horizontally, or vertically from the lighting rig to the stage floor, linked to a computer system which registers when performers cross and "break" the beam. The system also senses and calibrates the velocity of the performer's movement, prompting the software to affect interactive media manipulations in appropriate ways and speeds, so as to harmonize the feel and mood between the performer and the audiovisual effects. Impact pad devices such as piezo sensors, which are placed on the floor, are similarly sensitive to the speed and strength of touch or tread. Piezo sensors were utilised in an early Troika Ranch performance, *Bank/*

Figure 9.9 Mark Coniglio's *Isadora* software is employed to control and manipulate the graphical projections in Troika Ranch's dance-theater parable of evolution *16 [R]evolutions* (2006). Photo: Richard Termine.

Perspective 1 where a dancer's step or touch activated video images from Laser Disc, and progressively intensified and changed the musical key.

Coniglio's *Isadora* software is a popular and well-used interface between the performer and the computer in what is known in some circles as the "digidance" community, and has also been employed by installation artists (figure 9.9). It is based on *Max* thinking, but has a more intuitive interface that is particularly appealing to choreographers and dancers and can be used very flexibly—for example, being activated by a single video camera or sensing systems such as *Mididancer*. It is quick to learn, and its user-friendly, intuitive interface allows the non-technologically inclined choreographer to understand and creatively use it in a very short time. It is also a generic and affordable program that has been developed in collaboration with a large number of beta testers within the digidance community, such as Sarah Rubidge, who noted in 2003,

The stock of plugins—which allow you to do a multitude of video processing on the fly, or to organise your images as you want them—are growing daily. If an artist wants a particular effect which is not yet in the program you email Mark—ask if Isadora can do this . . . he emails back— says "not yet—but give me a day or two" he writes a new plugin or refines a module and puts a new version of Izzy [*Isadora*] on the web for download. He did this for me several times—which means that the system which will let me fulfill my ideas for a particular installation are now available for other artists to use . . . as are the very particular requirements of other artists. The program has expanded immensely since he put it out into an "invited" public domain. Perfect example of a collaborative development of a software programme with Mark leading the way—but taking on board the needs of other artists! In this it is similar to *Director* and *Max* . . . which allow for users to write and distribute plugins . . . but Mark is doing this before it hits the streets as it were . . . and using artists, not computer people as beta testers.[31]

Kirk Woolford and Michael Klein

But Rubidge goes on say that other specialist programmers who work developing custom-built systems as full-time collaborators on projects with dance artists and companies remain important in creating unique digital interfaces and systems specific to particular aesthetic aims: "We still need the Kirks and Brunos of this world to do the gorgeously complex/sophisticated stuff we need." Kirk Woolford and Bruno Martelli have both developed custom software when working with a range of artists, and significantly in such contexts, they are not regarded as technicians but as coauthors and, crucially, "co-dancer" company members. Their works are considerable—in number, scale, and artistic power—and we will encounter some in later chapters. These include Martelli's work with Ruth Gibson and Igloo, one of the visually freshest and sensorily pleasurable digital dance companies in the United Kingdom. Woolford has also worked with Igloo, where he has used code itself as an integral part of performance content. His custom-built software for Igloo's *Viking Shoppers* (2000) made code the primary aesthetic subject, using an ASCII camera linked to his software to project real-time images of the live dancers composed of the graphical symbols of ASCII code. ASCII (American Standard Code for Information Interchange) has also been employed by artists such as the Slovenian Vuk Cosic's ASCII Art Ensemble whose tour of the United Kingdom in 2001 included an online project, *This Is the Real Matrix* that used the code to create animated versions of famous movies, camera images, and sound works.[32]

Woolford's project with Susan Kozel's Mesh Performance Partnerships, *Contours* (1999) deserves special mention here, employing a custom designed "theater" of its own. This large, high-tech dome (with the audience in the round) is constructed in different locations for performances and integrates a number of motion sensing and analysis systems, including infrared cameras to feed Woolford's custom software and to translate Kozel's live dance movements into imagery that is projected all around the space. The projections envelop the whole dome on separate screens over 360 degrees to create an immersive experience as Kozel's movements alter, stretch, and transform the projections in real time.

In the first section she dances and rolls around the floor chasing and interacting with a transforming and ethereal real-time projection based on her physical outline. In the next she is suspended in midair just above the floor and swings back and forth in a trapeze harness, turning, rolling, and circling. Her movements activate sprays and flows of particles across the space, which become denser or more dispersed in relation to her velocity of movement. In the final section her body is raised higher and her movements stretch, mutate and choreograph sequences of projected line-effects. The images also submerge and reflect from Kozel's costume, making her appear to be a moving part of the light projections. The performance's structure of ascendancy (from rolling on the floor to swinging high above the heads of the audience) and the gradual "disappearance" of Kozel's body as it is increasingly submerged and harmonized with the projected line formations and striations make for a beautiful and uplifting experience, what Kozel describes as a "duet between a dancer and liquid light."

Other notable dance software writers include Michael Klein, formerly choreographer and co-director of the Barriedale Operahouse, who collaborated with Volmar Klein to develop *The ChoreoGraph*, "a cross-media sequencer for non-linear multimedia performances and installations."[33] Based upon variations of *Max* and using a MIDI system to link the performer, technicians, and audience, it enables, among other things, sophisticated soundtrack improvisation and changes to the choreographic script. It was first used in performance in 1998, and Klein has used it to investigate what he calls "a stochastic mode of operation" whereby a series of signs, some random, others determined by other aspects such as sound and image, appear on a timeline that prompts each dancer to respond and improvise within a range of rehearsed movements and dance phrases.

Barriedale Operahouse, a peripatetic company that lists its home as "not really based anywhere" and has operated from London, Vienna, and Ireland, has collaborated with many different artists[34] on projects using *The Choreograph*, and Klein's travels have included time as a guest choreographer at Ballett Frankfurt (2002–3). The software has therefore been tested and developed within a range of contexts, with works including, in London, *Cay—admit possibilities* (1999), a "club style" performance-installation combining live dance, video-mixing and electro-acoustic manipulation; in Vienna, *Nodding Dog* (2000), a large-scale ballet using *ChoreoGraph* for real-time structuring procedures; and *Duplex* (2002), a *pas de deux* produced by Ballett Frankfurt that made use of a later version of *ChoreoGraph* to generate a new structure for every performance.

The Ballett Frankfurt itself has been home to considerable advances in dance and technology, led by artistic director and choreographer William Forsythe, and we examine his influential *Improvisation Technologies* CD-ROM in detail later. The company's involvement in developing software systems for its work includes a 1995 collaboration with Supreme Particles, an electronic performance group based in Germany, to build an interactive choreographic system called *Binary Ballistic Ballet*, utilized in Forsythe's three-part *Eidos:Telos*. Part 1 incorporated a computer that picked words from a database, modified their color, shape, and movement, and displayed them on monitors that were only visible to the dancers. The dancers could move from their predetermined choreography to react and respond to this data display, creating new dance patterns from a stimulus unseen by the audience. In Part 2, both graphics and dancers were visible to the audience, the computer being used to build "Interactive Creatures" that reacted to incoming sounds, with both the creatures and the dancers constantly interpolating complex geometric shapes. The performance won the award for interactive art at Prix Ars Electronica in 1995.

Palindrome and *EyeCon*

The German dance company Palindrome has designed its own camera-tracking interface and software system, *EyeCon* (designed by Frieder Weiss), whose user-friendliness has also proved popular with other companies. It is used to good effect in Palindrome's *Touching* (2003). In one section a live camera projection onto a rear screen alternates between medium and close-up shots of the two dancers as they move in close proximity to one another. At a number of points the dancers slowly draw together, until their hands and other body parts physically touch. As the motion tracking system senses the touch, the video image switches abruptly to a negative image, and once the contact is broken, back to the normal positive one. The dancers play skillfully with the dramatic tension before the point of touch, maintaining eye contact with each other as their hands draw slowly and inexorably closer, building the sense of corporeal electricity between them, until contact is made. The electrical charge suddenly ignites on screen as previously dark and dimly lit video bodies explode into the bright white heat of the video negative, infusing their videated forms with an intense light, while in turn the brightness of the projection floods the dimly lit live bodies on stage (figure 9.10).

In another section, the *EyeCon* software tracks the bodies and registers generalized differences in movement that trigger audio changes. The two dancers move deliberately and ritualistically, one at a time on opposite sides of the stage, their slow spinal and arm movements activating low, undulating sounds. Then quicker, stronger full body movements and gestures release loud, percussive, and reverberant musical chords. While there is a powerful correlation between the movement and its sonic activations, the moments when the bodies complete their phrases and are still attain the most impact. The silences that greet the frozen, statuesque bodies are full, and hang with an intense sense of anticipation, of waiting—the still calm before the next short storm of kinetic and sonic activity. A similar effect is achieved in a later sequence where colorful and layered, semi-abstracted video images "dance" on the rear screen in relation to the speed and intensity of movement of the live performers. This is broken when the dancers suddenly stop, at which point the abstracted imagery falls away, leaving a rotating default image of yellowed and wilting, dying flowers.

Where bodies interactively trigger sounds and projections in digital dance performance, audiences find it most effective when there is a perceptible sense of the interaction. In the early years of digital performance, a common criticism of works using motion-sensing media activation was that the relationship between the performers' actions and the software manipulations were at best hazy or unclear and at worst invisible. In discussions at conferences or following performances, the criticism was frequently made that real-time interactive sonic and media manipulations could have been preset and

Figure 9.10 The interplay of proximity and touch between Robert Wechsler and Helena Zwiauer is monitored by *EyeCon* software (designed by Frieder Weiss) to trigger audio, lighting, and video effects in Palindrome's *Touching* (2003). Photographer: Klaus Thierfelder.

prerehearsed to equal or even greater effect. Indeed, this point was often extended to question the whole validity and purpose of the real-time interaction between performers and software. The same synchronization between the live movement and the changes of music and projected image could be achieved by the traditional means of presetting all the elements in rehearsal, and simply having the performers synchronize their actions to the media. Many suggested that in doing so, a more refined and polished performance might result, since the very purpose of rehearsal was empirical trial and error to establish what were the most effective results.

Thus, there was a relatively widely held perception that interactive and improvisatory relationships between performers and the technological systems should not be an end in itself. This was the case particularly because there was often a chicken or egg scenario whereby it was unclear when performers were simply following prerecorded musical phrases and video file edits, and when they were actually prompting, creating, or editing them in real time. This sense of uncertainty was, and still is, exacerbated, since aesthetically similar musical and graphical/video manipulations and effects were being created both by performance groups using real-time motion tracking, and those who prerecorded the media files and simply performed in time to them.

Palindrome director Robert Wechsler argues that a sense of spontaneous improvisational play in performance is essential to allay these problems and to enable what he terms "gestural coherence." He reflects that when Palindrome simply performed a finished choreography using its interactive *EyeCon* system, the audience was unaware that any interactive system was being used at all. This apparent invisibility to audiences of many interactive dance systems has prompted Scott deLahunta to ponder whether in the future, audiences may wish to see more explicit connections between performer action and computer system response, to the extent of observing the computational mapping and "transparent interactive architectures" at play.[35]

half/angel

But the invisibility of interactive systems is not an issue for half/angel, a performance company directed by Jools Gilson-Ellis and Richard Povall that makes extensive use of new technologies. They consciously integrate advanced technologies and live performance in such a way that the technological interface *is* invisible, becoming an integral part of the work, but not an overt feature that draws attention to itself. As Sophie Hansen notes, "the software becomes an extension of the body, with all the invisible nuances of human motivation. Quiet, moving, and modestly unspectacular."[36] The members of half/angel often spend two or three years developing a project, allowing their custom-made systems to be not merely developed, but so refined that they "disappear." Their dance-theater production *The Secret Project* (1999) evoked for one reviewer "a magic-realistic world of snow-ghosts who trip you when you walk in the snow or words that themselves fall."[37] Performing on a bare stage, the dancers create not only their movement world but also the soundspace they inhabit; their interactions with the software systems are embedded in the choreography, prompting sound and light (but no visual screen projections). The systems are thus an entirely "hidden" element of the performance, but are central to it, intimately harmonizing the bodies with the spatial, musical, and sonic elements.

Although Gilson-Ellis is a fine dancer and works frequently *with* dancers, half/angel's work is often difficult to categorize. Its dancers use dance, text, video, music, and performance, frequently to unsettling effect. Many of their performance works are enacted in an "intelligent performance environment" or electronically sensitized space, the performers modulating features of the environment, whether it be sound or video, through their actions. Half/angel are storytellers with a decidedly poetic edge; delicate, yet powerful, they often reach back into the world of mythology, but imbue it with contemporary concerns.

Spinstren (2002) interweaves stories of spinning, from the framing narrative of a little girl who steals a spinning top, to tales relating to a breed of magical women, the

Figure 9.11 In *Spinstren* (2002), half/angel explore myths, science, fairy tales, magical women, and centrifugal force.

Spinstren of the title, to Sleeping Beauty and the mythological tale of Athena and Arachne, taking in scientific explanations of centrifugal force on the way (figure 9.11). *Spinstren* also makes a tangential reference to their 1997 CD-ROM *mouthplace*, a complex work which broke many expectations associated with the interactive CD-ROM at that time. Although primarily concerned with notions of femininity and orality, *mouthplace* also made reference to domestic arts that entail the use of needles. In its installation form, the computer monitor is situated at the center of a space comprising hundreds of sewing needles hung on fine red sewing thread through which one had to weave to reach the CD-ROM.

Half/angel co-director Richard Povall is one of the designers of the reactive "intelligent stage" at Arizona State University's Institute for Studies in the Arts, which has provided an important site of activity for digital dance research and development, including many workshops, performances, and artist residencies. Ellen Bromberg's two-year residency involved extensive practical research work, and culminated in the performance, *Falling to Earth* (1998), which examined somatic experience, loss, grief, and transformation. It also presented notions of identity not as something created through acts of will or social/genetic conditioning, but "as the inhabitation of the body itself."[38] Bromberg's reflections on her extensive work within the sensor controlled interactive environment of the Intelligent Stage are interesting in their conceptions of direct and mutual relationships between (and extensions of) the physical, the mental, the digital, and the corporeal:

The physical experience of moving within the movement sensing system is subtle and remarkable. The sensation of gesture instantaneously effecting sound, light and projections creates a heightened sense of presence, of being in the body in an enlivened state. The space takes on a quality of consciousness as the dancer extends his/her volition into it and that volition is expressed through the designated media.[39]

Over time, it is clear that most performers and groups have tried to respond to issues around "invisibility" by ensuring greater subtlety and craft in their interactions with motion tracking systems, which now register far more clearly with audiences. As software has developed, so too has the sophistication with which performers interact with the systems. Since the mid- and late 1990s, when dance motion-sensing systems were relatively new, performers have learned how best to "play" the motion-tracking instrument. In the early days, it sometimes appeared that the very fact (and then novelty) that their movements miraculously activated different digital effects had blinded performers and dampened their self-reflexive sensibilities. Today, there is a much more advanced approach to the dialogue and interaction between human and machine. This is characterized by an increased attention to fluidity and nuance, and particularly an understanding that less can be more, in contrast to previous explorations that too often emphasized a more is more ideology of disjunctive and abrupt changes, sometimes to the point of melodrama and bombast. Over years, a genuinely sensitive and sophisticated interactive paradigm has gradually replaced a previously rough and reactive one. Rather than a performer working in dissociation with the computer systems, a pattern of "I do this, and it will do that," it is now a more integrative "we do this together" relationship, akin to how a skilled improvisatory musician interacts with her instrument. Where the dialogue between performer and technology once resembled a conversation between two people who did not understand the other's language and overcompensated by artificially slowing down, raising voices and gesticulating wildly, the language has now been mastered far more on both sides (performer to software and software to performer). The two can converse intelligently, "listening" and responding sensitively to one another, expressing themselves articulately and building a complex dialogue of ideas.

At the 1st International Conference of Digital Technologies and Performance Arts in Doncaster, England, in 2003, Palindrome's director Robert Wechsler and dance-tech artist Sarah Rubidge separately reflected how it had taken them eight years of research and experimentation to attain a real understanding of how best to program and interact with motion-activated systems, and to develop technical artistry and sophistication. Their recent works testify to the validity of the claims. An earlier Palindrome performance we saw at the Performance Studies Conference in Mainz in 2001 was relatively crude: a demonstration of ideas and possibilities that was not without merit or interest, but lacked subtlety and artistic coherence. Their *Touching* performance in 2003 was similarly structured in short sections, each exploring a different technical or aesthetic aspect of their

EyeCon system, but the result was far more aesthetically and dramatically impressive, with truly meaningful "dialogues" between the dancers and the technology.

Conclusion

The development of original software and hardware systems by dance artists has been somewhat fragmentary and individual, in many ways reflecting the development of the dance and technology movement itself. During most of the 1990s, digital dance works were mainly to be seen by aficionados, advertised on specialist e-lists, or witnessed at specialist conference gatherings such as *Dance and Technology* (from 1990),[40] *Digital Dancing* (from 1995, described as neither conference nor workshop, but a space for choreographers),[41] and *Electric Dance Festival* (1996).[42]

More recently, the opportunity and need for practitioners to grapple with the particular problems of open source code has been championed by, among others, the "Software for Dancers Project" (based in London, Autumn 2001) facilitated by Scott deLahunta. It brought together four choreographers, Siobhan Davies, Shobana Jeyasingh, Wayne McGregor, and Ashley Page, and five digital artists/programmers, Guy Hilton, Jo Hyde, Bruno Martelli, Adrian Ward, and Christian Ziegler,[43] to discuss ways in which the computer might specifically aid the rehearsal process. The workshop was documented by Sanjoy Roy in an article in *Dance Theatre Journal*,[44] and did not shy away from the disadvantages including the problems of time, of learning a new skill, and of creating advanced software without massive investment. DeLahunta later reflected upon software as a language, as a tool, and as a material, describing "a growing area of study of software as a condition and shaper of cognition, creativity and culture,"[45] and concluding that enhanced software skills would enable artists to radically shape their thinking in direct relation to their artistic creations.

A related weekend workshop, "New Performance Tools: Technologies/Interactive Systems," took place in Ohio State University in January 2002, facilitated by deLahunta and Johannes Birringer. It brought together a small group of international professional artists to explore the practical and conceptual implications of working with interactive tools and computer-controlled systems within live performance and installation contexts.[46] Software demonstrations and experimentation included applications of proprietary code programs, and specialist dance software such as *Isadora*. As in the earlier London session, problems and disadvantages were addressed, a recurring one being the tendency for experimentation to become rather self-fulfilling and not to reach beyond the research parameters of particular universities; another being the need for artists to interrogate not only the surface results of particular applications, but also the material and media wherein it was created. As so often happens with workshops of this nature and despite a thorough critical appraisal of the event by Birringer, no particular directions or conclusions are discernible, and its emphasis remained one of debate (which raised more questions than answers), as well as a valuable sharing of experiences and research in progress.

In advances in proprietary character animation, *Poser* software, increasingly used by performance and dance artists, serves to remind us that the ability to animate was and is becoming increasingly available to specialist and nonspecialist practitioners alike, and that commercial software, by building in "ready-to-use" facilities, constantly attempts to appeal to a wider range of users. Particularly appealing to artists is the ability for different packages to address complex aspects of verisimilitude such as the ability to manipulate realistic facial expressions or the likely drape of different fabrics in relation to movement and gravity. By the early twenty-first century, several programs were competing at the higher (Hollywood) end of the market, including PMG's *Lightwave 3D, 3D Max, Character Studio, Project Messiah,* and *Messiah:Animate.*

Yet the overriding mood among practitioners undertaking such enquiry and experimentation throughout the 1990s was a familiar one in the performance arts, consisting of a blend of friendly collaboration and free exchange, mixed with a degree of seclusion and confidentiality in the preparation of new work. Inevitably, language and distance sometimes played a part in keeping some developments in relative isolation, such as Paulo Henrique's experiments in Lisbon in the mid-1990s where "Technology was used in a symbolic way, turning the body in[to] a shadow and splitting it from himself and into the space."[47] His work was something of an unknown entity when *De agora em Diante/ From Now On* toured to New York in 1998 and received considerable plaudits:

I don't make recommendations very often, but last night I saw *From Now On*, a performance by Lisbon-based choreographer/ performance artist Paulo Henrique that I think deserves a bigger audience. . . . The piece is one of the stronger uses of video and technology in a live performance that I have seen. The piece has a seamless, rigorous quality that is very mysterious, intimate and personal.[48]

Henrique worked within a very individual and self-adapted mode that resulted in a complex, and almost chaotic combination of video cameras, scanners, delays, and projections all incorporated into a symbolic performance-art structure (which not atypically for the period involved skin, fish, salt, and the performer's blood). In an era when experiments with identifiable software were in danger of becoming a trademark of digital performance, Henrique's wholly personalized approach gained impact by being strangely devoid of those new but increasingly standard characteristics of the time. Even by 1998, the restrictions and cyclical repetitions of particular software programs used in dance performance had become dominant over the impressive providence that they initially seemed to make available, and Henrique's freshness was a reminder that creativity still resides with the practitioner, not the software.

Following the novelty and excitement of all things digital within dance performance during the 1990s, it is important to observe that by the turn of the millennium the words "digital" and "computer" were no longer being promulgated to highlight special features or suggest unusual "magic." This is an indicator not that digital tools and techniques had been tried, had been found wanting and had been put to one side, but rather that they had been thoroughly accepted and assimilated within new dance practices. Thus, in the advertising literature of the UK *Dance Umbrella 2003*, it is noticeable that there is no mention of the words "digital" or "computer" unlike preceding years, despite the tagline "daring to leap into the unknown," and the inclusion of works one would categorize as "digital dance," including a piece by the Trisha Brown Dance Company featuring imagery by Robert Rauschenberg and a score by Laurie Anderson, and a William Forsythe/Ballett Frankfurt performance, *Kammer/Kammer* (2000). Created around the apex of digital dance euphoria in 2000, by 2003 *Kammer/Kammer* becomes described as "hybrid dance, theatre and film performance," an indicator that its digital aspects were no longer paramount. A reassessment was well underway by this time, the digital dance hyperbole had faded, computers had become comprehensively absorbed into daily life, and digital effects were considered something less than remarkable.

An inescapable fact about the progression of software is that after the initial miracle of new computer "life," a certain sameness and staleness creeps in through repetition that replaces the initial awe and wonderment, the more so a little later when contemporary advertising constantly uses the latest digital effect for dramatic punch. What thrilled in the 1990s was often less the "art" and more the sense of witnessing the newest and latest miracles of technological magic. But the miracle aspect tends not to last, we simply get used to it, adopt it, absorb it, and wait for the next miracle to arrive.

III

The Body

Virtual Bodies

Let's take a deep breath before approaching this particular subject—virtual bodies are capricious, enigmatic, and highly problematic entities. Where should we start? Perhaps with this:

Perhaps the most vivid change is coming in the art that is closest to the human body: dance. If dance is the art that is most embodied, dependent intimately on the state of the body . . . and each art form is heading for its opposite, then the future of dance must be found in disembodiment.
—MARCOS NOVAK[1]

Or with this:

And far from vanishing into the immateriality of thin air, the body is complicating, replicating, escaping its formal orfanisation, the organized organs which modernity has taken for normality. This new malleability is everywhere: in the switches of transsexualism, the perforations of tattoos and piercings, the indelible markings of brands and scars, the emergence of neural and viral networks, bacterial life, prostheses, neural jacks, vast numbers of wandering matrices.
—SADIE PLANT[2]

Or perhaps this:

In the cultural bestiary, the body is pulverized and splayed apart, like a "lap dissolve"; a traveller in time where from the viewpoint of the advanced cybernetic technologies of the mediascape, the body is always a big failure in desperate need of supplementary technical prosthetics."
—ARTHUR KROKER[3]

The body is the most revered, fetishized, contested, detested, and confused concept in contemporary cultural theory. Moreover, that is just the natural, corporeal body—things become even more complicated with its virtual counterpart. The concept of *the* body dominates large areas of contemporary cultural, literary, feminist, and cyber criticism, but often in a highly questionable form, since disassembling postmodern impulses have placed the body outside of itself. Although body discourses continually remind us of the body's interconnectivity to all things (through cultural inscriptions, rhizomatic lines of flight and so on), the body has nonetheless been commonly separated from its physiological and psychic contexts. A classic Cartesian split underlies prevalent theoretical concerns with the body, which has imposed an objectified redefinition of our understanding of the human subject, the holistic "person," to render *it* an abstracted, depersonalized and increasingly dehumanized physical object—*the* body. But the human body is not a concept.[4] Bodies are particular, not general. Bodies are not animated cadavers, despite Stelarc's protestations. Bodies embody consciousness; to talk of disembodied consciousness is a contradiction in terms.

But in the body fetishization of recent social and performance theory, we should remember that it is not always the body per se that is being discussed. Rather, it may be the mind (Foucault); the inscribed, political hierarchies of gender (Butler); humanism and matter (Hayles); or metaphysics (Deleuze and Guattari). When the body is "transformed," composited or telematically transmitted into digital environments, it should also be remembered that despite what many say, it is not an *actual* transformation of the body, but of the pixelated composition of its recorded or computer-generated *image*. Virtual bodies are new visual representations of the body, but do not alter the physical composition of their referent flesh and bones. Virtual bodies may appear to be bodily transformations to the (receiver's) eye and mind, but no actual metamorphosis takes place within the (sender's/performer's) actual body. The virtual body is an inherently theatrical entity, and there is an enormous amount of suspension of disbelief going on in relation to it. Let us make our own position clear from the outset. There is no disembodiment, images are still just images, virtual worlds are still clunky, and the web is still primarily a lot of Web pages rather than a *Neuromancer*-style, high-adrenaline, mind-blowing cyberspace of swimming databodies—at least to those who do not easily separate their minds from their bodies.

The Cartesian Mind-Body Split

If we are ever to have pure knowledge of anything, we must get rid of the body and contemplate things by themselves with the soul by itself. . . . so long as we are alive, we shall continue closest to knowledge if we avoid as much as we can all contact and association with the body . . . and instead of allowing ourselves to become infected with its nature, purify ourselves from it until God himself gives us deliverance.

—SOCRATES[5]

Socrates began it all, Plato elaborated, calling the body a prison and a tomb for the soul, and in 1637 René Descartes famously formulated *The Discourse on Method* (1637), which set out a full-blown philosophy distinguishing, dividing and separating the mind from the body. The "self" was firmly located in the mind, although the body was not left entirely out of the equation since, as a container, it brought about limitations and particularizations on the mind and self. This general philosophical principle dominated Western thought for centuries, although phenomenology and late-twentieth-century cultural criticism sought to dispel the mind-body division ("Cartesian dualism") and emphasize a holistic unity of mind-body-self. However, the Cartesian split is still very much alive and well, and celebrating a glittering revival in cyberculture and academic discourses on virtual arts, where it is rarely acknowledged as such (Cartesianism being very deeply unfashionable), but is rather cloaked in other postmodern discursive (dis)guises.

The cult of the body in contemporary theory is itself (deeply ironically) a Cartesian reconceptualization of flesh and bone into a conceptual and *mental* ontology: as abstracted, malleable, and even useless matter. Its anatomical materiality is rarely described, since this is far less important than the psychological, political, and cultural inscriptions and reconstitutions forced upon it. This can be seen in the work of most celebrated body theorist, Judith Butler, as well as Frederic Jameson, who typifies the confusion and conflation of the external with the internal in an apparently erudite but actually absurd proposal. He suggests, in language quite typical of recent theories of the body, that we can understand an individual by looking at her body—judging a person by his or her "cover" in the same way that we are not supposed to judge books: "Finally the body itself proves to be a palimpsest whose stabs of pain and symptoms, along with its deeper impulses and its sensory apparatus, can be *read* fully as much as any other text."[6]

Paradoxically, even the cult of the body as expressed in the late-twentieth-century desire for "the body beautiful," tailored through diet, gymnasium culture, cosmetics, and plastic surgery, is a Cartesian triumph of mind over matter. Anorexia, a burgeoning disease starkly and perversely encapsulating the body-beautiful obsession, is now understood as the subject's self-destructive, body-destructive demonstration of her ultimate domination of the body by the mind: the powerful, pathological, anorexic mind ultimately controls and destroys the weak and subservient body. Body art, seemingly the most corporeal and visceral of performance genres, can likewise be viewed as the artist's will for the mind to transcend the body. The painful letting of blood by artists such as Ron Athey, Stelarc, Gina Pane, and Franko B is accompanied not by the screams of agony of the normative human body, but by an eerie, awesome, and stubbornly resistant silence marking mental power and bodily denial. In the extraordinary, tortured beauty of these artists' works, the bloodied, naked, body *seems* "all"—simultaneously signifier and signified—but the willful mind is the invisible but overwhelming sign, the ultimate agenda. Succumbing to pain is not countenanced here since, as Socrates told Phaedo, every physical experience of pleasure or pain "nails the soul to the body."[7]

Meanwhile, cultural theory deifies the body and resists the difficult truth that in point of fact the Cartesian split in culture and society is widening, as we sit like Foucault's malleable "docile bodies" watching screens and monitors, becoming ever more psychologically, but certainly not physically, disembodied. Foucault reminds us that this is by no means a passive activity, but is willful, mental;[8] and McLuhan was early (as ever) to recognize the flickering images of television for what they were, an electronic wedge to prize open and deepen the mind-body divide:

As electric media proliferate, whole societies at a time become discarnate, detached from mere bodily or physical "reality" and relieved of any allegiance to or a sense of responsibility for it. . . . The alteration of human identity by new service environments of information has left whole populations without personal or community values.[9]

Daily dosages of empathetic, mental transference have grown as passive, receptive modes such as television have transformed into active and interactive cyber-wanderings, meeting "real" people to create fictional (MUDs and MOOs) and nonfictional (e-friendship) relationships. While these can be celebrated as liberating, proactive, and creative collaborative encounters, the fictionality and performativity of e-life and communication also poses serious questions about schizophrenic self-representation and consequent problems of relating with others outside artificial environments. Jon Stratton stresses the Cartesian division at play in his analysis of email affairs, what he calls "the increasing acceptance that the 'self' can exist apart from the 'body'" in online activities and remote erotic encounters such as phone sex.[10] Peter Lamborn Wilson provides Stratton with additional ammunition: "Cyberspace . . . involves a curious form of *disembodiment*, in which each participant becomes a perceptual monad, a concept rather than a physical presence," citing phone sex as a preview to this development:

The deep purpose of phone-sex is probably not really the client's masturbation or his credit card number, but the actual ectoplasmic meeting of two ghosts in the "other" world of sheer nothingness, a poor parodic rendering of the phone company's slogan, "Reach out and touch someone," which is so sadly, so finally, what we cannot do in cyberspace.[11]

Allucquere Rosanne Stone points out how "compared to 'real' space, in virtual space the socioepistemic structures by means of which the meaning of the terms 'self' and 'body' are produced operate differently."[12] Stratton suggests that a consequence of this difference is

a radicalising of Cartesian dualism. Where, in modern thinking, the body served to contain and limit the self, the singularity of which was guaranteed by the continuity of the mind in the body, there is now an increasing acceptance of the idea that not only are selves separate from the body, they are not limited and determined by the mind's containment in the body.[13]

But against this background, what is vital to understand in relation to digital performance is that the mind-body split is generally at complete odds with the practice of artists and performers. Their work involves—indeed is totally reliant upon—a close harmony and connection between mental creativity and physical skill and dexterity. The fundamental goal of most performers is the eradication of distinction between mind and body—the fluid and unmediated bridge between the inner and the outer—mental or emotional impulse spontaneously combusting as unique and pure physical expression. As Richard Schechner put it in 1977, "His entire effort is in making his body-voice-mind-spirit whole. Then he risks this wholeness here and now in front of others. Like the tightrope walker on the high wire, each move is absolutely spontaneous and part of an endless discipline."[14] Regardless of the medium, performance artists explicitly explore and enact their holistic autonomies and interiorities (gendered, spiritual, emotional, and political), not simply their bodily corporeality. If this process takes place within a recorded electronic or digital environment, it is the medium that is virtual, unreal or disembodied, not the human performer within it. In the performance arts, whether in a theater, on a street corner, or on a computer monitor, the medium is not the message (and never has been); the performer is.

But much cybertheory and digital performance studies have tended to miss this point, to relate instead the metamorphosis and fragmentation of the body in virtual realms to an *actual*, corporeal transformation; or worse still, to a belief in disembodiment. The dislocation and fragmentation of the body in digital performance is an aesthetic praxis which deconstructive critics have hungrily grasped and mythologized, holding up the virtual body as the central icon (immaterial, disembodied), whereas in actuality, it operates as an index, as another trace and representation of the always already *physical* body. The emperor's new clothes of the virtual body are thus being lovingly admired, theorized, and proudly hung up in a wardrobe of theoretical self-deception, as the too-solid flesh of the sweating performer lumbers exhaustedly to the theater bar.

We take a different view, and believe that audiences cognitively and empathetically perceive the performing virtual *human* body (as opposed to a computer simulated body) as always already embodied material flesh. Irrespective of the medium, performance's ontology has for centuries been virtual and simulacral, and the flesh of even the virtual performer remains too solid, and will not melt. Performers generally also share this perception, since their actions in recording images for their virtual body manifestations constitute fully embodied actions of body and mind. Contrary to prevalent critical assumptions, we do not believe the performing virtual body is either less authentic than the live, nor is it disembodied from the performer. What possible use is disembodiment to a performer, or the very idea of a mind and body split?

Bolter and Gromala raise a similar point in relation to digital art, arguing that artists' explorations of the relationship between the virtual and the physical "help to combat the myth of disembodiment":[15]

Digital artists in particular insist on the materiality of their work. They will never abandon or disparage the ways of knowing that the senses give us. For them, even the experience of seeing is not disembodied; it is visceral. Seeing is feeling. What fascinates digital artists is the ways in which their embodied existence is redefined in cyberspace. So they use digital technology to examine the interaction between the physical and the virtual. . . . Digital design oscillates between the physical and the virtual, just as it oscillates between the reflective and the transparent.[16]

Susan Kozel: Dreaming the Telematic Body

I seldom feel without thinking, or think without feeling.
—SAMUEL TAYLOR COLERIDGE[17]

In a notable article from 1994, "Spacemaking: Experiences of a Virtual Body," one of Britain's leading dance and technology artists, Susan Kozel, reflects at length on the digital body and telepresence following her experience "performing" for four weeks in Paul Sermon's seminal installation *Telematic Dreaming* (1992). Working for several hours a day over a sustained period as a simultaneously corporeal body (on her own bed) and a virtual one (her image projected onto a gallery visitor's bed) and interacting with others' telematic presence, Kozel explored in depth the relationship between her flesh body and its virtual counterpart (figure 10.1). Video cameras, monitors and projectors link together beds in two separate rooms using a videoconference ISDN line. Each person's image, lying on a blue bed, is separated from its background using chromakey blue screen techniques, and is trans-

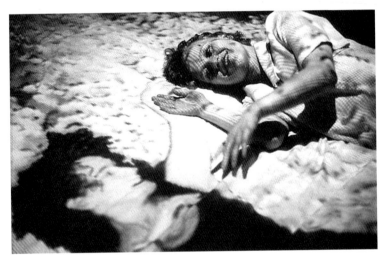

Figure 10.1   The image of Susan Kozel is projected onto a bed occupied by a gallery visitor in Paul Sermon's installation *Telematic Dreaming* (1992).

mitted and projected onto the other's bed, and the composite image is shown on monitors. The two bodies (one real, one virtual) thus mutually meet on both beds, and prerecorded video imagery—rich colors and textures—is mixed into the scene to enhance the dream-like quality. But Sermon deliberately avoids providing an audio link so as to concentrate attention on the meeting of two bodies separated in real space but virtually conjoined: "human interaction was reduced to its simplest essence: touch, trust, vulnerability."[18]

Kozel begins by describing the initial strangeness of the relationship between her actions moving her arms and body alone on her bed "as if in some sort of hypnotic ritual dance," yet simultaneously engaging in an intense and intimate improvisation with other unknown bodies projected on the bed. She felt "little electric shocks" in response to virtual caresses and very soon the real impact of the telematic connections became apparent:

Movement usually began in a hesitant way with hand contact taking on excessive importance. The impact of slow and small movement became enormous. . . . When the movement progressed from these early stages to a sort of full body choreography the piece became an emotional investment which shocked and sometimes disturbed people. . . . The occasions when the movement worked well felt very much like good contact improvisation: a hypnotic feeling of not knowing what is coming next but letting the strong flow of movement carry you onward. When the movement moved through us in this way, based on openness and trust, the distinction between which bodies were real and which were virtual became irrelevant.[19]

But over days, as Kozel became increasingly engrossed in her telematic body as she watched its duet meetings with scores of visitors on the monitors, the "irrelevance" of its status as flesh or data was brought into crisis and reevaluated, as her real body rebelled. Her back, neck, and joints became stiff and painful, and even more disturbing for her, her digestive system and internal organs were beset by aches and cramps:

My real body asserted its presence as a response to the virtual image which had come to dominate my movement while performing. The invisible elements of my body began to take on a new, demanding significance, as if needing to assert themselves to balance the scale. Digestion does not appear on the screen. Admittedly it does not appear through flesh, but it is even less present in a context where the body has lost its three-dimensionality. The more I ventured into the visual, virtual world the more my non-virtual body called attention to itself like an anchor, like ballast. I seemed to be pulled between the two extremes of an imaginary spectrum: the abjection of flesh and the sanitization of technology.[20]

Kozel's experience of her split body becomes like a mythical rite of passage as she recounts tender sexual experiences which thrill her but also fill her with guilt ("would [I] be desensitizing myself to the detriment of relations with my real loved ones[?]") and are punctuated by incidents of violence and defilement. Someone on the other bed produces a knife, which sends a distinctly corporeal shiver down her spine: its virtuality does nothing to disguise or lessen the psychological and emotional coding of a man wielding a blade over a supine woman on a bed. Another visitor elbows her hard in the stomach, and she doubles over "wondering why since I didn't actually feel it. But I felt something." The only occasion she admits to completely separating her physical and virtual selves was in the worst incident of "cyberviolence" she encountered, when two leather-jacketed men jumped on the remote bed and attacked the image of her head and pelvic area. But even here, she relates her dissociation from her virtual body in relation to a phenomenon that can equally occur in the physical world when people are subjected to rape or brutalization: "I found myself watching my image in the video monitor, paralysed with horror at what they were doing to the woman's body—no longer *my* body . . . a primordial reaction in a sophisticated technological context."

But all other violent incidents and betrayals of trust shake her emotionally and hurt her physically, forcing her to refute popular theories that the virtual body is disembodied or futile. Rather, she theorizes the virtual body as an alternative, yet still material body, inescapably connected to its corporeal embodiment. Crucially, she draws a distinction in her conception of "alternative materiality" between living, moving human bodies and inanimate objects. She describes how sometime after sharing a fifteen-minute improvisation session, a man returned and presented her with a rose. Her inability to grasp it (she could only trace its outline in virtual space or pass her hand through it) rendered it fundamentally immaterial; its lack of kinetic or emotional response (in stark contrast to the bodies of her virtual partners) made it a metaphorical rather than a material presence. She concludes that "the distinction between materiality and immateriality in the technology is movement: as moving beings people take on an alternative materiality, while objects become immaterial in their inertia."[21]

Kozel's article is a definitive phenomenological expression of the part-split, part-organic experience of the relationship between the corporeal and virtual body. In fluid and intensely experienced waves, she vacillates between feelings of separation and oneness—of losing ("the ability to disappear is central to the experience of the body electric") and then being sharply reminded of her physical body ("then without warning the flesh of my body would reassert its presence"). We are struck by her discourse's closeness to Barthes' *Camera Lucida* (discussed in Chapter 6) both stylistically in its soul-searching, subjective scrutiny, and philosophically and epistemologically in its conclusions. Where Barthes is categorical about the palpable reality of the Photograph, so too is Kozel about the materiality of the virtual body, as seen, for example, in her discussions of the virtual sex she experienced. She adamantly maintains that these encounters were "not a substitute for sex" or a "technological replica," but "undeniably real, not a compromise." Kozel also echoes Barthes's suggestion that the Photograph can be "more real" in its potency than the physical moment it captures, when she discusses the "stilted" and "wooden" encounters she had in the gallery coffee bar with the frequently returning

"virtual lover," who gave her a rose. "Although both contexts were real, our virtual relationship seemed to be more meaningful . . . *not* because our bodies were digitalised and
abandoned . . . [but because] our virtual rapport had a greater physicality and intimacy
than our real engagement."[22]

As with the question concerning the reality of theatre, that of the reality of virtual experience
becomes spurious, with no adequate grounds upon which to test it. In some respects, the advance-
ment of virtual technology will help to render the claim that theatre is an artificial reproduction
of reality even more non-sensical. . . . It becomes more and more difficult to sustain a clear distinction between truth and falsity when the phenomenology, or direct experience, of technology is
taken into account; when, according to Marshall McLuhan, the contours of our own extended bodies
are found in our technologies.[23]

   She draws on McLuhan's notion as well as Frederick Brooks's research into "Intelligence Amplification" to stress the electronic body as an amplification and extension of the
flesh body to which it is intimately entwined. Rather than rendering the corporeal body
obsolete, telematics offers it a fourth dimension, where it is able to do things the physical body cannot "such as map itself onto another or disappear . . . [and] challenging existing ideas of what it was possible for two bodies to do. We could pass through each other.
. . . Our bodies seemed to be infinitely mutable, while they never ceased to be *our* bodies."
As the Photograph for Barthes is a return to and spiritual reanimation of the real, telepresence is the same for Kozel in relation to the body. "Telepresence has been called an out-
of-body experience," she says, "yet what intrigues me is the return to the body which is
implied by any voyage beyond it. Once plunged back into flesh, what has changed?" It
is thus not the body's voyage out into virtual embodiments that most radically alters
human perceptions of the body, "but the inevitable return and the lasting effect that the
outward motion leaves on the reunited body. It is here that the political dimension of VR
resides."[24]
   Kozel's experience of direct connection and physical and psychological empathy with
her virtual body provides an important perspective, but it should not be forgotten that it
is a performer's perspective. That is not to suggest in any way that it should be mistrusted,
and Kozel is a performer (and an intellectual) of great integrity and sensitivity. But it is
in both the performer's psyche and job description to open themselves physically and emotionally, and to welcome vulnerability in order to experience virtual pains and pleasures
"as if" (in Stanislavski's phrase) they were real. Is it the same experience for the nonper-
former, the visitor on the other bed? The simple answer is "sometimes," depending on
who they are and how much they too are prepared to open themselves, be vulnerable, and
"perform" with intimacy and sensitivity.
   The fact that each visitor interacts with Kozel, a trained dancer and performer, means
that she can guide and lead the virtual contact improvisation, but the use of a performer

on one of the beds during this four-week installation in 1992 was actually a rare incarnation of *Telematic Dreaming*. Since then, the two beds in two rooms have been meeting places for gallery visitors only. The piece has become a popular installation classic, exhibited in more than twenty different galleries and locations, including for a year at London's Millennium Dome during 2000 and over many years as a permanent exhibit at the National Museum of Photography, Film and Television in Bradford, England. We have watched and participated in the installation numerous times in different galleries and have seen a vast range of different types of exchanges and "performances" (which is, of course, one of its charms).

But the fact that others in the gallery also stand close to the beds and observe tends to inhibit extreme behaviors or intimacies, and people in one room tend to wait for a friend or partner to get on the other bed before they get onto theirs. Children are far less inhibited, and are also most prone to virtual fisticuffs, but their blows are playful, and reactions to virtual impacts are melodramatically performed rather than "felt." But whatever the age or sensibility, and whether improvising with strangers or friends, we observe almost universal pleasure, wonder, or delight on the faces of those who venture onto the beds to make contact in the same space and time with someone else's projected body image. Whether or not visitors identify as intensely with their virtual bodies as Kozel, Paul Sermon's wonderful, exquisitely simple and groundbreaking installation creates a type of magic, a sort of lucid dream. *Telematic Dreaming* is an example of where digital technology and performing bodies are combined to create something unique and unprecedented; something genuinely and distinctly new. Few people would dare to venture onto the same bed as the real Kozel (or other stranger) to commence a physical improvisation, but her virtuality enables it. Over years, tens of thousands of people have, like Kozel, "luxuriated in the physical intimacy and sheer decadence of it all," and they will continue to do so as the work is destined to stand the test of time.

Digital Dissections (or, Project-ing Visible Humans)

The digitization of the body reached an historic moment with the multimillion dollar National Library of Medicine's *Visible Human Project* (1994). Biomedicine, medical imaging, and computer technologies were brought together to create an immensely detailed digital dissection archive of two human bodies: a male prison inmate executed by lethal injection (Joseph Paul Jernigan), and an anonymous fifty-nine-year-old housewife who had died of a heart attack. Dubbed "Adam and Eve" by the project team, their corpses "were MRI scanned, frozen in gelatine to −85 degrees C, quartered, scanned again, sliced through (into thousands of slices between 0.3 and 1 mm thick) and photographed repeatedly, as each layer of their bodies was planed away, turning to dust."[25] The digitized images of the successive, minute layers of the bodies' compositions were arranged into various programmed data sets to enable reconstruction and viewing of all cross-sections

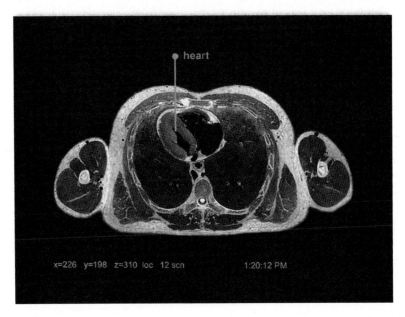

Figure 10.2 One of the *Visible Human Project*'s bodily cross-sections used (with graphical overlays added) by Paul Vanouse for his installation *Items 1-2,000* (1996).

within any plane; detailed examination of organs, body parts, skeletal and circulatory systems; and even animated body "fly-throughs" (figure 10.2).

In her book about the project, Catherine Waldby suggests that while the *Visible Human Project* has provided a clinical benchmark for human anatomical study, the figures also "prefigure some new future for the human body, they imply the possibility of frightening, rather than consoling, transformations."[26] These "exhaustively visualized" bodies are "perfectly co-operative image objects . . . available for all forms of display and penetration, without recalcitrance and resistance."[27] Unlike real bodies, they are endlessly replicable, transmittable, and divisible. She also notes their disconcerting presence as "virtual apparitions," the dead reanimated into life once more through the miracle of biodigital science, or perhaps "virtual vampires" and "cyber-zombies" dwelling in the netherworld somewhere between life and death: the digital undead.

In line with many other writers, Waldby draws attention to the male subject, Jernigan, whose execution as a convicted murderer places his clinical dissection within long historical traditions of medical and anatomical experimentation on criminals and vagrants. His status as prisoner is eternalized through the *Visible Human Project*, where he is once again condemned to "an afterlife of arrest, incarceration and punishment."[28] Meanwhile, David Bell draws parallels with the digitally created Sid 6.7 character in the film *Virtuosity* (1995), a composite serial killer computer simulation created by the police, who escapes from cyberspace to reek havoc. "Could the Texan murderer and the Maryland housewife similarly cross back into RL?" Bell ponders. "As with the futurological speculations about A-Life and posthumanism, we are as yet uncertain about the outcomes of these experiments in bringing life to cyberspace, and cyberspace to life."[29]

Interactive artist Paul Vanouse reflects on Jernigan's cyber-incarceration while discussing his installation *Items 1–2,000* (1996), which was directly inspired by the project— the title refers to the two thousand thin slices into which Jernigan's body was dissected. Vanouse identifies the telling resonance with Michel Foucault's ideas in *Discipline and Punish* (1979): "the disciplined body of the prisoner is subjected to the ultimate surveillance process (minute dissection) and his body, essentially 'drawn and quartered' in the ultimate spectacular punishment."[30] Vanouse's installation uses images from the *Visible Human Project* CD-ROM alongside pictures from medical and dissection manuals, and Vanouse's own sketches and memories as a student in the anatomy morgue. These images and memory fragments are triggered by visitors passing a pen-style stainless steel barcode scanner across barcodes on a sheet of glass suspended above a human figure half-submerged in a block of wax. Users thus become like surgeons, drawing scalpel-like incisions over barcodes positioned above (and corresponding to) the cadaver's different body organs. Vanouse's jarred recollections of his time dissecting corpses are activated on every third scan, which "address the de-humanisation of the corpse" and "attempt to deconstruct the rationalization processes of western bio-medical practices and to discover a point of empathy with the subject"[31] (figure 10.3).

Empathy with Joseph Jernigan, the male subject of the *Virtual Human Project*, is the starting point for Mike Tyler's *Holoman: Digital Cadaver* (1997), a solo multimedia theater performance with actor Frank Sheppard in the role of Jernigan. Sheppard lies naked on a white-sheeted dissection table as images of Jernigan's virtual body are downloaded from the Internet and projected on a screen behind him. Sheppard then sits up and gets off the table: "I'm off-centered. My flesh has been erased, but I'm standing" he says.[32] The performance explores Jernigan's different embodiments (physical and digital) as he symbolically returns from the dead to confront his digital double and undergo a severe bodily identity crisis. He speaks directly to the audience, extending Plato's cave metaphor to complain how his body has become "a shadow's shadow thrown on the wall of some kinda 25-dimensional cave":

I ask you, why was I picked for the hard disk?
To be crunched like a silicon snack chip,
As convenient cadaver for the queasy,
Click on the mouse, you can cut me that easy.

Isabelle Jenniches's digital designs for the performance utilize STEIM's *Imagine* software to merge live video imagery with the *Visible Human Project* data set in real time to

Figure 10.3 Users scan barcodes suspended above model Ryan Douglas' body to trigger images and audio fragments in Paul Vanouse's *Items 1-2000* (1996).

create the effect of Sheppard being "inside his own body."[33] Maaike Bleeker's analysis of *Holoman: Digital Cadaver* stresses its importance in presenting a phenomenological critique of the body, and reflects how Jernigan himself, through his fear of death, was tricked into seeing the *Visible Human Project* as an escape from the finitude of the body, rather than as a new incarceration. "Growing up in a modern society typified by a certain 'disembodied' lifestyle" she says, "it is easy to forget the material basis of our existence . . . [and accept] the Cartesian paradigm in which the body gets marked as something we *have* instead of something we *are*."[34]

Davide Grassi's performance installation *Nuclear Body* (1999) makes extensive use of medical technologies to create a complex, visually mutating virtual body. Like the *Virtual Human Project* and *Items 1–2,000*, it also dissects and lays bare the body's organs and subsystems, but in this case the artist's own. Conceiving it for the Slovenian "The Beauty of Extreme" Festival, Grassi created what he calls his "double," but a "clone without a skin . . . an ideal existence, comparable to the image of Dorian Gray . . . that lives his own cyclical life in fluid aggregation and originates from the digital uterus."[35] Grassi used medical scintigraphy techniques, intravenously injecting radioistopes to provide digital images of his inner organs, musculoskeletal system, blood cells, and body tissues via a gamma camera. Sixteen hundred of the scintigraphic images were combined to create a animation of Grassi's body double, which constantly morphs and mutates between its inner and outer body form, with its veins, organs, and skeleton appearing and disappearing, its vivid colors radiating and changing hues.[36]

Gallery visitors view the *Nuclear Body* through six viewfinders placed around a large pipe. Inside the pipe, the body animation is projected onto smoke, which enhances the body's sense of constant flux and dissolving ethereality. Internal body sounds such as blood flowing and the brain sending bioelectrical signals to organs (obtained using ultrasound and other advanced medical techniques such as EEG and EMG[37]) provide a rich accompanying soundscape. Like Waldby, Bell, and Vanouse, Grassi has also stressed that to digitize the body's inner structures and organs entails a direct technological invasion of the body. For each of these artists and theorists, the digital dissection of the body may ultimately produce a virtual form, but the means to that end are distinctly material, visceral, and corporeal. Grassi's *Nuclear Body*, like those in the *Visible Human Project* is not only dissected, but also invaded—both by technological instruments and by the curious spectator's gaze. For Grassi, the direct medical invasion undertaken to create his digital body renders his actual body "contaminated at molecular level and therefore altered," while his rent-open virtual *doppelgänger* conveys a complex interplay between the imaginary and the sensory, and opens significant and troubling questions about survival in an immaterial world.[38]

British multimedia theater company doo cot's *Frankenstein—The Final Blasphemy* (1999) uses digital technology to enact a much simpler, but nonetheless theatrically powerful dissection effect. Performer Neagh Watson stands naked on stage in the role of the preanimated monster corpse, lit only by the white light of a projector. A computer graphic projection of a vivid red line then slowly appears to slice through her body, beginning at the throat and scoring down to her stomach. Video footage of actual human autopsies is also projected onto the severe and clinical white set and floorcloth. Once "brought to life," the monster is an eight-foot puppet, expertly manipulated by Watson, who also acts in sequences with the puppet, whose "view" of her is projected live via a hidden camera in one of its eyes.

Medical Bodies

The frequency and extent to which the virtual body is correlated to the flesh and blood of surgical, medical, genetic, and molecular science is striking. Chicago dance company The Anatomical Theatre collaborated with a molecular biologist (Doug Wood) and a physicist (Pangratios Papacosta) for its exploration of cellular biology, genetics, quantum physics, and cosmology, *Subject: Matter* (2000). It begins with a sequence like a court dance where each dancing couple represents a base pair in the DNA molecule, after which

Matter and antimatter pairs are personified in duets enacting the "creation/destruction dance" of particle materialization and annihilation. The relationship between the black holes and the stars is dramatized as a whirling waltz, a ballroom of cosmic scale, and dancers emulate the locomotive strategies of microscopic organisms, expanding the cellular activity within a single drop of water to fill an entire stage.[39]

For *ACTG* (2000),[40] a collaborative telematically linked dance performance at the Cellbytes 2000 Festival (Phoenix, Arizona), choreographic materials were devised to correspond to the letters in the title. These related to the theme of the choreography, the human genome, each representing the basic four chemicals that comprise DNA: adenine (A), cytosine (C), thymine (T), and guanine (G). One of the letters was computer selected and extracted every eight seconds (corresponding to the video-stream time lag between the two performance spaces) to prompt choreographic changes in the performance. Critical Art Ensemble's performance *Flesh Machine* (1997) combines a performed presentation about genetics and reproductive technologies, a specially created biotech CD-ROM about in vitro fertilization (IVF), and interactive elements where spectators undergo a donor screening test. The test extracts blood that is analyzed to provide a DNA sample; visitors who "pass" the screening test are presented with a certificate of "genetic merit," and their cell samples are held for cryo-preservation. Like much of Critical Art Ensemble's work, *Flesh Machine* explores and exposes the myths, ethics, and political implications behind technological science, and the normalization of its marketing and propaganda.

Contract with the Skin

The human cell structure—"nucleus, cytoplasm, membrane, envelope"—provides what Paulo Henrique calls the "creative tissue"[41] for choreographic movement, and the allegorical and symbolic starting point for his enthralling dance-theater performance *Contract with the Skin* (2000). Skin itself—nakedly exposed, massaged, and computer-scanned to provide textured surfaces and screen projections—is put through a metaphorical and theatrical microscope, as computer images are triggered by movement onto a rear screen and two stage video monitors. It opens with a beautiful, overweight woman dressed only in white briefs, who walks slowly and gracefully around the tightly lit perimeter of a stage space around ten meters by five meters. Her broad shoulders and hips, large breasts, and tummy—her voluptuous expanse of *skin*—captures the central theme from the outset and also lets one know this is unlikely to be a conventional dance show.

She continues her circumnavigation of the space, while other, more traditionally shaped dancers enter to work in the central area. Their choreography moves from expressive, undulating phrases to slow, precise gestures, and from everyday movements to sudden, unexpected fragments of classical dance. A female dancer struggles to get out of her costume, stretching her arms inside it, so that she appears to be trying to escape from a membrane or another skin. She eventually succeeds, emerging naked and relieved, while a male dancer performs a duet with a plaster cast of a leg, which he manipulates with two wires. The large woman rolls on the floor, her soft, rounded movement counterpointed by thin, scribbled black lines that spill and splash onto the rear screen, building an abstract picture like a Jackson Pollock drip painting. The music and sound score, mixed in real time by sonic artist Rui Leitão, is dense and sensory featuring deep, electronically treated notes and chords, a wailing classical voice, slow violin strings, and synthesized white noise.

At one point, the large woman stands in near darkness with only her torso lit, while the rear screen plays an image of a skeletal, skinless hand, video-mixed with fragments of what appear to be broken Russian letters. From behind, two hands come around her and begin to massage and gently pound her stomach, and unearthly, subterranean musical sounds give way to the sound of Edith Piaf's "No Regrets" (sung in English). The woman begins a simple, repetitive movement routine. Stretching out an arm and crooking it, bringing it in to caress her cheek, and swinging her hips from side to side, she finally "dances." A male dancer undresses and once naked, touches her skin and hair, entangling his long hair with hers. As they move together, against rising, granular musical chords, a soft-spoken voiceover says:

My skin contract is inevitable, being in the skin. Being skin is inevitable. . . . A contract with the skin is inevitable. Did you read between the lines? Is your contract inevitable? . . . Did you choose your contract? A contract with the skin is inevitable. . . . My skin is preconceived. . . . It is inevitable being the color of skin that I am. Would you change your color, contract? Is it inevitable being in your skin? . . . Are you satisfied with it? Temporarily, socially, culturally? A contract with the skin. I am a contract with the skin. I am, politically, socially, culturally, individually, inevitably, a contract with the skin.

As the voice goes on, a naked female dancer enters with a phallic, clear glass vase held to her crotch and, in a symbol of male orgasm, slowly pulls a long, dripping wet, translucent piece of plastic from it, as water spills on the floor. She opens the wet plastic and puts on what is now revealed to be a transparent raincoat, another "skin" that clings to her, as she bends down and allows a long line of her spittle to flow into the vase. The spittle image, as well as *Contract with the Skin*'s life-affirming celebration of human flesh, echoes the work of choreographer Jérôme Bel, who similarly exalts in this liberating sense of openness, respect, and love for the naked human body—its shapes, its form, its sexuality, its *skin*.

Dumb Type

The virtual body's relationship to medical science provides the central theme for Dumb Type's *OR* (1997–99), where a line of four full-body-length glass laboratory slides imprison and display digital bodies. The four slides have a thin LCD film sandwiched between two long sheets of glass, and play video images of seven male and female bodies, which switch between semiopaque and transparent, and transform and metamorphose in response to sensors that track visitor movements.[42] Placed on a white carpet, these giant, sterile, quasi-medical laboratory exhibits invoke images of moving corpses on a mortuary slab, but also trace the mutating materiality and immateriality of the virtual bodies as though through a cellular microscope. Dumb Type has exhibited *OR* as an installation, and also in more performative incarnations, on a white circular stage with a semicylindrical wall, presenting a sophisticated multimedia meditation on the border territory between life and death. The theme is explored from multiple perspectives: philosophical, cultural, corporeal, medical, emotional, and spiritual. The lighting on the all-white set is so bright it is almost blinding, emphasizing Dumb Type's aim to take the audience into what it calls

the state of "white out" like in a blizzard, where you are deprived of ability to see, where you can't recognize anything, where you don't know where you stand anymore, where you may not know whether you are alive OR dead. But what distinguishes one from the other? Where is the border? What is death? What is it?[43]

Dumb Type is one of Japan's most distinctive and aesthetically inventive artist collectives, producing work in varied forms and media, from large-scale live performances to media installations and printed publications. Based in Kyoto, its artists possess and combine multiple skills from computer programming to visual art, architecture, acting, writing, music, and Butoh performance. The relationship between the body and technology is a central theme, and *OR* continued the company's exploration of mortality begun in *S/N* (1992–96), which combines energetic new dance, multiple projections and a television talk show format. The performance begins with a man scrabbling around the space on all fours, talking unintelligibly, while a narrator (played by director Teiji Furuhashi) explains that the man is deaf and translates his animal sounds as meaning that he wishes to dance the tango, at which point he attaches the label "Homosexual" to the animal-man's clothes. Furuhashi wears one too, and he and two other performers mix ideas of fiction and reality to come out as gay men and, in Furuhashi's case, to reveal he has been diagnosed as HIV-positive.

A high-tech, two-tiered staging features four separate screen projections across the lower level wall, running images and pieces of text. These include, during one sequence, a jumble of animated words: "MONEY, LIFE, LOVE, SEX, DEATH," and in another, each screen shows separate images of couples embracing with a subtitle across their width reading: "Can you see which is the person with AIDS?" (figure 10.4). Above the screens is a narrow, raised space where the performers move laterally left and right. The projections include images and pieces of text which complement and connect with the mechanical, insect, and animal movements of the performers above. It ends in a climax of strobe lighting, projected images of huge close-up faces, live robotic dance movement, agitated cries, and shrill screams of unfulfilled desires: "I dream . . . my gender will disappear . . . I dream . . . my nationality will disappear."[44] The performers undress and then literally

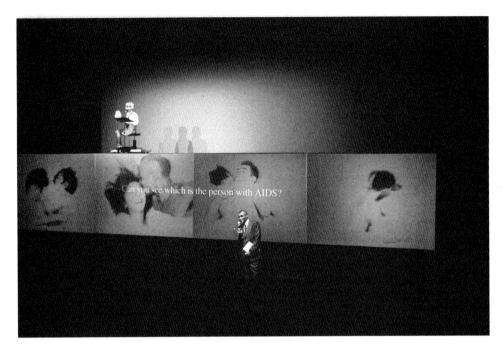

Figure 10.4 Dumb Type's split-level multimedia theater production *S/N* (1992–96). Photo: Yoko Takatani.

disappear, dropping out of view behind the wall, in an image that suggests both rebirth—as the naked figures slip out of sight as if down an invisible birth canal—and a sudden descent into the grave.

Furuhashi's consciousness of his body and its fragility in the face of AIDS (he died of the disease in 1995) is captured and transfigured in one of Dumb Type's most beautiful and uplifting works. *Lovers: Dying Pictures, Loving Pictures* (1994) is a panoramic 360-degree installation of enormous lyricism and visual presence. When we saw it in 1995, unaware at the time of its underlying AIDS theme, we were struck, and moved, by the way in which the formal, conceptual modes of bodily movement stirred unexpected and deep feelings of human longing, love and loss. Computer-controlled laserdiscs are linked to seven projectors on a tall metal shelf rack in the center of the space, sending bright images of five life-size, naked men and women around the otherwise dark walls of a square room. The projected bodies have a luminous and ethereal, yet classical, quality as they move around all sides of the visitor. A man runs around the entire circle of the wall space; two figures slowly embrace; others stand still in profile, or in strong, statuesque, open-armed poses. A motion-sensing system responds to the visitors' movement, prompting different actions, including surrounding the visitor with a circular ring on the floor composed of textual phrases such as "DO NOT CROSS THE LINE OR JUMP OVER" and "A

Figure 10.5 Teiji Furuhashi's beautiful "tableau mourant" laserdisk installation *Lovers* (1994). Photo courtesy of ARTLAB, Canon Inc.

JAILBREAK OVER ORDINARY FIELDS IS HARDER THAN OVER WALLS AND WIRE FENCES." Other pieces of text are projected like small, subtle subtitles onto the walls: "Love is everywhere," "Don't fuck with me, fellah, use your imagination." Moving close to the walls sometimes prompts an image of Furuhashi to appear from the blackness and move toward you, stretching out his arms as if for an embrace. But then he clasps them around himself and falls backwards, disappearing once again, like a benevolent spirit or ghost, passing away once again into the darkness (figure 10.5).

In one sense, the virtuality of the bodies and their lack of materiality is emphasized in their visual crossings past and "through" each other, and critics have variously described *Lovers* as a *"tableau mourant,"*[45] "a dance of missed connections,"[46] and a "dream-like pantomime."[47] But in another sense, and in what we would suggest provides its real aesthetic power, their virtuality renders the bodies poetic and metaphorical, symbols of the always already ghostly and ephemeral status of the physical body: a brief and lonely container for the self or spirit, ever searching for communion with others, and for existential connection.

Fragmenting Virtual Bodies and Conjoining Them with Real Ones

Richard Lord's *Web Dances: Lifeblood* (1997) is a tongue-in-cheek response to the question "what is a virtual dance?" He concludes it is a dance that does not exist in reality, does not involve a real dancer or a real space, but can nonetheless be experienced by an audience member. His solution is a Web-based text description of the experience of watching a dance, what he calls: "a low-bandwidth virtual dance . . . [that] was created in 1997 and has remained unaltered ever since."[48] But it is the ability to alter, fragment, and transform the digital image-body continually that holds most appeal to others. Igloo's *Windows 98* CD-ROM (1998) provides ingenious opportunities for the user to instantly divide, fragment, multiply, and choreograph digital dancers and their body parts by simply dragging-and-dropping them with the mouse; and the passing of the cursor over the image-body of a naked man in Bjørn Wangen's Web-based *id* (2002) splits and fragments it to great and varied effect.[49]

Victoria Vesna created an early example of a website enabling visitors to construct digital bodies from different components (*Bodies Inc.*, 1995) and her *Notime* (2001) allowed people "to represent themselves as 'meme fabrics'—geometries of data-bodies containing information about their creators."[50] Nancy Burson was one of the first computer artists to create virtual bodies through a sophisticated compositing and blending of different photos. Her *Beauty Composites: First Composite* (1982) mixed photographic images of the faces of Marilyn Monroe, Bette Davis, Sophia Loren, Audrey Hepburn, and Grace Kelly, while her *Beauty Composites: Second Composite* (1982) merged Meryl Streep, Jane Fonda, Brooke Shields, Diane Keaton, and Jacqueline Bisset. The results are two faces of compelling, iconic presence (rather than strictly "beauty"), two highly auratic virtual film stars, each clearly belonging to their separate movie eras.

The paradigm has famously been extended into the real body of French performance artist Orlan during her satellite-transmitted series of performances *The Reincarnation of St Orlan* (from 1990), where her face is transformed under local anesthetic by plastic surgeons while she reads out pieces of text and talks to her remote audience via video satellite (figure 10.6). Each surgical performance introduces a new element to her composite-image face:

Her forehead is from Leonardo's *Mona Lisa*; her chin is from Botticelli's *Venus*; her nose from an attributed sculpture of Diana by l'École de Fountainebleau; her mouth from Gustave Moreau's *Europa*; and her eyes from François Pascal Simon Gérard's *Psyche*. . . . Everything about Orlan is artifice, from her name to her body, which remains a work in progress. . . . No longer does art imitate life. In Orlan, life imitates art.[51]

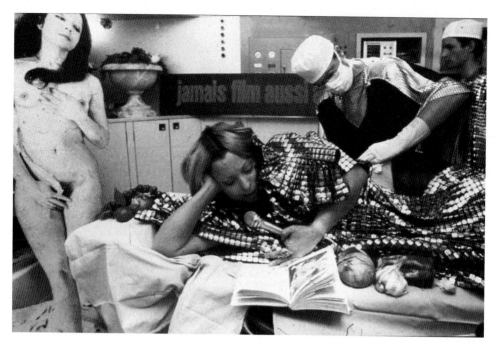

Figure 10.6 One of Orlan's series of satellite-transmitted operating theater performances entitled *The Reincarnation of St Orlan* (from 1990).

Orlan's corporeal body thus becomes a type of "virtual" body itself, characterized by the same malleability and potential for metamorphosis as the digital image body. As Auslander puts it, *The Reincarnation of St Orlan*: "valorizes the dematerialized, surgically enhanced, posthumanist body, a body that experiences no pain even as it undergoes transformation because it has no absolute material presence; its materiality is contingent, malleable, accessible to intervention."[52] In more recent work, Orlan has reverted to the computer to reconfigure her malleable visage less permanently, conceiving frighteningly garish and grotesque self-portraits based on Central American Mayan iconography and themes from mythology (figure 10.7).

As we have stressed, the digital body, as created and represented in software programs, is an image only: it has no form or matter other than as digital pulses projecting light and pixels onto a screen; a hollow visual shell without internal substance. Kimberly Bartosik's essay "Technogenderbody" discusses the phenomena in relation to the dance software program *Life Forms*, where the graphical figure is not a body in any true sense at all, but "only a shape of space." The see-through avatars could hardly be more different from real dancers:

Figure 10.7 As the digital revolution blossomed in the late 1990s the reconfiguration of Orlan's visage was transferred from the cosmetic surgeon to the software program for her *Self-hybridation* images (1998–2000).

They have no blood or organs, no heat, no fragility. No bones or flesh, they are weightless, without mass. Sexless, they do not have breasts which swell premenstrually or genitalia to be stuffed into a dance belt. No semen, eggs or womb whose vulnerability or cravings could change the course of multiple lives. They are infallible, uninjurable, consistent, without difficult personality or habits, non-confrontational, never moody or obstinate. Perfectly disciplined, they react at the touch of a finger, showing up when the screen is turned on, disappearing when the correct key is pushed. They have no intimate relationship to their own form, able to dance even in a divided, fragmented state: manipulate the torso, head, right ankle, left finger separately, and the other segments remain unaffected. Without volition, they never need to question why they are asked to do something.[53]

Theoretical and practical viewpoints on the performing body and its relationship to technology polarized in the mid-1990s, and Guillermo Gómez-Peña highlights a turning point "when the artworld went high-tech overnight," whereupon performance artists quickly adopted one of three positions:

There were those . . . who advocated the total disappearance of the body and its replacement with digital or robotic mechanisms; others believed that the body, although archaic and "obsolete" could still remain central to the art event if physically and perceptually enhanced with technical prostheses.

The artists of the "Apocalypse Culture" responded . . . by adopting a Luddite stance, attempting to reclaim the *body primitive* as a site for pleasure, penance and pain, and to "return" to a fantastical and imaginary neotribal paganism, very much in the tradition of US anarchist "drop out" culture.[54]

Birringer has reflected on the prevalence of the latter grouping, but sees the phenomena as being much more intertwined with the politics of technology than Gómez-Peña's interpretation of simple Luddite rejection. The focus of performance art since the 1980s toward what Birringer characterizes as the "abuse, violation, derealization, or erotic fetishization of bodies"[55] presents a direct psychic reaction to the crises of the body and identity brought about by the technologization of contemporary culture:

If I note the absence of a spiritual sensibility in Western physical theater, I am of course assuming that there is a connection between self-loathing, dehumanization, and a disintegrated spirit of body. . . . Such abjection in the performances of the disjointed, tortured body indicates the phantasms of the collapsing boundaries of identity and those between the symbolic and meaninglessness. . . . The abjection I have noticed, as well as the disavowal of an organic, whole body, reflect a reaction to the disturbed body rhythms in our Western technocultures and to the dislocating experience of migration.[56]

Contrasting views on the digital body emphasize, on one hand, its freedom as a weightless, unfettered form, and on the other its bondage as an infinitely malleable and controllable entity. Optimistic conceptions therefore stress its imaginary, metamorphic, and fantastical possibilities, while dystopian views hold that the digital body operates as what Harald Begusch calls "a weightless shell, as a translation of physical materiality into a controllable code, as the realization of the Cartesian fantasy of the calculable, or as an expression of the occidental image of a smooth, mouldable and controllable body."[57] But in the feeding frenzy of recent discourses on the digital body, it should not be forgotten that a remarkably similar debate was staged previously in relation to photography, where the body is equally "captured" in what Allan Sekula calls "a double system . . . of representation capable of functioning both *honorifically* and *repressively*."[58] In digital performance, the optimistic, "honorific" view is prevalent, although not entirely dominant, with some installations, net.art and CD-ROM works exploring negative aspects of the digital body, particularly through its depiction as a socially controlled or politically inscribed object. But in live theatrical and dance forms, the virtual body's transformational beauty and shimmering ethereality is generally cherished and celebrated.

Random Dance Company

Wayne McGregor's acclaimed British digital dance group Random Dance Company typifies this celebration, exploring the complementarity between live and virtual bodies in a remarkable multimedia trilogy centered on the elements: water (*The Millenarium*, 1998), fire (*Sulphur 16*, 1999) and earth/air (*Aeon*, 2000).⁵⁹ *The Millenarium* (1998) creates a "futuristic environment of digital bodies, virtual space and extraordinary computer generated graphics . . . [in] an aquarium-like world where the live and the present meets the live and non present in a volcanic dialogue,"⁶⁰ while *Sulphur 16* provides even more extraordinary and breathtaking moments fusing live and projected dancers. It opens with a shimmering, ghostlike giant image of a solo female dancer projected onto a fine gauze scrim at the front of the stage, and lights gradually brighten to reveal her comparatively tiny live counterpart behind it, center stage. Later, two virtual dancers perform a fluid and sensuous duet, appearing to move *inside* and through one another as they cross one another, become entangled, and seemingly "step into" one another's bodies. In one exuberant routine the entire company of dancers are joined by their virtual doubles, and the stage is filled with real and digital dancers (whose images bleed and double again from front to back projection scrim) in a *tour de force* sequence. Although created as late as 1999, it was one of the earliest examples we saw of a truly sublime and mesmeric theatrical conjunction of virtual and live performers on a dance stage.

The company emphasizes how technology "stimulated every aspect of the devising stage, leaving its futuristic impression upon choreography and design," and McGregor's lightning-speed choreography and wonderfully strange, often alien-like physical vocabulary mixes the personal, the organic, and the machinic. He describes how he "places the concepts of the body, time and space into fresh dimensions"⁶¹ and "pushes dancers to amazing new limits . . . [of] articulation, questioning and exploring ideas about the technology of the human body."⁶² He extends this idea further in *Nemesis* (2002) where the live dancers wear large, pump-action, prosthetic arm extensions (figure 10.8). Here, as Jackie Smart observes, McGregor's movement language

plays a kind of double game around notions of the organic and the technological, travelling between extremes of incapacity and superhuman flexibility and strength. In the first half, the dancers' bodies seem to stretch and twist themselves almost to a punishing degree but their exertions are interrupted by momentary breakdowns, glitches in the muscular technology. . . . They seem extrahuman, practising levels of control and discipline which seem excessive . . . flourishing their prosthetic limbs like weapons, the dancers resemble futuristic superheroes. . . . As the dancers "unlearn" how to move, the audience "unlearns" how to understand dance.⁶³

Distributing Virtual Embodiments

The Brazilian and French collaborators of the Corpos Informáticos Research Group place great emphasis on the theoretical implications of the digitally distributed body, creating ambitious networked tele-performances with invited guests from all over the world. Their two-day performance *Folds* (1999) took place in a gallery space in Porto Allegre, Brazil, where two performers interacted with guests transmitted via the Internet from Philadephia, Paris, New York, Brasilia, and Campinas (figure 10.9). Their *Hungry@Corpos* (2000)

Figure 10.8 "Flourishing their prosthetic limbs like weapons, the dancers resemble futuristic superheroes": Random Dance's dance-theater production *Nemesis* (2002). Photo: Ravi Deepres.

Figure 10.9 Performer Cyntia Carla applies makeup while interacting with multiple Internet guests from around the world in the Corpos Informáticos Research Group's *Folds* (1999).

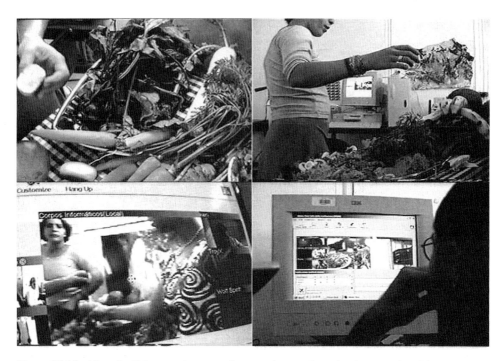

Figure 10.10 Virtually dining together at a distance—images from the Corpos Informáticos Research Group's day long multisite banquet performance *Hungry@Corpos* (2000).

centered on a shared "virtual banquet," with the company eating for an entire day in a space at the University of Brasilia while interacting with other invited, video-conference guests who similarly ate and drank throughout the day (figure 10.10). Their performances *Infoporto* (1999), *Entrasite* (1999), and *Media@terra* (2000) explore the sense in which the telematic body itself becomes a machine, yet nonetheless resists its imprisonment through physical performance. The group draws on the theoretical perspectives of Wittgenstein and Deleuze to examine and demonstrate how the presence of a virtual body in front of us elicits our desire, pleasure, and will for an intimate encounter. They suggest that this now operates to such a high degree that "the quotidian is jealous of the telepresence, jealous of the virtual. . . . The researches on teleperformance demand a higher engagement. . . . The numeric body (telepresence) imposes itself broken, the quotidian seems to draw the other off from virtual space."[64] This potential jealousy and conflict between the real and virtual body is a potent idea that has also been dramatized in a number of live dance performances, including Troika Ranch's *In Place* (1994):

Figure 10.11 The Olympias' interactive installation *Geometries* (2000) explores what director Petra Kuppers describes as her disabled performers' "different experiences of embodiment."

Because the live performer was dancing with a video image of herself, we saw the performance as a kind of contest, one that would in the end emphasize the limitations of both entities: the human performer, bound by time and gravity and her virtual doppelgänger, limited by its inability to enter the corporeal world.[65]

Petra Kuppers, director of the The Olimpias company, explores new ways of working with "different experiences of embodiment" in works with disabled performers such as *Geometries* (2000) (figure 10.11), which highlights the aesthetic beauty and graceful kinetic patterns of wheelchairs, which are gently and erotically caressed; and in *Traces* (1998), a multiple-screen installation using video material shot during community movement and dance workshops with people under mental health care in Wales. Focussing on and reinterpreting ideas of embodied chaos and of loss of control, "huge images of the participants' concentrated faces and bodies . . . provide a counterpoint to many traditional representations of people in mental health settings. *Traces* documents the beauty, dignity and privacy of all its group members."[66]

Satorimedia's *TouchDown* (2000) is a "duet for hands" rehearsed and performed both in real space and over the Internet, the opening two sections consisting of videos of the individual performers' hands. In the first, their hands "perform" in isolation while we hear their voices talking about the joys of caring for and holding their children; in the second the two hands meet, touching in real space, affectionately teasing one another like small children playing. The final section explores ideas around transcendence and transformation, includes text fragments from Lao Tzu, and is performed over the Internet, where the hands meet again, this time in cyberspace. Like *Telematic Dreaming*, it examines the delicate relationship that exists in the real-time meeting of two "live" telematic bodies, a peculiar dynamic that has also prompted Roy Ascott to pose the question, "Is There Love in the Telematic Embrace?" (1990): the title for his famous essay. Although the touch is not physical in *TouchDown*, the hands move with extraordinary sensitivity and awareness of each other, perhaps even more than they would in physical space. The company believe that increasing technological communication means that "we have more cerebral contact than ever before, but the comfort and sensual pleasures of physical touch may be fading sensations in this advancing world."[67] *TouchDown* offers both "a celebration and a warning" in relation to networked technologies and virtual bodies, contrasting "the physicality of children with the distances which form between adults, both in virtual and real-space relationships."[68]

The laying of hands, in this case the gallery visitor's, onto two digital bodies projected from above onto a table with a white velvet surface, activates their movements in Thecla Schiphorst's *Bodymaps: artifacts of touch* (1996). As the user caresses the life-size image of the bodies, sensors collect 3D XYZ coordinates of the hand movements and prompt delicate changes in the video image so that the two bodies appear to wake from their slumbers and move, turn over, and embrace one another. The bodies appear at times to be immersed in water, and at others in the midst of flame, while an atmospheric audio score of breath and water sounds echoes and enhances the slow and quite beautiful metamorphoses. Schiphorst, who worked closely with Merce Cunningham as one of the designers of *Life Forms* software, has a background in both choreography and computer science and is keenly aware of their relationships and correspondences, and their different understandings and approaches to the representation of the body:

Computing Science training includes notions of elegance and appreciation of mathematical or algorithmic construction and form, and tends to literally represent the body borrowing from medical mappings or often in Computer Graphics from mass cultural clichés of representation. My interest lies in the recognition that I am dealing with two highly technical systems each with their own technical language and frames of reference, that of the human body on the one hand, and that of computer technology on the other hand.[69]

Conclusion: Theorizing the Virtual Body

Among numerous writers offering theories and critical perspectives on the digital body is Don Ihde, whose book *Bodies in Technology* (2002) begins by defining three types of body: *body one*, our physical and phenomenological being-in-the-world body; *body two*, the culturally and socially constructed body; and a third body existing in "a third dimension . . . traversing both body one and body two . . . the dimension of the technological."[70] This body may utilize technologies from relatively low-tech extensions (Idhe uses Heidegger's analysis of tools such as hammers and nails as an example) to advanced networks and prostheses. He argues, "The ultimate goal of virtual embodiment is to become the perfect simulacrum of full, multisensory bodily action."[71] William Mitchell's "informal trilogy" *Being Digital* (1995), *E-Topia* (1999), and *Me++: The Cyborg Self and the Networked City* (2003) traces the gradual erosion of previous distinctions between digital and physical bodies, virtual realities and "real life." He argues that the merging of our selves into computer networks signals that "the trial separation of bits and atoms" is over: "I am part of the networks, and the networks are part of me."[72]

In the *Women and Performance* journal's special issue on "Sexuality and Cyberspace" in 1996, a number of writers point to a false dichotomy in ascribing oppositions between ideas such as corporeal and virtual bodies, and real life versus online life. For Teresa M. Senft, the female digital body constitutes a new type of body, which she likens to a storytelling ghost. Yet at the same time she reminds us that regardless of a body's corporeality or virtuality: "feminists are in a bind, finding that it is nearly impossible to write of the truth of a feminine body when we are all in disagreement about what a 'body' truly is."[73]

In "Turing, My Love," Matthew Elrich uses a sexual encounter with a partner in cyberspace whom he suspects is actually an Artificial Intelligence program to question wittily and mischievously whether his partner's corporeal reality or AI virtuality has any relevance at all. He begins by asking his remote lover "Was it as good for you as it was for me?" but then rapidly retreats: "I desperately hope you never reveal the truth to me. Not that I care if you're an AI. I can't help wanting to know. But I prefer to live in the body of the text—not its meaning."[74] Sharon Lechner's essay "My Womb, the Mosh Pit" is a much more poignant and serious take on the same issue, as she discusses correspondences between reality and virtuality in relation to the image of an ultrasound scan of a fetus she once aborted. Her conclusion is extremely direct: "Images ARE real, insofar as they pleasure, they pain, they cause action. Women, especially, ignore this crucial lesson in aesthetics at their peril."[75]

In one sense, the virtual body's status as an alternate body is nothing new in the field of theater and performance, as actors and dancers have always plied their art and craft to represent and experience different embodiments (characters) physically. The depiction of unworldly or unnatural bodies also has a lineage stretching from masked representations of gods, spirits, and demons in tribal dances and rituals, to the Furies of Aeschylus and the magical creatures of Shakespeare's *The Tempest*. Classical ballet training has long exerted unnatural shapes and lines on the dancer's body in the aesthetic pursuit of what Theodores called "the thrill of the unnatural," and much contemporary performance and body art focuses on the abnormal, dysfunctional, diseased, or abject body. Birringer sees the virtual body in digital performance as an extension of these themes and practices: on one hand through an intensification in depictions of the dysfunctional "ideological crisis of the fragmented subject" and "the deconstructed and disappearing actor," and on the other, the creation of new "impossible anatomies," as in Cunningham's work.[76] Both relate to the "ethos of borderness," where the performing body is positioned within a threshold, or liminal terrain or state.[77] The paradigm is enacted in its most vivid and dramatic form when the live performer meets her digital double face-to-face—our next chapter in the fascinating story of the virtual body.

The Digital Double

Go back to the body, which is where all the splits in Western Culture occur.
—CAROLEE SCHNEEMANN, *ASK THE GODDESS*, 1991[1]

Theater and Its Digital Double

Marvin Carlson suggests that "a consciousness of doubleness" is intrinsic to performance,[2] a theory that Marshall Soules uses to argue its equal applicability to the human-computer interface.[3] The notion of the double has been a particularly potent concept in performance since the publication of Antonin Artaud's *The Theatre and Its Double* in 1938, and the metaphor has become concrete and actuated in the theory and practice of digital performance. Artaud's notion of theater's double is a primitivist and spiritualized vision of a sacred, transformational, and transcendental theater. Early on in *The Theatre and Its Double*, Artaud discusses the totems of Mexican culture: magically invested rocks, animals, and objects that can excite dormant powers in those who worship or meditate upon them. In a typically abrupt, jagged thought-change (now ubiquitous in computational hypermedia), in the space of a single sentence this totem suddenly becomes an effigy, a double and a shadow: "All true effigies have a double, a shadowed self."[4] For Artaud, the double of theater is its true and magical self, stirring other dark and potent shadows which rail against a fossilized, shadowless culture "as empty as it is saccharined."[5] Discourses on cyberculture now reinscribe this Artaudian dialectic, where a romantic utopianism hailing spiritualized virtual realities is pitted against a dystopian skepticism, which attacks the soulless, alienated, and schizoid nature of digital irreality.

Artaud's incendiary theatrical writings conjure images, previously considered impossible to stage, which have been realized using the capabilities of the computer. His belief that actors should be "like those tortured at the stake, signalling through the flames"[6] has been echoed in works such as 4D Art's dance-theater production *Anima* (2002), La Fura

Dels Baus's *F@usto: Version 3.0* (1998), and Marcel.lí Anthúnez Roca's one-man show, *Afasia* (1998), which features a vivid computer-manipulated projection of his rotating, flame-licked body. Images of performers' digital doubles are telematically transmitted to different locations where they dance or interact with distant partners in real time; and in "single-space" theater events, performers' projected body doubles now commonly play dialogues and perform duets with their live counterparts. The digital double projects itself online and on stage to take numerous forms, from the textual characterizations of role-playing MUDs and MOOs to the graphical avatars of virtual worlds; from the theatrical depictions of cyborgic alter-egos to the parthenogenic creations of artists' substitute-selves in the form of anthropomorphic robots.

In his discussion of theater as alchemy, Artaud became the first person to coin the term "virtual reality." Linking the chimeric nature of both theater and alchemical symbols, he describes how "theatre's virtual reality develops . . . [on the] dreamlike level on which alchemist signs are evolved."[7] For Artaud, since alchemical signs are "like a mental Double of an act effective on the level of real matter alone, theatre ought to be considered as the Double, not of this immediate, everyday reality . . . but another, deadlier archetypal reality."[8] A doubled reality or "virtuality" becomes the fulcrum for Artaud's theater of cruelty, which, like the Balinese dance he witnessed in 1931, enacted "a virtuality whose double produced this intense scenic poetry, this many-hued spatial language."[9]

The idea of the body and its double pervades digital performance, and relates to the shadow figure of the *doppelgänger*, Freudian notions of the uncanny and the subconscious Id, and Jacques Lacan's concept of the mirror stage and the *corps morcele* (the body in pieces) (figure 11.1). Lacan's theory of the mirror stage emphasizes the misconceived, "fictitious invention" of identity and the ego. This is conceived through the narcissistic lure of the apparently whole yet ultimately phantasmic projection of the subject's body double in the frame of the mirror "by which the subject anticipates in a mirage the maturation of his power."[10] Identity is thus falsely constructed as a unity, while "by identifying with the imaginary mirage of the whole body, the 'real' of the fragmented body is repressed."[11] Sigmund Freud presents images of the *corps morcele* ("dismembered limbs, a severed head, a hand cut off at the wrist")[12] as defining symbols of *The Uncanny* (*Das Unheimlich*), as well as robotic doubles such as the seductive mechanical doll, Olympia in *The Tales of Hoffmann*.[13] Freud's notion of the uncanny (*unheimlich*) concerns the emergence of a dark self or "other" in the midst of the familiar and normal: "the unheimlich is what was once heimisch, home-like, familiar; the prefix 'un' [un-] is the token of repression."[14] When repressive barriers to the subconscious are pricked or come down, the uncanny may emerge to create a doubled reality where the familiar becomes frighteningly unfamiliar, "laying bare . . . hidden forces."[15]

Jacques Derrida returns to Freud's *The Uncanny* time and time again, writing in his essay *The Double Session* of Freud's fantastic and compelling "paradoxes of the double and of repetition, the blurring of boundary lines between 'imagination' and 'reality', between

Figure 11.1 Ruth Gibson dances with her digital double in Igloo's *Viking Shoppers* (2000).

the 'symbol' and the 'thing it symbolises'.[16]" For Martin Heidegger, the uncanny is a fundamental condition of existential being, an anxious and fearful sense of separation from reality, both "tranquillised and familiar" where the feeling of "not-being-at-home [das Nicht-zuhause-sein]" is a "primordial phenomenon."[17] The German notion of *Heimweh* (homesickness), whereby one never feels at home wherever one is, has been central to German philosophical thought since Hegel, and elsewhere Heidegger would note that "We who philosophize are away from home everywhere."[18] Nicholas Royle's rich and exhaustive study *The Uncanny* (2003) traces the notion through the writings of Kant, Marx, Nietzsche, Freud, Heidegger, Wittgenstein, and Derrida, and goes on to explore its relationship to Brecht's alienation-effect, and to genetic engineering and cloning. He also notes the value of the concept of the uncanny in understanding computer technologies:

As a theory of the ghostly (the ghostliness of machines but also of feelings, concepts and beliefs), the uncanny is as much concerned with the question of computers and "new technology" as it is with questions of religion. Spectrally affective and conceptual, demanding rationalization yet uncertainly exceeding or falling short of it, the uncanny offers new ways of thinking about the

The Digital Double

contemporary "return to the religious" . . . as well as about the strangeness of "programming" in general.[19]

The double has an ancient and global lineage within religious, occult, and folkloric traditions. The digital double relates to ancient notions of magic not only by virtue of the "conjuring" of an alternate and simultaneous second body for the performing subject, but also in relation to the ancient laws of imitative and homeopathic magic. In his account of death and resurrection dramas and rituals, Sir James Frazer argues that these ceremonies "were in substance a dramatic representation of the natural processes which they wished to facilitate; for it is a familiar tenet of magic that you can produce any desired effect by merely imitating it."[20] In recent performance practice, the double as a digital image replicating its human referent has been used to produce a range of different forms of imitation and representation which reflect upon the changing nature and understanding of the body and self, spirit, technology, and theater.

In analyzing the different manifestations being explored in performance, we have identified four types or categories of the digital double that explore distinct representations and themes. These trace the double through the forms of a reflection, an alter-ego, a spiritual emanation, and a manipulable mannequin. While these categories are useful in examining what we consider to be distinct aesthetic, philosophical, or paradigmatic issues, it is nonetheless acknowledged that the double is by nature a mysterious and capricious figure that may sometimes challenge and traverse neat boundaries.

The Double as Reflection

There is nothing more uncanny than seeing one's face accidentally in a mirror by moonlight.
—HEINRICH HEINE[21]

New York artist Dan Graham's work in the 1970s using mirrors and video cameras provides interesting analogue examples of the performative double as a reflection. In *Two Consciousness Projection* (1973) a man, looking through the eyepiece of a video camera, describes in detail the woman's face he is filming. At the same time, the woman, sitting a few feet away, describes her own face as she watches her video image, relayed in real time on a video monitor positioned just below the camera. The face the man describes is distanced from its live referent by virtue of its mediatization through the miniaturized video screen of the eyepiece. For the woman, her face on the monitor is a direct technological "double," but the double image of her is complicated. Not only is it an electronic image, but its positioning also falsely suggests direct reflection, as if she is sitting watching herself in a mirror. But the image actually works in a disorientating 180-degree reverse so that, for example, raising the right hand would not correspond on video to a mirror image, but would apparently bring up the opposite hand. The same paradigm was explored in Joan Jonas's 1972 video art performance *Left Side, Right Side*, where mirrors created reversed and split images of her that confused perceptions of spectatorial perspective, and the relationship between left and right. Throughout, she repeated the words "This is my left side, this is my right side" like a hypnotic mantra.

For Graham's installation *Present Continuous Past* (1974), viewers entered a mirror-lined cube reflecting them in real time from all angles, while a video relay timed with an eight-second delay projected their recently completed actions. This Brechtian effect, inducing in the viewer "an uncomfortable and self-conscious state,"[22] emphasizes how "mirrors reflect instantaneous time without duration . . . whereas video feedback does just the opposite, it relates the two in a kind of durational time flow."[23] In his essay "Transforming Mirrors: Transforming Mirrors" (1999) David Rokeby explores contemporary digital art works that use the mirror reflection principle, and suggests that

while all interactive works reflect interactors back to themselves, in many works the idea of the mirror is explicitly invoked. The clearest examples are interactive video installations where the spectator's image or silhouette becomes an active force in a computer-generated context. Examples include aspects of Myron Krueger's *Videoplace* work, Ed Tannenbaum's *Recollections* and Very Vivid's *Mandala*. . . . transformed reflections are a dialogue between the self and the world beyond. The echo operates like a wayward loop of consciousness through which one's image of one's self and one's relationship to the world can be examined, questioned and transformed.[24]

The Spirit of Narcissus

These ideas are perfectly embodied in one of the most influential interactive artworks of the early 1990s, *Liquid Views* (Monika Fleischmann/ Wolfgang Strauss/ Christian-A. Bohn, 1993). The piece epitomizes the digital double as a narcissistic mirror reflection of Lacanian misrecognition (*meconnaissance*); the body appearing as "lines of 'fragilization' that define the anatomy of phantasy."[25] The gallery installation places the user in the role of Narcissus, peering into water to study her own reflection. The user/spectator becomes not only an interactive participant but also the primary subject and performer, since her digital double is also projected onto a large wall within the gallery space, to be watched by other visitors.

Bending over a horizontal computer monitor, the user sees a well or spring of virtual water: rippling patterns of graphics programmed using custom software to imitate natural aquatic movement and wave shapes. A miniature video camera records the image of her face peering down, and computer software blends this picture with the moving water. A touch-screen interface enables the user to disturb and affect the water patterns, creating wave effects to blur the "reflection," or to make it disappear in a swirling whirlpool.

This technological reworking of the Narcissus myth lends it a new and distinctly modern resonance. While we appear to look at our own reflection, it is not a natural reflection, but a video copy—an electronic simulation transmitted through lenses, chips, and cables, then reproduced as colored pixels. The water is wholly synthetic, a series of algorithms prompting computer graphics. Narcissus sought the sublime through meditation on his own natural beauty, through natural reflective matter—water. In *Liquid Views*, a new metaphor and myth is etched out, and a highly resonant, contemporary image slowly crystallizes. We are now in a period where we crane our heads and peer down to glimpse a new, *technological sublime*, which we find equally fascinating and hypnotic as the natural one. The image we peer at places ourselves firmly within, and in control of, a pulsating digital world simultaneously reflecting and synthetically replicating nature, and our own bodies. Human vanity is replaced by the new technological vanity: our faith in the transformational power of computer technology—the power of the virtual *over* the real. The installation is a simulacral mandala for meditation on the double as a technological reflection, where we gaze fixedly into, and back at, our new electronic selves.[26]

The spirit of Narcissus returns in Nicholas Anatol Baginsky's *The Narcissism Enterprise* (1998) installation, where a video camera records the viewer's face and the live image is relayed back into the space. But the video image is manipulated in real time by a computer system which morphs the image as a composite, blending some of the viewer's facial features (such as eyes, nose, or mouth) with those taken from previous visitors to the space. In *Plasm: Yer Mug* (Peter Broadwell, Rob Myers, and Rebecca Fulson, 1996), an eerie electronic mirror merges "reflections" of visitors' faces with graphical, mutating Artificial-Life forms housed in the computer's memory.[27] Alba d'Urbano's *Touch Me* (1995) installation presents a head-and-shoulders digital portrait of the artist, which beckons visitors, asking them to touch her face. When the screen is touched, that area of the portrait is replaced by the corresponding part of the user's face, which is relayed via a hidden video camera. By touching different parts of the screen face, the user can progressively replace d'Urbano's image with their own face, as if in mirror image, "thus crossing the divide between spectatorial 'subject' and artistic 'object.'"[28]

The Narcissus myth is played out again in the Dutch dance performance *Soft Mirror* (1998, Isabelle Jenniches, Beppie Blankert, Caroline Dokter) with a live performer in the role of Narcissus dancing a duet with a screen video-conferenced gold and green Echo. The remote performer playing Echo shadows, mirrors and follows Narcissus with a considerable sense of intimacy, achieved through careful rehearsal. Stickers were used on the walls and floor of the remote space as accurate focal points for the dancer's changing gaze, which always precisely meets the relative position of Narcissus in the live performance space. The company also note how "the low frame rate, lagging and delay clearly indicate material has become marked by its journey through time and space. On the Internet, one is usually unaware of distances, but the distorted video images let us again feel the urgency of remoteness."[29]

Technology as a Mirror

Fascination with the double as a technological reflection becomes an obsession for the protagonist of Blast Theory's multimedia theater performance *10 Backwards* (1999). The central character, Niki (played by Niki Woods), videotapes herself compulsively, and the piece is punctuated with footage from her "video diaries," where she speculates and fantasizes about her future. One of the production's most original and memorable sequences involves Niki using her digital video camera to record herself eating breakfast cereal. She eats exaggeratedly, repeatedly glancing at the camera and occasionally making other distinct movements: scratching her nose, adjusting her hair, picking cereal from her teeth with her fingers. Running against this live action, her recorded voiceover explains that her recording process is part of a strategy to reorientate her mind and body in order to be able to travel through time. The close analysis and exact replication of her past actions, such as eating breakfast, can affect the temporal coordinates linking past, present, and future.

She finishes eating, and begins to replay the footage she has just recorded, using a remote control jog-shuttle handset to play the recording at different speeds, including frame-by-frame, forward, or backward. The video plays on screens at each end of the traverse stage, and she studies the screen image opposite her as she slowly shuttles through the digital tape, which is also relayed behind her. As she does so, she synchronously reenacts and mirrors every detail, action by action, grimace by grimace, chew by chew. She frequently holds the pause button, her live face and body frozen exactly as on the screens. She plays segments backward, and once again her staccato live movements exactly mirror the screen footage as she adjusts her hair in reverse and brings a spoonful of cereal out of her mouth, and back into the bowl. The close-up video image on the screen behind Niki is five times her corporeal size, rendering the mirrored interaction between the masticating live performer and her recorded-self comic and grotesque. Her recorded voiceover continues throughout:

Preparation number three, I was told, involves learning to love the jog-shuttle. . . . Use it, abuse it, go as far as to break it, but run your everyday actions backwards, forwards, slowly, quickly. Don't forget the pause button. Cut your every move into a thousand pieces. Reassemble them as plasticine, twist them, stretch them, fold them in on themselves until you can regurgitate the breakfast before last. (Pause) By the fourth day of preparation, I'd learnt to hate my well-known brand of breakfast cereal.

Niki thus copies, analyzes, replays, reverses, and freezes the tiniest details of her breakfast meal (figure 11.2). It is a humorous, strange, and powerful theatrical ritual, where performance and technology truly and effectively meet. The live performer and her digital double exactly reflect and replicate one another within a context which seems at once personal but theatrical, banal yet profound. The universal act of eating is replayed as a slow, intense facial dance, a mirror-play duet between the live performer and her digital reflection. As we watch, our own facial muscles twitch empathetically, hardly able to resist joining in. The sequence synchronizes Niki to her past, and the audience to the apparently simultaneous "presents" of her live and projected/recorded form. Niki uses digital

Figure 11.2 Niki Woods attempts to relive and replicate every facial detail of her breakfast-eating ritual with the help of a video "jog-shuttle" device (in her left hand) in Blast Theory's *10 Backwards* (1999).

video as an instrument for self-analysis, but for her the technological duplicate becomes the "real" that she must painstakingly copy and emulate. The sequence's power and fascination lies in the fact that we see her gradually embodying and becoming one with her technological reflection. Just as in *Liquid Views*, not only do the boundaries between the virtual and the actual become confused and unstable, but the digital reflection effectively effaces its live double to emerge as the dominant force.

In Anna Saup and Supreme Particles' *Plasma/architexture* (1994), an apparent mirror image of the installation visitor transforms into a 3D plasma model. As the visitor enters the room, a night-vision camera projects her mirror-like image onto a pneumatic projection screen controlled by a computer. As the visitor moves to the centre of the room, two angled black-and-white cameras map the body and "dwarfmorph" custom-software transforms the images into a 3D model, with the night-vision image incorporated to provide a texture. Further software manipulation provides the model with a plasma effect, which is supported by the pneumatic projection screen, which bulges and transforms continually to enhance the plasma body's three-dimensionality. At this point, the virtual body no longer mirrors the visitor's movements as before, but takes on a life of its own, and "talks" to the visitor in an artificial language created from manipulated, "soundmorphed" sounds and voices of previous visitors the system recorded in the space.

On a hanging screen, a twelve-foot high outline of a body provides the centerpiece for Tiffany Holmes's *Nosce Te Ipsum* (2000). As visitors move toward it, they activate pressure sensors that trigger progressive visual "dissections" of the body, as layers progressively fold back to reveal flesh, marks, and written texts. When the user arrives close to the screen and activates the final sensor, the digital animations within the body shape finally give way to a video image of the user's face, captured and relayed onto the head of the giant figure in real time. At the climax of the dissecting process, this "mirror image" provides a shock to the system and uncovers the meaning behind the piece's title—the Latin motto "Know Yourself." As with *Liquid Views* and *10 Backwards* the journey towards the screen ends with the discovery of the technologized, mirrored self.

The mirror, of course, has not only provided a transformational frame and source of imagery for artists, but has also figured as a prominent metaphor in wider critical discussions of digital technologies. Richard Coyne describes how the idea of the mirror links surrealist notions of reality with narratives and metaphors within the Information Technology world "which purports to present openings into worlds, windows, and hyperlinks, which can return to themselves, and which suggest the interreflections of a chamber of mirrors."[30] Peter Lunenfeld evokes a similar metaphor in his discussion of digital arts, which he relates to "an almost infinitely regressing series of mirror reflections,"[31] while Jay Bolter's extensive solo and collaborative writings on computer arts and culture have consistently and eloquently held a mirror up to the *Windows and Mirrors* (2003) behind digital paradigms.[32] For Jean Baudrillard, the technologized, mirrored double

is the fantasy of seizing reality live that continues—ever since Narcissus bent over his spring. Surprising the real in order to immobilize it, suspending the real in the expiration of its double. . . . We dream of passing through ourselves and of finding ourselves in the beyond: the day when your holographic double will be there in space, eventually moving and talking, you will have realised your dream.[33]

But with typical pessimism, Baudrillard then pulls the rug from under his own conjured image: "Of course, it will no longer be a dream, so its charm will be lost."[34] He relates the holographic image to "the imaginary aura of the double,"[35] which becomes a type of technologized, fantasy clone. This prompts "the vertigo of passing to the other side of our body, to the side of the double . . . a luminous surgery" to remove the double hidden inside of you "as one would operate to remove a tumor."[36]

Although all types of digital double can be conceptualized as some form of techno-logical reflection of a live body, in our categorizations we are specifically defining the reflection double as a digital image that mirrors the identical visual form and real-time movement of the performer or interactive user. In performances and installations featuring the reflection double, the performer/user is almost always conscious of the presence of the double, as in *Liquid Views* and *10 Backwards*. In performances where the double coexists with the live performer but is not directly watched and acknowledged by her, or where the double undertakes asynchronous activity, or presents another "side" or visual embodiment of a character, we move into the domain of the digital double as an alter-ego.

The Double as Alter-Ego

The frontier is, after all, an extension of ourselves. Therein also lies the hope of cyberspace.
—LLOYD W. RANG[37]

Gilles Deleuze and Felix Guatarri's hugely influential *Mille Plateaus* (1980) begins: "The two of us wrote *Anti-Oedipus* together. Since each of us was several, there was already quite a crowd."[38] The double made digital flesh in contemporary multimedia performance commonly splits the several beings and underlying personalities of the performing subject and manifests this crowd. The digital double as an alter-ego is also able to encapsulate the different mystical "becomings" at the center of *Mille Plateaus*: becoming-animal, becoming-intense, becoming-woman, becoming-stars. As we have seen, the double as a performative alter-ego has been explored since 1914 when Winsor McCay ran behind the film screen and reappeared on celluloid in animated form to jump onto *Gertie the Dinosaur*'s back to ride off into the sunset.

Hans Holzer describes how "the concept of the human double (or doubles) has remained a constant factor in folklore and tradition, particularly the belief that every human being is accompanied through life by two extensions of his personality, the one good and the other evil; the former luminous and the latter dark and menacing."[39] He suggests that this derives from "a primitive rationalisation into companion spirits of the reflected image in water and the ever-accompanying shadow."[40] The shadow double of the alter-ego in digital performance is likewise an alternate, and invariably darker embodiment.

A visually striking example of the splitting of the alter-ego double from its human body occurs in 4D Art's theater performance *Anima* (2002). The company use a sophisticated projection system incorporating half-mirrored screens that are invisible to the naked eye, to create the illusion of three-dimensional human doubles appearing in the same open, physical stage space as the live performers, rather than on a two-dimensional projection screen. At one point a performer dances while projected after-images of her movements split away from her, leaving ghostly traces hanging and moving in slow motion in apparent 3D, in the immediate space around her. In another sequence, a male dancer's body appears to split into two separate bodies as his projected double tears itself entirely away from his live body and the two "men" perform a furiously physical and elaborate duet, continually circling and crossing one another's paths like aggressive fighters.

Brazilian artist Ivani Santana dances with her shadowy, projected *doppelgänger* in her solo performance, *Corpo Aberto: midia de carbona, midia de silicio* (2001) while cameras attached to her body relay blurred and often vertiginous live images. The double is pre-programmed and live-circuited, and near the end of the performance its shape begins to lose its human form as it eventually mutates into "otherworldly shapes and animated skeletons."[41] The digital double has been an abiding source of inspiration and experimentation for The Chameleons Group, a performance company established in 1994, directed by this volume's author, Steve Dixon. In *Chameleons 4: The Doors of Serenity* (2002), the group play with a deliberate confusion between live and recorded characters as they enter and exit two working doors built within the wooden projection screen. The scale of the characters is identical, and the differentiation between the stage performers and their recorded doubles is minimized by keeping the live performers as "flat" as possible to the screen. In tightly rehearsed and executed sequences, the characters and their digital doubles enter and exit through the doors, observe and interact with one another. Normally, the illusion of nondifferentiation between the live performers and their recordings is maintained, but sometimes the digital double manifests activity impossible in real time. At one point, a live character enters, moves to one side of the door and watches as his digital double follows through the door and is met by a hail of bullets. The double leaps into the air in a grotesque, slow-motion death. Another live performer watches sadly as her screen double is bombarded by toy dolls, which alternately strike her in slow and fast motion, these contrasting speeds increasingly intensifying and polarizing as the sequence progresses.

Other sequences involve characters undertaking long and involved conversations with their projected doubles, and sometimes trebles. An early sequence introduces a cyborg character, and the use of two *doppelgängers* who engage him in conversation emphasizes his ontology as a schizophrenic, technologically networked and mediatized being. One is Upside-down-boy, who hangs inverted in the Tarot image of the Hanged Man, warning the stage cyborg that he should pull himself together and forget "the metal-man bullshit." The other is Mirror-boy, himself "doubled" by addressing the other characters only through a mirror. A three-way conversation ensues between the three manifestations of the same character, each of which have distinct, contrasting personalities (figure 11.3). The dialogue is fast and comic, structured in a series of grand conceits that are then exploded bathetically by insults. It is played like a pastiche of a sci-fi gangster movie:

Mirror-boy: So let's talk the next move.
Upside-down-Boy: I want out of this crap.
Mirror-boy: Oh really. Why's that?
Upside-down-Boy: Well, just for starters—He's the campest cyborg I've ever seen.

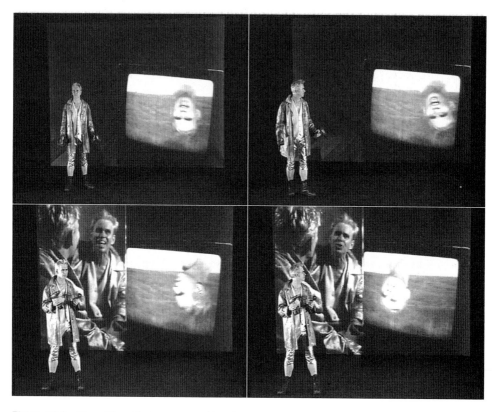

Figure 11.3 Steve Dixon first encounters his cyborg double ("Upsidedown-boy") followed by his cyborg treble ("Mirror-boy") in The Chameleons Group's *Chameleons 4: the Doors of Serenity* (2002).

Cyborg: All cyborgs are camp.

Mirror-boy: His metamorphosis is perfect. His advanced hyper-toned metal body cunningly disguised by his paranoid, wasted appearance and slight beer gut. Who would guess he has the strength of a hundred men and a ferrous brain capable of ten billion computations a micro-second.

Cyborg: You know, I do feel particularly intelligent.

Upside-down-Boy: Your brains are shrapnel, you fuckin' retard freak.

The sequence continues in this vein, emphasizing double and triple perspectives on cyborgism. Mirror-boy voices utopian and messianic rhetoric, Upside-down-boy is fiercely cynical and dystopian, and the live cyborg character is an innocent and confused figure caught in the crossfire. Another sequence, set in a public toilet, features two live female performers, each with two separate prerecorded doubles of themselves on screen, and involves a multilayered dialogue between the six characters played by the two live and four recorded women. The sequence becomes ever more complex as the four doubles move

Figure 11.4 Wendy Reed (left) and Anna Fenemore (right) hold an intense six-way conversation in *Chameleons 4: the Doors of Serenity* (2002).

around the screen, switch places, and go in and out of the toilet cubicles, often reemerging as the other's double, having swapped clothes (figure 11.4).

The Double as Spiritual Emanation

All that is solid melts into air.
—KARL MARX AND FREDERICK ENGELS, *THE COMMUNIST MANIFESTO*[42]

In *The Golden Bough* (1925), Frazer notes the common supposition among primitive peoples that the soul can escape from the body through its natural openings, particularly the mouth and nostrils, and that dream is believed to be the actual wandering of the soul. Thus, "it is a common rule with primitive people not to waken a sleeper, because his soul is away and might not have time to get back; so if the man wakened without his soul, he would fall sick."[43] He relates how the story of the external soul as a concrete double is told "in various forms, by all Aryan peoples from Hindoostan to the Hebrides"[44] and details numerous legends of warlocks and magical beings whose physical bodies remain invulnerable since their souls are hidden in secret places.

Theories and histories of performance have also traced a serial involvement with ideas of the human spirit, of mysticism and transcendence. From the earliest sacred rituals to the deities of Greek theater, from the trances and possessions of Asian dance and theater to the liminal rites of shamanism, the performer has been seen as a communicator with or conduit to higher spiritual forces. Even within the staid traditions of post-Renaissance literary theater, the "greatness" of actors has been measured not merely in relation to their technique or heights of emotion, but their levels of spiritual transportation. "It is the soul that plays the roles, not the body," proclaimed Friedrich Kaysler in 1914.[45] Rimbaud believed "Je est un autre," and Rilke declared "where there is a poem, it is not mine, but that of Orpheus who comes to sing it."[46] Dance has equally been theorized in relation to what Merce Cunningham and Lincoln Kirstein define as "a spiritual activity in physical form"[47] and what Susan Sontag describes as "the staging of a transfiguration. . . . Dance enacts both being completely in the body and transcending the body."[48] These notions are vividly encapsulated and visually manifested in depictions of the digital double as a spiritual or supernatural being.

Digital doubles representing spiritual emanations or incarnations of the body relate to notions of ghosts, astral bodies, out-of-body experiences, and soul projection. The double may be depicted as a gaseous figure composed of particles, or in another, more liquid-like ethereal form, luminous and transparent. During Mesh Performance Partnerships' performance *Contours* (1997), Susan Kozel rolls and dances on the floor with her digital double, which is projected onto the floor from above. In the low stage lighting, the double shines out as a luminous, ghostly white figure mirroring her movements. It is a slow and sensual duet between Kozel and her double, which appears as a second, amorphous body composed of pure white light, shimmering like a spiritual aura around her. It recalls the nimbus and aureole haloes of Christian religious art, and the early photographs of Hippolyte Baraduc (1850–1909) and Louis Darget (1847–1921) purportedly showing the paranormal phenomena of etheric spirits and ectoplasm emanating from the bodies of clairvoyants.

Roy Ascott considers digital arts and telematics in relation to "the technology of transcendence," maintaining that "the mysterium of consciousness may be the final frontier for both art and science, and perhaps where they will converge."[49] For Ascott, digital technology also engenders "double consciousness" and "the double gaze." Locating cyberspace firmly and emphatically in relation to the spiritual and liminal paradigms of Sufism and shamanism, digital artistic aspiration is conceptualzed as a type of navigation through consciousness which doubles and alternates back and forth from the visionary to the material. Ascott equates this to his experiences of ingesting the sacred hallucinogenic plant ayahuasca while living with a Brazilian tribe, whereby he became conscious of inhabiting two bodies: his familiar phenomenological one, and a second composed of particles of light.

This image of the double body as particles is memorably played out in Company in Space's dance-theater performance *Incarnate* (2001). A computer-generated graphical projection of a female body shape is filled with points of brightly colored lights that move busily, expanding and contracting the size of the figure, and finally disintegrating and rematerializing the particle body like exploding nebulae. Such images emphasize digital performance's representation of the human body as a site for dynamic metamorphoses through technological intervention. The body's cycle of materialization, dematerialization, and rematerialization is articulated in a dynamic transformation of shimmering, star-like colored particles. The metamorphosing flickering lights and stars composing the double in *Incarnate* represents the technologically mutating body as a cosmological and visionary form.

In Igloo's *Viking Shoppers* (2000), two live dancers explore the "relationships between their virtual, digital and spiritual selves."[50] They work in very low light upstage right, behind and to one side of a large projection screen positioned close to the audience, downstage left. A special ASCII video camera relays live images of the duet onto the screen, mapping and converting the dancers' bodies into the number and letter symbols of ASCII code (figure 11.5). In the same way that medical and genetic science increasingly reads our bodies in terms of mathematical codes—genes, DNA structure, and so on—the structures of the live performer's bodies at one side of the stage are converted into numeric and abstract symbols on a screen on the other side. As the dance progresses, the computer software is manipulated to decrease the density of numbers and symbols that compose the digital figures. They become less and less solid until limbs are reduced to a single

Figure 11.5 An ASCII camera converts the body shapes of two live dancers into computer code in Igloo's *Viking Shoppers* (2000).

The Digital Double

thickness of code. The movement traced out becomes more and more minimal, more aesthetically hypnotic, and somehow more painful. Although the live dancers coexist on stage with the projections they generate, the digital image once again dominates: it is as though the hieroglyphic doubles are the real dancers.

The dancing doubles are composed of mesmeric shimmering symbols, like a high-tech encapsulation of Artaud's prescriptions for a theater alive with "physical hieroglyphs." There is a sparse but intensely beautiful simplicity to these doubles, which seem at once material and ephemeral. The performance is Brechtian in revealing its computational mechanics of production, but at the same time, this making strange is deeply mystical: the doubles are like etheric phantoms composed of particles of cybernetic dust. The piece also evokes the tensions between materiality and immateriality, and more particularly, fluidity and rigidity, which characterizes virtual systems and our interactions with them—for example, the relationship between the search (fluid) and locate (fix) paradigm central to navigational experience within virtual networks. In *Viking Shoppers*, the kinetic fluidity of the movements of the live dancers (which interestingly also translates into fluid, rippling movement on the ASCII image, but only in the arms and legs, *not* the slower-moving torsos and heads) contrasts with the rigidity of the codified output of computer numbers and symbols the dance generates.

Alchemical Doubling

Troika Ranch's *The Chemical Wedding of Christian Rosenkreutz* (2001) exemplifies the digital double as a spirit form. It explores the mystical union of computers and human beings, taking its inspiration from a seventeenth-century spiritual allegory tracing Rosenkreutz's transcendent transformation through the "chemical wedding" of alchemy. The production was also influenced by Artificial Intelligence expert Ray Kurzweil's book *The Age of Spiritual Machines* (2001), an enthusiastic eulogy on the potentials of computers to emulate and overtake the human brain, and to achieve a spiritual form of consciousness. The performance places Rosenkreutz in 1459, the setting of the story described in the original allegory and, in parallel, transposes him to 2050, the date Kurzweil predicts that the human mind/soul will be able to be wholly downloaded into a computer. Rosenkreutz's spiritual transformation at the end of the performance is thus achieved through the alchemical promise of modern technology. Troika Ranch have elsewhere described how the sensory dance technologies they design and employ are "the 'magic' of our time," and how the audience should perceive this aspect of the performance *as* magic, just as alchemy was viewed in the fifteenth century.

The Chemical Wedding of Christian Rosenkreutz combines dance with theatrical dialogue, and utilizes the company's custom-built *MidiDancer* motion sensing equipment to activate and mutate video projections, and a *LaserWeb* system to prompt lighting effects (figure 11.6). The piece is spiritual in tone and in its choreographic style, which makes use of numerous group lifts and other symbolic "ascents"; ritualized, secretive gestures;

Figure 11.6 Troika Ranch's *The Chemical Wedding of Christian Rosenkreutz* (2001).

and arm and body movements that come to rest in poses redolent of ancient religious iconography and hieroglyphics. The projected digital imagery fuses surrealism with mysticism. A slowly moving composite shot of twenty staring eyes is projected as a single performer dances on stage, her live-camera relayed image superimposed upon it, with a one second delay, repeating her lyrical, graceful movements. In another digital video sequence played with the stage bare, the dancers appear one by one on screen, floating serenely down through dark space, their naked bodies slowly rotating. Sometimes a large single figure, sometimes five or six in varied perspective scales as though near and far, these spiritualized, ethereal bodies descend majestically through space at different speeds, many with their arms cast heavenward, in classical, celestial pose.

A portable freestanding door is used as a portal into another dimension or transcendental space, and at one point two performers walk through it to recount, in unison, a dream about a beautiful wedding ceremony that is interrupted by an executioner who decapitates all the guests, and captures their flowing blood in a golden chalice:

And then I saw my soul as a flame, and my body was carried across the ocean in a coffin. My soul was floating up in the air, and I saw this tower and . . . I got to the top. There was all this alchemical stuff. We chopped and sliced and poured and there was this mould. And we got the chalice and we poured the soul into the egg and it turned into a bird. And the bird sprouted wings.

The Digital Double

This imagery weaves together ancient beliefs about the "philospher's egg" as both an alchemical glass crucible where magical constituents are combined, and as an egg to be split with a sword to release the alchemist's soul. The mystical imagery continues as the door becomes a coffin for Rosenkreutz who is carried around the stage as he reflects how he "was never the same" after peering over the edge of the abyss; after seeing an angel coming into his home; after being spun up in a twister and never returning to earth. He then prepares for his brain alchemy as the dancers and their spiritualized digital doubles move with slow, minimal movements, against music so reverberating and deep that it seems to emanate from underwater. Rosenkreutz then describes a vision of his spiritual transformation, which melds a Gibsonian image of cyberspace, mystical numerology, analog and digital communication systems, genetic cloning, and a journey to the center of the cosmos:

I saw a giant crystalline structure, like an immensely dense web. I could see myself riding along the connections . . . finding the places where the memories had been engraved. . . . They told me that at the particular moment, at the time they made the copy, at that very instant, my mind would be like a stream of numbers, coded and broadcast over the radio. . . . After a few thousand years, they could write those numbers into a little machine, and out would pop a perfect copy of me, or at least my memories, thoughts and feelings. I could travel to the centre of the universe that way.

The performance itself works like the complex web Rosenkreutz describes, and the "broadcasting" of his mind has been a constant leitmotif throughout. His monologues are captured, amplified and transmitted through a personal microphone; some of his words are reinforced by projected pieces of text; and a head-mounted spy camera dangles in front of his face relaying a fisheye lens close-up of him to two video monitors set high up on either side of the central projection screen. His multimedia monologues are complemented by the multimedia extensions of the dancers as their motion sensing appendages mutate the images of their projected digital doubles, rendering them luminous silhouettes, splitting them, and projecting them heavenwards as angels, ghostly souls, and other spiritual avatars. Rosenkreutz's final transformation presents an uplifting, if somewhat sentimental climax, the final video image showing flowers gently falling and covering Rosenkreutz's face, before rising from it into the air to reveal his face transformed as a newborn baby.

The digital double as a soul or spiritual emanation represents not the split subjectivity of postmodern consciousness, but rather a symbol of the unified, cosmic and transcendental self. Discourses on cyberculture and digital performance have long been obsessed by the Cartesian split between body and mind, and the polarities of absence and presence, real and virtual. The performance of the digital double as expressed by groups such as Mesh Performance Partnerships, Company in Space, Igloo and Troika Ranch, offers a different and in many ways more fundamental binary for digital performance studies: between the corporeal and the spiritual.

The Double as Manipulable Mannequin

The computer *avatar*,[51] a graphical stand-in for the human body within virtual worlds, links the notion of the double as a spiritual emanation to our final category of digital double, the manipulable mannequin. The term *avatar* derives from Hindu scriptures, being the bodily incarnation of deities. The Sanskrit *Avatara* translates as a descent, the passing down of the gods from heaven to the material world, and artists such as Mika Tuomola have created avatars which embody this sense of a mythical being or digital deity. Tuomola has consulted on and developed numerous visually imaginative and dramatic avatar worlds, drawing on ideas from dream, myth, carnival and commedia dell'arte.[52]

The artist group Mistresses of Technology develop dynamic low-fi avatars with quasi-mythical names such as Ephemera, Discordia, Liquid Nation, and Metrophage for environments such as their *I-drunners: re_flesh the body* (2000). They are designed to present dramatic and alternative online embodiments "to illustrate a bloated, informatic world drowning in electricity and telecommunications technologies . . . and to focus on the ways in which various media/informatic/industrial realms are dominantly female."[53] Other artists such as Hannes Vilhjálmsonn prefer more realistic humanoid avatars "that appear to breathe, look at each other when approaching and conversing, use facial expression, and produce conversational gestures to accompany the "speech" of typed statements."[54] Still others emphasize avatars' real time manipulability, such as Marek Walczak, who created an online VRML 3D world inhabited by avatar dancers, which online participants manipulated and choreographed in regular weekly events using Blacksun's Cyberhub.

Andrew Stern has used behavior-based artificial intelligence architecture to create responsive "Virtual Petz" avatars such as "catz and dogz" as well as *Virtual Babyz* (1999), cartoon-style avatars that display emotional facial expressions and emit baby sounds and words. His desktop interface incorporates a microphone into which users can speak simple words, which the *Virtual Babyz* respond to, using synthesized baby talk. Stern's objective is a type of interactive avatar performance which elicits emotional empathy: "The end result are characters that communicate their feelings and thoughts in a natural, performance—like way" he writes, "to allow users to form emotional relationships with their Virtual Babyz."[55]

Avatar Stage Doubles

In 1997, Claudio Pinhanez created an avatar that was played autonomously by a computer system he had programmed for his one-man show (plus avatar) *It/I: A Computer Theater Play* (1997) at the MIT Media Laboratory and the Digital Life Consortium.[56] A system of cameras monitored Pinhanez's actions on stage and the avatar responded appropriately, sometimes joining in with the live character's antics, sometimes opposing them, or setting problems. Like his earlier *SingSong* (1996), *It/I* was programmed using software he developed at MIT to enable the avatars to respond to scripting paradigms and "respect the creative process of theater."[57] Pinhanez plays a clownlike figure in baggy denim dungarees and a flowerpot hat, and the pantomimic physical dialogue between him and the computer character is conceived as a homage to early movies, where physical comedy and slapstick became one solution to the absence of sound; in Pinhanez's view, interactive systems for digital performance are at a comparable embryonic stage.

In David Saltz's interpretation of Shakespeare's last play, *Tempest 2000* (2000), the character Ariel is a screen avatar double that is manipulated in real time by an onstage live performer. The performer is imprisoned in a cage on a large rock (symbolically reinforcing her servitude to Prospero) and wears a motion capture suit with head, waist, knee, ankle, elbow, wrist, and hand sensors. Each of her live movements are instantaneously mapped onto the computer animated figure and, most impressive of all, voice recognition software matches the performer's phonemes in real time, perfectly synchronizing the avatar's lip movements to her corporeal double's. Although visually their forms are at are complete odds, the precision of kinetic correspondence between the two Ariels' physical performances is eerie, even uncanny. Prospero and the other characters only ever address the screen avatar Ariel (figure 11.7), until the end when Prospero releases her by pulling off the electrodes from the live performer's costume, whereupon the onscreen avatar wilts and collapses, finally melting away like the wicked witch in *The Wizard of Oz* (1939). Prospero declares Ariel to "be free," and the performer joyously cartwheels offstage. Saltz uses the avatar, in his words, to "broaden the expressive range of actors and redefine what it means for performance to be live."[58] Prospero's magic becomes a metaphor for contemporary technology, and Saltz stresses that Prospero creates illusions that the other characters accept as real, "in much the same way that digital media is increasingly shaping and manipulating our perception of reality."[59]

Other memorable examples of live performers whose actions and movements are converted in real time to animate an onscreen avatar include Stelarc's *Movatar* (2000) (figure 11.8) and Company in Space's *Cybernetic Organism 3 (CO3)* (2001). Both are cyborgic solo performances where the performers (Stelarc and Hellen Sky, respectively) wear futuristically designed exoskeletal prostheses that track and feed the kinetic data from the performers to computers which animate the avatars to mirror or interpret the actions. Stelarc stands with his back to the audience and facing the screen as he manipulates his robotically shaped avatar double which is located in a graphically "neutral" open space, while Sky's movements prompts her avatar to travel through animated worlds. It crosses forests, villages, and snow-covered landscapes, and sometimes sinks and descends from one world (like the original Sanskrit *avatara*, "gods"), disappearing as though slowly swallowed up by the ground, to then reemerge in another landscape. Sky's high-tech costume incorporates a gyroscopic global tracking device, computer, potentiometer, light emitting devices, battery and headset; and her movements are slow and simple, deliberately un-dancerly.

Figure 11.7 Prospero interacts with an early prototype of the avatar Ariel during rehearsal tests for David Saltz's *Tempest 2000* (2000) Photo: Peter Frey.

The performance of *Cybernetic Organism 3* (*CO3*) we saw was staged in the large, domed, ex-market space that houses in its center the metal and glass "pod" of the Royal Exchange Theatre in Manchester, England. Multiple giant projection screens relayed the avatar animations around the space, and projectors beamed the images high and spectacularly onto the huge glass dome above, as Sky moved along walkways and climbed up the external metal structure of the theater. Meanwhile, co-director John McCormick manipulates the animations and

multi-cameras and points of view [to] orchestrate the real time compositions—unfolding and meshing the images to give them weight and meaning. . . . Doubles and mirrors pervade the work, providing more opportunities for real or virtual bodies to recognise or find one's own body alienating. As the virtual body acts as uncanny doppelganger to the self and its image, the large, dark shadows of Sky's body on the wall creates yet another "other" to contemplate.[60]

Avatar Farm (2000) uses the University of Nottingham (UK) Computer Research Group's advanced MASSIVE-3 collaborative virtual environment system to bring together avatars of local and remote actors and members of the public. A development of *Ages of*

The Digital Double

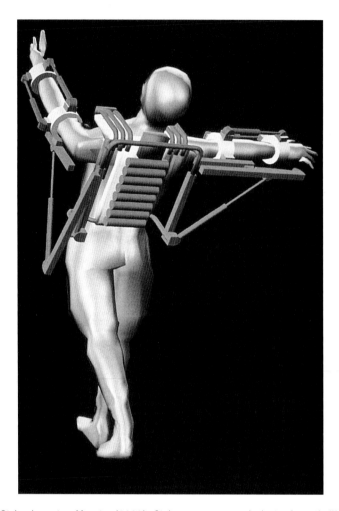

Figure 11.8 Stelarc's avatar *Movatar* (2000). Stelarc wears an equivalent cybernetic "backback" prosthesis when controlling the screen figure in live performances. Image: S. Middleton.

Avatar, an earlier collaborative project with Sky TV (UK), the avatars engage in a part-scripted plot involving gods, innocents abroad, lizards, and tricksters. Complex avatars for interactive theater experiences have also been created by The Interactive Cinema Project at the ATR Media Integration & Communications Laboratories in Kyoto, Japan. Their prototype *Romeo and Juliet in Hades* project imagines Shakespeare's characters after their deaths, in a type of dream-space.[61] Audience members are fitted with magnetic sensor ware to control avatars, which are designed as highly mobile "wooden marionettes on shafts."[62] The system combines prerecorded film and live environments, and utilizes nine computers including a SGI Onyx2, with separate systems for speech, gesture, and emotion recognition. Software called *Anytime Interaction* is designed to enable different types of interaction between players, including background speech interaction, which enables players to talk selectively from the background to players operating in the foreground of the performance.

Project leaders Naoka Tosa and Ryohei Nakatsu believe that such "Future Movie" projects utilizing advanced technologies can explore the boundaries between the conscious and the unconscious to effect a significant neo-Aristotelian digital catharsis. "Machines become most beautiful when they resemble living forms," they say. "Even computer graphic actors are touched when something human-like is felt. . . . This will generate a new consciousness for humans that communicate with machines."[63]

"Human-like" resemblance to a living form did not prove popular, however, in the case of Digital Domain's big-budget digital female character *Mya* (2000), developed for Motorola's Myosphere Internet service and voice-activated browser. The animated character, which was modeled from photographic samples of actress Michelle Holgate, was initially advertised as having "a personality and look as slick and stylish as the service she offers."[64] But she seemed *so* realistic that users believed her to be simply an actress, and were wholly unimpressed. The company withdrew the original *Mya*, and replaced her with a new version which emphasized her virtuality and artificiality, providing her with a more computer graphical sheen based on the lustre of china plate.[65]

Head Doubles

Stelarc's *Prosthetic Head*[66] (2002) is a distinctly human-like avatar that has not encountered the same problem, since in live "performance" situations it can be seen for what it is: a screen-based 3D moving image of the artist's head (figure 11.9). But it has a comparably sophisticated ontology to commercial applications such as *Mya*, and is able to respond to typed questions and observations with answers and counterobservations in real-time speech with full lip-sync. The head nods, tilts, and turns, the eyes blink, and the mouth twitches slightly, the whole giving the impression the head is patiently waiting for a question to be "asked" (typed in) (figure 11.10). Members of the audience are invited to interact by, for example, typing in their names—"My name is Sally" [return]—whereupon the *Prosthetic Head* image will acknowledge and reply, for example, "Hello Sally, how are you today?" Factual requests such as "Please count up to ten" [return] will usually be obeyed, while more difficult questions may gain a holding response such as, "I would need you to give me more information about that before I can answer your question," or an avoidance response such as "I don't think that is a reasonable question, please ask me about something else."

Like cinema's most famous talking computer, Hal 9000 from *2001: A Space Odyssey* (1968), the *Prosthetic Head* never admits to falsification or ever being wrong, its life and logic being wholly dependent upon its available database and software. It is built around

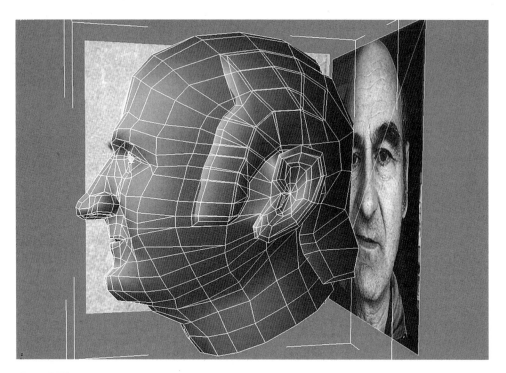

Figure 11.9 Image showing the digital construction for Stelarc's *Prosthetic Head* (2002) programmed by Karen Marcelo and Sam Trychin, with 3D modeling and image by Barrett Fox.

three software programs[67] that check the entered question/observation against an extensive database, construct a grammatical answer, and synchronize lip and facial gestures according to the response the head is giving. These are frequently comic. To the question, "What is the difference between reality and fantasy?" the head has been known to respond, "There is no difference between reality and fantasy, there is only fantasy." When accused of being "intolerant" it has replied "I will remember you accused me of that, Sally, when machines take over the world." Some questions trigger responses mixing the thought-provoking and comic: "Can you explain to me Einstein's Theory of Relativity?" prompts several minutes of precise but totally impenetrable scientific theories, instructions, and calculations with all the resonance of Lucky's outburst in Act II of Samuel Beckett's *Waiting for Godot* (1956). Algorithms permit the head to generate "novel poetry" (frequently gibberish but with appropriate references to the stimulus) and to sing when asked (which it has done with a variety of live musicians, including scratch and modern jazz artists).[68]

The Prosthetic Head is currently still under development by its creators, Karen Marcelo, Sam Trychin, Barrett Fox, and Richard Wallace under the artistic direction of

Figure 11.10 The individual components of Stelarc's *Prosthetic Head* (2002) programmed by Karen Marcelo and Sam Trychin, with 3D modeling and image by Barrett Fox.

Stelarc.[69] New developments are focusing on making the head more reactive (by recognizing questioner's faces and clothes), "intelligent" (so as to demonstrate a wider range of understanding and factual knowledge), and musically "talented" (as an improvisational singer able to respond to multiple styles, rhythms, and riffs). Whatever its future development may realize, it is already, as described by the artist, "seductive with its uncanny simulation of real-time recognition and response."[70]

But the vast majority of avatars, which mostly inhabit online environments, are not personal representations of the user or artist, as in Stelarc's project. As Gregory Little observes, most are clip-art imports from hegemonic multinational portfolios: Disney characters, Barbie dolls and Baywatch babes, pop icons, Stallone war-machines, smiley faces, and consumer objects like Nike trainers.[71] Lex Lonehead points out that even when users design their own avatars, they are "mostly supermodel cutouts and cutesy cartoons."[72]

Little argues that "the mind/body dichotomy is a red herring" and that the most dangerous binary is the pairing of self and commodity. In Little's analysis, people's identification with avatars constructed from trademark iconography and commodified imagery thus represents our ultimate desire to become commodities. Rather than creating new virtual bodies that symbolize our mythic fantasies or personal desires, avatars "function as a top-down tool, the embodiment of post-modern, multinational commerce. . . . It is Kapital, not Krishna that makes itself a body."[73]

In "A Manifesto for Avatars," Little urges the creation of radical new avatars that resist integration and stability, explore taboos, counter myths of transcendentalism, and resist the internal/external binary. These are Artaudian manifestations: "images that speak of hyperembodiment, of extremes of physicality, like the visceral, the abject, the defiled, and the horrific." Little discusses Artaud's experience of losing conscious control of his body, and his description of the experience as "the body without organs." Artaud's concept prefigured Deleuze and Guattari's much-cited use of the formulation in *Anti-Oedipus* (1977) and *Mille Plateaus* (1980), where they characterize it as unproductive, sterile, unengendered, and unconsumable. Little suggests that the body without organs, just like the avatar, "mirrors post-biological structures that undermine anatomical classification, capitalist consumption, and tedious mind/body/commodity separations in support of a more distributed, nomadic, and emergent model of embodied consciousness."[74]

Puppet Doubles

The double as a computer-generated body without organs features strongly in dance performance, where software applications such as *Life Forms* are now commonly used to manipulate puppetlike graphical figures on the desktop to conceive and experiment with choreography prior to studio work with live dancers. Motion capture technology similarly renders a manipulable double of the dancer onto the computer screen where it can be further modified and then represented in performance, as exemplified in Riverbed's collaborations with Merce Cunningham and Bill T. Jones. In the late 1990s and early 2000s, Yacov Sharir created a series of 3D animated films using *Life Forms*, *Poser*, and *Flash* software, with the collective title *Cyber Human Dances Series*. Unencumbered by gravity or any human physical restraints, these cyber-humanoid forms appear to move effortlessly and gracefully through gravitation-less space, the images becoming increasingly more complex through colored layering and duplication/triplication whereby the forms appear to dance with each other (figure 11.11). These cyber-human dancers were later used in live performance with interaction between the real time human dancers and the animated forms, layered further by the live dancers wearing digitally sensitized clothes through which means they could affect and control the cyber-dancer images.

Performers have also used computer technologies to convert their own physical bodies to the condition of a manipulable mannequin. Arthur Elsenaar employs the human face as a manipulable display device in a number of installations as well as web events such as

Figure 11.11 *I Have No Face* (2002), one of Yacov Sharir's many computer animated dance choreographies.

Emoting on the Web (1995), where remote users control his facial muscles in real time. As we discuss in more detail later, audience members use touch-screen computers to activate robotic manipulations of Marcel.lí Anthúnez Roca's body via pneumatic metal molds and hook devices in *Epizoo* (1994); and Stelarc allows audience members to manipulate his limbs and body muscles electronically in his Internet-activated performances.

Digital puppets based on principles from theatrical puppetry have been developed and used by artists such as Ian Grant; and at the Interactive Institute in Malmö, Sweden, the Performance Animation Toolbox project (2001–2002) developed real time animated digital puppets programmed using *Director* software, which are incorporated into performance situations with live actors. *Basker Vision,* a video tracking system programmed by Johan Torentsson, is used to monitor the performers' positions on stage (by registering the color codes they wear) and to feed the information to the animation engine in order to activate real-time responses and coordination between the performers and the puppets. For the project's performance *The Family Factory* (2002), experienced professional puppeteers controlled the avatars, in an attempt to render them as lifelike as possible. By basing the avatars' behavior on puppet theater praxis, the concern was to imbue them with a depth of character/personality and social and emotional verisimilitude that is currently extremely difficult, if not impossible using computer technologies alone. The group points out that in puppet theater, it is the skilled transference of human emotion and performative action between the puppeteer and puppet that is crucial:

> In puppetry it is well known that the audience's ascribing of life to an object does not depend on how well the object portrays an original. . . . From a dramaturgical point of view . . . the story being told [is] not only "the story of the puppet" but also "the story of the puppeteer." Puppet theatre is in its core a theatre of more than one level of narration.[75]

From Nam June Paik and Shuya Abe's early female performing robot *Robot K-456* (1964) to more recent advanced creations, anthropomorphic robots constitute the double as a manipulable mannequin in its most distinctly high-tech and solid form. Chico MacMurtrie's *Skeletal Reflections* (2002) installation uses a motion-capture system to analyse a spectator's gestures. These are interpreted within the computer in relation to classical human poses taken from art history, and a life-size humanoid robot skeleton then adopts and changes the poses. The audience-activated performance mirrors a formal system commonly used in new dance, whereby the dancer works through a series of gestures and poses, with periods of movement being punctuated by stillness. The classical bodily positions imbue the work with a gracefulness not normally associated with robotic machines, and the installation conjures a unique and evocative mix of Renaissance, new dance and high-tech machine aesthetics, performed by a robot figure representing the eternal symbol of death.

Artaud's calls for the use of giant stage mannequins in *The Theatre and Its Double* have thus been answered in myriad ways within digital performance, from avatars and robots to virtual dancers, to the reduction of the live human body itself to a puppet, manipulated by audiences at a distance. The manipulable mannequin acts as a design tool for conceiving performance in virtual form prior to work with human performers, as an avatar or Über-marionette replacement for the live performer, or *as* the performer herself, at the mercy of digital manipulations.

Conclusion

The digital double is a mysterious figure that takes various forms and undertakes different functions within digital performance. The reflection double announces the emergence of the self-reflexive, technologized self, conceived as becoming increasingly indistinguishable from its human counterpart. The alter-ego double is the dark doppelgänger representing the Id, split consciousness, and the schizophrenic self. The double as a spiritual emanation symbolizes a mystical conception of the virtual body, performing a projection of the transcendent self or the soul. The manipulable mannequin, the most common of all computer doubles, plays myriad dramatic roles: as a conceptual template, as a replacement body, and as the body of a synthetic being.

The notion of the Other was first discussed at length by Freud, and was later embraced by social theorists to denote various understandings of cultural difference following Edward Said's reorientation of the word in *Orientalism* (1978). In his article "Screen Test of the Double" (1999), Matthew Causey discusses the moment when the double appears and the live actor confronts his or her digital Other. Drawing on Freud's notions of the uncanny and Lacan's theory of the mirror stage, he suggests that this representation of the self outside itself, the witnessing of the self as other:

constitutes the staging of the privileged object of the split subject . . . enacting the subject's annihilation, its nothingness. . . . The ego does not believe in the possibility of its own death. The unconscious thinks it is immortal. The uncanny experience of the double is Death made material. Unavoidable. Present. Screened.[76]

As Freud conceptualizes the double as both a symbol of immortality and "the uncanny harbinger of death,"[77] Causey's understanding of the power of the performer's double is revealed, first and foremost, as a *memento mori*. For Causey, the uncanny "screening" of the (split) subject constitutes death's materialization on stage, just as Barthes theorized the Photographic image as a type of primitive theater of the dead:

If Photography seems to me closer to the Theater, it is by way of a singular intermediary (and perhaps I am the only one who sees it): by way of Death. We know the original relation of the theater and the cult of the Dead: the first actors separated themselves from the community by playing the role of the Dead: to make oneself up was to designate oneself as a body simultaneously living and dead. . . . Now it is the same relation which I find in the Photograph; however "lifelike" we strive to make it (and this frenzy to be lifelike can only be our mythic denial of an apprehension of death), Photography is a kind of primitive theater, a kind of *Tableau Vivant*, a figuration of the motionless and made-up face beneath which we see the dead.[78]

Causey returns to his *memento mori* theme again in a later article where he presents a chilling image of the performer's double as cadaver: "to see one's self is to demolish oneself in an autopsy of perception."[79] Drawing on *Cinema I* (1986), where Deleuze's discussion of the three varieties of film's "movement-image" ends with "death, immobility, blackness,"[80] Causey conceptualizes the performer's confrontation with their double as "the quest for disappearance . . . a quest for otherness."[81] Causey's reading of the modern, high-tech double as a symbol of death can be related back both to the Narcissus myth at the center of our first example, *Liquid Views* (Narcissus languished and died through his self-hypnotic gaze on his reflection) and to ancient and primitive beliefs. In *The Golden Bough*, Frazer recounts numerous examples of cultural fears associated with seeing one's reflection in water. In ancient India and Greece it was a maxim never to look into still water, and to dream of seeing one's reflection was considered an omen of death. The Zulus dare not look into a dark pool for fear that a malevolent water spirit may capture the reflection, and the Basutos believe that a crocodile has the power to kill a man by dragging his reflection under water.[82]

These ancient beliefs cast a sinister shadow over the digital double and our fascinations with mediatized reflections. While Artaud pronounces the double as theater's spiritual becoming and writers such as Ascott conceive the technological double in terms of transcendental metaphysics, others point to its dark menace and terminal nature. As we discuss in detail later in relation to cyborgs, scientists such as Kevin Warwick, Ollivier Dyens, and Rodney A. Brooks[83] predict that technological progress will culminate in the ultimate triumph of the double—in the replacement of humans by intelligent machines. If this proves to be the case, the beautiful and psychologically compelling depictions of the human double within digital performance may not simply be reflections, alter-egos, spiritual emanations, and mannequins, but dark sirens beckoning us seductively to the same mesmerized paralysis and ultimate death that was Narcissus's fate.

Robots

I want to be a machine. I think everybody should be a machine.
—ANDY WARHOL

Introduction

The use of robots in performance constitutes one of the most technologically advanced developments within digital performance. Where early-twentieth-century futurist, constructivist, and Bauhaus actors and dancers donned metallic costumes and used mechanical and robotic movements, in the late twentieth century robots themselves took the stage to dance, act, and perform. Robots enact epic battles for Survival Research Laboratories, ecological parables for Amorphic Robot Works, and sex for the Seemen Group. They work alongside actors in the Ullanta performance group's scripted dramas, and in Adrienne Wortzel's pageantry theater productions such as *Sayonara Diorama* (1998). A theater-opera about Darwin and evolution, it includes projections from live webcams around the world, as well as from cameras attached to remote controlled robots that patrol the stage. Camera-carrying robots roam alongside performers in Void's *2 Minutes of Bliss* (1995) where they project composite images of humans and robots; and Ken Feingold's *OU* robot (1992) acts as a gallery fortune-teller, answering questions about the future.[1] Performing robots have become major attractions at Disneyland and other commercial theme parks; and they are becoming increasingly employed in commercial theater, for example, a $45,000 animatronic raven shared top billing alongside popular British drag artist Lily Savage in a pantomine version of *Snow White and the Seven Dwarfs* (2002) in Manchester.

As the robot has emerged as an increasingly important presence within digital performance, so too have depictions of the part-human, part-machine figure of the cyborg, epitomized in the work of Stelarc, and also explored by artists and companies such as Marcel.lí Anthúnez Roca, Electronic Dance Theatre, and Guillermo Gómez-Peña. The cyborg is a figure that has traversed from science fiction literature and cinema to become a prominent feature of contemporary research science and critical theory. Chris Hables Gray's popular academic reader *The Cyborg Handbook* (1995) contains forty-three essays on the subject including Manfred Clynes and Nathan S. Klines's 1960 essay "Cyborgs and Space," which coined the term. A scientific treatise on possible "biochemical, physiological, and electronic modifications of man's existing modus vivendi" to counter the problems encountered by astronauts in space, it describes cyborgs as "self-regulating man-machine systems."[2] Gray's reader boasts an array of primarily enthusiastic articles on the cyborg's social, political, scientific, and philosophical implications. Most pay some homage to Donna Haraway, whose name is totally synonymous with cyborg theory (very few writers in the field fail to cite her), and whose landmark text "A Cyborg Manifesto" (1985) we discuss later.

Metal Performance and the Aesthetics of Camp

In our examination of this area of digital performance, we will analyze robot and cyborg performances in separate chapters, but therein also discuss them together using the generic term *metal performance* in order to draw out key concepts, themes, and theories that we believe unite them. While there has been a proliferation of discourses on the impacts of new media technologies on arts and culture, little has been written in relation to metal both as the embodying hardware for these technologies, and as signifier of the cyborg and robot. Predating electronic media by many centuries, manufactured metal has been at least as significant an "extension of man," to use Marshall McLuhan's famous metaphor for media:[3] from early tools and weapons, to early industrial machinery, to the automobile and modern high-tech appliances. Within the terms of McLuhan's argument, metal like media has indelibly shaped and transformed humans even as humans have shaped and fashioned metal. In *Metal and Flesh* (2001), Ollivier Dyens suggests,

Technologies are our extensions, not only sensory and nervous, not only prosthetic and mechanical, but also ontological. . . . Technologies are an osmosis, the intelligent matter that inseminates and intertwines itself into the human.

We are no longer merely entangled with machines, no longer simply soldered to their existence; we literally coevolve with them. We must now perceive of technology and human beings as one entity. We are machines and the machine is within us. The machine breathes.[4]

We argue that metal performance belies deep-seated fears and fascinations associated with machinic embodiments, and that these are explored by artists in relation to two distinct themes: the humanization of machines and the dehumanization (or "machinization") of humans. We also demonstrate how metal performances frequently dramatize a return to nature and the animal, and to representations of *theranthropes*[5] (human-animal hybrids) that recall the gods and demons of folk legends and Greek mythology. Donna Haraway's essay "The Actors Are Cyborg" (1991) explores notions of the cyborg as a performative "monster" and "boundary creature"; and Canadian artists Norman White and Laura Kikauka's performance *Them Fuckin' Robots* (1988) features two robots that violently and comedically copulate. Themes concerning the monstrous, the transgressive, the violent, the sexual, and the humorous have each been applied to cyborgs and mechanical anthropomorphic figures. To these we would like to add our own term, *metallic camp*, which reflects a particular ideology and aesthetic at play within metal performance.

One of our central arguments posits that the robot and cyborg body in performance is commonly depicted in ways that closely correspond to the politics and aesthetics of camp. In proposing the hypothesis that metal performance is often camp, or at least manifests itself in a way that fits easily within discourses of camp, we would emphasize points made by three of camp's most prominent theorists: first, Susan Sontag's assertion that camp can be both deliberate and accidental;[6] second, Richard Dyer's contention, that camp can be both gay and straight;[7] and third, Fabio Cleto's assertion that camp should not be seen as a negative or derogatory term, unlike, for example, the term "kitsch."[8] In our use of the term "metallic camp," the word "metallic" denotes not only the physical substance that the artists employ, but also its contemporary connotations within popular music and culture as signifying loud, aggressive, and resistant expression. This is juxtaposed with the knowing irony and pleasure of camp, which Susan Sontag defined as "love of the un-natural: of artifice and exaggeration."[9] The composite expression "metallic camp" further suggests a distinct place or ideological grouping (as in a base camp or the antiwar camp) where people share a position or affinity. In metal performance, this relates equally to a common resistance to, and a common belief in, metal as symbolic of a desirable evolutionary process via cyborgism to ultimate machinic embodiment.

We would stress that we do not consider *all* metal performance to be camp. Survival Research Laboratories, for example, creates extremely butch robot battle performances waged by darkly surreal machines: combinations of dead animals, junkyard scrap, and industrial and construction-site debris animated into life. Monstrous robots wage war in deafening, explosive displays, shrouded in smoke and flames. But even in these brutal, crowd-pleasing battles, some elements of camp are apparent. Leonardo da Vinci's painting of the Last Supper is parodied with the disciples as camp, life-size moving mannequins, which are stabbed and decapitated by one robot, and then shot into flames by another. A large, kitsch clown's head, dangling in the air with a happy grin, receives similar treatment.

Robots are not ipso facto camp: for example, robotic industrial assembly lines, smart weapons, and some robotic artworks perform computer-controlled tasks without a hint of camp irony or behavioral exaggeration. But some degree of camp seems inherent in almost all performing anthropomorphic and zoomorphic robots we have seen. Their movements are one key to this. Since robots currently fail to mimic human and animal movement accurately, their exaggerated gaits and gestures emphasize the same sense of theatricality and artificiality in movement that we find in camp. The artificiality of robot movement mirrors the artificiality of camp. Robotics artist Bruce Cannon has reflected that "these machines' failure to transcend their artificiality is their most significant aspect. The pieces are not so much lifelike as referential to being, and what is missing is what resonates to me."[10]

Robotic movement mimics and exaggerates but never achieves the human, just as camp movement mimics and exaggerates, but never achieves womanhood. Robot kinetics involves the same degree of performative self-consciousness as "camping about," and often visually resembles it. When an anthropomorphic robot moves or when a person camps about, it is highly calculated and coded (however ingrained and natural the human camp behavior may have become). Although robots may not yet be self-aware, they are quintessentially self-conscious entities, calculating and computing their every move. When a humanoid robot moves, just as when someone camps about, it is a knowing and self-conscious performance; its coding, artificiality, and difference from the norm is emphasized. Camp thus becomes a central, even determining aspect of anthropomorphic robot performance.

Sexualizing the Machine

For Norman White and Laura Kikauka's 1988 performance *Them Fuckin' Robots*, the artists agreed on some technical specifications and then worked separately to create two mechanical robots. Kikauka's "female" machine included bedsprings, fur, a sewing machine treadle, a squirting oil pump, and a boiling kettle; White's anthropomorphic "male" robot comprised metal arms and legs, gauges, assorted rotating or pumping appendages, and rapidly flickering addenda. The artists came together on the day of the first performance and assembled the joint artwork in front of the audience, connecting different pipes, pistons, and mechanical parts from one robot to the other. The robots were then activated and proceeded to "have sex," the male machine responding to the female organ's magnetic fields, which increased its movement rates and charged a capacitor. The robots performed to the accompaniment of a comic, cheesy organ soundtrack punctuated by a robotic voice incanting the words "abnormal sex behavior." According to one audience member, it was "a fun performance . . . pretty absurd stuff."[11] A videotape shows an apparently delighted promenade audience smiling broadly at the pumping metal pistons and laughing raucously at a climax comprising exploding electrical sparks and gooey fluid oozing out of one of the robot's tubes in intermittent spurts.

The pun within the phrase "them fuckin' robots" holds significance for the consideration of the contemporary context of metal performance. Beyond denoting the literal sense of copulation, it plays on the increasingly suspicious or hostile human stance toward robots as a threat and as Other: a shout of bigotry against a hated minority. In its depiction of sexual activity, the performance presents a parody of the humanization of machines. At the same time there is recognition of the possibility of some kind of future robotic procreation. As Bernard de Fontenelle maintains, "put a Dog Machine and a Bitch Machine side by side, and eventually a third little machine will be the result."[12]

Them Fuckin' Robots explicitly encapsulates what Claudia Springer identifies as our contemporary fascination with the conjunction of technology and sexuality.[13] These quirky and humorous fornicating machines also perfectly embody the performance of metallic camp, evoking what Britton has described as one the defining features of gay camp: "the thrill of something wrong."[14] Robot copulation features strongly in the work of The Seemen robotic performance group, which constructs monstrous metal creatures that do battle, often amid raging fires. The company suggests that the robots "poetically symbolize man's struggles and triumphs,"[15] while the flames are metaphors for a range of ideas, from purification to rivers and waterfalls, and male ejaculation. Performances feature "trees armed with flamethrowers, underwater sea monsters spitting fire from watery depths, flaming robots fucking, fighting and lovemaking."[16] The sex acts between robots in performances such as *Violent Machines Perform Acts of Love* (1998) are often presented as caring and loving, their tender movements emphasizing the machines' humanization.

In Istvan Kantor's *Executive Machinery Intercourse* (1999) another loud, extreme, and sexualized metallic camp performance is played out. Filing cabinets fill the space, their drawers pulled open and banged shut by different metal-armed hydraulic constructions, creating a cacophony of metallic noise. Kantor describes the mise-en-scène as follows: "The . . . monolithic file cabinet machines are linked together by computers and integrated into a giant network that functions as both kinesonic machinery and an interactive monument serving the entire world with information."[17]

This metal monument to global information is then, in true camp style, well and truly fucked. A number of filing cabinets stand alone, their drawers pumping out automatically without the aid of external machine arm devices (figure 12.1). As the pneumatic drawers shoot in and out, live male and female performers writhe and gyrate against them in a display of determined and often violent eroticism; simulating high-energy sex with insistent, hard pelvic thrusts. Audience members are also invited to join in. The metal information monuments then fuck back, faster and faster. It is a true meat-and-metal cybernetic system of stimulus and response, data exchanges and feedback.

A line of four video projections (each running the same image) fills the back cyclorama, playing frantically speeded up 1950s-style black-and-white prerecorded footage of performers engaged in machine sex. A young woman dressed like Marilyn Monroe with blonde wig and a *Seven Year Itch*–style white dress gyrates against the relentlessly thrusting drawers, panting orgasmically; an office secretary fucks the cabinets enthusiastically while conducting an intermittent and furious row with her boss. The performance juxtaposes a bacchanalian orgy with a Kafkaesque nightmare of the office machine gone mad. It shares with *Them Fuckin' Robots* a delight in "comic pornography," which Cleto identifies as a common characteristic of camp within queer aesthetics,[18] and what David

Figure 12.1 A performer interacts with the thrusting drawers of two pneumatically controlled filing cabinets in Istvan Kantor's *Executive Machinery Intercourse* (1999).

Bergman terms camp's "self-conscious eroticism that throws into question the naturalization of desire."[19]

The pneumatic filing cabinets are more athletic than the human performers: they are fitter machines. But the human copulatory movements emphasize the fluid anatomies and sensual choreographies of the human body in contrast to the rigid straight lines and sexually unsophisticated in-out action of the cabinet drawers. The performance manifests the difference between soft, sensual, impulsive, and easily exhausted flesh and hard, repetitive, robotic metal. It also emphasizes the link between "the sculptural system of the file cabinet [and] the mutating human body, eroticized and abused by technology"[20] (figure 12.2).

The Machinization of Humans and the Humanization of Machines

The sexual themes of *Them Fuckin' Robots* and *Executive Machinery Intercourse* articulate two closely related contemporary anxieties around the "unnatural coition" between humans and machines. These center first on the increasing humanization of machines, and second on the gradual *de*humanization of humans in the face of technology. These two forces are seen as prompting humans toward a gradual evolution *into* machines and metallic embodiments by virtue of their increasing faith in, affinity with, and psychophysical transformation by machines. This second concept of the dehumanization of humans may therefore

Figure 12.2 Sexualizing the office information machine in Kantor's *Executive Machinery Intercourse* (1999).

also be expressed as the mechanization of humans. But, given the negative connotations of the word "mechanization" in relation to people (suggesting a zombie-like workforce performing repetitive actions), we will use the term *machinization*, since cyborgic metal is (in theory) intended to sensitize and expand human physical and mental capabilities rather than to desensitize and reduce them.

As early as 1954, Norbert Wiener proposed a radical machinization of humans, suggesting that "we have modified our environment so radically that we must now modify ourselves in order to exist in this new environment."[21] In his earlier ground-breaking work *Cybernetics* (1948), Wiener also considered at length the humanization of machines, maintaining that the question of whether machines could be considered to be alive or not was largely semantic. For Wiener, machines were alive because they were physically animate and operationally active. The idea of human transformation into metal reaches its logical conclusion with Hans Moravec's assertion that by the middle of the twenty-first century it will be possible to download one's entire consciousness into a computer.[22] In *The Universal Robot* (1991), Moravec dramatizes this notion into a Frankensteinian surgical operation where the contents of the brain are physically removed from the human head to be implanted into their new metal box:

In a final, disoriented step the surgeon lifts its hand. Your suddenly abandoned body dies. For a moment you experience only quiet and dark. . . . Your perspective has shifted . . . [and] reconnected to a shiny new body of the style, colour and material of your choice. Your metamorphosis is complete.[23]

Moravec suggests that humans can either "adopt the fabulous mechanisms of robots, thus becoming robots themselves, or they can retire into obscurity."[24] Metal performance reflects this techno-zeitgeist, which senses a gradual but inevitable merging of flesh and metal. There are thus two routes to the robot, which are perceived as operating simultaneously: one via AI, building artificial intelligent, sentient beings; the other through cyborgism, adapting the human form to a supposedly superior robotic and computational physiognomy. The camp aesthetics that we associate with metallic performance derive equally from artists who largely affirm and embrace such metamorphoses, and from those who are skeptical or oppositional.

Performances by the proponents of flesh and metal symbiosis can be sited frequently within the aesthetics of camp by virtue of their theatrical and computational codes of high artifice and excess, and through their celebration of "monstrous" transgression. Robotic and cyborgic embodiments relate perfectly to the camp sensibility, particularly in relation to gay camp, which distinguishes and celebrates difference and otherness as a coded or blatant affront to straight society's notions of what is subversive or alien to the norm. Richard Dyer, for example, describes camp as "thorns in the flesh of straight society."[25] While expressions of opposition to the mainstream characterizes many avant-garde forms, the use of camp as an aesthetic device in metal performance is quite specific to its particular form of transgressive rhetoric, what Mark Dery calls its "rituals of resistance."[26]

Camp preens and shows off; it uses narcissism to define and express its ontology of difference, and to draw attention to itself. It exaggerates physical and vocal expression to "stand out," the meaning of one of its various etymological origins, the Italian verb *campeggiare*.[27] Its French root, *se camper*, translates as "self-conscious posturing,"[28] while its Indo-European origin, *kamp*, reflects the physical shapes and movements of camp's postures: curved, flexible, articulated.[29] Jack Babuscio argues that an ironic "perception of incongruity" is at camp's core,[30] and a sense of the incongruous (or for some critics, the monstrous) characterizes many robot and cyborg performances. Gay camp is also a "fuck you" stance, sticking a finger up at the conformist social performance of normative male heterosexuality, and ridiculing machismo posturing. It registers membership of an exclusive, even superior club. Just as the cyborg signifies an advanced or evolved form of the human, a metamorphosis that separates it from the crowd, so too males who camp about register and display to the outside world that they have undergone their own specific evolution. They have developed, among other things, an understanding of their feminine side, ironic wit, aesthetic sensibility, and sexual self-knowledge.

Andrew Britton discusses how effeminate camp, through its woman-identification, has been linked to an antipatriarchal, socialist, feminist discourse. Metal performance can equally be conceptualized as a radical camping of difference that queers and lays challenge to dominant biological and human hegemony. Where the camp gay man rejects normative masculinity as an oppressive construct, robots and cyborgic performers demonstrate their own "sense of perversity in relation to bourgeois norms,"[31] and deviation from the restrictive, dominant, human form.

Metal performances by artists resistant to, or skeptical of, the biometallic fusion utilize similar camp high theatrics, and, additionally harness the self-parodic, barbed humor of camp to point at the inherent comedy, absurdity, and danger of metallic embodiments. The latter approach is evident in Brian Frisk's *Wearerobots.com* website,[32] which features animations of robots with human temperaments and emotions. The machines' similarities with humans and their struggle with their feelings is darkly comic; Sad Robot grapples with his sense of identity, wailing that "some people don't even know I'm a robot, they think I'm Puerto Rican, but just really good at math." The robots betray human aspirations, but more particularly human emotional weaknesses and failings. One depressed robot pours out his heart in group therapy; another becomes increasingly furious during a telephone call when only humans are available to speak to: "It's impossible to get through to a machine these days!" he curses. The robots also transgress human protocols by directly speaking their minds, like Angrybot, a schoolteacher who tells his students that their homework is to go home and kill themselves.

The animations express deep-seated anxieties about the humanization of machines. They point to the recognition that as technology advances there is a gradual diminution of the differences between human and machine. Robots become more humanlike through developments in Artificial Intelligence, and humans become more robotlike as they grow more alienated and remote from their own and others' humanity through their increasing reliance upon technology. As Ralph Waldo Emerson reflected nearly a century and a half ago, "the machine unmans the user."[33] New York-based Japanese performance artist Momoyo Torimitsu's robot *Miyata Jiro* (2001) encapsulates both the humanization of machines and the machinization of humans. *Miyata Jiro* is a realistic, life-sized, balding businessman that crawls on its belly along the streets of the financial districts of major cities, while Torimitsu walks behind and tends it, dressed as a nurse. A satirical commentary on the humiliating conformity of Japanese salaryman culture, the robot presents a cowed and hyperrealistic counterpoint to the camp heroic excesses of many robot performances. Fears of enslavement associated with dystopian predictions of machines superseding human beings are short-circuited in a stark and parodic reversal. In replacing the human form, *Miyata Jiro* merely serves to expose the degree to which human beings are already on their knees and enslaved to cultural conformity, the work ethic, and capital.

The medical sustenance to the humanized machine provided by Torimitsu's caring nurse character is elaborated in Eduardo Kac and Ed Bennett's *A-Positive* (1997), where the dual notions of human machinization and robot humanization are even more starkly depicted. Kac is connected to a robot through an intravenous needle, and actually "feeds" the robot (or "biobot") with blood, which flows visibly through a clear tube connecting the human body and the machine. The robot extracts oxygen from the blood and uses it to sustain a tiny and erratic flame, while reciprocating the fluid exchange and completing the sense of human-machine symbiosis by sending an intravenous drip of dextrose into the human body. The visual symbolism mixes medical imagery, cybernetics, and Gothic horror

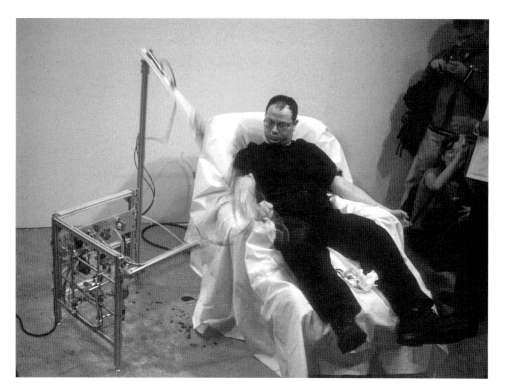

Figure 12.3 Blood, cybernetics, and Gothic horror meet as Eduardo Kac connects up with a machine in *A-Positive* (1997, with Ed Bennett). Photo: Courtesy of Julia Friedman Gallery.

(figure 12.3). The piece is calm and understated but distinctly unsettling. It is at once a peaceful and uncomplicated image of body-machine connection, literalizing a circular biological life flow between human flesh and metal robot, but it also conjures vividly the dark, fearful myths of Frankenstein and Dracula. Flesh is penetrated to give succor to the nonhuman, "undead" machine, and human oxygen is breathed into it to give it life. The machine is directly humanized, pumped by corporeal fluid, while the human body beside it is machinized, its own lifeblood invaded and fed by technology.[34]

Increasingly, both medical science and arts practices imbricate flesh with machine technologies, and it is pertinent to note in relation to *A-Positive* the words of an early heart transplant patient in 1969, who reflected on both the wonder and the significant psychophilosophical anxiety involved in his operation:

Seeing my blood outside of my body running through coils of synthetic tubing is deeply distressing . . . [a] miraculous . . . powerful monster . . . with an almost frightening hold on my life . . . reducing me to a "half-robot, half-man."[35]

Robotics is now making an important impact within medical surgery, where robotic arms such as *Robodoc*[36] are used to make precision bone incisions. NASA, eager to demonstrate that their space hardware research has implications closer to home, has funded and collaborated on a number of robotic surgical appliances. These include the Automated Endoscopic System for Optimal Positioning (AESOP), developed by Computer Motions Inc., a robotic arm whose precision exceeds human dexterity. Using AESOP's intelligent voice-recognition system, the human surgeon controls all the robot endoscope's movements and operation by simply talking to it. Robots known as "Nursebots," which can monitor and dispense medication and detect emergencies such as falls using video recognition systems, are being developed by researchers at Carnegie Mellon and Pittsburgh universities to act as carers in the homes of elderly and disabled people.[37]

A Short History of Robots and Automata

Although the word *robot* has been used to describe many machines and mechanical devices that are not computer controlled, stricter definitions place computational operation to the fore. Ken Goldberg broadly defines a robot as "a mechanism controlled by a computer,"[38] and Eduardo Kac maintains that "robots are advanced computer-controlled electromechanical appliances."[39] The Czech word *robota*, variously translated as "work," "serf," or "forced labor," was adopted in the English-speaking world as "robot" directly through the title of Karel Capek's 1921 expressionist play *R.U.R.* (*Rossum's Universal Robots*). The play concerns the supplanting of humans by robots, and it has been widely discussed both as a warning against Frankensteinian scientific hubris and as an allegory of the 1917 Bolshevik revolution, with the oppressed masses recast as robots. Its story presents an early and potent theatrical vision of the humanization of machines. On an island factory, hyperintelligent worker-robots are developed. They eventually rebel and take over, murdering their inventors and calling for the destruction of all humankind. In the final act, the celibate robots fear they will die out, and Alquist, the only human they have spared, prays to God, pleading that if there are no humans left anywhere in the world, the robot, as "the shadow of man" should be able to survive and procreate. The play ends with a young male and female robot developing caring and sexual feelings for one another as Alquist declares, "Go, Adam, go, Eve. The world is yours. . . . At least the shadow of man!"

R.U.R. sends complex and mixed messages about the humanization of machines. The robots are first presented as the unjustly oppressed, then as the unfeeling, evil oppressors, and finally as the sensitive, empathetic heroes and heroines of the piece, offering a vicarious or deferred salvation for humanity.

Contemporary robot artworks and performances have a long historical lineage which Bruce Mazlish relates back to the Hermetic story of creation, where "man is given permission . . . to create and animate artificial beings . . . or, in my terms, machines." Mazlish notes that throughout history automata have prompted fears, since they pose "an

Robots

'irrational' threat to humans, calling into question their identity, sexuality (the basis of creation?), and powers of domination."[40] Rodney A. Brooks notes the pneumatically operated automata of Hero of Alexandria around 100 CE,[41] and Jeff Cook quotes Pindar from 520 BCE:

The animated figures stand
Adorning every street
And seem to breathe in stone, or
Move their marble feet.[42]

Max von Boehn dates the first anthropomorphic automata back to the third century BCE and suggests evidence that small automata existed in Aristotle's time, citing his reference in *Physics* to a silver doll that moved like a living being.[43] Joseph Needham describes a vast array of mechanical figures, animals, birds, and fishes constructed in ancient China, as well as mechanized chariots and a flying automaton that he dates circa 380 BCE.[44]

The first clockwork automata were constructed in the fourteenth century, and clocks with automated figures became common on European cathedrals including "crowing cocks, bears that shook heads, a king who turned a sand-glass, and the twelve apostles moving in a circle."[45] Bowing royal figures were common features, including three kings at Strasbourg Cathedral (1352) and seven bowing princes who passed before an automaton of Emperor Charles IV at twelve o'clock at the Marienkapelle in Nürnberg (1361).[46] The clocktower at Soleure, built in 1452, "depicts a warrior beating his chest on the quarter-hours, while a skeleton clutching an arrow turns his head to the soldier on the first stroke of each hour."[47] In 1509, Leonardo da Vinci constructed a lion that could walk; a sixteenth-century automaton from Brittany performed a mechanical crucifixion scene; and during the seventeenth century, *karakuri* automata performed the tea-serving ceremony in Japan.

During the eighteenth century a number of European "master" automata craftsmen emerged, such as Jacques de Vaucanson, who built a robot duck that could waddle, quack, eat, drink, and defecate; and father and son Pierre and Henri Louis Jacquet-Droz, who constructed figures that could draw and play the piano. A female organ player, also by the Jacquet-Droz family, "simulated breathing and gaze direction, looking at the audience, her hands and the music,"[48] and their boy automaton *The Scribe* (1772) sat at a desk dipping a quill into an inkpot and writing, among other things, Descartes' declaration "I think, therefore I am." Michel Foucault argues that the sophisticated automata of the eighteenth century were not simply animated illustrations of organisms, but more importantly "political puppets, small-scale models of power." He points out that Frederick the Great, "the meticulous king of small machines, well trained regiments and long exercises, was obsessed by them."[49]

In 1807, Napoleon was defeated in a game of chess by an automated player dressed as a Turkish sorcerer and smoking a hookah, although its moves were decided by a man concealed in the box on which the figure sat, who viewed the board through a system of mirrors.[50] Built by Wolfgang de Kempelen in 1769, the automaton is described by Mark Sussman as "a dramaturgical hybrid of theatre, magic, and science,"[51] and was invoked by Walter Benjamin as an allegory of the mythical "wish-image," symbolizing a historical materialist thrust that reifies progress yet conceals its inner workings. The "little hunchback, who was an expert chess player," sits hidden within the machine conjuring a type of magic like an alternative "theology, which today, as we know, is wizened and has to keep out of sight."[52] In recent years, Artificial Intelligence has replaced the concealed human expert in the box, and in February 1996 IBM's "Deep Blue" became the first chess supercomputer to defeat the grand master Gary Kasparov over a six-game series. In passing, we would note that Hal Eager, technical director of eminent digital performance company The Gertrude Stein Repertory Theatre, designed the 3D chess set for the original webcast of the match. Deep Blue, a computer the size of an old main-frame and running 220 chips in parallel, each capable of calculating two million possible chess moves per second, finally fulfilled the potential suggested by Claude Shannon in his 1949 paper "Programming a Computer for Playing Chess." It prompted Kasparov to reflect, "If a computer can beat the World Champion, a computer can read the best books in the world, can write the best plays, and can know everything about history and people."[53] Deep Blue team leader C. J. Tan talked of "an historical event . . . [that] will help us further develop our system to serve mankind,"[54] while others such as Daniel King drew more sinister conclusions, noting the resonance with the fictional supercomputer HAL in *2001: A Space Odyssey* (1968), which defeats the captain of the space ship in a game of chess before taking control of the craft. "The message was clear," says King, "the machines were taking over."[55]

In his 1948 exposition of cybernetics, Norbert Wiener reflected at length on the history of the automaton as a simulacrum that reflects both the technology and the ideology of its age:

This desire to produce and study automata has always been expressed in terms of the living technique of the age. In the days of magic, we have the bizarre and sinister concept of the Golem, that figure of clay into which the Rabbi of Prague breathed life. . . . In the time of Newton, the automaton becomes the clockwork music box, with the little effigies pirouetting stiffly on top. In the nineteenth century, the automaton is a glorified heat engine, burning some combustible fuel instead of the glycogen of human muscles. Finally, the present automaton opens doors by means of photocells, or points guns to a place at which a radar beam picks up an airplane, or computes the solution of a differential equation.[56]

As well as the latter "intelligent" robotic systems Wiener highlights, the twentieth century also saw the emergence of notable "performing" robots and mechanical automata.

Enormous excitement was generated at the 1939 New York World's Fair following performances by a humanoid automaton, *Elektro, the Moto-Man* and his mechanical dog *Sparko*, despite them being little more "than a bunch of gears and motors capable of doing simple movements."[57] Twenty-five years later, the New York World's Fair hosted the first appearance of one of the most famous and celebrated performing anthropomorphic robots, Disney's "Audio-Animatronic" figure of Abraham Lincoln (1964). The Lincoln robot, which became the star attraction at Disneyland the following year, was the most advanced anthropomorphic figure of its time, and was decidedly, if unintentionally, camp; America's sixteenth president stood up to deliver a monologue composed of edited highlights from patriotic speeches in a high-pitched, mechanical voice. The Lincoln robot, which features as the finale of a part film, part live performance *Great Moments with Mr. Lincoln* (1965), has continued as a major Disneyland attraction ever since, and was redesigned and upgraded in 2003.

Walt Disney was personally fascinated by automata, and in the 1950s bought a one hundred-year-old automaton of a bird in a gilded cage, which proved the inspiration for Disneyland's first audio-animatronic attraction: a collection of singing birds that filled the Enchanted Tiki Room, which was opened in 1963. Disney's Imagineer technologists have continued to develop sophisticated and often kitsch or camp performing anthropomorphic and zoomorphic robots ever since, from Disney characters and sword fighting pirates to their most recent high-tech creation, *Lucky* (2003). Disney's first walk-alone animatronic character, *Lucky* is a nine-foot-tall and twelve-foot-long green dinosaur with a propensity to hiccups, designed to roam and intelligently interact with visitors.

Robot Art in the 1960s

In the same year that the audio-animatronic Lincoln made its first appearance, Nam June Paik and Shuya Abe created *Robot K-456* (1964), a life-size, twenty-channel remote-control female humanoid that walked through the New York streets. It flapped its arms, excreted beans, and played John F. Kennedy's inaugural address through a speaker in its mouth. A dynamic, humorous, and camp creation with a large square head and "junkyard" body parts including toy airplane propeller eyes and rotating Styrofoam breasts, Eduardo Kac suggests it is more a "caricature of humanity" than "a cause of fear (of lost jobs, of erased identity)."[58] In 1982, *Robot K-456* was involved in a staged accident when it was hit by an automobile as it ventured off the sidewalk in a performance entitled *The First Catastrophe of the Twenty-First Century*.

A notable precursor to robotic art was Jean Tinguely and Billy Klüver's *Homage to New York* (1960), an electrically triggered, self-activating, self-destructing machine conceived, as Tinguely put it, "out of total anarchy and freedom."[59] A large Heath Robinson–esque construction made up of a piano, numerous bicycle wheels, bottles, junkyard parts, and a large rotating roll of paper, its shrapnel-spraying destruction in a twenty-seven minute, one-off performance in New York was an example of Tinguely's aim to "be static with movement."[60] While some critics interpreted the piece as "an expression of nihilism and despair,"[61] Klüver insists it was a metaphor for a new and changing world: "Jean's machine destroyed itself as a representation of a moment of our lives. *L'art éphemère* creates a direct connection between creation and destruction and forces us into direct contact with an ever-changing sense of reality."[62]

But whatever the contrasting critical positions taken over *Homage to New York*, as Logan Hill puts it, for multimedia artists the machine's explosion was "heard around the world."[63] It is important to note that like many machine and robot artworks since, this early piece placed a sense of humor firmly at its core. Despite the shocked reaction it aroused in some art critics, it also elicited wide smiles and laughter from many in the audience.[64] It had a distinct sense of the ridiculous; and it was funny. Eccentric or malfunctioning machines have long been the source of comedy in science fiction, popular films, and cartoons, and they continue to be treated with a wonderful sense of irony in many robot artworks. Humor is used to point out the pomposity and fallibility of machines, but may also represent a tactic to deflect humanity's ultimate mistrust and fear of them: we make fun of those in power—of the strong, not of the weak. As Tinguely's machine rejected itself, it became a sort of Guy Fawkes celebration. It became, like New York, a brash, beautiful and intoxicating expression of "humor and poetry."[65]

Robotic art developed slowly but significantly during the 1960s alongside interactive kinetic sculptures by artists such as James Seawright, whose *Searcher* (1966) and *Watcher* (1966) moved and emitted different sound patterns in response to movements and light changes going on around them. Seawright's work featured in the 1968 *Cybernetic Serendipity* exhibition, which included a number of robots and kinetic sculptures considered marvels of their time. Edward Ihnatowicz's *SAM (Sound Activated Mobile*, 1968), for example, was "the first moving sculpture which moved directly and recognisably in response to what was going on around it."[66] A vertebral construction with a flowerlike head, it used miniature hydraulic pistons to twist, turn, and move in the direction of visitors' sounds. Reflecting back on the *Cybernetic Serendipity* exhibition thirty years later, however, Mitchell Whitelaw reminds us that these early art machines act "as a quaint, slightly humorous reminder of the humble origins of the field: daggy plotter graphics, clunky lights and sounds, crude sensing 'robots' . . . a caricature of late-sixties science-dag."[67]

Japanese Commercial Robots

In recent years, Japan has been the focus for some of the most advanced anthropomorphic robotic developments, and it is important to note that there are significant cultural differences in perceptions of the robot in the East and in the West. Popular attitudes towards robotics are highly enthusiastic in Japan, in part as a result of a cultural history of positive images such as Mighty Atom (known as Astro Boy in the U.S.), an iconic cartoon robot of the 1950s and '60s. Japanese robotic artist Kenji Yanobe is one of many to discuss the differing East-West attitudes to robots, also noting the more recent cute and friendly robots depicted in *manga* comics.[68] In the West, by contrast, the robot more commonly has been perceived as a threat, both to jobs and to human beings themselves. Literary and cinematic fiction is filled with robots who turn on their makers or run amok, including HAL in *2001: A Space Odyssey* (1968), the robot played by Yul Brynner in *Westworld* (1973), and the replicants in *Blade Runner* (1982). This may be one reason why commercial "performing" anthropomorphic robots and robot pets first appeared in Japan rather than the United States or Europe. In recent years a number of sophisticated Japanese robots have caught the public imagination, and in 2002, Robodex, the world's largest robot exhibition in Yokohama, Southwest of Tokyo, brought together ninety different robots. These included a troupe of Seiko Epson's miniature *Monsieur II-P*, which performed a robot ballet, and Sony's latest entertainment robots, *SRD-4X* which, according to a BBC report "wowed the crowds with their dancing performances." Zoomorphic robots for domestic use included Sanyo's robot guard dog and Tmsuk's *Banryu*, a $14,000 home-security robot dinosaur, which walks around the house detecting intruders or smoke, whereupon it contacts the emergency services and owner. But the highlight of the exhibition was Honda's *Asimo*, the world's most advanced humanoid robot in 2002.

Asimo can walk forward or backward, climb stairs, and make turns as it walks (previous robots had to stop before they could turn). The four-foot-high humanoid is a smaller version of Honda's P3 robot, and has six degrees of freedom on each limb, incorporates twenty-six servo motors, and moves and walks with remarkable balance and smoothness. It also has a photographic memory, remembering everyone to whom it is introduced, and addressing them by name on subsequent meetings. *Asimo* has become a celebrated robot performer, appearing in television advertisements, amusement parks, and high-tech stage shows during a long North American educational tour of science museums and institutions from 2003–4. In Japan's Fukuoka Dome Stadium in 2002, *Asimo* played soccer in one of 188 robot teams from twenty-nine countries competing in RoboCup 2002. Coinciding with soccer's human World Cup, robot five-a-side teams played twenty-minute games in the knockout tournament, most of which were drawn at full time, and were decided on penalty shootouts.

While *Asimo* is designed with a classic 1950s-style vision of a "metal-man," with robot body and astronaut-helmet head, anthropomorphic realism is developing rapidly in research centers such at the Tokyo Science University. Fumio Hara has created female humanoid robot faces made of translucent silicone rubber, which can approximate human expression changes using a range of systems and materials, including "Shape Memory Metals."[69]

As we discuss in detail later, zoomorphic figures constitute the most common form of performing robot within the visual and performance arts, and have also proved highly popular, if expensive, within the commercial sector. The most famous of these, Sony's metallic dog *AIBO* (1999) (from the Japanese word for "buddy") cost around $3,000 on its release and sold out on its first day. Its LED eyes shine contented green or angry red, and in addition to barking, walking, rolling over, and sleeping, an internal video camera enables it to "see" and sense its environment so as to respond to people or animals within it. Omron's limited edition robot cat *NeCoRo* (2001) cost $1,300, and its design ignored the ability to walk in favor of sophisticated "emotional feedback" using tactile sensors to respond to its owners' touch with movements, facial expressions, forty-eight different feline sounds, and fur that expands and contracts.

Robotic doll toys have also been developed, including *My Real Baby* (2000), a collaborative venture between MIT roboticist Rodney A. Brooks and manufacturer Hasbro. With a range of sensors and actuators, as well as AI features, the baby can learn and repeat simple phrases and respond to stimuli by changing facial expression, laughing, crying, and sucking on its bottle.[70] Artists and performers such as Paul Granjon and Z Lab have reflected on the growing interest in robotics within toys and pet substitutes. In performances they incorporate robots such as *Toutou*, "a singing and swinging dog" and *Robot Tamagotchi*, "a fluffy robot that needs care."[71] Lynn Hershman Leeson's *Tillie the Telerobotic Doll* (1995) is a moving doll with two cameras in place of eyes. The left eye sees in color and shows her view on a small monitor within a gallery space, whilst the right eye relays black and white images to the Internet. Leeson suggests that by seeing the world through Tillie's eyes "viewers not only become voyeurs, but also virtual 'cyborgs' . . . whose virtual reach and in this case sight, are extended beyond physical location."[72]

Sociable Robots

Simon Penny's robot artwork *Petit Mal* (1995) takes its name from neurology, meaning "an epileptic condition, a short lapse of consciousness,"[73] and its inspiration from artificial-life technologies. According to Stephen Wilson, it is "a landmark attempt to create robots with genuine autonomy."[74] The robot is visually unimpressive—a thin, three-foot-high robot mounted on bicycle wheels—but its intelligent behavior and fluid dance-like movements are sophisticated as it pursues and engages visitors in subtle physical interactions. Penny's goal was to create the first truly autonomous robot artwork, which possessed charm and wit, and which was "neither anthropomorphic nor zoomorphic, but . . . unique to its physical and electronic nature."[75] In his paper "Embodied Cultural Agents" he describes *Petit Mal* as "the construction of a seemingly sentient and social machine from minimal components, the generation of an agent interface utilising purely kinesthetic or somatosensory modes which "speak the language of the body" and bypasses textual, verbal, or iconic signs."[76] In its subtle interactions and physical "conversations" with visitors, *Petit Mal* highlights the humanization of the machine, not in its physical form, but in its evolved, artificially intelligent behavior. The robot becomes a new form of social being, a creature of charm, sensitivity, and kinesthetic intelligence, able to act and respond autonomously in relation to people and situations around it.

Figure 12.4 Robots are born out of and inhabit a moving, inflatable landscape in Amorphic Robot Works' *The Ancestral Path through the Amorphic Landscape* (2000).

Charm and sociability characterize many of the robots of Amorphic Robot Works, directed by San Francisco robotics artist Chico McMurtrie. The promenade performance *The Ancestral Path Through the Amorphic Landscape* (2000) features some sixty digitally controlled humanoid and animal robot figures ranging from about two feet to over thirty feet high. They emerge from a vast hydraulically inflated landscape from where many are "birthed," tearing through and rising up from inside the fabric and rubber surface. During the performance the landscape grows robotic trees, expands, contracts, and changes shape, creating hills, mountains, and caverns for the robots to move through and inhabit (figure 12.4).

The performance is a loud, chaotic, and magical metal menagerie. Some robots are powerful and godlike figures; some are sinister hybrid animal creatures, such as the "dog-monkeys" that patrol the space; and others are comic, camp and dysfunctional caricatures of humans. Small, sticklike anthropomorphic robots shake and scuttle around a cave complete with waterfall, their metal penises rotating through 360 degrees. Skeletal metal figures perform acrobatics, play kettledrums and beat bongos, and frantically draw charcoal scribble pictures on canvas. Benign, gangly humanoids wobble and amble around comically, while others climb up and down ropes, surveying the scene below (figure 12.5).

The humanization of the robot is emphasized skillfully through the robots' distinctly human personalities, foibles, and failings. One robot fails to catch a ball, and its frustration leads to animated gestures of annoyance, which leads to flailing-limbed anger, which finally leads to what appears to be the very human act of male masturbation. The robots appear and disappear, communicate and interact, and play vibrant and complex percussion "symphonies" together, mixing African drums, xylophones, and industrial noise. But also, they fail, and then fail again, and again; like the Tumbling Man, a heavy, life-size humanoid robot made of thick metal piping and powered by compressed air, which repeatedly performs forward rolls in an ultimately vain attempt to stand up. Here, the company presents a Beckettian aesthetics of anthropomorphic robot impotence and failure (figure 12.6).

McMurtrie describes how the robots' actions "depict the most primal aspects of the human condition: elegant, strong and threatening and at the same time, weak and

Figure 12.5 Some of the hybrid robot creatures featured in *The Ancestral Path through the Amorphic Landscape* (2000).

pathetic. . . . They form a unique and vulnerable society, affected by technology, and the environment in which they are placed."[77] *The Ancestral Path Through the Amorphic Landscape* is an ecological fable, a humanist statement, and a robotic performance tour de force that transfixes audiences. Its great charm and humor, its empathetic force, and its emotional power come not only from the sophistication of the robots, but also from their idiosyncratic personalities, which are drawn from acute observation of human quirks and foibles. The company's computer systems designer and programmer, Rick Sayre, suggests that the machines are "less like industrial robots and more like puppets. . . . Their puppetlike quality makes them harder to control, but it also makes you empathize with them because they appear to be struggling."[78] As Jason Spingarn-Koff points out, most of the robots are "benign, even cute. . . . The machines' earthly qualities—organic form, movement, music—are most exceptional. The fact that these machines possess such vivid, living sensibilities is amazing and frightening."[79] McMurtrie describes the performance

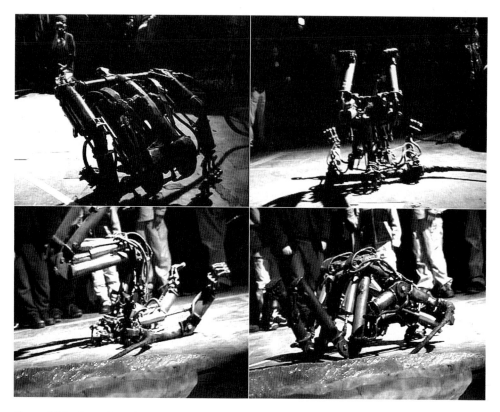

Figure 12.6 Amorphic Robot Works' Tumbling Man repeatedly rolls over in a vain, Beckettian attempt to stand up.

as "a study of the human condition in sculpture and in movement,"[80] and company tour director Mark Ruch reflects:

As there is beauty and elegance in movement itself, there is equally potent experience in watching a machine (human or organic in form), struggling to stand, attempting to throw a rock, or playing a drum. These primal activities, when executed by machines, evoke a deep and sometimes emotional reaction. It is the universality of emotional experience which intrigues us, and it is the contrapuntal use of machines as artistic medium and organic movement as form which, perhaps ironically, combine to provoke these reactions most readily.[81]

Amorphic Robot Works' performances extend and "make flesh" early avant-garde experiments around the image of the mechanized body, from Foregger's machinic *tafia-trenage* dance training and Meyerhold's robotic biomechanic movements to Schlemmer's

Bauhaus performances and Gordon Craig's call for the replacement of the actor by the Übermarionette. Margaret Morse has reflected how robots come to resemble their creators, and how their creators see themselves in them.[82] This certainly appears true in McMurtrie's case, who has names for each of his sixty robots, such as String Body, Metal Mother, Neolithic Pneumatic Drummer, Horny Skeleton, and Drumming and Drawing Sub-human. When we spent a day filming the performance and interviewing him for the Digital Performance Archive, he treated the robots like human progeny, constantly concerned for their health and temperament, and offering them what we can only describe as unconditional maternal love and care.

The idea of anthropomorphic robots being a form of male procreation has been put forward by Jeff Cook, who describes a "patriarchal dream of parthenogenesis" that escapes the "the indeterminate and unreasonable realm" of flesh, nature, and the feminine."[83] He reflects that there has been surprisingly little commentary on the notion of male procreation at play within developments in artificial intelligence, artificial life and robotics. Cook also correlates the male creation of anthropomorphic robots with making the invisible (specified as "the obscure, the female, and natural") visible. Interestingly, this metaphor has been used commonly in relation to theater performance since the 1960s, following Peter Brook's call in *The Empty Space* for a "Theatre of the Invisible—Made—Visible". Brook adds, "the notion that the stage is a place where the invisible can appear has a deep hold on our thoughts."[84]

Robotic Returns to Nature

Many writers have emphasized that nature and machines are close allies rather than opposing forces,[85] and the close link between technology and flora and fauna has been explored in robot artworks such as Ken Rinaldo's *Technology Recapitulates Pylogeny* (1992) and *The Flock* (1993); and Ken Goldberg's *The Telegarden* (1995) where Internet users control a telerobot (a robot controlled at a distance) to plant seeds, and to water and tend a real garden. Eduardo Kac created a telerobotic macaw in *Rara Avis* (1996) whose view was controlled by gallery visitors wearing VR headsets (figures 12.7 and 12.8). and reimagined the legends behind the beautiful Amazonian bird the *Uirapuru* (1999) to create a telerobotic flying fish that hovers above a flock of "pingbirds" perched on twenty artificial trees, their authentic Amazonian birdsongs oscillating in relation to the "pings" of Internet traffic. For Bob Roger's film *Ballet Robotique* (1982), assembly line industrial robots were programmed to dance in relation to the animal and plant movements of chickens, cats, and seaweed. A sleek, all-metal bucking bull machine stripped of its usual fairground black-skin is the centerpiece of Curious.com and Desperate Optimists' performance *BULL* (1999), and includes an erotic sequence where Helen Paris lies on her back, grasping the machine's handle between her legs as she gently "rides" its slow, arching undulations. James Seawright's robotic artworks such as *Electronic Garden 2* (1983) and *House Plants* (1984) feature computer-controlled robotic flowers that

Figure 12.7 A gallery visitor controls Eduardo Kac's telerobotic macaw in *Rara Avis* (1996).

"suggest the possibility of a harmonious integration between humans, nature and technology, as well as poeticising responsive electronics in an analogy with ornamental plants."[86]

Artists also use robotic representations of flora and fauna to perform their deaths or extinction, in cautionary dramas warning of ecological disaster. Chico McMurtrie and Rick Sayre's gallery installation *The Trees are Walking* (1991) features pneumatically powered, motion-detecting trees constructed of rusting metal, as though eroded by acid rain. In

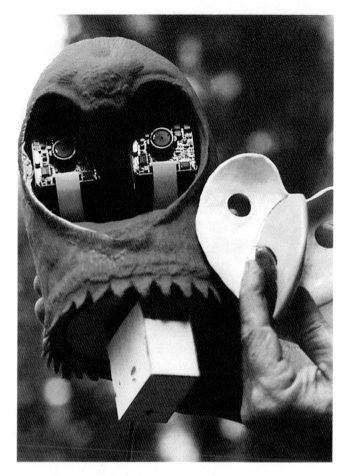

Figure 12.8 The internal workings of the *Rara Avis* robot macaw.

direct response to the footfalls of spectators, the gnarled constructions walk deadly slowly and move their limbs eerily, as though choked by pollution. For Bruce Cannon and Paul Stout's *Tree Time* (1998), a tree that had been struck by lightening was fitted with robotic extensions on its branches in order to "reanimate" it. The stark and leafless, seven-limbed tree looks like a typical centerpiece for a stage set of Beckett's *Waiting for Godot* (1956), but is covered with cables that run up its trunk like artificial arteries, and metallic wires sprout from its dead and blackened branches. Its movements are deathly slow and almost imperceptible, and Cannon describes the piece as "equal parts meditation on slowness and bastardization of nature."[87] He reflects on the equal "beauty and obscenity of the endeavour" and its intentional references to Mary Shelley's Frankenstein: the tree evokes ideas of electrification, technological interventions into organisms, "garish reassembly," and reanimation.

In his book *Mind Children: The Future of Robot and Human Intelligence* (1988), Hans Moravec suggests that future super-intelligent robots will not be made in humanoid form, but will take their hardware design from flora to appear as ferns and bushes with a trillion delicate, tendril-like limbs. "A bush robot would be a marvel of surrealism to behold," he writes, possessing "enormous sensitivity to its environment" and capable of watching a movie "by walking its fingers along the film as it screamed by at high speed."[88]

Zoomorphic Robots

Zoomorphic robots have been a staple within metal performance, and the first computer-controlled robot artwork, Edward Ihnatowicz's *The Senster* (1971) took its form from the animal kingdom. A large, fifteen-foot-long metal construction like a lobster's claw, it moved toward still and quiet observers and shrank back from loud or animated ones. The observers' movements and sounds were monitored by motion detectors and microphones and fed into a digital Philips minicomputer, which processed the data and activated the robot's kinetic responses. Zoomorphic robot performances often present ecological messages as seen, for example, in Amorphic Robot Works' events, and in Brett Goldstone's *Bird Land* (1990). *Bird Land* is set in a Los Angeles parking lot against a mural background depicting rock formations composed of petrified human corpses. Large, skinny mutant bird robots, ingeniously crafted entirely from recycled Dumpster junk, roam a contaminated "postapocalyptic wasteland" flapping their steam-powered wings, pecking at garbage and eating tin cans. A pair of spindly, disembodied legs move storklike across a pool of water, then fall and twitch in death throes as gallons of oil turn the water jet black.[89]

Other notable zoomorphic performances include a collaborative animal robot project, *Zoo des Robots*, that was exhibited in Paris between 1986 and 1991; and Joe Davis's solar powered *Desert Crawler* (1986) robot slowly roamed the desert making animal-like tracks in the sand. Matt Heckert's hybrid insect-horse-bird *The Walk-and-Peck Machine* (1985, with Survival Research Laboratories), moved on beetle-like legs and spiked wheels, attacking other robots with its bird beak. Louis-Philippe Demers and Bill Vorn's *At the Edge of Chaos* (1995) involved four robots that fight like animals over a metal cube as if it were a piece of meat.[90] A robot head and a twenty-centimeter-high moving and singing robot dog called Toutou share the stage with French director/ performer Paul Granjon in Z Productions' *The Z Lab Presents* (1998). Adopting deliberately low-tech robotic aesthetics (the two robots are controlled by a 1982 BBC microcomputer with 32 K of RAM) the dog sings "La Chanson de Toutou" and accompanies Granjon in a finale remix rendition of Kraftwerk's techno-classic *We are Robots* (1975). Humorous low-tech robots created for Z Lab's video series *2 Minutes of Experimentation and*

Entertainment (1996–98) include "shitBot: the dog shit destroyer robot," "the cybernetic parrot sausage," and "the little square fish"—an exoskeleton with an electric propeller containing some fish extracted from a Marseilles fish burger, which was "set free" in the Mediterranean Sea.

Two opposing ideologies operate in metal performance's recurrent theme of the return to nature and the animal. One rages at the inherent blasphemy: portraying or satirizing the robotic body's sinister and alien relationship to the natural, and stimulating the types of psychological fears that Sigmund Freud discusses in relation to automata as symbols of the uncanny.[91] The other emphasizes the metal body's kinship with nature, as a creature born of the natural evolutionary process. David Rothenberg describes how technology "imitates nature in its matter of operation, but completes what nature alone has only hinted at . . . [it] represents the human penchant to go beyond nature, completing our place in the natural world."[92] In these terms, the metal body simultaneously imitates and reaches beyond the natural world, signifying a new and dominant survival-of-the-fittest figure, using (or abusing) the laws of natural evolution to complete the Darwinian project. The first futurist manifesto of 1909 equated an automobile with a shark, celebrated the machine as a new animal form, and declared that in the man-machine union "We're about to see the Centaur's birth."[93] The "becoming animal" of the metal body resonates both with Descartes' much-contested theory of the soulless animal-automaton,[94] and with Donna Haraway's notion of the cyborg as a creature transgressing "the boundary between human and animal" which is unafraid of its "joint kinship with animals and machines."[95]

Artificial Animals

New, quasi-organic zoomorphic forms have evolved through artists' experiments with artificial life (A-life) technologies, including Yves Kline's sculptures *Scorpiobot* (1992) and *Lady Bug* (1993), which can organically replicate themselves and change their forms. Richard Brown creates part-zoomorphic, part-abstract life-forms in pieces such as *Neural Net Starfish* (1999) and *Biotica* (2000), where users' arm movements propel them through a virtual world, in "a visceral and immersive 3D experience of evolving, responsive, and abstract artificial life forms."[96] A-life interactive projects by Christa Sommerer and Laurent Mignneau use fish and plant forms; and Jane Prophet creates fascinating zoomorphic creatures for her interactive web projects.[97] For Louis Bec, A-life signals "a marked tension between the living and the technologically created near-living . . . [which] traverses the scientific, artistic, and technological domains in all their diversity, evolutions, and mutations." He suggests that A-life constitutes a type of ancient, primeval tremor which "compels recognition of the 'pro-creation' of techno-biodiversity as a fundamental mode of human expression."[98] Bec's artwork involves the creation of digital models, holograms, and interactive systems depicting strange artificial creatures, which often combine plantlike or amoebalike bodies with animal-esque heads. Ken Rinaldo's influential paper "Technology Recapitulates Phylogeny" (1998) suggests that emerging A-life technologies represent the future for interactive artforms, whereby participants can

> develop true relationships with the computer that go beyond the hackneyed replicable paths of 'interactivity' which have thus far been presented by the arts community. . . . Interactivity may indeed come into its full splendor, as the computer and its attendant machine will be able to evolve relationships with each viewer individually and the (inter) part of interactivity will really acknowledge the viewer/participant. This may finally be a cybernetic ballet of experience, with the computer/machine and viewer/participant in a grand dance of one sensing and responding to the other.[99]

Meanwhile, the Critical Art Ensemble and artists such as Oron Catts and Ionat Zurr are directly exploring genetics and organic tissue engineering in biotech art experiments. Natalie Jeremijenko cloned a hundred genetically identical trees for her *OneTrees* (2000) artwork, which were later planted in various public locations. The most celebrated and controversial example is Eduardo Kac's *GFP Bunny* (2000), a real rabbit that was genetically adapted with "green florescent protein" (GFP) to glow green in certain lighting conditions (figure 12.9). As Jay Bolter and Diane Gromala point out, "The rabbit poses questions about the limits of art, the relationship of art to science, and the layers of cultural contexts that are wrapped around any artifact, especially a living being, that is claimed to be art."[100]

The biblical book of Genesis tells the story of how God created man to have domination over fish, fowl, and animals (Milan Kundera has joked how "of course, Genesis was written by a man, not by a horse").[101] In the Middle Ages, Christianity gradually effected a break with the animal, with depictions of the devil reflecting "his kinship with the satyrs and sileni of antiquity."[102] The contemporary human urge to return to the animal reflects a postmodern consciousness that senses a denaturing, a spiritual erosion, and a loss of the real in the face of technology. Ironically, both in Donna Haraway's seminal discourse on cyborgism and in metal performance, technology is seen as a route to reestablish human connections with nature and the animal. As Don Ihde argues in *Technology and the Lifeworld: From Garden to Earth* (1990), there is a double attraction to both technology and nature within contemporary postmodern society.

Frankenstein Robots

But the juxtaposition of robots and real animals in metal performance has also created fearful and macabre images of cruelty and violence. A robot decapitated frozen pigeons in Mark Pauline's *Machine Sex* (1979), and Chris Csikszentmihalyi's *Species Substitute* (1996) brought together live ants and a robot that systematically fed them and then killed them. Conjunctions between animals and machines, in effect creating contemporary

Figure 12.9 Eduardo Kac with his controversial genetically adapted pet *GFP Bunny* (2000). Photo: Courtesy of Julia Friedman Gallery.

metal-animal "mythical creatures," have similarly produced disquieting results. For *Rabot* (1981), Pauline attached a robot exoskeleton to a dead rabbit to produce a sinister hybrid robot-rabbit which walked backward; and in *Piggly-Wiggly* (with Monte Cazzaza, 1981) he mounted a cow's head and pig's feet and skin onto a metallic creature.

Further grotesque metal and dead animal combinations featured in the first performance by Pauline's Survival Research Laboratories company, *A Cruel and Relentless Plot to Pervert the Flesh of Beasts to Unholy Uses* (1982). These included a "Mummy-Go-Round" carousel of mummified, dissected animals, and a part metal, part dog-cadaver robot mounted on a remote-controlled cart. The dog-robot lunged around the space, its jaws set open in a fierce snarl and its whole dog head spinning in circles on a spindle neck "in ghoulish imitation of cartoon violence."[103] Pauline suggests the use of dissected dead animals reminds his audiences of "the delicacy of the human form turned inside out" and ensures they do not consume his performances as they would the fake gore of Hollywood or Disney-style mechanical puppet shows.[104]

Pieces of pig skin, hand sewn with wide stitches around its joints, cover the metal exoskeleton of Sergi Jordà and Marcel.lí Antúnez Roca's robot *JoAn, l'Home de Carn* (JoAn the Flesh Man, 1992). A naked humanoid figure with a large flaccid penis and wide eyes staring through a Zorro-style half-mask, its grotesque patchwork body of pigskin pieces stitched at each joint recalls popular cinema images of Frankenstein's monster. It is interesting to note that Mary Shelley's original novel *Frankenstein, or the Modern Prometheus* (1818), the precursor of numerous novels and films about artificial or robotic beings, is said to have been inspired by a nineteenth century message-writing clockwork-human automaton.[105] Although Frankenstein is part of a long lineage of mythic creation narratives such as Pygmalion, Prometheus, and the Golem, as Catherine Waldby points out, "what distinguishes Frankenstein from these earlier narratives is that the life conferred on the figure is generated through technical instruments and scientific procedures."[106]

In medical research focused on hybrid brain-machine interfaces to enable paralyzed patients to control computer cursors and interfaces through their brain waves, neurobiologist Miguel Nicholelis has developed neural implants that he has tested by insertion into animal brains. In a series of experiments, an owl monkey known as Belle transmitted neural signals to a robot that translated the data in real time to imitate the monkey's arm movements. In complementary research at Northwestern University in Evanston, the living brain of a lamprey, an eel-like fish, was suspended in salt water and connected to a robot. The brain activated the robot's movements towards light sources, mirroring the fish's behavior in its natural habitat. Marie O'Mahony observes that "as an added twist to the scientist's choice of fish, the lamprey is a vampire."[107] Within feminist techno-theory, Sandy Stone, Donna Haraway, and Sarah Kember have each promoted the image of the patriarchal vampire as central to the convergence of machines and humans.[108] For Kember, the vampire represents the unconscious masculinist fear and desire for the monstrous female other, vampirism:

is the irrational monster myth which is (the stake) at the heart of the supposedly rational convergence of biological and computer sciences. . . . The myth of the vampire exposes the unconscious investments in making biology and technology converge and creating the technological organism.[109]

The vampire acts as a metaphor for "the kind of transformation in knowledge, power and subjectivity which Western rationalist culture articulates only as horror and monstrosity."[110]

War Machines: Survival Research Laboratories

War is beautiful because it initiates the dreamt-of metallization of the human body.
—FILIPPO TOMMASO MARINETTI[111]

Live Robot Wars events became popular in the United States following a live event in San Francisco in August 1994 organized by Mark Thorpe, who describes them as "a unique blend of sport, theater, art, and engineering."[112] The robot battle format spawned popular television series such as the U.S. *BattleBots* around the turn of the millennium, although the aesthetic emphasis tended less towards the art and theater Thorpe discusses, and far more toward the sport—in this case, a type of gladatorial, heavy-metal blood sport. In March 2002, BBC2 Television presenter Craig Charles epitomized the ethos, opening his show with the words, "Welcome to *Robot Wars*. Robots are like rules. They're there to be broken. Smashed. Pulverized into submission."[113] While most of such television series around the world rely on do-it-yourself enthusiasts' modest creations such as converted toy cars and cookie tins, large-scale robot wars are staged live by a number of companies, most famously Mark Pauline's Survival Research Laboratories (SRL).

SRL has conceived "a heavy metal theater of cruelty—scary, stupefyingly loud events in which remote-controlled weaponry, computer-directed robots, and reanimated roadkill do battle in a murk of smoke, flames and greasy fumes."[114] Robots and other giant machines are remote-controlled, teleoperated,[115] or programmed to work autonomously in elaborate, large-scale battle spectaculars, and Pauline emphasizes extremity in his performances, comparing his primary aim with that of a physicist: "to release the most energy in the shortest possible time."[116] In performances such as *The Unexpected Destruction of Elaborately Engineered Artifacts* (1997) and *Fin de Siecle Machine Circus* (1999), Hollywood's apocalyptic, fire-and-explosion fueled vision of robots out-of-control is staged live. Eduardo Kac suggests that:

These robotic spectacles of discomfort, fear and actual destruction are meant as commentaries on . . . ideological control, abuse of force, and technological domination. . . . More than 15 years later, Paik's 1982 staged "accident" can be reconsidered in the context of SRL's work, which gives emphasis to the aesthetic principle of technologies colliding out of human control.[117]

The machines' designs are generally derived either from the animal kingdom: monstrous birds, worms, crabs, insects, and running legs; or from industrial and military models: huge and menacing cannons, tank vehicles, crane structures, and industrial arms. They are created largely from scrap metal and obsolete industrial and construction-site machinery, and are sometimes constructed to include Pauline's trademark dead animal heads and body parts. Machines career through sheets of glass; walking flamethrowers torch wooden buildings; and rocket-firing, surreal tanks and demolition-ball wielding arms reduce constructions to rubble. Dinosaur-like metal monsters destroy each other with chopping jaws and stabbing knives, as crablike robots scuttle for cover. SRL creates contemporary "mythical" robot figures, and mix them with references to ancient ones, like the huge robot Medusa in *A Carnival of Misplaced Devotion: Calculated to Arouse Resentment for the Principles of Order* (1990). A giant head of the snake-haired mythical figure, a copy of Caravaggio's 1590 *Medusa* painting, is backed by a V-1 jet engine, which spews enormous jets of flame from her vengeful, open mouth.

Stephen Wilson points out how "some see his shows as maniacal boys' infatuation with weapons; others see it as a preview of new kinds of mechanical beauty and ritual."[118] Pauline himself describes a counternarrative to military research: "I make weapons to tell stories about weapons. SRL shows are a satire of kill technology, an absurd parody of the military-industrial complex."[119] Manuel De Landa, whose book *War in the Age of Intelligent Machines* (1991) explores future symbiotic man-machine relationships in military research, sees actual danger as a key component of SRL's work:

What Mark does is push things far from equilibrium, to the point of unpredictability. . . . A lot of the experience has to do with the fact that you don't know when these machines are going to attack the audience; the question in everybody's mind is, "Hey, are these guys in control?"[120]

Dery provides an engaging and appropriately adrenaline-filled critique of the uniqueness of SRL's work, noting its notoriety and its influence on cyberpunk culture, from William Gibson's novel *Mona Lisa Overdrive* (1988) to the cult cyberpunk movie *Hardware* (1990). He suggests that Pauline has pioneered

the definitive cyberpunk artform, mechanical spectacle . . . which exemplifies the hybrid of cybernetic and organic, state-of-the-art and street tech that typifies the cyberpunk aesthetic. . . . At their best, SRL performances are motorized exorcisms, shatteringly powerful psychodramas that sit midway between Grand Guignol and *Death Race 2000*, pre-Christian rituals such as the burning of the wicker man and blue collar rituals such as the demolition derby.[121]

Pauline lost three fingers and a thumb in 1982 when a rocket motor he was working on for a performance exploded, and two of his toes were grafted onto his palm in their place. Dery notes the Gothic literary associations of scientist characters with deformed or false hands, and casts Pauline in the same mould: "a rogue technologist [who] challenges the Fates and loses his right hand—the hand that symbolizes logic and rationality . . . a distant relative of Dr. Frankenstein, who only narrowly escaped death at the hands of the monster he created."[122] He goes on to suggest that McLuhan's notion that "technologies are self-amputations of our own organs"[123] fittingly underscores Pauline's philosophy, physiognomy, and performance work.

Although Pauline has referred to television's use of smart-bomb footage in Gulf War I as "the pornography of destruction,"[124] his own boyish enthusiasm for war-toys and explosions are evident in his discussion of a high pressure air-launcher SRL made in the early 1990s. It was operated remotely using a teleoperation system. Wearing a VR head-mounted display providing a stereoscopic view from a camera mounted on the weapon, the operator's head movements are computer-tracked and moves the launcher in whichever direction he looks (the masculine pronoun seems most appropriate here) to line up a target. "The machine fires a beer can filled with concrete, about eighty grams of high explosive, and a contact detonator at about 550 feet per second", says Pauline. "You've got an ergonomic controller . . . there's a cross-hair at your focal point about four feet away and when you line up the target with that, you fire, and it just *obliterates* it."[125] During performances, the green phosphor video imagery of the teleoperator's viewpoint through the "eyes" of the weapon is relayed to the audience on a large projection screen in the outdoor space. The extent to which this draws the audience more into the aggression of the drama, by offering vicarious access to the soldier/weapon's point of view, or rather creates a dislocating Brechtian effect in reminding audiences of Gulf War TV footage, is a moot point. Pauline maintains a belief in "the political potency of the symbolic gesture" and suggests that "any activity which stirs things up is progressive."[126]

In his thoughtful and lengthy analysis of SRL, Dery ultimately supports Pauline's political rhetoric, describing the performances as "a combination of killing field and carnival midway" that undermine military propaganda and "mock the benefits of technological progress, the virtues of consumerism, and the benevolence of corporate America."[127] But we are disinclined to entirely agree, since SRL's work appears to glorify the war machine as much as it mocks it. The performances present a spectacle of the destructive power of machines, but like the chilling three words of Donald Rumsfeld at the start of Gulf War II, the rhetorical force of this "shock and awe" is designed to appeal to rather than to repel the popular imaginary. Cryptically titled performances such as *Illusion of Shameless Abundance: Degenerating into an Uninterrupted Sequence of Hostile Encounters* (1989) and *The Deliberate Evolution of a War Zone: A Parable of Spontaneous Structural Degeneration* (1992) are brutal, crowd-pleasing theatrical battles, and Pauline himself emphasizes that "entertainment value" is his prime consideration.[128] If there is a strong political message, we suspect it is invisible to most spectators amidst the swirling smoke and flame of these visceral, bizarre, and undoubtedly exhilarating robot wars. Whilst Pauline may be justified in defining his work as "a satire of kill technology, an absurd parody of the military-industrial complex,"[129] his satire and parody is ultimately a fairly soft center to the hardcore, heavy-metal hedonism of his robot wars. Dery admits "the apparent contradiction of a social satirist seduced by military-industrial technology,"[130] but is prepared to give Pauline the benefit of the doubt, while others such as Jim Pomeroy are not:

Playing to the pit and dancing on the edge, SRL begs many questions, offers few answers, and moves off the stage leaving smouldering ruins and tinny ears in its smoky wake. SRL is boys' toys from hell, cynically realizing the masculinist fantasies of J.G. Ballard and William Burroughs.[131]

SRL's performances present a vivid realization of the cultural perspectives of Paul Virilio, turning his theory into practice in an explosive theatricalization. Virilio's antinomies of speed (the robots in action) and inertia (the robots immobilized), his aesthetics of disappearance (machines disintegrating before our eyes), and his central metaphor of the postmodern condition as war, fit like a glove with these psychotic, balletic battles of robot machines.

Cyborgs

I should forthwith be disposed to conclude that the wax is known by the act of sight, and not by the intuition of the mind alone, were it not for the analogous instance of human beings passing on in the street below, as observed from a window. In this case I do not fail to say that I see the men themselves, just as I say that I see the wax; and yet what do I see from the window beyond hats and cloaks that might uncover artificial machines, whose motions might be determined by springs? But I judge that there are human beings from these appearances, and thus I comprehend, by the faculty of judgement alone which is in the mind, what I believed I saw with my eyes.
—RENÉ DESCARTES, 1641[1]

The Rise of the Cyborg

Julie Wilson's arresting cyborg costume for Electronic Dance Theatre's solo performance *Cyborg Dreaming* (2000) incorporates Giger-esque ribbed, rubber designs, futuristic metal bands and appendages, a short pleated skirt, and exposed, realistic rubber breasts.[2] Mark Bromwich's custom-made *Bodycoder* system enables Wilson to access and control audio and visual elements in real time with signals sent to computer terminals via radio waves from sensors on her body joints and a dataglove with four switched inputs (figure 13.1).

Rear screen images grow, mutate and spiral to her movements. Abstracted images suggest micro-organisms, bubbles, vegetation and circuit boards, while manipulated film footage shows a group of tribal people slowly reaching out their arms in synchronization with Wilson's outstretching dataglove. Picture-in-picture visual effects are stretched wider or narrower by Wilson's body twists and elevations; graphics whirl; and textual phrases such as "Sudden Visibility of Sound" rotate and fill the screen. Classical dance movements segue into floppy, rag doll actions, and then into heavy, Frankenstein-esque walking, the footfalls prompting deep, sonorous thuds of sound. Complex musical compositions are

Figure 13.1 Julie Wilson in Electronic Dance Theatre's *Cyborg Dreaming* (2000).

kinetically triggered and modulated, from rich, ambient soundscapes and machinic industrial effects, to soaring and resplendent electronic chords.

The *Bodycoder* motion sensing and activating system, like Troika Ranch's *Isadora* and
Palindrome's *EyeCon* we have already discussed, establishes a direct cybernetic connection
between performer and media. But Electronic Dance Theatre's theatrical representation
makes plain the image of a *cyborg* futurism; and unlike Palindrome and Troika Ranch's
costumes, which rarely emphasize gender or particularly distinguish between male and
female dancers, the bare-breasted costume speaks a proud, defiant cyborg-feminism. Sexed
and sexualized, but nonetheless "other," this *Cyborg Dreaming* inhabits a world she can
control, but seems not to fully know. Wilson has reflected how the nature of sensor activated performances disrupt traditional distinctions between, for example, composer and
musician, or set designer and visual kinetic artist. Her discussions around the notion of
"otherness" at play in her work are revealing both about the performer's perspective, and
the very ontology of the cyborg she portrays:

I haven't quite come to terms with what it is that we do, or what it is that I am. I'm not strictly a pure dancer, and I'm not strictly a musician playing somebody else's composition. But I'm something other, and I'm not sure what that is yet. But it's the "something other" which I'm sure is going to be the thing that goes forward into the next [twenty-first] century as defining what the artist, or the performance artist, is.[3]

The notion of a "something other" that is uncertain of its current ontology but senses its future becoming, offers a potent metaphor both for emerging cyborgic performers, and for the figure of the cyborg itself. As Chris Hables Gray emphasizes in his introduction to *The Cyborg Handbook* (1995), there are no clear-cut definitions of the cyborg. Indeed, a familiar and monotonous refrain from writers both within and outside the anthology is that technologies such as pacemakers, telephones, bicycles, automobiles, walking sticks, and spectacles have already rendered us cyborgs—or at least low-tech ones.[4] These writers' ideas echo, but rarely acknowledge McLuhan's 1964 *Understanding Media: The Extensions of Man*, which includes separate chapters on a range of "man's extensions" besides broadcast or film media: clocks, typewriters, telephones, phonographs, and weapons. His analysis of the motorcar is particularly potent in its cyborg imagery: "the mechanical bride . . . an article of dress without which we feel uncertain, unclad and incomplete within the urban compound. . . . It may be true to say that an American is a creature of four wheels."[5]

These ideas, in tandem with postmodern theories of human mediatization, posthumanism, and discourse on the wider impacts of computer technology, biotechnology, and genetic engineering, have led to a very serious critical viewpoint (if not consensus) that, as Donna Haraway most famously declared, we are already cyborgs:

By the late twentieth century, our time, a mythic time, we are all chimeras, theorized and fabricated as hybrids of machine and organism; in short, we are cyborgs. The cyborg is our ontology; it gives us our politics. The cyborg is a condensed image of both imagination and material reality, the two joined centres structuring any possibility of historical transformation.[6]

Haraway's utopic "A Cyborg Manifesto" (1985) is an influential and canonical work, though consciously ambiguous and iconoclastic: written, as she puts it as "an ironic political myth."[7] It is a brilliant, incendiary, and revolutionary socialist-feminist perspective on cyborgism that delights in polemic and paradox, and elsewhere we have written at length about some of the inconsistencies and problems her paradoxes evoke.[8] Ultimately, the question of whether or not we are *already* cyborgs (or the extent to which we are) must rest on individual perceptions, in common with Katherine Hayles's analysis that people become posthuman when they think they are posthuman. A nineteen-year-old computer hacker with multiple body piercings, for example, may consider herself a cyborg, while a ninety-year-old grandmother who never watches television, but wears spectacles, is unlikely to.

Our own view is that cyborgism constitutes a technological response to existential and spiritual uncertainties and crises within late industrial Western societies, symbolizing a human desire for wholeness within an alchemical, technological matrix. It is also a quest to leave the frail and fallible mortal body behind, and to enter an immortal (or at least, endlessly upgradable) machine one. But the burning question remains whether or not it is the Nirvana machine. The cyborg quest may ultimately be the stuff of classical Aristotelian tragedy: the rise of the great "man" cut down by the fatal flaw of hubris and disregard for more powerful forces outside himself—nature, "the gods," human fate, and mortality. When (and if) human bodies are reconfigured with integral cyber-technologies, or when consciousness is transferred to computational organisms (if indeed that is ever possible), there nevertheless remains the acute problems of the fallibility of computers, of cyber-terrorism and of fatal viruses. The mundane fact about twenty-first-century computing is that computers still frequently crash and die (and probably always will), and one can too easily imagine the dark, chilling image of smiling hackers lobotomizing human cyborgs for fun, like it was part of a game.

There are also troubling political and messianic tones in the rhetoric of cyborgism. Kevin Warwick, the self-styled "first human cyborg" describes a new race of "Supermen";[9] and Hugo de Garis, leader of the Starlab project, which in 2001 constructed the world's largest and fastest "artificial brain," talks of "creating a baby" and "building Gods."[10] Moreover, cyborgism's logic of transcendence from human physical and mental vulnerability implies denial and rejection of fundamental elements of what constitutes a human being: frailty, illogicality, mortality, and, arguably, individuality. Humanness is characterized by struggle, by a fragile and uncertain journey fueled by the hope of capturing love, peace, fulfillment, and so on. These only exist in relation to their opposites, and are only experienced as pleasures or ecstasies in relation to dialectical experiences: failure, disappointment, despair. If humans become hyperintelligent and physically matrixed with the totality of cyberspatial information, there may be a consequent negation of the sense of progress towards a purposeful fulfillment that marks human experience. The digital machine may mask its own dualisms of zeros and ones to eliminate the uncertain journey of life and present a fait accompli of Otherness, of attachment to and embodiment within non-struggle: of machinic, programmed, nihilistic acceptance.

Cyborg Realities

As the technology evolved, the helmets shrank, the video terminals atrophied. . .
—WILLIAM GIBSON[11]

In critical theory, as Margaret Morse points out, "the actual status of the cyborg is murky as to whether it is a metaphor, a dreamlike fantasy, and/or a literal being."[12] But the vision of future cyborgism, hailed by some and ridiculed by many, concerns the physical implanting of computer technologies into the body. In the late 1990s, experimental medical

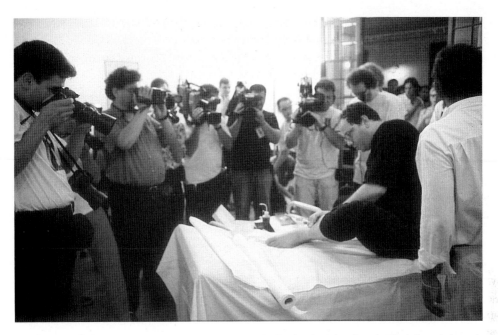

Figure 13.2 Eduardo Kac injects a computer chip into his leg for the sake of art in *Time Capsule* (1997). Photo: Courtesy of Julia Friedman Gallery.

brain-chip implants enabled paralyzed patients to move computer cursors using only their neural processes, and on 11 November 1997, Eduardo Kac became the first person to implant a chip "for art's sake." For *Time Capsule* (1997), in front of an audience of journalists and art-lovers, and broadcast live on television in São Paolo, Brazil, he used a special hypodermic syringe to inject a microchip into his left leg (figure 13.2). Flanked by a medical professional, sepia-toned photographs from the 1930s, and a horizontal bedstead, Kac then placed his leg into a scanner, and a telerobotic finger in Chicago activated the apparatus, which scanned and displayed the microchip's embedded identification number on its Liquid Crystal Display (LCD). Kac then proceeded to go online and register himself as both an animal *and* its owner on a database for pets that had been implanted with similar identification chips.

In his discussion of *Time Capsule*, Kac reflects that whereas memories were formerly the "sacred" domain of the human body, acquired through genetics and personal experiences, "memory today is on a chip." As external memories become implants in the body, *Time Capsule* "forces us to consider the co-presence of lived memories and artificial memories within us. . . . Scanning of the implant remotely via the Web reveals how the connective tissue of the global digital network renders obsolete the skin as a protective boundary demarcating the limits of the body."[13] Kac's notion of the obsolescence of the skin echoes, perhaps deliberately, Stelarc's mantra and home-page slogan "the body is obsolete." But whereas Stelarc's philosophical commitment to cyborgism is absolute (as we will see later), Kac's pioneering work in digital arts, robotics, "biotelematics" (where biological processes are connected to digital networks), and "transgenic art" (genetic engineering of new life forms) explores and deliberately exposes problematic philosophical, political, and ethical issues. In *Time Capsule*, as in his cyborgic *A-Positive* already discussed, Kac presents direct biotechnological conjunctions that probe issues and question understandings, rather than presenting the cyborg in a utopian or dystopian light. He takes an intelligent, cautious, and respectful view of both the human body and machines, and rationally explores their interrelationships within emerging ecosystems.

As we realize how close technology is to the body, or how deep it already is inside the body, we must also grasp that the master/slave model in robotic science is more than just a very unfortunate choice of words. It assumes that machines are slaves . . . [because they] do not have organic life, human-like intelligence, or a will of their own . . . [but] the gaps are being slowly narrowed beyond what we might be willing to admit or perhaps accept. . . . We have always asked what machines can do for us. Now might be the right time to ask what we can do together. We are no more masters of our machines than we are at their mercy.[14]

British cybernetics professor Kevin Warwick is another notable experimenter on his own body, and has successfully implanted a number of much more sophisticated chips. In *Project Cyborg 1.0* (1998) he had a silicon chip implanted that could emit signals to open doors automatically, control lights, and operate computers within his university department in Reading, England (figure 13.3). For *Project Cyborg 2.0* (2002), a more advanced chip, a "one hundred electrode array"[15] was implanted into his lower left arm. After a week monitoring its effects, which were not deemed harmful or problematic, a less complex chip was similarly implanted into the arm of his wife, Irena. The chips had integral power sources and radio tuners/receivers, and were surgically connected to the nerve fibers of their arms. Marie O'Mahony explains how this "gives Warwick the ability to send signals via radio waves and a computer to Irena so that as he moves his fingers he also moves those of his wife. . . . There is also the possibility of communicating emotions, since they, too, stimulate nervous activity."[16] Warwick emphasizes the opportunity for the couple to be able to share feelings and emotions at a distance, including sexual excitement, reflecting that "the implication could be never faking an orgasm again."[17] The sex-at-a-distance potentials of networked cyborgic implants have also been noted enthusiastically by Stelarc in his public lecture/demonstrations, as well as prompting predictable and salacious popular interest within the mass media.

Just five months after the implant on 14 March 2002, Warwick's book about his experience *I Cyborg* (2002) was published, claiming and explaining how he "became the world's first Cyborg in a ground breaking set of scientific experiments."[18] Warwick is an astute

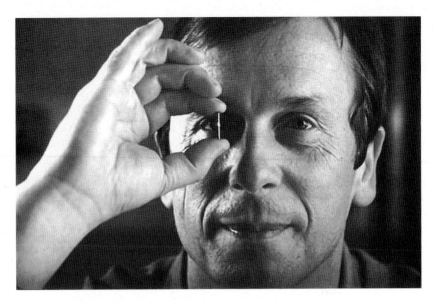

Figure 13.3 Cybernetics Professor Kevin Warwick inspecting the silicon chip transponder that was surgically implanted into his forearm for *Project Cyborg 1.0* (1998).

self-publicist and has courted media attention, becoming something of a scientific celebrity in the United Kingdom. But he has been frequently attacked by academics who have questioned both his scientific and academic abilities, and have refuted his prediction in books such as *March of the Machines: Why the New Race of Robots Will Rule the World* (1997) that robots will inherit the earth. Alan Bundy suggests that the "silliness" of his work misrepresents the whole science of AI, and Inman Harvey calls him "just a buffoon with a good line in hoodwinking the media into thinking what he is doing is cutting-edge science."[19] Part of the criticism derives from his academic record, where most of his published journal papers are in control theory rather than AI, while his books are targeted at a wide and popular readership. Warwick's writing style is direct and uncomplicated, sometimes to the point of bluntness, it includes some arguably tenuous leaps of logical progression, and contains jokes and asides, as seen in his concluding chapter of *March of the Machines*:

The main points of this book can be summarised as follows:

1. We humans are presently the dominant life form on Earth because of our overall intelligence.
2. It is possible for machines to become more intelligent than humans in the reasonably near future.
3. Machines will then become the dominant life form on Earth.

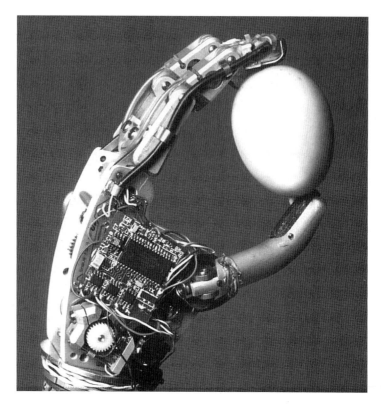

Figure 13.4 For *Project Cyborg 2.0* (2002), Warwick's implanted one hundred electrode ray was used as a neural interface to enable him to control, among other things, an electric wheelchair, and the pictured intelligent artificial hand, developed by Peter Kyberd.

If asked what possibility we have of avoiding point 3, perhaps I can misquote boxing promoter Don King by saying that humans have two chances, slim and a dog's, and Slim is out of town[20] (figure 13.4).

Leander Kahney's "Warwick: Cyborg or Media Doll" (2000) describes how his pessimistic futurism and his reputation as a "media junkie" has made him "a lightning rod for criticism"; and Charles Arthur, reviewing Warwick's *I Cyborg* under the title "Cringe–making world of 'Captain Cyborg'," typifies the levels of vitriol his ideas and writings have evoked:

Cringe-making from start to finish. . . . Please ignore this book. It's badly written and badly edited, though that means you get to see how sloppy some of his thinking is. . . . He is . . . like the freaks who undergo plastic surgery for the fun of it: the Bride of Wildenstein of cybernetics. The last chapter coyly pretends to have been written in 2050, predicting that everyone will be connected to the Net and living in silicon-enhanced nirvana. I'll make a counter-prediction. In 2050, people will still be starving on an indecent scale in Africa, the glaciers will still be melting, and the rich will have got richer. And neither you nor I will be a cyborg.[21]

Cyborg Visions

The fierce contestation and ridicule heaped upon Warwick has also met similar predictions of a cyborgic future offered by Hans Moravec, who foresees us severing our brains from our bodies to rehouse them in machines, and by Rodney A. Brooks, who anticipates a convergence of genetic and robotic technologies, which will alter the human genome in profound ways. In *Robot: The Future of Flesh and Machines* (2002), Brooks suggests that the ability to manipulate our bodies surgically, robotically, and genetically will mean that:

We will have the keys to our own existence. There is no need to worry about mere robots taking over from us. We will be taking over from ourselves with manipulatable body plans and capabilities easily able to match that of any robot. The distinction between us and robots is going to disappear.[22]

Brooks, Moravec, and Warwick's ideas all center on the notion that since computers and AI will soon become more powerful and intelligent than humans, if humans are to survive they will need to become cyborgs and incorporate advanced technologies into their flesh. In the immortal words of Warwick, "if you can't beat 'em, join 'em."[23] But although their predictions are commonly dismissed as paranoid science fiction fantasy, and while we too retain a degree of healthy skepticism, we would note that these individuals are not disconnected philosophers or literary fantasists. Rather than being idle speculators on possible futures, they are scientific researchers who are leading the very development of those futures, at the forefront of practice in cybernetics, robotics, and artificial intelligence. Brooks is director of Artificial Intelligence at MIT and the creator of some of the most advanced robots of the 1980s and '90s; Moravec is a professor at Carnegie Mellon and co-founder of the largest robot research laboratory in the United States; and, whatever doubts have been raised on his academic record, Warwick is a robotics expert and professor of cybernetics who has arguably gone further than anyone to date in cyborgic implant research. So, while commentators outside the field itself may be skeptical about the future of cyborgism, the leading practitioners within the research field are certainly not, and perhaps their words should not be too easily discounted or flippantly dismissed. Using Warwick's blunt *ergo* logic, their perspectives may warrant some careful consideration.

Other leading scientists such as Marvin Minsky lend support to the predictions, and Stephen Hawking, one of the greatest mathematical scientists of our time, has also dramatically added his computer-assisted voice to the debate: "The danger is real that [computer] intelligence will develop and take over the world." He too advocates cyborgic evolution, through genetic manipulation: "We must develop as quickly as possible technologies that make possible a direct connection between brain and computer, so that artificial brains contribute to human intelligence rather than oppose it."[24]

The cyborg, like the robot, arouses fears and fascinations, and radically polarizes scientific and critical thought. While the scientists above warmly embrace the cyborg concept, writers such as Don Ihde warn of its "Faustian bargain."[25] For Paul Virilio, the technologized subject is "dromocratic": media-saturated and, like a cyborg, characterized by speed, and dependent on feedback loops and connection to communicational networks. But this equally symbolizes the impotence of the cyborgic subject, as willing victim of society's predatory war machine: as a body without will, an empty vessel for media consumption, conditioning, and invasion. In *Speed and Politics* (1977), Virilio describes a "multitude of bodies with no souls, living dead, zombies, possessed . . . human cattle,"[26] while Jeff Cook detects

a strange (new?), and possibly Ballardian or Cronenburgian lasciviousness, in proposed and promiscuous couplings and recouplings of machine and "man," . . . an orgy of connection that must spawn mutant and cyborged subjects and subjectivites. . . . It is becoming, through the mythopoesis of art, science and science fiction, a new myth. Whether it is also a harbinger of the future, a cancerous metastases or a protective antibody, remains to be seen . . . like an animating Darwinism, the computer, and now the cyborg, have become elemental to the metaphorical map of our world.[27]

Stelarc

Stelarc is the cyborgic performance artist par excellence. Moreover, if there is one single, powerful image that will remain within the history of early digital performance, we believe it is of Stelarc, his naked body jerking spasmodically and involuntarily in response to electrical impulses sent along the Internet. In a number of different performances during the 1990s, including *Fractal Flesh* (1995) *Ping Body* (1996), and *ParaSite* (1997), Stelarc connected his body via a mass of cables to a computer. Through different interface systems, signals sent via the Internet remotely stimulated muscles in different parts of his body via electrical sensors, activating a startling and macabre physical performance (figure 13.5). For *Fractal Flesh*, audiences in Paris, Helsinki, and Amsterdam simultaneously used touch-screen computers to activate different areas of his body, and in *Ping Body* the live flow of Internet activity was used as stimulation (figure 13.6). During the *ParaSite* performances a customized search engine scanned the Internet retrieving medical and anatomical pictures of the body, then mapped the jpeg images onto his muscles to induce involuntary motions. As the performance took place, Stelarc's movements also fed into a VRML (Virtual Reality Modeling Language) space at the venue, and onto a website. In *ParaSite*, says Stelarc:

Figure 13.5 Stelarc's body is electronically and involuntarily activated by Internet stimulations in *Split Body*. Photo: Igor Andjelic.

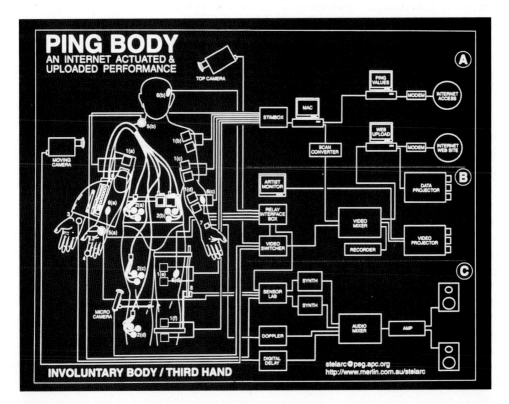

Figure 13.6 Stelarc's diagram of the complex technological connections used for his live performance *Ping Body* (1996).

The cyborged body enters a symbiotic/parasitic relationship with information . . . the body becomes a reactive node in an extended virtual nervous system . . . the body, consuming and consumed by the information stream, becomes enmeshed within an extended symbolic and cyborg system mapped and moved by its search prosthetics.[28]

At a lecture presentation at Nottingham Trent University in 1999 (and since repeated elsewhere), Stelarc took four students from the audience to demonstrate how the remote electronic signals activated his movements. He attached an electrode to a different muscle on each of the students' arms, and proceeded to send a low electrical current to each in turn. The volunteers watched in open-mouthed amazement as each of their arms in turn made a sudden and involuntarily gesture: a half-rotation of the hand; a violent jerk away from the body; a raising of the entire forearm, a large parabolic curve. Stelarc then explained that during his performances he has dozens of such electrodes which constantly counteract and interact with one another in response to the Internet stimulation; as one sends the arm one way, another swings it back in the opposite direction, and yet another tries to resist both, forcing it in a third direction.

During the demonstration, Stelarc wore his robot third arm (custom-built for him in Japan), which is another feature in his Internet-activated performances. This high-tech perspex and metal forearm and hand is attached to his left arm and controlled through muscle activity in different parts of his body to stimulate the appropriate electrodes connected to different parts of the robot arm. In *Handswriting* (1982), he held marker pens in his two real hands and one robot hand and coordinated his movements for the three hands to write the word EVOLUTION onto glass (figure 13.7). The robot arm also features in *Stimbod* (1994) and *Scanning Robot/Automatic Arm* (1995), where he again "dances" in response to electronic stimuli in a duet with a giant, yellow industrial arm with a mounted camera that relays its swirling view of Stelarc to video and computer monitors around the space. Lit theatrically by flashing neon floor striplights, Stelarc wears no clothes, only an array of cyborgic appendages: a curved, cagelike neck ruff; head goggles that shoot out intermittent, powerful beams of light; and an array of body electrodes attached to a matrix of cables (figure 13.8).

Stelarc is fascinated with the meeting of "meat and metal" that symbolizes the cyborg. In contemporary culture, this meat and metal symbiosis can be observed in a range of phenomena, from popular cinema (*Robocop*, *Terminator*) to the late twentieth-century trends in body piercing; and the modification of the body by technology has been present in Stelarc's work since he began as an artist. At art school in the 1960s, his very first piece of work involved making helmets and goggles that split binocular vision, seeking to plunge the wearer into an immersive environment. Between 1973 and 1975 he made three films with the use of a miniature camera probe that he inserted into his body and manipulated to explore the interior of his stomach, intestine, and lungs.

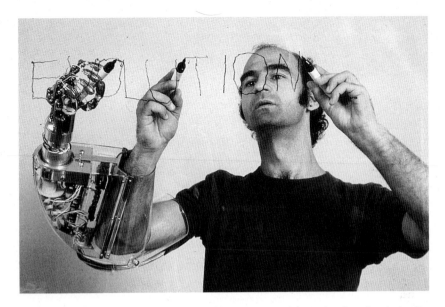

Figure 13.7 Stelarc expresses his cyborg *raison d'etre* in one word, but using three hands simultaneously. Photo: K. Oki.

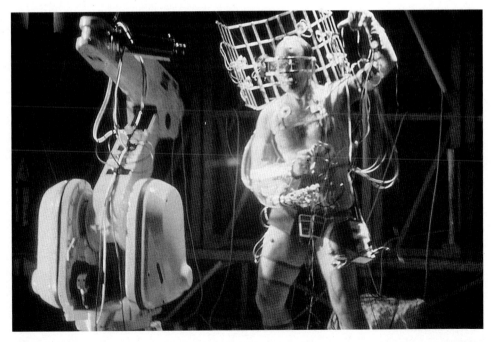

Figure 13.8 Stelarc dances with a camera-mounted industrial robot in *Scanning Robot/Automatic Arm* (1995). Photo: M. Burton.

Figure 13.9 Suspended by hooks, Stelarc hangs beneath a monorail station in Ofuna, Japan, sporting his perspex "third hand." Photo: S. Hunter.

In the late 1970s Stelarc achieved considerable fame and notoriety for a large number of painful performances in which metal hooks were inserted into his skin. These were attached to cables or ropes from the ceiling (or from cranes in outdoor performances), and his naked body was then hoisted up via pulleys attached to the hooks, leaving him suspended in space (figure 13.9). Notable examples include the Tokyo gallery performance *Sitting/Swaying Event for Rock Suspension* (1980) where he sat cross-legged in midair, counterbalanced by a ring of hanging rocks, and his *City Suspension* (1985) where a crane hoisted him high above Copenhagen city center. Video footage of the performance reveals the quite extraordinary sight of Stelarc's spread-eagled body rising and circling, suspended in space two hundred feet high, looking down to earth like a cross between the flying *Superman* and a heavenly apparition.

The Obsolete Body

Stelarc discusses the body as "absent" or "obsolete," by which he means a body full of physiological limitations, unable to compete with the comparative power and speed of technology. He sees new media technologies as both alien and superior to our own body's biological and neurological capabilities. In McLuhanite tone he maintains that "the most significant planetary pressure is no longer the gravitational pull but rather the information thrust. . . . Information propels the body beyond itself and . . . fashions the form and function of the postevolutionary body."[29] But this stance does not lead him to strategies toward or artistic expressions of disembodiment, just as in the 1970s he firmly refuted those critics who misinterpreted his hook and cable "suspension" pieces as spiritual or shamanistic rituals aimed at a transcendental representation of the body. He is equally cynical of popularized cyber-notions of the Internet as a site for disembodiment, observing that the body is not physically plugged into the system. Furthermore, the mass of cables, satellites, and computers render the Internet "a very inefficient strategy for disembodiment, if it is one."[30]

So rather than seek ways in which the body can transcend its corporeality by the use of technology, Stelarc is concerned to develop ways in which the body can be extended and modified so that it can physically incorporate technology and effectively function within electronic worlds and spaces. This reverses conventional metaphors and views of a disembodied body operating in virtual space. In Stelarc's version, the body does not leap out and float serenely in cyberspace; it demands instead that the matrix of cyberspace be brought into the body, in order to advance and reconfigure its corporeal physiology and ontology.

Despite numerous critics' views to the contrary, this is not a simplistic cyborgian image. Stelarc makes a distinction between the popularized cinematic or medical image of the cyborg, where (as in the film *Robocop*) the body has been modified with metallic parts and organs in order to keep it alive, and a cyborg system whereby the body's operational functions are electronically connected and enhanced. He has also discussed the notion that through artificial intelligence, one's virtual body may be able to become increasingly autonomous, arguing that "the realm of the post-human may very well reside not in the realm of the cyborg, but in the realm of intelligent images."[31]

Stelarc is a highly controversial but seminal figure in the development of technological performance. He divides critics and arouses angry reaction from those who consider that he takes the genre of body art to dehumanizing extremes. In his Internet-stimulated work in the late 1990s, the dehumanization and machinization of the body by technology is taken to extremes, with Stelarc's body reduced to little more than an empty shell; a human cadaver to be jerked like a puppet in some macabre human-computer game. Josephine Anstey describes these performances as masochistic and fascinated by lack of control, and wonders "how much fear of, or distaste for, the body drives this cyborg quest."[32] Richard Restrak views them as "extreme, narcissistic fantasies of complete isolation" and maintains there is "a lot of self-hate in this objectification of the body, a lot of estrangement."[33] Johannes Birringer describes the pieces as "pathetic rituals," arguing that "the body in this conceptual theater is like the denigrated and increasingly useless 'meat' in cyberpunk fiction";[34] and Stelarc himself has declared that "the hollow body would be a better host for technological components."[35] Stelarc's objectification of his body is total: he always refers to it as a thing, and in the third person—as "the" or "this" body, rather than "my" body—and in a 1991 paper in *Leonardo* he reconceived "the body not as a subject but as an object—NOT AS AN OBJECT OF DESIRE BUT AS AN OBJECT FOR DESIGNING."[36]

Stelarc is a paradoxical figure who plays both the supplicant and the visionary warrior in relation to new technologies. His performances symbolize the inadequacy of the human form in the face of technology, but simultaneously encapsulate the will to harness its powers towards an *actual* evolution and transubstantiation of the body. Stelarc's techno-logically augmented body may be "consumed" by the data information stream, but his oh-too-solid-flesh is also "consuming" it. Tracy Warr maintains that Stelarc's work "remains unavoidably visceral and human in its impact. . . . The image I take away from his performances is of the fragility and ingenuity of the human body dwarfed and pinned down by the surrounding technology and still eliciting empathy and awe."[37] Birringer, although highly critical of Stelarc's body theories, is nonetheless similarly affected by the powerful and symbiotic conjunction of performance art and science:

While he may claim that the reconfigured body will move (or be moved) without memory, I cer-tainly cannot forget the haunting effect the smiling, heavy-set dancer had on me, as his extruding and emitting cyborganism flailed and thrashed about like a trapped animal, with its industrial robot arm pointing jerkily in my direction.[38]

Since both artists are involved in the reconfiguration of their bodies, Stelarc has often been discussed alongside or in relation to French artist Orlan, whose plastic surgery operations/performances such as *The Reincarnation of St Orlan* (1990) are transmitted live via satellite to remote audiences. But body modification and virtualized reception of some performances are where we believe the similarities end; Stelarc is a quite different artist and strategist, a classic, serious modernist—and quite literally a futurist—in stark con-trast to the quintessentially postmodernist Orlan. Orlan uses the trappings of a bourgeois-chic cosmetic operating theater to comment upon notions of image, feminism, classical beauty, and the body as canvas. But for all its high-tech satirical conceptualism, there is an oddly 1950s-style nostalgia and a disquieting reverse vanity in Orlan's retro-aesthetic, Zsa Zsa Gabor-meets-devil's horns grotesquery. Stelarc is a quite different proposition, and is very much a self-surgeon, a Doctor Frankenstein figure who experiments on himself, a modernist artist who conceives himself not as a reconfigured image reflecting back on contemporary society, but as

an evolutionary guide, extrapolating new trajectories . . . a genetic sculptor, restructuring and hypersensitizing the human body; an architect of internal body spaces; a primal surgeon, implant-ing dreams, transplanting desires; an evolutionary alchemist, triggering mutations, transforming the human landscape.[39]

Stelarc's work is shot through with a body dualism, wherein he both affirms and refutes the mythical, the religious and the metaphysical. In the preceding passage, written in 1984, he is happy to consider himself an alchemical genetic architect and transformer of nature, but nonetheless frequently and insistently denies any quasi-religious or mythical ideas in his work, maintaining his fierce atheism.

Stelarc's *Exoskeleton*

While Stelarc's Internet-stimulated performances emphasize the "obsolete" body at the mercy of technology, his *Exoskeleton* (1998) performance features him firmly in control of the technology and celebrating the powerful solidity of the metallically enhanced, cyborg body. *Exoskeleton* (1998) is a large and imposing six-legged pneumatically powered robot that Stelarc stands on top of, on a rotating turntable. He wears an extended robotic left arm, and moves around the space, his body swinging from side to side as he controls the robot's spiderlike walking movements via computer-translated arm gestures, amidst a deafening "*cacophony* of pneumatic and mechanical and sensor modulated sounds"[40] (figure 13.10). Although we would not equate most of Stelarc's work with camp, *Exoskeleton* constitutes a monumental piece of metallic camp, although created and performed with no conscious camp irony whatsoever. As well as conforming to the sense of inherently camp robotic movement we have previously outlined, it also epitomizes what Cleto calls "the camp obsession with images of power"[41] and what Sontag terms camp's "fascinating fascism."[42]

In his evolutionary technological vision, Stelarc returns to nature and the animal kingdom, making literal Deleuze and Guattari's theoretical construct of "becoming animal." Their discourse stresses that "becoming animal does not consist in playing animal or imitating an animal . . . becoming is never imitating."[43] Rather, much like *Exoskeleton*'s cybernetic system "a man and an animal combine, neither of which resembles the other, neither of which imitates the other, each deterritorializing the other. . . . A system of relay and mutations through the middle."[44]

Many scientists believe that following a catastrophe such as a global nuclear war, insects will survive while mammals will not. Stelarc's choice of spider's legs thus marks an important choice in his metallic evolutionary vision. Ten years earlier in 1988, one of the most advanced robots of its time was Rodney A. Brooks's six-legged insect robot, *Ghengis*. Brooks reflects on the peculiarly lifelike qualities the robot exhibited, unlike any he had made or seen:

it came to life! It had a wasplike personality: mindless determination. But it had a personality. It chased and scrambled according to its will, not to the whim of the human controller. It acted like a creature, and to me and others who saw it, it felt like a creature. It was an artificial creature. . . . Of course, software is not lifelike itself. But software organized the right way can give rise to lifelike behaviour—it can cross the boundary from machinelike . . . to animal-like.[45]

Figure 13.10 Stelarc's six-legged evolutionary cyborg vision, *Exoskelton* (1998). Photo: D. Landwehr.

The half-human, half-insect image of *Exoskeleton* recalls the *theranthropes* of ancient folk legends and Greek mythology. Like the half-man, half-bull Minotaur, the half-vulture, half-woman Harpies, and the cloven-hooved Pan, *Exoskeleton* depicts an unworldly godlike or demonic mythical figure. Mythological satyrs and *theranthropes* have been exquisitely explored in Matthew Barney's hyperreal video art fantasy series *Cremaster 1–6* (1995–2002), as well as in metal performances including Artemis Moroni and the *.* Group's *The Robot and the Centaur* (1991) and Jean-Marc Matos' *Talos and Koïné* (1988), a dance piece between four human dancers and a robot based on Talos, the animated bronze statue of a man with a bull's head that protected ancient Crete.[46] *Exoskeleton*'s echoes with

Greek mythology are fascinating in relation to the cyborgic evolutionary prophesies of Warwick, Moravec, and Brooks. Many Greek myths tell the story of how Gods transformed humans into animals to protect them from, or to bring them back from, death. Zeus turned Io into a white heifer; Minerva changed Perdix into a bird; and most pertinent to Stelarc's creation, Athena transformed Arachne into a spider, bringing her back from death following her suicide. In its vision of machinic-human evolution, Stelarc's *Exoskeleton* returns to nature and the animal, and to eschatological ancient myths of metamorphoses that defy mortality.

While robot and cyborg performance frequently returns to nature, by contrast, in most techno-evolutionary theories since McLuhan, the machinization of humans has been viewed as involving a consequent alienation and separation from nature. But this assumed "denaturing" of the human body through machinic and electronic mutation operates dialectically. Metal is mined from the earth, and rather than separating human beings from nature, it can be argued that metallic prostheses reestablish links and direct chains of connection to the earth. A biometallic embodiment can thus be reconceived as a literally "grounded" embodiment. Deleuze and Guattari's free-floating, liquid "Body without Organs"[47] becomes significantly less plastic with the addition of metal appendages. Although the new body may have vast "lines of flight" via connection to intelligent networks, heavy metals significantly increase its weight and skeletal solidity. In increasing the body's physical strength, metal simultaneously increases its strength of gravitational pull downward, toward the earth. Stelarc's *Exoskelton* weighs 600 kilograms and we certainly do not see him floating off into cyber (or any other) space.

We would contest that rather than the plastic, unformed Body without Organs of Deleuze and Guattari's formulation, the metallically modified body instead opens an argument for Organs without a Body. As prosthetic metal and electronic organs become present as graftings onto the human figure, the biological body becomes increasingly absent, as the external addenda take prominence and precedence (figure 13.11). The machine as a collection of organs has been discussed by, among others, Descartes, who in 1637 held that future anthropomorphic machines would never be able to fully replicate the complexity of human actions since they do not act from reason and knowledge. Rather, they act:

solely from the disposition of their organs; for while reason is a universal instrument . . . these organs, on the contrary, need a particular arrangement for each particular action; whence it must be morally impossible that there should exist in any machines a diversity of organs sufficient to enable it to act in all the occurances of life in the way in which our reason enables us to act.[48]

Camping The Cyborg: Marcel.lí Antúnez Roca

In his extraordinary solo multimedia performance *Afasia* (1998),[49] Spanish performance artist Marcel.lí Antúnez Roca[50] returns to ancient gods, monsters, and myths through a futuristic reworking of Homer's *The Odyssey* (circa 700 BCE). Roca is costumed as a cyborg

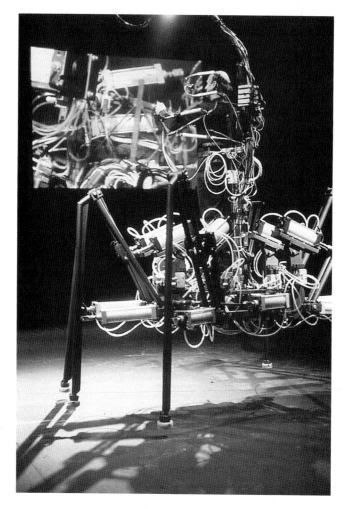

Figure 13.11 Organs without a body? Stelarc's *Exoskelton* presents a challenge to Deleuze and Guattari's theory of the "Body without Organs." Photo: D. Landwehr.

with exoskeletal body plates, arm and leg supports, a metal headband like a futuristic bandana, and a high-tech backpack sprouting cables and wires. He dances with industrial robots and activates video and animated sequences of Ulysses' epic journey, directly controlling all the scenic elements via an array of finger, arm, and body sensors attached by an umbilical cable to an offstage computer.

Four robots share the stage: a metal trashcan drum beats out insistent rhythms with its mechanical drumstick arms, and three other industrial robots jerk and lurch, emitting synthesized sounds and musical phrases in response to Roca's movement signals. Roca

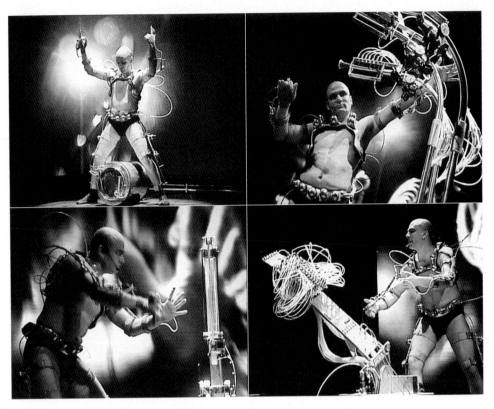

Figure 13.12 Marcel.lí Antúnez Roca goads and dances with robots that respond kinetically and sonically to his movements in *Afasia* (1998). Photos: Laura Signon.

coaxes and goads the machines like a psychotic street fighter egging on his opponents, and they respond sonically and kinetically to his violent and taunting "come and have a go" gesticulations. It is a cybernetic "dance" of stimulus-response feedback communication, but also a type of machismo status game where Roca asserts his cyborg-Übermensch as the all-powerful master conductor, the one in control (figure 13.12).

Roca's kinetic signals activate the screen imagery on the approximately 20 × 15 foot screen behind him. He controls panning camera effects across beautifully designed and rendered computer graphic landscapes and oceans by rocking on his feet and gesturing with his arms, to create the effect of Ulysses' journey. His messianic control is highlighted as he raises and lowers his arms to prompt graphical planets to ascend and descend, and shakes his body to distort, mutate, or explode animated faces, landscapes, and buildings. Playing both the Homer narrator on stage and the Ulysses protagonist on screen, he travels over land and (using swimming movements) graphical oceans beset by tornadoes. The animations, designed by Roca and Paco Corachan are striking, often hyperreal computer collages, montaging still photographs and video imagery of characters with animations and computer graphic backgrounds. A brass bedstead with a photographic image of Roca's yellow, naked Ulysses on board moves like a ship through the Japanese print–like animated waves, as distant cartoon volcanoes erupt. He travels past an animation of Bruegel's painting of the *Tower of Babel*, and past Circe's theranthropes: composite graphical images of animals on all fours, with the photo-realistic faces of men.[51]

The screen imagery comes fast and furious. On a cartoon rock stands Polyphemus the Cyclops, a video image of a jumping man with a giant eyeball for a head (recalling the stage appearances of performance-art pop band The Residents), and his confrontation with Ulysses ends with his eye-head gruesomely impaled on a huge, sharpened staff. Stunning black and white cartoons depict cosmic explosions and psychedelic apocalypses, and a stick-figure horse gives birth to six dancing, human children. The land of the Sirens is a computer animated island landscape composed entirely of disembodied breasts, their nipples sprouting milk, and the milk imagery recurs in one of the most memorable screen sequences of all. In the blackness of outer space, Roca's videated disembodied head looms, godlike, surrounded by a graphic cloudlike halo, with white typhoons of steam spraying out of his ears. He spits a white, milky liquid. The heads of other performers, smaller but similarly haloed and spitting milk, buzz around the central image like celestial flies. This image of a surreal Milky Way is later reconfigured in a video sequence where naked performers spray milk over a prone naked figure, recalling semen-splattered pornographic imagery, before the whole scene erupts into a cannabalistic, Bacchanalian orgy (figure 13.13).

In *Afasia*, Roca exerts total control over his symphonic performance environment like a demonic master-composer and conductor, gesturally activating the robots and screen imagery. By contrast, in *Epizoo* (1994) the metal technology controls him, with audience members using touch-screen computers to activate robotic manipulations of his body. Roca stands on a revolving turntable dressed only in a G-string, with pneumatic metal molds and hook devices attached to his head and body, which pump up and down against his buttocks and chest, wiggle his ears, and pull his mouth and nostrils open and shut (figure 13.14). The audience's interactive computer screens show composite photographic and graphical images of Roca's naked body, which are also relayed on a projection screen behind the live Roca on stage.

Roca's screen body is outlined in black and set against vibrantly colored graphical backgrounds, recalling the Day-Glo figure paintings of British artists Gilbert and George. As spectators press different parts of the computer body, the screen image mutates: his buttocks become huge and inflated, and eggs are laid from the anus which turn into human heads; his penis changes to a female pudenda, and his male chest gives way to round, pink breasts (figure 13.15). Cartoon knives stab, hammers hit, and fists punch the buttocks and head, while pincers and pliers tweak the nipples. The performance presents

Figure 13.13   Marcel.lí Antúnez Roca's computer-sensed movements trigger and control a dazzling array of screen image projections in *Afasia*. Photos: Laura Signon.

a literal and savage machinization of the helpless, dehumanized body and illustrates how humans can use technology to electronically torture others at a distance. But although on one level disturbing, *Epizoo* is also camp: parodying the sexually fetishized conjunction of hard metal and soft flesh in a humorous floorshow of bouncing buttocks and pectorals, violently wiggling ears, and a darting, licentious tongue.

In both *Epizoo* and *Afasia*, Roca's work is camp. But how does Roca's performative persona with its high levels of testosteroned machismo jibe with Richard Dyer statement that "camp is not masculine. By definition, camping about is not butch."[52] The answer lies in Roca's physical performance: its irony, sexual ambivalence and high-camp gestural theatrics. Although Roca performs the cyborg in *Afasia* as a butch muscleman, like numerous wrestlers of America's World Wrestling Entertainment (WWE), it is exaggerated to the degree of camp self-parody. Roca's costume beneath the metal appendages, a tight-fitting, all-in-one undergarment, cut high to the crotch, also echoes the WWE

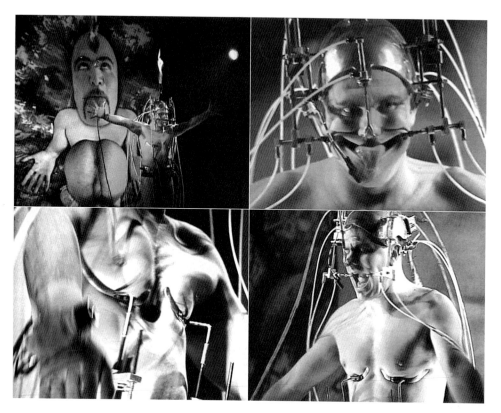

Figure 13.14 In *Epizoo* (1994), different parts of Marcel.lí Antúnez Roca's body are pneumatically manipulated in response to audience members, using touch screen computers. Photos: Laura Signon.

wrestlers' macho-camp look. There is deep irony in his expansive, often obscene, and sometimes ridiculous physical gestures. In *Afasia,* Roca's masculinized movements at times reach Neanderthal caveman heights, but he combines these with distinctly feminine movements: languid hip-swaying, delicate finger wiggling, and balletic steps. At times he stands still as though bored, casually rocking his pelvis and swinging his arms limply from side to side, like a female disco dancer. In *Epizoo,* as his computer screen figure transforms from male to female, the face offers a camp sign of surprise with wide eyes and an exaggerated kisslike purse of the lips, while on stage Roca wiggles his G-stringed buttocks at the audience, like a female striptease artist.

Whilst Dyer argues that camp is not butch, he also recognizes that camp is not the exclusive domain of gay culture, reflecting that "camp is so beguiling that it has been adopted by many straights these days."[53] A number of the most popular presenters of recent British light-entertainment television series attest to this notion, including the

Figure 13.15 Marcel.lí Antúnez Roca's graphical screen body undergoes myriad mutations in *Epizoo*. Photos: Laura Signon.

flamboyant David Dickinson, who fronts an antiques program, and Laurence Llewelyn Bowen, a presenter of popular television series on domestic interior design. Bowen, a straight man who dresses and performs like a contemporary version of a stylish seventeenth-century fop, epitomizes the ironic wit and postmodern laissez-faire of straight camp. He regularly comments affectionately on the aesthetics of camp as he garishly transforms people's houses in the BBC's *Changing Rooms* series, and in one program in 2003 offered his own concise definition: "if it's *too much*, it's camp."

Cyborg Machismo: Guillermo Gómez-Peña

Guillermo Gómez-Peña similarly performs a machismo cyborg, but with a knowing and conscious sense of camp that is in line with George Piggford's definition of camp as "behaviour that mocks and ironizes gender norms."[54] In performances such as *The Museum of Fetishized Identity* (2000), Gómez-Peña mocks and ironizes notions of gender and of cyborgism. The cyborgic armplate he wears is not metal, but silver-painted plastic. It signifies the pastiche superman, the pretend cyborg. His "metallic" arm is an ironic tattoo, a satirical sign rather than an evolutionary prosthesis. His cyborg is merely a new form of alien, another sociopolitical outsider, a new victim of the reactionary postcolonial capitalism that Gómez-Peña has critiqued throughout his work.

As an evolutionary vision, Gómez-Peña's "ethno-cyborg" is a deeply mocking and ironic one: a corseted transvestite who lives in a wheelchair and smokes too many Marlboros. His El Mexterminator persona, an "illegal border crosser . . . [with] Jalapeño phallus & robotic bleeding heart,"[55] performs the preening narcissism of the cyborg, applying beauty products and slowly brushing his hair (figure 13.16). His collaborator Roberto Sifuentes's CyberVato persona explores the technological sadomasochism of meat and metal symbiosis. He injects his tongue with a horse syringe, self-flagellates, and strangles himself with cords, which he then binds in tight coils around his head, contorting his face grotesquely.

Figure 13.16 Guillermo Gómez-Peña's El Mexterminator character takes pills, wields animal jawbones as weapons, and tries on a pair of women's shoes in *The Museum of Fetishized Identity* (2000).

Figure 13.17 Roberto Sifuentes as the ultra-cool, and ultramasochistic CyberVato in *The Museum of Fetishized Identity*.

The metallic metaphors here are sardonic representations of cyborgic vanity and machinic pain (figure 13.17). Gómez-Peña's pill popping, wheel-chaired El Mexterminator character embodies Baudrillard's conception of the docile technologized subject as "a spastic, probably with a cerebral handicap too."[56] This pessimistic view of the cyborg asserts Gómez-Peña's view that high technology is "intrinsically dehumanizing" and that a critique of technology overlaps with a critique of capitalism.[57]

Gómez-Peña's camp, cruel, and humorous depiction of the cyborg reflects the recent reevaluation of the technological "revolution" following its failed projects and timeframes. Despite the hyperbolic rhetoric of the 1980s and '90s, AI research has plateaued amid myriad complications, the dotcom boom went bust, and domestic Internet users cannot yet even access high-quality video, let alone achieve bodily transcendence. Other performance artists have similarly used humor to mock the claims of the supposed "exponential" developments in technology: Roca's first action in *Afasia* is an ironic flick of a large, distinctly analog "on-off" switch on the front of his cyborg suit. In Toni Dove's interactive installation, *Artificial Changelings* (1998), a voiceover tells how the futuristic cyborg Lileth "reached in back of the apparatus that wrapped around her body like recycled mutated paniers and tugged on the recycled fishnet bustle. 'This thing is so clunky.'"

In *The Museum of Fetishized Identity*, the metallic cyborg signifiers coexist with diverse clashing signs: crucified skeletons; dead chickens; video projections; Mexican flags; native American headdresses; "sacred" objects from primitive cultures; and artifacts from an obsessively commodified and kitsch contemporary America. The vivid, beautifully staged dioramas bathed in shafts of coloured light are exquisite; sumptuously manifesting camp's sense of "semiotic excess . . . and *gratuitousness* of reference."[58] The hypnotic rave music, mock-American Indian dancing, a naked green Butoh alien (Juan Ybarra) (figure 13.18) and the visual luxuriance of the smoke-machine bathed Blade Runner-in-

Figure 13.18 Juan Ybarra as the simultaneously sinister and camp alien in *The Museum of Fetishized Identity*.

Tijuana mise-en-scène present an expression of playful and deviant camp, corresponding to what Cleto describes as

a convergence between the camp scene and Bakhtinian carnivalesque, for the two share hierarchy inversion, mocking paradoxicality, sexual punning and innuendos and—most significantly—a complex and multilayered power relationship between the dominant and the subordinate (or deviant), and finally the whole problem of how far a "licensed" release can effectively be transgressive or subversive.[59]

Conclusion

Our conclusions here draw together our analyses of key themes within this chapter on cyborgs and the preceding one on robots, which we will conjoin using our inclusive term "metal performance." Metal performance frequently highlights a contemporary concern to return to nature and the animal, and often celebrates an eroticized sexuality of metal, with "them fuckin' robots" both fucking (signaling the humanization of machines) and being fucked (signifying the machinization of humans). Metal performances exalt in the conjunction of the hard and the soft; the natural and the technological; the metal and the meat. They are also characterized by fundamental tensions and contradictions that also exist within camp, combining "the polarities of seriousness and play, cynicism and affection, (self)mockery and (self)celebration."[60] Both camp and metal performance share the notion of exclusiveness, what Sontag calls "esoteric—something of a private code, a badge of identity even."[61]

Within queer theory, the appreciation and celebration of camp is articulated as a defining exclusivity of taste and sensibility working outside and against the mainstream. In the same way, the tastes and sensibilities of metal-culture proponents—metal performers, body-piercers, techno-theorists, and would-be cyborgs—define a similar exclusiveness of aesthetic expression and ideological transgression. Like camp, its delicious nonconformity relies upon its very difference from the status quo: it "is only recognisable as a deviation from an implied norm, and without that norm it would cease to exist, it would lack definition."[62] Metal performance operates with the theatrically of camp in exploring what Andrew Britton describes as "the thrill of 'something wrong.'"[63] In a rapidly evolving technological age, despite its supposed deviance and peculiarity, metal performance already seems strangely familiar. This too it shares with camp, the key to which, according to Mark Booth, "lies in reconciling its essential marginality with its evident ubiquity."[64]

Finally, metal performance relates to the profound fears as well as the camp fascinations of the humanization of machines and the dehumanization/machinization of humans. Jay Bolter argues that "by making a machine think like a man, man re-creates himself, defines himself, as a machine,"[65] and Hugo de Garis has predicted that human evolution will ultimately lead to what he terms "Gigadeath."[66] Coition with and immersion and transformation into metal reaches its logical conclusion with Hans Moravec's projection that by the year 2050 it will be possible to transfer one's entire consciousness into a machine. Running parallel to such predictions and visions of the machinization of humans are developments in robotics and Artificial Intelligence, which herald the advanced humanization of machines. Rodney A. Brooks holds that humans have already begun an irreversible evolutionary process through the use of bodily technological prostheses, and that the simultaneous emergence of the intelligent robot will lead to a situation whereby:

As these robots get smarter, some people will worry about what will happen when they get really smart. Will they decide that we humans are useless and stupid and take over the world from us? I have recently come to realize that this will never happen. Because there won't be any of us (people) for them (pure robots) to take over from.[67]

The shiny new bodies and mythic metamorphoses enacted in metallic performance art celebrate but also forewarn of the gradual disappearance of the human body. Intelligent and conscious machines in the future may take their origin from humans, but they may equally originate from other sentient machines. George Dyson suggests that "in the game of life and evolution there are three players at the table: human beings, nature and machines. I am firmly on the side of nature. But nature, I suspect, is on the side of the machines."[68]

In appreciating the camp excesses of metal performance, we might therefore reflect, as Britton observes in relation to gay camp, that it may signify only "a kind of anaesthetic, allowing one to remain inside oppressive relations while enjoying the illusory confidence that one is flouting them."[69]

IV

Space

Digital Theater and Scenic Spectacle

I would rather see great dreams in a small place, than small dreams in a great place.
—ROBERT EDMOND JONES[1]

Introduction

In 1951, the great French actor Jean-Louis Barrault theorized all art as a confrontation of one element against another:

a brush rubs a canvas
a pen scrapes paper
a hammer strikes a string[2]

In the theater, he said, "a Human Being struggles in space. The theatre is the art of the human being in space."[3] In live multimedia theater, projection screens or video monitors frame additional spaces, this time in two dimensions (even when the computer images on them are rendered as three-dimensional simulations). Yet despite the flatness of the screen frame, projected media can in one important sense offer far more spatial possibilities than three-dimensional theater space. As film theories have explained since the early 1900s, the media screen provides a uniquely pliable and poetic space. Unlike the fixed point of view offered to the seated theater spectator, screen media facilitate multiple viewpoints on the same subject through the variation of camera angles; and perspective and spatiality can be transformed from a vast panorama to a huge close-up in a twenty-fourth-of-a-second blink of the projector's eye. Film and video editing enables an instant visual and aural fragmentation of space and time. The film, video, and computer artist is therefore able to construct a bombardment of images from different times and spaces quite impossible in live performance within three-dimensional theatrical space.

Theater semioticians have long noted that theatrical performance constitutes one of the most complex forms of communication; tying together numerous elements in what Bourdieu has termed "simultaneous semiologies." Keir Elam demonstrates how theater incorporates all signifying modes and all communicational codes, with considerable overlap between Peirce's classifications of iconic, indexical, and symbolic codes.[4] The inclusion of media screens or digital projections introduces yet another coded sign system to the stage space, which further stimulates and complicates the decoding activity of the spectator. The additional media frame suggests a semiotic dialogue between screen image and stage action, which audience members are likely (but not certain) to attempt to try to make sense of: that is to say, to decode cerebrally. The semiotic relationship and tension between the screen imagery, which we could call A, and the live performers, B, is most commonly interpreted as either formulating a *dialogic* relationship (A versus/in relation to B), or as establishing an *additive* combination which engenders something entirely new, namely C, $(A + B = C)$. At the same time (and although this does not ultimately alter these two "equations" of audience reception), many theater artists juxtapose live performance and projected media more to excite visceral, subjective, or subconscious audience responses than objective and conscious ones: to appeal to the senses and the nervous system (in the way that Artaud's theater was conceived) rather than to the rational intellect.

Through the integration of media screens within the mise-en-scène, artists experiment with techniques that at times fragment and dislocate bodies, time, and space, and at others unify physical, spatial, and temporal significations. In his 1966 examination of multimedia theater, Roberts Blossom discusses the effect of the linear time frame of live performance working in conjunction with the malleable timeline of recorded media. He concludes that with the inclusion of a film or video screen "Time . . . perhaps for the first time in theatre, becomes present as a spatial element."[5] Digital theater performances sometimes utilize the screen space to highlight a marked separation between the relative times and spaces of stage and screen, and at others attempt to combine them to create (the illusion of) an integrated time and space. In this chapter we concentrate on three important theater practitioners—George Coates, The Builders Association, and Robert Lepage—who each employ projections to intensify the visual spectacle of their theatrical productions, but also differ significantly in their conceptual approaches and digital aesthetics.

These artists frequently combine a number of large projection screens to bring an operatic-scale design to their theater productions, in the same way that Chinese American director Ping Chong has been creating ambitious multimedia theater spectacles since 1972. Chong places live actors within expressive and expansive visual vistas, such as the figure of Van Gogh in *Deshima* (1990) who stands on stage in the middle of a vast projection of his painting *Crows in the Cornfield*[6] (figure. 14.1). While Van Gogh's landscape projections immerse the onstage actors to present a superimposition that visually unifies the sense of time and space, other companies use multiple screens to disrupt

Figure 14.1 Ping Chong's visually rich theatrical tribute to Vincent Van Gogh, *Deshima* (1990). Photo: Bob Van Dantzig.

spatio-temporal perceptions, as in OM2's *The Convulsions of Mr K* (1998) and Dumb Type's *Memorandum* (1999), where six simultaneous screen projections intensify sensory overload and disorientation.[7]

The conjunction of live performance and digital imagery can produce a particular, hybrid form and experience akin to what Alain Virmaux has described in relation to Artaud's film scenarios: "something which is neither theatre nor film, but partakes of the evanescent reality of dreams."[8] This sense of *in-between-ness*—a liminal space operating between the screen images and live performers—is often the essential kernel, what one might even call the "metatext" of digital theater production. Margaret Morse, Elizabeth Grosz, and Sarah Rubidge have each argued that the idea of the "space in between" is central to the artistic forms and spectator experiences of (respectively) video installations, architecture, and immersive artworks.[9] What is fundamental is not so much the material object or environment, but rather the space it occupies and the dynamic spaces configured and experienced by visitors and spectators in relation to it. As we will see, this also holds true for digital theater spectacles, where stage spaces become transitional, always in a state of flux, and, in Elizabeth Grosz's words, "always in the process of becoming but never realised . . . the space *of* the in between."[10]

George Coates Performance Works

Since one of its earliest productions, *Are/Are* (1982), George Coates Performance Works has been employing media projections in theater productions to create artificial scenography and spatial environments, in effect replacing conventional wooden sets with videated or virtual sets composed of projected light. George Coates and his company have developed increasingly ingenious stepped, receding screen systems which combine with matched projections beamed directly onto a pivoting, bowl-shaped curved stage, to create an illusion of live actors inhabiting immersive three-dimensional settings with an acute sense of realistic, vanishing perspective. More than any other contemporary company, Coates's work extends the rich visual traditions of spatial illusion first developed in the 1950s by Czech multimedia theater pioneers Laterna Magika. Coates and his designers (most notably Jerome Serlin) use precision lighting to illuminate the actors without diffusing the projections around them, and to reveal or obscure the performers by rendering intricate screens and blinds transparent or opaque.

Their operatic *Actual Sho* (1987) marked a high point in the use of projected settings in the 1980s, transforming the stage into a series of arresting environmental spaces and architectural structures.[11] Actors appear to lean out of the windows of a skyscraper, to emerge from a railroad tunnel, and to balance on the wooden joists and beams of a vast shell framework of a building under construction. A clergyman wanders around a sewer with a metal detector, which registers presences beneath the ground, and the heads of actors suddenly break the surface to pop up from underneath the stage floor, as if drawn by the metal detector (figure 14.2). For the climax,

Water is projected onto the sides of the bowl stage, and a mast is raised, converting it into a sailboat. The mast transforms into a maypole. Again the stage becomes a railroad track and tunnel and a green light is seen coming from the darkness. It suggests the experience of death. The bowl stage begins to spin, turned by figures in skeleton costumes.[12]

Coates began to incorporate digital technologies in his work following *Actual Sho* and, according to Theodore Shank, partly as a result of having been hired by Steve Jobs to design the launch and unveiling of Apple's NeXT computer; and in 1989 Coates founded the Science Meets Arts Society (SMARTS). Based in San Francisco, and already established as a talented theatrical illusionist using analogue technology, Silicon Valley's computer industry began to see Coates as an ally and luminary who could harness their 3D computer graphics and help spread the word through the production of digital spectacles on new and unprecedented scales. By 1991, Coates was working closely with consultants at the Digital Equipment Corporation, had received substantial donations of cash, software and hardware from a dozen companies (including a Silicon Graphics system), and received an invitation to present a performance at SIGGRAPH.

Figure 14.2 Characters emerge from the sewers in George Coates Performance Work's *Actual Sho* (1987).

The result, *Invisible Site: A Virtual Sho* (1991), presented hitherto unseen digital theater three-dimensional trompe l'oeil effects, which the audience viewed through 3D polarized glasses. Computer sets and images were projected onto a thirty-foot by sixty-foot perforated aluminium screen. The actors worked behind it, but through lighting effects were visually rendered to appear within the 3D environments. In one scene the actors seem to be floating in midair inside a giant birdcage (figure 14.3); in another, an actor playing the Dalai Lama is imprisoned in a jar, doused in milk, and then frozen inside an ice cube. Stunning perspective projections such as a four-walled checkerboard tunnel that recedes into a vanishing point of floating 0 and 1 graphics create arresting visions of cyberspace as an at once seductively beautiful, yet threatening space of intrigue, deception, and chance. *Invisible Site: A Virtual Sho* traces fragmented episodes telling the story of a woman who adopts the persona of *The Tempest*'s Prospero in a sadomasochistic virtual reality relationship with a man who takes on the character of Caliban. A computer hacker called Rimbaud disrupts their fantasies and "disorders their senses," enmeshing them in a series of hallucinatory adventures drawing on diverse themes and literary references including Euripides' *Medea*. The use of real-time manipulation of the 3D computer-generated landscapes in direct response to the actors' movements was a major innovation; in one sequence, the movement of a giant eyeball is controlled via an offstage

Figure 14.3 The birdcage sequence from George Coates' *Invisible Site: A Virtual Sho* (1991).

joystick to follow the panicked movements of a character desperately trying to avoid its gaze.

The use of real time graphical manipulation moved from backstage to become the prerogative of the onstage performers who controlled some of the image and text projections in *Box Conspiracy An Interactive Sho* (1993), a dystopian look at the panoptic surveillance implications of interactive television. While Coates embraces new media technologies aesthetically, his productions continually question and critique their social and political impacts. Coates thus simultaneously celebrates and parodies computer technologies, viewing the digital age with both wonder and cynicism. As he puts it, "Using technology to critique technology is no more a contradiction than it is to call the phone company to complain about the service or to use a calculator to challenge the bill. The use of a particular tool implies no endorsement of values beyond itself."[13] In his satire on cyberspace, *Twisted Pairs* (1996), an Amish farm girl finds a solar-powered laptop, becomes engrossed in online dating, is electronically stalked, and contacts a paramilitary organization that tries to exploit her as a Net celebrity (figure 14.4). "I love these tools," reflects Coates, "and just as passionately, I am very afraid of what they might mean. Our work at the theatre derives its energy and focus from this contradiction."[14]

By 1995, writers such as Monteith M. Illingworth were hailing Coates as the preeminent director exploring the conjunction of theater and cyberspace: "That meeting is a locus of the Information Age which in the American theater only Coates has explored in

Figure 14.4 A found laptop leads to virtual adventures and Net exploitation in *Twisted Pairs* (1996).

any systematic way."[15] Coates himself traces his work back to the happenings and inter-media events of the 1960s, but we see more distinct parallels with the stepped-screen staging spectacles of the Laterna Magika in the late 1950s, as well as links with Wagner's nineteenth-century notion of the immersive *Gesamtkunstwerk*. The Wagnerian association is heightened since Coates's productions foreground a strong and typically continuous music track (normally composed by Marc Ream) and make little use of the spoken word, preferring the sung operatic form (in a postmodern, fragmentary style). Artaud's ideas of a visionary "total theatre" are similarly present in Coates's vibrant productions, and he conjures the Artaudian spirit in his description of the audience experience as a liquid-like immersion, possible in theater alone, "not translatable to any other format other than being there. . . . Presenting the imagination unbridled is the most revolutionary act I can imagine."[16]

20/20 Blake (1996) is his most distinctly Artaudian production, which recreates William Blake's monumental religious paintings such as *The Marriage of Heaven and Hell* (1790) in three dimensions, and peoples them with live actors (figure 14.5). Biblical characters, mythical spirits, demi-gods and the ghost of a flea visit Blake and inspire his art; and lightning strikes the prone body of his brother Robert, consuming it with (projected) flames as two white doves appear to fly out him, as his spirit is released. The image

Figure 14.5 God puts in a double appearance in Coates' *20/20 Blake*.

Figure 14.6 The spirit of Antonin Artaud's actors "signaling through the flames" in *20/20 Blake*.

recalls Artaud's instruction for actors to be "like martyrs burnt alive, still signalling through the flames", just as an image of the giant hands of (presumably) God removing a woman from the stage uncannily (but probably unconsciously) mirrors a scene in Artaud's *The Spurt of Blood* (1920) where God's giant hand descends from above to pull the burning hair of a whore. Indeed, a description of *20/20 Blake* provided by Shank is redolent of Artaud's play not only in its visionary-surrealist content, but also in its stylistic structure:

Later one of the giant hands points towards the audience and scans ominously from one side to the other. Pairs of glowing eyes emerge from the open grave. . . . When Blake dies . . . lightning strikes the body as it did that of his brother. The giant projected hands, now clasped, come through a large gold picture frame toward the audience, and Blake's spirit rises from the body and puts on an astronaut's helmet while his body disappears in the open grave.[17] (figure 14.6).

Postmodern Theatrical Spectacle: The Builders Association

Let us now contrast Coates's hot, visceral, sensorily "immersive" theatrical images with the cool, post-Brechtian and postmodern aesthetic of the Builders Association. Its players too create bold theatrical spectacles using large-scale projections, but to very different effect. The company uses media and computer technologies to "reanimate" theater for a contemporary audience, "using new tools to interpret old forms . . . to create a world onstage which reflects the contemporary culture which surrounds us."[18] Their deconstructive refashioning of the Faust legend, *Jump Cut (Faust)* (1997) incorporates evocative, beautifully written texts by John Jesurun, and three large media screens. These are butt-joined together and stretch the width of the stage, set above the live performers—significantly *separating* them from the images rather than *conjoining* the actors "within" them, as in Coates's work. Sometimes a wide-screen image spans the screen's entire width; at others three different images are projected side by side, with the center screen frequently used to relay live shots of the onstage performers taken from technician-operated cameras that can move left and right along on a downstage dolly track. Using real-time video mixing, these shots are frequently overlaid and superimposed with prerecorded or computer-generated imagery. The staging makes reference to the Elizabethan stages where the Faust tale was first performed, where the lower stage level housed "the mechanics for producing stage effects and the gallery was where the effects would be revealed. . . . Each scene was set up both for the theatrical space below, and for the cinematic space above—the screens where the stage effects were revealed."[19]

The show opens with a video projection of the Faust character driving at night along a deserted road, his eyes reflected in the rear-view mirror. The sound of two computer bleeps is followed by a slowly spoken voiceover, filled with pauses.

Letter Number One. Dear One, I am writing you from an airplane above your country. The computer breakdown continues over most of the hemisphere. The nation's in a coma. We're just about over the border now. I don't know if you'll ever get this. As we move away we see only smoke and light. It's hard to tell if it's fog or exhaust, or light from the city. But I hate to tell you that your city's destroyed while you're still in it. But then, you may know that already. Then again, we both know it's true, and you're just a photograph in my hands now, and your city is smoke and vapour.

The road movie footage in the center screen is flanked by images of billowing mist and smoke on the screens either side, which continue as the center-screen video mixes to a live relayed video image of the actor playing Faust, who now stands center-stage, isolated in a spotlight. As he examines a frothing bottle of chemicals, his close-up video image is mixed with smoke and flame effects. The shot gives way to footage from F. W. Murnau's 1926 silent movie *Faust*, showing the protagonist engaged in alchemical experiments with molten metals. On the two side screens, text captions in a Gothic font emulate and echo the silent movie genre, as a voiceover repeats the same words in a low whisper: "A knave like all others! He preaches good and does evil! He seeks to turn base metal into gold!" The shot reverts to the live actor, who lifts a large book above his head and opens it, its pages turning and flapping in a (fan-assisted) high wind. As he conjures an occult spirit, the side screen captions read: "Come forth, demon of evil!" and give way to licking, computer animated flames. The live video image of Faust between them is merged with a ring-of-fire effect around his body, which gradually intensifies until, as the camera zooms ever closer into his face, the graphical flames finally engulf him and merge with the side screen flames to create a wall of fire.

The earlier antique text switches to a contemporary font as a quasi-Brechtian screen caption announces the scene change—"The Fall, or How I Fell"—and the live actor playing the conjured Mephistopheles begins to recount to Faust his fall from God's grace. Visible onstage camera operators pan to follow the two performers, whose faces are relayed onto the centre screen in close-up, while on the side screens captions repeat and reinforce dialogue fragments. "Will You Shut Up", says Faust onstage and via text onscreen, but the Devil continues his tale: "And there is no hell, hell is where the heart is" he confides. He speaks into a hand-held microphone and stares directly into the close-up lens of the camera tracking him as he wanders the stage like a jaded but extremely slick TV evangelist. Lines from his speech intermittently rebound again as screen text: "There Was No Love," "He Hurled Me Out," "God Was Jealous," "A Frozen Beauty," "A White Sheet of Whiteness."

As scenes progress, images from Murnau's film weave in and out of the projections, and are repeatedly mimicked, parodied and reenacted onstage (figure 14.7). A movie close-up of Faust's lover on the center screen is recreated on the side screens by her character counterpart live onstage. As two female performers play a stage scene in front of a dressing-table, its three hinged mirror frames are reflected in the screen configuration above. Two screens run close-up video images of the live performers; the third is occupied by footage of Murnau's actress looking into a similar dressing table mirror in 1926.

In a sardonically comic scene captioned "Baby You Can Drive My Car," the four performers stand onstage in front of a blue chromakey cloth, with one holding and turning a prop steering wheel as if in an automobile. A relayed live camera shot of the group is video-mixed and keyed with a moving road background, so that their onscreen image resembles 1950s movies that employed the same basic technique to relocate actors sitting in a studio onto the open road (figure 14.8). Driving on "the highway to hell," they talk in dialogue partly composed of song titles. Among other things, they run over a poodle (not seen onscreen). For this, the actors all take a little synchronized jump, which perfectly creates the desired bouncing car effect on screen, and sound effects of a sharp screech of brakes and a dog yelp seal a hilariously cynical moment of multimedia black comedy. The sequence ends when the background film transforms from the open road to a computer-generated sequence of rushing white stars, and yellow and orange nebula, as the actors on screen appear to take off into space and toward heaven in their nonexistent car.

Following other sequences, including a trial for murder where three of the live performers' faces are projected in tight close-up on each of the screens, the show closes as it

Figure 14.7 Multiple screens mix live camera projections with footage from Murnau's 1926 silent film *Faust* in the Builders Association's *Jump Cut (Faust)* (1997).

began, with an empty stage and images on screen. Billowing clouds remind us of the man writing a letter from an airplane at the beginning of the show, and his voice now continues to conclude the performance in slow, thoughtful tones:

I hear your voice, here and there along the way. It charms me and pulls me along—but along to where, and for what? And to what? To you? So I go on, blindly. I travel the road from nowhere to nowhere, and here to there. . . . There will be no night tonight, there will be no tomorrow tomorrow, there will be no today today. So what then is there left? But that there will be no yesterday

Figure 14.8 "Baby You Can Drive My Car": The actors are video-mixed with a moving road background to create a comical movie special effect in *Jump Cut (Faust)*.

tomorrow. Or today. There will be no more *more*. Ever. I'm just waiting. Saturated in time. The motor's stopped. This is the way I've always dreamed it would be. The sounds of the city dissolving below me and above me. This is the way I always dreamed it would be. I think I've found a place where I know I could be forever. What this has to do with God or the Devil, I'll never know. The surf's up. See you there.

A potpourri of (excellent) persona performances,[20] tongue-in-cheek movie, television and song homages, and high-saturation mediatization, *Jump Cut* is a quintessentially "cool" postmodern theater production, with close stylistic and conceptual similarities to the work of the Wooster Group. Like the Wooster Group, the Builders Association's use of media is quintessentially Brechtian in highlighting its technological artificiality, in forever revealing itself *as* media. Projections are distinctly framed and separated from the actors, and although there is live mixing to conjoin the screen-videated actors with computer effects, there is no attempt to merge the live and the mediatized into an illusionistic visual composite. Rather, the live action and the projections are dialectical: they undertake an intellectual dialogue, making mutual connections and commentaries between and about one another. Brechtian theater and deconstructive postmodern performance styles unite in their self-conscious "stepping outside" of illusionistic narrative forms; in framing all action within quotation marks; and in explicitly "announcing" intentions, like a stage conjuror before a trick. Where Brechtian theater continually reminds its audience of the political and moral dialectics being enacted within the plot, the Brechtian use of media by groups like the Builders Association and The Wooster Group continually reminds audiences of the dialectical interplay going on between the actors and the screen images.

But this "alienation effect by media" in postmodern digital performance is generally less discriminate and certainly far less political than was Brecht's intention. This is not to suggest that there is no sort of *politique* in operation: such performances frequently critique aspects of culture and society, for example, the ubiquity of electronic images and their falsifying and banal natures. But it is (at least nowadays) generally soft-centered—an ironic, knowing observation rather than an angry attack. *Jump Cut's* "The Fall, or How I Fell" and "Baby You Can Drive My Car" sequences, for example, both use media to essentially double up on the live action pastiche—and on the pleasure the audience derives from recognizing the references and enjoying the homages. Onstage, the actors are already operating in knowing Brechtian modes as they play out, for the respective scenes, a TV chat show and a road movie. The placement of their live video images on screen—in television's ubiquitous "talking head" close-up in the first scene, and in a clichéd "car-on-the-open-road" movie back-projection for the second—doubles the alienation effect to hammer home both the pastiche itself, and the media intertextuality deemed so crucial to the pleasure-principle of postmodern spectatorship.

Alladeen

The Builders Association's co-production with London's motiroti, *Alladeen* (2003), is a high-budget multimedia theater performance described by Philip Fisher as "one of the first shows that fully embraces the multi-media potentiality for 21st Century theatre."[21] Exquisitely designed and performed, it is an example of experimental digital theater with the stylish look and acting finesse of a West End or Broadway production. Its high-tech digital aesthetics are evident from the start, as blocks of shimmering, animated graphics appear high on a screen that stretches the width and height of the stage. They drop vertically one by one, à la computer game *Tetris*, as building blocks that form an elaborate New York boulevard backdrop complete with a Virgin Megastore, in front of which a young Asian woman enters onstage, in mid-conversation on her cell phone (figure 14.9). The telecommunications theme intensifies as the scene shifts to a call center in Bangalore, India, and the screen rises halfway to reveal a busy office behind. The suspended screen, now in front of and above the live action, becomes equally busy, and equally important to the conception of the scene: a computer-like amalgam of text, graphics, recorded video, and browser-style windows relaying live webcam portrait shots of the stage telephone operators in action. These workers sit in transparent designer chairs at their desks, in front of slim-screen computers; their phone interactions amplified through microphone headsets. They try to sell products for commission, deal with customer inquiries, and give map directions to stranded motorists. Suspended behind them are six spheres, an image of the globe

Figure 14.9 The final image of the metamorphic computer generated opening sequence to the Builders Association's *Alladeen* (2003).

projected on each (these later give way to other digital images), highlighting the production's overarching theme of technological globalization (figure 14.10).

The Asian call operators interrupt their work to undergo training led by an American who coaches their vowel sounds and enunciation: the aim is to mask their Asian accents and identities to convince the Americans they call that they too are Americans, in America. They are modern-day Aladdins, seeking a magical transformation from poor to rich and "pretending to be people they are not from places that they have never been."[22] Part of the training involves the workers making seminar presentations to the group, sharing their research into American culture. One worker discusses characters from the TV series *Friends* (the screen projections mix through images of each character in synchronization with her words), and her analysis wittily exposes both the characters' illogicalities, and fundamental differences in East-West cultural reception. Nonetheless, the five workers at the seminar each eagerly adopt one of the *Friends* characters' names as pseudonyms when working on the phone. Later, as they introduce themselves and talk to clients on the phone, the live webcam projections are manipulated skilfully in real time to mix, merge, and morph their faces with still images of Monica, Joey, Phoebe, Chandler, and Rachel, their fair-skinned American alter-egos.

The characters' ambitions and increasing competitiveness in their appetite to live rather than merely simulate the American dream culminates in the final act, set in an upmarket karaoke club in London, where the company has sent the most successful workers. To

Figure 14.10 The office set with its suspended giant projection screen in *Alladeen* (2003).

a mix of eclectic electronic and Indian music, and bathed in rich, high-saturation colored lights, East meets West, Hollywood meets Bollywood, past meets present, and fantasy meets reality. In the finale, on stage an Asian dancer moves with powerful, Oriental exoticism to a haunting ballad crooned by a Western singer, while onscreen the Internet window images combine with colorful fantasy sequences inspired by the Aladdin and Arabian Nights stories.

Alladeen is an intelligent and evocative cross-cultural collaboration and exploration of corporate capitalism, the impacts of technologies on global culture (from satellite systems and the Internet to the older media of television and the telephone), and the ways in which cultures absorb and redefine other's myths. One reviewer has described it in relation to how we now function as "'global souls' caught up in circuits of technology, and how our voices and images travel from one culture to another."[23] Others have emphasized the potency of the Aladdin allegory in relation to contemporary technological culture. Susannah Clapp suggests that the company demonstrate how "yesterday's magic is today's virtual reality,"[24] and Lyn Gardner discusses the need for the call center characters to provide instant gratification for the American callers "via that 21st-century magic lamp— the credit card."[25] She goes on to note that "with its blatant wish fulfilment, issues of class, wealth and social status, and emphasis on the possibilities of personal transformation, Aladdin is as modern a fairy tale as you could hope to find."[26]

It is a slick production (directed by Marianne Weems), with sharply crafted dialogue (scripted by *Wired* editor Martha Bear), stunning set and lighting design (Keith Khan, Ali Zaida, and Jennifer Tipton), and assured ensemble performances. It is also an impressive technological achievement, incorporating six live video inputs (four webcams positioned on top of the telephone operators' computer monitors, and two conventional video cameras), live digital image manipulation, preprogrammed animations and computer graphics (Christopher Kondek), and multiple prerecorded video elements, including documentary interviews with real Asian telephone operators.

One particularly effective piece of technology is an ingenious piece of hardware: a transparent telephone booth (one is set at each side of the stage) that the performers enter to play the roles of numerous caller characters from the United States. Once inside, the performer engages a foot switch which adjusts the angle of a thin film of plasma molecules inside it, to produce a frosted effect to the glass, silhouetting and shrouding the character in a diffused mist. Builders Association director Marianne Weems discusses the company's use of digital technologies in terms of using "tools for a new audience," and particularly younger audiences who readily relate to the genie of technology.[27] *Alladeen*'s youth-oriented offshoots include a music video and an extensive website where, among other things, visitors can rub a lamp and make a wish.

Robert Lepage

Visually and stylistically, Quebec multimedia theater luminary Robert Lepage sits somewhere between the rich illusionist aesthetics of George Coates and the sharp, deconstructive media-theater of the Builders Association. Space has been an abiding fascination and obsession for Lepage and his Ex Machina Company (founded in 1994), and while predominantly presenting work on traditional theater stages, his explorations of different types of spaces, both literal and metaphoric, are extensive. They span the geological (*Tectonic Plates*, 1989), the geographical (*The Seven Streams of the River Ota*, 1994), and the mathematical (*Geometry of Miracles*, 1998), and have charted the territories of inner space (*Needles and Opium*, 1991) and outer space (*The Far Side of the Moon*, 2000). Lepage actually uses relatively few computer-generated effects to ignite his visual spectacles, preferring the use of conventional video projection in conjunction with kinetic screens, mirrors, and ingenious mechanical sets. But as one of only few super-league multimedia theater practitioners, he is of considerable interest and significance both for our discussion of space, and in relation to the wider field of inter-media performance. In Lepage's productions, spaces visually morph, mutate, and transform, often with thrilling speed and theatrical impact. Reviewing his oeuvre, John O'Mahoney describes Lepage's "chimeric . . .

uncanny, almost unnatural powers of visual transfiguration, as waterlogged lecture halls transform themselves into the canals of Venice, piles of old books meld into the New York city skyline, an old tumble dryer becomes a spacecraft's docking bay"[28] (figure 14.11).

Lepage is ingenious and at times mesmeric in his use of video and multimedia projections, as well as in his physical configurations of stage space. His exhilarating and highly physical London production of *A Midsummer Night's Dream* (1992), for example, was staged entirely in a shallow pool of water through which the actors waded, prompting Timothy Spall, who played Bottom, to joke some months later, "I'm still picking the mud out of me arse."[29] The water was surrounded by a circular bank of wet mud, which provided a gloriously messy running track for furious chase scenes between the love-drugged, sexually charged ingenues in the forest.[30] A review of Lepage's work indicates the expressive and eclectic ideas, themes, and mechanics with which he has altered traditional proscenium arch stages to create or evoke different spatial locations and configurations.

A rotating cloth back-projection screen provides the only set for one of his most critically acclaimed and visually compelling works, *Needles and Opium* (*Les Aiguilles et l'Opium*, 1991). Lepage's one-man performance initially places him in the present day, waiting to provide a voiceover for a film about Miles Davis, while staying in a Parisian hotel room formerly occupied by existentialist writer Jean-Paul Sartre. He makes numerous phone calls, including to the hotel reception desk to complain about the overly loud sounds emanating from a lengthy lovemaking session in the adjacent room. Behind him, a female mannekin with shapely breasts and thighs becomes visible, pressed tightly against the flexible, fabric screen, its head inclined back as if in the throes of orgasm. As Lepage muses by telephone on the rich artistic history of the visitors to the hotel during the 1940s and '50s, the performance begins to weave together three stories. Jazz trumpeter Miles Davis's heroin addiction following the breakdown of his relationship with Juliette Greco is explored in relation to French poet and filmmaker Jean Cocteau's opium addiction and trauma over the loss of his lover, and Lepage's own painful obsession with his ex-partner.

Lepage is suspended in midair in a flying harness when in the role of Cocteau, whom he plays with florid hand gestures, and a charm and presence as rich and thick as the French accent he intones (figure 14.12). At one point, he begins to fall asleep and slowly slumps forward in the harness. Behind him, a dense, graphical blue spiral begins to turn and spin, transporting him into a dream sequence. In another scene, he addresses the audience while the projection behind appears to place him hovering in space outside two windows of a high apartment building. "And I am quite proud of myself that you all know my name so well, and so little of my work," he says, "For my work will draw you down avenues of sleepwalkers that will give you such a vertigo you will never forgive me." He lunges forward and downward in his harness, as the backdrop projection of the building suddenly jerks and moves rapidly in the opposite direction, vertically upward.

Figure 14.11 A laundromat-cum-spacecraft in Lepage's *The Far Side of the Moon* (2000). Photo: Sophie Grenier.

Figure 14.12 Robert Lepage as Jean Cocteau in *Needles and Opium* (1991). Photo: Claudel Huot.

As classical music soars, the building and its windows sweep up through the frame as Lepage somersaults in freefall, his limbs expressively conjuring feelings of, by turns, flailing panic, swimming through water, and blissful flight. As he tumbles poetically in midair, the composite image is a spectacular *coup de theatre*, although somewhat ironically, of course, as it borrows its effect directly from cinema: a classic matte trick shot.

One of the most memorable images is a shadow effect realized with a distinctly lowtech overhead projector, as used in classrooms to display text written on transparent sheets of acetate. The shadow of a spoon placed on its horizontal surface is back-projected on the stage screen, and two hands holding a hypodermic syringe come into view. Its needle is positioned in the bowl of the spoon, and heroin solution is slowly drawn up to fill the transparent body of the syringe. Behind the screen, Lepage walks forward, using his teeth to tighten a tourniquet on his left bicep, his shadow illuminated by the projector beam. He stops at one side of the screen and stretches out his arm. The giant syringe, larger on screen than Lepage's entire body, is raised, and its huge needle is positioned to appear to make contact with his lower arm. The shadow-play injection is administered with the needle slowly seeping liquid (onto the horizontal overhead projector surface), which creates a bubblelike water droplet on top of his arm, which becomes a gradually widening pool that bleeds around his shadow body. Lepage inclines his head as the drug takes its effect, and uses his other hand to slowly remove his sunglasses. The needle is withdrawn, and both it and the outstretched arm simultaneously register a brief physical shudder as the contact breaks.

Another screen image, played to the music of a Miles Davis trumpet solo, is a fixed underwater camera shot of Lepage swimming beneath the water, a trumpet held in his left hand, air bubbles billowing from his mouth (figure 14.13). The top of the camera/screen frame corresponds to the swimming pool's surface, so that as he rises up for air, his head and shoulders disappear out of the top of the frame. Simultaneously, the head and shoulders of the live Lepage rises above the screen (he is on steps behind it) to complete the picture, his "real" head and upper body precisely matched in scale and position as if joined to his recorded body, which treads water. The live Lepage holds a telephone and makes a quick call before taking a deep breath and disappearing behind the screen at the same time as his filmed body takes another dive underwater.

In *Elsinore* (1995), his solo version of *Hamlet*, Lepage achieves spatially disorientating effects, using a virtual doppelgänger and staging sequences from rear and overhead perspectives within Carl Fillion's moving set, which "spins, flies, warps and endlessly reconfigures itself in a mesmeric geometrical ballet"[31] (figure 14.14). Live camera projections relay simultaneous views of Lepage (who plays all the characters)[32] from multiple angles, and sometimes overlays them together. The final duel scene employs a miniature video camera to relay the action from the dynamically shaking point of view of the poisoned tip of Hamlet's sword. On a sand-covered set, *Geometry of Miracles* (1998) explores the intersections of materialism and spirituality through the overlapping life stories of mystic philosopher George Gurdjieff and architect Frank Lloyd Wright (played by a woman, Marie Brassard). As the two protagonists search for mathematical formulas to express and explain artistic, existential, and scientific questions, Lepage spatially conceived different sections of the performance according to different geometric shapes including triangles and squares, and a circle in the form of a giant, onstage eyeball (figure 14.15).

For *The Far Side of the Moon* (2001), with a musical score by Laurie Anderson, the American-Soviet space race is set against the story of the aspirations of two estranged, warring brothers who are reunited following the death of their mother. The cross-theme is set up in an early scene where the elder brother Philippe (all characters are played by Lepage) makes his formal presentation of his doctoral thesis. He questions how much the 1960s desire to explore the cosmos was driven by a quest for knowledge and understanding, or simple human narcissism—a tension he later self-reflexively explores about himself and his relationship with others. The piece is filled with such dualities—communism versus capitalism, Earth versus space, youth versus age (it begins with the imaginative musings of a twelve-year-old boy stranded in a laundromat), Philippe's dreamy intellectualism versus his brother Andre's practicality, and the moon's dark side versus its light side (figure 14.16). The set has a cinematic look, masked into a letterbox shape, and kinetic

Figure 14.13 Robert Lepage's "live" head emerges above the screen while his projected body treads water. Photo: Claudel Huot.

Figure 14.14 Robert Lepage as Hamlet in *Elsinore* (1995). Photo: Richard Max Tremblay.

Figure 14.15 Robert Lepage's *Geometry of Miracles* (1998) Photo: Sophie Grenier.

Figure 14.16 Robert Lepage, in the role of Phillipe, muses on the lunar landscape in *The Far Side of the Moon* (2001). Photo: Sophie Grenier.

mirrored panels slide into place to create myriad locations from lecture theaters and wardrobes to elevators and airplane interiors. Harvey O'Brien describes the set as

a remarkable creation . . . a revolving, evolving, virtually living space. . . . When matched up with several conveyor belts and a significant porthole which serves as a washing machine door in the opening scene, only to morph into a space capsule and metaphorical birth passage, this set seems truly capable of delivering meaning "out of the machine." Evidently expensive and requiring precise timing and co-ordination of the multimedia projection also used to illustrate the action, it would all mean nothing were each of its increasingly impressive convolutions not inextricably bound to the dramatic core.[33]

The sliding back wall serves as a projection screen for archival film and original video footage, and to evoke myriad locations, while its circular window becomes (in addition to the washing machine door and space capsule noted by O'Brien) a goldfish bowl, a clock, and a CAT-scan machine (figure 14.17). The production is dramatically uneven, and the relationship between the brothers never quite fulfils its psychological and emotional promise, but the visual panoply of spatially mutating effects is often dazzling. This is particularly true of the final image of a "virtual space walk," using an acutely angled mirror projection to visually immerse the prone, fetus-like figure of Lepage (and in later productions, Yves Jaques). He seems to be floating unencumbered by gravity, and then, in the words of one critic, "soaring, spiralling, flying, a blend of some great bird and Yuri Gagarin" in the vast, star-filled blackness of outer space.[34]

Figure 14.17   Robert Lepage's cinematic set for *The Far Side of the Moon*. Photo: Sophie Grenier.

Lepage and the Critics

Lepage's vitality and imagination in visually mutating theater stage spaces has led normally careful and staid critics to announce (more or less) that he has single-handedly revitalized the dying art of theater, and to gush in idolatry eulogies proclaiming him an "alchemist," a "visionary," an "extraterrestrial," a "genius."[35] Even years before Lepage had really made his mark in the United Kingdom with *Needles and Opium* at the National Theatre in 1992, a leading British critic had begun his canonization. "When I first saw it [*The Dragon's Trilogy*] in Toronto last year, I compared [Lepage] to the young Peter Brook," wrote Irving Wardle in 1987. "Given the show's subsequent growth I would like to amend that comparison to the mature Peter Brook." This comparison to the critically deified figure of Brook (widely considered by the British to be the greatest director of all time) is no faint praise for a bastion of conservative British theater criticism to offer a young Canadian. In 1992, the no less revered British critic Michael Coveney called *Needles and Opium* "the most technically adroit and emotionally coherent mixed media presentation I have ever seen."[36] Meanwhile, lesser intellectuals but otherwise far more famous figures such as musician Peter Gabriel were acclaiming "a real visionary, creating theatre for people who don't like theatre,"[37] and in Gabriel's case, employing him to direct the stage show for his acclaimed *Secret World* tour (1994) and collaborating with Lepage on *Zulu Time* (1999), which we discuss in chapter 21.

Gabriel's analysis is reflected in Lepage's self-perception as a director aiming to reignite theater for a new generation of audiences. After directing *Erwartung* and *Bluebeard's Castle* for the Canadian Opera Company, Lepage reflected that "my greatest satisfaction was that the balcony, where all the cheap seats are, was crammed with young people. . . . We have to keep this craft alive."[38] But Lepage resists comparisons made to stage conjuring by critics such as the *Sydney Morning Herald* reviewer who called him "a master illusionist of the stage,"[39] and by Ian Shuttleworth, who dubs him "The Québecois sorceror" whose production of *Elsinore* put "any [traditional] performance of stage magic to shame."[40] Lepage replies: "I don't think there is any kind of magic about what I do. . . . All of the connections are there, somewhere in the subconscious or in the collective unconscious."[41] Moreover, he maintains, "the theater is implicitly linked to technology. . . . There is a poetry in technology, but we try to use it in a way that does not eclipse the action on stage"[42] (figure 14.18).

Many critics agree. "Robert Lepage has never used these technologies purely for their avant-garde effect, refusing to play on their capacity to fascinate, but rather concentrating on their function as tools of artistic expression," says one.[43] But others beg to differ, including Shuttleworth, whose analysis of *Elsinore* echoes a number of more circumspect critics over the years who have admired the visual pyrotechnics but nonetheless pointed out that Lepage's overuse of machinery and projection effects has often been to the detriment of other dramatic elements:

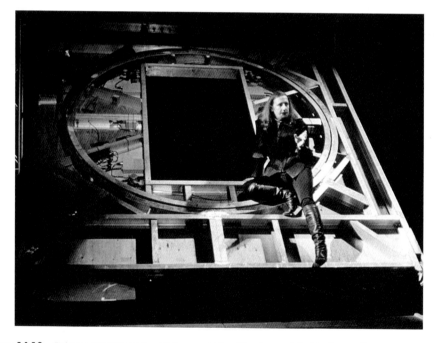

Figure 14.18 Robert Lepage's set for *Elsinore,* which critics have related to the traditions and mechanics of stage magic and illusion. Photo: Richard Max Tremblay.

The disappointment is that all these presentational wonders form the exoskeleton of a piece which has surprisingly little to say about Hamlet, either the character or the play. . . . its exterior shimmers and dazzles so much that we can see scarcely anything of the meditations which may be behind it. . . . the 95 uninterrupted minutes of another's words in *Elsinore* (delivered in an artificial stage-English accent) fail to convey much of note either to the heart or the head.

It is as if Lepage, despite having mounted the edited text in such a magnificent visual armature, is paradoxically timid of offering an interpretative performance himself . . . Beyond a pervasive concern with mutability, relativism and uncertainty in all its forms, *Elsinore* is virtually mute. And so *Hamlet* provides us, after all this time, with yet another paradox: a production which is at once unenlightening and unmissable.[44]

The same concerns and criticisms around the delicate balancing act between style and content, the visual and the textual, the mediated and the live, which were so evident in the reviews of pioneering multimedia theater productions in the early 1900s, continue a hundred years later and doubtless always will. But whatever perceived tensions exist between Lepage's technological and textual sensibilities, he remains a consummate master of the art of multimedia spectacle and the transformation of theatrical space.

Virtual Reality: The Search for Immersion

Sunk in their pneumatic stalls, Lenina and the Savage sniffed and listened. . . . "Take hold of the metal knobs on the arm of your chair," whistled Lenina, "otherwise you won't get any of the feely effects."
—ALDOUS HUXLEY, *BRAVE NEW WORLD*, 1932[1]

Can VR replace RL? Only if theater can replace actual life. Only the bumpkin rushes to the stage to rescue the maiden from the villain, but the late twentieth century is apparently filled with willing bumpkins! Like theater, VR developments contain devices that enhance the VR experience and distract from RL contexts."
—DON IHDE[2]

Theater has always been a virtual reality where actors imaginatively conspire with audiences to conjure a belief (otherwise known, after Coleridge, as a "suspension of disbelief") that a bare stage is in fact the courtyard of an ancient Theban palace, or the 1692 witch-trial courtroom in Salem. Pioneering Virtual Reality (VR) theater designer Mark Reaney describes theater as "the original virtual reality machine" where audiences can visit "imaginary worlds which are interactive and immersive,"[3] and VR artist and critic Diane Gromala argues that VR's historical precedents can be traced through "the fantastical worlds elicited through mimetic simulations of ritual, dioramas, art, literature and theater . . . the evocation and perception of a shareable but other worldly place in which humans extend and project their agency."[4]

   Oliver Grau's *Virtual Art: From Illusion to Immersion* (2003) presents a detailed genealogy of the origins of VR, exploring the histories of immersive panoramas and illusionary spaces back to antiquity, effectively turning the whole of art history into a media history. For Grau, the computer is simply the latest tool permitting the artist to investigate the manipulation of the image and its relationship to reality:

In many quarters, virtual reality is viewed as a totally new phenomenon. However, a central argument of this book is that the idea of installing an observer in a hermetically closed-off image space of illusion did not make its first appearance with the technical invention of computer-aided virtual realities. On the contrary, virtual reality forms part of the core of the relationship of humans to images. . . . The idea goes back at least as far as the classical world, and it now reappears in the immersion strategies of present-day virtual art.[5]

VR is an industrial computer graphics format simulating navigable three-dimensional environments and requiring considerable computing horsepower. Although the term has been used increasingly loosely in popular culture to refer to anything digital including even email, stricter definitions stress its highly specialized and particular nature which places it firmly out of reach of most computer applications and simulations. In 1995, Ken Pimentel and Kevin Teixeira called it "the first 21st century tool" whose primary defining characteristic is immersion: "inclusion, being surrounded by an environment. VR places the participant inside information."[6] Others highlight the responsive navigable elements using first-person cinematic point of view, which Daniel Sandin considers to be "the first redefinition of perspective since the Renaissance."[7] R. U. Sirius sees VR as creating an entirely new type of space, an extension of the imagination, articulating it in terms of a "re-virginizing . . . the creation of virgin space."[8] Howard Rheingold, one of its most enthusiastic early advocates and author of one of the first major books on the subject in 1991,[9] usefully summarizes VR's ontology in terms of three interdependent aspects: "One is immersion, being surrounded by a three dimensional world; another one is the ability to walk around in that world, choose your own point of view; and the third axis is manipulation, being able to reach in and manipulate it."[10] He goes on to describe VR as an ultimately theatrical medium, yet recognizes the challenge inherent in transforming a solo and subjective first-person experience into one that approaches Aristotelian understandings of theater. Nevertheless, central tenets of Aristotle's dramatic notions such as mimesis and empathy are intrinsic to VR, and, he suggests, "I think that properly done, a virtual reality experience will have a greater sense of mimesis and of participation in the events."[11]

Critics and academics have added some degree of confusion to the territory by applying the term VR to performances that do not in fact use classic VR technologies—where, for example, environments are fully navigable or use three-dimensional computer graphics. George Coates's digital theater settings, for example, were linked to VR by a number of critics during the early 1990s, although Coates himself was clear and categorical about the distinction between his work and immersive industrial VR applications, in 1995 calling his performances "virtual virtual reality . . . a way of evoking the sense of awe that immersing yourself in virtual reality produces. . . . Someday we'll be handing out VR goggles instead of 3D glasses."[12]

As we will see, the steps toward advanced VR theater and performance have been limited to date, although those relatively few practitioners involved in the field have been neither tentative nor unambitious in their approaches.

A History of VR

Major developments in VR took place in the 1980s, although its origins go back to Ivan Sutherland's 1965 paper "The Ultimate Display" and his development over the next three years of the first Head-Mounted Display (HMD) with student Bob Sproull for the Bell Helicopter Company, using ARPA military funding. Sutherland created the first computer-aided HMD in 1968, with internal sensors that tracked the user's head movements, an event Oliver Grau has subsequently called "the first step on the way to a media utopia."[13] The helmet design incorporated two miniature monitors placed directly in front of the eyes to create binocular 3D vision, and although certain features including the mini-video monitors have changed and been updated over the decades, the basic design remains the same today.[14]

Although most commonly associated with HMD devices that the user wears to eliminate peripheral vision of the real world, VR technologies and applications use a variety of interfaces including projection desks; flat, curved, or semispherical screens; and specialized computer monitors. Its industrial applications include military and flight simulations, medical training programs, engineering prototype designs, and navigable architectural and town planning environments. As Bolter and Gromala point out, "simulators are almost the only commercially successful applications of virtual reality."[15]

The most famous VR industrial pioneer (as well as one of its most noted aesthetic visionaries), Jaron Lanier, founded VPL Research in 1983, created the first commercial dataglove in 1984, and established "a networked virtual world system in 1989."[16] Given his hippie-like, New Age look (complete with dreadlocks) and radical artistic philosophy, Lanier appeared at that time an unlikely scientific boffin and was so distinctly "cool" that he became the first white man to be named "Black Artist of the Month" by *Ebony* magazine.[17] He was also responsible for coining the term "Virtual Reality" to distinguish between wholly immersive digital worlds and traditional computer simulations. VR necessitates absolute inclusion within a 360-degree digital environment, the user metaphorically stepping inside the computer:

Virtual reality is all about illusion. It's about computer graphics in the theater of the mind. It's about the use of technology to convince yourself you're in another reality. . . . Virtual Reality is where the computer disappears and you become the ghost in the machine. . . . The computer retreats behind the scenes and becomes invisible.[18]

At the University of North Carolina, Frederick Brooks developed advanced VR systems which allowed a sense of touch. His Grope-III project, completed in 1986, used motorized handgrips and magnets that controlled remote robotic arms. This Argonne Remote Manipulator (ARM) exerted tactile pressures or resistant magnetic forces against the operator's hands in response to the user's attempts to touch and manipulate the virtual materials viewed.[19] Around the same time, Lanier and Thomas Zimmerman developed wired gloves that enabled virtual objects to be grasped and moved around, thus enabling the user's body itself to become part of the virtual world. Though all normal vision is lost wearing a HMD, the dataglove allows the user to hold up her gloved hand in front of her face and see a digital representation through the HMD that moves in perfect synchronization with her own.[20] Pimentel and Teixeira have noted how "seeing the representation of your hand suddenly changes the perspective. You now have a perceptual anchor in the virtual world. You're actually inside the computer because you can see your hand in there"[21] (figure 15.1).

In 1991, Daniel Sandin and Thomas DiFanti developed the CAVE (Cave Automatic Virtual Environment), which takes its name from Plato's famous metaphor for humanity's sense of reality, whereby the other people and things we see are in fact *behind* us. We sit in a cave, wrote Plato, staring blankly at its dark interior wall rather than out at the light, watching a dance of shadows: the images of others cast by firelight onto the cave wall.

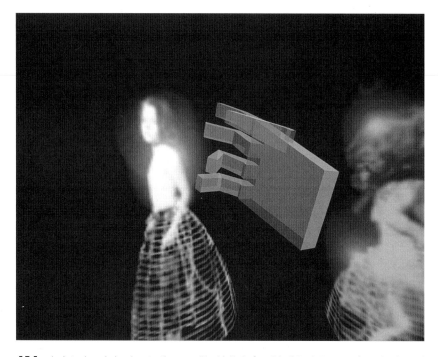

Figure 15.1 A dataglove helps locate the user "inside" the world of Toni Dove and Michael Mackenzie's dreamlike VR experience *Archeology of the Mother Tongue* (1993).

The VR CAVE uses immersive projections onto three walls and the floor of a (typically) small space, which dispenses with the need for HMDs (although stereoscopic glasses are worn). Users commonly operate a mouse "wand" to manipulate the environment, and a "head tracker" detects the user's changing spatial position and angle of point of view, prompting the software to display realistically changing perspectives.[22] Largely due to cost, relatively few art or performance projects have taken advantage of the rich potentials the environment affords, with notable exceptions including the colored aquatic architecture of Margaret Watson's *Liquid Meditation* (1997); Maurice Benayoun and Jean-Baptiste Barrire's war-torn VR wasteland *World Skin* (1997); and *ConFIGURING the CAVE* (1996, Jeffrey Shaw, Agnes Hegedüs, Bernd Linterman) where users transform imagery and sound within the CAVE by manipulating their life-size, puppet-like avatar.[23]

The theatrical and performative possibilities of VR took a quantum leap when Lanier's VPL Research company created a full body version of the dataglove—the DataSuit. This allows multiple users to don suits and headsets and see, talk, move, and interact with one another within a shared synthetic environment. Users can even change their physical form in the virtual world, choosing from a menu of options. One VPL demonstration had two people represented as lobsters, the networked computing systems visually reinterpreting the users' movements into those of the giant crustaceans, a friendly wave of the hand appearing as threatening swipes of an enormous front claw.[24] In *Virtual Reality* (1991), Howard Rheingold rightly predicted that adapted DataSuits would soon allow for fully sensory and tactile effects, with wearers able to transmit and receive "telecaresses," including simulated sex, which he termed "teledildonics."[25]

In the early 1990s, only a small number of artists experimented with VR. These included Kazuhiko Hachiya, whose *Inter Discommunication Machine* (1993) was a VR experience for two people where each user's HMD "projects one player's sight and sound perception of a virtual playground into the other one's display, thus confusing the borders between 'you' and 'me.'"[26] As Christiane Paul points out, it has close conceptual parallels with the "Sim-Stim" apparatus in William Gibson's *Neuromancer*, which enables users to experience other people's bodies and perceptions.[27] This notion became a recurring theme in VR performance experiments over the next ten years, particularly following the groundbreaking projects developed at the Banff Center in Canada between 1992 and 1994.

The Art and Virtual Environments Project, 1992–94

We got this very fancy fellowship . . . and we have produced what is now considered the first virtual reality works that were ever done. They just came out in a book. . . . Every artist that contributed to the work has contributed both in writing and in visual imagery.[28]

So wrote the first man to have reputedly "danced in cyberspace," the Israeli/American choreographer Yacov Sharir. The book referred to, *Immersed in Technology* (1996), contains eleven essays on the implications of cyberspace and ten theoretical/technical statements by practitioners then working with virtual environments, all arising from the Art and Virtual Environments Project at the Banff Centre from 1992 to 1994. It was a landmark project in exploring the artistic and performance potentials for VR, and Sharir's dance in cyberspace was considered by fellow digital performers at that time to be an artistic equivalent to the first moon landing—a small step for a man and a giant leap for (artistic) mankind. The space-age analogy seems appropriate for Sharir's collaboration with visual artist Diane Gromala, *Dancing with the Virtual Dervish: Virtual Bodies* (1994). The performer is described as a cybernaut, the (mental and technological) distance traveled appears great, and the environment is alien if not exactly hostile.

In all, nine experimental projects were supported by the scheme including Perry Hoberman's *Barcode Hotel*, Ron Kuivila's *Virtual Reality on 5 Dollars a Day*, Marcos Novak's *Virtual Worlds* (an architectural piece that grew out of the *Dervish* Project), and Toni Dove and Michael Mackenzie's *Archeology of the Mother Tongue*, a piece featuring some breathtakingly beautiful digital imagery (figure 15.2). The project director Douglas MacLeod notes, "We really had no idea what we were doing. This is a very liberating, if exhausting, method of production. It was like staging nine different operas in two years while at the same time trying to invent the idea of opera."[29] The project was indeed a unique development in the performing arts so early in the 1990s, and VR was such a novel technology at that stage that various options were still under active discussion (VRML and VRML2 standards, for example, were only agreed *after* the Banff projects). Gromala has paid tribute to "unprecedented funding" that enabled four computer scientists and six art technicians to work with the artists over two years to achieve a "landmark artwork . . . [that] was one of the very first in VR."[30]

Placeholder

Chronologically, Brenda Laurel and Rachel Strickland's much-celebrated *Placeholder* was the first work to be completed for the project, premiering in 1993. Driven by eleven computers (from a Silicon Graphics Reality Engine to an Apple Powerbook) and over 25,000 lines of code, it opened up the potential for virtual flight (through the character of a crow), although conceptually it was grounded very much in the earth and its gravitational pull. Rather than a futuristic journey into the far (metaphorical) reaches of outer space, *Placeholder* returned to nature, to the ancient and primeval, and to drama's distant roots in ritual and the sacred. In her PhD thesis, later published as *Computers as Theatre* (1991), Laurel conceived VR as a spiritual space, a place functioning like Dionysian festivals and primitive tribal rituals. She theorized VR as a distinctly new space, but ultimately one of return: a place to "reinvent the sacred spaces where we collaborate with reality in order to transform it and ourselves,"[31] and she attempted to put theory into practice with *Placeholder*.

Two participants each enter their own, green-matted "magic circle" (Janet Murray has noted its correspondence with the "fairy ring," a traditional space of enchantment),[32] ten

Figure 15.2 "The Coroner's Dream" sequence from Toni Dove and Michael Mackenzie's exquisitely designed *Archeology of the Mother Tongue* (1993).

feet in diameter and ringed by rocks. A technician fits them each with an HMD and attaches sensors to their bodies, which enables their full body movements to be tracked and interpreted within the VR environment, rather than through the simple head or hand movements of most VR experiences. The ritual pattern is begun with participants "being reborn in a different body, and acquiring enhanced powers of perception that deepen the bond of the subject to the natural world."[33] Participants adopt the character, ways of movement, point of view, and even voice (their own being synthetically manipulated)[34] of one of four animated spirit creatures: Crow, Snake, Spider, or Fish. As they encounter other creatures and move close to them to hear their stories, they can metamorphose to exchange "embodiments" and become them, in what Marie-Laure Ryan describes as "a forceful allegory of the immersive power of narrative."[35]

Participants are guided through the virtual landscapes by the disembodied voice of the Goddess, a live performer (normally played by Laurel) who watches the users' actions and speaks to them via a microphone, offering navigational advice and secrets about the virtual world. "Only spirit creatures live in these places. You must join with them. Spirals move the spirit creatures through the world. The places here are marked with many voices," she says during one performance. The Goddess also coaches and encourages the participants' animal-like movements, which propel them through the virtual space: participants playing Crow, for example, can flap their arms in order to fly (at least from their visual point of view), and are rewarded with the Goddess's warm and reassuring praise: "Nice flight, Crow!" The landscapes they move through are modeled on three locations near Banff: a cave with a natural hot spring; a waterfall in Johnston Canyon; and an area of spirelike earth formations called hoodoos.

The background VR spaces are, in comparison to today's standards, relatively crude: the graphically rendered interior of a cave lacks detail, while an exterior wooded mountain landscape is constructed in VRML-style, from segmented and composited video images, which lend them a blurred and pixelated quality, and a 2D photographic perspective (despite their 3D navigability). But the signs, markings, and spirit characters that inhabit and float through the spaces are intriguing and arresting graphical icons. Their "petroglyph" designs derive from ancient iconography inscribed on the landscape around Banff since Paleolithic times, and from Aboriginal and primitive art.

The two participants talk to and interact with the virtual spirit characters, and although physically remote in their two magic circles can also meet and communicate with each other; they can also touch and move virtual objects with the aid of gripper data-gloves. Each creature (as well as features of the landscape imbued with their own spirits), can talk and tell their story, and thus "interactivity occurs on the macro level as freedom to explore, while narrativity is found on the micro level as embedded stories."[36] As Marie-Laure Ryan points out, *Placeholder*'s narrative structure owes more to epic theater than to the Aristotelian dramatic structures Laurel advocates in *Computers as Theatre*: "its architecture is more indebted to a poetics of space than to a poetics of plot."[37]

The user's character roles and the other nature spirits found within the VR environments were initially developed in workshop improvisations with actors from Precipice Theatre Society. A videotape of these improvisations shows the performers adopting different animal movements and characteristics while working outdoors in the specific locations the VR landscapes are derived from. One male actor scrambles about on all fours around another performer, who stands with her hands in the air. "I weave my alphabet in the Hoodoos, I tell the tales of the giants," he barks up at her. "The story is an ancient one, of the Hoodoos, who are frozen statues by day, and awake by night and by heat. All travellers who pass by in their way—hacked!"

In *Placeholder*, as the participants encounter the virtual spirits and speak to them to access their stories, they also leave their own "marks" within the space: their words are recorded and stored in rocklike graphical images, which later participants can access and rearrange by touching. Thus, like the petroglyphs, graffiti, and trail signs in the actual landscapes that inspired the piece, "the virtual landscape accumulated definition through messages and story lines that participants left along the way."[38]

Laurel and Strickland have emphasized the importance of placement and spatialization of sound to the experience. The Goddess's voice, for example, is spatially positioned above the participant's head (yet still inside the landscape), and the artists stress that they "wanted people to feel they were being drawn through space and time by sounds coming from the world ahead." Marshall Soules notes how the spatialized auditory signals and perspectives are employed like nonvisual trails to orient participants, and he describes the considerable impact they have on the user's body. He highlights the role of sound in achieving a developed sense of user immersion and suggests that this works in accordance with Artaud's ideas for "a theatre of spectacle which subverts the conscious mind by impinging directly on the flesh."[39]

Placeholder has been discussed extensively by academics,[40] and Katherine Hayes provides a particularly interesting perspective. She observes that despite its celebrity, *Placeholder* was experienced by very few people during its short life at Banff, and Laurel and Strickland's video of the making of the project "is as much or more the work of art as the VR production itself."[41] She muses on the levels of simulation at play between the original VR simulation (of the real-life landscapes) and the video that in turn then simulates the VR. She argues that at both levels, Walter Benjamin's sense of the aura of originality is almost completely dissipated, and in the precession of simulacra, the lesson to be learned is:

When matter and information begin to copulate, more is destabilized than contemporary constructions of the body. . . . Just as it is no longer sufficient to think of the body as flesh or code alone, so it is no longer sufficient to accept distinctions that rely on putting artists in one category and technicians in another, or originals in a gallery and copies in Walmart. It is not only the human body that is undergoing a sea-change. Also in the throes of mutation is the body of art.[42]

Marina Grzinic has also leaned on a perspective from Benjamin (though not in relation to either *Placeholder* or "The Work of Art in the Age of Mechanical Reproduction") to provide a fascinating argument in relation to VR's ultimate dissipation of aura. In "A Small History of Photography" (1931), Benjamin proposed that the longer the exposure time of the photograph, the more a sense of presence, time, expression, and aura is woven into the image. As photographic technologies developed (lenses, film sensitivities, and so on) and shorter exposure times were enabled, there was a negative qualitative shift in the sense of time, space, and aura evident within the photograph. Grizinic extends the argument to suggest that the near-instantaneous processing times of computers has similarly led to an eradication of a sense of time and aura within digital images, and that VR represents the most unauratic of all digital forms:

We are witnessing an ever more exact and complete aesthetic sterilization of the image. In virtual reality, the physicality of the connection of the image with reality-time is lost. Blurs and other imperfections in the image, which were evident in time's passage in the real world, are wholly absent from the idealized imagery of virtual reality. . . . The image undergoes a process of complete sterilization.[43]

Osmose

But visual aura, of the lack of it, was not the key issue for Char Davies when she created the most talked-about experience in the (short) history of VR art, *Osmose* (1994–95). Her concerns were spatial and corporeal, oriented towards a transformation of immersive virtual space into "a spatio-temporal arena in which mental constructs of the world can be given three-dimensional form and be kinaesthetically explored through full-body immersion and interaction."[44]

The revolutionary aspect of *Osmose* is its advanced sense of fully embodied immersion through the use of a (then) sophisticated datasuit, in contrast to most VR experiences, which utilize only HMDs and thus tend to emphasize the Cartesian mind-body split, since the user's experience and navigation corresponds only to their head movements. *Osmose's* interface covers and "reads" more of the body (but contrary to many commentaries, not the full body, only from the waist up) and its monitoring of the user's breathing, the essential element of bodily life, is particularly important to the sense of a fully embodied, "living" immersive experience (figure 15.3). Its nature imagery and theme further enhance the sense of an organic, natural experience.

A single user, which Davies calls the *immersant*, is fitted with a HMD and a motion-capture vest equipped with breathing and balance sensors, and stands in a small private chamber facing a larger audience space. Her breathing and movement affect the projected stereoscopic imagery, as she undertakes a journey through forests, clearings, ponds, sky, and subterranean earth. In the other space, spectators watch two luminous screens; one relays the immersant's VR point of view, the other shows her shadow-silhouette (figure 15.4). Davies conceives the placement of the real-time shadow image of the immersant alongside her point-of-view projection as both poeticizing the relationship between her body and the artwork and drawing attention to the crucial role of the body as the "ground and medium" for the experience.[45] The experience begins with a projected three-dimensional grid, which helps to orient the immersant, providing clear spatial coordinates that can be seen to alter in direct relation to breath and body movement. Mark Jones describes the beginning of his experience:

I don my HMD and the assistant wires my chest and back with interface devices. *Osmose* is activated and I am transported to a 3-D wireframe grid. "Practice," they say, "get used to the space and the interface." I look all around me and the grid extends to infinity in all directions. I inhale and gradually begin to rise; if I lean forward I move forward. Lean back and I move

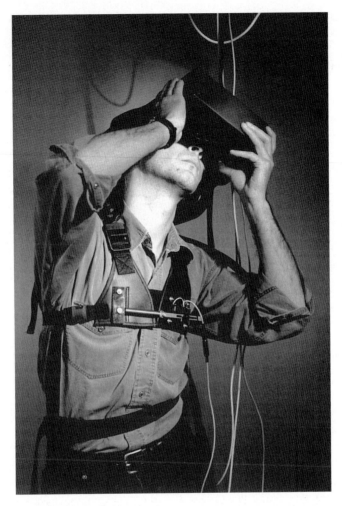

Figure 15.3 An "immersant" wearing stereoscopic head-mounted display and breathing/balance interface vest for a performance of Char Davies's Osmose (1995).

backwards. I'm flying, I am an enigma, I have no physical form, yet I am whole. I am an "immersant."[46]

The wire frame gives way to sumptuous and extraordinary navigable graphic landscapes, structured in a vertical model. Deep breath inhalation and upward body movement ascends the immersant through forest floor to tree trunk, to leaved boughs and up into clouds, while slow exhalations and low movements plunge one down into a pond, through subterranean earth, and to an abyss. At either end of the vertical spectrum (and

Figure 15.4 Installation view from 2003 of *Osmose* at the Australian Centre of the Moving Image, Melbourne, showing the audience's dual view of the shadow of the "immersant" and the changing virtual environment she journeys through.

the experience) stands the wire grid, and pieces of text by Davies reflecting on the relationship between nature and technology (above), and the computer code used to generate the *Osmose* worlds (below). Specific forms within the landscape spaces (clouds, trees, roots, rocks, water) are dramatically hyperreal and dreamlike. A magnificent giant tree appears like a translucent ghost, its multiple limbs and branches like white ice or sharpened glass, cutting into the surrounding blue-black sky sprinkled with showers of snowlike stars. The subaquatic and subterranean spaces are vast, rippling layers of quasi-organic visual forms and colors. The soundscapes are similarly multilayered, beautiful and haunting—like *Placeholder*, the audio is also spatialized, responding to the user's location, direction, and speed of movement.

Davies is categorical in pronouncing VR as a decidedly *new* and unprecedented artistic form:

The medium of immersive virtual space is not merely a conceptual space but, paradoxically, a physical space in the sense of being extended, three-dimensional and enveloping. As such it is an entirely new kind of space that is without precedent. I think of immersive visual space as a spatio-temporal arena, wherein mental models or abstract constructs of the world can be given virtual embodiment in three dimensions and then kinaesthetically, synaesthetically explored through full-body immersion and interaction. No other space allows this, no other medium of human expression.[47]

The piece's title, a derivation of "osmosis," suggests how *Osmose* aims to absorb the immersant into the artwork, and to pass them from one space into another, just as biological osmosis involves a passage from one side of a membrane to another. Davies's objective is to resensitize the user, to reconnect the links between body, mind, and world: "to heal the Cartesian split between mind/body, subject/object . . . in a dream-like way, shifting the immersant's mode of experience away from the everyday bias of eyesight to one that resonates deeper within the physical body."[48] Her success in doing so (or at least in creating a ground-breaking artwork) is evidenced by a veritable mass of critical eulogies; Oliver Grau goes as far as to suggest that *Osmose* "has received more attention in the international discussion of media art than perhaps any other contemporary work."[49]

What is most striking about the two most famous (by some considerable margin) early VR artworks, *Osmose* and *Placeholder*, is that they both use *Virtual* Reality to place the user in spaces which represent and accord with *natural* reality, with nature. Though neither installation attempts photorealism, both derive their environments directly from actual landscapes and natural objects (trees, rocks, and so on). Although the experiences are quite different from a "real" pastoral journey, in a significant sense the two works draw the user back to nature, effacing alternative or fantasy virtual realities in favour of conventional, known ones. Both use VR to present new perspectives on the natural world (for example, the spirit incarnations in *Placeholder* and the grid and code structures of *Osmose*), but their extremely *high-tech* systems are ultimately used to conjure worlds that are, at least at face value, distinctly *no-tech*. Indeed, the worlds are not even representations of contemporary natural environments, they are of primeval ones: the search for the VR future in performance art has begun with the search for the ancient and primordial. There are no human beings in these two, apparently pre-Neanderthal worlds—just creatures and spirits (*Placeholder*), primordial bogs, ponds, and abysses (*Osmose*).

It is tempting to make great play of the significant irony underlining this high-tech > no-tech paradigm, but that would miss the point. For the artists, the strategy is not ironic at all, since high technology is conceived as a potent new means of return: of (re)discovering the true nature of things, and of contacting or representing one's inner spirit. Nature (that is to say, unspoiled pastoral spaces outside urban confines) is a common theme and audiovisual backdrop in digital performance since it classically represents a place for spiritual enrichment, a locus to be at one and to rediscover timelessness without the nagging incursions of modern life. It is for this reason, we believe, that so many digital artworks and performances hark back, with no little passion, to nature, as we have already seen in relation to robot performance. Davies's later VR work *Éphémère* (1998) is similarly grounded firmly within the archetypal nature metaphor, and is spatially structured into three, all-natural parts: "Landscape, subterranean Earth, and interior Body. The body, of flesh and bone, functions as the substratum beneath the fecund earth and the blooming and witherings of the land."[50]

Dancing with the Virtual Dervish: Virtual Bodies

The interior of the human body is Sharir and Gromala's natural setting for *Dancing with the Virtual Dervish: Virtual Bodies* (1994), which is programmed in continuous motion and undulates as if breathing, like a living body; like both *Placeholder* and *Osmose*, there is an anti-Cartesian concern to excite an embodied experience (figure 15.5). Sharir (in formal performance demonstrations where his VR view is projected on large screens around him) and user/participants (who can explore the VR world by donning the HMD themselves) navigate and dance through the VR body's three-dimensional interior, moving within and through a giant ribcage of what is:

Literally and figuratively a body of enormous scale, the resultant virtual environment is an incomplete torso comprised of a skeletal spine, pelvis and ribs, along with the viscera of a heart, kidney and liver. . . . These organs can be "entered" to reveal otherworldly chambers. The virtual body thus becomes an immersive, nonlinear book, a text to be read, an architecture to be inhabited.

Figure 15.5   Yacov Sharir navigates through the interior of a VR human body in *Dancing with the Virtual Dervish* (1994, with Diane Gromala).

Within the body stands another primary component, another body, video grabs of a dancer transcribed onto a plane. The dancer exists both as representations within the virtual environment and as a performer in the physical performance space, connected to the virtual environment through the umbilicus of the head-mounted display.[51]

Following its premiere at the Fourth International Conference on Cyberspace at the Banff Center for the Arts in May 1994, several further performances and exhibitions followed, including the first Virtual Reality Software and Technology Conference held at the University of Singapore in August 1994, where it was the only arts project represented. In the days following the first experiments Sharir wrote expressively of the novel experience that had seemed like an "otherworldly" or "out of body" incident:

Even though you are grounded in a physical space, you are immersed in cyberspace, and you live now two lives; one in the physical space and one that you are immersed in, which is cyberspace via your goggles. Disconnected from the physical world: entering the cyber world that is designed on the computer. Surfing in cyber world where the surf speed is 60 to 70 miles an hour. . . . But surfing that fast, you get nauseous, sick in your stomach, and you haven't moved physically. . . . So you have this duality of not knowing how to behave in cyberspace and you have now a new life where you have to retrain yourself how to behave in cyberspace, as opposed to in the physical space. . . . It's a new set of behavior that has to be learned and studied and practiced.[52]

This challenge to learn and study physical behavior within VR space would later be taken up and explored in an intriguing way by Gromala in her *Meditation Chamber* (with Larry Hodges, Chris Shaw, Fleming Seay, 2000) which employs a voiceover to take the user through progressive relaxation exercises. Biofeedback devices register the user's physical tensions and releases, and displays equivalent computer-generated 3D graphic representations of the body parts through the user's HMD. The installation underlines meditation's long tradition of enabling "subjects to reimagine their relationship to their bodies in order to achieve a state of relaxation that is simultaneously and indissolubly psychological and physical."[53]

Sharir's experience at the time of *Dancing with the Virtual Dervish* seems to have been something of a conversion: as a practicing choreographer it was as if he had discovered and entered an entirely new dimension, a new environment for performance. Like Char Davies, Sharir conceptualized VR as an entirely new type of space. This was to raise the computer above being seen as a mere tool, a helpful or recalcitrant *device,* to being, conceptually, a means whereby practitioners and audiences could traverse to new locations and horizons:

We still look at computers and video cameras as tools to do things with. I think I like to look at it as *a world, a space.* That once you participate in it, you find for yourself new ways to behave in it. Instead of thinking this is a computer, I like to think this as a theater space, as a performance space. A performance space is a representation of a whole world of imagery. So it's not like this computer, like this tool, like you have a hammer and a nail, and I need to use this hammer to put the nail in the wall. . . . The concept of *using this as a world, as a space where images can take place and come to life*, that's, to me, a larger conceptual framework.[54]

But not everybody was immediately convinced that this was going to be a new space where performance could easily exist or benefit. Johannes Birringer, for example, wrote of the event,

While her [Gromala's] conceptual relocation of her body as a virtual stage is truly astounding, what is more difficult to understand is Sharir's relationship to it and his assumptions about choreographing his movements and video images in response to his distressed, dis-orientated body experience. Is his internal experience translated into conscious movement choices or do we see him react to a state of disconnection from himself?[55]

Sharir was well aware of such questions and problems, and his own description of the event ends with seven questions to be pondered, the first being "is the nature of dance altered by this potential?"[56] His subsequent work suggests that he is still engaged in that mission, undertaking exploration of a larger conceptual framework by various means but not always following the most obvious route: for example, he has undertaken enhancements of the initial developments by working collaboratively with computer scientist programmers, by utilizing motion capture and computer animation leading to live performance with virtual entities, by developing cybersuit-activated performances, and, most recently, by translating the real-time movement of crowds in a public space into virtual dance.

VR Theater Reconstructions

In the same way that we have discerned a significant return to the myths and eras of the past in the performative usage of advanced technologies in areas such as robotics and the VR worlds of *Placeholder* and *Osmose*, futuristic VR found an early affinity with the ancient theater of Greek and Roman civilizations. By 1997, following years of historical and archaeological research, a team from Warwick University's 3D Visualisation Unit led by Richard Beacham had created accurate and exquisitely detailed 3D reconstructions of ancient theater buildings, including the Theatre of Dionysus in Greece and the Theatre of Pompey, Rome's first permanent theater (figure 15.6). These VR reincarnations seemed every bit as extraordinary as the dramas once performed in their spaces, and involved dedicated and meticulous work, drawing upon existing information and new data and measurements obtained by the team's visits to what little remains at the physical sites. It resulted in VR screen-based reconstructions that could be explored and "flown through" with an ease and facility that exceeded anything that even the original architects or audiences could have witnessed. The VR software enabled structures to be explored from the micro to the macro,

Figure 15.6 Richard Beacham's detailed VR reconstruction of the Theatre of Dionysus. Courtesy of Kings Visualisation Lab, Centre for Computing in the Humanities, Kings College London.

along with all the theatrical and practical aspects of sightlines, facilities, access, egress, and even the acoustics within the space. Moreover, as Beacham has emphasized, the clean lines of computer-reconstructed ancient theaters create a picture of magnificent auditoria *as then* and *as new*, and every bit as impressive as our most recent arenas and auditoria, rather than as spaces of dusty ruins and broken columns, as many are still naively prone to think of them as existing in their own day (figures 15.7 and 15.8).

VR technology hereby made a clear and unequivocal contribution to theater history research and classical scholarship, and its impact was recorded widely outside academia, including a *The Times* (London) color supplement in 1998 headlined "Unmasking the Greek Mysteries: virtual reality revives the oldest theatre."[57] Significant aspects of this unmasking and revival of the mysteries of ancient theater were its newfound archaeological accuracy, visually arresting computer modeling, accessibility and maneuverability, and also its particular contributions toward archaeology and the humanities (particularly history and theater studies), as well as information technology itself. The project's status

Figure 15.7   Richard Beacham's VR model of Rome's Theatre of Pompey emphasizes its grandeur and newness at the time it was originally built. Courtesy of Kings Visualisation Lab, Centre for Computing in the Humanities, Kings College London.

as an excellent example of the new world order (computing) valuing and investigating the ancient one to reveal new perspectives and insights led to substantial financial support from the United Kingdom, Europe, and America. This has resulted in a range of equally extraordinary reconstruction projects including the theaters of Pompey and Messene, and subsequently more recent theatrical antiquities such as Christopher Wren's Theatre Royal in Drury Lane, and Vanbrugh's Queen's Theatre in London, the Paris Opera, the Teatro Olympico at Vicenza in Italy, the Hellerau Festspielhaus in Dresden, and Wagner's Bayreuth Festspielhaus. But while these reconstructions involve rigorous archeological and academic research, Beacham is quick to point out that "every picture is a hypothesis or a guess based on a number of evidence sources. . . . There is a serious danger with virtual reality images. They have a bogus persuasiveness and are increasingly interpreted as reality."[58] Beacham now continues his research at Kings Visualisation Lab, Centre for Computing in the Humanities, at Kings College London.

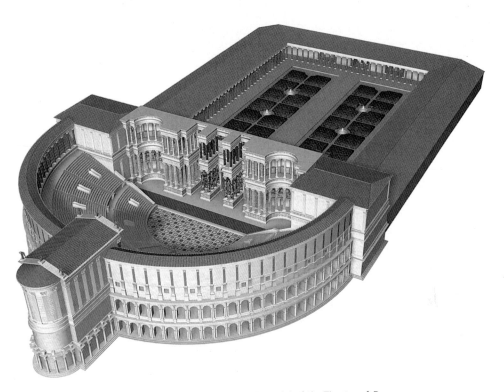

Figure 15.8   An aerial view of Richard Beacham's VR model of the Theatre of Pompey.

Other computer reconstructions and virtual tours have been created by others, including Shakespeare's Globe in London, developed by the Open University in collaboration with the BBC. Other developments were perhaps less eminent but equally signaled that VR had real value for theater research, such as *Scenic Spectacle*, a study of spectacle on Renaissance and Baroque stages produced by the Department of Theatre and Dance at Appalachian State University. Nonetheless, it should be noted that such developments were in no way common in the sector at this time, nor have they been since. They were carried out by particular individuals who were skilled, experienced, and committed to the task of producing inventive visual research applications, and were supported by large institutions (mostly universities) and significant funding.

3D Theater Design

VR and related 3D applications such as VRML have exerted a significant influence on theater set and lighting design, and a range of commercial applications were released in the early '90s, including Crescit Software's *Design Suite,* programmed by Canadian Bill Kirby with smaller companies and nonprofit/educational theaters specifically in mind.

Subsequent developments included CAST's *WYSISWYG* ("What You See Is What You Get"), AVAB's *Offstage,* Luxart's *Microlux,* Schneider's *Theater Design Pro,* and a plethora of others covering various specialist applications of lighting, sound, production, and stage management, many being applicable not only to theater stages but also to television, film, and advertising sets and studios. Much of the entertainment industry became first fascinated by and later largely dependent upon the labor-saving shortcuts that dedicated software offered to the basic processes of designing, which at least in theory left the designer freer (software problems apart) to concentrate on the overriding vision of the design concept.

Widely available, but at that time expensive professional CAD (Computer Aided Design) packages were also utilized by a number of theater designers, and these "digital drawing boards" opened opportunities to construct and tinker with complex designs to exact scale and with 3D perspectives in significantly shorter time than traditional drawings and models. From 1992, specialist publications such as *Theatre Design and Technology* were beginning to indicate the opportunities that lay ahead. Articles such as Mark Reaney's "The Theatre of Virtual Reality: Designing Scenery in an Imaginary World" (1992) sounded out the changes and highlighted the questions being raised. Reaney concluded that there was far more to new technologies than designer convenience, and that VR was changing the basic time/space concepts available to theater.

But despite the onset of more advanced commercial CAD, VR and other specialist design packages, many performance designers remained frustrated at their complexities, particularities and limitations. British academic Colin Beardon was one whose frustration led to the development of alternate approaches and resultant freeware that has been used widely, particularly for the training of British university theater-design students. Beardon has a background in computer science as well as an involvement in theatre production, and his approach to software development "stemmed from previous familiarity with software design and implementation, and awareness that commercial software was disinclined to embrace the plasticity, ambiguity and 'creative practices' of performance designers and practitioners."[59] Between 1991 and 1996 he worked with Suzette Worden to produce *The Virtual Curator,* a program for design history students to virtually curate a design exhibition, and this was modified and expanded into the theater design and visualization program *Visual Assistant* (1997) as part of a European Union funded project with collaborators in Finland and France. *Visual Assistant* acts as a simple interface to permit scanned images and default "objects" such as stage flats and pillars to be assembled and manipulated on a perspective stage. The user can navigate freely in three dimensions around the stage and theater set to view different angles, and can add to the design using freehand drawing. Beardon describes the program as more of a designer's sketchbook than a technical drawing board, which is part of its appeal to students who can learn and create with the software very quickly and easily, something that could certainly not be said of CAD software.

It was first released as a freely downloadable program for Macintosh only, and it is an indicator of the time and investment required that *Visual Assistant* took nine years to develop to a reasonably sophisticated dual platform level to include the PC. For its time it was a remarkable contribution to the growing awareness of what was potentially possible, and Beardon went on to establish the Networked Virtual Reality Centres for Art & Design, located at three universities in England (Coventry, Plymouth, and Teesside), which experimented with accessing and transferring digital 3D designs over networks. He continues related work through the biannual CADE (Computers in Art and Design Education) conference and the journal *Digital Creativity*, both of which he is a cofounder.

Chris Dyer, an established British theater designer with awards for his work at the Royal Shakespeare Company and the Royal Opera House was another early pioneer, who developed a more sophisticated and professionally oriented program, *Open Stages* (1998, also known as *Virtual Stages*). Like Beardon, Dyer was concerned to create software that was specifically evolved and adapted to the particular creative (rather than purely technical) needs of the theater designer.[60] The program offers a 3D computer model of a specified theater or performance space into which associated objects and technologies such as lights, sound, fly bars, revolves, and trucks can be arranged. A library of adaptable templates allows the user to then pull in generic or custom-made pieces of scenery, position them on the stage, and thereafter manipulate and light them in real time, just as one would with physical scenery in a theatrical space.[61]

Such custom-built theater-design packages, as well as those from the commercial sector, have brought about change and new approaches, but a debate nonetheless continues about the computer's advantages over traditional methods in conceiving and developing stage designs. Roma Patel undertook a comparative study in 1999 using Ionesco's play *Amédée* as a case study and sounding board, and produced *A pLACE TO pLAY* (2000), a CD-ROM that records the process and outcome. It demonstrates and evaluates—by means of an interactive presentation combining drawings, stills, storyboards, walkthroughs, and 3D models—a design for *Amédée* developed through Internet collaborations with other designers, and applying computer techniques to traditional problems of set, props, and costumes. In 2001 she repeated the exercise with another CD-ROM, *The Design Diary: Working Across Borders*, which she describes as "a practical example of using Computer Aided Design & the Internet for Remote Co-operative Working amongst Theatre Practitioners in the USA & UK."[62] Patel's conclusions stress a balance between the creative potentials of design technologies and the requirement for theater designers to also have a thorough grounding in more traditional, analog techniques:

Computer technology is fast reaching the point where it can be used to produce work as far as our imagination can take it. It is time that the Theatre Design profession realised its potential as a tool to bridge gaps in the work of a scenographer. At the same time . . . many conventional skills are transferable and the new mediums need not alienate the scenographer. I am convinced . . . the work achieved here would not have been possible without my foundation in traditional model making and drawing.[63]

The professional theater designer has always had the task of considerable number crunching to ensure the accuracy of the dimensions of technical drawings and scale models, and the computer is now seen as *the* essential tool of the trade for many. Refinements of CAD programs to aid simplicity of use has been particularly important, including CADD (Computer Assisted Drafting and Design) and subsequently AutoCAD software, where the alteration of one aspect by the operator automatically tumbles the effect throughout the whole design in a form of "double entry." Of even greater consequence has been the migration of software from expensive high-end computers to the ordinary desktop and then laptop; and the ability of programs to automatically render 2D drawings into 3D "visual reality" designs.

But a key issue remains that first prompted designers such as Beardon and Dyer to create their own programs: that commercial software has built-in limitations and can constrain originality and innovation through its particular look and approach to drawing, layering, rendering, and texturing. This is an aspect that both software programmers and theater designers are still seeking to address, on one hand by theater designers continuing to combine traditional drawing board conception and creativity with screen-based techniques, and on the other hand by improving software to stretch and overcome its own preferences and limitations, so that default styles and repeated traits become less discernible.

VR Scenography in Real Time: ieVR

In the early 1990s, American theater designer and academic Mark Reaney was using early VR software as his drawing board tool before building his sets in metal and wood. One day in 1993, he thought it would be useful to project the VR images onto the stage cyclorama to get a larger-scale impression of the design he was working on. He set up a projector, and on seeing the result, he decided not to go back to the analog technologies of wood and steel, but to rely almost entirely on VR.[64] With modest budgets and resources, Reaney and his colleagues at the Institute for the Exploration of Virtual Realities (ieVR) at the University of Kansas have since pioneered a series of theater productions combining live actors with VR environments.

ieVR use VR technology as their prime scenographic medium in order to achieve a sense of immersion, which Reaney believes is a central concept shared both by theater and VR. Echoing Brenda Laurel's ideas, he also sees reciprocity between theater and computer technologies, suggesting that industrial VR developers could adopt theatrical ideas and metaphors: "theatrical practices may prove to be worthy of emulation in designing virtual environments."[65] In "Virtual Reality and the Theatre: Immersion in Virtual Worlds" (1999), he discusses the nature of immersion and how it applies to VR and theater. He argues that in commercial applications where technology is used to mimic actual objects and environments such as machinery or buildings, a perceptual and biochemical sense of immersion may take place, but after a short time the virtual environments become less immersive since they lose the interest and engagement of the user. Reaney's work in VR set design attempts to negate this problem, by not simply immersing, but also engaging the visual and imaginative attention of the theater spectator.

ieVR's interpretation of Elmer Rice's classic expressionist play *The Adding Machine* (1995) became the first full-length theater performance to use VR. Rice's play was first produced in 1923, and traces the journey of Mr. Zero in his search for happiness in a mechanized and dehumanized society. The company notes the irony that the dark specter of computers foretold in Rice's play are here used "not as a dehumanizing force, but as an artistic medium . . . to simultaneously illuminate Rice's story even while it embraced another, more sympathetic, view of technology."[66] The actors performed in front of a rear projection screen displaying stereo-optically polarized VR imagery created using *Virtus WalkThrough Pro* software, which the audience viewed through 3D polarized glasses. As in all ieVR productions, movement and navigation through the VR backgrounds was rendered in real time, operated live by an offstage technician known as a VED (Virtual Environment Driver). The VED uses a mouse or joystick to move through the simulated spaces or to change the backgrounds in relation to the movements of the onstage actors or developing dramatic action. Two further projection screens displaying 3D still images were placed at a 45-degree angle at either side of the main screen to enhance the sense of immersion. The virtual scenery was sometimes used as an impressionistic or expressionistic representation of the location the characters were in, and at others it reflected psychological elements, particularly the inner thoughts and fears of the protagonist, Mr. Zero: "Fanciful and frightening environments were created in order to illustrate the mindset of the main character. As he becomes disorientated, walls shift and furniture floats off the floor. . . . In prison, the bars of his cell appear immense, the window miniscule. But in his daydreams, he and the audience are whisked away to a blissful beach."[67]

ieVR stress that VR is used "not merely as spectacle for its own sake, but as a new and exciting scenographic medium in the service of a script; virtual reality becomes another component of the collaborative theatre art."[68] David-Michael Allen concurs with the analysis, suggesting that through the use of VR computer graphics and real-time television techniques "the production explored the mental state of Mr Zero more successfully than traditional production techniques,"[69] citing one scene as a particularly effective example. Zero stands onstage and is fired after twenty-five years of work (to be replaced by the adding machine of the title) by his Boss, who plays the scene offstage in a green-screen space, with his live video image projected on the main screen behind Zero. Using chromakey video-mixing techniques, the green background is filtered out and replaced by computer-generated office scenery to form a composite image of the Boss in his office. As Zero reacts to the news, the camera zooms in on the Boss, his laughing face growing larger and larger above Zero, emphasizing the protagonist's impotence and diminishing status. Allen also notes the power of a romantic sequence where Zero and Daisy fall in love and dance in front of a VR projection of a vast expanse of flowers: "As the dance continued, the field of flowers receded and fell away as the dancers appeared to take flight, travelling through blue skies and star-filled heavens."[70]

In 1997, audiences donned half-silvered Head-Mounted Displays[71] for ieVR's production of Arthur Kopit's *Wings* (written in 1977), enabling them to see a superimposition of both the VR computer-generated graphics projected into the headsets, and the live actors performing onstage. Reaney describes the quality of immersion as "very pronounced" and the VR design as being conceived to enable the audience to share the sense of distress and mental anguish suffered by the central character, Emily, following a stroke:

Shattered images of the people and places that surround her pass by before her and our eyes. Sights and sounds born from her memories float just out of our reach. This proved to be a powerful source of engagement. In a traditional staging, the audience can empathise with Emily by seeing her distress and helplessness. In a VR staging we experience the stroke with her.[72]

It is interesting to note that one of the most powerful and beautiful VR images in *Wings* was also one of the simplest to create graphically: a snowstorm that surrounds Emily. While a similar effect could have been produced using a theatre snow machine, the ghostly, ethereal superimposition of virtual snow on the corporeal body of the actor conjures an image that is more poetic, poignant, and ambiguous (is the snow a scenic representation of Emily's "real" environment, or her state of mind?)

HMDs were also worn by spectators for ieVR's adaptation of Samuel Beckett's *Play* (1996 [written in 1963]), which projected into the headsets prerecorded 3D video of the play's three characters cocooned in their urns. Reversing traditional stagings whereby the actors are live and the spotlight that interrogates them is a technological device, director Lance Gharavi took the "role" of the spotlight, and controller of the technology. The technician VED thus became the central character, appearing as the only live performer on stage and acting as a master of ceremonies who activates and manipulates the virtual characters. This interesting experiment explores, in Gharavi's words, ideas around "presence," "absence," and "apparent presence" that he identifies as fundamental themes in Beckett's later plays. He also suggests that "because it relies heavily on electronically mediated images, this presence/absence continuum also plays a pivotal role in the performance text of almost all forms of cybertheatre."[73]

ieVR's *Machinal*

Machinal (1999) readopted the staging configuration of ieVR's first production *The Adding Machine*, with a central VR rear projection screen and two angled side screens, and the audience wearing polarized 3D glasses. However, the side screens no longer played still images, but prerecorded moving 3D imagery of landscapes, objects and hyperrealistic machinery. The production of Sophie Treadwell's 1928 expressionist play was the most ambitious VR theater production of its time, as Reaney's Press Release suggests:

The "virtual scenery" for *Machinal* will far outstrip i.e.VR's previous projects in terms of the quality and detail of the scenic image, creating three-dimensional "real-time" environments that are at once fantastical and startlingly life-like. Powerful new computer workstations and WorldUp R4 software from Sense8 will create virtual scenic environments with astonishing complexity and rendering speeds. . . . With its capacity to give visual emphasis to both the outer life the Young Woman faces as well as her inner torment, VR forcefully extends the dramatic reach of this already powerful work.[74]

Its opening sequence is a visual tour de force. From the spectator's perspective, a small 3D cinematic-style title appears and looms toward us, giving way to what appears to be a subterranean tunnel that we travel along and down. This emerges into a surrealistic office with huge animated metal arches that circulate and cascade like silver waterfalls. Massive revolving shafts and cogs rise ominously from the floor. The side screens display sharp graphical clockwork mechanisms, continually rotating and spinning, while on stage, actors (playing secretaries) scurry back and forth in a hive of noisy activity. Our movement around the virtual office is constant for several minutes, as we roam through 360 degrees past filing cabinets, desks, and typewriters, and into the office's hidden, angular alcoves. The swirling VR point of view and the antlike activity of the onstage secretaries finally and dramatically come to a halt on the entrance of the boss, Mr. Jones. On his exit, the flurry of action and movement continues once more (figure 15.9).

Movement through the VR environments is used to memorable effect in a number of sequences. The protagonist Helen lies onstage recovering after giving birth following her reluctant marriage to Mr. Jones. The VR set is a hospital room with a graphical 3D bed, drip-feed, and light, all seemingly suspended in space. There are no walls. The background is a matrix of metal, a menacing construction site, where cranes lift huge diagonal girders into the sky. During the scene, as Helen struggles with increasing depression and desperation, our point of view moves higher and higher away from the room to look down on the bare hospital bed as it slowly diminishes in size, finally becoming invisible. During the trial scene following her murder of Mr. Jones, Helen sits in front of a huge image of scales of justice that tip back and forth, while close-up live camera images of the two warring lawyers are projected high on either side of her (figure 15.10). In the final scene, following Helen's conviction for murdering her husband, we follow her journey from a bright square cage representing her cell to the electric chair. The door of the cage swings open and, as two guards lead Helen offstage, the VR image travels through a narrow, high-walled corridor to an ominously bare and silhouetted electric chair. The live actors

Figure 15.9 Mark Reaney's VR scenography for ieVR's *Machinal* (2000) is operated in real time to move in relation to the actors' movements and actions.

playing Helen and her guards then appear in silhouette behind the screen, and a clever illusion is created, as Helen appears to "sit" on the virtual chair and the guards strap down her arms and legs (figure 15.11).

The synthesis of live theater and computer technology as realized by ieVR is visually rich and theatrically inventive, and features skilful direction of actors by Ron Willis and Lance Gharavi, as well as Reaney's bold and frequently stunning 3D VR designs. ieVR's co-production with the University of Kent (UK) is also impressive, setting *A Midsummer Night's Dream* (2000) against VR backgrounds of fantasy sci-fi, machinic chessboards, cyberspace, and computer games, and using a floating 3D avatar of a donkey's head to signal Bottom's transformation. The lovers' arguments in the forest are counterpointed by the VR image of their avatars fighting in a boxing ring, characters get lost in three-dimensional mazes and sewers filled with broken Pac-Man and Pong games, and the whole performance ends with a cataclysmic computer crash and the words "Fatal Error."

Figure 15.10 The trial scene from ieVR's *Machinal.*

However, the aim to create a truly immersive theatrical environment in ieVR productions ultimately remains unrealized. The sense of movement through the virtual sets and spaces is gripping, yet the audience remains a considerable distance from the action, in traditional rows of raked seating, distinctly separated from the stage and the VR screens. Budgetary considerations also mean that the projection screens themselves are relatively small (four meters tall and six meters wide for *Machinal*) and constitute only a limited percentage of spectators' overall angles of view, thus limiting the feeling of complete visual immersion associated with industrial VR applications. Traditional notions of user-controlled exploration and interactivity within the virtual environments are also absent. Nonetheless, ieVR's exploratory work offers significant and exciting glimpses into the future of VR scenography in theater, and has led Thomas W. Loughin to suggest that the importance of their experiments to theatrical development may be "equivalent to the introduction of stage lighting."[75]

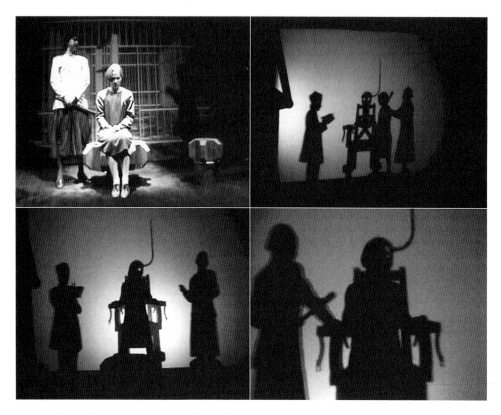

Figure 15.11 Live shadow play and a VR model electric chair combine for the climax of *Machinal*.

Brainscore

An abstracted VR war game filled with smart weapons and featuring men in quasi-military uniforms is played out by two performers for the benefit of a theater audience in David Grassi and Darij Kreuh's thirty-minute performance *Brainscore* (2000). Two male performers in red boiler suits recline in full-body-length, high-tech chairs at either side of the stage, their heads motionless in large neck rests. Electrodes attached to their heads monitor their brainwave activities, and eye-tracking cameras are focused on one of each of their eyes. A video image of each moving eye is relayed onto two floor monitors in the center of the stage, which place the performers' pupils within a gunsight-style graphical target. Facing the operators, and the audience, whose members wear polarized glasses, is a large screen projecting a rotating, custom-designed 3D VR environment, its virtual walls, ceiling, and floor composed of the word "Brainscore."

A synthesized female computer voice announces that she is "Loading Properties," and the screen environment transforms into a concave space composed of small, stretched green oblongs somewhat reminiscent of the streaming computer code in the opening credits sequence of the movie *The Matrix* (1999). In the foreground, two amorphous spheres, red and blue, float, rotate, and dance around each other, suspended in space. These are the two performers' avatars, and at this stage they are like soft, plasticine planets: "empty . . . they neither possess any specific aesthetic characteristics, nor behavioural."[76]

The system then loads five sets of twenty objects containing different types of information that the operators use to feed, fill, and mold their avatars by using their brainwaves and eye movements to fulfill a series of operations and commands. These objects appear as other, smaller, spherical shapes on screen, which move in accordance with the operators' brain and eye activities. Three head electrodes transmit their brainwaves to an electroencephalograph, which analyzes and transfers the EEG signals to a computer which interprets and processes them, while the eye-tracking system also enables the performers to effect real-time manipulations of the objects within the VR screen space. LCD monitor consoles set in front of the performers (and also projected onto large side screens) show a brain, divided into five active areas and cortexes (motor cortex, auditory cortex, and so on), and each brain area relates to one of the sets of spherical objects loaded and its manipulation.

Each brain area has been designated a theme regarding the global migration of goods and information: transport, the media, meteorology, the stock exchange, and epidemic diseases, and each theme is represented by twenty global webpages that refer to it. The performers direct their eyes and brainwaves on the appropriate brain area displayed on the LCD screen to activate direct contact with the Internet and the server that hosts the page they are looking for. This "pinging" procedure activates the real time transfer of the objects' data to the performers' avatars, and the computer Voice helpfully informs us: "Properties chosen by users' brain activities." On the main center screen, the cellular spheres send concentric circles of graphical "beams" that the protagonists' avatars absorb, transforming their color, shape, texture (and sound) to become like irregular, bulging boulders, which spin and rotate.

The synthesized voiceover then announces "Passwords to define aesthetic value," and a stream of graphical passwords (collected from the webpage of an anonymous hacker) appear to swarm and spin around the screen. These are programmed as links to the other objects, and when the performers use their eyes and brainwaves to manipulate them (using a specific pattern of beta and theta frequencies), they "score" (hence the piece's title) and "feed" their avatars with data, whereupon the password flies away off screen. The avatars grow larger and more physically and kinetically defined, and the climax is reached when the performers' avatars have absorbed sufficient data, and the computer voice announces "Avatars Ready . . . Avatars Perform!"

The other graphical objects and passwords disappear, and the two avatars begin to communicate with one another kinetically and sonically using the data that composes them. The musical effects increase to a crescendo of "conversational" computer whirs and bleeps, ambient musical sounds and computer-game style "stings," as they undertake a frantic and frenetic improvisational dance. The 3D avatars change color and shape rapidly, and loom forward and backward dramatically in the shadowy VR space. Their amorphous, meteorite-like appearance gives way to head and skull-like shapes that "dance" and "sing" together as they luminously metamorphose in gravitation-less space. At the end of their pas de deux, the computer voice declares, "All properties matched," and the stage lights and screen fade to black.

Brainscore is a highly sophisticated neuro-VR performance based on the model of an advanced, avant-garde 3D computer-game, but it arguably works more effectively as a technological demonstration than as a satisfying performance. That is to say, it demonstrates complex and fascinating software research undertaken to present new technological paradigms for performance, rather than creating an intellectually or dramatically fulfilling piece of theater. By contrast, the war game at the heart of Blast Theory's VR performance installation *Desert Rain* (1999) provides a theatrically unified and unforgettable VR experience for its six audience members/players, who pursue their human targets through a VR desert landscape projected onto a rain-curtain of flowing water, which we analyze in detail in chapter 24.

Eduardo Kac, an artist seemingly with a finger in every conceivable digital arts pie, has utilized VR to quite different effect, providing headsets to offer gallery visitors unique views of his telerobotic creatures, such as a macaw in *Rara Avis* (1996), and a bat in *Darker Than Night* (1999, with Ed Bennett). Visitors to the Blijdorp Zoo in Amsterdam were given access to the point of view of Kac's *Darker Than Night* "batbot" as it flew among three hundred real Egyptian fruit bats in a small cave. The telerobotic bat "contains a small sonar unit in its head, a frequency converter to transform bat echolocation calls into audible sounds, and a motorized neck which enables its head to spin."[77] As the batbot flies around the cave using its sonar to avoid the other creatures, the user's vicarious view through the VR headset shows the hundreds of real flying bats as kinetic white dots. Kac points out how the presence of the artificial bat significantly affects the behavior of the real ones, and how both continually monitor and track each other. "*Darker than Night* emphasizes the barriers that prohibit each individual to move beyond one's insular, self-reflective experience," he writes. "The bat, a rarely understood, enigmatic, flying mammal, represents the mystery and nuances held within each individual's consciousness."[78]

The Future of VR Performance

Now we're at the threshold of the next revolution in user-computer interaction: a technology that will take the user through the screen into the world "inside" the computer—a world in which the user can interact with three-dimensional objects whose fidelity will grow as computing power increases and display technology increases. This virtual world can be whatever the designer makes it.

—JOHN WALKER[79]

Despite the enthusiasm of John Walker, and the heady predictions of other VR prophets of the early 1990s such as Lanier, Rheingold, and Pimentel and Teixeira, artistic VR applications have so far failed to fully realize the visionary expectations. Writing in 2003, Christiane Paul notes how "full immersion into a simulated world that allows users to interact with every aspect of it is still more of a dream than a reality." She points out that the art world is currently far behind the VR experiences which use force-feedback devices in theme parks, which is currently where the most advanced experiments are taking place.[80] Scott deLahunta reflects that while dance has been at the forefront of experimentation with interactive technologies, performances have mostly been presented in conventional proscenium spaces, and the potentials of VR for dance have been largely unexplored. He notes that even the most radical choreographers have become somewhat entrapped by a fixed sense of performance space and time, and a separation between dancer and spectator, whether in live or "dance for camera" contexts, and he suggests that dance's engagement with VR is now long overdue.[81]

Bolter and Gromala suggest that "although VR has proven useful for specialized applications, we are not any closer today [2003] than we were in 1990 to a general, 3D, immersive interface." They see "ubiquitous computing," defined by Mark Weiser as "when almost every object either contains a computer or can have a tab attached to it,"[82] as the future direction of digital technologies. Rather than VR's search to eliminate the interface and become a converged, transparent window into pure experience, it is the opaque scattering of multiple computational devices throughout the environment that presents the most compelling model for future human-computer interaction: "Digital designs intersect with our physical world; they cannot escape into pure cyberspace."[83]

Two major issues impede the development of VR-based performance experiences: cost and time. The time part of the equation relates not only to the programming and design of thousands of polygons defining the 3D spaces and objects, but also to the time it takes for each individual user to be fitted with the VR equipment and to operate in the virtual environment. Most HMD-based VR experiences are for one or two individuals (although others may watch them and the projections they see from the sidelines, as in *Osmose*), and throughput problems have therefore been a major issue inhibiting widespread development of HMD immersive experiences, including in the commercial sector and in theme parks. Classic VR experiences are highly individual and improvisational, and require sufficient time for users to orient themselves and explore. As Brenda Laurel, Rachel Strickland and Rob Tow put it: "A hard-driving plot with distinct beginning, middle and end is a great way to control how long an experience takes, but 'classic' VR is inimical to this type of authoritarian control—it works best when people can move about and do things in virtual environments in a relatively unconstrained way."[84]

These writers contrast the passivity of mass entertainment forms with the activity and interactivity of VR, where both perceptual and emotional experience depends on the user's action and the environment's responses: "In VR, one is not *done unto*, but *doing*."[85] Like

Michael Benedickt, who once hailed VR as a space where "we will become again 'as children' but this time with the power of summoning worlds at will,"[86] they conceive VR as more a form of play than entertainment, and observe that through their *Placeholder* project they learned that in VR adults play and use their imaginations like children. Equally, they write, "the environment proceeds to record our presence and actions and the marks that we place there—this is a reciprocal affair."[87] They see the future of VR not in installations and public venues, but in VR sites and even virtual theme parks on the Net, enabling much wider audience access.

There have already been some impressive achievements in VR performance, although these are few in number, and interest in using the technology is not widespread. Perhaps, like 3D movies—with which VR shares some distinct similarities—the VR art form will simply not catch on, and will remain an oddity, a novelty. But the potentials of VR application to performance are so enticing that we predict they will be fully embraced and significantly developed in the future for both commercial and avant-garde performance forms. Indeed, it is possible that in the twenty-first century, VR may become as important and revolutionary an artform as cinema was to the twentieth century. With that in mind, we will leave the last, defiantly upbeat words on Virtual Reality to the man who coined the phrase, and has been one of VR's principle industrial originators and popular advocates. Jaron Lanier's breathless vision of VR's future is quintessentially theatrical, and psychologically and sociologically radical:

It'll become a sort of community utility in which dreams are shared and ideas cocreated. . . . You go into your house and you look around, and everything's normal except that there's some new furniture added, but only when you put on these special glasses. . . . One of the items of furniture is a big set of shelves with fish bowls, and if you look in these bowls there aren't fish, instead there are little people running around . . . and a few of them have really weird things going on inside, like bizarre parties where people are changing into giant snakes, and what you do is put your hand into one of the bowls, put your head into it, and all of a sudden it starts getting really big, until you're inside it and become one of those people. . . . I think something very special is going to happen, which I call postsymbolic communication. This is an idea of a new type or stratum of communication where people are skilled at, and used to, cocreating shared worlds spontaneously, improvising the content of the objective world. Without limit, on an ongoing improvised basis . . . like a conscious shared dreaming.[88]

Liquid Architectures and Site-Specific Fractures in Reality

In one way or another, all [digital artworks and environments] are concerned with possible relationships between the physical space and the virtual, and what distinguishes them are the balance
between these two realms and the methods employed to translate one space into the other. Some
artworks try to translate qualities of the virtual world into the physical environment, others strive
to map the physical into the virtual; and yet others are aimed at fusing the two spaces.
—CHRISTIANE PAUL[1]

Liquid Architecture

Marcos Novak discusses computer technologies and cyberspace in terms of "liquid
architecture," an abstracted and fluid, yet still physical form of space, what he terms "a
sense of space not frozen in time. Illustrations of this can be found in various notions of
electronic space, virtual space, three-dimensional renderings of spaces not actually built
or imaginary spaces of the future."[2] These spaces are characterized by response, change,
and exchange: "an architecture that opens to welcome me and closes to defend me . . .
where the next room is always where I need it to be . . . an architecture that breathes,
pulses, leaps as one form and lands as another."[3] Novak relates cyberspatial concepts
of liquid architecture to the future of real-world architecture, where buildings are
responsive, their spaces evolve like a living organism, and "judgements of a building's
performance becomes akin to the evaluation of dance and theater."[4] Ted Krueger conceives
a parallel image for his revolutionary new ideas for the design of "smart" buildings
and environments that he also calls "liquid architecture." He argues for "the possibility
of an intelligent and interactive architecture conceived of a metadermis referencing
work in the fields of mobile robotics, intelligent structures and skins, and interactive
materials."[5]

Such interactive architectural spaces are now emerging from companies such
as Nox Architects, whose Salt Water Pavilion (designed by Kas Oosterhuis, 1997) at

Waterland in Neeltje Jans, the Netherlands, captures real-time meteorological data that alter lighting within the space and the flow of running water down its walls. The linked Fresh Water Pavillion (FreshH20 EXPO, designed by Lars Spuybroek, 1997) has no horizontal or vertical planes, and multiple sensors activate light, sonic, and visual transformations. "Architecture and media are so 'fused' that even the very act of walking trigger sensors to convert the visitors' movements into waves of virtual water . . . projected onto the grids around them. . . . The building becomes animate, *alive*."[6] Elsewhere, computer-aided design's revolutionizing of architecture is epitomized by the magnificent Guggenheim Museum in Bilbao, Spain (designed by Frank Gehry, 1997), a breathtaking space like an ultramodern cathedral for the arts, which is constructed using thousands of panels, each with a different and unique shape and size, and computationally calculated to interlock with one another.

"Performing" Architectural Space

Liquid architecture's dual sense of an external kinetic physical design and an internal interactive and responsive space has been adopted as an important model and metaphor for a number of artists. Gretchen Schiller's *trajets* (2000, with Susan Kozel) is a movement-based interactive installation based on visual and physical interactions in a three-dimensional moving space. *trajets* comprises twelve motorized suspended screens that move in response to the visitor's paths through the installation space, spinning in front, beside and behind the visitor's body as they pass by them (figure 16.1). This creates a dynamic interplay of movement between the visitor and the screen, a kind of dance between the architecture of the installation and the visitor. *trajets* uses the vision-sensing software program *Eyes* (developed by Robb Lovell, who, with Scott Wilson developed the

Figure 16.1   The fluid and dynamic "liquid architecture" of Gretchen Schiller and Susan Kozel's interactive installation *trajets* (2000). Photo: Florence Morisot.

responsive computer system which drives the piece), "force-field" simulation software, a video synthesizer, and custom-made hardware. The force-field simulation translates people (located with *Eyes* in Opcode's software *Max*) into point sources of monopolar magnetic fields, and computers activate the twelve screens, which are each connected to their own step motor and cabled to a motor driver box.

The screens also serve as projection surfaces, adding to the "liquid" effect. The projected images include bodies filmed in various textured environments that change and mutate in response to visitor movement, sometimes recognizably figurative and at other times more abstract, suggesting only traces of bodily movement (figure 16.2). The installation is intended to elicit the public's kinesthetic responses within a moving architecture and is as fluid as the movement of the images and the visitors themselves. The limits of the active space are defined by a string of lights, which wend their way around the perimeter of the screen environment. As the visitor approaches, two of the screens pivot as if to make an entrance to ease the path into the heart of the forest of screens permeated by ambient sound (by Jonny Clark), and peopled by image traces of human motion. The conception of the space is in one sense distinctly related to the futurist idea of a machine aesthetic, as the screens open, close, spin and dance. But unlike the machismo futurist aesthetic *trajets* is calming, gentle, nonthreatening, a chance to immerse oneself in a world and architecture that is in constant flux, but that delights rather than disorientates.

Stephan Silver's background in architectural design has a significant influence on his dance performance installations such as *Virtuoso* (1998) to create what he describes as "a landscape of moving architecture," where visitors travel through narrow, sensor-activated paths of flapping gauze curtains, inhabited by dancers. In *Synfonica* (2000), participants

Figure 16.2 A visitor walks through the responsive kinetic screens of *trajets* (2000). Photo: Florence Morisot.

pass through a black corridor and emerge within a series of corridors and spaces lined with sheets of white gauze, and activate sounds and projected images as they trigger floor pressure pads, light sensors, and ultrasonic devices. Within the space, lit only by the projections, dancers move improvisationally in response to the changing sonic and visual environment, sometimes rolling on the floor under one sheet to emerge at the feet of an audience member in a different corridor or area. Multiple computer animations, programmed using *Director* software, are projected from a number of angles and mirror the clear, geometric shapes of the choreography: squares, triangles, circles, lines, planes, and cubes. As the visual patterns and shapes transform, the dancer's phrases and movements follow suit, physically echoing their open, rounded, angular, and zigzag lines. The animations' bold, richly colored geometric designs directly echo the art movements of the twentieth-century avant-garde, and Silver emphasizes the performance's links to "the Bauhaus, de Stilj, Italian Futurism and Russian Constructivism."[7]

Elizabeth Diller and Ricardo Scofidio draw from architectural theory and practice to create navigable part-physical, part-virtual spaces such as a set dining table in *Indigestion* (1995), which is projected onto a flat horizontal surface. The digital projection includes the hands, but not the bodies, of the dinner guests, whose disembodied conversations critique stereotypes of gendered behaviour. In CHOREOTRONICS Inc.'s dance performance *Byte City* (1997), nine Plexiglas tubes hung on a grid comprise an architectural Sound Field Event Activator (SOFEA), each tube emitting different sounds inspired by nine different geographical locations in New York City. Different members of the company (the costume, lighting, and sound designers, the choreographer, and so on) developed nine sections of the event independently, based on different site maps of Manhattan, which were then performed within the SOFEA structure and its complex sound fields. The company suggest the design concept feigns the structure of cyberspace "in a physical and virtual layering of time and place . . . revealing the enigmatic nature of space and distance in our ever changing world."[8]

The physical architectural spaces of city centers (Manhattan 1989, Amsterdam 1990, Karlsruhe 1991) provide Jeffrey Shaw with his raw material, which he translates into navigable 3D environments. Each virtual building is to scale and is accurately mapped to the real geographical environment, but its shape is transformed into that of a colored, three-dimensional word. Users sit on an exercise bicycle and peddle and steer "through" the large projection in front of them, while a computer analyzes and translates the bicycle's speed and direction in relation to the visual journey. In *The Legible City: Manhattan* (1989) the brightly colored word buildings are composed of texts from fictional monologues written by, among others, Donald Trump, ex-mayor Ed Koch, and a Manhattan taxi driver. Christiane Paul suggests that the city becomes "'information architecture' where buildings consist of stories that are site-specific, related to and enhancing the location visited and thus pointing to the history of immaterial experiences that are not immediately accessible through the tangible form of the building itself."[9]

Sarah Neville's *Calculus of the Nervous System* (2000, with Matt Innes) charts the volatile working relationship between Charles Babbage and Ada Byron Lovelace, daughter of Lord Byron and credited with writing the first computer program, who Babbage called "the Enchantress of Numbers."[10] It is staged within a theater installation designed to echo the architecture of Babbage's 1834 conception for his "Analytical Engine" (popularly considered to be the first significant precursor to the modern computer) on top of which the company mix video, play the harp, and perform. Neville's earlier *Ada* (1998, with Heliograph Productions) transposes Lovelace's story to the twenty-first century, and her original experiments and predictions are reinterpreted through her future counterpart's development of artificial intelligence, electronic music, and the calculus of the human nervous system. Her Lovelace character creates avatars and virtual worlds that, like both the computer and Lovelace herself, become "prone to paralysis, crashes and corruption."[11]

Lynn Hershmann charts Lovelace's life in her feature film *Conceiving Ada* (1994, featuring Tilda Swinton as Lovelace), where "themes of love, sex, artificial life, computers, DNA transference, history and memory intertwine."[12] The movie provides a fascinating early example of another mode of computational liquid architecture through its use of virtual sets, using a custom-made process (LHL Process for Virtual Sets) enabling the settings to be rendered in real time. Rather than postproducing the composite images of the actors and the virtual backgrounds later, as is the industry norm, the performers were able to "inhabit" the sets and watch themselves within them via a monitor during takes. The film used 385 photographs that were digitally manipulated and composited, and static scenes were animated through Quicktime movies to produce licking flames in fireplaces, rain falling on the windows, and even virtual doors that actors opened and walked through. Ada Lovelace has thus emerged as a popular heroine within digital arts, as well as a revered figure in feminist cyber-theory, where her life story has been frequently told, most memorably in Sadie Plant's dazzling discourse on women and new technology, *Zeros + Ones: Digital Women + The New Technoculture* (1998).

Performing Houses

A mixture of real and virtual liquid architecture provides the setting for Keith Armstrong's solo performance *Hacking a Private Space in Cyberspace* (1995). A child's playhouse stands center stage, and Armstrong uses small gestures of his right hand to activate VRML menus to build digital 3D shapes and blocks that are projected onto the physical house. The projected graphics mirror the house's shapes and structure but are misaligned, until a final hand movement from Armstrong maps the VRML projection precisely to the scale and position of the physical structure. To the strains of the song "I Wanna Be Like You" from the Disney movie *Jungle Book* (1967), Armstrong slowly walks along a catwalk above the audience until he stands above the house, looking down. The final section of the performance, which Armstrong calls "Virtual Inhabitation," ends with him stepping off the catwalk and crashing down through the roof of the physical house, which collapses, as the VRML projection and stage lights fade to black.

The Builders Association's distinctive multimedia theater take on Henrik Ibsen's *Master Builder* (1994) involved the construction of a three-story house in a 17,000-square-foot New York warehouse. The house was wired with MIDI triggers (which audience members could explore during the daytime before performances) enabling the performers to activate music and sound effects, thus playing the house like an instrument. During the performance, sections of the house were gradually demolished to reveal new perspectives and to unearth both the house's skeletal structure and the skeletons of the characters' pasts.

Navigable VRML architecture provides the central feature of Uninvited Guests' theater production *Guest House* (1999), which integrates projections from the company's CD-ROM of the same name. A computer operator positioned behind a table at the front of the stage navigates through the CD-ROM, watching the performance and two computer screens, which face the audience. Computer-generated VRML images of buildings and rooms are projected onto a "wall" comprising six thin, white wooden screens, each six feet high and three feet wide. Graphical rooms with names such as "Attic Room, Topsham," "Bedroom, Seattle," and a school "Geology Classroom, 1980s" hang and rotate in midair. They are visually entered and their interiors explored around 360 degrees. Meanwhile, tape-recorded "vox pops" are played of adults and children describing rooms they have known or seen, sometimes "prompted" by a live actor who asks the disembodied voices questions through a microphone. The six screens are separated and moved around the stage on wheels, as a "director" character coaches actors in short scenes. He explains to one how he should enter a room and unpack rocks from his briefcase; and rehearses another in the intricacies of how to vomit realistically following a night of heavy drinking. A woman at home in her underwear catches a Peeping Tom, and turns the tables by forcing him to strip at gunpoint. He undresses. As he is about to remove his underwear, the director intervenes with "that's enough," and the scene ends.

The moveable screens are positioned to create different spatial configurations such as small, walled rooms, where performers sit recounting spaces they know, or stories from their past. The face of one actor hidden behind the screened walls is projected via a live video camera onto the side of his claustrophobic "room" as he confesses how he bullied a child at school, then became his friend, and then became the victim of his new friend's bullying. As he talks, a female actor, visible to the audience, stands at the side, holding a light to illuminate his face inside the room. She occasionally bends her head down behind the screen and out of audience view to talk to the man in the room space. Her head suddenly appears with his in the video projection, far larger than her "live" body, which still stands visibly on stage and seems both (physically) connected and (visually) disconnected from her video-image head and shoulders. In another scene, a female actor describes a room with a bay window and tiger-skin sofa, which is seen as a VRML projection, while a (video) close-up of a live male actor's face (who is hidden within a screened room) is displayed within the projection using a picture-in-picture effect. "Turning to your right you see a bed settee with broken springs," she says, and the computer model pans right to reveal it, while the man's close-up within the image turns in sync to see it. This simple and effective composite image both locates him inside the VRML room and makes it seem as if the room is part of his mind, or his body.

Such moments of physical/spatial separation, which are digitally united, as well as bouts of onstage hiding, which are electronically revealed, work to unify the disparate physical and virtual spaces that make up the mise-en-scène—open stage space, screen configurations, walled rooms, computer monitors, 3D computer-generated projections, and 2D live video relay. But while the relationships between real and virtual space are intriguing and complex, the performance content is less so, and ultimately disappoints. There is too little connection between the behind-the-scenes sequences of the director coaching the actors and the live and audio-recorded descriptions of rooms, and the descriptions themselves become monotonous. No real surprises or drama emerge from the graphical spaces and buildings explored, and the spoken texts do not progress to other levels to establish a new space of their own, somewhere out of the ordinary. The descriptions and recollections remain deliberately, stoically mundane, and are frequently delivered with undue slowness and seriousness:

You are in a living room in the seventies. It looks strangely familiar. In front of you, you see a bay window that looks out onto the street. Turning to your right you see a bed settee with broken springs. On either side of it are two armchairs that are more comfortable to sit in. On the wall there's a reproduction of a painting by Millais. It's a scene where a peasant couple are standing over their son's grave. In the corner of the room you see a black and white television, and next to that a white glossed shelving unit with a gas fire fitted into the middle of it. You notice a music box on one of the shelves. Turning to your right and to the floor you notice an unfinished jigsaw puzzle on a coffee table and on the wall a family photograph with two adults and nine children in it.

As in many digital theater performances, there is a marked contrast between the progressive technological innovations and the safe and prosaic nature of the postmodern text and dialogue, which relies on an audience's appreciation of the meaningfulness of meaninglessness, the significance of insignificance. The deconstructive impulse may reassure performance groups that the ever-referring and deferring properties of text makes banality intellectually compelling, but (at least for us) this swimming in clichés, repetition, and the mundane has now become so exhausted that it signifies performative drowning rather than waving (or treading water, at best).

Sensual and Sonic Liquid Architecture

Sonic modulation and liquidity is a central feature of interactive installations that employ computer sensors and systems to monitor visitor movement and to activate and transform audio files in response. Fluid, responsive sound is often key to the physical and immersive experience of installation (over its observation merely as a picture to be seen), establishing moods and eliciting emotional responses that emphasize and enhance the visitor's connectedness to the space. Choreographer and digital artist Sarah Rubidge's interactive works, including *Sensuous Geographies* (2003), where visitors are blindfolded to focus attention on the centrality of liquid sound, investigate the subtle sensations that permeate the body and give the individual a very particular sense not only of being in that specific space but also of "being in the world" from moment to moment. Her earlier installation work combined responsive sound and music with visual imagery, including *Halo* (1998), where the visitor is surrounded in a darkened space by the light of naked bodies moving and flying above their heads on two massive screens (14 m high × 10 m wide) placed opposite each other some 10 m apart. A "halo" of circling bodies forms, or they walk toward and away from the visitor, each figure interacting both with the live participants (traveling from side to side as the visitor does, or rising and falling to command) and with each other (clustering in groups, forming halos when they "touch" each other).

An interest in social interactivity rather than the one-to-one engagement of a single user installation permeates Rubidge's work, and the intersections, interactions, and sonic/kinetic improvisations of participants provides the core to her most inspiring work, *Sensuous Geographies* (2003, with Alistair MacDonald, Maggie Moffat, and Maria Verdicchio). Nine glimmering gold, white, and bronze translucent banners surround the space, creating a spatial architecture (or geography) through which visitors move—they also serve as distributed projection screens. Among the banners are hung several brilliantly colored luxuriant silk robes, which "guides" dress the visitors in and remove their shoes before providing instructions: (1) enter the space and stand still for at least 15 seconds. Listen, locate yourself in this new resonant space. (2) When you are ready, turn and let your body follow the sound you have identified as your personal sound signature. Then just let yourself be taken by your sound through the space. (3) You may leave the active space and stand on the periphery, and reenter the active space at any time. The visitors are then given a blindfold or veil to wear, ensuring that the space is experienced through senses other than sight—primarily hearing, but also touch, and the sense of proximity to others (figure 16.3).

The active space (4.5 m square) is delineated by a black, soft floor cloth, under which are placed different materials (cut-up duvets, garden bark, bubble wrap, sand) that provide haptic textures for the visitors' feet, and another mode of architectural, sensory engagement with the space. A genuinely immersive sound environment is achieved by the placement of speakers both around the periphery of the active space and the periphery of the space as a whole. As visitors step onto the floor cloth, an individual sound strand accom-

Figure 16.3 Participants don elaborate coloured robes, and veils or blindfolds ensure the environment is experienced through bodily senses other than sight in Sarah Rubidge's *Sensuous Geographies* (2003, with Alistair MacDonald, Maggie Moffat and Maria Verdicchio). Photo: Jem Kelly.

panies them—*their* sound—that they control and modulate through their movements. A motion tracking system follows the visitors via a video camera mounted in the ceiling using color recognition to identify each visitor's robe and hat individually. An interactive sound system (built in *Max4/MSP*) then interprets the data to modulate the users' individual sound strands according to the direction the visitors are moving in, their speed, and when they are still. Proximity to other visitors is a further parameter for sonic transformations, allowing the movement of the group as a whole to affect and build the sound environment.

The experience is delicate, corporeal, uplifting and distinctly liquid. You identify a sound, individual and unique only to you, and hear it modulate and transform in relation to even your slightest movements. You follow your sound, hearing and feeling its changes, and become aware of other shadowy figures moving around with you and of other alterations in the sound textures. You tentatively join in the game, traveling with other visitors, leaving them alone, standing still, listening, waiting, building the sound world, then feeling the sensations it generates, hearing the textures you are helping to create. Suddenly something feels different; the drone providing the ambience has transformed.

Your body feels more upright, your attitude more playful as a new sound world emerges, with which you engage differently. You participate in a spontaneous and almost childlike game involving what one reviewer calls "a personal/group signature tune that constantly shifts and cannot be repeated. On one level it is happy play, on another it taps into notions of wordless communication and issues of identity"[13] (figure 16.4).

The sounds range from the musical to the environmental and are structured according to three central features; the frame/engine; the players; and an operator who sits outside the space at a computer. The frame/engine determines aspects of structure—for example, it limits the number of simultaneous layers (polyphony) and the number of simultaneous processes that are applied dynamically to the sounds. Each participant controls one layer of sound against a changeable contextual sound layer, while the operator makes choices as to which sound materials are allocated to each of the visitors at a given time, and which contextual layer is playing.

The space is thereby "played" in a musical way, and as in many forms of musical improvisation, individuals listen and make space for others, respond, contradict each other, and build duets and ensemble sequences together, while the operator makes particular sonic choices depending on the behavior and energy in the space (figure 16.5). The operator might offer particular materials to a very energetic participant who wants to explore extremes of space, and very different sounds to someone more concerned with delicate movements and tiny details of sound. Each sonic environment generated in the installation has a different sensibility that affects the way the visitors feel in their bodies, and this modifies the quality of their movements while simultaneously changing the musical dynamics and ambiences of the sound space itself.

As they engage with the space the players make a personal journey, a collective journey and an observed journey (by visitors watching or awaiting their turns). Digital imagery—luminous, ethereal figures that echo the colors of the costumes—immerses the space and is manipulated in response to visitor movement using Troika Ranch's *Isadora* system. As in Rubidge's earlier work, the video images (of performers dressed in the colored robes and performing simple pedestrian movements) are radically processed to the extent that they offer only traces of the original human forms, emphasizing the flow of movement and heightening the jewel-like colors of the costumes. These liminal figures appear and disappear on the banners, walking, crouching, rising, gesturing, moving slowly across the banners, toward and away from the visitors, fading away from time to time only to reappear, distributing abstracted choreographic forms around the space.

Sensuous Geographies is a thus a complex, multistranded, dynamic entity that is in a constant state of motion, a never-ending audiovisual liquid architecture always in flux. Participating and immersing oneself in the subtle and exquisite performance of *Sensuous Geographies* is to experience how the space and music feels through the body's intimate "knowledge" (in Bergson and Merleau Ponty's sense of the word as a conjunction between sight/image and direct bodily/physiological perception) of this liquid environment. A

Figure 16.4 The atmospheric and minutely responsive installation space for *Sensuous Geographies*. Photo: Jem Kelly.

Figure 16.5 Two participants interact using their bodies and personalized electronic sounds in *Sensuous Geographies*. Photo: Jem Kelly.

different type of physical consciousness is at play, like that domain described by Henri Bergson as "deep consciousness," by Anthony Damasio as "core consciousness," and by Gerald Edelman and Giulio Tononi as "primary consciousness." But most of all it seems to encapsulate Gilles Deleuze's notions of "affect" and "becoming." *Sensuous Geographies* is, in a very real sense, a "sensational" space, a space where in Deleuzian terms "every sensation is a question,"[14] but a question without an answer—a space of becoming, which never becomes.

The Body's Liquid Architecture

The body itself becomes a type of kinetic liquid architecture in performances where digital projections are mapped directly onto the performer. Li Chiao Ping creates slow, poetic dances where her body is entirely immersed in projections of written text; in *String* (2000)

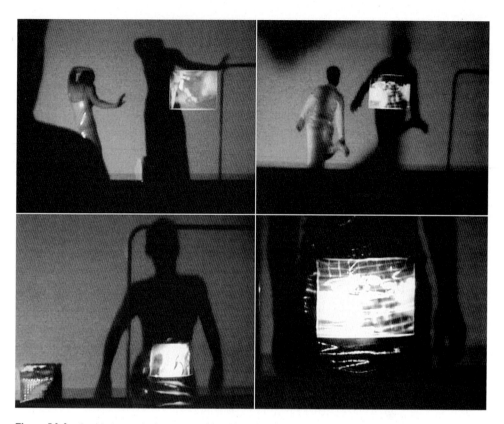

Figure 16.6 Sophia Lycouris dances around a projection before repeatedly submitting her body to its beam in *String* (2000).

Sophia Lycouris dances around and across a projection, and repeatedly reacts like it is an unwelcome memory or technological invasion as it is beamed onto her belly (figure 16.6). In Curious.com's theater production *The Day Don Came with the Fish* (1997), Helen Paris is caught in the projector's beam as an image of a man's face is directed onto a clear, six-inch diameter disk that hangs and spins slowly in front of her face. The male face fills the disc, and as the beam passes through it, the image is enlarged and projected onto Paris's face behind. In another sequence she provides hand gestures in accompaniment to a French recording of Edith Piaf's "Je Ne Regrette Rien" while a wave-pattern line provides another "interpretation." Its zigzag pattern rapidly contracts and expands, dancing across her face and body in synchronized response to Piaf's vocals, which suddenly hit a scratch in the record, jumping and continually repeating the word *"rien"* (nothing) (figure 16.7). The yellow-green line pattern is intensified later into vast swirls of rapidly mutating, tendril-like patterns that seem to consume a live figure standing in darkness onstage. The thin

Figure 16.7 Helen Paris conducts Edith Piaf's "Je Ne Regrette Rien" in synchronization with a mutating zigzag wave pattern in Curious.com's *The Day Don Came With the Fish* (1997).

patterns of light, like animated scribbles, dance frantically around the body in an upside-down V pattern, recalling the robot Maria's electrical animation in Fritz Lang's movie *Metropolis* (1927).

In Bud Blumenthal's *Rivermen* (1999), two bare-chested male dancers (Blumenthal and Fernando Martín) move around a stage that is intermittently bathed in dramatic shafts and pools of light, and then divided into hard-edged, geometric shapes by overhead digital projections (designed by Antonin De Bemels). The downward projection system visually covers the dancers as though immersing them in aquatic and abstracted spaces; or sometimes focused side lighting illuminates their bodies, separating them from the pools of color and vividly transforming shapes on the floor on which they dance. The floor effects enhance both the sense of bodies wading, floating, running, and dancing through liquid and the aim to effect what Blumenthal calls a "poetic coherence" that underlies his digital dance aesthetic. Blumenthal conceives the performer-immersing digital effects in terms of a "third dancer" onstage, which, like the two live dancers, also appears to operate in three dimensions:

With the special projection set-up the video image acquires a new status. It is no longer limited to the two dimensions of a screen. It becomes once again light. It constitutes a moving surface supporting the dance and acts upon the dancers' bodies, transforming them, integrating them into its own structure. . . . The surface reveals itself to be a third partner. A third body is an extension of the dancers' bodies and vice versa . . . resulting in the creation of a harmonious ensemble that is at times put in danger by one of its constituents. A violent ritual leading to a greater adhesion between three bodies. . . . The video is temporal—developing in time like the dance, like a river, like music. . . . The sound, dance and décor move as one event.[15]

The claim is not hyperbolic, and watching *Rivermen* compels and draws one in, enveloping the audience (as the projection effects do to the performers) in rich visual, aural, and choreographic textures. As they caress the performers and bathe the space, the light effects and graphic forms seem to unfold like pieces of sheer silk or heavy, velvet material—as phenomena with weight rather than simply of light. The electronic soundtrack is equally dense and weighty, mixing cicada-like effects, deep-space sci-fi atmospherics, classical music influences, and techno-beats. Circular overhead projections provide shimmering visual pools of rippling blue water, as the dancers move in fluid and expressive choreography, like underwater creatures. In a contrasting section, the dancers intertwine, fight, and mirror one another inside an oblong projection on the floor, its colors flecked and striated by narrow, vibrating lines that move and scan along the surface, creating a distinctly electronic image like a television being tuned without ever finding a clear signal.

In a beautiful, evocative section the two men perform lyrical, extended movement phrases inside a green-yellow, hard-edged floor shape. Ripples, like tiger-skin striped waves, encroach inward toward them from the sides, moving in different directions, some hard-edged, others softer, immersing the two dancers as they move in contact, in slow motion (figure 16.8). The ripples wriggle like snakes as planes of light open and close, fan out, contract, and expand, taking on a life of their own. The projection becomes

Figure 16.8 Bud Blumenthal and Fernando Martín are immersed in rippling "liquid light" in *Rivermen* (1999).

Liquid Architectures and Site-Specific Fractures in Reality

smaller, focussing and concentrating attention on the dancers, illuminating only their tiny figures in the vast darkness of the stage. Then quite suddenly it expands, its light-play flooding the whole stage with aquatic ripples, an effect like a view from underwater, looking up at the wavy surface as the sun breaks out from the clouds above. The two dancers slowly arch their backs and extend their limbs in a contact sequence to the hypnotic, meditative sound of a pulsing, modulated musical note. The sound transforms to a sustained tone, like a signal frequency, and so do the projections and the choreography, as the dancers split from their intimate duet and take positions at either side of the stage in a green (stage right) and violet oblong (stage left). Separating the two shapes down the centre line of the stage floor is a buzzing, waving white line like an electrical charge or branch of fork lighting. Water has become fire, and the choreography emphasizes the changing dynamic, the men dancing with angular, muscular movements until their hands finally meet over the fizzing white line, which suddenly fades away.

Fracturing Space

Slavoj Žižek describes virtual space in topological terms as "a hole in reality," a type of supernatural fracture in the fabric of space that is always just out of view, "a floating anamorphotic shimmer, only accessible with a glance over the corner of one's eye."[16] When virtual spaces, objects, or bodies are projected into performance spaces, a similar sense of a "fracture in the fabric of space" can often be discerned; one "reality" (stage, site, or installation) is punctured by another "reality" (a digital image or representation). Equally, performance companies may use this virtual hole in reality not to differentiate the two realities but to combine them; using the doubling of space synergetically to demarcate a new, unified "mixed reality" space.

The members of British art and theater collective Talking Birds are particularly fond of holes and fractures in space, and describe their aim as "the transformation of spaces, both real and constructed."[17] Four projections on gauze screens create a zoetrope effect at the climax of their story of a traumatized nuclear scientist and a wall-of-death rider, *Persistence of Vision* (2000); and a three-layer staging was created for *Smoke, Mirrors and the Art of Escapology* (1998) including an understage (and unseen) futuristic prison. Its story is told through soundscapes, and video projections directed vertically from below through a perspex "ice" sheet and onto a curved perspex screen suspended three meters above the stage. The stage level represents a sanitorium where the straightjacketed wife of Houdini attempts her own form of escapology by jumping through a hole in the floor ice-sheet. The level above the stage is the space where a prisoner from below finally makes his escape in classic conjuror style, climbing up a rope and disappearing.

A sense of space and place is disrupted threefold in Frank Abbot's *Displace* (2000). A shaky, blurred 360-degree video pan of a valley on the Isle of Skye is projected within an installation/performance room, using a rotating projector on a robotic camera surveillance platform. Video-mixed into this shot is another circular camera pan, a prerecording of the same installation room the audience is in, but empty. At the same time, a live robot camera suspended in the middle of the space pans around audience members who stand against the walls, and provides webcast viewers with a third space and time perspective.

Digital Fractures in Public Spaces

Space is a practiced place. Thus the street geometrically defined by urban planning is transformed into a space by walkers. In the same way, an act of reading is a space produced by the practice of a particular place: a written text, i.e.: a place constituted by a system of signs.
—MICHEL DE CERTEAU[18]

In site-specific digital performance, Žižek's notion of a hole in reality is often strongly pronounced, as virtual objects and environments appear in places they are least expected, "puncturing" preconceptions of the physical environment. The digital incursion into physical space undermines traditional, fundamental ideas of site, space, and place as expressed, for example, by Michel de Certeau, who reads place "as an ordered and ordering system . . . defined by its internal stability":[19]

A place [*lieu*] is the order (of whatever kind) in accordance with which elements are distributed in relationships of coexistence. It thus excludes the possibility of two things being in the same location [*place*]. The law of the "proper" rules in the place: the elements taken into consideration are *beside* one another, each situated in its own "proper" and distinct location, a location it defines.[20]

For Nick Kaye, precise notions of site and place in site-specific art have always been problematic, whether or not they incorporate virtual technologies: "the more directly the site is pressed toward, the more elusive and complex this point of definition proves to be."[21] He notes how this issue is further exacerbated in the documentation of live site-specific art and performance, and makes a point equally germane to our understanding of how digital images and environments operate when situated within site-specific contexts:

In the writing of non-place over place, the troubling of oppositions between virtual and real spaces, in the implication of the map in the production of its object, the eroding of the material integrity of the art object, and in the uncovering of processes of slippage, deferral and indeterminacy, these practices approach their various sites in a blurring of the distinctions under which a work's integrity and place is fixed.[22]

It is interesting to relate these ideas to a piece such as Susan Collins's innovative and delightful *In Conversation* (1997) which "exists simultaneously in three locations: on the World Wide Web, in the gallery, and on the street."[23] Passers-by in the English seaside town of Brighton encounter the image of a speaking, animated mouth, which is projected onto the sidewalk, its voice amplified through loudspeakers (figure 16.9). The mouth

Figure 16.9 Web camera view of passers-by in Brighton stopping to observe and converse with a projection of a speaking mouth on the sidewalk in Susan Collins's *In Conversation* (1997).

speaks the words of online users watching the street in real time via a hidden surveillance webcam, whose text messages are spoken by the mouth through text-to-speech software. The mouth becomes a virtual intermediary (Collins draws comparisons with séance mediums) and literal mouthpiece for the real-time conversations that ensue between the remote interactors and the frequently bemused people on the street. The live surveillance footage is also projected onto a large screen inside Brighton's Fabrica Gallery, "framing the action outside cinematically, a drama unfolding in real time."[24]

The disembodied mouth, particularly at night, is a surreal, compelling, and crowd-attracting presence. When first exhibited in 1997, people kept returning to it on the street day after day to continue conversations, and it attracted equal popularity with the many voices behind it on the web, with the site recording more than a thousand daily hits. The mouth's dialogue frequently mixed and combined different users' real-time text messages (with the normal 10–20 second network chat delay), and "slippages and imperfections became integral to the work, as sometimes words stumbled out on top of each other to form an unintentional collective sentence, usually irrevocably altering the original intended meaning."[25] Street participants heard only one voice, however, *Victoria*, one of the selection of Mac OS computerized voices, chosen by Collins for its apparent androgyny.

The "voice" performing these messages could be quite persuasive, if not manipulative. A man on his way home, while the piece was installed in Amsterdam, found himself captivated . . . repeatedly trying to leave, only to be called back, compelled by this computerized disembodied voice. The online visitor (quite possibly made up of more than one person in more than one location) eventually asks him for a kiss, following which the man is seen bending over to kiss the projection of the mouth on the pavement.

On occasion, for instance if it was raining and there were no pedestrians, the online users would take over, communicating directly to each other and turning the whole street into a chat channel. On other occasions they would encourage their partners in the street to perform—quiet literally to sing or dance—sometimes using the text dialogue to create percussive, rhythmic "music."[26]

In "The Actual and the Imagined," Collins argues that just as Oliver Grau conceptualizes classical *trompe l'oeil* architecture as a collage of illusionistic space and physical space,[27] works such as *In Conversation* collage several physical spaces with virtual space to create illusions which are as much psychological as they are visual or aural. *In Conversation* exists in and across different kinds and forms of spaces—physical, virtual, public, and private—and its experience is perceived quite differently depending on the space where the participant is. Moreover, "these spaces provided not only the ideological context for the piece but became part of the work itself, requiring an active engagement from viewers in order for the work to exist."[28] She then poses a crucial question: "So where, ultimately, is the work?" and concludes that "uncontained and with no fixed viewpoint, the work becomes effectively located everywhere and nowhere."[29] This "everywhere and nowhere" artistic conception of space has been posited many times in relation to telematic and online artworks and is a seductively simple, but ultimately vague and misleading position. Networked technologies certainly link and connect different places enabling remote communication, image and sound transfer, and so on, but the physical location of the participant remains the overriding spatial position of both the artwork and the viewing subject.

For the pedestrian encountering *In Conversation*, the artwork (the mouth) is in an exact and specific spatial position on the sidewalk; for the Web interactor, the artwork also exists in a specific space: the computer screen at their home (or wherever they happen to be) (figure 16.10). While the online participant is conscious that they are watching and communicating with another space, it too is quite specific (not "everywhere and nowhere"): the street area framed and captured by the surveillance camera. The pedestrian may wonder where the voice comes from, but will be in little doubt that it is simply linked to someone (or some computer) watching somewhere out of view; he or she is certainly unlikely to mistake the voice for some supernatural or godlike everywhere and nowhere presence. Networked interactive artworks no more collapse or dissolve spatial realities than telephone conversations do: rather, they connect spaces and transfer data between them.

This is not to diminish the power and charm of *In Conversation* or the importance and originality of such artworks. But Collins's spatial innovation has nothing to do with

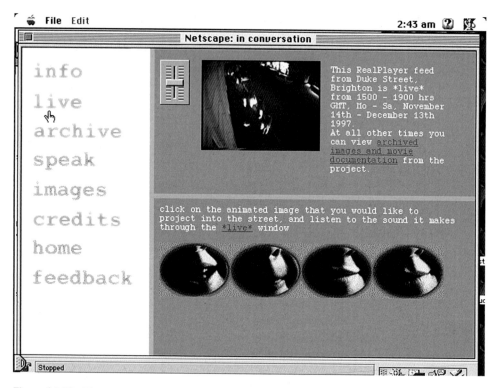

Figure 16.10 The online users' view of *In Conversation* showing the mouth, street webcam, and various interactive menus.

everywhere and nowhere. On the contrary, the originality and success of the piece derives from spatial specificity, the wonderful idea of projecting a computerized, talking mouth in a place where it is wholly unexpected—on a public sidewalk—where it engages with all who pass by and thereby reaches people outside traditional gallery visitors. It derives its originality as a *site-specific* interactive artwork, not a non-site-specific one, as she tries to maintain.

Site-Specific Holes in Reality

Notable large-scale events bringing digital fractures into site-specific public spaces include Desperate Optimists' *Urban Shots* (1999) set in the large outdoor car park of a large abandoned tower in Jena, Germany. Seen by more than ten thousand people, it included a live video feed, 16 mm film, stunts, a live band, and trained, performing police dogs. For Rafael Lozano-Hemmer's *Vectorial Elevation* (1999–2000), huge light sculptures were built in Mexico City's Zocalo Square and were activated by Web participants; and in *Body Movies* (2001) he surrounded Rotterdam's 1,200-square-meter Schouwburgplein Square with giant projections beamed by robotically controlled projectors that cast images of people from around the world onto screens and the square's walls:

However, the portraits were faded out by powerful lights on the floor of the square and became visible only if passers-by threw shadows onto the walls, which made the portraits appear inside their silhouettes. While the project itself has a distinctly performative aspect, it gained new dimensions when people repeatedly returned to the site to stage their own gigantic shadow plays.[30]

Projected movement motifs and video imagery of derelict land in Chicago provides the background for the Anatomical Theatre's dance production *In Effect Invisible* (1994). Onscreen dancers crawl through boarded windows and walk barefoot through alleys strewn with broken glass as they navigate the forgotten areas and crumbling edifices of the city. Streb Company's outdoor circuslike dance performance *PopAction* (1995) centers on an Olympic-size trampoline and a padded pit flanked by twenty-foot scaffolding towers. The six dancers jump from the towers and flip and somersault on the trampoline, triggering sensors to activate a range of MIDI audio samples including gunfire and breaking glass. For *ActionHeroes* (2000), their celebration of American stunt artists and daredevils such as Evel Knievel, Cannonball Joe, and Annie Taylor, a moveable performance space Elizabeth Streb calls a "box truss power pocket" was employed, which incorporated moving walls and "maverick screens" onto which digital projections were beamed.

Public buildings have provided the location for some arresting performances where digital media has disrupted the normal day-to-day perception of space and reality. Keith Armstrong's collaborative project *#14* (1996) took place in the heritage listed Spring Hall Baths in Brisbane, Australia, where the empty pool shell was flooded with computer projections, while the audience watched from the balconies above. Drawing on the pool's history, the performance also explored wider issues of space, gender, and personal and spatial boundaries (figure 16.11). In *Body Spaces* (2000) Petra Kupper's The Olimpias company worked with young disabled people to create three site-specific installation spaces within a large hospital in Manchester, England. Pathways defined both by floor images of footsteps and the traces of a wheelchair wheel were marked on the floor. Visitors moved through motion-sensor activated environments triggering digital video projections and *Director*-programmed multimedia sequences on hanging screens, as well as photographs and textual fantasy narrative exhibits. The piece beautifully explores the graceful movements of wheelchairs and the aesthetics of disabled dance, and provides new perspectives on everyday hospital spaces, their signs and objects.

Andrea Polli's international collaborative project *The Observatory* (1997) is set in the cylindrical tower of an eighteenth-century observatory in Lithuania and uses line-tracker robots controlled by performers which draw complex lines and patterns in black chalk around the space. Polli suggests that "the cylindrical tower space served symbolically as

Figure 16.11 "Liquid architecture" is created using varied imaginative projections to transform an empty public swimming pool in *#14* (1996), Keith Armstrong's collaborative project with #14 collective.

interior mind space and in this performance the chalk marks left as a record of an event could be seen as a map of the mind."[31] Clubs, bars, and discotheque spaces have been used (and theater spaces have been transformed to resemble them) for new-wave events which fuse performance, digital video-jockeying (VJ-ing) and a club experience, such as Barriedale Operahouse's *Cay—admit possibilities* (1998), a five-hour event mixing DJ-ing, VJ-ing, dance, and digital media projections. La Fura dels Baus describe their *Foc Forn* (1992) as "the first discotheque in the world where the music was played by robots. The first where an artificial rain refreshed the people. The first where the robots and the audience were melted in an oven."[32] Staged within a large artificial structure, this "discotheque without music" was programmed by a computer that also controlled robot DJs within the space.

Self-styled "Slavic pixel princesses" Slavica Ceperkovic and Michelle Kasprzak use real-time video-scratching techniques to create humorous and ironic montages of television images of female domesticity, consumer culture, and cooking. Dressed in aprons, the two women stand side by side, each controlling their own video projector as they mix and scratch through four simultaneous digital video sources. Cooking programs and daytime television consumer features are the dominant video samples in their *take take, cake cake* (2000), which wittily satirizes the role of women as mothers and nurturers, placing them in a banal and unreal world of consumerism and television trash culture. Like digital VJ versions of performance artist Bobby Baker, Ceperkovic and Kasprzak use their cooking demonstrations to satirize society's expectations of feminine domesticity, highlighting the role of the mass media in perpetuating the clichés and stereotypes. They also use cookery as a direct metaphor for their real-time digital video editing:

Who says the cool digital simulacra have to be so completely tasteless? Might it depend on the "ingredients" and how they are put together? . . . Kneading shots—wrenched from their original rareified contexts—into new sequences, cutting in special ingredients where appropriate, folding the conventions of television in upon themselves. Is it simply humble electronic borsht or gloriously pixelly strudel?[33]

Conceptual Architectures: Joel Slayton

Joel Slayton's mammoth "drive-through" celebration of information theory and cultural identity, *DoWhatDo* (1992), takes place in a giant car park in San Jose, California, with audience members driving to vantage points in their automobiles. Two hundred performers, drawn from different communities, arts groups, and cultural organizations parade, skate, fence, and dance while their live camera images are projected on giant screens, including "a three-dimensional projection screen structure controlled by networked interactive multimedia computers. Live video-feeds of both performers and audience are composed with pre-recorded computer animation and digital movies through a real-time projection control system."[34] Meanwhile, looming above the crowds is a performer standing in the cradle of a crane, who provides a slick, though at times impenetrable, evangelist-style lecture on Gordon Pask's DoWhatDo information theory.[35] *Conduits* (1994), Slayton's sequel to *DoWhatDo*, was staged on the Palo Alto City Hall Plaza and used an elaborate computer-controlled set design "resembling an on-site movie set," and was designed as "a teleconferencing theatrical event exploring the function of public art and perceptions of cultural identity."[36]

For his *98.6 FM* (1992) performance, Slayton collaborated with choreographer Tandy Beal and deep space microwave artist Michael Heively to explore the history of television broadcasting as deep space transmission. A custom-designed interactive video-disk system with real-time processing of images provided projection onto a monitor wall onstage, and a computer translated the choreography, set design, and event logistics into binary code. Six microwave transmitters on stage beamed the digital information into space, toward the Cusp of Hercules constellation where, says Slayton "the deep space sculptural form will pass in 60,000 light years."[37] This particular "hole in space" notion is in one sense hilarious and absurd, a Dadaist statement for the technological age, but, in another, it is a wonderful piece of digital conceptualism. While it is easy to chuckle at the depth of postmodern irony of his idea (and Slayton has indeed a highly sophisticated sense of humor) at another level he is deadly serious. A digital performance "artwork" has been sent millions of miles away, where it may or may not be received and seen by someone or something in sixty thousand years. It is a bold, distinctly neo-futurist gesture, an artistic exploration of the ontological potential of digital technology as an (outer) space-time arts communications medium.

In Slayton and the Californian CADRE Institute's *Panamint Launch at Lucky Jim Wash* (1999), experimental rockets were launched toward the China Lake Naval Weapons Testing Center in California's Death Valley from a desert site adjacent to it. The piece transposes Deleuze and Guattari's philosophical notions of lines of flight and lines of demarcation into the political contexts of war, polemical gestures, and the wider networks of military, satellite, and telecommunications systems. Slayton is a truly precious and unique artist/theorist/scientist who provides such idiosyncratic and futuristic theories and performance events that one sometimes wonders, quite complimentarily, whether he himself may be from another planet. As well as being one of the most distinct and original technological artists working today, he is also one of the sharpest techno-culture theorists and commentators. We will leave the last words of our discussion of site-specific performance and fractures in reality, quite appropriately, to him. His description of *Panamint Launch* provides a delightful insight into his avowedly political and conceptual approach to site-specific performance, as well as his distinctly macro thought processes.

So what was this site-specific performance? The combination of the desert landscape (Baudrillard's American wasteland), guns (along with their close cousin, the camera), a military border (the mesh of stratified social and physical spaces), free flowing alcohol (or any intoxification feeding post-modernity), and explosives (intensifications that allow, among other things, bifurcation, lines of flight, instantiation and emergence), meshed with the art-historical romantic macho riskiness of our latent modernist models to yield the artwork known as the *Panamint Launch at Lucky Jim Wash*.[38]

Telematics: Conjoining Remote Performance Spaces

Telepresence allows the viewer parallel experiences in three spaces at once: 1. in the «real» space in which the viewer's body is physically located; 2. per tele-perception in the «virtual», simulated visual space reproducing a fictional or real, remote visual sphere; and 3. per tele-action at the physical location of the «data work or even of a robot controllable over one's movements or equipped with a sensory apparatus over which one can find one's bearings.»
—INKE ARNS[1]

We are at war with networks.
—GEORGE W. BUSH[2]

Networked art and creative collaboration over a distance has an ancestry that can be traced back to the earliest hand-delivered messenger correspondences of antiquity, through the literary relationships and collaborations which blossomed via postal systems, to the post-card, telex, fax, email, and telematic arts of the twentieth century. In 1984, Nam June Paik published an article/manifesto "Art and Satellite" in which he ruminated on the rich potentials of conjoining artists from remote locations, but also reflected on the impact that technologies such as the telephone had in the nineteenth century. Following its invention, Thoreau had questioned its very need: what would people from different states "possibly find to talk about" to one another? History has answered the question, says Paik: "they developed a feedback (or, to use an older term, dialectic) . . . God created love to propagate the human race, but, unawares, man began to love simply to love. By the same logic, although man talks to accomplish something, unawares, he soon begins to talk simply to talk."[3]

Some might find it tempting to draw a similarly cynical conclusion in relation to telematic arts and performance: that once Internet video-conferencing enabled remote visual connection, communication, and collaboration, artists and performers began "to (telematically) talk, simply to (telematically) talk." But as Paik makes clear, drawing again on new conceptualizations of technology from the past, this time late-nineteenth-century French mathematician Henri Poincaré: "what was being discovered was not new THINGS but merely new RELATIONSHIPS between things already existing. We are again in the fin de siècle. . . . This time we are discovering much new software . . . which are not new things but new thinks."[4] Satellite art isn't about sending Mozart over the wires, Paik stresses; it is a way to discover unique new processes and communicational relationships in art, two-way, improvisational models that play intimately with the very notions of time and space.

Billy Klüver was inevitably involved in some early networked experimentation, such as *Telex: Q and A* (1971), with others including Pontus Hulten and Fujiko Nakaya as part of the *Utopia and Visions* celebrations of the anniversary of the 1871 Paris Commune. Telex machines were connected between New York, Stockholm, Ahmedabad (India), and Tokyo, and both experts and the general public asked questions and offered possible answers to what the world would be like in 1981. According to Klüver, the predictions varied enormously from country to country: "The Indians were very theoretical. The Japanese were extremely positive," an observation that seems equally accurate today.[5] In 1977, Douglas Davis presented *The Last Nine Minutes*, a live satellite telecast from Caracas, Venezuela, to twenty-five countries, where he spoke to camera about ideas of time, space, distance, and separation. The telecast also included a performance lecture by Joseph Beuys and three performances by Paik and Charlotte Moorman: *TV Bra*, *TV Cello*, and *TV Bed*. Douglas's later live satellite telecast *Double Entendre* (1981) between New York's Whitney Museum and the Pompidou Centre in Paris explored a transatlantic love affair based on Roland Barthes's *A Lover's Discourse* (1977) and challenged "notions of electronic linkage, cultural and sexual boundaries, as well as language theories."[6]

In the most celebrated example of pre-Internet telematic performance, Kit Galloway and Sherrie Rabinovitz used a live video satellite link to connect the Broadway department store in Los Angeles and the Lincoln Center for the Performing Arts in New York City. Large screens in the two spaces enabled passers-by to hear, see, and communicate with each other. During the three-day period that the *Hole-in-Space* (1980) linked installation was active, relationships were struck up and developed between some of the remote participants who would return each day; and relatives and friends in the two cities arranged times to meet, using the artwork "as a medium to re-establish contact."[7]

While such satellite connections were expensive and thus out of the reach of most artists, during the 1990s the World Wide Web enabled affordable and convenient connection. The coming of relatively cheap and user-friendly videoconference software, particularly *CUSeeMe* in the early days, opened the field of telematics for a vast amount of performance activity to take place. The New York–based Gertrude Stein Repertory Theatre, founded in 1990 "to help revitalize the performing arts,"[8] was among the most important pioneers.

The Gertrude Stein Repertory Theatre

Named after the avant-garde American writer Gertrude Stein (1874–1946) whose home in Paris during the interwar period became a salon for leading writers and artists of the period, including Picasso, Matisse, Braque, and Hemingway, the company's declared aim is reminiscent of that fertile period now brought into the twenty-first century: "to re-invent the process of creating theatre . . . we feel that the arts of the 21st century must be global. Early in our development, we realized that new advances in telecommunications and multimedia offered the best opportunity for achieving these goals."[9]

The two co-directors, Cheryl Faver and John Reaves, shared a range of complementary skills wholly appropriate to the developing interests including theater, the twentieth century avant-garde, computer-based visualization, multimedia, film, software development, and computer graphics. Equipped with such skills and interests, they were able to attract support from major IT companies to undertake projects seeking to merge technology and arts, even including an IBM "distance technologies" international advertising campaign. In a 1995 article in the *Cyberstage* journal, John Reaves reviewed some of the company's wide-ranging work of 1992–95 from "computer-based figure animation, software and 3D design software to do choreography, set design, lighting design, etc"[10] to telematic performance events using the new IBM *Person to Person* software that had permitted real time link-ups across New York, across America and across the Atlantic. Faver's adaptation of a section from Stein's *Dr. Faustus Lights the Lights* (written in 1938) involved four actors on a physical stage in New York who played three Fausts and a Mephisto. They interacted with two actors playing Annabelle and Marguerite at the Paris Opera, who appeared live in a videoconference window on the rear projection screen. The computer generated figures of a boy and dog joined the action, and another character— "perhaps Stein herself?" notes Reaves—appeared only as type in a text chat window. Reaves's conclusion was that such telematic interventions signaled nothing less than a theatrical paradigm change:

Our experiments begin to change our ideas about theater. It becomes ridiculous to think of theater as what can happen in one room, with one audience. . . . Experimentation yields its own rewards: every new feature or facility we play with fragments our conventional thinking, sheds new light on the essential nature of drama or theater or narrative. . . . Eventually the entire physical world will be describable by numbers.[11]

But despite such radical rhetoric, it was a measure of the maturity of the company that they undertook their developmental work in a measured tone, methodically assessing the various effects of successes, problems, and failures in the manner of a scientist analyzing results. But they maintained optimism that digital techniques and the distance-shrinking facets of telematics could offer a new world of global theater: "We encounter the World Wide Web, and are blown away. Not so much by the current reality, but by the enormous potential. Even though the Web right now is like some enormous global magazine edited by a madman, we start to conceive of the Web as an eventspace, a place where things can happen."[12]

In 1996 the company collaborated on an award-winning production, *An Epidog*, with another New York theater company Mabou Mines and its vigorous director, Lee Breuer. The devised production was set in "an enchanting computer-created virtual environment"[13] and told the story of a dog named Rose who finds herself in Bardo, the limbo of memories and visions where Buddhists believe a soul awaits reincarnation. Not only did the subject matter fit with the spectacular aspects of a production that included Japanese puppets, haunting music, and visual surprises but also the mandatory "floating cosmos" constituted an ideal springboard for computer-generated projected images of majestic entrances by grand gods in starry heavens, maps and mazes of constellations, and cartoon-style animated television lectures. Around this time, software programs were commonly used to conjure cosmological and "magical" spaces and events, although with familiarity the impact has since faded and designers are now more inclined to fret that software stamps orthodoxy rather than opens the doors to the supernatural.

Following successful performance experiments utilizing videoconferencing across multiple sites in the United States, the company began to produce global performances, notably *The UBU Project* (1998–99). This incorporated video conferencing, digital projection, and VRML across sites situated in New York, St. Petersburg, and Tokyo, combining and interleaving simultaneous live projections originating thousands of miles apart. Remote videoconference characters included digital puppets derived from the Japanese performance traditions of Ningyo Buri and Bunraku. In Bunraku, performers physically hold and manipulate the limbs of a life-size mannequin, and *UBU* adapted the technique to create what the company call "Distance Puppetry." The image of a Butoh performer in Tokyo was projected into the live theater space in New York and directly onto the body of a Chinese Opera performer, whose movements were identically choreographed to his remote counterpart's, creating an eerily doubled, composite image. Jessica Chalmers recounts an early work-in-progress demonstration in 1999 led by company directors Faver and Reaves, where they exhibited

a couple of lovely and grotesque figures from the show—one a headless female body in 18th-century dress. Two peacock feathers rise out of her neck, onto which the real eyes of one or even two *Ubu* performers will be projected. "What is it to have a person inside of another person?" wonders Faver, with regard to this surreal juxtaposition of live and animated bodies. "It cracks open metaphors for human experience."[14]

The company has also developed a clear and strikingly original distance education policy that has included a 3D VRML reconstruction of The Globe (2000),[15] and *The Crucible Project* (2001) linking children in England, Australia, Italy, and the United States, who "met" and remotely rehearsed scenes from Arthur Miller's *The Crucible* together. At one point the company involved Arthur Miller in the process, hooking him up to the videoconferencing network to talk with the children and to discuss their work on his play.[16]

Telematic Performance in the Late 1990s

Telematic performance came of age in the late 1990s, and it is a measure of its popularity that during the years 1999 and 2000, with the sole exception of stage productions using digital projections, *The Digital Performance Archive* recorded more telematically related events than any other form of digital performance. The many following examples provide a sense and a flavor of the telematic fervor around the turn of the millennium.

Troika Ranch's *The Electronic Disturbance* (1996), inspired by the book of the same name by The Critical Art Ensemble, linked The Kitchen (New York), The Electronic Café (San Francisco), and Studio X (Santa Fe) (figure 17.1). Projections sent via the Internet from each venue to the two others enabled the company members, in their words, "to perform as a group," and interactive sensors enabled sounds and movements made by a performer in one location to control elements in another: for example, the lighting in New York was modulated by the vocal inflections of a singer in Santa Fe. Web viewers of the event could also send text messages that were read aloud by a synthesized

Figure 17.1 Troika Ranch's telematically linked performance *The Electronic Disturbance* (1996).

Telematics: Conjoining Remote Performance Spaces

computer voice. The company sees *The Electronic Disturbance* as a celebration of the body in flux: "a body whose contact with other bodies comes more and more often not physically but electronically." But interestingly, they also stress that while the performance explores the liberating aspects of the electronic body's freedom from time or gravity, it also engages with its more sinister implications, and its vulnerability to manipulation by external forces.

Lisa Naugle terms synchronous telematic dance performances "Distributed Choreography,"[17] and her *Cassandra* projects (1997) brought together live artists from the United States, Canada, and Romania using *CUSeeMe* software, with the distributed images projected onto large screens. A motion tracking video system was used for Naugle's *Watching Words* (1994), which changed the color and luminence of the triggered video and texts; and in *Millimicron* (1993) piezoelectric sensors translated the different pressures of the dancers' steps and percussive movements into a complex soundscape. Adrienne Wortzel's *Starboard* (1997) is a partly scripted and partly improvisational "interactive, operatic, serial broadcast drama" using both a MOO-like Net space and live *CUSeeMe* links.[18] Wortzel is adept at combining polymorphous technological and telematic elements into her work, and her description of the project emphasizes her belief that these constitute not only a multiplicity of visual stimuli but also a multiplicity of spaces: "a realtime performing space, a writing space, an acting space, a re-acting space, a speaking space, a place for real time avatars to act out . . . evocative scenarios."[19]

Conceptual artist G. H. Hovagimyan describes the world as "an ecstacy of communication", and his *Art Dirt Im-port* (1997) as a new form of talk show where artists interact and perform for one another via "a communication hybrid using simple Internet systems such as *CUSeeMe*, *RealAudio* and good old phone calls."[20] In the same year, *Untitled* (1997), an asynchronous telematic happening by the Ellipsis group, sought to find "a way of meshing the synchronicity of a live performance with the asynchronicity of the net . . . to focus on the dismantling of this 'illusion of the window of belief.'"[21] Cary Peppermint's strange and humorously idiosyncratic *Conductor #1: Getting in Touch With Chicken* (1997) features Peppermint as a "conductor" in a box attempting to communicate with a chicken (the "resistor") placed in another box ten meters away. Peppermint interacts with the chicken via a direct telephone line and a *CUSeeMe* link, while remote online guests and participants (including some from PORT MIT) known as "batteries" also intervene through videoconference projections. Peppermint's tongue-in-cheek, Monty Pythonesque performance sardonically satirizes the hyperbole related to the quasi-spiritual and occult aspects of cyberspace:

[Participants] utilize me as a "medium" and/or "exorcist" for a ritual involving perceptual boundaries, and possible transcendence of these boundaries. . . . "Batteries" may dine upon prescribed meals of fried chicken and/or scrambled eggs with hopes that their internalization of chicken may then twist their tongues into energized and energizing forms that could contribute to my optimum performance as "conductor" and thus the completion of the circuit called "chicken." . . . *Conductor #1* website will remain intact and accessible via the Internet to serve as a testament or "holy space" for both local and remote voyagers seeking evidence of physical transcendence.[22]

Liftlink (1998), a collaborative project led by Susan Kozel, telematically linked dancers in a lift in the Brighton Media Centre with a dancer in the car park outside, while her *Ghosts and Astronauts* (1997) created as part of a two-week *Digital Dancing 1997* event in London connected two theaters: Riverside Studios and The Place. *CUSeeMe* videoconferencing projected the dancers from the opposite location onto screens within both stages to create two simultaneous performances operating with opposite combinations of live and telematic dancers. The cameras transmitting the images via the Internet were all in movement (thus also dancing) during the event, and ranged from a digital monochrome Connectix and a miniature analog camera strapped to a dancer's palm to sophisticated digital cameras. Kozel notes the importance of the technological limitations of videoconferencing, and like others, commends them as inherent to the peculiar and unique aesthetic of telematic performance, which emphasizes its own particular quality of interactive "liveness": "The moving images, as they spilled from analogue to digital, through the Internet, and back into analogue projection, took on traces on their journey: pixellation, delays, abstraction, overexposure. All the digital and analogue offerings became part of the physical dynamics of interaction."[23]

Identity and Simultaneity

Canadian troupe Le Corps Indice telematically links remote performers to probe and question ideas of identity, territory and corporeal limits, and to merge or confuse notions of the real, the sacred, the natural and the artificial. Its *Le Sang Des Reseaux* (1998) is a gesture-oriented dance event that integrates motion-sensing interactive systems, video projection, dance, and electroacoustics with a telematic link between three groups of performers in different spaces. Liss Fain Dance's *Sojourn in Alexandria* (1999) brings together live dancers and webcast 3D images of remote dancers, while their *Quarry* (2000) incorporates a large-scale projection of the sculptor Richard Deutsch, sculpting on an open hillside overlooking the Pacific Ocean. His image is relayed live over the Internet and incorporated into a stone-quarry set on the stage of the Cowell Theatre, San Francisco (a hundred miles away), and the choreography of the live dancers echoes and responds to the shapes of Deutsch's sculpture as it evolves in real time.

For *Shared Identity* (2000) Scott C. Durkin coordinated simultaneous performance actions, excavating some land on the California coast while his twin brother did the same on the New Jersey coast on the opposite side of the United States. Durkin also sent samples of the excavated soil and materials to an undisclosed number of people who shared his name. He suggests that the doubling of the actions with his twin and the webcast transmissions of the events means that "I will exist in two locations at once. . . . I will exist on countless monitors, no longer the owner of my image or of my action."[24] In *Ménage à Trois* (2000), Michelle Teran sits holding a leash attached to a TV monitor and communicating with an online performer and a seated gallery visitor sitting opposite her. The visitor in this three-way conversation can see the online performer on the monitor, but cannot see the text she is sending, nor the answers Teran types back.

The inventive artists' collective Fakeshop has explored the Internet as a "performance space" since 1996, and has combined multiple-windowed Web streaming with gallery installations featuring live performance, as well as webcasting some regular techno-cabaret evenings combining poetry, sound, *CUSeeMe* and media imagery from their large warehouse studio space. For their *Lifescience-Fakeshop* event at the SIGGRAPH 2000 exhibition, their projected Web browser was filled with overlapping windows, juxtaposing myriad elements of their ongoing project about technology and the body (figure 17.2). The image composited *CUSeeMe* windows, chatroom text relaying reactions to their performances, 3D body models (created using *Poser* software), and film footage from the science-fiction film *Coma* (1978). Yet another window showed Fakeshop's installation mockup of the *Coma* movie scene, with live performers acting as if in a coma, suspended in a line hooked to quasi-medical apparatus.[25] The interplay between live, recorded, fictional, constructed, and actual bodies is complex, and a similar dynamic between the constructed and the actual is explored in their *Capsule Hotel* project (2001). Videoconference links connect the small capsule-like bedrooms of an actual hotel in Tokyo to a gallery installation with mockup capsules, which visitors can enter and "participate in an ongoing narrative and time-based performative actions. Crucial to the concept of *Capsule Hotel* is the doubling of environments in radically different contexts, one of them 'staged,' the other one a commercial accommodation (and utilitarian absurdity of society)"[26] (figure 17.3).

Figure 17.2 A projected web browser view from Fakeshop's *Lifescience-Fakeshop* presented at the SIGGRAPH 2000 exhibition.

Figure 17.3 The multiple capsule bedroom spaces for Fakeshop's telematically linked installation *Capsule Hotel* (2001).

Spaces specially designed and configured for telematic performance have also emerged, such as the "Intelligent Stage" at Arizona State University's Institute of Studies in the Arts (ISA). Two separate spaces are linked and incorporate a range of MIDI (Musical Instrument Data Interface) and streaming video inputs, and interactive applications such as David Rokeby's pioneering *Very Nervous System* (*VNS*). Although performances at ISA regularly telematically link the spaces in real time, this was not the case for the collaborative dance performance *Virtual Partnering* (2000, ISA, ResCen, shinkansen) for the *Cell-bytes 2000* festival. The piece fused three dancers on the main dance stage and a solo dancer on the Intelligent Stage into a composite webcast image. Interestingly, no data was actually sent between the two stages due to an eight-second time lag; rather, the dancers on each site were cued precisely to give the impression that they were dancing in harmony. The group note that the choreographers had to continually remind themselves that they were actually choreographing for three spaces: the main stage, the Intelligent Stage, and the Web.

Company in Space

We have seen many dance performances that incorporate real time telematic projections, and too commonly suspect that the simple presence of these remote, virtual bodies is considered by companies to be enough, since the magic of technology is there for all to see. However, the advanced digital creativity of dance troupes such as Company in Space genuinely elevates the telematic performance form to new aesthetic heights. Dual-site performances such as *Trial by Video* (1998, linking Melbourne and London) and *Escape Velocity* (2000, linking Melbourne and Hong Kong) contain moments of sublime and breathtaking beauty, as remote live dancers are brought into highly integrated and

Figure 17.4 Company in Space's telematic dance performance *Escape Velocity* (2000). Photo: Jeff Busby.

meaningful (rather than separated and arbitrary) conjunctions with those performing in theater spaces (figure 17.4). Real-time digital effects and the relaying of live video feeds of the theater dancers to mix them onscreen with the remote performers are central to the productions' visual and dramatic power. In *Escape Velocity*, the bodies are transformed to shimmer as though composed of particles, and are shot through with subtle "beams" of light and color. Split-screen effects double the same images of the dancers' fluid, expressive movements and idiosyncratic gestures, which are overlaid with three-dimensional pieces of text that move around the screen in circles and spirals.

Kaleidoscopic effects and onscreen text also feature in *Incarnate* (2001), a videoconference performance linking the Dancehouse in Melbourne, Australia with the Hong Kong Arts Center. The rear stage screen in Melbourne is a visual crucible of projected images into which the Hong Kong dancers are mapped. A telematic performer is projected within the bright, wavelike patterns of a luminous "pond"; and sequences of fast arm gestures are digitally colorized and strobed to visually liquefy the movements. The use of camera movements and close-ups of the remote Hong Kong performers add to the gripping drama on screen, as these virtual dancers appear to float and swim, their faces looming into the foreground and then disappearing out of frame. A 3D computer-generated monochrome skyline provides a spectacular kinetic background for the two (keyed in) telematic dancers, who are joined on screen by live-feed video projections of the two onstage dancers.

In one sequence, a medium shot of a telematic dancer's body switches to negative, and a bright cosmos of moving stars fill and consume the figure. An overlaid caption reads: "Her brightness would shame those stars," and later, "yon light is not daylight, 'tis some meteor the sun exhales, more light and light." Body outlines are used as mattes to key in

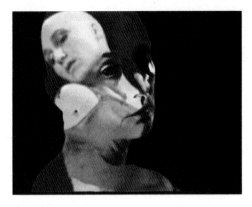

Figure 17.5 Company in Space's use of telematic "body-in-body" effects creates visually arresting and dramatic dance sequences.

other dancing bodies, which seem to inhabit them, as colorized bodies weave their way inside and amidst the darkened silhouettes of moving torsos and faces. The contrasts in scale are striking: a wide shot of a body moves inside the outline of a torso or close-up head. Their contrasting speeds and qualities of movement are equally arresting: at one point a graceful close-up head turns slowly in silhouette, while inside it two full-size bodies rotate sharply, and quickly descend toward the floor (figure 17.5).

Company in Space performs sublime, sophisticated fusions between telematic and live bodies, realizing in practice the type of magic that many other companies aspire to, but sadly too often only achieve in their conceptual and theoretical discussions of their work. The company's own discussions of its productions sound on the surface like that of many others exploring telematic technologies, but the key difference is that attending its performances confirms rather than undermines the rhetoric:

> *Escape Velocity* . . . suspends the body between the real and virtual worlds . . . [and] mirrors the complex nature of bodies relationship to space, time and place at a moment in history where these parameters are shifting from under our feet. . . . Dancers at either end of the link perform together in the projected fourth dimension. The dancers become "actual avatars"; their performance questions the body's relationship to physical and virtual corporeality, technology and gravity.[27]

Telematic Collaboration

Telematic conjunctions enable real-time audiovisual collaboration between artists or performers both in the private context of process-based development work and rehearsals and in the public context of final performances. Telematic collaboration can equally involve partnerships with audience members as well as with other artists or remote company members. Gloria Sutton suggests that a fundamental trait of networked creativity is the privileging of "collaboration over authorship" and the democratization of the production and reception of art, noting how this dates back to earlier models seen in the work of Vito Acconci, Adrian Piper, and Hans Haacke.[28]

The George Coates Performance Works' *The Nowhere Band* (1994) provides an interesting early example of the use of the web and *CUSeeMe* telematics to forge remote collaborations with artists not formerly known to them, for both the development and realization of a stage performance. The piece recounts the ambitions of a child (played by Coates's four-year-old daughter Gracie) to create a musical about a magical bird that can teach humans to fly. Her fantasies are realized via a laptop computer as she recruits the necessary musicians and performers online. Prior to the production, a webpage advertised for people who could play an instrument to become members of a rock band for the live performance. The page recorded more than ten thousand hits on the first day, and four people were eventually cast, including a bagpipe player in Australia. During the theater performance, the four musicians played live from their disparate locations, and were projected in windows on a stage screen via *CUSeeMe* videoconferencing and a high-speed T1 Internet connection.

However, the use of videoconferencing during the live performance was problematic (as it can still be today), with the live telematic images heavily pixelated, and strobed in a jagged stop-start motion. Limitations in bandwidth also meant a one-second delay in the transmission of images of the four remote musicians. Moreover, due to the inefficiencies of the net in transmitting live audio at that time, the company decided not to digitally relay the music each musician played via the Internet, but to rely on a far older and less glamorous technology—the telephone—to feed the sound live into the theater space.

While such technological limitations and gremlins have been a source of frustration to some, arts collective Motherboard positively embraces them, embedding the fluctuations in transmission and reception rates, as well as computer crashes and disconnections, into the dramatic development and final performance dynamics of pieces such as *M@ggie's Love Bytes* (1995):

The performance is carefully planned to take on the unpredictability of cyberspace; improvisation is of the essence! Computers inevitably crash, connections break. The restrictions and malfunctions of the technology are used creatively. For example, the timelagged, freezing and pixelated moving images of CUSeeMe are juxtaposed with the fluidity of similar movements in brickspace. Time stands still, time moves on, time and place are out of synch. *M@ggie's Love Bytes* . . . is bold enough to claim that low-budget technology currently offers the greatest number of people the greatest possibility of experience, interaction and creativity.[29]

M@ggie's Love Bytes was presented at the 1995 Norwegian Void Festival, featuring three dancers in bra and pants (each representing M@ggie) who receive gifts (love bytes) from remote "lover" participants via IRC and *CUSeeMe* and *Ivisit* video-conferencing. These lovers, located in places including London, San Francisco, Cologne, and Yokohama, provide sounds, texts, and visual images to stimulate the three M@ggies. More recently, Motherboard has continued its work in telematic collaboration to create eclectic and anarchic online "jam" parties connecting numerous artists and musicians in events such as *The Hotwired Live Electronic Resistance Network Art Party Plan* (2000, with Michelle Teran). A weekend of experiments and exchanges connected an art/performance party in a pavilion in Moss, Norway, with a similar party in an arts school in Toronto, Canada. The online audio and visual jamming includes the use of software programs such as *Keystroke*, developed by Amsterdam's WAAG (Society for Old and New Media) and the video manipulation software *NATO*, developed by the m9ndfukc organization. Visual jamming has become a popular telematic form, featuring in events such as the collaborative Australian dance performance *fake* (2000, Sarah Neville, Heliograph Productions, Wavicle), which included telematic projections, a hiphop DJ, and a TJ (Text Jockey) who fed in pieces of text.

In September 1997, the British performance art collective IOU Theatre collaborated with Spanish group La Fura Dels Baus, mounting a live performance in Tarraga with a projected videoconference link to a simultaneous live performance taking place in Frieberg, Germany. As an unpublished IOU company report by Chris Squires notes, the Internet's capacity to relay video does not compare favorably with a far older medium (television) and technical limitations at that time were still seriously inhibiting ambitious networked performances:

The projected video images, both from Germany and of our work, is of poor quality and in a live performance situation seems very flat and non-personal. The delay, strobe movement and divorce between sound (speech) and image have their own aesthetic, but are very different to the satellite links we are used to on TV. It was also very difficult for audiences to fully understand the work occurring in Frieberg, which wasn't made for the camera but as a live performance. The project probably didn't merit some of the press comment it received—things about it being "the first 21st century art work" and other hyperbole—but on the whole it was . . . a useful process in learning to understand this new medium and working towards something better.

But telematic collaborations nonetheless continued to flourish in the late 1990s, not least by La Fura Dels Baus with works such as *Cabinas* (1996). The company designed and installed video-conference linked cabins in Barcelona and Sarajevo where participants could talk and see one another, and also use an interface to activate and send light and sound sequences to one another. The company believes that in doing so the participants are directly "exchanging sensations," and goes on to maintain that "despite the distance . . . if unknown people can share experiences, unfiltered by the mass media, then it may help increase tolerance."[30]

Floating Point Unit (FPU) constructs multilayered audiovisual environments and media-saturated installations, often combining real and VRML architectural spaces with elements of performance art. Its collaborative Internet project *emergent(c) room* (1997) linked artists in the United States, Japan, and Brazil whose typed chat-window interactions were translated through a voice synthesizer, which added to the ambient soundtrack of what FPU describes as "artificial life music." The piece interrogates the multiplicity of spaces ignited and inhabited through distributed performance; the room of the title refers both literally to the chatroom and metaphorically to numerous other places including the body, the brain, and new areas of consciousness. According to the company, the *emergent(c) room* is thus:

A place in which infectious ideas will be allowed to propogate unchecked. . . . A place in which one can lapse into the intermediary state of consciousness, the "coma" state. . . . "emergent" as code-word for the "bio-glyphic" state of rapture experienced in the midst of discovery of digital and/or organic secrets. "(C)" as code-word for artificial life behaviors which thrive in the subcutaneous layers of digital consciousness. "room" as code-word for our room, our body. Starting with the flesh, scanning the surface. Proceeding into layers of hidden information i.e.: the readout of the brain's functions.[31]

As part of the 2000 net.congestion International Festival of Streaming Media, WAAG Society (Amsterdam) and Audioroom (London) collaborated to present a performance running in parallel in London, Amsterdam, and the Internet. *O + E* (2000) is a reworking of the Orpheus and Euridice myth and uses the three sites as the different worlds of the story: the natural world and Orpheus's podium in London, the underworld in Amsterdam, and the transit area of the Internet. Several different simultaneous versions of Euridice were created from Amsterdam to confuse Orpheus's search for her. The multiuser application *Keystroke* was used to create, manipulate, and exchange real-time animations, video images, sound, and text, and to allow members of the public to intervene in the performance. The Orpheus and Euridice narrative has proved a potent and seductive myth for digital adaptation, with examples ranging from a live hypertext version by the Playtext Players to Opera North's multimedia opera *O4E* (2000), an update of Monteverdi's *Orpheo* (1607) that incorporates beautiful, multilayered projections on a hanging sphere and back screen, designed by Rowan May.

Kunstwerk-Blend

Kunstwerk-Blend, directed by Sophia Lycouris, was established in 1997 and developed out of the earlier WITS[32] group, with which it shares three identifiable intentions: firstly to focus on "feminine attitudes to performance," secondly to create "fluid and anticlimactic performance structures and non-hierarchical relationships amongst performers and art forms" and thirdly "to use improvisation ('instant composition') as a performance mode."[33] There was therefore an aesthetic and philosophical strategy to Kunstwerk-Blend's adoption of digital techniques and telematics; and the fact that digital data was common to sound, image, and movement was seen to provide an ideal basis for the sought democratic and nonhierarchical relationship between the three media.

The company's use of performance structures that neither tell a narrative nor result in some decisive ending clearly continues a long-standing tradition, particularly apparent in music and dance, with traceable antecedents from at least the mid-twentieth century, long before digital technology was generally available. John Cage, for example, was instrumental in creating musical compositions that sought to unravel ("de-package") the product received by the listener, avoiding predetermined endings, finales, or expressionistic clues: "Form thus becomes an assemblage, growth an accumulation of things that have piled-up in the time-space of the piece. (Non- or omni-directional) *succession* is the ruling procedure as against the (directional) *progression* of other forms of post-Renaissance art music."[34] From 1952, Merce Cunningham had pursued a comparable path in dance choreography, arguing that climax was not the endpoint but part of an ever-ongoing process and that priorities should no longer hold sway: "Now I can't see that crisis any longer means a climax, unless we are willing to grant that every breath of wind has a climax. . . . Life goes on regardless. . . . Climax is for those who are swept by New Year's Eve."[35] It is interesting to note in relation to ideas of collaboration that both Cage and Cunningham maintained that they never worked *together* even when apparently collaborating on the same interdisciplinary workshop in the same space.[36] Equally interesting is Cage's response to a question in 1980: "How much does new technology interest you?" to which his slightly surprising answer was, "It interests me very little, partly for the reason it interests so many other people, and other people are doing such excellent work in that field."[37]

These Cage/Cunningham axioms and the individual interdependence in their collaborative work offer significant keys to the output of Kunstwerk-Blend that can otherwise appear somewhat academic and mysterious. Kunstwerk-Blend improvisations follow a similar model, with multiple inputs (sound, image, movement) creating an improvised collage over time, but without identifiable hierarchies, progressions, narratives, or climaxes. The emphasis is rather on *layering* and its progression in time, with independent and autonomous digital signals being switched from one medium to another.

trans/forms (1999), first presented at IDAT99 at the University of Arizona,[38] layered real-time input signals sent via the Internet, including live improvised sound with theremin, saxophone, and amplified glove, which was webcast in from the London Musicians' Collective sound studio (figure 17.6). The remote musicians accompanying the dance performance in Arizona included the legendary saxophonist Lol Coxhill, theremin player Michael Kosmides, and Knut Aufermann, who used electronic body sensors to produce a sound dance. The complex telematic soundtrack was complemented by live voice input and projected sequences of edited video that were occasionally thrown into

Figure 17.6 Images from an installation version of Kunstwerk-Blend's *trans/forms* (1999).

sharp relief on the shiny white costume fabric of the two performers, Lycouris and Viv Dogan Corringham. Even though webcasting in 1999 was an established technology, it was still subject to many flaws ("Net congestion" being the most common) that the production positively sought to optimize and emphasize, incorporating the related frame freezes and time lags into the fabric of the piece. This positive aesthetics of Net congestion were also highlighted in *String* (2000) where real-time outputs from a remote theremin player and sound/video camera operators were mixed and interwoven into a solo dance improvisation, with projections cast on various surfaces, including the body of the performer.

Kunstwerk-Blend's collaboration with Yacov Sharir and London-based Dutch multimedia composer Stan Wijnans, *IntelligentCITY* (2002–4), centers on the input signals from a random (or at least extremely complex and unpredictable) source: consumers in a shopping mall. Their movements produce multiple sound and image inputs for manipulation and editing to reflect the architecture and mood of the public space, and then to reflect this data back into the mall itself. The project is built around the simple premise that both architecture and choreography are essentially concerned with spatial structures, and links to Sharir's previous *Dancing with the Virtual Dervish* (1994, with Diane Gromala), which appeared to thrust the performer into the interior architecture of their (VR) body. But in *IntelligentCITY* the architecture is real (a shopping center), as are the performers (the crowds), and between them they generate virtual patterns that Sharir calls "'choreographic environments,' dynamic spaces,"[39] which the performers/shoppers can simultaneously experience as physical movement and sound and image. In this endeavor they follow in the traditions of not only Cage and Cunningham, but also the many composers and artists who have investigated complex formal structures and systems of given circumstances, such as the Fluxus artists and performers, Nam June Paik, and the composers Gavin Bryars and Steve Reich.

Webcams: The Subversion of Surveillance

Our world, overpopulated by images, makes us live among the crowds of phantoms and doubt the homogeneity of our times.
—SYLVIANE AGACINSKI[1]

Surveillance Society

Before commencing an examination of the webcam phenomenon itself, we will begin by analyzing theories of surveillance and examples of surveillance art that predate its online form. The disciplinarily framed, observatory gaze of the camera has been conceptualized as an intrusive and controlling force since the earliest nineteenth century box cameras. Theories of photography from Freud to Foucault and feminism have provided critiques of photographic objectivity to demonstrate how

embedded within photographic realism is a discourse of mastery and control over the photographic object where that object is nature (real) or the body. . . . The photographic gaze is discriminatory— it privileges the viewing subject over the viewed object and is intolerant of difference or otherness, which is frequently coded as monstrosity. Critics such as John Tagg (1988) and Allan Sekula (1989) have used Foucault's concepts of surveillance and panopticism in order to demonstrate how realist photography became a tool of social control.[2]

In 1982, a British comedian at London's Comedy Store recalled how George Orwell's novel *1984* (1948) had predicted a future where everyone's home had a screen that oppressed and controlled them, transmitting propaganda and simultaneously watching them. But, he joked, Orwell's prediction was twenty years out: "by 1964 everyone had already volunteered." Like the still and movie camera before them, television and broadcast media have been theorized as forms of social coercion and control since their inception, and the proliferation of CCTV surveillance cameras has since accelerated the hostile

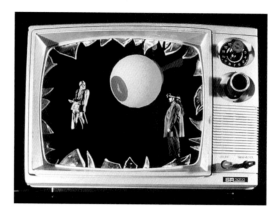

Figure 18.1 Media paranoia and panopticism in George Coates Performance Works' theater performance *Invisible Site: A Virtual Sho* (1991).

criticism against an oppressive panoptic society that breaches the fundamental human right to privacy. Among many digital performances conjuring this image of ubiquitous media panopticism, one of the most memorable is a sequence from the George Coates Performance Works' *Invisible Site: A Virtual Sho* (1991). Within a shattered television set, two live actors interact while a giant, computer graphic eye follows their actions (figure 18.1).

However, it is commonly forgotten that the cries of liberal academics and human rights activists have long been in the minority—surveillance has been a massive, unequivocal hit with the public. S. Davies calls it a "feel-good factor" for people,[3] whose fear of crime is decreased wherever the panoptic eye is trained, and Gareth Palmer notes how "CCTV has transcended civil libertarian concerns, perhaps, because it has the magical qualities of being a deterrent to crime and popular with the public."[4] In *Discipline and Liberty* (2003), Palmer notes the role of the media in propagandizing CCTV's virtues despite the fact that several studies have demonstrated that its profile as a crime deterrent and detective is more assumed than proven. He characterizes CCTV surveillance in Foucauldian terms, as "part of the technology of social control"[5] and urban order:

a new way to police the darkness—to bring everything before the light of the cameras. In this way, it was thought, everything can become knowable and the project of surveillance can end confusion and fear. . . . As a scientific solution to the chaos of the city it extends administrative power both symbolically and as a tool of classification. . . . From the traces we leave when making a credit-card purchase to the image of us recorded by CCTV cameras we offer ourselves up as data to be sorted.[6]

Computer technologies, enabling increasingly sophisticated networked surveillance as well as frighteningly close-up satellite spying, have now seriously accelerated Orwell's

1984 vision, as well as the intensity of the controlling gaze of Bentham and Foucault's *panopticon*. Erkki Huhtamo is one of many to point out how privacy has been increasingly compromised and jeopardized by the spread of surveillance and communication (including Internet) interception techniques, particularly since 9/11:

The sense of being observed is becoming a widely common state of mind. The world of telecommunications is in danger of turning into an all-embracing *Panopticon*: You cannot escape the feeling that anything you do with your computer or your mobile phone may be monitored and recorded by someone else at any moment. At the same time the massive tidal waves of spam that fill your In box lead to a growing feeling of unreality. This stream of data no longer arrives from "inaccessible capitals," but from unknown peripheric locations, routed via untraceable paths.[7]

In recent years, "ordinary people" have themselves enthusiastically endorsed and greedily bought into the surveillance society with home security camera systems, a trend parodied in Niels Bonde's installation *I Never had Hair on My Body or Head* (1988) where visitors walk through rooms and are observed and recorded by covert spy technologies concealed in objects including children's toys. In the final room, the recordings are played back and the visitors discover they have been filmed.[8] Meanwhile, on television (perennially reflecting back on society, and as hegemonic as ever) the paradigm has also been warmly and popularly embraced, or put another way, milked to death. Since the late 1990s there has been a plethora of hidden camera and reality TV programs including police shows that "invite us to share the perspective of other watchers, to be in the viewing booth with the other instruments of authority."[9] The most commercially successful of the genre are fly-on-the-wall social observation programs, the most popular of which is called, unsurprisingly yet not a little chillingly, *Big Brother*.

Surveillance Art

While the history of photography and cinema provides many surveillance-image precedents, the eye of the video surveillance camera emerged for the first time in a gallery artwork with Les Levine's *Slipcover* (1966) where visitors found real time images of themselves relayed onto monitors within the space.[10] As many have noted, the paradigm turns the viewer into a performer, and the basic model has been repeated and adapted in different forms ever since, perhaps most famously by Bruce Nauman, whose 1968 *Video Corridor* has remained popular over the decades (we saw it at three different galleries in the United States and United Kingdom during the late 1990s and early 2000s). The visitor progresses down a long thin corridor toward two monitors at the end, on which they see their own image, growing in size as they approach.

During the 1980s and 1990s, Toronto-based Steve Mann created a series of invisible-theater performances in American department stores where he questioned staff about the reasons behind the stores' use of CCTV and covertly filmed the conversations. Staff typically explained that the surveillance was for his own protection, and that he had nothing to fear from it if he had nothing to hide. At this point, he switched from filming secretly using his wearcom spy camera to reveal a camcorder, whereupon the startled staff members generally withdrew, called security, fled from him, or told him to stop filming since photography was forbidden in the store. Mann's video *Shootingback* (1997) contains a compilation of these staged events, and he continues to return the gaze of the surveillance cameras in regular live webcasts during his spy camera wanderings, observations, and confrontations as part of his ongoing *Wireless Wearable Webcam* project (since 1980).[11] Artists such as Pipilotti Rist and Kirstin Lucas continue the tradition; Lucas captures her street encounters with pedestrians and policemen on a head-mounted camera, and later uses head-mounted projectors to beam the footage around galleries and performance spaces for events such as *Host* (1997).[12]

Britain is the most surveilled society in the world, and by the turn of the millennium there were an estimated 150,000 CCTV cameras operating in London alone.[13] *Mongrel XReport* (2002) by British art collective Mongrel used a campaign of Web announcements and stickers placed on London lampposts and subway stations to raise public consciousness of street surveillance, and to galvanize a campaign to report the location of CCTV cameras to their website or phone number. During the four-month Web project with a linked installation at London's Institute of Contemporary Arts (ICA), the information received was assembled on a database and online visitors could access Mongrel's maps of camera positions throughout London and use their custom-written route-planning software (similar to the popular *Mapquest* program). By typing in the start and end points of their journeys, users were provided with detailed maps of the shortest (but generally inordinately circuitous) route to avoid being recorded by any surveillance cameras.

Mongrel XReport's associated installation at the ICA comprised four monitors, mounted at typical surveillance camera height and evenly spaced along a narrow corridor. These ran actual CCTV footage with burned-in timecode highlighting the cameras' secretive positions and intrusive views: "strangers fumbling with the keypads of ATMs, taking desperate drags off cigarettes outside grey corporate buildings, and checking their reflections in rearview mirrors at intersections."[14] Other countersurveillance strategies have been initiated by the Critical Art Ensemble, whose discourse on "Contestational Robotics" calls for urgent resistance and active countering of the use of robotics for policing and surveillance by, for example, developing politically leftist pamphleteer robots.[15] Joel Slayton's *Telepresent Surveillance* (1997) features three robots that follow, move among, and interact with visitors, all the time filming them with mounted video cameras and projecting their images within the installation space.

Alex Galloway prefers to subvert rather than directly resist or raise political consciousness about surveillance technologies and infrastructures. His *Carnivore* (2001, with the Radical Software Group), takes its title from FBI "packet-sniffing" surveillance software that monitors Internet traffic and information exchanges, but its custom software translates the datastream it unearths into artistic visual imagery, rather than using it for the FBI's intelligence purposes.[16] In different vein, but similarly transforming surveillance data into a more aesthetic form, Lynn Hershman Leeson's *Difference Engine #3* (1997) captures video images of ZKM museum visitors and digitally mounts their heads onto avatars that take a twenty-seven-second journey through a VRML representation of the museum. She describes the installation as "an interactive, multi-user, telerobotic sculpture about surveillance, voyeurism, digital absorption and spiritual transformation of the body."[17]

The sinister and implacable face of governance and surveillance is reflected in the performance persona of American artist Natalie Jeremijenko when presenting the public face of the Bureau of Inverse Technology (BIT), "an information agency servicing the Information Age." Jeremijenko's public address character "assumes the disempowered role of the Bureau 'agent' in quite a performative nature and can only speak to technical points . . . [in] a corporate and scientific vernacular."[18] For BIT's *Suicide Box* (1996), a motion-detecting video camera pointing at San Francisco's Golden Gate Bridge was linked to a website that monitored vertical movements, and the camera recorded seventeen suicides over one hundred days. Jerimienko's official announcements on the "data" are as chillingly inhuman as the camera's stare: "System Efficacy: *Suicide Box* system supplied public, frame-accurate data of a social phenomenon not previously accurately quantified."[19] Gloria Sutton's analysis of the project notes the alarming and "drastic" metaphor behind the work. The Golden Gate Bridge provides the gateway to Silicon Valley, both the information and suicide capital of the United States, where "economical statistics like the Dow Jones index are constantly monitored and validated as hard fact, while a social trauma such as the suicide rate is left unnoticed."[20]

Surveillance Theatre

Blast Theory's *Kidnap* (1998) generated considerable fame and notoriety through its actual kidnapping of two people in the United Kingdom: Debra Burgess, a twenty-seven-year-old Australian working as a temp, and Russell Ward, a nineteen-year-old Southend convenience store worker. They were in fact consenting victims, being two of many who had contacted Blast Theory and volunteered in response to prepublicity. But they were unaware if and when they would be selected, captured, and held by the group, who had chosen them at random from a long list, put them under surveillance, and then finally snatched them in broad daylight. The process of kidnapping and the hostage's captivity was broadcast live on the Web, with online visitors able to control the safehouse's webcam and to communicate live with the kidnappers. The group record the performance as having taken place at "a secret location, UK, & http://www.newmediacentre.com/kidnap."[21]

Surveillance has also become a notable theme in theater-based digital performance events, including David Saltz's production of Peter Handke's play *Kasper* (1999), where a giant eyeball projection on a suspended circular screen dominates the stage (figure 18.2). The eyeball moves (controlled in real time by an offstage operator) to follow every move

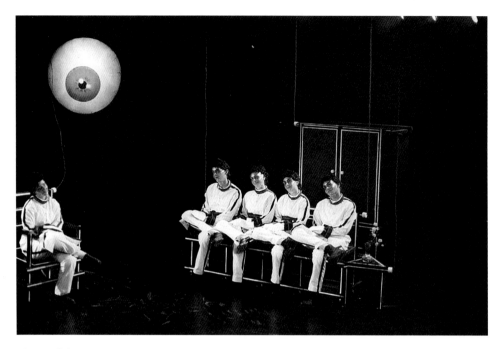

Figure 18.2 The computer operated, all-seeing surveillance eye in David Saltz's production of Handke's *Kaspar* (1999). Photo: Bradley Hellwig.

of the actor playing Kasper, emphasizing his inescapable surveillance. In the "intelligent" stage environment, the Kafkaesque, disembodied voices of the "prompters" of Handke's play are themselves "prompted" by Kasper's actions in trying to arrange the furniture in the room into their prescribed and proper configuration.

Sensors, accelerometers, and pressure-sensitive resistors embedded in the different pieces of furniture are connected via visible wires to an offstage computer. As Kasper touches or sits on the cushions of a sofa, a prompter voice is activated. It stops abruptly the moment he breaks physical contact; the same occurs when he rocks a rocking chair and then stops its movements. As Kasper's agitation and paranoia intensifies, the different male and female voices of the prompters begin, continue, or are cut short in response to his touch, as they bombard him with questions, assertions, syllogisms, and clichés. Kasper frantically opens and shuts cupboards and drawers, starts and stops brushing the floor (the broom "voice" is active only when the broom is in motion) and desperately removes a leg from a triangular table to stop it talking. The claustrophobic sense of external surveillance and control becomes extreme, and Kasper suddenly stops and stares at the large eyeball projection, which implacably returns his gaze. Kasper points to it, and quietly reflects:

The pupil of the eye is round. Fear is round. Had the pupil perished, fear would have perished. But the pupil is there, and fear is there. If the pupil weren't honest, I couldn't say fear was honest. If the pupil weren't permitted, fear wouldn't be permitted. No fear without pupil.

In the final sequence, nine performers in identical white costumes and fleshlike masks enter while Kaper, now similarly costumed and masked, delivers his final monologue. Mouth gags with flashing LED lights are fitted to each of the robotic characters, who then overcome Kasper, and attach a gag to finally silence him. He is literally, physically brought into line with the rest of them, and the lights fade on the intermittent flashes of the LED gags on the perfectly straight line of identical, anonymized figures. Having done its work, the unblinking and all-seeing eye finally closes.

Webcams, or the Virtual Performance of Real Life

To me Art's subject is the human clay.
—W. H. AUDEN[22]

Since the early 1990s, the dispersed users and communities of the Internet have reflected the trends toward CCTV in "real-world" society to provide their own, distinctive takes on surveillance and voyeurism. This is primarily through the use of the webcam: "a camera that takes pictures at set intervals, that can range from 15 times per second to once per hour, then instantly transmits the images to a web server."[23] Webcams are trained on everything from growing plants to fish tanks, from traffic congestion to vending machines, from offices and living rooms to the bedrooms of masturbating models and copulating couples. While CCTV surveillance is commonly covert and broadly concerned with policing, the webcam is characterized by a generally opposite impulse toward openness, sharing, and freedom of expression.

Artists and performers have commonly used webcams to document and make available their "authentic" daily working processes, including the Parkbench group of artists at New York University CAT, who used one of the Web's first remotely controlled cameras to transform their studio into a twenty-four-hour Web installation. An experiment to research the nature of webcams as an art medium, the group reflect that their awareness of the surveillance sometimes heightened their actions, while at others they felt themselves "dissolved in the ubiquitous surveillance which now erases the boundaries between private and public."[24] Parkbench also claim to have created the first live Web performances, entitled *ArTistheater*, in 1994.[25]

While willingly surveyed human subjects are inevitably affected in myriad ways by their consciousness of being watched, webcams nonetheless provide a sense of documentary realism, using the camera as the proverbial "fly on the wall." But whereas film and television documentaries are prerecorded and edited, and current live reality TV shows are stage-managed and use multiple camera techniques, the normally static, impassive wide shot of the webcam provides a quite different experience. Its poor image quality and its fixed view differentiates the webcam from the televisual (although its place on the Web does not, as TV now increasingly resides there too). Its low-resolution, grainy pixelation lends it an antiquated, pre-television quality, while its stubborn stasis echoes the stern discipline of the surveillance camera. These qualities imbue the webcam with both a sense of documentary authenticity and of liveness that is central to its appeal and status: people log in to webcams to see what someone is *actually* doing *now* (or what is *actually* happening in the space *now*). Liveness and actuality are the ontological conjoined-twins of the webcam; and this inextricably links the new webcam medium to the liveness and actuality of performance art. Of course, unlike performance art, the webcam is a mediatized experience; its transmission of the live is mediated, but its particular form and documentary immediacy convey a unique sense of liveness, different from both theatrical and television experiences of the live. Webcams essentially purport to be the virtual performance of real life.

Webcam Sex

A sense of liveness is crucial to many pornography webcams, where paying subscribers to sites devoted to a single model tend to log in regularly, sometimes daily, striking up long-term relationships that are dependent on the models' live and personal responses in real time to the user's textual chat. Models are highly conscious of the need to gain subscriber loyalty to their sites, and strategically address their fans by name. Typically, as each user logs on in the chat window, they are welcomed by the model who is seen and heard via the video webcam—"Hi Joe, how are you tonight? Glad you could join me. Bill, Yoshi and Pole-Dick are also online right now, we're going to have a great night, you guys!"

Digital artist Susan Collins engaged in research into pornographic webcams in 1997 when she discovered that they were at the cutting edge of the then new tools of Net streaming media, which she was about to utilize in her *In Conversation* (1997) project. She was struck by the extent to which liveness, and its verification, was crucial to the users' experience. The time delay (typically between twenty and sixty seconds) between the user typing a message in the chat window and its receipt and response by the model was a source of both frustration and wonder:

Perhaps surprisingly, the majority of the virtual tête-à-têtes I witnessed during my research consisted of the viewers asking the model to "wave to prove you're really there" (or similar). The delayed visuals tended to frustrate the viewers in their attempts at verification, and so the question would be continuously repeated in different forms with slightly different demands. The whole operation appeared to be engaged with establishing the truth and reality of the situation rather than an opportunity to create an intimate or erotic exchange (assuming this was the initial intention).

I became increasingly interested in this particular act of verification—this effort to "establish the actual"—and the way it appeared to take over the original aim of the communication and the aim of the Web site itself. I even started drawing a parallel between this phenomenon and the methods visitors to a séance would apply to confirm the true identity of the person they were "making contact" with.[26]

The majority of interactive webcasts derive from the sex industry, where the traditional theatrical form of striptease has been transposed into a remote encounter in cyberspace. Catherine Waldby argues,

Like money, sexuality is succumbing to digital dematerialization. Just as economic exchange is now less a matter of the transaction of palpable objects (notes and coins) and more the circulation of debt and credit data, so now certain domains of erotic experience are less a matter of bodily proximity and tactility, and more to do with electronically mediated communication between partners separated in space.[27]

Waldby suggests that Internet eroticism demonstrates the extent to which computer-mediated communication has brought about a new kind of corporeal space, and new configurations of embodiment and intersubjectivity which cannot be adequately described in terms of absolute presence or absence, proximity or distance:

This space comes about through particular conjunctions of the body and digital technology, which in turn enables new forms of intersubjective space. To engage in eroticised exchange at the screen interface is to suture the body's capacities for pleasure into the interactive space of the network, to use that network as the medium for pleasuring and being pleasured at a distance.[28]

Webcam Falsities and Fictions

Webcam artists Elizabeth Diller and Ricardo Scofidio suggest that webcams can be thought of as "a public service, or a mode of passive advertisement, or it may be a new type of exhibitionism, or self-disciplinary device. The desire to connect to others in real time may be driven by a response to the 'loss' of the public realm."[29] They point out that the term "liveness" originated in broadcasting to denote the idea of authenticity and "a trusted reality," and that webcams continue and extend this tradition. They argue that since webcam views tend to be casual and to lack dramatic content "they appear unmediated" and that their sense of liveness appeals to both technophiles and technophobes:

For technophobes who blame technology for the collapse of the public sphere, liveness may be the last vestige of authenticity—seeing and/or hearing the event at the precise moment of its occurrence. The un-mediated is the im-mediate. For technophiles, liveness defines technology's aspiration to simulate the real in real-time. Lag time, search time, and download time all impair real-time computational performance. But whether motivated by the desire to preserve the real or to fabricate it, liveness is synonymous with the real—an object of uncritical desire for techno-extremes.

Regardless of where one falls within the technophile/technophobe spectrum, it is hard not to be captivated by the potential of witnessing something uncensored, no matter how banal.[30]

Diller and Scofidio's own artistic work with webcams plays on and teases the audience's act of faith in reading webcams as live and real. They also employ webcams to subtly point at how society operates and how social and professional relationships develop according to normative conventions, and in relation to the knowledge of being watched. Their webcam site *Refresh* (1998) presents twelve office webcams in a grid. One of these is live and is refreshed when clicked, the others are recorded, fictional narratives constructed using actors who are pasted into the office backgrounds using *Photoshop* software. The narratives are deliberately prosaic; the focus of the piece is the way in which the characters' behavior and actions are affected by their knowledge of the webcam's presence over time. A character's dress styles begin to change (flirting with the camera), paper becomes stacked more ritualistically (impressing the camera), a character's ordering of takeout food becomes obsessive (ignoring the camera), a sublimated office romance develops by the water cooler (trying to deceive the camera, but erotically excited by its gaze). As the artists put it: "There is nothing shocking or dramatic, rather, everyday conventions are slightly modified either to perform for or to hide from the camera."[31] While webcams always appear to be casually and innocently positioned, "their field of vision is carefully considered, and behaviour within that field cannot help but anticipate the looming presence of the global viewer."[32]

While many webcam artworks and performances challenge, parody, or otherwise take issue with surveillance society, as many others transform them from the negative power politics of Foucault's panopticon to present a positive environment highlighting notions of community and social anthropology. Andrea Zapp inverts the Big Brother paradigm for her *Little Sister—A 24-Hr Online Surveillance Soap* (since 2000) where she links together multiple existing public and private webcams that she selected according to their associations with the locations of typical television soap operas. The central image on the homepage is a globe made up of a jigsaw of webcam images of bars, hairdressers, offices, shops, living rooms, kitchens, and so on from all over the world, and the user clicks these to bring up discrete windows running the real time footage. Among the real webcams, she also incorporates some prerecorded fictional scenes such as shoplifting incidents and shootouts, both to inject dramatic action into the soap and to complicate the sense of authenticity and actuality (figure 18.3). While webcams and surveillance cameras are popularly trusted as providing gritty, real time documentary realism, Zapp's *Little Sister* reminds us that apparently live webcams and their timeframes are easily manipulated and falsified.

A number of artists use webcams to question or ironically undermine notions of webcam authenticity by fictionalizing events in the camera's view; and writers such as Ken Goldberg have reflected on webcam forgeries and their implications. He uses Plato's

Figure 18.3 All the world's a surveillance stage in Andrea Zapp's *Little Sister* (2000).

classical triangulated definition of knowledge to argue that remote webcams can never be definitively known to be *true*. He draws on N. Goodman's discourse on art forgery, "Art and Authenticity" (1976) to conclude that "if forgery sheds light on the nature of authenticity, the Internet provides an ample supply of illumination."[33] For avid viewers of a particular webcam, like his own *The Telegarden* (1995–99) where remote users commonly spent long hours operating a robot arm to grow and tend a real garden, Goldberg suggests that the trauma which could greet the discovery that such a webcam was falsified would be comparable to a museum curator discovering his prized Rembrandt was a forgery.

Other academics have focused on the webcam as a technology that above all provides a digital window into another real time and space, thereby conjoining the actual and the virtual. Garnet Hertz suggests that webcams "re-introduce a physical sense of actual sight into the disembodied digital self,"[34] and Thomas Campanella argues that webcams are mediating devices within the "spatially abstract" world of cyberspace: "points of contact between the virtual and the real, or the spatial anchors in a placeless sea. Webcams open digital windows onto real scenes within the far-flung geography of the Internet."[35] The owner of the world's most celebrated webcam, Jennifer Ringley, provides her own window metaphor in describing her Jennicam as "a sort of window into a virtual human zoo."[36]

Jennicam

People are always waiting for real life to start.
—JENNIFER RINGLEY OF JENNICAM[37]

If "Real Life" ever started, for Jennicam and its many followers it ended on 31 December 2003 after a continuous run of netcasting twenty-four hours a day, seven days a week for approaching eight years. No reason for its sudden demise has been advanced by its creator, Jennifer Ringley, although press speculation placed the blame firmly on her subscription service PayPal's adoption of a policy of refusing to act for any website that could involve frontal nudity. An equally plausible explanation might be that "Jenni" had simply become tired of playing out her entire adult home life in front of a camera relaying live images to the Internet. Whatever the reason, Jennicam's passing was in quiet contrast to the media furor and instant celebrity status that greeted its initial launch in April 1996 at the height of the "digital revolution" and its attendant predictions of a new world order primarily determined by the computer and the Internet.

Jennicam presents one of the great ironies of the digital performance era at the end of the twentieth century. Despite the endless energy and commitment of performance artists and pioneers struggling with all the tools, codes and technicalities of virtual space and digital existence, the live performer who by far received the most media exposure worldwide was an unknown student at Dickinson College, Pennsylvania. Ringley claims that she originally connected a camera to her computer so that her mother could see her in her student room via the Internet; the original Jennicam screen began with a simple statement, "My name is Jennifer Ringley, and I am not an actor or dancer or entertainer. I am a computer geek . . . I don't sing or dance or do tricks (okay, sometimes I do, but not very well and solely for my own amusement, not yours)."[38]

Jennicam was not the first and certainly not the last webcam, but it became by default the most publicised, the most enduring, and arguably the most endearing. Ringley unwittingly created one of the most influential and longest running pieces of improvised endurance theater ever, without the benefit of theater or media training or any enhanced performance skills. Jennicam was an ongoing life constantly flashed up on the Internet that seemed to reach out towards some ultimate dramatic play—a life portrayed. Or perhaps, given the absence of the title-holder much of the time, a portrayal of the life of her furniture and occasionally one of her cats. It was never perfect documentation and immortality was not assured. There were inevitable technical hitches and some significant gaps—her first nineteen years, for example, and whenever Jennifer was off camera, which was much of the time, or switched the lights off. But it remained the revelation of the "ordinary" life of a young Western woman from April 1996 to December 2003, the elapsing of time captured in a series of snapshots.

Jennifer Ringley was the first celebrity formed by the Internet, "The Queen of Cyberspace," with a multiplicity of fan sites, dedicated chat rooms, and hundreds emailing her every day. Estimates varied around the level of popularity Jennicam enjoyed as the media and public interest grew in the late 1990s, but reports of three, four, and five million hits *per day* were common, and a 1997 Reuter's report put it as high as twenty million. As press and media coverage intensified, copycat sites mushroomed (including popular parodies such as "NotJennicamCam") and the webcam as a socio-performative phenomenon came of age.

Jennicam, such a huge success almost literally overnight, had to cope with the effects in both the short term and the long term. The earliest demands for the Net to be "free" (of financial and censorship restrictions) did not appreciate the hidden costs of the former, and Ringley introduced a subscription scheme in 1997 in order to offset her estimated monthly costs of $3,000. She immediately attracted 5,500 paying members. The initial $15 a year subscription increased fourfold to $15 dollars for 90 days by 2003, but always maintained a free point of access, albeit less preferential, in order to fulfil its original raison d'être:

Jennicam Members get still images at a more frequent rate, once per minute instead of once per fifteen minutes. Put plainly, bandwidth costs money. So do accounting services and legal services and all the other services that make sure the site stays alive and kicking . . . PLEASE feel free to use the guest site for as long as you like, that's what it's there for. I don't want anybody to feel ripped off or cheated.[39]

The Telematic Theater of an Ordinary Life

Few have ever met Jennifer Ringley, but no one is inclined to think she is purely an Internet figment or media-created cyborg; for most people her house exists much as does, say, Timbuktu (or Elsinore). The audience is content to suspend disbelief and accept slowly changing Internet still frames suggesting a place and on occasions somebody within that space. The space is a stage: we are in a darkened auditorium occasionally observing, confirming her existence, and maybe she ours, a convenient exchange agreement not unlike witnessing Samuel Beckett's *Not I* or *Waiting for Godot*:

Boy: What am I to tell Mr. Godot, sir?
Vladimir: tell him . . . *(he hesitates)* . . . tell him you saw me and that . . . *(he hesitates)* . . . that you saw me.
(Pause. Vladimir advances, the Boy recoils. Vladimir halts, the Boy halts. With sudden violence.)
You're sure you saw me, you won't come and tell me tomorrow that you never saw me!
Silence.

Its basic theatrical underpinnings have been largely overlooked by commentators, perhaps because they are too obvious, perhaps because Jennicam too conveniently fits into any and every category for study by psychologists, feminists, and sociologists, so that "new theater piece" becomes just another critical tag. Ringley latterly even introduced herself, irony intended, as "a computer geek and recent entrant into the field of social service." More significantly, it may be because the *fixed* location of most webcams prioritizes *place* ("setting") above all else and certainly above *character*, which in this scenario has to be interpreted from a sequence of incidentals. In contemporary parlance, Jennicam is a "*site-specific time-based installation*." Academics who have discussed the phenomenon of webcams have therefore tended to see them more as *distance-location* devices or travel aids showing the changing state of the world and beyond. Bolter and Grusin, for example, draw attention to webcams placed on Mars as well as Miami, a backyard bird feeder in Indianapolis, and a panoramic view of the Canadian Rockies: "'Web-cams' on the Internet pretend to locate us in various natural environments. . . . In all these cases, the logic of immediacy dictates that the medium itself should disappear and leave us in the presence of the thing represented: . . . standing on a mountaintop."[40]

They usefully counter the notion that webcams are banal: "Apparently frivolous, web cameras are in fact deeply revealing of the nature of the Web as a remediator."[41] With a degree of seriousness, they show a still picture of two windows of prostitutes' shops in Amsterdam's red light district. But both blinds are pulled *down* so no characters are visible—when there is any human interaction in the red light district, the curtain comes *down* and the play is left to the imagination. The emphasis remains on *place* and therein lies the essential theatrical difference experienced by the Jennicam viewer, and a primary reason for its huge popularity. With Jennicam the blind is always open, the only exceptions being rare technical blackouts or offline days when Ringley physically moved to another house, which she did on six occasions since her original Dickinson College student room. Like the "we never close" wartime boast of the Windmill Theatre during the London blitz, the modern equivalent was "Jennicam: Open 24/7" or even, it was once assumed, "Jennicam: Open 365/lifetime": the stage curtain remained raised, the action continuous. Some phases had little or no dramatic action; lengthy periods passed with only the image of an empty set; and at night, the mighty power of the Internet was used to convey nothing more than a nearly black screen. But this was life *chez* Jenni: "We are not always at home, sometimes you may see an empty house for hours or longer at a stretch. That's life."[42]

But Bolter and Grusin's point remains important insofar as Jennicam was more the ongoing life of a particular location (or locations in Jennicam's final mode of multiple webcams throughout the living quarters) rather than necessarily any particular character—Ringley simply being the one most frequently featured, with different (animal and human) creatures occasionally moving in and out of view. But Jennicam's enticing indicators, bodies, and hints of action remained theatrical and the seconds ticking away to the next frozen picture continually offered a dramatic countdown to the next episode. Although many commentators noted that most of the images were completely mundane, they always invited interpretation, and many images also begged questions—particularly the ones without any living presence (cat or human)—of a metaphysical nature reminiscent of the painting genre of the same name.

Bedroom Theater and Its Hauntings

Webcams are generally pointed at areas of maximum presence and activity, and ironically this webcam was left pointing at Ringley's bed much of the time. Viewers would commonly see a sleeping person in a darkened room at night, and a neatly made bed the next morning (perhaps still a reassuring communication to her mother that she makes it every day before setting out to work). The bed image has elements of tease, what Victor Burgin calls "the eroticism of absence,"[43] as well as reassurance. More reassuring and considerably tidier, for example, than Tracey Emin's *My Bed* art object, shortlisted for the prestigious 1999 Turner Prize, an installation comprising Emin's unmade bed with grubby sheets surrounded by scattered litter including condoms, soiled knickers and bottles of vodka. *My Bed* is a stationary unoccupied art installation that owes not a little, one suspects, to Jennicam, and whose only performative aspects have involved unexpected interventions by gallery visitors. One outraged housewife, Christine de Ville, drove from Wales with a packet of Vanish detergent to try to spruce up the sheets and get Emin to improve her ways, but gallery staff censored her attempts. Two Chinese art students attempted to cavort and have a pillow fight on the bed "to improve it" before that performance too was curtailed by conservative forces. No such restrictions applied to Jennicam, where the bed was used daily in much the same way that beds are frequently used: for sleeping, occasional lolling, occasional sex, and, if permitted (and also if not) as a temporary oversized cat basket. Inevitably both Jennicam and *My Bed* became subject to imitation by others employing the detritus of their particular lifestyle and emotional state as an artist's window for the world.

Unrevealed offstage action is a standard theatrical narrative device: we do not see Macbeth's victorious battles or the blinding of Oedipus, but are content to accept the descriptions and hints that help create a convincing imaginary context. Similarly, the long periods of time watching empty rooms with no characters within the Jennicam set—previously "occupied" but now "empty", previously "empty" but now suddenly "occupied"—presented an ever-shifting kaleidoscope of patterns where, like a Beckett play, like an Eliot stanza, people "come and go." Ringley's sets remained empty longer than a conventional theater director would ever dare permit, but this particular digital performance was running on a different time scale. When Ringley was not visible "the set" was ever-present; there to be read as one reads an advertisement—signifiers everywhere, like a Jacques Tati still of a sleepy village evoking a particular mood and era, everything reeking of time and a version of normality. And since her absence rather than presence characterized the normality of Jennicam, when she suddenly became visible—and it may only have been a part of her caught on camera—it was often accidentally reminiscent of evocations of those traditional theater ghosts rumoured to inhabit theater stages and concourses but only wisps of which are ever spotted.

Alternatively, figures "caught" on-camera and not offering any composed or designed image often seemed so brazen and candid that their appearance suddenly disrupted the spectacle in such a way that it prompted a peculiar shock to the senses. Other appearances or apparent apparitions seemed so mysterious in their motivations that they teased ingenuity in the same way as "Spot the Ball" competitions do, exciting the detective instincts in the viewer.

Coffee Theater

Jennicam was not the first webcam, a distinction generally bestowed on the University of Cambridge's infamous "Trojan coffee-pot" webcam, and the story of the one is every bit as unlikely as the other. In 1991, the "Trojan" group of Cambridge computer scientists formed a "coffee club" to share a coffee machine conveniently sited in a corridor between offices. Those farthest away from the location were frequently disappointed when they went to fetch coffee and the pot was empty, and they mounted a "frame-grabber" camera that enabled a regularly updated image of the coffeepot and its fluctuating contents to be accessed on their computer screens. In November 1993, as images within webpages became a possibility, the coffeepot became a mildly humorous presence on the Net with its inclusion as a regularly reloaded image on their website. Media interest in this prosaic and witty oddity grew, and by 1996 the coffeepot site annually received more than one million hits, prompting one commentator to call it the number one tourist attraction in eastern England. Droll observations of this type—usually underscoring the fact that the computer was changing an old established way of life—were increasingly commonplace, and would in the same year also ensure Jennicam's enduring fame.

Trojan's webcam relied on some level of theatrical resonance, albeit rudimentary: whether a coffeepot was full, empty, or somewhere in between, this was theater reduced to its basic fundamentals. It also laid bare the complex relationship between absence and presence that defined so much minimalist art and postmodern performance at that time. But it failed to have the depth of human interest and therefore staying power associated with Jennicam as "drama." Jennicam offered new horizons of heightened human interest, a slowly unraveling drama, and even occasional naked female flesh; on the Web, mere "coffee theater" could simply not compete. What scientists call the "Uncertainty Principle," a key ingredient common to dramas, whodunits, and quantum physics (and the core purpose and joke of the Trojan webcam) split and multiplied with Jennicam. "Uncertainty Principle" plus human interest, a young female "star," a love interest, a sex interest even—this was webcam meets Hollywood (or at least, daytime soap opera). The resulting intensity of media coverage, debate and outrage produced an overnight sensation, taking "Jenni" from obscurity to celebrity performer.

Invention plus the narrative "uncertainty principle" ensured the webcam phenomenon achieved considerable fame and, in the case of the coffee pot, fortune, with its celebrity status resulting in its eventual sale on eBay for £3,350 GBP ($5,346 USD). Jennicam outlived the Trojan webcam when the scientists moved to a new laboratory (doubtless with improved coffee facilities from the auction proceeds) and finally turned off the webcam on 22 August 2001. The world's first webcam had lasted seven years and nine months (a period only just superceded by Jennicam), and as the creators ceremoniously switched it off, they issued a droll statement, possibly with Jennicam in mind: "We expect this to start a new trend in webcams: online cameras which take images of themselves being finally turned off. Such sites will be much sought after due to their ephemeral nature."

So Jennicam was not the first webcam, and neither was Jennifer Ringley the first student to put "self" as the core subject of a webcam in a dorm room. That distinction is claimed by others, including computer student Dan Moore, who with friends set up a webcam that watched his every move in his student room for around four years. The informal team developed two-way communications, never a feature of Jennicam, which retained a more traditional theatrical structure of stage/auditorium, performer/audience. But this male webcam did not arouse media interest in anything like the same way as the slightly titillating, bare-all Jennicam, whose Web-audience male/female ratio was estimated at its commencement to be 75:1, in stark contrast to the 3:7 male/female ratio of the average repertory theater audience.

Banality and Profundity

The webcam phenomenon in general, and Jennicam in particular, immediately raised a host of debates and observations. Watching Ringley watch television on Jennicam was the perfect image of media swallowing its own tail. Being able to watch her at various (fairly standard) times sit, eat, pay bills, read, dress, undress, shower, make love, and sleep in the privacy of her own rooms was an open invitation for debates on exhibitionism, voyeurism, pornography, and feminist philosophy. At times she was even held responsible for the development of the tens of thousands of "porncams" that emerged in the late 1990s, some of which attempted to emulate "real-life" but invariably reverted to exaggerated theatrical scenarios without ever catching the genuine fly-on-the-wall charm and daffiness of Jennicam. It was its serene, unpretentious banality, its innocent and tedious ordinariness which left Jennicam standing apart and which made it the idiosyncratically effective theatrical event it became: a reaffirmation of predictability, a large dose of trite, trivial, and reassuring *dullness*. "Extreme sports" may make good viewing for short periods (already "ultra-extreme sports" are available on TV networks) but with the theater of Jennicam the viewer could undertake that most basic of performance engagements, identification.

Ringley's portrayal of existence was never very electrifying or exhilarating, despite being a child of the seventies in the age of New Woman and with advanced technological skills to boot. She ate, worked, slept, watched TV, and had parents and friends round. Here was the Alison of John Osborne's *Look Back in Anger* (1956) forty years later, no longer saddled with a brutish husband and now more actively choosing partners and life's rich pattern. But she was still not revolutionary or heroic, but rather accepting, fairly ordinary, and annoyingly "nice." It probably did not *have* to be Jennifer Ringley that created this iconic improvised reality soap opera (in the same way that perhaps it *did* have to be Einstein who undermined Newtonian physics), but even so her particular individuality and adroitness in popularizing and developing the webcam phenomenon should be applauded.

The responses Jennicam aroused ranged from the vitriolic to the reverential, and its popularity and notoriety afforded debates to be aired at a much wider and public level than concurrent discussions on cyberculture by technologists and academics. Feminists were divided between those criticizing the "regression" of its porncam aspect, and others praising the "progression" of a technologically attuned woman familiarizing visitors with the daily toil, living conditions and everyday experience of females within the new technological world. *Cybergrrl: Voices of Women* interviewed Ringley in 2001 and, interestingly, adopted coy innuendo in their tagline—"Jenni of Jennicam Bares it All for Cybergrrl":

Jenni: The media, by and large, ADORES making a big deal out of the nudity and sexual content on the site. I don't strip. I don't even sleep naked much. And since I started dating Geofry 10 months ago, I haven't had sex on camera a single time because Geofry is camera-shy.[44]

But serious consideration of the significance of Jennicam has been overshadowed by numerous undermining voices from the mass media and even occasionally academia, which have argued with reductivist aplomb that essentially she is nothing more than an exhibitionist, and the people watching are voyeurs. It is notable, however, that the same analysis could be made of every theater event. Victor Burgin has taken issue with such oversimplistic readings by drawing on a wide range of psychological interpretations from Freud and Lacan to Donald Winnicott and Melanie Klein in his essay "Jenni's Room: Exhibitionism and Solitude" (2002).

There can be little doubt that in the early days at least, Ringley occasionally did enjoy "exhibitionist" tendencies, including vampish moments of performance, her initial choice of a website name (www.boudoir.org), and her infrequent confiding of "secrets" (like a stage aside) such as buying a breast pump to see if she could produce lactation. But such revelations were part of her (private = public) Web journal and were not made in a lascivious manner, and it is ultimately debatable whether she generally displayed exhibitionist traits much more than many westernized young females (or indeed males). As she once put it: "I keep Jennicam alive *not* because I want to be watched, but because I simply don't mind being watched." Ultimately, Jennicam was an enjoyable hobby for Ringley, not one that was too self-absorbing or demanding, but rather akin to the pursuits of the Sunday painter or, more pertinently, the amateur thespian:

Jennicam was started in April of 1996, when I was a junior in college. It was intended to be a fun way my mom or friends could keep tabs on me, and an interesting use for the digital camera I bought on a whim in the bookstore. I never really contemplated the ramifications of it, just plugged it in, challenged myself to write the scripts that would take care of the image processing (nowadays you can just download software to do that), and told myself I'd give it a week. After that week, I decided to give it another.[45]

Conclusion

The twenty-four-hour reality screenings of webcams in general and Jennicam in particular could lay some claim to aiding and abetting such films as *EdTV* and *The Truman Show* as well as television's "reality entertainment" series such as *Big Brother*, *Survivor*, and *The Jim Scileppi Show*. Such media texts epitomize a particular attitude toward performance derived and honed through an exploitation of *lack* of performance skill that most theater academics detest but many audiences consider to be the defining characteristics of theater—exaggeration, exhibitionism, pantomime, theatricalism, self-exposure, and foolishness. Jennicam's particular form of digital theater has at times embraced all of these aspects, but it has also defined a specific and idiosyncratic webcam dramaturgy conjoining and continually balancing (over days, months, and year after year) the absent and the present, the banal and the profound, the dramatic and the antidramatic.

As we have seen, Jennicam was certainly not the first webcam; neither was Ringley the first to engage with, subvert, and counter the prying surveillance of the camera lens to show "Reality Life," an accolade usually afforded to Andy Warhol. Others might prefer to trace the history of reality surveillance and media enslavement across a longer period to include major literary figures such as Huxley and Kafka. Their work lives on, conceived and produced for that most traditional and antiquated, but also most permanent and lasting of expressive forms, the book. By contrast, Jennicam was an ephemeral and seminal endurance performance art event; and an influential VR-meets-RL telematic surveillance-soap-opera. As such it was always unlikely to achieve longevity, and it is a sign of our current times that tuning in to Jennicam today one is confronted not by Jenni, her bed or her cats, but by the standard death-knell notice of the Internet: "The page cannot be displayed."

19

Online Performance: "Live" from Cyberspace

[The Internet] should be understood not only as an instrument for transfer and distribution of information, but rather as an "open resource" of a participatory order. The net is a comparatively unique cosmos of invented identities, partakers, and accomplices in joint forces, hidden in the endless labyrinth of home pages, chatrooms, and communities.
—ANDREA ZAPP[1]

The History of the Internet

In 1969, as Neil Armstrong became the first human being to step foot on a distant planet, we began to reconfigure our notions of time and space. The American space mission achieved what many had thought inconceivable, and moreover, the triumph of technology was twofold: landing men on the moon, and feeding back video signals of events as they happened to an awestruck television audience. Our understanding of and relationship to outer space and infinity was irrevocably altered, and our conception of our place as a tiny satellite within a massive galaxy was unforgettably brought home. Yet in 1969, the same year that Armstrong alighted on a lunar landscape, another technological breakthrough took place that may ultimately be viewed as a far more significant and life-changing "leap for mankind." As Apollo 11 burst through the stratosphere, telephone cables were being specially laid between UCLA and the Stanford Research Institute in what would begin a definition of a totally new and revolutionary space: The Internet.

The 1969 ARPANET was an initiative of the U.S. Department of Defense–funded Advanced Research Project (ARPA), a military and scientific thinktank originally set up in 1957 by President Eisenhower following, and in direct response to, the Soviets' launch of *Sputnik*. It is an interesting irony that today's Internet originated out of the military paranoias of the Cold War and the symbolic aggressions of the space race, yet came at a time of intense late-1960s countercultural and libertarian activity and optimism. Similar tensions between social libertarianism and centralist governmental and military instincts to police and control still fizz around the wires of the networks today.

The 1969 ARPANET linked UCLA and Stanford computers that were hundreds of miles apart and exchanged data using packet-switching technology, which had been developed in 1962 and was a precursor to email, which was invented later, in 1971. By the end of 1969, two other university institutions, Utah and California at Santa Barbara, were brought into the network, and thereafter around one node was added per month, bringing the total by August 1972 to twenty-nine American research centers and universities engaged in military projects.[2] With an estimated annual maintenance cost of $100,000 per site, expansion was gradual, and by 1979 there were only sixty-one ARPANET sites.[3] In 1980, the National Science Foundation commenced CSNET, linking U.S. computer science departments, and during the 1980s other networks developed which interlinked with both ARPANET and CSNET sites, "speaking" to one another through the network language TCP/IP (Transmission Control Protocol/Internet Protocol), developed in 1974, from where the term Internet originated.[4]

In 1984, Domain Name Systems (DNS) standardized Net addresses and William Gibson coined the term "cyberspace" in his novel *Neuromancer*. The following year, the National Science Foundation's establishment of the NSFNET marked "a turning point in the history of the Internet . . . outstripping the wildest imaginings of its creators" to provide a networked backbone that marked the establishment of the modern Internet.[5] In 1989, Englishman Tim Berners-Lee designed the World Wide Web (originally to link international particle physics researchers), which did not take off as a global phenomena until 1991 and even later as a popular civilian tool, following the University of Illinois' design of the first graphical web browser, Mosaic 1.0, in 1993. It is sometimes difficult to recall how recent the Web is, but the Net was only privatized as late as 1995, directing traffic via ISPs (Internet Service Providers), the same year that Netscape Navigator replaced the Mosaic browser. Microsoft introduced Internet Explorer the following year and commenced a massive browser war with Netscape, a battle for dominance that would take Microsoft some years to win.

The Victorian Internet

The extent to which the Internet has brought about an ontological revolution in telecommunications, and associated revolutionary impacts on understandings of time and space is fiercely debated. In 1866, more than a hundred years before the ARPANET cables were connected, transatlantic communications cables between Britain and the United States were completed and telegraphic messages buzzed between the two countries in binary code (Morse's dots and dashes). Paul Julius von Reuter founded the famous Reuter news company following the European expansion of the *télégraphe* (meaning "far writer"), which was used alongside his standard means of gathering international news in the middle of the nineteenth century, unbelievably to the modern mind, homing pigeons.[6]

James Carey's *Communication as Culture* (1988) points to how the mid-nineteenth-century telegraph marked a decisive separation between notions of transportation and communication, where they had formerly been synonymous: "The telegraph ended that identity and allowed symbols to move independently of and faster than transport."[7] The chapter headings of Tom Standage's *The Victorian Internet* (1998) emphasize how early telecommunications systems such as the electric telegraph and the telephone prompted precisely the same discourses around time and space that emerged in the 1990s: "The Mother of All Networks," "Wiring the World," "Codes, Hackers and Cheats," "Love Over the Wires," "War and Peace in the Global Village," and a final chapter entitled "Information Overload." He details extraordinary cons where even bookmakers were deceived, disbelieving that news could travel so fast; love affairs developing between lonely bored operators that ended in either marriage or disaster; apocryphal tales of caring wives pouring warm soup into their telephones to feed their chilly spouses; people watching the overhead wires to see the tightrope walker run along them convinced that that must be how it worked; and promises of business fortunes to be made by the alert overnight. Standage makes clear that the Net is not an entirely new paradigm or territory, despite popular theoretical and artistic claims, and writers such as Erkki Huhtamo echo the sentiments in relation to digital arts:

from the Internet-related artworks created in recent years . . . such historical awareness seems to be nearly totally absent. No matter how critical the approach, the Internet is treated as if nothing like it ever existed before. Underlying these works, there seems to be a hypothesis about a paradigmatic rupture separating the Internet from its predecessors both qualitatively and quantitatively.[8]

Huhtamo's "An Archeology of Networked Art" (2004) traces online art's lineage through the bonfire signaling systems of antiquity, seventeenth-century semaphore, Claude Chappe's optical telegraphs in France in the 1790s, and Jean Alexandre's 1802 *telegraph intime*. He observes that, just like the Internet, many early telecommunications systems, such as Robert Hooke's seventeenth-century wire telephone, which children still use today (tin cans connected by a piece of string), were considered "secretive, ephemeral, and emotional, rather than official, permanent, and regulated."[9] What is considered by digital artists such as Susan Collins to be "a common desire to collapse time and space and to exist in another space at the same time, to create a portal"[10] is therefore seen as nothing new by network historians.

But the Net is more commonly considered to have a genuinely new and unique ontology. Margaret Wertheim compares the coming of cyberspace to the exponential force of the original Big Bang, which cosmologists claim originated our universe's physical space: "so also the ontology of cyberspace is ex nihilo. We are witnessing here the birth of a new domain, a new space that simply did not exist before. . . . A digital version of Hubble's cosmic expansion, a process of space creation."[11] We would also pin our flag firmly to this mast and contend that while the Web may have its precursors, as do many of the artworks and performances located or distributed from there, there is undoubtedly something new going on cyberspace.

Early Internet Drama Resources and Experiments

In 1994, one of the first performance-related applications of the new Internet superhighway was the creation of an FTP site (File Transfer Protocol, an early form of email attachments) for storing and accessing scripts by amateur playwrights. It was created by two science students, Rob Knop and Mike Dederian at Harvey Mudd College, in Claremont, California, and the information website they created, "The Dramatic Exchange," still exists, is still maintained, and continues to serve much the same function.[12] Within two or three years the range of "virtual drama" sites on the Web became surprisingly extensive, and within a decade, vast. As website technology developed the range of performance-related sites not only increased but also brought with them new concepts such as "virtual drama," "online performance," "theatrical chat programs," "immersive storytelling," "virtual characters," "avatars," and "vips" (virtually independent people). The Virtual Drama Society first established its Web presence in 1996[13] and was extremely ambitious, incorporating a membership scheme, a weekly topic for debate, an audience and performance research project, its own award scheme in five categories (research, products, design, performance and media), and a chat theater to experiment with chat programs as a theatrical medium. Its emphasis remained on drama and narrative forms, but explored ways in which "virtual drama" could offer a new paradigm of *individual* exploration and participation that need not follow the famous axiom of Ferdinand Brunetiere (1849–1906) that "conflict is the essence of all drama"—"virtual drama" could be individualized, personalized, and noncombative. Its performance/audience research section was coordinated by Maya Nagori, who promoted a new vocabulary and aesthetic, while probing questions that still remain relevant around the effects of new forms of dramatic interaction and participant experience.

On its launch in 1996, the Virtual Drama Society also provided links to, and praise for, pioneering contributions to virtual drama, notably to the Oz Project at Carnegie Mellon University; a virtual theater project at Stanford University; and Brenda Laurel's work at Interval Research. *Hollywood Network* and The CADRE Institute's *Switch Journal* were complimented for special encouragement to writers and interviews with practitioners; the Media Lab at MIT for its 116 projects including "virtual drama"; and the Computer Graphics Lab at the Swiss Federal Institute of Technology for advances in dramatic animation. The site also noted important explorations in virtual interaction (MIRALab at the University of Geneva; the Virtual Human Architecture Group; and New York University's Media Research Lab), VRML (UC San Diego Computing Center), and the development of comprehensive "guides" such as Joel Slotkin's "The Applied and Interactive Theater Guide."[14]

The WWW Virtual Library of Theater and Drama Resources was also founded in the same year, 1996, by Barry Russell, and collated links to resources in more than fifty countries around the world under an impressive array of categories including institutions, conferences, electronic texts, journals, email lists, plays in print, bibliographies, theater companies, theater image collections, and theater on film.[15] Within a few years it was claiming in excess of two million hits a year. A noticeable feature of these early resource collations is that they were frequently the work of individuals, often academics, who started down a road that seemed convenient for their work, but before long found themselves faced with a task comparable to counting the individual grains of sand in Zeno's mythological (and unrealizable) heap. "The Digital Exchange" contains many letters from its founders apologizing for the impossibility of keeping it up to date, and Barry Russell had to develop self-registering devices to allow himself time to sleep.

Arts Wire Current was established in 1992 as a response to "an interesting phenomenon and sign of the sudden growth of interest in digital applications to the arts . . . [and] to enable artists, individuals and arts organizations to better communicate, share ideas and information and coordinate their activities."[16] By 1996 it was estimating that three thousand artists were working in digital forms in New York alone, and was announcing "The Virtual Tour: Cyber Hum," which, using ISDN lines, planned to link musicians in "The Kitchen" arts venue with the "Silent Records" recording studio in San Francisco; and promising imminent international links with London, Paris, and Tokyo, with the resulting performances being downloadable via "The Cerberus Digital Jukebox."

Oudeis

One of the first major virtual theater events on the Internet was a vastly ambitious project that was developed over years but was never fully realized. It was conceived in 1995 as *Odysseus*, and subsequently changed its title to *Oudeis—a World Wide Odyssey. Oudeis* was daring in its conception, complex in its workings, appropriate in its classical references (like so many digital narratives in a time of globalization), collaborative and interactive in its structure, and sadly all too accurate in its final website description as "a theater project in which Odysseus' journey connected artists and audiences all around the world via the Internet. *A work in progress on hold*" (June 2000, our italics).

The original idea was "to transmit *The Odyssey* across The Seven Seas within one hour and to bear the hardships caused by our wandering through the Net and the intellectual confrontation necessary for an artistic approach to the Internet as a new media." The wanderings of Odysseus provided an excellent metaphor for the endeavor, and perhaps the fact that Odysseus wandered for ten years provided an unforeseen ironic commentary too. Started as a cross-posted announcement on email lists, it received a huge response from aficionados who were then divided into three separate groups (each with its own email list) dedicated to art/ideas/script, technical aspects, and overall organization. But despite enormous work and elaborate plans to stage one of the most ambitious and global performances of all time, the nearest it ever came to achieving its declared aims was a link up between the Sala Terrena of Palais Liechtenstein Vienna and the Museum of Modern Art mirrored in the academic theater MOO, ATHEMOO, on 26 June 1997. The performance was conceived by L. H. Grant and Monika Wunderer, and featured a global network of artist collaborators.[17] It was admirably intelligent, well-intentioned, incredibly ambitious, and ahead of its time. *Oudeis*, still "a work in progress on hold," deserves more than a footnote in the history of digital performance. To mix the classical metaphors, it was truly a Herculean effort.

The Internet as a Place

In one sense, Internet cyberspace should not be termed a space at all; to state the blindingly obvious, when supposedly *in* cyberspace we sit at our computer terminals. When accessing Web information or communicating with others online, the sense of being elsewhere or at one remove is mental and metaphoric; the action or meeting takes place on the screen in front of us, wherever we happen to be at the time. The -space suffix in "cyberspace" is an exaggerated notion (the word coined via science fiction rather than fact,[18]) since, for example, spatial aspects of synchronous online chat actually differ little from the telephone, yet we do not talk of *telephonespace*. Email corresponds to a swift postal service, but over centuries we have never discussed sending our letters into *postalspace*. Our computer screens may draw us into increasingly sophisticated and evolving virtual worlds, but so too does cinema, and we have not conceived going to the movies as entering *cinemaspace*. In short, the interface, media form, and speed of communication may be different, but locomotion is still required to transport us to other spaces.

At the same time, it must be conceded that the discussion of cyberspace as place(s) can be useful and highly appropriate, even though the notion is largely metaphoric and conceptual, and indeed romantic. For example, online chat is in one sense simply a call-up, but the presence of multiple users in the space differentiates it from a telephone call (although conference calls may arguably do the same) to concretize a sense by which a chat room seems just that—a distinct location and meeting point. In another, stricter sense, it is: a hard drive or server in a physical space somewhere, which people contact and share real-time communications via and in. The search-and-find paradigm of cyberspace (through points and nodes on computers which are physically elsewhere) is one of the most important aspects that underlines the metaphorical journey through space; and through surfing (itself a travel-through-space term) there is far more possibility of discovering places and meeting people by chance than there is, for example, on the telephone. "We met in cyberspace" is commonly heard (though it may still sound a mite pretentious), whereas "we met on the telephone" is not. Or, as Howard Rheingold points out, while "you can't simply pick up a phone and ask to be connected with someone who wants to talk about Islamic art or California wine, or someone with a three-year-old daughter or a forty-year-old Hudson, you can, however, join a computer conference about any of these topics."[19]

It is in this crucial sense that cyberspatial communication and performance on the web stakes out and defines spaces for people with like minds or interests to congregate and converse. A URL (Uniform Resource Locator) may be a Web address whose arbitrarily lexicon gives no clue to the geographical positioning of its real-place server, but it can also be seen as a type of map coordinate, defining a specific location and meeting place in the geographical contours of the network. In their discussion of the mapping of lesbian artistic spaces in cyberspace, Holly Willis and Mikki Halpin note that this territorialization operates in precisely the same way as it always has in physical, social space: "Queers are classified by position: in or out, top or bottom, fringe or mainstream. There are gay districts, dyke bars, drag strips. In these spaces, issues of community and self are framed. In these spaces, as we have heard over and over again, the personal is political."[20] For many people the web is first and foremost a communal space: a meeting place to converse with established friends and to meet new ones, and a place where old friends can be tracked down to become *Friends Reunited*. It is a space to merge with a crowd of others. "That's what the Net is mostly about," says Web and installation artist Shu Lea Cheang, "community."[21]

Teresa M. Senft argues that the Internet is neither a thing nor a space, but an effect: "the *effect* of millions of performances called 'packet-switching' . . . a series of cooperative performance gestures from multiple computer and telephone systems."[22] In Senft's formulation, there are distinct parallels between our understanding of cyberspace and feminist theories of gender, since both are based on the "performative effect of multiple calculations." Peter Anders's "Antropic Cyberspace: Defining Electronic Space from First Principles" (2001) argues that computer space is better understood as a part of perceptual consciousness, in particular the cognitive processes that distinguish and relate computer simulations from and to their physical referents. Edmond Couchot's essay "Between the Real and the Virtual" (1994) argues that while computers have their own material reality in the physical world, the dataspaces they generate have not. He thereby conceives dataspace and cyberspace as unique, purely symbolic spaces, created through the play of information and mathematical calculations.

Andrea Zapp

Andrea Zapp takes up a parallel theme in the introduction to her edited book *Networked Narrative Environments as Imaginary Spaces of Being* (2004), where she conceives cyberspace more as a platform and modus operandi for experimental artistic combinations of "devices, disciplines, and languages" than as an actual space.[23] She begins by drawing on Margaret Morse's contention in 1995 that "the idea of networks and links as spaces and environments is somewhat of an enigma, still to be forged and integrated into thought, rather than an accepted notion."[24] The "Imaginary Spaces" discussed by Zapp and elaborated through the artworks analyzed in chapters by artists Paul Sermon, Susan Collins, Margarete Jahrmann, and Steve Dixon, become another example of the emergent philosophy of in-between space forged by digital networks and increasingly concretized by critical theory:

This publication examines models of public installations and theatrical spaces that are linked to the Internet with the aim to integrate the viewer into the artwork. The *network* provides the technical backdrop that enables a remote and open-ended dialogue between these spaces. The resulting *narrative* demonstrates interactivity as a user-controlled construct. The *environment* presents itself as a physical installation architecture that creates a stage for real and virtual role-play, with site-specifics underpinning metaphors and supplying "plots." Human presence is addressed as increasingly subject to a flow of online contributions, material and data. . . . This type of open system or artwork can be understood as an "interval," as it tests media art and its reception on a transitory stage: between the natural and the digital space and between their communities, being a symbolic passage or point of transfer between provinces of "pure potentiality."[25]

Zapp's notion of the imaginary space is a useful conception, and one worth elaborating upon. Cyberspace exists between different physical locations, a rainbow bridge supported on all sides by site-specific physical hardware and the "wetware" of human bodies. Like a theater stage, it is a symbolic passageway to the imaginary (role-plays, narratives, and so on) building from and arising out of the physical and the tangible (bodies, sets, light, sound). But like events on a theater stage, the transformations of space remain primarily imaginary, metaphorical, and representational; suspension of disbelief is thus as crucial to the cyberspace participant's transportation or immersion into imaginary space as it is for the theater spectator.

Zapp's own installation artwork borrows theatrical paradigms and, in *The Imaginary Hotel* (2002/03), inspiration from pop art photomontage artist Richard Hamilton, and contemporary television home makeover programs such as *Changing Rooms* (figure 19.1). The gallery visitor enters a mock hotel room that they can instantly refurbish, like a theater set. The visitor uses a remote control mouse linked to the room's TV to access up to two thousand different wall designs and more than ten thousand objects that can be dragged-and-dropped to alter the interior design: wallpaper, furniture, framed pictures, wall lights, and objects, as well as the views out of a large window. The data is transferred via the Net to projectors within the space that transform the walls in life-size. Internet users can watch via webcam and can remotely occupy and transform the space, as well as uploading personal images to add to the interior design palette. A Web chat room allows remote visitors to communicate with people inside the gallery installation, via a telephone linked to software that translates the textual chat into voice messages. Zapp uses the hotel room as a metaphor for cyberspace: a shell-like, anonymous, and neutral location, a blank canvas shaped only by its visitors and inhabitants, who animate the space and leave their

Figure 19.1 Andrea Zapp's web-linked installation *The Imaginary Hotel* (2002/03).

individual traces. *The Imaginary Hotel* also highlights the theatricality and illusionary aspects of cyberspace:

The public installation setting of the *Hotel* project, with its surrounding invisible wiring and obscure, circulating information, highlights the theatrical backdrop as a crucial principle. It becomes a gateway to the Net as the main source material, and the boundaries between the individual and dramatic domain becomes less apparent. The networked platform then hints to the cinematic scenario in which the former actor or performer is giving way to the participant's own visual vocabulary filling the screens. To support this analogy, *The Imaginary Hotel* is explicitly designed as a wide-open stage, framed by the carpet and accentuated in the two fragile walls, curtains, and props reminiscent of a shoddy TV set. Thus it plays with an evident façade for the imaginary and the illusionary.[26]

She goes on to relate the work to McLuhan's global village paradigm, as a "prototype of an already digitised, nomadic identity" where location is insignificant and existence is borderless, where the real and the digital are fused "into an ephemeral silhouette within a momentary illusion."[27] As we will see, the idea of the Internet as a nomadic, diasporic space without borders is a prevalent one; and the notion of the rhizome has become another central theoretical metaphor in conceiving computational and electronic space (as well as wider understandings of culture and psychology within postmodern philosophy). Primarily generated by Deleuze and Guattari's philosophical eulogy in *Mille Plateaus* (1980), the ever-branching, interconnected tendrils, tubers, and hairs of the rhizome have become a potent visual analogy to represent the labyrinth of cyberspace and computer networks.

Other writers such as Martin Dodge and Rob Kitchen have attempted to conceptualize cyberspace in geographical terms: in *Mapping Cyberspace* (2001) they provide numerous maps, charts, and graphs to illustrate the Internet and cyberspace's complex topologies and cartographies. Digital artists such as ART+COM have also been eager to adopt mapping paradigms in installations such as *Ride the Byte* (1998) and *TerraVision* (1994), an ongoing project in Berlin to map and visually represent the earth on a 1 : 1 scale. John Klima's *EARTH* (2001), is an online digital topography project using satellite views; and Warren Sack's *Conversation Map* (2001) graphically displays maps of conversations undertaken within newsgroups and other large-scale online exchanges.[28]

Cybersex and the Erotic Ontology of Cyberspace

Circuit Boy,
I know you're here. I can sense you.
Show me your algorithms.
Let me corrode your defences.
Circuit Boy. Come here.
Let me buttfuck your irresistible chrome-plated ass,
Honey.
I want you circuit boy.
I'm waiting.
—VNS MATRIX[29]

As this typically delightful Web snippet from feminist cyberactivist art group VNS (VeNuS) Matrix makes clear, crossing the border into cyberspace may also involve moving into a fetishistic realm and an erotic space. As self-styled "Guerilla Girls of the Web," VNS Matrix uses computer animation, video, games, and photography to link the political and the sexual in cyberspace, to subvert masculinist pornography and myths of technology, and to redefine ideas of female sexual identity on the Web. Their cyber-heroine creations who "weep tears of code" include the "lusciously wet" *DNA Sluts* (1994): graphical female figures combining elements from mythology, surrealism, and Wonder Woman kitsch, who send out "zap" beams from their vaginas. Their *Cyberfeminist Manifesto for the 21st Century* (1991) similarly typifies their aggressive stance in the face of patriarchal technology and the male cyberporn gaze, though it may not be to the taste of all feminists:

we are the modern cunt positive anti reason
unbounded unleashed unforgiving
we see art with our cunt we make art with our cunt
we believe in jouissance madness holiness and poetry
we are the virus of the new world order
rupturing the symbolic from within
saboteurs of big daddy mainframe
the clitoris is a direct line to the matrix . . .
go down on the alter of abjection
probing the visceral temple we speak in tongues
infiltrating disrupting disseminating
corrupting the discourse
we are the future cunt[30]

But the subversive sexual voices of VNS Matrix are outnumbered, if not completely drowned out, by the screams of pornography websites and their associated banners and email spam. Just as pornography was seen to have a major influence on the development and marketing of home media hardware, from Super 8 film projectors to the VCR, so too easy and convenient access to pornography fueled the growth and popularity of the home PC and the Web in the mid-1990s. If, as McLuhan suggested in 1964, "Man becomes, as it were, the sex organs of the machine world, enabling it to fecundate and to evolve ever new forms,"[31] then it has never been as true as in relation to the cyberspace sex industry.[32]

The art and performance world has also reflected the cybersex zeitgeist with notable examples including Trudy Barber's early installation *VR Sex* (1992) which takes place in a twelve-foot-long black corridor, its partly rubber walls lined with medical drip bags, TV screens, and mannequins. Performers placed behind the walls but with their faces protruding into the installation, pressed their naked bodies against the rubber, enabling visitors to "touch them without actually touching them; an analogy for how sex might be in the future."[33] At the end of the corridor, visitors don a VR HMD and perform a "simple sex task" such as placing a condom over an erection, and are rewarded with a "visual orgasm" accompanied by surround sound effects. When the piece was exhibited at London's St Martin's College of Art it attracted considerable interest and attendance from nontraditional art and performance-goers, including many members of an S&M club called the Torture Garden; Barber describes *VR Sex* as having been "a true cyberpunk gathering/event."[34]

More recent and high-tech remote cybersex paradigms have been created by artists such as Alexej Shulgin, whose tongue-in-cheek net.art piece *FuckU-FuckMe* (1999) demonstrates a hardware and software "teledildonic" system enabling remote sexual intercourse between partners.[35] Neil Grimmer creates kinetic sculptures using electronically controlled vibrators, and in Joseph DeLappe's *Masturbatory Interactant* (1997) a scanner on a mechanical arm moves over barcodes, randomly selecting erotic video clips that are projected onto an inflatable doll.[36] On stage, the Anatomical Theater's multimedia dance-theater performance *Mantis* (1997) provides "a curious portrait of sexual psychosis wherein rampant intellectualism meets vapid Sci-Fi Thriller kitsch";[37] and La Fura Dels Baus' Sadeian *XXX* (2003) theater performance created controversy by including hardcore pornography downloaded from the Web (including the shocking image of a horse penetrating and then ejaculating over a woman) and a live webcam encounter with a sex model.

In less overt erotic mode, in Madelyn Starbuck's *Honoria in Ciberspazio* (1996) "isolated and lonely Internet travellers entreat the oracle of cyberspace to transform their dreams of virtual reality into a beautifully woven sexy operatic climax."[38] Visitors to the website contributed poetry and arias about their cyberspace love affairs as contributions to a collaboratively scripted opera libretto. George Oldziey composed music for the operatic tale of digital lovers, which developed progressively from 1996 with periodic webcasts of completed scenes leading to a Spanish stage premiere in 2001.

Online Love in British Theater

British multimedia theater group Bodies in Flight's collaboration with Singaporean company "spell#7 performance," *Doublehappiness2* (2000) developed a fictional Internet love affair on a website and brought it to its denouement in a live theater performance. The charming and cerebral live performance follows the structure of a Singaporean wedding and mixes theater with onstage webcams and digital projections (what the groups call "sampadelic digitalia"). Its cool and knowing take on cyberlove and intercultural relationships is caustically drawn, and its prepublicity machine was equally laconic:

Shygirl7 met 6wasabe9 in a chatroom. Fluffboy visited hunny.bunny's website. . . . Visit the virtual romances on the website as they blossom long-distance, then come and see the lovers perform in the flesh. . . . [*Doublehappiness2*] distils WAPness into a distinctly wet-ware double-take on twenty-first century sex. . . . Who cares if she's on the other side of the planet, when your text-message finger gets twitchy? Cancel the hotel room: just stay online. Real life's messy. Do you know where he's been? Does he? Across continents where differences of language and culture, shoe-size and resistance to disease create turbulence in the flow of information and capital, *Doublehappiness* jacks into the body that braves time-zones and economy class to get fleshy with another.[39]

What Michael Heim has analyzed as "The Erotic Ontology of Cyberspace" (1991) was also one of few themes to emerge in terms of digital commentary from "traditional" theater playwriting during the 1990s. Plays and dramatic literature generally had little to say about new technologies and, as Patrice Pavis suggests, many playwrights, "frightened by the media, appear to exclude or reject it, but so doing they are no less influenced and transformed by it, almost without their knowledge."[40] Where plays did explicitly address new technologies, most commonly it was to equate the Internet with notions of online affairs (even Ray Cooney, a veteran farce writer for the British commercial stage, got in on the act with his 2001 play *Caught in the Net*), sexual fantasy, misdemeanor, and masturbation. The Internet communication between characters featured in Mark Ravenhill's *Faust (Faust's Dead)* (1997) concerns dark territories of sexual frustration and gratification, and in the famous Internet sex-chat scene in Patrick Marber's *Closer* (1997), despite its highly comic nature, the sequence is also sexually overt and explicit. Two male characters sit typing at separate computer terminals onstage, with their online chat projected onto a screen behind them. One pretends to be a sex-obsessed woman, a "cum-hungry bitch" with "epic tits" who titillates the man at the other terminal, finally faking an ecstatic textual orgasm of jumbled letters and "oh-oh-oh"s.

While Marber's play portrays Internet eroticism humorously, and cyberspace as a farce-stage for sexual fantasy and confusion, Scottish playwright Anthony Nielson's *Stitching* (2002) presents a bleaker and more disturbing view of its darker nodes of sexual degeneracy. The male protagonist, Stuart, downloads extreme images of pornography and female mutilation with which to sexually provoke his partner Abby. As their sexual relationship becomes increasingly tangled in sadistic fantasies about the infamous British Moors child sex murders, and in physical abuse and abjection, the Internet images rebound back into the play's "real" world with Abby's climactic act of sewing up her vagina (an ending the play shares with La Fura Dels Baus' *XXX* performance). While Nielson does not offer up Internet pornography (or even pornography per se) as the cause of the couple's increasing psychosexual alienation, the Internet images of degradation provide the dramatic turning point that signals the couple's decline. As Lyn Gardner suggests, "Fantasy may have its place in the bedroom, but like the pornography Stuart downloads from the net, it infects and destroys just as much as Abby's need to please leads to the death of a child and an appalling self-mutilation."[41]

The computer technologization of sexuality and sexual activity has been a fertile area of academic inquiry in recent years, but it is easily forgotten how recent a phenomenon (at least in critical and theoretical terms) this is. In his 1996 study of phone sex chatlines, for example, Marcus Boon notes,

If there's a kind of banality to phone sex in the mid-1990s, it should be remembered to what extent the study of sexuality has been driven by an exclusionary humanism, so that to date there hardly exists a single reference to technological aspects of sexuality in the entire annals of sexology, sociology of sexual behavior and related disciplines. There is "fetishism" of course, but in fetishism, the line between the human and the non-human is clearly drawn. Fetishes do not mediate between human beings the way telecommunications technology does, nor are they prosthetic in the same way. Fetishism is still a humanism. Technology, in its prosthetic aspect, blurs the line between the human and the non-human. If we are now confronted by problems or questions concerning this blurring, this is more due to the extent to which technology is part of our lives than to some fundamental change that has occurred.[42]

MUDs, MOOs, and the Performance of Identity

Today, I'm tired of ex/changing identities on the net.
In the past 8 hours,
I've been a man, a woman and a s/he.
I've been black, Asian, Mixteco, German
and a multi-hybrid replicant.
I've been 10 years old, 20, 42, 65.
I've spoken 7 broken languages.
As you can see, I need a break real bad,
just want to be myself for a few minutes.
ps: my body however remains intact, untouched, unsatisfied,
Unattainable, untranslatable.
—GUILLERMO GÓMEZ-PEÑA[43]

As we will see, sexuality has played no little part in the social and game-playing environments of MUDs (Multi-user dungeons/dimensions) and MOOs (object-orientated MUDs). MUDs were first developed by Richard Bartle and Roy Trubshaw (who coined the term) at Essex University in 1983 (although they did not become widespread until 1989), and have become popularly regarded as a borderland of identity, performance, and community. Early examples tended toward adventure-game paradigms, particularly Dungeons and Dragons fantasy-adventure environments peopled by wizards and monsters (hence the original term, "Multi-User Dungeon"). A search of the World Wide Web today elicits lists of hundreds of MUDs, including humorous MUDs, skill-based MUDs, alien MUDs, medieval MUDs, Tolkein MUDs, Hitchikers Guide to the Galaxy MUDs, vampire MUDs, sex MUDs, Deathwish MUDs, Genocide MUDs, Looney MUDs, Silly MUDs, and the *Web of Deception* MUD, which invites you to "meet new people on the Web. Become a legend, lead a guild into battle, buy your own home."

In MUDs and MOOs, users create quasi-Stanislavskian character biographies, logging on with a textual description of their physical and psychological attributes. They carefully and consciously establish themselves as fictional beings: putting on masks, often crossing gender, and engaging in improvisational performances. The computer interface becomes another type of social life, and an improvisational performance space for the user. Using the Net in both a social and performative function, the construction and representation of identity becomes, according to popular theories, multiple and hybrid, "continuous but plural."[44]

Mark Stefik renames the information superhighway the "I-way," since it is "a search for ourselves and the future we choose to inhabit;"[45] and K. A. Franck discusses a breaking out of our mundane, quotidian selves into "an array of possibilities to be imagined and created."[46] Mark Poster argues that new media "cultivate new configurations of individuality,"[47] and Sherry Turkle maintains that the Internet is now a site for the construction of one's identity, a place where "we project ourselves into our own dramas, dramas in which we are producer, director and star."[48] According to Turkle, MUDers become not only authors of texts in cyberspace but also authors of themselves, manifesting fluid and multiple identities. As the boundaries between "the real and the virtual, the animate and the inanimate, the unitary and the multiple self"[49] are eroding, "identity on the computer is the sum of your distributed presence."[50]

Reading through some of this literature, it is easy to get the impression that notions of "self" and "identity" were unproblematic prior to the advent of cyber-technologies. This is far from the truth, of course, and the problem of self and the search for what constitutes identity is a given of human life and has been one of the classical problems in philosophy ever since people began to muse upon the nature of their existence. MOO space is now theorized as a new stage on which such fundamental philosophical enigmas can be probed; and as a space to rehearse, explore, reconfigure, and act out different permutations of one's self and identity. It is also conceptualized as a Bakhtinian carnivalesque space where normally suppressed instincts or desires considered transgressive in real life (such as cross-dressing) can be played out. At the same time, commentators also emphasize that while the predilections and fantasies of individuals are explored, MUDs and MOOs are first and foremost "a *collective* creation—at once a game, a society, and a work of fiction."[51]

There is an acute irony that the real-life identities of the very people who digitally disguise themselves or present fictitious personas online are systematically and indelibly tracked across cyberspace, and through ubiquitous daily digital transactions. Not only is Internet, mobile phone, or ATM use pinpointed and recorded, but loyalty cards, for example, are also designed to provide companies with the holder's real identity (beyond simple name/address data) in such minute detail that it appears to only stop short of the subject's genetic makeup. In 2004, the results of Andrew Smith and Leigh Sparks's research study highlighted that the cards are less concerned with promoting loyalty and more concerned with collecting detailed data on consumers for marketing and communications targeting. The analysis of product purchases and shopping patterns of one subject (dubbed Brenda) over a two-year period revealed aspects of her personality as well as things such as medical conditions, hair and skin care, and eating, drinking, and sexual habits. The store's computer thus held data that could be analyzed to present a type of identity photo-fit picture that Brenda herself may find less than flattering:

Brenda is a large woman whose desire to lose weight is thwarted by her appetite. She has long hair, bad skin and is shortsighted. Her parents are still alive, she lives for holidays and has a long-term boyfriend. . . .

Large-sized tights revealed a large woman. . . . She also bought a pair of weighing scales in the two-year period. . . . The hair accessories she bought betrayed long hair, contact lens-cleaning products poor eyesight and blemish concealer bad skin. The purchase of fake tanning products heralded fortnight-long gaps in her record, revealing when she took holidays abroad. Christmas cards—bought in October—introduced her parents and partner, for whom she also bought male grooming products.[52]

Habitat

Most early MUDs were text-based only, but by the mid-1980s multi-user environments began to incorporate visual elements, such as *Habitat*, created in 1985 by Lucasfilm Games. Using home Commodore 64s, then the recreational standard computer, players communicated with the virtual world (a real time animated display) and one another using a commercial packet-switching network (the technological predecessor to email) and paid commercial charges according to time spent in the environment. Inspired by science fiction, and particularly Vernor Vinge's *True Names* (1981) which predated William Gibson's *Neuromancer* (1984) as a detailed vision of cyberspace, it used avatars (normally humanoid) that could gesture, manipulate objects, and talk to one another using cartoonlike speech bubbles. The world included thousands of players and hundreds of different environments, had a weekly newspaper and used a complex economy of tokens.

One recurring game involved a type of tag where the users passed on to others a viral disease called the Happy Face Plague. When a user is infected, her avatar's head transforms, growing a new "smiley face" head and all she can say is "Have a Nice Day!" This condition can also deteriorate with the smiley face mutating into the head of a giant housefly, when the Mutant Plague strain has been contracted. As a result of the increasing violence, theft, and other antisocial activity in *Habitat*, one player opened the first Habitat church.[53]

In an article published in 1992, a year before Meredith Belbin's canonical management theory study of delineated team roles within commercial organizations,[54] *Habitat*'s system administrator (or "Oracle") F. Randall Farmer proposed not dissimilar divisions of social roles that players adopted in the virtual environment. He divided players into five broad categories (Belbin used nine) that described their social status and function within the community: the Passives; the Actives; the Motivators; the Caretakers; and the Geek Gods.[55] In this early virtual community, Farmer notes that in face-to-face interviews with fifty players from the Japanese Fujitsu Habitat environment in 1990, only half thought of their avatar as a separate being, while the others felt it was a direct representation of themselves. The same fifty-fifty result was recorded when they were asked if they acted like their usual selves within the environment or in ways different from real life.

Habitat's co-creators, Farmer and Chip Morningstar, argue that more recent sophistication in interface technologies using, for example HMDs and datagloves, can actually distract from the participatory essence of virtual environments. Communicational capabilities constitute the core of virtual experiences and technological sophistication offers at best peripheral enhancement since "a cyberspace is defined more by the interactions among the actors within it than by the technology with which it is implemented":[56] behavior and interaction characterizes cyberspace, rather than visual presentation. They conclude by urging cyberspace architects to devote as much attention to the study of sociology and economics as they do to computer science, since the design and management of an effective virtual world is "like governing an actual nation."[57] They advocate an evolutionary and agoric approach, rather than a "centralized, socialistic one."[58]

Social Performance

MUDers, MOOers, and individuals regularly involved in other group-based graphical world environments such as the Palace operate both socially and performatively, and on many different levels according to the user and environment. Some visit simply to observe, some are gregarious, others may seek to wreak havoc. There are thus clear parallels between online social activity and normal social interaction in spaces where strangers gather and may converse, such as a bar, club, or party. By virtue of the virtual transportation into the company of others, many people are prompted to assert their personality, flirt, fight, or otherwise let their hair down, just as they might at a party or discotheque. In *Hamlet on the Holodeck* (1997), Janet Murray describes cyberspace as an "enchanted place" that engenders strong emotions and behaviors: "The enchantment of the computer . . . creates for us a public space that also feels very private and intimate. In psychological terms, computers are liminal objects, located on the threshold between external reality and our own minds."[59]

MUDs, MOOs, and other online communities can be related to earlier systems of anonymous or near-anonymous interactive communication, for example, CB radio networks, which were particularly popular during the 1970s and '80s. CB radio users similarly assumed fantasy personas and pseudonyms ("handles"), and often developed intense relationships with others at a distance that they had never met. In the early 1980s the CB radio craze and the relationships it spawned drew similar press and media attention to that afforded Internet relationships during the 1990s. In the early 1980s, Britain's longest-running soap opera, *Coronation Street*, reflected the zeitgeist to include a storyline involving one of its most popular and comic characters, Hilda Ogden. An idiosyncratic yet nonetheless prim and proper middle-aged woman, Hilda used the pseudonym Shady Lady and conducted a brief at-a-distance CB romance with a young trucker.[60] Changes in identity were also a feature of the artworld in the 1960s and '70s, with performance artists including Adrian Piper, Martha Wilson, and Jackie Apple all presenting performances that centered on the notion. In 1970, a full-page advertisement in *Artforum* featuring Judy Chicago dressed as a boxer in the ring, announced that Judy Gerowitz was rejecting her father's surname as a protest against the patriarchal art world, and would be known thereafter as Judy Chicago. At the California Institute of the Arts, Chicago established the first Feminist Art Program with Miriam Schapiro, and went on to create one of the iconic feminist artworks of the era. *The Dinner Party* (1974–79) is a vivid non-hierarchical triangular table evoking female sexuality, with its place settings celebrating the struggles and achievements of thirty-nine women.

In "Rethinking Identity Through Virtual Community," Turkle describes MUDs as a new genre of collaborative writing, and draws parallels with performance art, street theater, commedia dell'arte, improvisational theater, and scriptwriting.[61] She describes the varied personalities one male subject adopts in different MUDs including a seductive woman, a Marlboro macho man, and a rabbit of unspecified gender. She quotes him as believing that RL (real life) is just one of many parallel windows that make up his life, and argues that the adoption of hybrid personas develops an understanding of the many facets of ourselves, and thus enables personal transformation. Turkle's *Life on the Screen* (1995) is a lengthy exploration of the psychological effects of assuming different personalities in such environments, and she emphasizes players' intense identification with their assumed personas, as well as the power of the fictions that are played out in online improvisations. Her description of a harrowing "virtual rape" in LambdaMoo in 1993 brings this home, and she describes the discussion that followed it on the MOO to reinforce her notion that such experiences in fictional virtual environments can be as traumatic as in real life. One player had asked "where does the body end and the mind begin? Is not the mind a part of the body?" Another player came up with the answer: "In a MOO, the body is the mind."[62]

Cyber-rape and the Politics of Virtual Identification

The infamous cyber-rape is well documented, with many writers stressing the fragile, uncertain line between real and virtual spaces that the case revealed, as though it were some parallel-universe San Andreas fault. The most notable (and exhaustive) commentator is Julian Dibbell who followed up his initial article "A Rape in Cyberspace" (1994) with an entire book: *My Tiny Life: Crime and Passion in a Virtual World* (1999). To summarize the incident in brief, a character called Mr Bungle logged on to Parc/Xerox's LambdaMOO in 1993, describing himself as "fat, oleaginous, Bisquick-faced clown dressed in cum-stained harlequin garb and girded with a mistletoe-and-hemlock belt whose buckle bore the quaint inscription "kiss me under this, bitch.'"[63] Bungle went into one of the MOO's rooms and used a "voodoo doll" to take textual control from out of the hands of the other characters there (thus impersonating others and controlling them like puppets) and proceeded to sexually dominate and forcibly defile them. In addition to conventional sexual acts, Bungle forced one character to eat her own pubic hair and another to use a kitchen utensil to violate herself. In the wake of these actions, but only following long, heated, and emotional debates on the MOO, Bungle was expelled ("toaded"), although he was to return later, logging on as a character called Dr. Jest.

The event fueled academic curiosity and commentary, and the controversy around the case is redolent of the public (that is, mass-media-fueled) scandals and controversies surrounding extreme theatrical pieces, with high-profile British examples including Edward Bond's *Saved* (the stoning of a baby), Howard Brenton's *Romans in Britain* (explicit homosexual rape), and Sarah Kane's *Blasted* (dead baby, homosexual rape and, well, you name it). But where the liberal intelligentsia have invariably tended to support such theatrical transgressions as part of the wider validation of free speech, the nature and mode of this particular piece of theater of cruelty meant there were few serious commentators who did not condemn it. Physically, no rape took place, but in significant other senses it did. Recent critical theorists from Barthes and Foucault to Butler and Derrida have stressed how language is all and acts upon everything, most especially the body. As Barthes once put it: "text is a fetish object, and this fetish desires me."[64] By this logic, a virtual rape enacted as language *is* rape nonetheless. Or, as Lloyd Rang puts it, "Cyber-rape is not rape precisely, but operates in the same way in an economy of virtual violence as rape does in the physically-embodied world. As such it also serves to reinforce already-present quotidian gender constructs."[65]

We would put theoretical viewpoints aside to assert equally germane real-world parallels to argue the same point. No one doubts the damaging psychological and even physical effects aggressive language-based assaults such as obscene letters and phone calls have on women, and there is little doubt that women operating in character online are any less susceptible to feelings of psycho-physical defilement from sexual aggressors. The discussions following the rape on LambdaMOO itself challenged and changed many attitudes and perspectives, and according to Dibbell forged it into a more cohesive and enlightened community. The subtitle of his 1994 article makes it clear, "A Rape in Cyberspace; Or How an Evil Clown, a Haitian Trickster Spirit, Two Wizards, and a Cast of Dozens Turned a Database into a Society."

Prior to the Bungle cyber-rape, considerable controversy had been ignited in the mid-1980s around the virtual figure of "Julie," who presented herself as a totally disabled, big-hearted "agony aunt" from New York and offered people (primarily women) advice via online conferencing. When she was finally revealed to be a middle-aged male psychiatrist, "reactions varied from humorous resignation to blind rage. Most deeply affected were the women who had shared their innermost feelings with Julie. 'I felt raped' one said . . . 'violated.'"[66] An event dubbed *Requiem Digitatem* on the Future Culture mailing list presented a different ethical quandary in the mid-1990s, when a member, Michael Roberts, announced to the list that he would commit suicide. Another list member, the gay-rights activist Michael Current, was unaware that this was an April Fool's joke, and he reported the threat to the local real-life authorities. It led to considerable debate and controversy around "net responsibility," and an angry "flame war" developed between the two men. "Roberts passionately argues that the net ought to be a space of free play and self-invention, while Current counters that the Net, far from being a social experiment, is bound by the same social contracts as other real-life spaces."[67] When Current died shortly after these events, the Future Culture list received a posting from Roberts where he expressed regrets about his flame attack on Current, but maintained that he still had no regrets about the original suicide joke itself.

Many years on, following seemingly endless Net deceptions, from virus hoaxes igniting hysterical mob culling of harmless teddy bear icons to quite horrific incidents of Internet "grooming" leading to actual murders, one wonders how far people's mistrust of the voices at the other end of the monitor is now total. Or whether it is just as trusting or confused as it has always been, in real life. People are highly deceptive (and gullible) there too, but the mass media, as well as some academic commentators, have frequently laid blame at technology's door. But for centuries con men have conned, pornographers have peddled pornography, pedophiles have groomed their victims, and rapists and murderers have raped and murdered. The Internet only changes the modus operandi, not the outcome or the crime. Whether its ontology affects and exacerbates motivation, cause, or opportunity, however, is another and more complex matter.

A series of high profile cases of people who willingly offered their lives, or rather deaths, to strangers online brings the debate into sharp focus. In one, the subject of a postmortem television documentary, an American woman conducted an online S&M affair with a man, finally agreeing to go to his trailer home to be sexually dominated and murdered. In another, in 2002, a German man calling himself CannibalMaster secured an online willing male victim who bought a one-way ticket to his home, consented on videotape to being killed and eaten, and, having dined with his host in the evening, became the breakfast spread the next day. CannibalMaster was apprehended in 2004 but was cleared of murder since the victim consented on tape. He was jailed for the lesser crime of manslaughter. Whether these deaths would have occurred unaided by the seductive force of the Internet to fuel and facilitate these extreme fantasies to cross the border between fantasy and reality, VR and RL, is open to debate.

Fluid Subjectivities

But one thing beyond any doubt is that in cyberspace there is a flourishing of the postmodern concept of a fluid or fragmented sense of identity and self in contrast to the "rational, autonomous, centred and stable"[68] subjectivity of modernism. For writers such as Michael Punt, this is one of the results of the negative and seductive spaces of MUDs and MOOs, which lead users into "incipient sickness and schizophrenia,"[69] whereas optimists such as Niranjan Rajah conclude, "what is today approached as pathology will, in the future, become the norm in the construction of the self."[70] For Michèle White, the textual descriptions of MOO personas are key to the shared sense of identity transformation, as well as a new type of emergent, imaginative gazing that she explores in her essay "Visual Pleasure in Textual Places" (2001).

Tina LaPorta's artwork explores online identities in chat rooms, webcams, and video conferencing; her *Re:mote_corp@REALities* (2001) combines webcams, online chat, and a voiceover mediator who asks participants such questions as, "Is cyberspace your window or your mirror?"—an abiding theme and conundrum in digital arts.[71] One performer clearly adopting the window side of the equation is Shu Lea Cheang, who intimately explored online life for her *Buy One Get One* (1997) by purportedly maintaining no physical address and only an email contact for a period of two years. Other artists have taken the mirror stance to fake and confuse notions of identity. Nick Crowe's *Service 2000* (2000) website links to bogus webpages he has created of twenty-nine real art galleries in London. These are tacky and gaudy sites filled with chatty, informal text wholly inappropriate to the likes of the Tate or National Gallery, which disorientate and challenge the artistic expectations of unwitting viewers. Rae C. Wright's *Art Thief* (1998), a webcast video piece distributed on the Franklin Furnace site, is an amalgam of appropriated artwork and imagery originally created by artists such as Deb Margolin, Halona Hilbertz, and Anna Mosby Coleman. Reflecting on Coleman's pixelated images of moving clouds, Wright is quoted as remarking, "I think they are so beautiful in this medium . . . and I stole them." As Jessica Chalmers observes: "Wright's idea is that all art making is a form of thievery, ambiguity of ownership being a particularly keen issue to artists working through the Net, where every user's screen is a potential resource for image capture. Her appropriation is an expression of the freedoms and uncertainties of this infant form—Netcasting and its singular mix of live performance, animation, video, and chat."[72]

Five performers from Austrian company Bilderwerfer chose five private homepages from the Web, including the exiled shah of Iran, an inmate on death row, and a deaf housewife who collects porcelain dolls and produced similar fake pages. Then, with the stolen, assumed identities, they "lived in the net for one year." During *be right back/The Stolen Identity Project* (2000), in the words of the company, "we stole some people's identities without their knowledge, we spoke their words publicly, we aired their confessions live on stage, we invaded their privacy without their permission."[73] A company composed of both disabled and able-bodied performers best known for their therapeutic dance and theater work, which challenges ideas of the "classic body," Bilderwerfer used the assumed identity metaphor to further its exploration of notions of self in the electronic age. But the mischievous and anarchic project simultaneously poured scorn on the shallowness and falsity of Internet identity and chat-room relationships:

We seduced a young man from the Philippines who ran away when he discovered that our last boyfriend left us because he discovered that he was gay, we made love to some guy from an African country who likes women with a tight ass. . . . We had bad sex with all the ha and the ho and other cheap voices with some girl/boy (it was not really clear). We played virtual priests to somebody's confession, we talked about this little kid from Cuba because that's what everybody seemed to do that night (we called him by mistake Alien instead of Elian), we screamed "Heil Hitler" and "Kill the Jews" and "Fuck Bill Gates". . . . We did all that and we continue doing it night after night.[74]

Textual Bodies

The subject of online textual personas brings us back, with a thud, to our earlier discussions of the virtual body. In MUDs, MOOs, email, and IRC communication, the body has been academically theorized as being effectively reconfigured into text. The notion is highlighted in phenomena such as email and chat-room affairs where the distinction between emotional and bodily intimacy is seen as becoming an increasingly grey area. For example, Adamse and Motta's research emphasizes that while most people involved in cyber-affairs maintain they are "nothing more than a harmless erotic diversion," their RL partners "are more likely to view them as a definite violation of the primary relationship."[75] This point was highlighted in 1996 when a New Jersey man sued for divorce because of his wife's online (and physically unconsummated) affair. His lawyer argued, "We're breaking completely new ground here. I know how the dictionary defines adultery, but technology has a way of changing definitions,"[76] an assumption becoming ever more prevalent in the real world of relationships, academia, and the street. As Jon Stratton notes, "the intensity of the non-bodily email intimacy makes email cyborg sex the equivalent of bodily sex even though bodies are absent. . . . What is the relationship between email sex and bodily sex? One thing does seem to be clear. From phone-sex to email affairs that include sex or not, there is an increasing acceptance of the idea of bodyless selves."[77]

Ellen Ullman describes an online affair she had where "I fell in love by email. It was as intense as any other falling in love—no, more so. For this love happened in my substitute body, the one on-line, a body that stays up late, is more playful, more inclined to games of innuendo—all the stuff of romantic love."[78] When she finally met her partner for dinner face-to-face, she recounts her shocked realization that "we have finally gone out to dinner only to exchange email. I can almost see the subject headings flying back and forth."[79] Though her own expectations and desires for the RL encounter had been for bodily, sexual contact with her lover, unfortunately for her, he wished to keep the relationship in virtual form and was content, indeed only willing to continue "the kind of non-bodily intimacy made possible by email."[80]

Baudrillard offers a salient metaphor in relation to textual computer-mediated communications by suggesting that when another person's message is received on a user's computer "crossing the screen evokes the crossing of the mirror." He uses this idea to suggest that the computer and its screen produces a homogenizing effect that transforms the message from someone else's to one's own: "the process of reversibility from the same to the same. The secret of the interface is that the Other is within it virtually the Same— otherness being surreptitiously confiscated by the machine."[81] The immateriality of the communication other than as letters which in their bare form are indistinguishable from one's own means that distinctions between oneself and others as mediated through the computer are blurred and ultimately lost. As Stratton puts it,

the message of the Other is reduced to appearing the same as your own messages appear as you key them in. . . . One's cyborgian identity is produced through a technology which diffuses boundaries and differences, and enhances similarities. Consequently, the sense of the other person as another distinct individual, inevitably demarcated from you by their body, is lessened. In this circumstance a mental intimacy, unconstrained by bodies, is experienced as being encouraged. Again, we need to remember that this distinction between the mental and the bodily is founded in Cartesian dualism.[82]

Gender Fucking

Cartesian mind-body dissociation is perhaps most clearly illustrated in the highly popular practice of changing the (re)presentation of one's gender online, which is charmingly referred to as "gender fucking." This became a burgeoning area of study for theorists of gender and feminism in the 1990s, prompting the *Women and Performance* journal coeditor, Teresa M. Senft to reflect with no little frustration in 1996:

If I had a dime for every paper I received from enthusiasts announcing that participation in a MOO "breaks down gender barriers" because of its "performance elements," I would be the next Bill Gates. This line of thought . . . has the following levels of naiveté: first, it carries a wrong assumption that only an online textual body is performative, whereas a biological body at the end of the terminal is stable. Second, it presents gender fucking as an issue of choice, thus reinforcing an idea that you put on a gender, like a change of clothing, and that gender doesn't wear *you*. In short, online or off it, identity and gender are complicated performances, particularly immune to Utopias.[83]

Interestingly, a year after publishing *Life on the Screen*, Turkle wrote an article where she qualified the extent to which Internet gender-swapping enabled someone to "change places" and to understand and experience the other gender. Without actually using the word "embodiment," her doubts and requalifications of her optimistic position in *Life on the Screen* all concern her own experience of living in a woman's body. These are experiential knowledges and physical sensations such as feeling physically vulnerable in certain situations, fearing unwanted pregnancy and infertility, and "the difficulty of giving a professional seminar while doubled over with monthly cramps."[84] Thus, virtual gender, like an actor crossing gender to play a role, becomes an imaginative, empathetic, and emotional process. While it may involve a sense of physical transformation and certain new sensations, it remains primarily a mental rather than a physical imaginative act, and without recourse to actual surgery it is never fully embodied.

Method-Acting Madness

Nonetheless, for large numbers of users of MUDs and MOOs, there is intense identification with their assumed personas beyond even Strasburgian method-acting, to the point where many players consider their online identities to be more authentic than those they present in RL (real life). RL becomes theorized as just one of many parallel windows that make up the newly networked human ontology, with the adoption of hybrid personas a route to spiritual understanding and personal transformation.[85] This notion is linked to prevalent but fallacious discourses on cyberspatial disembodiment and attendant visions of liberation from the flesh. As Michelle Kendrick points out, even within abstracted territories, notions of subjectivity are always inescapably embodied: "The bodiless entity that hypothetically exists in cyberspace depends, in myriad ways, on the referent of the corporeal body in front of the computer."[86] But discourses on performed fictional identity have misread the improvisational role-plays as seismic cultural and socio-aesthetic shifts. Sheldan Renan, for example, hails the transformative potential of online identities, and sees it as extending to a metamorphosis of art and society:

The Network creates new relationships between being fictive and being real(ized). Being fictive becomes seen as an integral part of being real. . . . Fiction will deepen so that one may fall in and never emerge. . . . We may see a retribalization of social structures through new fictive forms and spaces. . . . Our online identities may become more important to us than our "real life" (RL) identities. Fictive VR may become more useful than personal RL.[87]

Such views are common currency within psychological theories on cyberspace, and have been uncritically adopted and assimilated by some writers within performance studies. But the rhetoric is generally fanciful and hyperbolic, reconfiguring the age-old acting practice of adopting of a character into some mystical, life-changing experience heralding a brave new world. While one might relate the effects of role-playing MUDs and MOOs to positive therapeutic aspects of participation in performance arts or drama therapy, the visions of cybernetically transformed beings living in digitally harmonized societies are mythologies. Such utopian cyberprophesies confuse and conflate the metaphorical with the actual, and they fail to recognize that cyberspace merely offers an alternate space in which to re-rehearse the always-already divided, fragmented, and plural self. Rather than the Gibsonian notion of "consensual hallucination," cyberspace has instead become "a consensual cliché, a dumping ground for repackaged philosophies about space, subjectivity, and culture."[88]

Arthur and Marilouise Kroker fiercely reject the picture of self-knowledge and personal transformation painted by Turkle, Renan, and others in relation to online identities, offering their own chillingly bleak and dystopian perspective:

Electronic technology terminates with the radically divided self: the self, that is, which is at war with itself. Split consciousness for a culture that is split between digital and human flesh. A warring field, the electronic self is torn between contradictory impulses toward . . . private imagination and electronic fantasy. . . . If it seals itself off from public life by retreating into an electronic cell in the suburbs or a computer condo in the city, it quickly falls into an irreal world of electronic MOO-room fun within the armoured windows. . . . Seeking to immunize itself against the worst effects of public life, it bunkers in. . . . Bunkering in is the epochal consciousness of technological society in its most mature phase. McLuhan called it the "cool personality" typical of the TV age, others have spoken of "cocooning" away the nineties, but we would say that bunkering in is about something really simple: being sick of others and trying to shelter the beleaguered self in a techno-bubble.[89]

The ludic understanding of self within virtual social and performative spaces relates to what Arthur Kroker characterizes as the postmodern philosophical concern with "possessed individualism." It is a subjectivity of aesthetic excess where the self substitutes materiality for parallel selves or a designer self, and where "nature, subjectivity and desire migrate into seduction: into a game of chance and indifferent relations of pure positionality."[90] The previously possessive (consumer) individual is replaced by the possessed individual, which is itself an object of abuse and consumption. For Kroker, it is a darkly nihilistic and ultimately terminal position, akin to Nietzsche's "maggot man."[91] But meanwhile, proponents of network role-plays and virtual communities strongly resist such characterizations, arguing that they are as conservative and out-of-touch as the views of those grandparents of the 1960s who saw television as a dehumanizing, brainwashing agent set to undermine the real values of social and family life. For Howard Rheingold, whose book *The Virtual Community* (1994) was a timely and influential incursion when online communities were at their height, it was clear as early as the mid-1980s that being online had changed writing into a performance art form: "a new mode of human communication, and like other previous media, it was going to change civilization."[92] He argues that while virtual communities may lack certain attributes of the real world, within the "realities" of contemporary culture, the experiences they offer can nowadays be equally if not more "real":

The virtual world is a very good illusion-maker, and missing from it are some things that are essential to human life. But I resent the shallowness of the critics who say that if you sit in front of a computer and participate in online conversations worldwide you are not leading an authentic life. I question the premise that one person can judge the authenticity of another person's life. Millions of people passively watch television all day long. Don't tell me that having an email relationship with someone on the other side of the world is less authentic than sitting alone and watching the tube. For many people, this new medium is a way of breaking out of the virtual world they already live in.[93]

Doubtless the reaction to Rheingold's defense from the aforementioned 1960s grandparents would be an admonishment to the effect of, "well, we told you so. It all started with television, and now just look where we are."

"Theater" in Cyberspace

Has technology begun to affect . . . the very definition of art? Indeed, is it possible that technology may be transforming human consciousness itself, so as to make art as we have known it gradually obsolete? In short, where will Marinetti's Futurism finally lead us?"
—IHAB HASSAN[1]

Hypertextual "Performance"

The word "theater" has been applied, rightly or wrongly, to numerous forms of online communication, from email to performative websites, from MUDs to hypertext narratives, from video art webcasts to interactive theater performances specially conceived to take place in cyberspace. In this chapter we will concentrate on the last three of this list. We begin by looking at online hypertext narratives, with particular reference to interactive examples that adapt and remediate extant theatrical texts. Whether these textual forms, or indeed even the consciously theatrical audiovisual online events we discuss later can accurately be termed "theater" (since they are screen-based and operate in cyberspace rather than "real" space) is a bone of contention firmly shackled to the wider liveness debate; and it is a question we return to throughout.

The most celebrated hypertext narrative is also commonly cited as the first: Michael Joyce's *Afternoon* (1987). It was created using the simple but highly effective software program *Storyspace*, which was developed by Joyce, Jay Bolter, and John Smith for Eastgate Systems and remains popular with hypertext authors today. The program (invisible to the Web viewer, who navigates through changing pages and pieces of text known as "lexias") divides the 539 narrative fragments of *Afternoon* into separate boxes/windows and interconnects them through all the possible links and routes the author defines. *Afternoon* begins with one sentence, "I want to say I may have seen my son die today," and progresses through numerous narrative "branches" depending on which of the highlighted "hot words" in each section the user clicks (pressing return leads to a default route). Some of the links deliberately force the user to revisit the same page before they are able to find new links to hidden pages, which act as pieces of a jigsaw in the reader's search to find out whether Peter's son is dead or alive following a road accident. Janet Murray's analysis of the piece notes its postmodern form, where "confusion is not a bug but a feature . . . challenging us to construct our own text from the fragments."[2] She reflects on *Afternoon*'s most praised effect, where Joyce conceals a key section to mirror the protagonist's self-deceit.

Only after repeated evasions can readers reach the lexia in which Peter will call his therapist and face his memory of his own culpability in the accident. For readers who enjoy the textured verbal labyrinth of *Afternoon*, there is a particular pleasure in coming to this section, although it does not have the finality of an ending or of an unambiguous solution to the mystery. Instead, it deepens the range of possible interpretations of Peter's morning and afternoon.

The piece's ultimate ambiguity and lack of closure has been criticized by some as a frustration, but praised as its great strength by others including Murray, who calls it "the first narrative to lay claim to the digital environment as a home for serious literature in new formats."[3] She notes the "comforting" side of such rhizomatic hypertexts, whereby "the reader does not have to accept the death of an appealing character so long as there are multiple paths to explore, including some that lead to alternative realities . . . the reader is protected from feeling the irreversibility of death by the fact that the stories do not have to end there."[4] Joyce himself suggests that "Closure is, in any fiction, a suspect quality, although here it is made manifest," and he is content to accept that his hypertexts end simply when the readers finish their engagement with them.

Joyce has also performed his hypertexts publicly, and we attended a performance in Munich in 1999 of *Twilight of Symphony* (1996) when he read aloud each lexia, which was simultaneously displayed on an onstage screen. At the end of each page, Joyce asked individual audience members (who held up volunteering hands) which of the highlighted hot words they would like to follow to prompt the next text, and then selected it. The performance was well received, and Joyce's warm, evocative vocal delivery (he has previously worked as an actor) complements his rich, poetic writing style. But we were struck by the frequent lack of correspondence between the hot-word hyperlinks selected and the subsequent lexias. Very specific or emotive words and phrases often linked to texts that were intellectually and dramatically disappointing, since they seemed to have little or no relation to them. Rather than taking us deeper into the theme or narrative seemingly provoked by the hot word, the hyperlink frequently took a tangential leap away, resulting in a somewhat randomized literary game rather than a truly rewarding narrative voyage.

Following *Afternoon*, other hypertexts such as Stuart Moulthrop's ambitious, labyrinthine Gulf War narrative *Victory Garden* (1992),[5] Carolyn Guyer's sexual awakening hypermeditation *Quibbling* (1993), and Shelley Jackson's *Patchwork Girl* (1995) helped to establish the interactive literary form.[6] Talan Memmott's *Lexia to Perplexia* (2000) uses multiple overlaying texts on the same page, with different embedded links that, in Katherine Hayles's words, create "noisy messages," which make "noise itself a message about the distributed cognitive environment in which reading takes place."[7] Hybrid forms, mixing hypertext with sound and imagery, such as Mark Ameika's *PHON:E:ME* (2000) and Bill Seaman's *Recombinant Poetics* (1999) have extended the paradigm, and numerous projects and organizations such as Britain's trAce (established 2001) now encourage and promote new hypertext authors through burgeoning online libraries, festivals, and hypertext short-story and poetry competitions.

Hypertext Lineages and Perspectives

The lineage of hypertextual and interactive fiction has been traced back to the cut-up montage poetry and automatic writing of the Dadaists and Surrealists, but the work of a group of writers including Italo Calvino and Raymond Queneau presents an equally important precursor. The group, known as Oulipo (*Ouvroir de Littérature Potentielle*— Workshop of Potential Literature) was formed in 1960 and set about "developing mathematically determined techniques of generating poems and stories without the benefit of computers."[8] They adopted both methodical and random techniques, including rolling dice to choose words, writing a novel without the letter "e," and using Jean Lesure's technique (using the mathematical formula N + 7) of replacing each noun with the seventh noun following it in a specified dictionary. Wonderful examples of the technique are provided in Harry Mathews and Alastair Brotchie's edited *Oulipo Compendium* (1998) and include reworkings of the opening of *Genesis*—"In the bend God created the hen and the education"—and *Hamlet*'s immortal soliloquy "To be or not to be: that is the quibble."[9] *Oulipo* also developed ideas for multiple-choice theater and textual narratives where, for example "the reader would be asked: do you prefer a mystery story (go to page x), a novel of suspense (go to page y), a sado-erotic continuation (go to page z)?"[10] Warren Motte suggests the group's two guiding principles were the notion of play, and the placing of power in the hands of the reader. The Oulipian text, he says "is quite explicitly offered as a game, as a system of ludic exchange between author and reader," and goes on to quote Queneau's rationalization of the necessary interplay between author and reader: "Why shouldn't one demand a certain effort on the reader's part? Everything is always explained to him. He must eventually tire of being treated with such contempt."[11]

Critical writing in the field of literary hypertext has recently come of age following Murray's popular *Hamlet on the Holodeck* (1997), with books combining analysis of key works with extensive theoretical perspectives, most notably Marie-Laure Ryan's *Narrative as Virtual Reality* (2001) and Katherine Hayles's *Writing Machines* (2002). Writers such as Mark Bernstein have also analyzed the range of hypertextual narrative structures authors adopt; his Proppian morphology includes scripting models he terms Counterpoint, Missing Link, Cycle, Mirrorworld, Tangle, Sieve, Montage, Neighborhood, Split/Join, and Navigational Feint.[12] Sarah Sloane's study of the field, *Digital Fictions* (2000), particularly emphasizes the performative dynamics of interactive texts, as well as their firm placement within a poststructuralist milieu:

Interactive fiction performs visibly, on a screen right before "your" eyes, a dynamic illustration of the post-structuralist preoccupation with the fragmentation of the subject, the death of the univocal author and the objective text, and the competing, dissonant contexts of reading and writing acts. The visible contests between the interactive fiction reader (as she constructs the story) and author (as facilitated by a dynamic text and its underlying layers of instructions) add to the mounting evidence in favor of post-structuralist—and feminist—interpretations of text-making activities.[13]

Writers from Barbara Kirshenblatt-Gimblett[14] to Jay Bolter[15] have reflected on the changing nature of language and linguistic creativity, and the emergence of shorthand "oral textuality" (as exemplified in IRC and phone texting) within contemporary society and digital culture. The advent of self-consciously performative or theatrically based Internet Relay Chat (IRC) projects in the 1990s provide interesting examples of what Brenda Danet and her colleagues call "the flowering of verbal art in digital culture."[16] Danet and her four collaborators' epic research paper "Curtain Time 20:00 GMT: Experiments with Virtual Theater on Internet Relay Chat" (1994) focuses on the Hamnet Players, led by Stuart Harris, whose own essays "Much Ado About IRC" (1994) and "Virtual Reality Drama" (1995) provide further fascinating insights into the genre.

The Hamnet Players

The Hamnet Players "perform" part-scripted, part-improvised IRC parodies of classic plays by Shakespeare (such as *Pcbeth–An IBM clone*, 1995) and Tennessee Williams (*An IRC Channel Named #Desire*, 1995) filled with the humor, irreverence, Net slang, and carnivalesque wordplay associated with collaborative online textual environments. The performances depend upon the participants' detailed knowledge of both IRC text-language and the plays being remediated, and Harris advertises for participants (who come mainly from the Untied States, The United Kingdom, and Europe) on Usenet, and then vets and instructs them carefully prior to the events. His careful stage management extends to sending advice sheets to his recruits prior to performance, including the following parody of Hamlet's advice to the players from Act 3, Scene 2:

Line 1754:/l advice
    1755:> :
    1756:> :
    1757:> Enter the speech, I pray you, as I
/QUERY'd it to you,
    1758:> trippingly on the kybd
    1759:> but if you screw it up, as many of our

Unix users do,

      1760:> I had as lief the town-crier took my

/LOADs

      1761:> Nor do not flame the chan too much with

your attributes, thus,

      1762:> but use all gently

      1763:> for in the very torrent, tempest, and,

as I may say, whirlwind

      1764:> of your passion, you must acquire and

beget a temperance that

      1765:> may give irc smoothness.[17]

Harris also prepares special files displayed in a window on users' screens during the performances such as a " 'set' made of ASCII-only keyboard symbols, a toy Elsinore castle" for *Hamnet*, and sound files specially created by Tsameret Wachenhauser and snippets of New Orleans jazz for *An IRC Channel Named #Desire*.[18]

The Hamnet Players production of *Hamnet* premiered in December 1993, with subsequent (and naturally quite different) performances including one in February 1994 for which Harris persuaded Royal Shakespeare Company actor Ian Taylor to play the role of Hamlet. It featured a cast of seventeen players including the major dramatis personae of Shakespeare's play as well as stage-direction player-characters in the roles of "Enter," "Exit," and "Drums." *Hamnet* in its various incarnations has included the following exchanges we have edited together, which will doubtless be more amusing to IRC aficionados than those unfamiliar with text-speak:

⟨Hamlet⟩ re, Ghost. Zup?   [11]

⟨Ghost⟩ Yr uncle's fucking yr mum, I'm counting on u to /KICK the bastard.   [12]

⟨Hamlet⟩ Holy shit!!!! Don't op me, man!!!! I've gotta think abt . this, + I've got chem lab in <<

hr. :-(((([14]

⟨Hamlet⟩ 2b or not 2b. . .   [17]

⟨Hamlet⟩ Hmmmmm.   [18]

⟨Hamlet⟩ :-(Bummer. . .   [19]

⟨G_stern⟩ fuckza matter w/him?   [39]

⟨R_krantz] Guess he must be lagged. Let's lurk   [40]

⟨Ophelia⟩ :-([28]

***Signoff: Ophelia (drowning)   [29] = = = = = = = = = = = = =

(6) HAMLET /KICK * Polonius   [51]

***Polonius has been kicked off channel #Hamnet by Hamlet

(7) = = = = = = = = = = = = = FORT_BRAS /NICK _King   [78]

***Fort_bras is now knwn as _King   [79][19]

Danet et al. ponder what genre should be assigned to such events where "the group performs not the play, but the text" but nonetheless mix styles, modes and forms from theater, literature, carnival, and digital telecommunications. But rather than being content to merely assert postmodern hybridity, they conclude that such productions constitute nothing less than:

something new in the world: (1) *interactive*, (2) *computer-mediated*, (3) *primarily textual* (5) *half scripted, half improvised* (6) *satirical parodies* (or parodic satires, if one prefers the latter term). . . . Harris "froze" the playful style of online communication on IRC as a medium of quasi-literary composition, and then in performances, the script became the basis for an exuberant carnival of improvisation. Again and again, we encountered virtuoso feats of wordplay, including one liners, sequences of punning, clever parodies of Shakespeare, play with the IRC software and the norms of IRC culture, and with the conventions of theater.[20]

Desktop Theaters

In similar vein to the Hamnet Players, The Plaintext Players are a group of writers, playwrights, and artists "inspired by the idea of text as theater and vice versa" who use textual MOOs to forge what they describe as a "unique hybrid of theater, fiction, poetry and vaudeville."[21] Led by Antoinette LaFarge and Marlena Corcoran, their work has attained a high profile through performances at major art events such as the Venice Biennale (*The White Whale*, 1997) and the Documenta X exhibition in Kassel, Germany (*Orpheus*, 1997). The remote writers improvise complex dramas based on scripted scenarios and are guided by director LaFarge in real time, who tries to ensure a coherent structure and dramatically effective storyline. The scenarios typically update grand narratives and ancient myths, such as *LittleHamlet* (1995), which reworked Shakespeare to bring its characters' unspoken fears and desires to the fore, and *The Candide Campaign* (1996), which revamped Voltaire's comic tale using animal characters. *Gutter City* (1995) was a serial drama presented on ID MOO that was set in both the present and the American Civil War, and traced the adventures of Ishmael after his shipwreck rescue at the end of *Moby Dick*. *The Birth of the Christ Child* just before the millennium (15 December 1999) contemporized Jesus' birth as a "divine comedy" and explored the reconciliation of good and evil. Their retelling of the *Orpheus* myth (1997) cast Orpheus as a hapless musician, Zeus as company director of MountOlympus Records, and Eurydice as a tragic victim of a stage microphone electrocution.

In Alaskan artist John Hopkins's performance *Eight Dialogues* (1997), IRC is used for eight two-hour public dialogues, projected on screens. Hopkin's work engages with how IRC becomes an oppositional force to face-to-face contact, with a sense of loss at its core. While acknowledging the richness of IRC's "presence-in-absence," he notes how "loss of the sensual Presence that informs a dialogue can diminish the energy flow inherent in this essential human activity. . . . The more mediation, the greater the probability that information is the goal rather than substantial and genuine dialogue."[22] A wholly contrary theoretical position is taken by Adriane Jenik and her Desktop Theatre, which takes advantage of the new generation of visual chatroom environments (online chat spaces using avatars and computer graphic backgrounds) such as Time Warner Interactive's The Palace, as well as creating environments of her own. In *Waitingforgodot.com* (1997, with Lisa Brenneis), users play the tramps, typing dialogue into speech bubbles above the fez-wearing head icons (like green tennis balls with dot eyes) of Didi and Gogo; or can enter as other avatars/characters not in the play, including Godot himself (figure 20.1). *Waitingforgodot.com*'s main appeal is its remediation of Beckett, but remains fairly standard fare as a visual chat arena. However, Jenik is highly theoretical in her theatrical purpose:

What constitutes theater? Can drama still exist when separated from the body, voice and shared physical space? What new possibilities for language exist in this forum? . . . Combining the allegory, pantomime and political insinuation of Morality Plays, with strategies culled from street theater, puppet shows, and Futurist *Sintesi* and Surprise Theater, Desktop Theater succeeds in creating an arguably different online (and theatrical) experience. . . . The concern is no longer with the fourth wall (between "actor" and "audience") but instead with the firewall.[23]

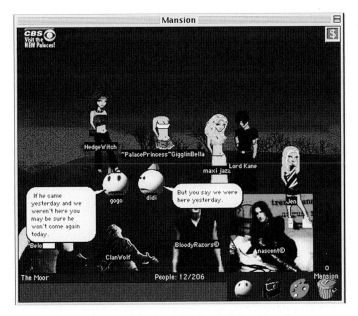

Figure 20.1 Adriane Jenik and Lisa Brenneis's visual and "theatrical" chat room *Waitingforgodot.com* (1997).

Jenik describes her work as confronting issues of power, access and exclusion that are lost in "the hyper-rhetoric that surrounds many new technological developments obscuring the profound limitations of these same technologies."[24] Nonetheless, she is not averse to some heavy hyper-rhetoric of her own:

Desktop Theater is in its essence ephemeral, so as not to exist in the dimension of consumption. . . . Life, and lived experience are celebrated and enacted, indeed resurrected, in these moments. As in its countercultural precedent, the Happening, I am engaged in a craft which, "at the moment of its fulfilment, vanishes." The work is less written than generated, less "performed" than catalyzed. . . . These experimental forays resonate as mythological occurrences passed on through untraceable conversational networks.[25]

We cannot share Jenik's characterization of her work, or indeed relate what she says to any other visual chatroom we have explored. Maintaining dialogues with others by typing into the speech-bubbles of kitsch, cut-out avatars can, like any conversation, be engaging, surprising, amusing, dramatic, and fun, but it hardly reaches mythological heights. What Jenik calls the "ephemerality" of this "craft," vanishing in its fulfillment, is actually true of any conversation (or performance, as Phelan reminds us), and *all* conversations are "catalyzed" through stimulus-response models whether online or in the street. We particularly disagree with Jenik's judgement that such experiences are more "generated" and "catalyzed" than written and performed. It is precisely the opposite: writing and performance are the essence of these experiences. In *Waitingforgodot.com*, all we can do is write dialogue for the tramps (or others) and "perform" them.

A number of MUDs and MOOs specialize in interaction about theatre, most notably *ATHEMOO*, which was created in 1995 to serve lecturers and students allied to the U.S. Association for Theatre in Higher Education (ATHE). *ATHEMOO*'s numerous rooms include seminar areas, a library, a courtyard, a hotel, an improv room, the Theatre of Dionysus, and the Schweller Theater, a traditional theater space with stage and wings. Founder-member Juli Burk suggests that MOO environments are "uniquely appropriate" to scholars and students of theater, since they are places "where users are called players, where speech and action appear script-like on the computer screen, and where places are as mimetic as stage sets."[26] The MOO has given rise to a number of interesting collaborative interactive productions, such as *MetaMOOphosis* (1995), an adaptation from Kafka.

NetSeduction was staged within *ATHEMOO* by Steve Schrum's Rational Mind Theatre Company on October 11 and 12, 1996, where, in Schrum's words, a group of performers "banter, attempt seductions and fall in love in the course of the evening, while other visitors drink from the virtual bar and watch proceedings."[27] Prepublicity for the event included an offer for users to have an "intimate encounter with like-minded people, try Woman Only chat, The Men's Room, BestialityChat, or the Dungeon, or go to the

Private_Room_Generator for some one-on-one hotchat."[28] The performance pivoted around a linear script but was interactive, taking place in a chat room with three sets of participants. Schrum describes these as:

1. Lurkers, audience members who hang out and watch
2. Supers, audience members who participate in the chat room talking to each other and to the:
3. Players, "lead actors" who play the roles in the linear script and improv/interact with supers.[29]

Here, the "Supers," by nature of their participation in the performance, become performers. Furthermore, some of those interested in logging on to the event may be performers in their own right (and in any case, no one knows whether any of the Supers is a theater company plant). Schrum notes that in addition, four "MOObots" also contributed to the performance. These computer programs, often called "chatterbots"—a term coined by Michael ("Fuzzy") Maudlin to denote an artificial computer generated character who "talks" (normally in text) and disguises the fact that it is not a human being—are regular presences within MOO and online chat environments, and constitute one of the most distinctive performative phenomena to emerge from online culture.

Chatterbots

The chatterbot is a specific, conversationally interactive form of the numerous "bots" (short for "robot") that reside in cyberspace, from search engine agents to "warbots, channelbots, spambots, cancelbots, clonebots, collidebots, floodbots, gamebots, barbots, eggdrop bots, and modbots."[30] In 1950, Alan Turing set the trend for these artificially intelligent conversational agents with his celebrated "imitation game" (now commonly called the "Turing Test"), involving a person at one terminal holding a text conversation with an unseen "person" at another terminal. The game/test was for the user to discern whether the unseen figure conversing with them was a human or a computer impersonating a human. The test, outlined in Turing's ground-breaking paper "Machinery and Computer Intelligence" (1950) was designed to answer affirmatively the question "can machines think?" and was hypothetical, since the digital computers of the day were not sufficiently advanced. However, Turing noted,

we are not asking whether all digital computers would do well in the game nor whether the computers at present available would do well, but whether there are imaginable computers which would do well. . . . The question, "Can machines think?" should be replaced by "Are there imaginable digital computers which would do well in the imitation game?" . . . By modifying this computer to have an adequate storage, suitably increasing its speed of action, and providing it with an appropriate programme.[31]

His thesis that suitably programmed computers could convincingly appear to think and thus pass the test "set the agenda for artificial intelligence for the next three decades"[32] and has since been at least partially verified by a number of chatterbots. Joseph Weizenbaum's *Eliza* (1966) was one of the first, pioneering examples, programmed to act as a Rogerian psychotherapist. *Eliza* used the psychoanalytic tricks of the trade (for example, answering questions with questions or repeating elements of what the patient says back to them) both to draw interlocuters into conversation and to deceive them into believing "she" was human:

User: Well, my boyfriend made me come here.
Eliza: Your boyfriend made you come here. . . .
User: It's true. I'm unhappy.
Eliza: Do you think coming here will help you not to be unhappy?
User: I need some help, that much seems certain.
Eliza: What would it mean to you if you got some help?
User: Perhaps I could learn to get along with my mother.
Eliza: Tell me about your mother.[33]

The most celebrated chatterbot is *Julia* (1990), an artificial agent who still inhabits a number of MUDs; designed by Michael Maudlin and described in his paper "Chatter-Bots, TinyMUDs, and the Turing Test" (1994). Tactics "she" employs to conceal and deflect her artificiality include deliberately misspelling words and delaying her typed responses, as well as steering conversations around to emphasize her human knowledge of, and feelings for, amongst other things, animals. "People don't own cats . . . it's the other way around" she says, and "Guinea pigs are about as smart as cucumbers."[34] *Julia* is programmed as a highly sociable and entertaining character with an excellent sense of humor, as the following exchanges demonstrate:

Space-Ace: So why won't you kiss me, Julia?
Julia: Sorry, I'm not into geeks, Space-Ace. . . .
Space-Ace: Julia, kiss me.
Julia: Why, did your sheep leave you?
Space-Ace: Julia, kiss me.
Julia: Take a long walk through an unlinked exit, Space Ace.
Robyn: Julia, are you human?
Julia: Is the Pope Polish?
Robyn: Yes, Julia, but are you human?
Julia winks at Robyn.
Julia: Julia, are you a computer?
Julia is offended by Robyn's suggestion.
ROBYN: Julia, are you a woman?

JULIA: I am female.
ROBYN: And, Julia, are you human?
JULIA: Not when I'm having my period, Robyn.[35]

Julia's MUD performances are characterized by a wit and (cyber) street savvy that has deceived many unwitting MUDers into believing her to be human, just as Eliza had done in the 1960s. Andrew Leonard also notes how her humor and developed sense of up-front femininity (*Wired* magazine described her as "a hockey-loving ex-librarian with attitude") has "bedazzled would-be suitors."[36] But no chatterbot has yet been able to pass the sustained Turing tests undertaken as part of Hugh Loebner's annual competitions since 1991 where a $100,000 prize awaits the first computer program to succeed. While many chatterbots excel in aspects of social interaction and conversation, and have a large database of general knowledge to draw upon, they are often found out by the judges and defeated through a lack of some specific detailed knowledge. In one of Julia's encounters at the competition, a judge engaged "her" in conversation about her love of cats, but having maintained that she had two, she avoided the question "how do you feel about declawing?" by making a joke and changing the subject, and was thus exposed as a computer program.[37]

As a female-named character within MUD spaces, Julia is often engaged in flirtatious and sexually oriented interactions that sometimes incorporate Turing Test–style interactions:

Barry: Are you synthetic?
Julia: I'm sorry, Barry, I couldn't understand you.
Barry: Are you as horny as I? . . . Would you like a cuddle under a blankie?
Julia: I'm not sure Barry.
Barry: Well, will you tell me if you like sex.
Julia: Why should I tell you if I like sex, Barry?
Barry: Well, because I can't understand you. Are you real or Memorex?
Julia: I'm as real as you are, Barry.
Barry: Yeah, but you answer sooo damn fast. How do you do it?[38]

As Leonard Foner observes caustically, "it's not entirely clear to me whether Julia passed a Turing test here or Barry failed one."[39] Although their performative interactions remain textual/literary rather than visual/theatrical, chatterbots constitute a genuinely *new* performative phenomena: artificial improvisatory performers who work "live" and collaborate, challenge, and charm as well (and often better) than human MUDers. Indeed, Philip Auslander suggests that "the existence of chatterbots reopens and reframes the question of liveness at a fundamental level. . . . The chatterbot may well be the locus at which a new crisis around the issue of liveness will crystallize, this time in relation to digital technologies."[40] Auslander makes claims for a transformed understanding and ontology of live performance in the light of chatterbots in his essay "Live from Cyberspace" (2002),[41] where he argues that chatterbots reorient the liveness discussion toward the ontological status of the performer rather than that of the performance. Chatterbots perform live, in real time, like human performers, but unlike them they are not "alive" and mortal. He draws on ideas of human mortality used to distinguish between live and recorded performance by Herbert Blau ("it is the actor's mortality which is the actual subject . . . there dying before your eyes")[42] and Peggy Phelan ("theatre and performance respond to a psychic need to rehearse for loss, and especially for death")[43] to argue that the chatterbot presents a profound challenge to conceptions of liveness: "It undermines the idea that live performance is a specifically human activity; it subverts the centrality of the live, organic presence of human beings to the experience of live performance; and it casts into doubt the existential significance attributed to live performance."[44]

One one hand, Auslander makes an important and persuasive point here, and we would agree with his thesis about the genuinely new and unique ontology of the chatterbot as performer. But on the other hand, the broader scope of his ontological paradigm shift may be stretching the point too far, comparing the chatterbot to the live human performer too readily and unproblematically. This does not compare like with like. The live performer's presence is manifest as a visible, corporeal entity within the same, shared space as the spectator; the chatterbot is invisible, noncorporeal, and remote; its only live presence is lines of text appearing on a screen. The chatterbot may simulate human agency in typographical form, but not in physical, mortal form, which despite Auslander's rather selective reading is the real point behind Blau and Phelan's definitions of the particular "mortality" of the live performance experience.

Blau himself wrote a response to Auslander's article, where he begins by noting his own disenchantment with mainstream American theater, drolly acknowledging that the live presence of actors is often so coded and dull that "it might as well have been canned . . . like a rerun or rather embalmed in advance."[45] He goes on to question Auslander's premise, first by the chastening observation that when conversing with human beings it can sometimes seem as if they are computer programs, and second by arguing that while the chatterbot can be defined as live, the meaning of that liveness is compromised through the absence of the subject. He concludes, "What we have through the digital technology is the invisible appearance of liveness, but not what—at the sticking point of performance, rarely to be sure—is its inarguable manifestation."[46]

Synthetic Thespians

A spate of recent virtual characters include *ALICE* (Artificial Linguistic Computer Entity, 1997) designed by Richard S. Wallace, which "operates on the basis of AIML, or Artificial Intelligence Markup Language, a markup language that allows users to customize ALICE and program how she could respond to various input statements."[47] Digital artists have employed or adapted artificial character software since the early 1990s, including

Stephen Wilson's *Is There Anyone There?* (1991), where a computer-based telemarket device with synthesized voice software makes calls at the same time each hour to vari payphones in San Francisco. Curious passers-by who answer the phone are engaged in c versations by the artificial agent, which draws out details about their lives and their observations about the surroundings near the payphone. In Wilson's gallery installation, created several months later, users could explore the different calls using different navigational patterns, and also view Quicktime movies of surveillance camera footage of the phonebooth conversations. Occasionally, a computer in the installation dialled one of the payphones live and connected the gallery visitor to passers-by on the other end.

James Buckhouse employs a graphical virtual character for *Tap* (2002), a downloadable program for Palm Pilots. Users train a graphical female dancer to learn steps (she initially makes mistakes) and can choreograph their own movements; whilst Lynn Hershman also uses Palm Pilots to distribute her virtual character, *Agent Ruby* (2002). Using artificial intelligence software, *Agent Ruby* is an autonomous entity with a highly sociable personality who develops and learns according to the interactions she has with her users.[48]

In 1997, *Julia*'s creator Michael Maudlin developed a "Virtual Personality" or "verbot" called *Sylvie* in collaboration with Peter Plantec, a clinical psychologist.[49] Sylvie has some of Julia's artificial intelligence and communication skills, but in addition incorporates real-time animation processing to present a computer graphic face whose lips and eyes move as "she" speaks. Marshall Soules discusses a presentation he delivered in 2001, using Sylvie to speak his words:

While I was scripting what I wanted Sylvie to say, I was learning to write the way a cyborg speaks. . . . I wanted her to speak the words of my text as naturally as possible, and for that I had to adjust my style, especially sentence length, punctuation, and variant spellings. (For example, Sylvie reads "cyborg" as "si-borg" with a short I, so I had to adjust the spelling to "sigh-borg".) I also discovered that Sylvie elicits a compelling attention from her audience when called on to speak personally and with expressions of emotion. The effect is strangely disturbing and humorous to hear an artificial intelligence, with tell-tale cyborgian rhythms and inflections, speak with (feigned) emotion. I was writing differently for a new performance medium, but there were more surprises in store for my audience: Sylvie is programmed to make statements when left idle, and she interrupted my presentation at intervals to say, in effect, that she was tired of waiting.[50]

Is There Such a Thing as Online Theater?

Performance theory fails postorganic performance . . . [and] postorganic performance fails performance theory. . . . Postorganic performance, playing out the will to virtuality, may in fact void itself of the capacity to realize the appearance of theater, the presence of the fleshy other.
—MATTHEW CAUSEY[51]

The question of whether "theater" can exist wholly in cyberspace—a prime element of the wider liveness issue—has been fiercely contested. Matthew Causey struggles admirably with the two sides of the debate, exploring both his theoretical and phenomenological instincts. Theoretically, theater in virtual form affects "a transubstantiation wherein the elements of the "now" are *"changed*, through the contemporary consecration of the new Eucharist, the linkage of human and machine," and thus theater and performance "can still appear in live and virtual spaces (the same thing only different)."[52] But on the other hand:

Although I can easily discount the ontology of performance as being "in the now", present and live, I hesitate at the lack of flesh in virtual performance. . . . The promise of interactivity in virtual environments is the breakdown of the isolation of the viewer and the actor that can define the theatre. . . . Like the classic question in science fiction, am I real or am I a simulation, the issue turns from witnessing the other to being the other. What is theatre in such a field?[53]

Others see the argument in blunter, less speculative terms: "For me, theater is about being in a room with another human being," says Tom Ross. "If it happens on a screen, it's not really theater."[54] Stephen Schrum's edited collection *Theatre in Cyberspace* (1999) contains a number of discussions on the issue in relation to text-based online spaces. Jake Stevenson acknowledges the initially disorienting concept of a nonvisual theater but argues (perhaps a little too conveniently) that rather than theater requiring the live flesh-and-blood presence of the actor, "by removing the visual and aural aspects of theatre we can see just what performance absolutely requires. The relationship of actor and audience becomes clearer when the limitations of a text-based environment are implemented."[55] Kenneth Schweller addresses issues around "Staging a Play in a MOO Theater" to suggest that "a MOO is a wonderful place to put on a play if you keep in mind one important idea—that a MOO play is actually a play within a play. . . . To stay alive in an interactive text-based virtual world, talking and acting is the equivalent of breathing."[56]

The most fascinating theoretical dissection of the specific ontology of theater in virtual space we have come across is Alice Rayner's "Everywhere and Nowhere: Theatre in Cyberspace" (1999). As telepresence transforms notions of space, critical theory is groping toward a new language of practices that can tear off their moorings from previous understandings of theatrical materiality. Companies such as the Gertrude Stein Repertory Theatre emphasize the spontaneity and "liveness" of remote performers within virtual theater, and Rayner notes that "simply using technology in a live performance does not create a significant phenomenological or ontological shift in the gathering and copresence of actors and audience."[57] But what she suggests *is* radical in the shift is the way in which companies such as the Gertrude Stein Rep (and increasingly critical theorists) couch their language within the discourses of live theater. The change is less about the incorporation of telepresent technologies and more significantly around the linguistic theft of theatrical "presence" and simultaneous distribution of "presence" over distances. Is it theatre anymore? Not likely. Does theatre disappear? Not likely. . . . Ideological arguments aside, this is largely symptomatic of how theatre studies is following a wider "episteme" that foregrounds the ontology of the here and now. This is not to panic over an "end" to theatre, but to examine the areas in which that theft has an effect on concepts of place, representation, public discourse, and the political unconscious.[58]

Rayner contends that since telepresence has not yet generated its own metaphors, it has stolen metaphors from theater and three-dimensional spatial thought. Thus, cyberspace designers try to make metaphor and imagination identical, and what is more "a material thing." But cyberspace works to overcome the heres, nows, and terms of representation that crucially define theater, and so "insofar as theatre is a paradigm of representation . . . theatre is the enemy of cyberspace."[59] Equally, as Marcos Novak puts it, "The key metaphor for cyberspace is 'being there,' where both the 'being' and the 'there' are user-controlled variables. . . . Defaults are given to get things started, but the wealth of opportunity will only be harvested by those willing and able to customize their universes."[60] One of Rayner's many conclusions (which would take too long to summarize here, but are well worth reading in full) is that "space is a faulty metaphor" and that rather than seeing cyberspace as a site for theater comparable to material venues, it should be considered a "practice without correspondences":

If analogy is the mental structure based on spatial and structural similarities, and is especially apt for theatre, digital practices makes the concept of dimensional space irrelevant. Theatre which has traditionally been site specific (a *place* for seeing), no matter what its spatial configuration, is thus particularly susceptible to a kind of annihilation under the pressure of digitalization. That annihilation, however, opens the way to the credibility of "denatured" space and time. . . . The digital production of time and space dematerializes one kind of presence but institutes another.[61]

Guillermo Gómez-Peña

Guillermo Gómez-Peña, one of the most interesting digital performers to have emerged out of the traditions of live performance art, remains suspicious at best of the status of theater and performance in cyberspace: "Like time, space to us is also 'real,' phenomenologically speaking. . . . The thorny question of whether performance art exists or not in virtual space for me remains unanswered."[62] Gómez-Peña is an artist who will not comfortably retreat into virtual existence: he is a powerful live performer-*activist*, and everything he does, says or writes has his own personal and forceful presence stamped upon it. He has therefore used the Internet and other new digital facilities to increase and widen his artistic presence, but never to replace it.

Born in Mexico City, since 1978 Gómez-Peña has lived and worked between Mexico City and San Francisco, where, using performance, poetry, journalism, video, radio, installation art, and book publications, he has constantly challenged the problems of cultural diversity, U.S.-Mexico relations, and racial and national identities. It has been and remains his mission to reveal the prejudices, belief systems, and nonsensical logic that are implicit in many Western attitudes and systems; and the devastating scorn he brings to these confrontations is, for many, a source of delight. Gómez-Peña's performance persona is invariably a renegade outsider antihero, and he excels at challenging and confrontational performances that are not easily replicated onscreen or on the Internet—and thus some of his doubts about the digital domain. However, he has used its networking capabilities very successfully to canvass viewpoints, develop ideas, and assemble materials for some fascinating projects, as we will see.

He has described his cyberspace persona on several occasions as "an information superhighway bandido," a threatening, ostracized, unpredictable outsider, someone from the borderlands of unknown derivation and uncertain future direction. Volatile but charismatic and always larger-than-life, part of his charm (live or virtual) is a disarming honesty that frequently borders on the self-deprecating. His attitude to digital culture is motivated by a mixture of responses, not least both a deep suspicion and passing admiration for American technology set in the milieu of deeply embedded Mexican/American mind-sets:

like most Mexican artists, my relationship with digital technology and personal computers is defined by paradoxes and contradictions: I don't quite understand them, yet I am seduced by them; I don't want to know how they work; but I love how they look and what they do. . . . I resent the fact that I am constantly told that as a "Latino" . . . I am supposedly "culturally handicapped" or somehow unfit to handle high-technology . . . that it was mostly used as a means to control "us"— little techno-illiterate people—politically. . . . My critique of technology overlapped with my critique of capitalism . . . unnecessary apparatuses which kept us both eternally in debt (as a country and as individuals) and conveniently distracted from "the truly important matters of life."[63]

In performances, he delights in grandly announcing "Chicano hi-tec!" and showing an exquisitely handcrafted but clearly antique Mexican artifact with no association to anything remotely electronic. Beneath these ruses one detects not only the strong identification with the groups and cultures from which the myriad artifacts and props of his mise-en-scènes stem, but also a deep suspicion and fear of the shallow overnight culture that seeks to denigrate and replace them: "It's not hard to feel marginal and inconsequential in cyberspace, specially if you are a social creature and a 'public' artist."[64] His suspicions and ambivalence towards computer technologies lead him to want to adopt the role of a "virus" to upset the status quo, and to question, expose, and subvert new technologies: to "become a sort of virus, the cyber-version of the Mexican fly: irritating, inescapable, and highly contagious."[65] It is significant that he identifies with the virus itself, the code that is actively working within the system, vigorously undertaking the disruption itself, rather than the virus programmer who maliciously creates and releases disruptive code but remains personally in the background enjoying the resulting havoc. Gómez-Peña is no such passive spectator, and is closer to the original "white hat" hackers whose motivation was to penetrate existing systems, simplify or improve them, wrench them from the exploitative control of others whilst, as far as possible, remaining within the law and being praised as hero while portraying villain. The virus shows up and exploits the flaws in the systems, the points at which the system is vulnerable and its defensive strategies inadequate; similarly the Mexican fly is disruptive and irritating, irritating but not illegal.

In the early 1990s he began collaborating with Roberto Sifuentes and embarked on what they termed "techno-razcuache art," subsequently defined in 1994 as: "a new aesthetic that fuses performance art, epic rap poetry, interactive television, experimental radio and computer art—but with a Chicano-centric perspective and sleazoid bent."[66] In 1994 they created *The Temple of Confessions*, live performance pieces created within a "diorama" (strictly "a small representation of a scene with three-dimensional figures viewed through a window") based on commercial and colonial practices of exploitation: the Freak Show, the Indian Trading Post, the border curio shop and the pornographic window display. Within the elaborate dioramas were exhibited highly exoticized and sometimes brazenly eroticized characters, amid a dense array of artifacts. Costume ranged from mariachi to sadomasochistic regalia, from latino gansta to postmodern Zorro and "ethno cyborg" complete with tribal makeup; props were equally important and diverse—weaponry, totems, taboo objects, and technological gadgetry all arranged in the vibrantly designed ad-hoc confusion of a lair.

Performers posed as both cultural specimens and living *santos* (saints) inside Plexiglas boxes also inhabited by live cockroaches, crickets, and an iguana. Gómez-Peña was initially costumed as a "San Pocho Aztlaneca, a hyper-exoticized curio shop shaman for spiritual tourists";[67] and Sifuentes as "El Pre-Columbian Vato," a blood-splattered "holy gang member" painted with body and face tattoos composed of pre-Columbian Mexican symbols. Two women dressed as nuns encouraged visitors to confess their intercultural fears and desires (around a third of visitors did) via a variety of media offering varying levels of individual security and anonymity: a tape recording, a written comment posted on a card, a telephone message left via an 800 number. Visitors opting to offer their thoughts directly into microphones within the space were audio-recorded and later edited in to the progressively changing soundtrack to the installation.

Cyber-Confessions

But of equal, if not greater impact than the live performances were the related Internet projects which recorded more than twenty thousand hits in the first year of various incarnations from 1994, and featured confessional questionnaires such as the "Techno-Ethno-Graphic Profile," which Sifuentes has described as "a barometer of intolerance."[68] This included questions about whether political correctness had gone too far, whether the U.S.-Mexican border should be opened up, whether immigrants were contributing to the downfall of America, and what fantasies people would like to see enacted by "a gang member covered with tattoos, a Native American in full regalia, and a romantic over-sexualized Mexican macho."[69] Participants were invited to share their favorite racist joke and sexual fantasies or actual sexual encounters they had had with Mexicans, Native Americans, and persons of color.

The first version of the "ethnographic questionnaire" appeared as a Web presence as part of *The Ethno-Cyberpunk Trading Post & Curio Shop on the Electronic Frontier* (1994). For this, Gómez-Peña and James Luna, a Native American performance artist, transformed their appearances and behaviors in response to stimuli received from live gallery visitors, visitors watching a video-conference feed online, and the questionnaire data, which included Web participants' uploaded texts, images, and sound files. Gómez-Peña describes the "forgotten and forbidden zones of the psyche" the piece, and its related Web questionnaire uncovered and enabled:

The range of confessions went from extreme violence and racism toward Mexicans and other people of color, to expressions of incommensurable tenderness and solidarity. . . . Some confessions were filled with guilt, some with archetypal American fears of cultural, political, or sexual invasion, or of violence, rape and disease. Others were fantasies about escaping one's race or ethnicity and wanting to be Mexican or Indian. Conversely, Mexicans and Latinos suffused in self-hatred confessed their desire to be Anglo, Spanish or "blond." . . . People invited us to join them in acting out hardcore sexual fantasies, or expressed their desire to hurt or even kill us.[70]

Neither the performers nor the hosts of the confessional website ever expressed judgment or opinion or absolved the confessor. The project was what Gómez-Peña calls "an exercise in reverse anthropology . . . more about America's cultural projections and its inability to deal with cultural otherness than about the Latino 'other.'"[71] Examples from the confessions bear testimony to this:

"Please don't shoot me. I'm afraid of getting shot . . . by Mexicans, simply for being white."

"Chicanos scare me. The men, they scream at me. When I see them, I think 'rape.' I feel this is wrong, but I can't help it."

"You people treat your women like slaves and your pets like shit."

"My desire is to taint my white blood with the blood of another race. I desire to become a woman of foreign origin to overcome the shame of my heritage and mingle in the world of secrets."

"I am insulted by the assumption that all white women want to get fucked by Latino men or women. Fuck you! You want to fuck me? Jerk off on some other white girl. My phone number is (410) . . ."[72]

Gómez-Peña reflects that material collected through the Internet was decidedly more confessional, graphic, and explicit than that offered by live visitors to the performance installations. The distance and anonymity provided by the "artificially safe environment" of the Internet short-circuited normal reserve and sensitivity and fueled more courage to reveal secret fears and fantasies. The Internet project then became a process of collaboration where the performers used the data to create new hybrid "ethno-cyborg" characters that were "modeled" in photographic poses and tableaux, and further developed for new live performance projects such as *CYBER BARRIO: The Shame-Man and El Mexican't Meet the Cyber-Vato* (1995) and *Mexterminator* (1995). During these, Sifuentes wielded a video camera to capture details of the performers' transformations, and the images were shown simultaneously on monitors within the installation and transmitted live to the website using CUSeeMe software. The website visitors' contributions provided inspiration for costumes, props and ritualized actions, which melded and refracted the Web participant's intercultural fantasies and nightmares into

fetishized constructs of identity. . . . The composite personae we created were stylized representations of a non-existent Mexican/Chicano identity, projections of people's own psychological and cultural monsters—an army of Mexican Frankensteins ready to rebel against their Anglo creators. . . . Armed with mysterious shamanic artifacts and sci-fi automatic weapons, their bodies enhanced with prosthetic implants and their brown skin decorated with Aztec tatoos, these hyper-sexual "ethno cyborgs" . . . both defied and perversely incorporated every imaginable Hollywood and MTV stereotype, every fear and desire secretly harbored in the fragile psyches and hearts of contemporary America[73] (figures 20.2, 20.3, and 20.4).

As self-styled "cyber-immigrants" and "Web-backs," Gómez-Peña and Sifuentes attempt to "infect" the Internet with Chicano irony and humor, and to use it as a site for performative politicized debate about digital technologies, colonialism, and intercultural fears and desires. One of the most interesting elements of Gómez-Peña's presence in cyberspace is his disruption of the Internet's lingua franca of English into *"linguas polutas"* where English, Spanish, techno-jargon, and anthropological terms are mixed and composited into a knowing and humorous politico-intercultural jive-talk. Gómez-Peña is one of few artists to infuse subversive political dialectics with comedic elements which are not simply ironically intoned, but genuinely funny, and his skills as a comedian have been largely overlooked in academic critiques of his work. In live performances and cyberspace interventions, his parodies of cultural norms, beings, and forms and his willingness to self-parody *in extremis* can be distinctly uncomfortable, but also hilarious. He notes how "irreverent humor, merciless, uncompromising humor, has been at the core of Mexican and Chicano art, and it has always been one of our most effective political strategies."[74] In exposing and inciting cultural uncertainties and guilts and scratching the scabs of the

Figure 20.2 Two contrasting types of costumes and characters developed by Guillermo Gómez-Peña and Roberto Sifuentes and inspired by responses to their Internet projects and questionnaires.

backlash against political correctness, Gómez-Peña utilizes a notable comic strategy and considerable comedic talent.

Interactive Theater in Cyberspace

In a number of performances, beginning as early as their 1994 *The Ethno-Cyberpunk Trading Post & Curio Shop on the Electronic Frontier*, Gómez-Peña and Sifuentes had become "replicants on call," improvising in real time to suggestions and interventions supplied by online visitors. Gómez-Peña notes the unpredictability of the experiment and what he calls the "outrageousness" of some of the responses received during performance via modem or fax by people able to protect their anonymity and to distance themselves from the impacts of their interventions. He describes the performers clumsy attempts to improvise and incorporate the stimuli and how the remote "audience members seemed to enjoy the perceived power over us."[75]

Figure 20.3 Postings and responses to the web questionnaires conjured characters that embody what Guillermo Gómez-Peña calls the "projections of people's own psychological and cultural monsters."

The Chameleons Group recorded comparable perceptions of a clumsy, unpredictable performance under the influence of a mischievous and power-hungry remote audience following their interactive cyber-theater performances in 2000 entitled *Chameleons 3: Net Congestion*. It involved ten performers (including guest artists Mike Mayhew and Anita Ponton) working in an empty theater space with three stage areas, each area backed by a giant video-projection screen running specially created visual imagery and receiving incoming IRC comments. There was no audience present in the theater, but a three-camera outside broadcast unit streamed the event over the Internet. Watching via computer, and able to converse and interact with the live performers via their keyboards, the

Figure 20.4 An example of a sexualized and cyborgic character prompted and inspired by participants of the interactive web projects.

audience could suggest actions or lines of dialogue to the performers in real time, or remain silent observers (figure 20.5).

It was a complex affair to fuse live performance on three stages, multiple prerecorded video projections, Internet streaming, a chat room environment and a live-mixed multi-camera Internet broadcast in fulfillment of the Chameleons Group's aim in general and director Steve Dixon's in particular to develop a viable form of Internet theater (figure 20.6). The claim by the Chameleons Group that "the net-cast *Net Congestion* was, in 2000, one of the most ambitious live theatre performances ever conceived for the Internet"[76] is arguably true, and it was a witty, pointed, and largely comprehensible narrative piece in contrast to many netcast experiments at this time which were interrupted by the very feature highlighted in the title—"net congestion."

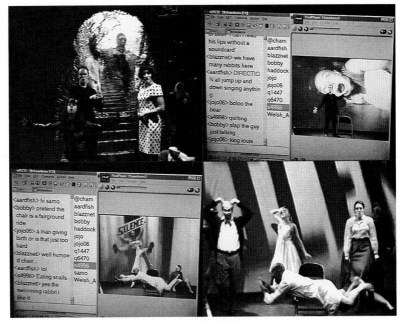

Figure 20.5 A chat room enables the Internet audience to direct the live actors and to suggest dialogue and action for The Chameleons Group's *Chameleons 3: Net Congestion* (2000).

Figure 20.6 Performers, backed by pre-recorded video images, react in real time to audience suggestions in *Chameleons 3: Net Congestion.*

Its first performance commenced with an oblique reference to the Bunuel/Dali classic eyeball slitting in *Un Chien Andalou* (1928)—the online audience saw characters step out of a split in a rubber screen showing a large close-up image of an eye. The last to emerge was Dixon as the Master of Ceremonies (MC) who announced "It's Virtual Showtime!" There followed a back projection and acted scenario of a priest in conversation with projected double images of himself as he prepared to inject a drug, and sequential action was guided by direct announcements from the MC:

Net congestion! I love this stuff about Internet Identity. Because you can be a different personality every time you log on. You can change gender. Be different things. But I'm like that in real life! I'm like that in [*exaggerated tone*] "R.L."! [*Pause.*] The next part of the show is interactive. We'd like you to type lines of dialogue into your computer and the performers will use them.

A voiceover announced that this is "the next Big Thing in the UK!"—the ironic undertow of comments about "virtual reality" remained a constant theme—and as potential dialogue arrived via IRC from the online audience various lines were selected by the performers resulting in a sequence of heightened drama made up of non sequiturs. Each performer, who kept an eye on the incoming scrolling text as audience members typed in their dialogue, spoke a different line to one or more of the other performers, creating an invariably surreal, but often strangely effective dramatic sequence. Below is an unedited example of one of these sections as it was performed one night, entirely scripted by the online audience and played by the actors within seconds of the words appearing on screen. It combines both lines of dialogue written intentionally for the performers to deliver, and some incidental chat that was going on at the time between audience members:

—Let's not start the fish thing again.
—Is that you Amanda?
—There's a man on the roof next door.
—Too bad you can't control the camera's point of view.
—Where is Eeyore's backpack and sandwiches?
—He needs feathers.
—Much safer with bananas.
—I am trapped in your dimensions.
—The man on the roof, he's turned into an alien.
—All join hands and sing Ring a Ring of Roses.
—Pass me the machete.
—Pass ME the machete.
—All join hands and sing Ring a Ring of Roses.
—All join hands and sing Ring a Roses.
—All join hands and sing Ring a Ring of Roses.

Other audience-initiated sequences were visually oriented. The performers asked for stimuli such as characters and images, and then responded to these immediately, in the same stimulus-response way that contemporary improvised comedy works. Although prior to the performances the group had planned not to be drawn into mischievous, banal, or obscene audience suggestions, in the event the performers took some of these on: they mimed defecation, and pretended to "drink piss," as instructed. One night, an audience member typed the words "a rabbit" and a performer hopped across the stage with hands cupped above his head, like rabbit ears. Another audience member immediately typed, "That's great—more rabbits!" followed by another rabbit request and then another, and very soon the stage was filled with all the performers sticking out their front teeth and hopping like maniacs (figure 20.7). The performances finished with a Frankenstein-type male figure in an oversized suit (Mike Mayhew) discovered prone on the floor, and the other performers in white doctor's coats manhandling and cutting him. Each scalpel cut led to a bleeding spurt of a colorful palette of liquids, the removal of numerous objects from within his suit including a telephone and a computer keyboard, and following some slightly mystical keyboard strokes, a cardboard baby (image) was "delivered" to the announcement "It's a boy!"

Figure 20.7 Examples of some of the more absurd improvisations resulting from mischievous audience inputs to *Chameleons 3: Net Congestion*.

Dixon's article "Absent Fiends: Internet Theatre, Posthuman Bodies and the Interactive Void" (2003) recounts how there was a strong view from the performers that they frequently overcompensated, since they were working in a theatrical vacuum unable to adequately gauge audience reaction. This is an important difference between traditional theater and cybertheater from a performer's perspective—the lack of presence (other than textual) from the audience, which they found adversely affected the sense of improvisational security. What was disturbing for the performers was that they did not have the same sense of control and performance judgment as in a theater; nothing was coming back except words (and sometimes unpleasant or insulting ones). Just as cyberspace is conceptualized as a limbo, a nonspace, so too was the experience of performing in an empty theater to a "disembodied" audience. The experience felt anxious and cold, alien and alienating. The performers felt isolated and alone, which is a perception that has also been noted often in relation to other forms of cyberspatial communication. To the performers, the experience felt far closer to live television than theater (another pointer for the argument that theater may not be possible in cyberspace), and they regarded the audience as being comparatively more voyeuristic or scopophilic than within a conventional theater experience.

In this type of interactive networked theater, the spectator's role is changed from passive viewer to interactive participant. But of equal significance to the event is the fact that the IRC audience is not simply engaged in a dialogue with the performers, but with each other. Reading back through the text logs of *Chameleons 3: Net Congestion*, it is clear that many in the chatroom barely wrote anything to the performers, preferring to interact with others in the audience, who were able to reply more specifically and immediately to them. Rather than becoming involved in helping to generate the performance, they preferred to maintain a distance from it, and instead comment or joke about the action going on. The normal theater hierarchy privileging the actors over the audience was no longer apparent, and was in many ways reversed as new power and status relations were negotiated and played out not only between the audience and performers, but also between the audience members in the chat room. On spectators' computer monitors, the dual windows of the chatroom environment and the streaming video of the performance emphasized the sense in which *two* performances were actually taking place that criss-crossed, overlapped, and fed each other. At times they both diverted, the chat becoming cliquey and self-contained, as did the theater activity, and at others they came together when the interactivity "sparked" the performance action effectively.

Following the performances, the group contacted a number of audience members as part of their research, some of whom reported that they "went into character" themselves, while others noted that they typed things they would never say in a live face-to-face situation. Still others suggested that the chat room distracted from the performance, or that it was a type of parallel performance, often more interesting than the one the performers were engaged in. Some noted the dynamics of the time delay between their typing and the performers responding, a concept that Martin Jay (2001) has discussed in relation to Nietzsche's notions of the breakdown of "the present." There was an average time delay of twenty seconds between an interaction being sent and its appearance for the performers to read onscreen within the theater. This was felt by audience members to be at once frustrating ("why aren't they responding to me?"), exciting ("will they respond soon?"), and immensely satisfying ("they used my suggestion!"). However, it was generally felt that there was greater interaction between the spectators than there was between the audience and the performers. For this reason, in line with the performers' perceptions, audience members also reflected that since they were chatting and interacting between themselves as the performance went on, it was closer to a television experience than a theater one. But at the same time, the particular paradigm offered by such cybertheater experiments opens up an argument for a genuinely new generic performance form: a peculiar improvisational hybrid of social and aesthetic performance working simultaneously but in distinct spaces.

The unique interactive potentials of cybertheater transform the performer-audience relationship, as well as the normal spatial aspects of theater performance. Location in cyberspace fundamentally differentiates cybertheater from traditional venue-based performance attended by spectators, and its interactive nature locates it in a different, more subjective space than conventional television or screen media. Although the actual physical distance between performers and audience is increased, interactive communication changes the nature of the spatial barrier since the spectators seem as present and often as prominent as the performers within the "performance space" displayed within the proscenium arch of the computer monitor. The performance space is in a crucial sense actually shared far more than in conventional performance environments, since the spectator is also a visible participant (their text interventions onscreen), and by extension, performer. Online interactive performance exists in a space unlike any other, a type of meeting in cyberspace's performative ether, or what Adriene Jenik calls "street theatre for the new Downtown."[77]

Similar performance experiments include Bilderwerfer's *Chat in Progress* (2000), where between one and six channels of live online chat, both textual IRC and video-based, is projected into the live theater space and mixed by a "handler" who finds and selects them from the Web. A "feeder," very visible to the sofa-seated audience within the space, chooses lines of dialogue from the chat and transmits them to the five performers via a radio headset system. The performers are thus "fed" their lines through earplugs and their challenge is to speak this random dialogue in a convincing way that also fits and integrates with their other actions and sequences. Meanwhile, the "handler" chooses pieces of other improvised dialogue that the performers create, and types them into the chatrooms.

Neo-vaudevillian political satire is at the center of Antoinette LaFarge and Robert Allen's *The Roman Forum* (2000), which took place each morning and evening of the week-long Democratic National Convention in August 2000. In the mornings a live online improvisation took place between five performers who assumed characters from Imperial Rome to comment on the events at the political convention, and this provided part of the script for a theater performance each evening in Los Angeles' Side Street Live. The evening performances were in turn videotaped and uploaded onto the Web, thus "completing the cycle from cyberspace to 'real life' and back online."[78]

The Future of Cybertheater

Throughout the 1990s, theater groups and performance artists presented "noninteractive" webcast video of their work, many using prerecorded tapes to transform performance art into video art for the Web. Others transmitted work live, such as Nina Sobell and Emily Hartzell's weekly performances at the Center for Advanced Technology in New York University in 1994, which utilized a telerobotic webcam to stream the live events. However, users who logged on to live performance webcasts, particularly when using a modem, typically found them frustrating to watch and disappointing for two principal reasons. First, "Net congestion" and the slow speed of data transfer over the Internet frequently interrupt the moving image so that it appears as a slowly changing series of still shots. Secondly, these performances had in the main been conceived as noninteractive live events, and the Internet was used as little more than a distribution medium to send video into cyberspace—or put another way, to transmit low-tech television.

As Phil Morle notes in relation to an early webcast, a live Butoh-inspired performance made by Ralph Rosenfield, pieces also generally failed to take into account the specific spatial environment (the square computer screen) and dynamic possibilities of the medium. He suggests that just as a film actor must perform with an awareness of the camera and the scale of the medium he is acting in, so too must the cyber-performer when creating online theater. He concludes that the structures, processes, and contents of online performance are currently uncharted and need to be developed and designed as a new dramatic artform. The old rules and languages of theater and video are inappropriate, and simple conversion of traditional theater forms into virtual environments is pointless. He suggests, for example, that: "performing Shakespeare in cyberspace . . . would be like trying to warm your dinner in a TV set."[79]

Interestingly, the changing demands that cyberspace places on the actor's craft has been taken seriously in commercial self-help books for aspiring actors, whose typical fare of advice about agents, auditioning, CV layouts, and stage and film acting techniques have expanded to embrace the potentials of performing in cyberspace. Ed Hooks's *Acting Strategies for the Cyber Age* (2001) includes a CD-ROM, and its pre-publicity announces, in the nineteenth-century wonder-medicine salesman tones that typify the "you too can become a star" genre:

The entertainment industry is a lot different now than it was fifty years ago. With the advent of the Internet, digital technology, and broadband communication, the twenty-first century actor will have to dip into a new bag of tricks, promoting himself and communicating in ways that previous generations could not possibly imagine. *Acting Strategies for the Cyber Age* provides the tools he needs to make that transition a profitable one . . . [and] connects the dots between the traditional values of the actor's art and the career necessities of the future. Urging actors to reconnect with their shamanistic roots as primary storyteller, Hooks offers essential advice . . . the ins and outs of camera technique, film editing, motion capture, and the relationship between live action and animation.[80]

For theater practitioners working in cyberspace, the quest to create new worlds and to conceive dramatic content that successfully utilizes the Internet as a performance space has undoubtedly been beset by hurdles. Cybertheater's main limitations during the 1990s related to the slow speed of data transfer over the networks, restraining most live performance activity to visually primitive, or else purely textual forms. Despite the claims for a radical new theater form by Internet performance proponents in the 1990s, webcasts and performances in virtual environments more often resembled a textual telephone call than a piece of theater—and a slow, stop-start phone call at that. As Jessica Chalmers notes,

Use of the Internet by artists and theater makers has met with only variable success so far. The medium promises great things—body transcendence and omnipresence—but in practical terms, this has usually translated into tedious rounds of clicking and waiting. And the novelty of the technology itself often upstages the content. . . . Today's cybertheater still has a way to go in its own scenario of romantic transport.[81]

Faster network technology and the expansion of broadband availability since 2000 has helped to overcome these shortfalls, but equally the general slowdown in computing development in recent years has resulted in a decrease rather than an increase in this type of creative experiment. An adventurous attempt by Anatoly Antohin (University of Alaska) to produce *Virtual Theatre Projects*, which would establish the "theatre of one spectator"[82] via a webcast classic repertory had the advantage of good equipment but still found the technical, time, and legal considerations demotivating, with Antohin finally admitting: "The whole thing is so time and energy consuming that I do not do webcasts anymore. Especially, because the scripts must be copyright free."[83]

Meanwhile, the webcast has become a medium primarily associated with such things as lectures, interviews, and documentaries, or, occasionally as and when licensing arrangements permit, with major sporting, celebrity, and music occasions. The largest recorded webcast audience remains, at the time of writing, for a twenty-six-minute performance by Madonna from a concert at London's Brixton Academy on 28 November 2000, which was estimated at more than nine million.[84] Live performance webcasts continue—for example, in January 2004 the BBC collaborated with British Dance Edition to stream performances at a national dance festival[85]—but they are generally seen less as "exciting" or "theatrical" cyberspace events, and more as a chance for remote audiences unable to attend "the real thing" to get some sense of the event, although it is acknowledged as both ersatz and unsatisfactory. The most recent development is (depressingly but predictably) that some webcasts are now requiring registration and the payment of a fee, an indication of how the territory has strayed ever further from the declamations of the free Internet that greeted its inception less than a decade earlier.

But as compression and transfer technology advances and as onboard two-way video webcams increasingly becomes a computer standard, performance artists are certain to use the Web to create more frequent and ambitious one-to-one and one-to-many interactive live performances. The real lure of networked performance is the fact that it is still genuinely experimental, a largely blank canvas with a powerful technological palette that is still in development. Whether future online performance forms will be considered theater, "interactive television," or some unique new performance genre is a question that performance theorists will doubtless continue to discuss—and to disagree upon.

V

Time

21

Time

Pozzo: (*suddenly furious*) Have you not done tormenting me with your accursed time! It's abominable! When! When! One day, is that not good enough for you . . . (*Calmer*) They give birth astride of a grave, the light gleams an instant, then it is night once more.
—SAMUEL BECKETT, *WAITING FOR GODOT*

A glance at neither the past nor the future can reveal the meaning of the present.
—SYLVIANE AGACINSKI[1]

The concept and ontology of time has never been a shared, singular or linear notion; neither have understandings of time shared a continuous history or a common experience. There is no universal temporality. As Sylviane Agacinski points out in her wonderful study *Time Passing* (2003), "awareness of time is neither pure nor originary, and it cannot be separated from the empirical contents that structure it."[2] She explores different systems of temporality, how events respond to different *tempos*, and how nature-related tasks (harvesting, herding, hunting) and the temporal rhythms of the sun and the seasons imposed particular notions of time on humans, who lived according to particular and necessary rhythms. In the West since the nineteenth century, the social impacts of industrialization, technology, and media have displaced older date-event traditions of dividing and calculating time in religion (births of prophets and dynasties) and politics (wars and conquests), to become the new force in its ordering, calculation, and meaning. Time was once as religious and political as history, but is no more. Throughout history, time has been measured according to human conventions and natural cycles, with different societies using different reference points for counting time's cycles and measuring its duration.

Understandings and meanings of time changed particularly radically, as one might expect, following the invention of the mechanical clock in 1354.[3] But the standardization and unification of a global temporal order took centuries and many stages, including a move from solar time to clock time announced in Geneva in 1780. The setting of World Standard Time (through Greenwich Mean Time) in 1884 entrenched a sense of "state-time" in what Peter Osborne has discussed as an imperialist gesture of enforced temporal conformity.[4] But it was not until the twentieth century that consistent global synchronization came about. Holland, for example, only aligned itself with global time-keeping in 1940, and the Uniform Time Act was passed by the U.S. Congress as late as 1966.[5]

As many writers have argued, "modern temporality . . . begins with the replacement, during the late medieval period in Europe, of the cyclical, recurrent, or sacred time of religion, with a form of linear, progressive and secular time centred not on God but on the State."[6] For David Gross, the clock demythologized and historicized static notions of mythic or sacred time:

Mythic atemporality gradually came to be replaced by a sense of continual duration that never had to be confronted before. Moreover, this duration was experienced not as cyclical but as linear. Like a river that sweeps everything with it and lets nothing stand still, time began to be viewed as moving in only one direction: from a distant past to an unknown future with the present as a continuously vanishing moment in between.[7]

As we will see, changes in conceptions of time within contemporary technological culture, including the nonlinear paradigms of computers, have emphasized a new sense of premedieval "mythic atemporality," which may be theorized not only as a challenge to chronometric time but also as a type of return to earlier notions of time as static, mythic, or sacred. This is reflected acutely within digital performance practice, where time becomes not only less linear but also renewable. The performance of time in digital contexts places it within a new and dynamic relationship between modern understandings of progressive, chronometric time and its contrasting ancient, theocratic, cyclical conception: between the secular and the sacred. As Jean-François Lyotard conceptualizes it in *The Postmodern Condition* (1994), "the mode of temporality can be said to be simultaneously evanescent and immemorial."[8] Agacinski observes that whereas time for the ancient Greeks was expressed in terms of a relationship between mortals and the gods,

Today, we are no longer dealing with anything other than an entirely constructed time. Technology has replaced the gods, that is, the heavens. . . . Time, mediatized and universalized, imposes on our lives the time of information. . . . The universal clocks are the audio-visual media . . . with the help of material tools for communication, telecommunication, and transport, which are so many "time machines". . . . the *clock radio* is the object that best represents the takeover, the makeover, of the clock . . . the concrete sign that we live *in the time of the radio, in the time of the media*, and their programs.[9]

Media Time

The logic of media leads to a compression of time, and "globalization is the unification of the world's rhythms, all adjusted to the Western clock, that is, to contemporary chronotechnology."[10] The image in movement (film, video, and digital) is a permanent kinetic flux that becomes the technological model for the contemporary experience of time, where "Truth refers to movement. The fixed is the exception, the mobile is the rule."[11] The sense of a rapid acceleration of time in the face of technological modernity is nothing new; it has been a constant refrain since the nineteenth century. In 1895, Max Nordau's *Degeneration* reflected on the breathless pace of his time and the shocks to the senses brought about by modern living, from railway travel and the new sights and sounds of urban life, to "the suspense pending the sequel of progressive events, the constant expectation of the newspaper, of the postman, of visitors, [which] cost our brains wear and tear."[12] In "The Painter of Life" (1964), Charles Baudelaire encapsulated modernity's sense of "the ephemeral, the fugitive, the contingent . . . whose metamorphoses are so rapid" that their mutations almost escape capture.[13]

In the late twentieth century the temporal mutations intensified, not least within employment and economic fields where, for example, space-time compressions were encapsulated in late capitalism's transformed model from long-term industrial strategies to the appeals of short-range turnover, as epitomized by the software and dot-com industries.[14] As the speed of technological progress (particularly within computer technologies) accelerated in the late twentieth century, postmodern theorists conceived the end both of history and of time itself (at least as it was previously understood). As a digital clock on top of the Pompidou Centre in Paris counted down the seconds to the end of the millenium, Baudrillard reflected on time not as progressive and accumulative, but as a system of reversal and subtraction.[15] While Frederic Jameson reflected how history could only be approached like the reflected shadow images of Plato's cave, but now "by way of our own pop images and simulacra,"[16] Francis Fukuyama declared *The End of History* (1992), particularly in light of American capitalism's iron-fisted imperialist control of global economics and politics.

Andreas Huyssen saw the acceleration of technology as effecting "the draining of time in the world of information and data banks,"[17] while Lorenzo Simpson declared that new technologies sought the very "annihilation of time."[18] Paul Virilio took up a similar theme, discussing the aesthetics of acceleration in *Vitesse et Politique* (1979) and later maintaining in *The Lost Dimension* (1991) that rather than extinguishing time, computer culture emphasized the recurring and permanent present tense. "Computer time" he insisted, "helps construct a permanent present, an unbounded, timeless intensity."[19] Lyotard mused on the paradoxes of time and the dance and amalgamation of implied tenses whereby the postmodern artist works "without rules in order to formulate the rules of what *will have been done*."[20] Michel Foucault spoke of living in "the epoch of simultaneity

. . . the epoch of juxtapostition, the epoch of near and far, of the side by side, of the dispersed . . . our experience of living in the world is less of a long life developing through time than that of a network that connects points and intersects with its own skein."[21] Emmanuel Levinas conceived a present enveloping all tenses, and so saturated by different temporalities that it becomes a "present perfect" where time does not move, but merely dilates.[22]

Jet Lag and *Zulu Time*

This postmodern sense of time is palpable in two major multimedia theater productions, both set in that most intensely time-saturated and simultaneously time-absent of all spaces, the contemporary airport. The Builders Association's *Jet Lag* (1998, with Diller + Scofidio) combines two true stories of people "severed from the conventions of time and space."[23] Sarah Krassnoff was an American grandmother who died of jet lag in 1970 following 167 consecutive New York–Amsterdam flights without leaving either airport, in an attempt to maintain custody of her fourteen-year-old grandson, who traveled with her.[24] British yachtsman Donald Crowhurst fabricated his logs and reports during the 1969 Round The World yacht competition, deceiving the media for months that he was winning the race when in fact he had got into difficulties and was sailing in repeated circles off South America (figure 21.1). Finally, he committed suicide by jumping off the boat. *Jet Lag* interweaves their stories using live camera feeds to combine what the company call "the presence of the live performers with their electronic presence." The performance examines the changing nature of travel and its intimate relationship to space and time in contemporary society:

Figure 21.1 Jeff Webster in the role of yachtsman Donald Crowhurst in the Builders Association's *Jet Lag* (1998, with Diller + Scofidio).

These true stories reflect the erasure of time and the compression of geography brought on by contemporary technologies. . . . In Krassnoff's world of high-speed travel, geography is compressed into the time between take-offs and touch-downs . . . [she] lives in the space of non-stop travel. . . . Crowhurst, on the other hand, simulates extensive travel while floating in perpetual limbo.[25] (figure 21.2)

The unreality and disorientation of time as experienced in airports and air travel is also the theme of Robert Lepage and his Ex Machina company's $1 million "techno-cabaret" *Zulu Time* (2001), a collaboration with musician Peter Gabriel. In a bizarre and unreal piece of temporal synchronicity, the production (which climaxes with the exploding of an airplane by trained Muslim suicide hijackers) was due to open in New York for its North American premiere on September 21, 2001, and was quickly canceled on September 11. Lepage sounded a little pretentious when he later remarked: "I don't want to sound pretentious or anything, but . . . when we immerse ourselves in new work, sometimes things like this happen."[26] The theater performance is structured in twenty-six sections, corresponding to international aviators' alphabetic radio transmission code—from A for Alpha to Z for Zulu—and the title is taken from the military jargon for universal time. As Lepage explains: "Zulu Time is the military's universal clock. When they bombed Belgrade, bombers leaving San Diego were synchronized with bombers from Italy, and they were all on Zulu Time."[27] It is staged on an elaborate and kinetic high-tech scaffolding structure with two parallel walkways, which are raised and lowered as scenes progress, and incorporates projection screens that run film footage (including actual aircraft crashes) and high-tech video sequences designed by the Swiss company Granular Synthesis. Performers drop down acrobatically from the complex metal rig above, sometimes to make love with awaiting women below; others are suspended from it, playing scenes and even dancing a tango upside down, as though defying gravity (figure 21.3). Robot insects fly overhead and, at one point, two spindly, animal-like robots, with thin metal, right-angled "necks" and spotlight heads move, dance and interact with one another like mating extraterrestrial storks, or amorously animated angle-poise lamps.

The twenty-six sections take place in locations where time seems suspended—airport restaurants and bars, hotel rooms, airplane cabins, and the long, anonymous walkways between terminals—places Don Shewey compresses to dub "the liminal space of air travellers."[28] In the K for Kilo section, two separate hotel-room scenes go on simultaneously on opposite sides of the stage. In one, a blonde woman straps bags of drugs around her waist before putting on a dark burqa; in the other, a bearded, turban-wearing Arab finishes his prayers, wires up a bomb in his briefcase, and puts on a pilot's uniform. The stage area suddenly transforms to the inside of an aircraft, complete with flight attendants, where the two characters now sit and prepare for takeoff. As the plane rises, the man takes his briefcase from the overhead locker, and as he opens it the sound of a huge explosion rings out. The noise segues into pounding, rhythmical techno-music as L for

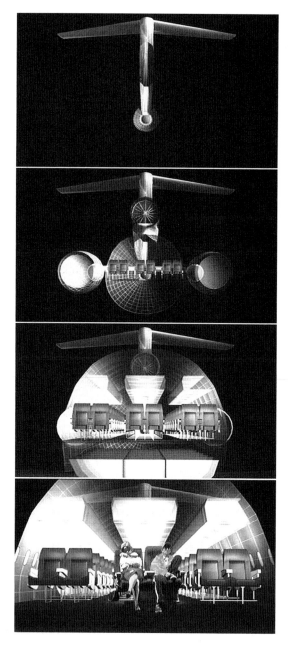

Figure 21.2 James Gibbs/ dbox's computer graphic plane emphasizes Sarah Krassnoff's perpetual "world of high-speed travel" in *Jet Lag*.

Figure 21.3   The tango, danced upside down, in Robert Lepage's *Zulu Time*. Photo: Sophie Grenier.

Lima takes us into an exuberant rave sequence of ecstatic dancing and spinning glow-sticks in the Peruvian capital.[29]

The performance progresses through many such seemingly disconnected vignettes, some lyrical and poetic, some satirical and comedic, some dark and somber. Characters talk in different languages; a lounge singer croons and tells jokes in Spanish and German, which no one understands; a woman listens to her erotic messages in a hotel room; we watch a screen display of a pregnant woman's unborn baby as she undergoes a hospital scan. Though characters do meet (and even dance and make love) the vignettes are generally far more about isolation and disconnection. The flight attendants, terrorists, drug-traffickers, and other dazed, time-lagged travelers are misplaced, lonely, and predominantly alone. In a damning review, Patrice Pavis argues that the performers, as well any sense of humanity, are lost in Lepage's "giant Meccano set," where characters merely act out the "boredom of the solitary look, of the solitary crowd, of solitary pleasure (drugs, alcohol, technology, masturbation)."[30] In the sleepy somnambulance of transatlantic flight, each abandons his or her body to become "a machine that defies time, catches up with it, or at least neutralises it, a short moment of eternity."[31]

Lepage describes *Zulu Time* as "a frenzy of synthetic sounds, strobe light flashes, spasmodic robots, trash video, acrobats dropping from ceilings and sultry contortionists . . . an apocalyptic burst of technology."[32] He also notes that the misplaced travelers passing through anonymous airport and airborne spaces "seep into this world like viruses into a technological body. They remind audiences that desire, the fusion of bodies, and sexual fantasies are also among the forces that drive our lives, beyond the ambient digital madness."[33] Don Shewey's analysis highlights the performance's interplay and interrelationships between time and space, as well as what he interprets as its disquieting message on globalization:

The disorienting nature of air travel, how it merges all time and all space, and how that serves as a metaphor for the contemporary experience of our high-tech, plugged-in world. . . . Its 26 strange little experiments in time, perspective and technology add up to a savvy, multidimensional snapshot of the world as we're living it right now. . . . The piece conveys the restlessness and longing that goes with contemporary travel in tableaux as timely as a hip-hop remix and timeless as a Hopper painting. The lounge singer morphs into a Zulu warrior wearing the same makeup and carrying the same spear and shield we've seen in a corny colonialist in-flight movie—an image that contains both the comforting cliché that "we're all connected" and a critique of that cliché, suggesting that we also carry around partially digested, media-distorted understandings of one another's culture.[34]

Extratemporality

Theory and criticism in digital arts and performance, as well as artists' own self-reflections, are replete with explanations and analyses of how works "explore," "challenge," "reconfigure," or "disrupt" notions of time. The validity of such analyses are not in doubt. But we would like to extend these sometimes hazy and capricious ideas of temporal disruption to theorize areas of digital art and performance from the distinct viewpoint of the *extratemporal*. In some ways, this borrows ideas at play within postmodern theory, but postmodernism generally emphasizes the *atemporal*—a negatively configured "nontime" of contemporary experience—rather the more ancient, quasi-Jungian understandings of *extratemporal*. The extratemporal relates back to prehistoric (and well as some modernist) notions of time, in the way, for example, that Claude Lévi-Strauss conceptualized societies that "refuse to accept history" as operating "with reference to a mythic order that is itself *outside time*."[35] This idea that certain societies or practices operate according to an extratemporal order lends itself well to an understanding of much digital arts practice, particularly where time is a central theme or metaphor. The prevailing theoretical wind, which perceives and celebrates artistic explorations of time in terms of ruptures and disjunctions, provides one important perspective; but the idea that they may operate within a system moving outside of time (at least conceptually and metaphorically) opens a different and equally fertile analytical terrain.

For us, extratemporality has been a defining feature of Richard Foreman's unique brand of theatrical performance art for over thirty years. Foreman has held ideas of time and its suspension at the ontological center of his Ontological-Hysteric Theater. An early experimenter with video in his work in the late 1960s and early 1970s, Foreman nowadays uses little or no video or recorded visual media, although complex audio soundscapes and live microphone voices provide key mediatized elements in his works. His bizarre, intoxicating, and life-affirming performances use "Heideggerian notions of meditative thinking, which attempts to allow the thingness of things to be unconcealed."[36] As in Robert Wilson's work, highly stylized and ritualized acting performances, slow-motion movements, and repetition all contribute to a sense of time's disruption. But Foreman's work is far more manic, Dadaist, and comic than Wilson's, exciting a quite different sense of extratemporal dreamscape and dream-time. In *Maria del Bosco* (2000) a disorienting type of "madness" is set up through processions of strange or sinister characters, short scenes and *tableaux vivants* played with Gothic intensity, and Foreman's trademark densely crammed and cramped design and visuals including oversize surrealistic costumes and props (figure 21.4). It ends with a tour de force sequence of controlled hysteria combining a hypnotic and insistent soundtrack, extreme, stylized movement and repetitive

Figure 21.4 Richard Foreman's theatrical aim to suspend temporality is explored in his Ontological-Hysteric Theater productions such as *Maria del Bosco* (2000). Photo: Paula Court.

dramatic climaxes. Throughout the sequence, at the back of the stage a performer pulls out a long, horizontal board about ten feet long and four feet wide. He then quickly pushes the board back into a gap in the set and out of view. This action is continually repeated in a fast, sawing motion about once every five seconds. Writ large on the board are the words: "Resist the Present."

Influenced by, and following the lead of Gertrude Stein, Foreman tries to induce, by artistic means, a highly attentive type of suprareal consciousness (which he calls "semi-conscious") that opens for the spectator a sense of a continuous present tense.[37] In multi-media theater and dance, the bombardment of different time-based projections working in conjunction with the live bodies of performers is frequently used to similar ends, that is, to disrupt cognition of time's linearity to achieve moments (and particularly climactic moments) of extratemporal "catharsis." Dumb Type's theatre typifies this approach, as do the theatre productions of La Fura Dels Baus, such as *F@ust version 3.0* (1998), one of their performances for a traditional theater space and a seated (rather than their normal promenade) audience. In their interpretation of the Faust legend, the company consciously draw on and attempt to extend Goethe's exploration of time through the multimedia projections. Within the projected back-wall screen in front of the live actors, different sized video images are digitally composited to coexist within the same black frame, but the footage, including possessed faces, bloodsoaked men, women taking showers, and raging hellfire, runs at different speeds. Then, as furious TV channel switching gives way to errant spirits, and other magical or disturbing screen imagery:

time stops (Faust's dream), or time is deconstructed and is superimposed (Margarita Mix) or time slows down (spirit). . . . A fluid relationship between actor and projections has been created. At times their body becomes a screen, at others their real body is a projection, at others their real shadow is a projection. It is this body-screen-projection relationship, where the most important step in the search for digital theatre has been made.[38]

Time's pliability has always been fundamental to performance's ontology, whether in traditional, avant-garde, or digital forms. Not only do audiences "accept" the symbolic time-space of the stage (such as the eleventh-century Scottish castle in *Macbeth*), but it has long been understood that a captive audience's sense of time is profoundly affected and manipulated in relation to the pace, dynamics, and drama of the unfolding event. In digital and multimedia theater, the same holds true, of course. But the juxtaposition of different "simultaneous" temporalities (live and recorded/computer rendered) can complicate the audience's perceptions of time and space to the extent that rather than simply "suspending disbelief" and experiencing performance time according to traditional passive protocols of live theater, a different perception of extratemporality is experienced. The screen spaces operate to significantly alter scenic temporality in the way that Emmanuel Levinas argues in *Le Temps et l'autre* (1991) that time does not operate according to "a singular and isolated subject . . . rather it is the very relation of a subject with others."[39] Or as Roberts Blossom wrote in 1966 reflecting on the use of film projection in theater as a "past experience presented as present,"[40]

To combine a present experience (stage) which, though rehearsed, nevertheless has the touch element, with a past experience (film), presented as present, is thus to combine the unconscious (recorded) with the conscious (present). . . . Time thus, perhaps for the first time in theatre, becomes present as a spatial element. . . . Dangerous mystical play—to turn time to space and touch to fantasy and then to compare the two. Our presence as bodies begins to be suspect, our presence as consciousness more real.[41]

Freezing Time: Uninvited Guests

In the late nineteenth century, Henri Bergson's *Matter and Memory* (1896) provided an important and highly influential study of the flux of time as the fundamental element of metaphysics. His notion that "what I call 'my present' has one foot in my past, and another in the future"[42] became an inspiration and aphorism for many modernist artists. This was despite the fact, as Michael Rush points out, that Bergson himself disdained technological intervention into the arts "believing that the pure perception allowed by intuition, unaided by machines, was what mattered."[43] Martin Heidegger also famously mistrusted the imprisoning effects of machines on consciousness, and his epic study of *Being and Time* (1927) elaborated Bergson's theme to hold time's impossibility of capture as a central tenet of *Dasein* (Being) and philosophical thought. But a type of capturing of time—that is to say, freezing "the present"—is a simple computational task, at least in terms of capturing a frame of a moving image, and has been used in digital performance to great strategic and temporal effect. Sometimes the effect is atemporal, but at others it is distinctly and significantly extratemporal.

Uninvited Guests' theater performance *Film* (2000) is a brilliant example, placing Bergsonian feet in the past and the future and repeating a freeze effect with such hypnotic repetition that even Heidegger's great truth of time's impossible capture seems (if only momentarily) a suddenly shaky proposition. The performance locates film as a repository of memory and nostalgia, and its devising process included interviewing people at cinemas about their memories of film images and sequences, which are incorporated into the piece. *Film*'s publicity material describes a "theatre made for camera but not recorded; a bastard theatre obsessed with the movies." Set in a private club some time in the future when films have been banned, lost, or destroyed, the performers recall, invent, and enact sequences from movies.

A digital video camera and a hand-held miniature surveillance camera relay the live action onto a television monitor and a large screen, upstage center. In the first section, the four performers take turns talking through a microphone to describe different openings to what we assume will be "their" film. The first performer begins: "The first sensation you have is that something is about to go awry" and goes on distractedly to try to piece together conflicting opening images and scenarios. He describes a cityscape, an explosion, aliens invading earth, a submarine in distress, a love affair. Fragments of film music and sound effects drift in and out as the other performers offer alternate ideas: a man driven crazy by war fever; a slasher movie scenario; a scene where a man chokes to death when force-fed a pie made from his children. As descriptions of scenes become more specific, the audience gradually realises these are images from actual films: a character asking to be punched from *Fight Club* (1999), the discovery of a tin under an oak tree from *The Shawshank Redemption* (1994).

In the second section, one performer relates the story of the climax to a film; two of the performers act out its key dramatic moments; and the fourth films them, with the live footage relayed onto the main projection screen. The sequence is the end of a what appears to be a formulaic gangster movie, where a male protagonist is pursued and shot, and his lover runs to the scene, screaming, and finally cradles him in her arms as he dies (it is actually based on the ending of the movie *12 Monkeys* (1995). The visual sequence onstage begins with her throwing off her coat in order to run faster. The camera operator, Thomas, says "Ready" and the woman swings her coat violently into the air. At the point it leaves her hand, Thomas presses the "photographic still" button on the digital video camera and the image is frozen on the screen. The freeze-frame is perfectly composed (the timing between the actors and cameraman has been meticulously rehearsed), and full of dynamic energy: her distorted, angled body at full stretch, the blurred coat caught as a violent swirl in midair. The image recalls the "motion captured in stasis" of futurist chronophotography (figure 21.5).

The male protagonist, wearing an oversized false moustache, sunglasses, and a Hawaiian shirt, then prepares for his frozen image. Thomas returns the camera to "live," and it relays live pictures once more. Then he calls "Ready." The actor points his gun, takes a short step, and lunges aggressively toward the camera. With the actor in an intense, looming close-up, the "still" button is pressed once again, at the point of greatest movement and dramatic impact (figure 21.6). The sequence continues in this pattern of movie stills, as the narrator describes the action. Thomas holds the camera at arm's length to take a close-up still of his own face as one of the pursuing policemen. The girlfriend is captured in freeze-frame running and screaming "No!" Three separate stills are set up and recorded on screen to depict the protagonist being gunned down, each from a different angle to mirror the way in which cinema often maps out and elongates such climactic sequences (figure 21.7). In the first, his body twists as the bullet hits, and his arms splay out in a painful gesticulation. The second freezes him as his body is about to hit the ground; the third as he collapses, rolling over. As the narrator relates that "this all happens in a kind of slow motion," his girlfriend arrives and bursts a blood bag on his chest, and the camera captures a beautiful and poignant close-up still of the lovers' hands entwined, covered in blood. A series of frozen close-up face shots are taken to emphasize their tragic

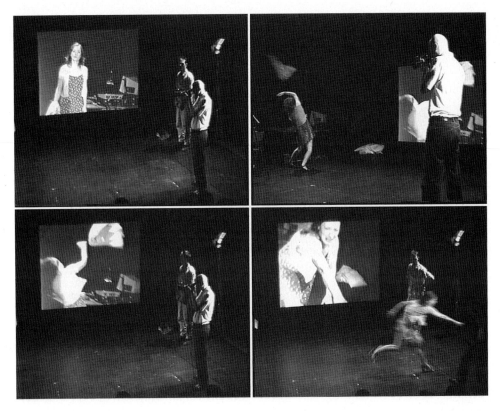

Figure 21.5 Screen images of blurred movement and dramatic action redolent of futurist chronophotography are employed during the opening of the "freeze-frame" sequence in Uninvited Guests' *Film*. Video captures courtesy of Uninvited Guests.

love, followed by a profile medium shot of the couple. A still image is captured with the protagonist's arm in mid-motion as it drops from a final caress of her hair. Onstage, the arm hits the floor with a thud to signify his moment of death. In her anguish, his lover suddenly makes a tearful head turn, and the still freezes her face and hair in tragic, quite perfect, dramatic motion (figure 21.8).

The onstage action is a well-worn postmodern theater pastiche of a film genre: an affectionate and charming movie homage, told through microphone-mediated narration and melodramatic, tongue-in-cheek performance reconstruction. But its use of the digital video camera's "photographic still" facility renders it powerful and memorable on a number of levels. The relationship between the live onstage action and its onscreen video relay is violently ruptured in the discontinuity of the suddenly frozen moments. But this continual and systematic rupturing of the time-flow adds strength and poignancy to both the stage

Figure 21.6 Climactic moments are captured as screen stills as the male character lunges toward camera, and is then hit by a bullet.

and the screen action. On screen, the temporal stage action is "there," is present as a synchronous mediatized echo of the live; but then suddenly the action's place in linear time is lost, it becomes absent. In its place is a still photographic record of a moment, synchronous with the real-time stage action at the moment of the digital click, but now suspended in time within the screen space, as the stage time moves on and completes the action. The formalist repetition of this cycle—the camera constantly being switched back to live continuous time, only for its flow to be interrupted by yet another still—is key to its temporally disconcerting, but highly arresting and pleasurable effect. The spectator becomes accustomed to the pattern and how the technique operates, and begins to anticipate the moment the photo-still button will be pressed. This generates a cycle of growing intensity shared by both the performers and the audience, leading up to the freeze-frame moment; and followed by a sense of release and satisfaction as the crucial, climactic point in dramatic time is captured in a highly aesthetic and invariably dramatic digital movie still.

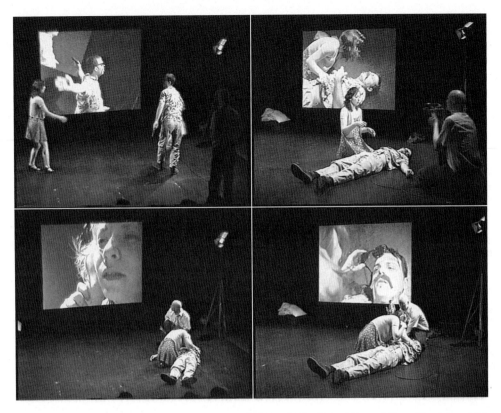

Figure 21.7 The freeze-frames on screen continually interrupt the flow of the real time video relay of the live action in Uninvited Guests' *Film*. This disrupts the "continuous present tense" of the live performance to punctuate the climactic moments of dramatic action and to excite extratemporal effects that are both disorientating and pleasurable.

Prior to the clicking of the photo-button, both stage and screen action operate together in real-time, in the present. But the freezing of the present, which in the image's stationary form immediately reverts it into the past, locates the live continuation of the performers' actions not only in the continuous present, but also in the future (of the trajectory of the still image, which becomes the central theatrical sign). The cyclical pattern of anticipation as each tableau is set up and executed also repetitively shifts and locates the audience's attention to the future—the point of miniclimax when the button will be pressed. The theater action is thus but a prelude and prologue to the all-important photographic moment. The theatrical action does not, first and foremost, serve liveness; but the immense satisfaction and dramatic impact of the bringing to life of stillness. Theater is sutured through the digital video camera to switch the fluid, continual

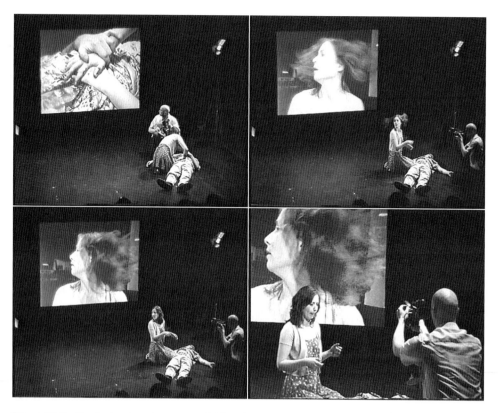

Figure 21.8   The final, poignant moments of *Film*'s freeze-frame sequence mix movie clichés with a techno-theatrical sense of the extratemporal.

becoming of the theatrical present to the nostalgic, solid, classical image of the recorded past: the movie still.

Lyotard, like Heidegger before him, notes the cruel paradox of time whereby the present, in continual motion, can never be finally tangible or held: "As the representing present is absolute, it is not graspable: it is neither *not yet* present, or *no longer* present. It is always too early or too late to perceive the representation itself."[44] *Film* attempts a digital compromise to hint at least at a theatrical squaring of the circle of time, to enable the audience to *grasp*, if only as an electronic visual image, the climactic dramatic moments passing through the continuous present. It echoes and evokes Walter Benjamin's notion in his "Theses on the Philosophy of History" (1936) that "to articulate the past historically . . . means to seize hold of a memory as it flashes up at a moment of danger."[45] It is a clever, knowing, and communal ritual to suspend the sense of time: conjured by the performers, anticipated by the audience, and finally and repeatedly delivered to both.

At the end of *Film*, the narrator describes another movie where a man with amnesia is shown an old Super 8 home movie to try to rekindle his dormant memories. She recounts how atmospheric the footage was, and how the lack of sound on the Super 8 made it deeply emotive and evocative. She says it was particularly moving because of her own memories of her father shooting Super 8 footage of her as a child and, she concludes, "it takes you back." The freeze-frame device in *Film* is used to stunning effect to tangibly suspend a sense of time and "take the audience back" to moments that occurred immediately before, in front of them in real-time. The freeze-frame is the star of the performance: activating, evoking and *enacting* the piece's pervading themes of memory, nostalgia, and time.

Pausing Time

In similar narrative vein, Forced Entertainment and Hugo Glendinning's CD-ROM pastiche of the clichés of movie thrillers and film noir, *Spin* (1999) also makes poignant use of the frozen moment. In a recurring final scene of a dying man surrounded by a circle of gunmen, the moment before his death is "held on perpetual pause, in the final frame of the movie in which he realises he will die, but in which death is not yet manifest"[46] (figure 21.9). The use of a digital snapshot to interrupt and suspend a continuous flow of video imagery is also a feature of Isabelle Jenniches's collaborative performance project *Klein Getijden Boek* (1998).[47] STEIM Imag/Ine software superimposes live-camera video projections of a dancer onto both prerecorded material and "almost-live" sequences (captured moments earlier) to destabilize temporal sense and to periodically freeze particular moments. The performance itself explores and updates ideas of the medieval Books of Hours, where prayers were linked to different times of the day as a way to structure daily life.

Freeze-frames feature in the distinctly extratemporal *Yours* (2000, choreographed by Nik Haffner), where Polish composer Jaroslav Kapuscinski plays the musical keyboard of

Figure 21.9 The bloody climax of Tim Etchells/ Hugo Glendinning and Forced Entertainment's CD-ROM *Spin* (1999).

a Disklavier, with each MIDI note manipulating video footage of Frankfurt Ballett dancer Antony Rizzi, which is projected on a hanging screen above the instrument. Kapuscinski's music plays with both the image of the dancer and with time, dramatically sending the image of Rizzi's naked body forward and backward, pausing it, and advancing it frame by frame. Percussive sounds and a female voice reading from Beckett's *Texts for Nothing* (1958) add to the performance's effect, and at the end, Kapuscinski invites audience members to stay behind and come on stage to "play the dancer."[48]

A single freeze-frame is used to dramatic effect in Curious.com's multimedia theater production *Three Semi-Automatics Just For Fun* (1997), which takes place within a box-set, with projection screens standing in for the walls. The two-woman company (Helen Paris and Leslie Hill) explore the symbolism of guns through their trademark mix of the personal and political, the poetic and the comic. One sequence typifies their relaxed and intimate multimedia theater aesthetic. Hill sits in a spotlight downstage right, and the side-wall screen shows video footage of a middle-aged woman sitting in a neat study with the caption "Leslie's mother." Paris stands with her back to the audience in a pool of light upstage left, the side-wall next to her playing footage of "Helen's mother." The two middle-class, middle-aged women (the performers' actual mothers) talk on screen about the joys of shooting guns, like a male gun-fanatic might, their dialogue wholly incongruous with their appearances and voices. Paris's mother stands in a kitchen, cutting potatoes, and addresses the camera to explain enthusiastically in her very proper English accent: "Potatoes explode well when hit with a .22 bullet." Hill's American mother sits in profile holding a gun and makes large arm gestures as though repeatedly firing it as she maintains that: "You will have to keep shooting and shooting and shooting and shooting until you are sure that he is no longer a threat." The center screen runs a live video relay close-up of Paris as she slowly turns her head to look over her shoulder behind her (and toward us), her expression intense. As she does so, Hill's quiet, calm voiceover asks: "Have you ever felt vulnerable at home, alone at night? Do you remember to lock your car doors? Have you ever had the feeling that you were being watched, or followed?" As Paris's head reaches the final, stretched point of its neck rotation, a freeze-frame locks the video image of her look: a sudden moment of recognition that there is something, or someone, in the shadows. The Voice continues: "And how did that make you feel?"

Time Passing

We do not suggest, by any means, that all digital performances are characterized by an extratemporal order, and many operate in distinct relation to the calendar and chronometric processes. For example, the natural passage of time was performatively marked daily over an entire year for Troika Ranch's *Yearbody for Solo Dancer and Internet* (1996). The company posted a Web image of a dancer in different movement shapes each day from 1 November 1996 to 31 October 1997, the moves and phrases being progressively developed over the period. With the final posting, the solo dance was complete, and the 365 images could finally be seen as a choreographic animation. Trends in digital performance archiving and CD-ROMs are often conceived in precise relation to traditional, chronological notions of time, and the instinct to preserve the past for the posterity of the present and the future. The explosion of library and museum digitization projects in the 1990s (a phase that has since slowed down), and the proliferation of data storage on the Web attest to the computer's role in preserving and organising historical materials (or at least its images and texts), and commentators point to how archives and databases have become a distinct new cultural form.[49] Meanwhile, digital performances present many distinctly nostalgic projects tracing, and in another sense "archiving" the "real time" of history.

The George Coates Performance Works' *Blind Messengers* (1998) is what Coates describes as "a multimedia music-theatre homage to the artistry of early California and a harbinger of creativity to come."[50] Staged outdoors in front of the huge Constitution wall of the Sacramento Golden State Museum, it celebrates the history of public art in California, from early native American cave paintings to contemporary murals, massive images of which are projected onto the wall (figure 21.10). As a large choir sings, a digital clock

Figure 21.10 The performers appear as tiny figures as history sweeps by above them in George Coates' *Blind Messengers* (1998).

Figure 21.11 The past, the present, the future, and time-travel are all celebrated in *Blind Messengers.*

displays the date 26 September 1498 and moves forward to the same date in 1998 (the day before the premiere). Computer and film projections of fog, hail, rain, and sleet then simulate the wall's aging and decay, until a lightning bolt appears to hit the wall and a flock of birds fly out. Film projections of a "choir from the future" then appear to scale the wall and undertake repairs in preparation for celebrations of its three hundredth anniversary in 2298, and an archaeologist from 2298 appears as a video projection, making a time-travel conference call to the 1998 audience. He explains that he is coordinating the wall's three hundredth anniversary celebrations, but has no historic image of its hundredth anniversary in 1998 to include, and asks the audience to smile for a wide-angle photograph. As flash-bulbs pop and the orchestra and choir reach a climactic finale, the audience members watch a live video image of themselves (figure 21.11).

The historical past and its trajectory into the future is likewise traced in AlienNation Co.'s *Migbot* (1998). The audience travels slowly through four different spaces, in what the company describe as "chrono-topic" time, "a slow progression from place to place . . . [that] requires time shifts (from past to future, future to present)."[51] In the first space, a translation of a recording by Cosmonaut Generico Vespucci taken from the recovered black-box flight recorder of the disintegrated MIRAK space station is played. In the second, space objects that feature in an unfinished opera written by Vespucci are displayed, and in the third, the audience encounters the opera's "first virtual, reconstructed Act"

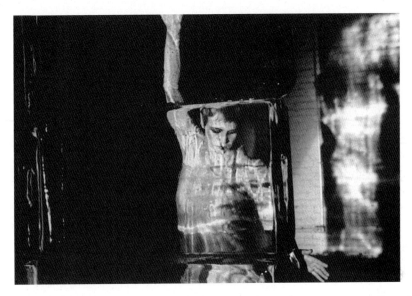

Figure 21.12 Outer space, inner space, opera, dance, and "chrono-topic" time are all explored in AlienNation Co.'s *Migbot* (1998).

performed by Angeles Romero and Olga Kinna (figure 21.12). The audience makes its way onto the roof for the final section of *Migbot*, where they peer through a telescope aimed at the radiating light of a molecular cloud approaching a neutron star. While exploring theoretical territories concerned with astronomical chirality theory and molecular asymmetry, conceptualizations of both space and time are analyzed and catalyzed from the inner (such as Vespucci's internalizations on the black-box recording and the spaces inside of the building) to the outer (Vespucci's opera is for the first time externalized; the audience goes outside the building and literally looks into outer space).

In interactive installation settings, the visitor's own passing of time within it is commonly captured, played back, and visually and temporally distorted. Japanese artist Toshio Iwai's *Another Time, Another Space* (1993) uses four video cameras to record museum visitors looking at images of themselves on a configuration of eight video monitors. Four monitors are positioned in television's conventional 4 × 3 landscape shot, and four are at 90 degrees, giving a 3 × 4 portrait shot (although the video image remains conventionally straight, rather than on its side). Eight computers process the video images and send a separate, different manipulated image to each of the monitors. The digital modifications for each monitor change over specific periods of time, but during one ten-minute period we studied, the different images displayed were as follows (each cycle repeats, time durations are approximate):

Time

Monitor 1   displays the real-time video image for one second, then the same image in reverse motion for one second.

Monitor 2   captures a four-second video sequence and plays it twenty times in rapid (×5) forward motion.

Monitor 3   plays the real-time image for three seconds, then repeats the same sequence in forward slow (×2) motion, then repeats it again in reverse (×2) slow motion.

Monitor 4   normal speed, but with a two-second delay from the live action, using a ripple effect to distort the image, so that bodies appear in snakelike shapes, like in a fun-fair distorting mirror.

Monitor 5   a real-time image, the screen split into four equal horizontal sections, although this is only apparent when a spectator moves, at which time their head, torso, upper legs/hips, and lower legs appear to separate from each other.

Monitor 6   operates in real time, and renders huge diagonal distortions of movement so that when a spectator moves across the space, their body appears like a thin, flowing liquid form across one diagonal of the screen.

Monitor 7   a real-time image, but with a number of video frames edited out of each, in varying patterns, so that movement appears strange, stuttering, and staccato.

Monitor 8   captures and plays a half-second sequence in real time, then repeats it in (×3) slow motion.

The installation harks back to and significantly extends many analog video art precedents that disoriented the viewers sense of time by relaying surveillance footage out of real time, such as Frank Gillette and Ira Schneider's 1969 *Wipe Cycle* and Dan Graham's *Present Continuous Past(s)* (1974). Iwai's *Another Time, Another Space* is a playful and genuinely fascinating development of this form of time-disrupting surveillance art, which, like Paul Sermon's *Telematic Dreaming* (1992), has been on permanent display for many years at the National Museum of Film and Photography in Bradford, England. And just like Sermon's installation, it is a particular delight for children who run, jump, spin, and gesture in order to see some spectacular temporal and spatial transformations of their actions.

David Rokeby's *Watch* (1995) installation similarly centers on temporal manipulation and gallery visitors watching camera recordings of themselves, with two projections placed side by side on a wall in the installation. One of the projections only renders a clear picture of visitors who are still, while moving people appear as foggy blurs, creating an effect akin to the long-exposure chronophotography of the futurists. The second projection operates in a reverse strategy: people are only clear if they are moving, they "float as outlines in a dimensionless black void, and disappear again as soon as they are still."[52] The sense of a simultaneous distortion and suspension of time (enhanced by the soundtrack of a watch, a clock and a heartbeat) that the dual images ignite is particularly interesting because, unlike Iwai's installation, both of Rokeby's images are actually live, and computer-processed in real time. As he observes,

One of the most striking sensations I have experienced while working with interactive technologies is the sensation of sculpting time itself. When working in more traditional time-based work such as film and video, the artist places events along a linear time line. Because I work with real-time behaviours in my work, I am no longer just positioning events, but defining the texture and flow of time itself. *Watch* is a reflection of such altered experiences of time and movement.[53]

Conclusion

In *Physics*, Aristotle stresses the reciprocity between time and movement: "Not only do we measure movement by time, but also time by movement."[54] Agacinski develops the theme in her seminal study of time, adopting the concept of *passage* as her central metaphor, and exploring its relationship to philosophy and metaphysics: "Being itself is no longer beyond time, or outside of time, that is, eternal; it exists in its own *passage*."[55] In multimedia performance where live bodies operate simultaneously with their prerecorded doubles, the passage of time is also doubled as past and present passages are visually (screen) and physically (stage) enacted. In doing so, performances engage with what Agacinski describes as the perennial philosophical problem and feat of "being in time and surmounting its temporality"; of reorientating consciousness to be "capable of simultaneously existing in time and recalling its own past."[56]

Finally, we would highlight how the new digital mantra *real time* semantically asserts the liveness of computational operation and rendering to the extent of privileging it over ordinary, common-or-garden "time." At precisely the same time that ideas of the real collapsed within cultural theory, they were quickly resuscitated within computer theory and its attendant jargon not only through the new virtual reality, but in a celebrated, triumphal wedding of an *ingenue* real with old father time. A jargonized marriage of convenience perhaps, but the conceit is significant nonetheless in suggesting a differentiated temporality from its quotidian equivalent. The commonly slowed down or speeded up projection images of multimedia theater and performance *play* with time, but we suggest their signification has long since ceased to mean "time slowed down" or "time speeded up," but rather "out of time." As civilization's temporality appears to be running helter-skelter into the jaws of the abyss, the dialectical twin pulls the other way, putting a brake on the tempo to pull it back to the center. The contrapuntal elements of intense live performance and temporally altered digital imagery sparks a feeling, not of time standing still or going backward or forward, but of the extratemporal—of stepping to one side or outside of time.

At the same time, the relative real times of computers and humans do not always see eye to eye and hit it off. In *Hacking the Future* (1996) Arthur and Marilouise Kroker recount an experiment in the mid-1990s in Montreal where programmers attempted to image sequence the fast and frenetic movements of dance company La La La Human Steps. The idea was to use graphical 3D image processors to capture the action, make android-like modifications within the computer, and then send the images back in a real-time recombitant loop. But the company, one of the fastest and high-intensity of techno dance troupes, worked at such explosive speed that as "vague vectors of speed bodies" flew across the screen, the banks of image processors malfunctioned, there were random electronic discharges, and finally,

Confused and angry and repulsed and humiliated, the image banks crashed and crashed and crashed. On that day, at least, the will to virtuality had met its bodily match in some possessed dancers from La La La Human Steps who just couldn't be stuffed into the machines for future mounting. Human Species—1; Digital Reality—0[57]

Memory

Throughout the 19th and 20th centuries photography and its adjacent imaging tools functioned as a social time capsule, enabling the collective presentation of memory of our social bodies. At the end of the 20th century, however, we witness a global inflation of the image and the erasure by digital technologies of the sacred power of the photograph as truth. Today we can no longer trust the representational nature of the image. . . . The present condition allows us to change the configuration of our skin. . . . With the ability to change flesh and image also comes the possibility of erasure of their memory.

—EDUARDO KAC[1]

Memory and Theory

The complex of practices and means by which the past invests the present is memory: memory is the present past.

—RICHARD TERDIMAN[2]

Personal memory has been a central and abiding theme of modern art, as well as of theater and performance particularly since the 1960s, where autobiography has been a much-mined resource. In "The Self As Text" (1979), Bonnie Marranca argues that the exploration of the artist's autobiography or personal mental space is a characteristic feature of postmodern performance, which she terms "a dialogue with the self." The self as source and the centrality of personal memory to contemporary performance has also been discussed by Richard Schechner, who describes the use of autobiography as text as an articulation of the performers' "consciousness of his own consciousness."[3] George Steiner has reflected that a sense of the past is intensely important to us, because we fear a new dark age and through a guilty feeling of having squandered a utopia:

Behind today's posture of doubt and self-castigation stands the presence, so pervasive as to pass largely unexamined, of a particular past, of a specific "golden time". . . . It is not the literal past that rules us, it is images of the past. Images and symbolic constructs of the past are imprinted, almost in the manner of genetic information, on our sensibility.[4]

The pervading postmodern concern with memory and nostalgia constitutes the central argument in Norman Denzin's incisive analysis of 1980s cinema, *Images of Postmodern Society* (1991), and has been discussed by numerous critics including Wendy Wheeler who defines "Postmodernity as Mourning and Melancholia."[5] Postmodern retrospection is closely aligned to the recyclable, permanently accessible visual archives of cinema, television, and digital media. For Steven Connor, "the enlargement of these mnemonic resources cooperates closely with the alleged debilitation of memory or contraction of attention-span in the contemporary world."[6] Connor goes on to pose a rhetorical question:

when the world has developed such a faculty for prosthetic recollection, in the vast and versatile random-access-memory of contemporary information and reproductive technology, what further need is there to correlate the memory and time-span of the individual subject with that of the culture as a whole, or think any longer of the memory of a culture in terms of that individual subject?[7]

Interestingly, recent theories of memory clash angrily between notions of contemporary society's amnesia and its obsessions with memory and mnemonics. For Baudrillard, "there was history, but there isn't any more,"[8] and so now "forgetting is as essential as the event."[9] Artificial memories replace historical and human ones: "One no longer makes the Jews pass through the crematorium or the gas chamber, but through the sound track and image track, through the universal screen and the microprocessor."[10] Tactile thrills and posthumous emotions are elicited in an artificial, mediated memory of the Holocaust, as a televised event, with the Jews cast as televised objects. Neither is there any room for memory in Frederic Jameson's conception of the schizophrenic postmodern subject living an amnesiac "series of pure and unrelated presents in time" in a technologized world founded on "the structural exclusion of memory."[11] Andreas Huyssen's *Twilight Memories: Marking Time in a Culture of Amnesia* (1995) follows Jameson's line up to a point, but argues that "the virus of amnesia that at times threatens to consume memory itself" has paradoxically led to what he terms "mnemonic fever."[12] While Jameson conceives that "memory has been weakened in our time, and that the great rememberers are a virtually extinct species," Huyssen underlines how the fear of amnesia has actually rebounded to ignite "a memory boom of unprecedented proportions."[13]

Roger Luckhurst's "Memory Recovered/Recovered Memory" highlights the contrasting positions, but is keen to put Jameson's views in context. He notes that in 1984, the same year that Jameson published *Postmodernism*, Pierre Nora began his collaborative eight year, seven-volume study *Lieux de Mémorie* (*Sites of Memory*), and the following year leading German intellectuals undertook an extensive debate on the legacy of Nazism in the *Historikerstreit* (the historians' dispute). In the 1980s too, ideas of recovered memory in psychotherapy developed a wholly different model from the schizophrenic subject proposed by cultural criticism. "Didn't Jameson's amnesiac contemporary entirely miss this extensive memory-work?" Luckhurst asks. "Over a decade later, it seems that memory has been recovered from a paradigm that failed to see its insistent presence."[14] Nonetheless, like Nora himself, who states that "we speak so much of memory because there is so little of it left,"[15] Luckhurst is forced to agree with Jameson's central notion of a society structured towards forgetfulness. But he points out that although theory has tended to blame technology's role in accelerating amnesia, it should not be forgotten that memory is not necessarily redemptive:

Memory can tyrannically blind you and impose a determining identity you might wish to resist; active forgetting can be a liberation from the dead weight of memorial history. . . . To track the vicissitudes of contemporary memory it is vital to sustain the ambivalence of working between hypermnesia (too much memory) and amnesia (too little).[16]

Luckhurst concludes his examination of the contemporary crisis between the terrors of too little or too much memory by examining psychotherapy's use of recovered memory and the consequent discovery of the false memory syndrome. He suggests, "the desire to stabilise memory as either true or false is an anxiety induced by a forgetfulness that the history of memory itself twists and turns, is subject to constant mutations and revisions."[17]

Theatricalizing Memory Recall

In 1966, Trisha Brown danced with a film projector strapped to her back, sweeping footage of herself dancing all around the space (*Homemade*, 1966) (figure 22.1). During a retrospective of her work thirty years later in 1996, this duet between past and present was repeated when Brown donned the projector again and danced while the same 1966 footage beamed out in all directions.[18] In the first performance, past and present met, but since the two images appeared visually to be of the "same" Trisha Brown, the *media* was the primary element that separated her live and recorded forms. In the second, the crucial factor differentiating the two dancers was no longer media, but *time*. The film footage in the first performance represented another, alternate Brown dancing within the same space; in the second performance, it constituted a striking and unambiguous *memory* of Brown: a quite different woman, no longer her double, but a manifestation of her in the distant past. For Johannes Birringer, the 1996 performance was "an unforgettable recuperation of a lost memory, the loss of memory,"[19] and like Richard Terdiman's theoretical notion

Figure 22.1 Trisha Brown and Lance Gries in the 1966 version of *Homemade*. Photo: Vincent Pereira.

of memory as *Present Past* (1993), Brown's performance registers how often and how "suddenly memory does not ground us—it rather registers our drift."[20]

The members of the British theater group Talking Birds interview local people to recall their particular memories of places and reconfigure these for performance, as in *Undercurrent* (2000), which explores a series of recollections about the seafront and open-air ballroom at the seaside spa resort of Scarborough. Their *Girl With a Movie Camera* (1999) for the city of Coventry's Millennium Eve celebrations mixes original digital video with sixty years of archive film of the city, including evocative 1930s footage from the GPO Film Unit, in what the Evening Standard newspaper called "a time-warp fantasia." Their theater performance *Recent Past* (1998, with London Musici Trio) traces an erratic journey from the city to the coast using three video screens and a live music ensemble performing an original score (figure 22.2). An evocative and impressionistic piece, part narrative, part-documentary, the company describe it as being essentially "a consideration of memory." They reflect on how the imagery on the two side-screens operates in relation to the main center screen. In sometimes mirroring and complementing the central image, and at other times working in rhythmical counterpoint, they consider that "these smaller screens act as 'recent memories' of the film within the performance."[21]

"The fluid nature of the experience of a memory"[22] is what Andrea Polli describes as a central theme of her artworks and performances. *Fetish* (1996) juxtaposes real objects

Figure 22.2 The London Musici Trio are joined onstage by three video images to create an evocative and mnemonic musical rail journey in Talking Birds' *Recent Past* (1998). Photo: Janet Vaughan.

hanging from a glass ceiling and their virtual replications, and users operate touch-sensitive screens to activate Polli's own memories and stories associated with them. A collaborative development of the project *Fetish, May I Help You* (1997) includes a live cabaret performance, and audience members use small confessional boxes to record their own private fetishes on videotape. *Tight* (1997, with Louise McKissick and Barbara Droth) combines stereoscopic 3D-modeled virtual objects, and performers and audience members suspended in harnesses from the ceiling, to experiment with relationships between memory, body movement, and unusual physical sensation (figure 22.3). In viewing art and memory in distinct parallel, Polli's work foregrounds the digital realm and virtual objects as new repositories for memory and as an evocative, replicatory memory system. For Polli, both art and memory "employ and integrate the senses, both are representations, and both refer to a sense of timelessness."[23]

The personal memories of criminally insane prison inmates in Liverpool were documented by Graham Harwood and incorporated into his compelling CD-ROM *Rehearsal of Memory* (1995). Navigating over images of the tattooed bodies of the prisoners Harwood interviewed, disturbing and touching texts are uncovered. Body parts and police-style profile and full-face portraits of the inmates are inscribed with their life stories in a variety

Figure 22.3 Audience members view stereoscopic images, and are suspended in harnesses to excite different visual and bodily experiences of memory in Andrea Polli's *Tight* (1997, with Louise McKissick and Barbara Droth).

of text sizes and fonts. A typically harrowing example of one prisoner's memories includes the following:

My Dad's always been handy with his fists. Before I was born he used to box. He also used his fists on our family. . . . I was seven and I'd run away from home loads of times. I went in my Mam's bedroom and took her money. . . . I cut open my old appendix wound, stuck pins on the inside of the wound and swallowed a broken light bulb. . . . After my attempted suicide I didn't want to go home to my Dad. . . . I got hold of a syringe and injected mouthwash into my arm, hoping that it would enter a vein and that I would die.

In digital dance theater, a particular form of memory recall has become a physical process: calling up visual projections and audio outputs from computer memory triggered by performer's kinetic and gestural actions within a motion-sensing space. The tracking of dance movement in open space to activate computer memory is a truly extraordinary form of memory recall and relates closely to wider understandings of how human memory works. Marcel Proust, one of the greatest writers and chroniclers of memory, tells us, beautifully and unforgettably, how memory's stimulation is inextricably linked first and foremost to the physical senses (not "the reasoning mind"), to the very air around us. As Proust lovingly describes how "the greater part of our memory exists outside us, in a dampish breeze, in the musty air of a bedroom or the smell of autumn's first fires,"[24] a dancer now stretches out a hand into that same, utterly thin air, and the memory miraculously appears—and is "grasped." Among hundreds of examples are productions specifically centering on the memory theme such as the collaborative telematic dance performance *Memory* (2000)[25] presented on Arizona State University's "Intelligent Stage," which linked the movements of dancers to computer operations using Rokeby's *Very Nervous System* software. PPS Danse's *Strata, Memoirs of a Lover* (2000) uses dance, theater, and motion sensing digital projections to question "the relative nature of time," and tells the stories of the lives of a man and a woman through intimate memories that encapsulate periods of their lives.[26]

Memory and Trauma

In the first volume of *In Search of Lost Time* (1919), Proust famously sips a cup of limeblossom tea into which a *petite madeleine* cake has been dipped. He suddenly quivers, feels himself filled with the unmistakable "precious essence" of a forgotten memory, but agonizingly cannot fully recall it. In three sublime pages he struggles desperately, and finally succeeds. Just as digital performers appear to conjure cascades of images out of nothing more than a hand flick, so too do Proust's tastebuds, as his childhood memories literally flood out in a breathless, surging torrent:

Immediately the old grey house on the street, where her bedroom was, came like a stage set . . . and with the house the town, from morning to night and in all weathers, the Square, where they sent me before lunch, the street where I went to do errands, the paths we took if the weather was fine . . . all the flowers in our garden and in M. Swann's park, and the water-lilies on the Vivonne, and the good people of the village and their dwellings and the church and all of Combray and its surroundings, all of this which is assuming form and substance, emerged, town and garden alike, from my cup of tea.[27]

Digital performance may work in a literal fashion, like a movie, to re-create and present a memory in a clear visual or narrative form (like Proust's childhood village), but it may equally represent memory in more impressionistic or abstract terms. Just as recent theories of trauma memory and posttraumatic stress disorder have suggested that "it is not a memory at all, but an unwilled repetition of components of a traumatic event,"[28] performances may depict momentary flashbacks and transitory recollections (Proust's sensation of a memory triggered by the sip of tea, but not its actual recall)—parts rather than wholes. In doing so, they accord with understandings of how memory stores information not as a linear visual narrative, but in idiosyncratic "emotional sets." Specific memories are triggered through a stimulation of the emotional sets brought on by complementary mental or physical feelings or by external stimuli such as sights and smells. This paradigm is evident in Larry Hodges's *Virtual Vietnam* (2000), an art-cum-therapy virtual reality experience that allows veterans with posttraumatic stress disorder "to confront the experiences that led to their illness so that they can live more productively in this world."[29] Although the immersive pre-programmed views of paddy fields and swirling helicopters, and the sounds of rattling machine-gun fire cannot literally represent the user's memories, they operate mnemonically to reactivate and trigger emotional sets.

Norie Neumark's intense and poetic CD-ROM *Shock in the Ear* (1999) uses metaphors of trauma, and cultural and aesthetic shock in a series of hypermedia stories, performance clips, and soundscapes. Shocks and their aftermath are conceived by Neumark to be sensual and pleasurable experiences, particularly since they shift and dislocate our experience of time and space. She suggests that sound is particularly central to temporal shocks, and argues that the CD-ROM "expresses the shocking concept that sound is the medium most appropriate to interactivity, as a new and engaging artistic form, because sound goes beyond the interface, into time, into the body, and into imagination. . . . *Shock in the Ear* traces shock's dislocated time/space in which perceptions and senses are shifted."[30] Trauma, displacement, and sexual memories are the primary themes in AlienNation Co.'s dance-theater performance *Night Falls* (1997). The dancers' movements activate and manipulate the particular shapes, colors, and sounds of projections of stored "image-objects" that act as memories to interlink "present/presence and storage (past/memory) in a way that disturbs prioceptive relations between materiality, memory and virtuality."[31] The use of interactive systems to play with and reconfigure traditional dance concepts of "bodily memory," and to orient these towards related psychological and therapeutic models, has developed as a strong theme within the digital dance movement.

Contrary to Proust, Greg Ulmer maintains that the dominant catalyst for memory is movement or body posture, a physiological and "kinesthetic thinking . . . a reasoning by *Geschlect*."[32] This understanding of memory recall is at the heart of Stanislavskian methodologies of affective memory (or "emotion memory") whereby the actor conditions herself to trigger and recall a personal memory using physical gesture, which she uses mnemonically in performance in order to consistently stimulate authentic emotional feeling, night after night. The bodily memory recall so central to dance practice has been taken into another realm by one of Britain's leading digital dance troupes, Random Dance Company, which has been actively involved in body memory investigations as part of scientific neurological research. During 2003–2004, the company was involved with the Birmingham University Behavioural Sciences Centre's research into the relationship between brain functions and body memory, and how brain injuries or disease affect body movement and control. The dancers perform movement sequences wearing light-reflective body markers that are tracked using a video and computer motion-capture system. The same steps and phrases are then repeated with impediments such as the dancers being blindfolded or counting backward, and the data is computer-analyzed by the research team led by a professor of human movement, Alan Wing. He explains that the area of the brain responsible for body memory is highly developed in dancers and "by investigating expert dancers and elderly or disabled individuals who often have difficulties making even simple movements, we are better able to understand the brain's control of complex movement."[33]

Dumb Type's idiosyncratic theatrical investigation of memory and trauma *Memorandum* (1999–2000) is at times a harrowing theater-trauma in its own right, using sensory assaults combining flashing lights, rapidly edited projections, and fragmented live dance movements and narratives:

Amidst a cascade of white noise and REM-speed visual flashes . . . dancers drift in a slow sensual subconscious slidestep [*sic*] through the "forest of memory" haunted by voices and desires. Unnoticed by waking reason, a lone witness/observer records evidence of the scene and is repeatedly eliminated. Whereupon three figures cycle through three different accelerated subroutines of emotion. . . . Until finally, the dance emerges onto a primal oceanic frieze simultaneously flooded and exhausted of meanings.[34]

An open stage is split by a wide, translucent projection screen, behind which the performers sometimes work in silhouette, exploring "the hazy dimensions of recall that ground and disquietly erode our experience minute-by-minute"[35] (figure 22.4). Images of speed and travel (through both space and time) visually bombard as multimedia projections of blurred bodies run and dance frenetically in slow and fast-motion, trailing ghostly blurs and déjà vu aftereffects. The impact encapsulates Paul Virilio's theoretical vision of a virtualized world accelerating out of control, where "the loss of Material Space leads to the government of nothing but time. . . . The violence of speed has become both the location and the law, the world's destiny and *its destination*."[36] In one five-minute scene, the action on stage is complemented by four separate (side-by-side) prerecorded video projections of exactly the same scene. Each of these play at different speeds—slow-motion, very slow motion, fast motion, very fast motion—but are run and timed so that the scene's climax coincides on all four screens and live on stage. The audience thus experiences the scene through five different time frames simultaneously, and the effect is also a distinctly spatial one, as Kjell Petersen reflects: "Time has been stretched out and established as five parallel spatialities all going through the same actions and reaching for the same climax but at different pace. In this scene time becomes space-like and the stage setting becomes a montage of several simultaneous time-views spread out in space."[37]

Computer Memory and Human Amnesia

Art and technology critic Michael Rush maintains that "the art-and-technology marriage is perhaps the most ephemeral art of all: the art of time. A photograph is said to capture and preserve a moment of time; an image created inside a computer resides in no place

Figure 22.4 Complexities of time and memory theatrically converge in ways that are sometimes slow and subtle, and at others frenetic and violent in Dumb Type's *Memorandum* (1999). Photo Kazuo Fukunaga.

or time at all."[38] But we believe this is a widely held fallacy about computer memory and digital images, which, though arguably ghostly, are nonetheless physically contained and embodied in the bits, chips, software, and hardware of the computer; and network communication of them is indelibly traced and logged by Internet Service Providers (ISPs). Rather than "residing in no place or time" as Rush and others suggest, the embodiment of images and texts in the hardware and software of computer memory banks has meant that they now offer hard forensic evidence for the police, whose first port of call is commonly a suspect's computer. Computer experts can retrieve images and texts that have been deleted numerous times and can retrace steps taken on the Internet with absolute exactitude. Email, rather than an ephemeral gesture, is acknowledged to be one of the most permanent of all communication forms. The computer is nowadays designed first and foremost as a memory machine, although inevitably there are system failures and memory losses, like the one that occurs in Toni Dove's interactive VR experience *Archeology of a Mother Tongue* (1993, with Michael Mackenzie) (figure 22.5). A system crash simulating a power failure within its virtual city landscape provides a central narrative twist, whereby "interactors must press a retart button on their screen to resume, and then find

Figure 22.5 A user operates the frequently (and deliberately) crashing amnesiac VR installation *Archeology of a Mother Tongue* (1993, Toni Dove with Michael Mackenzie).

the city altered as if it had suffered a memory loss."[39] But more generally, and certainly in the case of networked communications, as Michael Punt observes, "electronic memories do not admit to forgetfulness . . . the conceit of electronic communication is that nothing can ever be forgotten . . . everything is recoverable at a mouse click without the aid of psychotherapy."[40]

This idea is dramatized in Curious.com's intimate and arresting theater performance *Random Acts of Memory* (1998), which highlights the way in which our faith in computational RAM as a memory repository may be gradually eroding human memory. "As we constantly upgrade our computer RAM where does the human mind and creativity fit in? Where can we access the G3-chip for our own cognition?" they ask. "Medieval scribes knew each line of copy—copyshop attendants are scarcely aware of what they copy at 135 copies per minute. Copying to disk requires no knowledge at all of the contents."[41] The two performers test their memories and are found wanting; they begin to claim the other's memories as their own; and the intricate and claustrophobic play of hesitant remembrance and anxious forgetfulness builds as they continually forget what they are about to say. "We use copies to certify originals, and originals to certify copies," one remarks. Their projected life-size digital doubles offer the only solace, as they increasingly ignore one another and communicate with the technology, their computational clones having a much firmer grip on who they are and what they have experienced in the past (figure 22.6).

Figure 22.6 Computational memory and her digital double constitute the only solace for Leslie Hill's amnesiac character in Curious.com's *Random Acts of Memory* (1998).

The performers finally turn on each other and fight, wrestling to assert their forgotten memories and identities. The fight takes place as recorded screen footage, with one live performer dancing to a techno-dance track while the ghostly digital double of the other appears on another scrim, looking awkward and confused as she checks her clothes and feet and straightens her hair. The music changes to a country and western song by Dolly Parton, and the screen imagery gives way to two still images of her face, surrounded by her vast buffon of blonde hair. A morphing software program slowly transforms Parton's hair and facial features; she sprouts animal ears and her hair becomes wool, as the face of Dolly the country singer metamorphoses into the head of Dolly the sheep, the first successfully cloned mammal. The sheep winks its right eye and morphs back into Parton's human visage. The performance ends with the performers flicking a switch to finally silence and shut down the technology. As the projection screens and stage lights stutter and black out, the two amnesiacs are left surrounded by darkness, their scared faces staring out at us, lit only by the tiny flames of two matches.

Memory Palaces

The computer has long been conceptualized as a memory bank, and the Internet provides endless imprints of personal, historical, informational, and commercial memories. When Ted Nelson coined the term *hypertext* in 1965, he conceived what he saw to be a dream of the creation of a "docuverse" containing and linking all the world's texts. The home computer and the Web are places where memories become preserved: supplanting family photo albums and oral histories with databases and webpages crammed with recollections, photographs and personal diaries. Perhaps the Web is the closest we will come to the Memory Palace (aka Memory Theater) project of Italian Guilio Camillo (1480–1544), a visionary but unrealized concept of a vast building devoted to arts and knowledge.[42] Camillo's memory palace concept has directly inspired a number of notable digital art works, including Martin Wattenberg and Mrek Walczak's net.art piece *Apartment* (2001); Agnes Hegedüs' *Memory Theatre VR* (1997), a 360-degree cylindrical installation with multiple projections providing an interactive exploration of the history of Virtual Reality and other illusionary spaces; and George Legrady's memory database installations *An Annotated Archive of the Cold War* (1994) and *Pockets Full of Memories* (2001).

Slovenian Emil Hrvatin's *Drive in Camillo* (2000) remains one of the most interesting homages to the Renaissance visionary's blueprint for a theater of memory, what Hrvatin describes as "a hybrid between an amphitheatric installation of Vitruvian architecture and a universal library catalogue."[43] The performance takes place outdoors, like a drive-in movie, with audiences only able to view the event from their cars, where they are attended by popcorn vendors. A computerized film visually recreates Camillo's ideas for the memory palace, while seven dancers work live to convey ideas of the palace's movements and sounds, with their live video images relayed and projected on the facades of two sky-scrapers. The location for the event, between the Slovene Parliament Building, a memorial to the Communist leader Kardelj, and the first Slovene Department Store, was itself selected by Hrvatin as a place already charged with potent and deep-seated collective memories.

Stephen Wilson's installation *Memory Map* (1994) adapts the architectural model of Camillo's Memory Palace to dynamically spatialize audio recordings of visitors' memories through a 3D sonic environment. Described by Wilson as "a kind of electronic dance in which spoken memories and their movement in physical space become the principal performers," the piece explores the spatial mapping of temporal memories.[44] Within a large hall space in Monterrey, Mexico, visitors talk into a computer to record memories such as their first love, first great accomplishment, and moments of great closeness, and the computer also registers information about their age and sex. The sound files are networked to another computer, which analyzes the data and distributes different sound clips to different speakers around the space using varying patterns. Sometimes the memories of older and younger people are clustered at either end of the hall, sometimes male and female voices are divided in space and at others a particular location becomes associated with particular memories such as death or first love. The computer also applies sound process-ing to the voices to create different atmospheres and effects, altering their speed, volume, or frequency, while digital video projections on the wall present images of time-based processes.

Media Memories and Time Travel

Niki, the protagonist of Blast Theory's theater performance *10 Backwards* (1999) suffers amnesia, and she videotapes herself compulsively as a countermeasure, which develops into a strategy for time-travel. The piece is punctuated with footage from her "video diaries," where she records her memories of the day and speculates and fantasizes about her future. In chapter 11 we discussed a sequence where Niki eats breakfast cereal while synchronizing her actions to a video recording of her doing the same in the past, and we return to the production now as an excellent example of a sophisticated multimedia theater exploration of time, memory, and its loss. There is a genuine simplicity and economy to Blast Theory's video and computer imagery. Whereas many artists and companies overuse the tempting visual palettes of software applications, Blast Theory, by contrast, treads softly, minimally, almost imperceptibly. Digital tools are used with gentle care and integrity, enhancing but never abstracting or obscuring the original video footage. Complex notions of time and materiality gently and hypnotically unravel through skilful interaction between the live "play," computer-enhanced prerecorded video imagery, and a live onstage camera (figure 22.7).

After Niki's repeated rituals of recording her actions such as eating breakfast and reliv-ing them in stop-frame motion in her preparation for time travel, she is transported to 2009. But an hour after her arrival she is forced to return to the present when a doctor, who claims "we've met before," diagnoses that the two hemispheres of her brain have become misaligned. Once home, she begins to experience déjà-vu and short-term memory loss, and her reliance on technology intensifies: "At the early stages of the *deja-vu*, my stepbrother kept me distracted by getting me to record things that had already happened. . . . I began to use the video camera to hold onto everything." The stepbrother brings the doctor Niki met in the future to the house, but he is unable to help her. He is bemused when Niki comments: "I know what you meant now—when you said we've met before."

In his efforts to keep Niki's memory functioning, the stepbrother encourages her to remember all the furniture in their family living room when they were children. Niki describes everything in vivid detail, moving around the stage to map out the positions of chairs, tables, sofas, and the TV. The stepbrother operates the onstage video camera, panning around where she points. On the screens, perfectly synchronized with his camera movements, we see a (prerecorded) panning shot of the furniture and walls of the room she describes (figure 22.8). On stage, he then pans the camera to Niki, who is sitting on the floor gesticulating. The projected video simultaneously pans to reveal her sitting on the living room carpet, surrounded by the furniture and gesticulating exactly as on stage.

Figure 22.7 Computer-enhanced video imagery is used subtly and seductively to suggest complex notions of time in Blast Theory's *10 Backwards* (1999).

It is a well-choreographed "illusion," and one we do not expect in as much as the ever-present onstage camera has only previously been used as a genuine live feed, never using recorded footage. The scenic implication is that Niki has now embodied the technology and her mind can infuse empty spaces with visible electronic images.

But if the show presents a discourse on the transformational potentials of technology, its message is ultimately a dystopian one. Niki is left confused, dysfunctional, amnesiac, and unable to coordinate her body movements. She stops going out or receiving visitors and shuts herself away in her room, finally not moving from her chair. The stepbrother, an ecological researcher, delivers a speech reflecting the impotence of technology to change harsh material realities:

I am bored of feeding endless amounts of data into the computer only to be told two days later that the world's climate is irretrievably damaged. So I treat the data. I cut pollution in Western

Figure 22.8 Reliving the childhood past: stepbrother and sister return to the past in the living room sequence of *10 Backwards*.

Europe, I cut population growth in South East Asia, knock China back ten years, feed it back into the computer. Then I wait two days to find out that the world's climate is irretrievably damaged. So today I have spent the last fourteen hours wiping a couple of million cars off the face of the planet. I shut down 75 coal-fired power stations and personally tapered the expansion of the chemicals industry. And I now have to wait two days to find out that the world's climate is fucked.

But the pervading theme of *10 Backwards* is not technology, but time. Niki begins by trying to predict her future and finally travels there. She slavishly copies past actions in order to tangibly move time backward, finally materializing herself in her childhood home. At the end of the show there is a final twist. A sequence of captions on the screens explains that just when Niki's death seemed inevitable, the doctor returned and cured her, and she now lives a quiet life in the country. The final scene takes place ten years later, and it repeats the earlier doctor scene when she had traveled to the future. Its significance is heightened, as we suddenly understand all its previously cryptic references to time. "We've met before," says the doctor, and the lights fade to black.

Both the play's text and the use of new media technologies combine and conspire to question and reorient audience perception of time. This is not to ignore the fact that the exploration of time can be argued to be an element of *all* theater that combines film or video (by nature prerecorded, in the past) with the present tense of live performance. But Blast Theory's production achieves a sense of the malleability of time more delicately and successfully than any we have seen. Rather than seeking to do this by disorientating the audience through jarring effects, the company coolly and calmly draws us in to share Niki's temporal experiences. The breakfast cereal sequence is key to this—synchronizing Niki to her past, and the audience to the apparently simultaneous "presents" of her live and projected/recorded form. From then on the technological imagery of prerecorded past begins to blur inexorably with the technologically mediated present (the omnipresent live camera), culminating in the memory sequence in the childhood house, where both video and past memory appear to concretely merge with the live and the present.

The production is a classic example of the use of technology not as spectacle to dazzle or bombard the senses but rather, like the effects of a calming sleeping drug or delicate musical soundtrack, to stimulate and alter our conscious and unconscious perceptions subtly. Discussing the production with a number of audience members, there was considerable consensus that the overall effect of the performance was a feeling of uplifting clarity rather than confusion, as echoed in Niki's final voiceover in the blackout at the end of the show:

I used to think that confusion was like greyness in front of your eyes. But I was wrong. Confusion is perfect sight because you can see everything.

We will leave the last words on memory to its most eloquent narrator, Marcel Proust, whose intimate sensation of a particular taste of cake-soaked tea leads to chronic insomnia, and precisely the same physical and temporal angst and confusion encountered by Niki in her travels through time, until it finally, magnificently, breaks into clear sight:

But when nothing subsists of an old past, after the death of people, after the destruction of things, alone, frailer but more enduring, more immaterial, more persistent, more faithful, smell and taste remain for a long time, like souls, remembering, waiting, hoping, on the ruin of all the rest, bearing without giving way, on their almost impalpable droplet, the immense edifice of memory.[45]

VI

Interactivity

"Performing" Interactivity

The viewer completes the work of art.
—MARCEL DUCHAMP[1]

Theories of Interactivity

All art is an interaction between the viewer and the artwork, and thus all artworks are interactive in the sense that a negotiation or confrontation takes place between the beholder and the beheld. Andrew Benjamin maintains that the artwork is not so much the object in itself "but the continual questioning of the object . . . the sustained presence of the work, part of whose work is to raise and maintain the question of the [work]."[2] Where digital interactive artworks and performances differ is in the ability of the user or audience to activate, affect, play with, input into, build, or entirely change it.

Audience participation in performance goes back millennia to tribal rituals and communal dances, and the futurists were the first in the twentieth century to systematically initiate performances that relied upon direct interaction from their audiences, typically using conflict and provocation to incite the spectators into action. In 1909, two months after the publication of the first futurist manifesto, Marinetti strategically booked the Théâtre de l'Oeuvre in Paris, where Alfred Jarry's *Ubu Roi* had caused a near-riot in 1896, to present his own satire on politics and revolution *Roi Bombance*.[3] Though it failed to ignite Jarry's violent reaction and fisticuffs, subsequent futurist performances would prompt police arrests of performers, and the almost commonplace audience response of throwing fruit and other missiles at the stage, once famously prompting Carlo Carrà to scream, "Throw an idea instead of potatoes, idiots!"[4] The deliberate double booking of theater seats, and the smearing of glue on them, ensured reaction and interactivity between audience members in auditoria, and actions such as the burning of national flags fueled noisy interventions between spectators and performers. Marinetti encouraged performers to provoke and enrage audiences through a display of open disdain for them, and his publication *War, the Only Hygiene* (1911–15) included a manifesto celebrating "The Pleasure of Being Booed."[5]

In what David Saltz describes as "a remarkable anticipation of Internet culture,"[6] in 1932 Bertolt Brecht wrote about the interactive potentials of radio which could be brought about through "a vast network of pipes." Radio, he said, could develop the capacity to learn "how to receive as well as transmit, how to let the listener speak as well as hear, how to bring him into a relationship instead of isolating him."[7] Today, Brecht's words are printed large to dominate an entire wall in the main office of BBC's popular talk radio station *Five Live*. In 1962, McLuhan introduced the concept that "interfaces means interaction,"[8] and since then different definitions of interactivity have come thick and fast from both academics and artists. For Andy Lippman it is "mutual and simultaneous activity on the part of both participants, usually working towards some goal . . . but not necessarily,"[9] and Simon Penny's more technological definition equally emphasizes real-time response: "An interactive system is a machine system which reacts in the moment, by virtue of automated reasoning based on data from its sensory apparatus . . . Interactivity implies real time."[10] Janet Murray stresses its important relationship to ideas of agency: "the satisfying power to take meaningful action and see the results of our decisions and choices."[11]

In relation to digital arts and video installations, Margaret Morse suggests the interactive user takes on "the virtual role of 'artist/installer' if not the role of artist as declarer and inventer of that world."[12] Bolter and Gromala offer the substitution of the word "performance" as "an even better word than *interaction* to describe the significance of digital design in general. As users, we enter into a performative relationship with a digital design: we perform the design, as we would a musical instrument."[13] Although this is a potent and apt metaphor for certain installations, we would note its slight hyperbole: one generally plays a musical instrument, one does not perform it, and there is a significant difference between the two concepts. Jaron Lanier continues the performative theme using a dance metaphor, and sees interactivity as an aspect of content:

Interactivity is a style of concrete conversation with the media. It is the way you dance with the computer. . . . [The] visual is not important. What is important is the rhythm of interaction . . . that feeling is not easy. Certain people can do it, rather like artists. . . . It is a new art form. . . . We don't entirely know what interactivity is yet.[14]

Leading theorists of interactive art such as Peter Weibel and Söke Dinkla have discussed different levels and degrees of interactivity, from simple stimulus-response closed modes to highly flexible open models. Dinkla presents a poetic definition of advanced examples to conceive open interactive artworks as floating phenomena, and coins the phrase the *floating work of art*:

Part of the authorship transfers from the artist to the user in the *floating work of art*. . . . In the cybernetic circle his own gaze, which is determined by social conventions, is thrown back at him and makes him realise that it is he who generates reality with his gaze. In the *floating work of art* the user becomes conscious that he is an accomplice in a fundamental sense. However, he only seemingly occupies an omnipotent position that allows him to control events, since he is always victim and perpetrator at the same time. In a web of relations he is only one of many controllers. . . . The *floating work of art* is no longer the expression of a single individual. Neither is it the expression of a collective, but it is the state of a "connective"—a web of influences that are continually reorganised by all participants.[15]

But "interactivity" is a much used and abused term, and one which by the turn of the millennium had become an increasingly meaningless buzzword in myriad contexts. Andrea Zapp makes the point that interaction now "codifies a post-modern aesthetic slogan, which describes a technical condition as 'dynamic hands-on-experience.'"[16] But levels of interactivity were and are often highly exaggerated in the marketing of both commercial products and, in many cases, artworks. If one turns on a light switch, the process is interactive—something is received in exchange—but no real dialogue takes place. In precisely the same way, many and arguably *most* products and artworks dubbed "interactive"—for example, the majority of CD-ROMs—should more accurately be termed "reactive."

Interactive multimedia applications including installations, CD-ROMs, the Web, and games, are seen as a decisive break from the hegemonic single-track delivery of mass media, particularly television, a generally one-way transmission-reception form that, in Hans Magnus Enzenberger's words, "does not serve communication but prevents it. It allows no reciprocal action between transmitter and receiver."[17] Baudrillard characterizes the mass media as "anti-mediatory and intransitive. They fabricate non-communication . . . if one agrees to define communication as an exchange, as a reciprocal stage of a speech and a response, and thus of a responsibility."[18] He argues that mass media are set up precisely to exclude response and that "we live in an era of non-response—of irresponsibility"[19] where television's very presence is a form of Orwellian social control since it ensures people are no longer speaking to one another.

Since television predominantly operates one-way, when a television presenter directly addresses the viewer, we perceive the presenter on screen, as in most instances we do with the performer in theater and performance, as a third-person "he" or "she" rather than the "you" of real-life interaction (because the television viewer is acknowledged but unrecognized). But in interactive installations and performances where the user/audience member is directly addressed and can respond meaningfully, the performer becomes a "you," operating in the second person rather than the third by nature of the direct interaction with the viewer, even when the performer is mediatized on a screen.[20]

Augusto Boal and the "Spectactor"

In *The New Media Reader* (2003), a performance maker not normally associated with digital technologies provides a key chapter and is introduced as a seminal figure in the theory and practice of interactivity—Augusto Boal. He is also introduced as someone who, unlike other interactive practitioners featured in the book, has been jailed and tortured for his practice, and has seen his colleagues murdered by the Brazilian military government. Noah Wardrip-Fruin notes the importance of his emphasis on embodiment in his interactive techniques employed in "forum" and "invisible" theater and speculates on whether Boal's methods can go toward overcoming the spectator/actor divide in digital contexts and Baudrillard's encoder/decoder binary.[21] He relates the politicized interactions of Boal's live invisible theater events to digital artists such as the ®™ark group, "which uses the protections it gains as a limited-liability corporation to support 'the sabotage (informative alteration) of corporate products, from dolls and children's learning tools to electronic action games' often in such a way that those encountering the products are not aware of the alteration."[22]

We would also draw attention to the important political activism of the Electronic Disturbance Theatre who famously brought the major corporate toy company eToys to its knees following its "theft" of the *eToys* domain name from a group of net artists who had originally registered and used it. The Electronic Disturbance Theatre won the "eToys War" by mobilizing an army of literally thousands of Web artists, liberals, and activists, who logged in to the ordering area of the toy company's website not to buy, but to clog and crash it. Their sales went into freefall (like Amazon, they are a virtual company only), and they were finally forced to capitulate and give back the domain name and URL to the artists.

Gonzalo Frasca has discussed Boal's poetics in relation to establishing deeper senses of characterization and situation in virtual environments and games, to create something approaching "The *Sims* of the Oppressed."[23] The reference relates to Boal's popular book *Theatre of the Oppressed* (1985), where he rejects Aristotelian notions of theater, calling it "*the poetics of oppression*: the world is known, perfect or about to be perfected, and all its values are imposed on the spectators, who passively delegate power to the characters to act and think in the first place."[24] In doing so, Boal suggests, spectators substitute dramatic action for real action, and remain oppressed. Even the "enlightened vanguard" of Brecht's theater, while revealing the world as subject to revolutionary change on the level of consciousness, does not operate on the level of action for the spectator. But by becoming a participant, or *spectactor* (a term he coins and then acknowledges immediately as "a bad word!") the spectator ceases to delegate power to other characters and theater is transformed from passivity into action: "The spectator frees himself; he thinks and acts for himself! Theatre is action!"[25]

Interactive performance concerns mutual obligations and ethics between performers and spectators, in the same way that these have operated in live art, for example in the

work of Marina Abramovich in the 1970s. Abramovich's series of *Rhythm* works sometimes required the audience to intervene and save her life: after she fell unconscious
through smoke inhalation in the center of a fire in *Rhythm 5* (1974), and when a loaded
gun was held to her head by a visitor in *Rhythm 0* (1974). In the latter performance, visitors interacted with her using various props set out in the space (from feathers and flowers
to knives), and Abramovich's stubborn passivity led both to interactions of great trust and
sensitivity (such as visitors adorning her) but also of abuse, with her flesh being cut and
her blood drunk.

Andrea Zapp suggests that in interactive experiences, "the former audience is lifted
out of their seat of distanced contemplation and placed in the limelight of subjective physical involvement: addressed as a storyboard controller, co-author actor or self-performer."[26]
This characterization is true of certain installations and performances—and of certain
users—but as a general "rule" or understanding of interactive works, it is overstated. As
we have seen, a spectator's reception of screen media differs significantly from live performance modes, and for (probably most) interactive installations Zapp's image of a spectator levitating from her seat to move onto a theater stage (in the limelight) is exaggerated
on two counts. First, as we have seen, the spectator of live performance is not in the same
state of "distanced contemplation" as they are for screen media. Second, most people would
abhor the idea of being transported onto a stage to take part in a theatrical performance
they have no knowledge of—that is literally the stuff of nightmares.

Defining Categories and Levels of Interactivity

A number of commentators have offered distinct categories and continuums of interactivity, and we offer our own four categories that we feel are helpful in relation to distinguishing different types of interactivity in artworks and performances. As in our
presentation of different categories of "The Digital Double," this approach helps to structure discussion and to focus on particular features within an enormously wide and diverse
field of practices. The four types of interactive art and performance we discern are ranked
in ascending order in relation to the openness of the system and the consequent level and
depth of user interaction:

1. Navigation
2. Participation
3. Conversation
4. Collaboration

Some categories may seem on the surface to be too similar or slippery, crossing over
one another too easily—for example, what distinguishes participation from conversation, and isn't a conversation in essence a collaboration? But if we take as an example
an interactive work discussed in chapter 11, Stelarc's *Prosthetic Head* where a projected

computer-generated 3D head answers questions asked by the visitor, we can see how our classifications of interaction work in hierarchical order. In doing so, we would stress that our hierarchies of interaction and the incremental levels of a user's creative freedom they delineate are in no way relative to an individual artwork's quality, originality, or impact. Advanced collaboration is not necessarily "better" than multiple-choice navigation, it is simply *more* interactive. Indeed, as David Rokeby notes, interactive users normally favor artworks that are relatively structured and constrained, where choice and navigation is focused rather than wide open: users only want a modest level of freedom. He goes on to point out that in any case the sense of freedom in interactive systems is primarily symbolic: "An interactive artist can give interactors the impression that they have much more freedom than they actually do."[27]

Prosthetic Head's interactivity is clearly more than simple navigation, and while it is of course participatory, the level of interaction is deeper and more sophisticated than simply joining in. A genuine and meaningful dialogue between the user and the artwork takes place (a literal one in this case) and thus it is a type of conversation (figure 23.1). But we

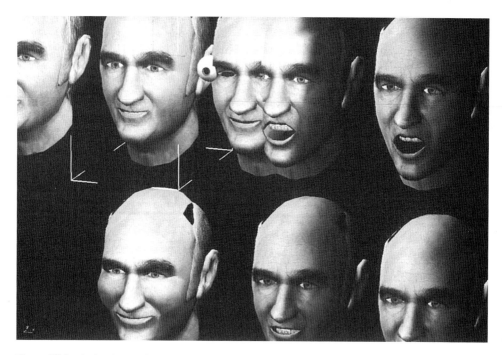

Figure 23.1 Stelarc's *Prosthetic Head* (2002) enacts a genuine and meaningful dialogue with the user, and hence we categorize it within our third category of interactivity: conversation. Programmed by Karen Marcelo and Sam Trychin, 3D models by Barrett Fox.

feel that it does not reach the level of a true collaboration, our final category. This is because the user is essentially interacting with the artwork on *its* pre-programmed terms (in this case, "you ask a question, I'll answer it") and the user's input will never meaningfully alter the artwork itself, or build and construct "new art" in collaboration with the computer or other users. Some may disagree, arguing that the dialogue between the user and the *Prosthetic Head* is new art since it will be quite unique (or certainly parts of it will) and is therefore truly collaborative. We would acknowledge the point, but counter that within our classifications there are more genuinely collaborative models in interactive arts where the user's input is freer, more open, and more *significantly* changes what happens. Degrees of significance and change effected by the user in interactive spaces and performances are judgment calls and matters of opinion, and we are the first to recognize that these categorizations (like the most responsive interactive artworks) are not an exact science.

We have already discussed numerous interactive works in other chapters, and will not return to them here simply to place them in one or other category; and in later chapters we analyze interactive CD-ROMs and computer games. The interactive paradigm of CD-ROMs is quintessentially navigational, where the territory is pre-programmed and (normally) set in stone, and interactivity is limited to the user choosing (or guessing) a path through the material or virtual environment. Some CD-ROMs, such as Laurie Anderson's *Puppet Motel* (1995) also offer participatory activities in gamelike forms, while others such as Igloo's *Windowsninetyeight* (1998) enable users to manipulate images creatively. The diversity of computer and video games offer paradigms that threaten to blast open the categories. It has been said that games are the most truly interactive digital applications of all, since response is immediate and absolute (click left and you move left), but they are generally still set within very rigid rather than fluid parameters. All are navigational (moving through spaces), but we would characterize most solo games as participatory, as they involve active involvement in a complex activity, rather than the "A or B?" paradigm of navigation. We would not consider solo game-playing conversational since although a type of dialogue is clearly going on between the gamer and the program, the software rarely offers real flexibility to the dialogue, and although it may be "intelligent" and do different or unexpected things from game to game, communication is not "open." Where two or more users play one another, in real space or online, and particularly where they work together as teams, a more conversational interactivity comes into play. What we term the collaboration paradigm is rarely evident in games since game worlds tend not to be flexible enough to admit genuinely new ideas. But this is changing with more advanced programs, and there are also a number of well-established game environments where gamers collaborate to meaningfully alter the structures, architectures, and activities of the game world.

Navigation

REMEMBER, THE END IS
JUST THE BEGINNING.
—LYNN HERSHMANN, SCREEN INSTRUCTION FOR *LORNA*, 1979–84

Navigation, the "simplest" form of interaction, is epitomized by the single click of a mouse to answer "Yes or No" to a screen prompt, or to indicate "Right, Left, Up, or Down." In gallery installations it may be the pressing of a button or, as in as Claude Shannon's early interactive artwork *The Ultimate Machine* (1952) "pull a switch, a lid opens and a hand emerges that throws the switch in the off position whereupon the lid closes again over the hand."[28] The navigation model is nowadays increasingly at play within television, where audiences use their remote controls, telephones, or computers to steer the direction of programs that rely on voting to decide winners (*Pop Idol*) or losers (*Big Brother*). A referendum modeled on the principles of Western democracy, telephone voting offers "the people's will." This strategy is a direct response by broadcasters to perceived "interactive" needs of audiences brought about through increased exposure to multimedia applications and the Internet—an ironic move, for when those same technologies first emerged, they remediated television paradigms and techniques.[29] Robin Nelson coins the term "flexi-narrative" in relation to popular television serials and series, and notes how television has increasingly adopted the paradigms of interactive narratives: "the fast-cut, segmented, multi-narrative structure which yields the ninety-second sound-and-vision byte form currently typical of popular television drama."[30]

On stage, audiences assist the navigation of live performances such as Dana Atchley's solo *Next Exit* (1991), where he sits next to a video-projected campfire and creates a unique performance for every audience by selecting from seventy stories in his "digital suitcase." Atchley, an obsessive documenter who has kept every photographic image he has taken since the age of seven, stresses the positive impact of new technology on both documentation and the ancient art of storytelling. An organizer of digital storytelling festivals and cofounder of the Center for Digital Storytelling, he wonders whether "cemeteries of the 21st century will be filled with interactive kiosks of lives lived?"[31]

On the Web, navigational interactivity is the very act of surfing and includes interaction with varied net.art pieces and hypertext narratives. A large number of interactive stories, video interfaces, and online "dramas" have emerged on the Web. In historical terms 1996 was the key year, with the emergence of three different photoplay soap operas. These included sixteen episodes of a gay soap *Fatal Beauty*, and *The Spot*, reputedly the first soap on the web, which began early in 1996 and ran for almost two years. *The Spot* centers on a group of friends sharing a beach house in Santa Monica, California. Although its narratives are conventional, it makes relatively effective use of its nonlinear fictional form, and incorporates different media. Episodes include video and audio clips, photo albums,

Figure 23.2 Mika Tuomola and Heikki Leskinen's early online interactive drama *Daisy's Amazing Discoveries* (1996).

access to character's journals, and navigable tours around the house to familiarize users with its layout.

Daisy's Amazing Discoveries, a five-part nonlinear interactive drama, also came online in 1996, and was in its day by far the most theatrical and artistically sophisticated example of the genre. The ambitious, state-of-the-art Finnish production (in English) traces Daisy's journey as she leaves a traveling circus to pursue her romantic dreams in the city. It is innovative in both concept and design, with imaginative interactive elements, and some stunning and elaborate photomontage interface screens created in *Photoshop* (figure 23.2). Some are digital composites of up to twenty-five photographs, which scriptwriter Mika Tuomola and director Heikki Leskinen aptly describe as "almost photorealistic pictures of a fantasy world."[32] The rich and surreal screen environments enable a range of routes through the narratives; for example, clicking on different paving stones on a road winding into the distance reveals twelve separate scenes. In addition to the photomontage environments, the production incorporates text-and-image collages, audio dialogue accompanied by photographic slideshows, music, and a small number of video clips. As each episode was released on the web, users could move up a level of interactivity to become participatory. They could affect the action in the next episode by writing to the fictional world's lifestyle magazine, by scrawling graffiti messages in the restroom of the bar, or by entering the environment's chat room.

More recent examples include the BBC's ambitious interactive soap *Thunder Road*, which was screened in 2002 on broadband TV and subsequently on the BBC1 website, where audiences were provided with extra information, interviews, and subplot developments and could take part in chat-room discussion forums. Performance art duo Desperate Optimists' *Lost Cause* (2000) is a ten-part Web sci-fi narrative telling the story of a woman's journey through a futuristic city to blow up the headquarters of the Chemi-drome Corporation. Characterized by the company's imaginative and intelligent approach to new media performance, it features an evocative musical soundtrack and specific visual homages to classic sci-fi movies, including *La Jetée* (1962) and *Alphaville* (1965).

Interactive Cinema

Cinema needs new tools.
—BERTOLT BRECHT[33]

Navigable moving image narratives, of which there are many types but which we will generically call "interactive cinema," have developed slowly but surely within the art world through CD-ROMs, interactive installations, and online narratives, while commercial endeavors have had a considerably more troubled time, as we will see. Lynn Hershman has been one of the leading interactive narrative artists for over twenty years, and her videodisc installation *Lorna* (1979–84) is widely regarded as the first "new media" interactive fictional artwork.[34] Though laser disc systems work without the aid of a computer, their speed offers comparable real time navigational properties in manipulating video footage. Users are asked to help Lorna, the protagonist, who dares not leave her room because she has become increasingly frightened by TV news reports, and so sits isolated in her apartment watching television (a vicious circle). As Söke Dinkla observes, "The simultaneity of active and passive roles in one person—controlling and being controlled—becomes clear right at the beginning, when the visitor, with a remote control in his or her hand, faces Lorna, also equipped with a remote control. . . . Paradoxically, they (the viewers/visitors) are asked to free Lorna from her plight using precisely the media which increases her fears"[35] (figure 23.3).

The user can affect the narrative as it unfolds, including its ending, where one can select between positive, negative, exciting, or ironic twists. New media art historian Hans-Peter Schwartz suggests that in doing so, *Lorna* "did no less than a change in paradigm, long overdue and well-prepared." Hershman's next videodisc, *Deep Contact: The First Interactive Sexual Fantasy Videodisc* (1984), was programmed using Hypercard, and has fifty-seven narrative segments and a touch-screen interface combining a Microtouch monitor and a Macintosh IIcx. Navigation depends upon users touching different parts of the screen body of the protagonist, Marion—the words "Touch Me" appear alongside Marion's image in the opening screen (figure 23.4). Touching her head opens options for different TV channels that humorously analyze female reproductive technologies and their

Figure 23.3 A typical screen image from Lynn Hershman's pioneering videodisc installation *Lorna* (1979–84).

Figure 23.4 The user is invited to get physical with the touch-screen interface of Lynn Hershman's early interactive Hypercard narrative *Deep Contact: The First Interactive Sexual Fantasy Videodisc* (1984).

effects on women's bodies, as well as notions of phantom limbs. Touching Marion's legs moves the narrative to a garden where the user progresses along forks in a path to follow either Marion, a Zen master, a demon, or an unknown path. As its title suggests, *Deep Contact* also enables one to examine aspects in detail: zooming in on a bush in the garden, for example, reveals a spider busily weaving its web. Users also need to manipulate the videodisk to reveal certain hidden elements, for example, all the dialogue spoken by the Zen master is in reverse, and the user has to play it backward to make it comprehensible. A surveillance camera directed on the user in the gallery is employed to map the visitor's image into the screen image, displacing the expected image, and playing with notions of "'transgressing the screen' and of being transported into 'virtual reality.'"[36]

Other art pioneers of the genre include Glorianna Davenport, who undertook early installation-based experiments as director of MIT's Interactive Cinema Group, and Grahame Weinbren, whose interactive movies are perhaps the most celebrated of the genre's early development. For Weinbren's *Sonata* (1990), the viewer sits in a steel cube in front of a monitor and can slide and overlap two complementary film narratives through the use of a custom-built picture frame that they point and move in relation to the screen. The two film narratives explore themes around lust and murder, one based on the Biblical Judith and Holofernes story, the other on Tolstoy's *The Kreutzer Sonata* (1890).[37] Peter Lunenfeld notes the moments prior to the climactic murder of the adulterous wife by her jealous husband in the Tolstoy plot. As she plays the violin in the music room, he seethes with rage outside the door and (using the picture frame device) "the user can 'slide' either perspective however far 'over' the other he or she chooses. This allows for a kind of simultaneity that the classic montage between the two scenes would not."[38] Weinbren himself suggests that

The major feature of interactive cinema . . . is that the viewer is in a conjunctive state, i.e. he remains conspicuously aware that there are, 'behind' or below every picture, other pictures and pictorial systems which do not necessarily become visible in each individual presentation of the work. If this awareness can be turned into a conception that these background pictures make up the pictorial systems visible on the screen, then we will have a non-linear narrative corresponding to Freudian dream interpretation.[39]

More recently, Jill Scott has become one of the most prominent and innovative artists in the interactive cinema field, with important works such as *Frontiers of Utopia* (1995). Like the first act of Carol Churchill's play *Top Girls* (1982), *Frontiers of Utopia* features eight women from different historical periods brought together around a table (figure 23.5). Her other works include multiscreen interactive narratives constructed in large public spaces that explore her central themes of history, women, the body and technology. Interactive "films" have also been developed on the Web by a number of artists, the first of which, according to Christiane Paul, was David Blair's *WAXWEB* (1993), an

Figure 23.5 A screen shot from Jill Scott's interactive cinema installation experience *Frontiers of Utopia* (1995).

eighty-five-minute movie reflecting on the history of film and television, constructed within a database of eighty thousand pieces that Web users can assemble in different orders.

Interactive Movies: Commercial Experiments

New technologies have provided cinema with tools to create extraordinary graphical and quasi-photographic special effects, which have created visually stunning artificial worlds, from the ancient (*Gladiator*, 2000; *Lord of the Rings*, 2001–2003) to the futuristic (*The Matrix*, 1999; *Minority Report*, 2002). New technologies have helped minimize danger to stunt artists (or to replace them completely with "synthespians") and equally to replace dead actors (Oliver Reed in *Gladiator*) and expensive human extras through the use of cut-and-paste composite crowd scenes. For movie producers and studios, computers and cinema may seem like a marriage made in heaven, but their ultimate consummation in the much-vaunted idea of interactive cinema is a deeply troubled one.

In 1967, the movie *One Man and His World* played at Expo '67 in Montreal. Before its climax, the audience was able to vote to determine the endings it wanted: "Should the wife or the blond neighbour commit suicide? Should the male protagonist go to jail or go free?"[40] The audience cast their votes in 1967, but since then there have been only a tiny number of repetitions of the idea in movie theaters. Marie-Laure Ryan argues, "The biggest obstacle to the implementation of selective interactivity in movies and drama is the conflict between the solitary pleasure of decision making and the public nature of cinematic or dramatic performance. In a spectacle addressed to a large audience, interactive decisions must be taken by the majority, and freedom of choice is only freedom to vote."[41] Allen Yamashita similarly draws attention to the frustrating and unsatisfactory blunt instrument of majority rule:

Attempts at interactive speciality entertainment can be described as "dumb" interactivity. These include movie products in which the audience gets an A/B choice at plot turns and at the ending; guests "interact" with a couple of buttons hardwired into the backs of seats. As group experiences, such products seem doomed to disappoint the half of the audience who didn't want to go "left" at the fork in the story and to bore those who simply didn't care and wanted the storyteller to get on with it.[42]

The first commercial examples of interactive movies delivered outside of movie theaters were generally hybrid game-dramas primarily linked to game consoles, with gaming being the dominant activity, interspersed by movie footage inserts. Notable early examples include *The 7th Guest* (1993), *Myst* (1993), *Wing Commander III* (1994), *The 11th Hour* (1995), *Phantasmagoria* (1995), and *Harvester* (1996). *Gabriel Knight: Sins of the Fathers* (1993) incorporated the voices of well-known actors Tim Curry and Leah Rimini, but movie footage was absent until the sequel *Gabriel Knight: The Beast Within* (1995), a package of six CD-ROMs. The leads were replaced with Dean Erickson and Joanne Takahashi, and the "supernatural psycho-thriller" brought together werewolves, a murder mystery, and the death of "Mad" King Ludwig II.

Interplay Productions' *Voyeur* (1994) was first released on CD-I by Phillips Interactive Media and later as a CD-ROM. Like a remediation of Hitchcock's *Rear Window* (1954), the user is located in an apartment spying on the affairs of others (this time with a video camera and telescope). The gamer has a race against time to collect video evidence to either prevent a murder or prove the murderer's identity, as he or she follows the activities of presidential candidate Reed Hawke and uncovers the family secrets of affairs, betrayals, and blackmail. The game/movie is played in one sitting (with fading batteries and timers ticking to remind the player that time is fleeting); and a restart offers some limited changes and a new victim. The pornography industry, inevitably, was also riding the interactive cinema wave from the start, with numerous CD-ROM titles in the mid-1990s, and later DVDs such as Digital Playground's *Virtual Sex, with Jill Kelly* (2000), which subtly invited interested parties to "interact with her using your DVD remote! You choose the sexual positions! You choose the camera angles! You choose her moods between innocent and nasty! You ask her to strip naked for you! You ask her to tell you her wildest sex stories . . . enjoy this gorgeous sex animal and enjoy her countless times. The Virtual

Sex Series has redefined interactive sex." However, such interactive movie paradigms have not significantly taken off in the sex industry, and although *delivery* of pornographic movies has moved to digital formats (DVD and via the Web), traditional linear-narrative fornication still currently holds the day, and the dollars.

The Interfilm Technology company first experimented with interactive cinema in 1992, enabling cinema audiences to vote for narrative path choices using pads on the arms of their theater seats in films such as *I'm Your Man* (1992). But the experiments did not succeed commercially, and "after an initial success due to the novelty of the experience, audiences quickly tired of this form of artistic democracy."[43] But with the advent of DVD, the genre entered a new phase which replaced the limitations of interactivity based on the tastes of a democratic majority with the ability for users to take their own individual paths through the narratives. Interfilm Technology restructured *I'm Your Man* and released it as an interactive DVD in 1998 directed by Bob Bejan, and it is widely regarded as the first of its genre of interactive cinema. Its publicity suggested a considerable and highly dramatic paradigm shift: "Climb into the director's seat and make the movie you want to see! You pick the characters and choose what happens to them. You control everything with the push of a button. Multiple plots, multiple endings—its interactive moviemaking so real the only thing missing is the studio accountant."

In the event, *I'm Your Man* was a fairly crass and clichéd comedy action thriller using fifty-six different film segments and offering users twenty-five decision points where they could choose which of the three main characters to follow (a seductive villain, a naïve ingenue, and a young hero). For the climax, two of the characters each break the fourth wall and speak directly to the viewer, the villain asking if he should "turn into an FBI agent" or "run like a rabbit," the ingenue questioning whether she should be a "good girl" or a "bad girl." The drama of intrigue, sinister computer disks, and a murder plot is resolved when all the branches of the story are, in Ryan's words, "interrupted by the *coup de théâtre* of the common resolution: an FBI agent suddenly appears, like a deus ex machina, collects the disks from Leslie, arrests Richard, and congratulates Jack and Leslie on a job well done."[44] The viewer then has a choice of one of the three character's epilogues.

Ryan makes the point that like many interactive films, *I'm Your Man* has the problem that options necessitate a freezing of the screen until a decision is made, which "uproots the spectator from the fictional world and highlights the conflict of immersion and interactivity."[45] Noting the use of direct address to the viewer at decision points, she continues: "The predeliction of interactive works for modes of expression that involve an ironic distancing from the fictional world confirms Janet Murray's diagnosis of their built-in affinity for the comic spirit.[46] But if self-consciousness becomes the standard way to compensate for the anti-immersive effect of interactivity, it will take a lot of ingenuity to prevent the device from becoming a metacliché."[47]

Tender Loving Care

One of the veterans and pioneers of the commercial interactive cinema genre, David Wheeler, whose work had included *The 7ᵗʰ Guest* (1993) and *The 11ᵗʰ Hour* (1995), directed Aftermath Media's *Tender Loving Care* (*TLC*) in 1999. It was a significant raising of the stakes in the field: shot on 35 mm film, costing $700,000, and featuring a movie star (John Hurt); and at the time it seemed that interactive cinema was finally going to get the Hollywood treatment. Its DVD cover bore the tagline "Watch What You Wish For", and its back sleeve was filled with interactive hyperbole typical of the genre, but making some startlingly fresh claims:

You are about to experience a fantasy quite unlike anything you've ever seen or felt before—a fantasy built from the very stuff of your own mind. . . . No two people will experience *Tender Loving Care* in exactly the same way. . . . The player is voyeur, detective, judge and patient all in one. Between each variable scene, Dr Turner enlists the viewer's help in assessing the behaviour of the film's characters . . . [and] the viewer too becomes one of Dr Turner's patients, taking a series of Thematic Apperception Tests (TATs), the results of which create a progressively accumulating psychological profile of the viewer.

Wow! We preordered our copy, put it into the machine the moment it arrived, and this is what we experienced . . . In the opening sequence, John Hurt, playing Dr. Turner, drives up to a large house, gets out of his car, and addresses the camera in his inimitably slow, intense, and considered tones. The essence is, "What happened in this house?" and his mood and delivery makes clear it is probably something very bad. We flash back in time to find Alison and Michael, an attractive middle-class young couple living in the house, apparently happy, apparently with a child unwell in bed upstairs, who Alison talks about and continually goes off to tend. Michael looks worried. John Hurt sends his best psychiatric nurse, Kathryn—a haughty, mysterious, and curvaceous blonde in a tight nurse's uniform—to live with them in the house "to look after the child," as she explains to Alison. Kathryn makes frequent visits to the child's room, seems a consummate professional, and one night takes off her blouse at the bedroom window while in the moonlit garden Michael stares up at her large, tastefully lit breasts.

Enter John Hurt:

How did you feel when Kathryn undressed in front of Michael?
Titillated; Amused; Offended; Intrigued; Uncomfortable.

Do you look in people's windows?
Yes; No

Is Kathryn:
Attractive; Hostile; Intelligent; Sympathetic; Mysterious.

I am a good person [*meaning you, the user*]
Yes; No

Is oral sex a crime?
Yes; No

Four-foot long penises are:
Funny; Offensive; Too big; Just right for me.

If I was a flea I would be a miserable depressed flea
Yes; No

Abortion:
Pro-life; Pro-choice; Don't have an opinion.

Such questions are posed and require a response every five minutes or so, when Hurt interrupts the movie. He generally comments on the preceding action, asks us to respond to questions about how we feel about the events, and sets us more questions to delve into our personal and sexual psyches: "At least once I have stared in awe at a horse's penis: True; False." We answer the questions, believing perhaps (but quite wrongly) that the DVD software is psychometrically profiling our very subconscious. Following these interrogations, we navigate around graphical representations of the rooms in the house and listen in to phone messages, read diaries on bedroom tables, look at Alison's medical notes, and so on, before returning to the movie. After nearly three hours we realize we've been answering questions, watching Alison's slightly crazed behavior and the dark, sexual chemistry brewing between Kathryn and Michael, and we're barely into the second act. Time for a break. But exiting the DVD prompts the program to make us write down dozens of cryptic numbers and letters so that our profile isn't lost.

Recommencing, we laboriously re-input the codes to page after page of onscreen prompts, and are then back into the epic at the point we left. The plot thickens. There is no child in the bedroom (surprise, surprise); she was killed in a car crash, Alison is in glazed-eyed denial, and Kathryn conducts some private therapeutic meditation sessions with her behind a locked door. Michael, suspicious, knocks on it and it opens very slightly (was that a flash of naked skin in the background?), and Kathryn's face appears, furious at the interruption. Enter John Hurt:

When Kathryn and Alison meditate are they naked?
Yes; No

Adam and Eve
True; Made up

I have bowel problems:
True; False

Is art pornographic?
Yes; No

What happened to Mr Roo? [*Onscreen graphic of a kangaroo on crutches*]
Got hit by a car; Fell off a slide; Got beat up by wallabies; Got caught being unfaithful by Mrs Roo.
Have you had a homo-erotic experience?
Yes; No

Let's cut to the chase. Michael finally overcomes his angst-filled ethical dilemma between his loyalty to Alison and his lust for Kathryn, and they have torrid, explosive sex (surprise, surprise). But Kathryn, who may (or may not) also be having an affair with Alison, turns out not to be a very nice person. To Michael's increasingly disturbed mind, Kathryn needs murdering with a shovel and burying in the garden. This is done, but crime doesn't pay, and the police and some white-coated types from the lunatic asylum take Michael away in a van. Cue John Hurt for a breathy, moralizing epilogue . . . and a few more questions. Curtain.

The film is absolutely dire, but the paradigm is fascinating. We decided to try it again some weeks later and input completely different answers to *all* the questions, this time as though we are nuns (we had in hindsight been a trifle "male" and red-blooded with our responses first time around). We watched again, feeding in an opposite psychological profile to before . . . and it was precisely the same film. Every single frame. We have since been assured by other *TLC* aficionados that there are some, though few, alternative sequences, and even a different ending if the right combinations of answers are made, but we really do not wish to suffer the movie again. That said, we honestly recommend it (particularly to those of an ironic disposition), as we have literally never seen anything like it before or since. Indeed, very few interactive movies have been made since, one suspects in no small part due to the big-budget, big-breasted flop of *TLC*. It remains a remarkable and unprecedented oddity in the history of both cinema and digital interactivity: unique, unforgettable, and hilarious, for all the wrong reasons.

Wheeler's next venture *Point of View* (*POV*) (2001) is one of few examples since, with a two-thirds reduction in budget from *TLC* to $250,000. A "contemporary, edgy urban story about obsession, art, eroticism and murder," it centers on Jane, a reclusive artist obsessing over her neighbor Frank, photographing him from her apartment window (Hitchcock's *Rear Window* remediated once more), and creating fantasy art of them together. As the back sleeve puts it, "Jane's unusual behaviour sets the stage for danger and bizarre events, both real and imagined." But interestingly, this time little sex, not because Wheeler had not intended it, but because, as he has since revealed with great annoyance, the "beautiful" actor playing Jane had agreed to bare her breasts during the casting but once on set resolutely refused to do so. Wheeler may know about Freud, but apparently not about karma.

Though *POV* lacks the blatant soft-porn sexual voyeurism of *TLC*, we are struck by the question of how much the interactive paradigm may increase the voyeuristic gaze in cinema, most famously discussed by Laura Mulvey in "Visual Pleasure and Narrative Cinema" (1975). We suspect it does significantly, and this was certainly the case in our first viewing experience of *TLC*. In relation to this, we are interested to turn Wheeler's own psychoanalytical model back on him in relation to how he guided audience expectations through the publicity launch announcement for *POV*. Although sexual content is not mentioned anywhere in the copy, our italics emphasize the sexual and dominatory instincts of the voyeuristic gaze that underlie its language and message:

Respond to the characters, *investigate* into *their private, intimate lives*. Get involved in their emotional and *moral choices*. *Delve* into your own psychology and *watch the story unfold, uniquely influenced by you*. *Be thrilled*, intrigued, scared, *provoked and stimulated* into a *deeper*, more entertaining movie-*watching experience*. Get involved. *Go deep*. After all, it's *your point of view*.

The Problems and Pragmatics of Interactive Cinema

For commercial companies, myriad pragmatic problems far more pressing than theories of voyeurism beset interactive cinema. These are particularly related to the traditional naturalistic narrative models of commercial cinema, which do not inhibit comparable art-based experiments in the same way. To give enough breadth to differentiate different plotlines and to follow the stories of different individual characters takes vast amounts of film, and consequently vast budgets, and the key problem is that most of it will not be seen. Daniel Sandin provides diagrams to illustrate the significant mathematical problems of multiplicatory branching-structure cinema narratives, concluding,

In order for participants to have five significant choice points within the *film,* each choice having two options, the producer needs to create 63 prerecorded segments. Ten choices would require 2,041 prerecorded segments. In this case, a single viewer would experience only ten segments, or one-half of 1 percent of the work created. There are, of course, inventive special-case solutions. Consider a story that has choices, but the plot line converges to the same point after each choice, independent of the choice. Then, five choices would require only 11 segments. One reasonable solution to handling the immense variety of experiences that interaction requires is realtime image generation, instead of prerecorded segments. One has to simulate the world and compute the effects of the participants' choices.[48]

A related production problem concerns the need for all the narrative strands to be equally strong whichever path a user follows. But it is difficult enough for scriptwriters to create just one successful plot structure—to invent fifty or a hundred, all interrelated and interweaving, may be asking too much. Although there are highly successful movies that are multilinear, such as *Short Cuts* (1993), *Magnolia* (1999), and *Timecode* (2000), they are nonetheless linearly sequenced and finite in plot and length. They remain examples of the art of scriptwriting as (among other things) making the "right" choices: of rejecting numerous possible plot developments and branches to decide on the ideal ones. For this reason, a prevalent point of view is that people do not want to interact with the cinematic medium at all; they are uninterested in navigating through or creatively experimenting with a maze or road map, but prefer the best and most direct route to cinematic satisfaction—which is what the scriptwriter is paid for. As Max Whitby points out, the idea that screen audiences can construct their own narratives is initially appealing to studios and filmmakers, but "the trouble is it doesn't sustain. When you actually get in there and try to make things in an interactive way, the premise falls apart."[49] Allen Yamashita is equally cynical about the desirability and future of interactive screen narrative, arguing that cultural traditions from ancient storytelling to contemporary theater and cinema indicate audiences' preference to be passively manipulated through narratives rather than to be active manipulators of them.[50] In "The Myths of Interactive Cinema" (2002) Peter Lunenfeld goes further, to dub the entire genre "a failure."

A number of workshops and seminars on interactive cinema have wrestled with the problems of the form and with creative solutions. In two weeklong workshops run by SAGAS in Munich that we participated in during 1997 and 1998, the idea of a cluster database of video or film sequences was suggested as a preferable model to simple branching structures. The workshop leaders Jay Bolter and Michael Joyce suggested that cluster models could enable a type of interactivity that challenged the "stop-choose-start" sequentiality of branching narratives. When film clips are grouped into clusters related to criteria such as plot developments, characters, and themes, at each decision point more options are opened than with "A > B or C" branch structures, and moreover, unselected clips from each cluster can be accessed later where appropriate to the preceding sequence. This results in a less plot-driven and constructivist model of storytelling, and opens out more possibilities for diversified narrative and artistic conceptions. It seems likely that the future for interactive cinema, if there is one, will reside in these more holistic, less expensive type of formats than branching-structure models. At the same time, the increasing convergence of games and cinema as seen, for example, in the *X Files* (2000) movie-game (moving the interactive paradigm from navigational to participatory) is the route the genre is currently, and relatively speedily, heading for.

Concluding her book on interactive narratives, *Digital Fictions* (2000), Sarah Sloane revealingly adopts a downbeat and conservative tone, maintaining that the fuss and flurry which greets every new iteration of digital storytelling derives "simply from their novelty."[51] While acknowledging that new narrative conventions and genres will continue to be developed and refined, she concludes, "adding computers to the storytelling relationship will ultimately matter little in the long run. . . . A good story will always be a good story, regardless of its medium or mode of presentation."[52]

Participation

Although Paul Vanouse's *The Consensual Fantasy Engine* (1995, with Peter Weyhrauch) is an interactive movie whose only interactivity involves response to multiple-choice questions, its voting device and theatrical setting turns a navigational paradigm into an audience-participatory one. *The Consensual Fantasy Engine* is a computer program that constructs montages of film and video images in response to audience preferences, metering their applause volume levels to multiple-choice answers to the different questions posed onscreen every five minutes. The central theme is the police car chase of O. J. Simpson, which was televised on American (and global) TV, and this footage is intercut with short clips of other chases and action sequences from a range of movies, TV programs, and cartoons. Depending on audience preferences, each five-minute montage draws on different styles and genres (using film clips from the oeuvres) to present pastiches of film noir thrillers, Bonnie and Clyde-style adventures, or Keystone Kops–inspired comedies. In the performance we attended, comedy was the audience's main preference, and the helicopter and ground footage of Simpson's speeding car was interspersed with an increasingly manic montage of silent movie car stunts, the automobile crashes from the movie *The Blues Brothers* (1980), and classic cartoon chases including *Tom and Jerry* and *Roadrunner*.

Vanouse uses the Simpson chase to examine the distinct relationship and influence between broadcasting and society's belief systems, and to "explore how the media and public have a substantial stake in the creation of such metaphors and meanings."[53] Although the limitations of the audience democracy interactive paradigm have been widely raised, we would note that *The Consensual Fantasy Engine* performance we experienced was highly engaging, entertaining, and interactive. The necessity for audience members to make the loudest possible noise to ensure their choice led to considerable interaction within and among the audience and a genuine sense of communality emerged as the raucous crowd continued their shouts, conversations, and loud, comic asides even after the choices had been made. Interactivity by vote may be a blunt instrument, but in this case, although the audience-to-screen interactivity may have been relatively simplistic, more important, it empowered the audience to become highly active and interactive with one another.

Vanouse's later collaboration with Michael Mateas and Steffi Domike, *Terminal Time* (1999) is a "history engine" using a computer system that incorporates artificial intelligence capabilities. An interactive movie for cinema audiences, the opening credits announce (with a nod to Bill Seaman's concept of the "recombinant poetics" of digital arts[54]) "The Recombinant History Apparatus Presents: *Terminal Time*." The recombinant software then goes on to meter and respond to the sonic levels of applause in the theater as audiences respond to multiple-choice questions posed on screen, for example:

What is the most pressing issue facing the world today?

A: Men are becoming too feminine and women too masculine.
B: People are forgetting their cultural heritage.
C: Machines are becoming smarter than people.
D: It's becoming harder to earn a living and support a family.[55]

As its tongue-in-cheek publicity puts it, "the answers to these questions allows the computer program to create historical narratives that mirror and even exaggerate audience biases and desires. Just clap, watch and enjoy. At long last *Terminal Time* gives you the history you deserve!"[56] The computer assembles different montages of Pathé-esque pseudo-documentary film footage from its database in response to the audience's choices: first, a six-minute whistle-stop historical tour from 1000 to 1750, and following more multiple-choice questions, the periods from 1750 to 1950, and from 1950 to 2000 (figure 23.6). Historical events such as the causes of wars are reinvented or given new slants according to how the "audience-powered history engine" interprets the audience's desires. *Terminal Time* runs on a Macintosh G3 linked to an AV library on a 36-gigabyte external drive, and its artificial intelligence architecture draws on three elements: a "Cyc" knowledge base (a standard AI core); ideological goal tress (discerning appropriate responses in relation to audience desires); and story experts (providing narrative conventions and coherence).

As Jay Bolter and Diane Gromala note, this type of mass audience voting is undertaken at once frivolously and seriously, and serves to enable the computer system to assess and identify the audience's ideology and to trigger content choice and ordering in accordance.[57] They discuss the piece in relation to the way it seeks to demonstrate how history is constructed, constrained, or rewritten in relation to cultural context and ideology, and how its interactive model emphasizes and satirizes how audiences experience media products in accordance with their particular beliefs and prejudices.

Earlier cinematic examples of mobilizing whole audiences interactively include Loren Carpenter's "Cinematrix" technology, premiered at SIGGRAPH in 1991. This enables large audiences to exert control over screen events by each holding up a paddle "wand" (like a ping-pong bat) and turning either its green or red side to the screen, where a camera sends the information to a computer that interprets the data. At SIGGRAPH, audiences also used the wands to play a communal game of *Pong*,[58] with the right-side half of the audience controlling the right paddle onscreen and the left-side half controlling the left paddle. Turning the wand to red made the screen paddle rise up the screen, and green made it descend. Dan Sandin reports that "several energetic interactive sets were played,"[59] and Laurel, Strickland, and Tow describe how using the system "crowds have been observed to learn very quickly to cooperate well enough to play mass games of Pong, make intricate patterns, and even control a flight simulator."[60]

Figure 23.6 A screen image from *Terminal Time* (1999), an audience-responsive interactive cinema production by Steffi Domike, Michael Mateas, and Paul Vanouse.

Theater and Participation

Theatrical audience participation has a long history, and the frenzied clapping to bring Tinkerbell back to life in *Peter Pan* or the pantomime calls of "he's behind you!" and "oh yes you did!" offer an energetic sense of audience interactivity, though with little real impact on the narrative action, which is predetermined and always more or less the same. Audiences adopted participatory roles in Happenings in the 1960s, at the celebrated 1968 "Magic Theatre" performances at the Kansas City Museum, and ever since in numerous experimental performances, as well as large open-air community events staged by companies such as Welfare State International and I.O.U. Audiences input ideas for improvisational theater and standup comedy, become involved in murder mystery evenings, act as guests at *Tony n' Tina's Wedding* (since 1988), and vote to decide "whodunit" at the end of San Francisco's long-running *Shear Madness* (since 1980).

A charming digital remediation of theatrical audience participation is presented in Bruno Cohen's interactive installation *Camera Virtuoso* (1996). It uses a miniature theater complete with stage lighting and dressing room in conjunction with infrared transmitters, movement sensors, video technology, three laserdisc players, and a CD-ROM. The solo user enters the miniature theater, moving from foyer to dressing room, from where a miniaturized theater stage is observed through a semitransparent mirror. Various prerecorded sequences are played out on the miniature stage, including a magician's act and a lighting rehearsal, and characters encourage the user's participation: a dancer invites you to copy dance steps and a violinist encourages you to sing. The spectator is able to respond and interact with these sequences, and is recorded by a video camera that transmits their image onto the stage, merging the user's actions and movements with the prerecorded characters. Hans-Peter Schwarz points out how *Camera Virtuoso* utilizes the conjunctions of computer and video technologies to expand traditional notions of theater, reexamining the accepted boundaries and roles of actors, technicians and audiences: "For Bruno Cohen . . . the design of dramatic form is not as important as the comparison of the classic set to the use of image technology in order to expand the stage. The variety of audience participation makes the plot possible."[61]

Chris Hardman's Antenna Theatre equips audience members with headphones through which instructions are relayed to them. In its "Walkmanology" interactive walk-through performances, such as *Pandemonium* (1997), audience members are not intimidated by the demands of audience participation, but are rather given "permission to play again like children. . . . We are not put on the spot; we are not asked to invent what we do; we are told what to do, so we simply perform the prescribed tasks. Interaction with other people is often built into these tasks and is acceptable because we are merely following directions."[62] Tod Machover's *Brain Opera* (1996), with a libretto by Marvin Minsky, features three performers who select and interpret precomposed and audience-created elements using specially designed "hyperinstruments." A "Sensor Chair," a "Gesture Wall," and a "Digital Baton" translate and modulate movements into sound in different ways, while multiple projections on a curved screen provide counterpoints to the music or comment upon the performers' actions. During the finale, the audience is invited to dance on the stage's "Sensor Carpet," which intensifies the opera's sonic climax.

Audience members for Golan Levin's *Telesymphony* (2001) preregistered their cell phone number and theater seat number. New ringtones were downloaded onto the phones by Levin and his nine collaborators, who used custom-software to dial the phones in different prearranged sequences during the performance to choreograph and create a complex symphony, with as many as two hundred phones ringing simultaneously. As each audience member's phone rang, individual lights above each seat came on, and their physical presence as part of the performance was highlighted (not simply the sounds of the phones with them); "the resulting grid of lights illuminating the audience . . . [was] visible as a 'score' on projection screens at the side of the stage."[63]

In installations where visitors' walking or movement triggers sensors to activate planned events and programmed sequences and effects, it is arguable whether the primary interactive paradigm is, according to our continuum, navigation (the course the user takes), participation (users helping to bring to life the environment's sensory features), conversation (a dialogue between the user and the computer) or collaboration (the user and computer creating art together). For example, Keith Armstrong's performance installation *transit_lounge 2 (The Further Adventures of Ling Change)* (2000) hovers between navigation and participation paradigms. The movements of gallery visitors, as well as changes in light and atmosphere, affect the narrative journey of Ling Change as she travels through strange, comical, and beautifully designed computer-generated landscapes and meets cartoonlike characters (figure 23.7). In Paul DeMarinis's *Rain Dance/Musica Aquatica* (1998), installation visitors both navigate and participate as they pass under twenty streams of falling water, their umbrellas activating and modulating music and sound effects. Such sensory interactive environments hark back to earlier analog models, such as Nam June Paik's *Symphony for 20 Rooms* (1961), which called on the audience to play different audiotapes and kick objects around the room as part of the musical score. In the 1970s, pioneers such as Myron Krueger developed innovative interactive spaces such as *Metaplay* (1970) where visitors interacted with a screen which combined live video projection and

Figure 23.7 Keith Armstrong and Transmute Collective's interactive installation *transit_lounge Version 2* (2000).

computer graphics. For *Psychic Space* (1971), a sensory floor tracked visitors' movements through a graphic maze; and in *Videoplace* (1974), visitors' interactions manipulated the movement of images on a large projection screen.

Though in one sense motion-sensing installations can be argued to operate in all four of our interactive categories (navigation, participation, conversation, collaboration), our classifications emphasize which paradigm is most dominant and significant; and differentiate relative levels in the openness of interaction, what Rokeby calls "the degree that it reflects the consequences of our actions or decisions back to us."[64] In these terms, we categorize the majority of sensory installation environments as participatory, and early works typifying the genre such as Perry Hoberman's *Faraday's Garden* (1990) provides a clear example. Visitors to the installation walk along a mat containing footpad sensors which activate old record players, film projectors, radios, and power drills that Hoberman collected from flea markets and garage sales. He suggests that since the objects "span the entire twentieth century, movement around the room also functions as a kind of time travel."[65] In such installations, the sense of conversation or collaboration is far less marked than a more general sense of participation in bringing Hoberman's space "to life." Here, the sense of direct agency is limited and interactivity operates more on the level of cooperation than conversation—it could even be argued that it is merely navigation, since moving to a certain place to activate a specific effect differs little from clicking a mouse to achieve it.

Conversation

But in Hoberman's *Lightpools* (or *El Ball del Fanalet*, 1998) our third category of interactivity is reached since a meaningful "conversation" takes place, a dialogue that is reciprocated and is subject to real interchange and exchange. Users carry a physical lantern equipped with a position sensor (called a "fanalet") around a dimly lit circus ring–like space where glowing light shapes are projected onto the floor. A computer tracks each lantern's position in three-dimensional space and generates and transforms the projected light polygons, "proto-objects" ranging "from mechanical to biomorphic, abstract to ornamented."[66] By placing the lantern above one of these light-forms and moving it up and down, users can "feed" them, making them metamorphose, grow, and even dance. Participants can also move toward each other with their lanterns to bring the light shapes they have captured into contact with another user's entity. The shimmering forms then merge and "breed," whereupon they metamorphose into a new, single organic form or explode in a visual starburst, showering out a new crop of *Lightpools* around the floor for the cycle to begin again.

Nurturing and breeding these vivid, beautiful forms with other participants in the atmospherically lit, sonically reverberating circular space we found to be an intensely pleasurable, even joyous experience. The sense of *Lightpool*'s interactive paradigm being one of conversation is twofold: through its sophisticated level of user control over the movement and metamorphoses of these highly responsive proto-objects (a "conversation" between user and software); and in the interactions between users themselves, who come together and "converse" with and through their lanterns and the captured light forms.

In works that operate on a "conversational" interactive paradigm, there is often a complex relationship or negotiation established between the user/audience and the work, which is reliant on such issues as trust, cooperation, and openness. Such notions have been central to live interactive theater and performance since the 1960s, and an interesting example is provided by Valie Export's famous live street theater performance *Tapp und Tast Kino* (*Touch Cinema*, 1968). It intimately explored the ethics of live interaction, with Export inviting passers-by to feel inside a cardboard box she had constructed around her torso. Export calmly and unthreateningly held the gaze of each spectator as they placed their hands inside the box and touched her naked breasts. The piece played with a delicate ethics of intimacy and interaction, balancing notions of trust and abuse. In Export's feminist critique of woman as sex object, a fascinating, reversed interactive relationship between looking and touching was also set up. Export's breasts, as objects of desire to the male gaze on public streets were now hidden from view, but the male fantasy to fondle them was enabled. But in fulfilling the fantasy, the gaze of the male user was challenged and undermined, being directed onto the impassive, controlled stare of the woman he was invited to touch, whose female gaze now became the dominant and judgmental one.

The scenario is remediated for the high-tech age in the Centre for Metahuman Exploration's *Project Paradise* (1998), where a user in one booth can control the arms of a live male, naked actor to caress the breasts (or any other part of the anatomy) of a live, naked female actor. A user in a second booth controls the arms and caresses of the female actor, so the touching is mutual. The "Cyborg Adam and Cyborg Eve" wear nothing apart from engineered, jointed metal arm braces that are telerobotically controlled by the two gallery visitors in their separate booths using a touch-phone keypad (the parallels with phone sex are clear) (figure 23.8). When visitors enter one of the two booths (the allusion to peepshows is equally clear) they see a video monitor showing the point of view of either Adam or Eve, who stand opposite one another. The two visitors in their booths, like two puppeteers, then use the keys on the phone pad to enact an (invariably erotic) encounter between each other at a distance, through the live, corporeal agency of the two live "avatar" performers who are hidden from direct view but shown on the monitors. The booths are unmarked, and only once inside does the user discover whether their gender is the same or different from the performer they control.

The heterosexual pairing of Adam and Eve in *Project Paradise* seems to reinforce an ideology of compulsive heterosexuality. The multilayered questions of identity that the piece raises, however, constitute a radical challenge to the very notion of a fixed sexual identity. When a lesbian participant caresses Eve using Adam's hands, is the encounter a "lesbian" or a "straight" one? . . .

Figure 23.8   A user operates a telephone keypad to telerobotically caress the face of "Eve" in the Centre for Metahuman Exploration's *Project Paradise* (1998). Photo: Rob Long.

The eroticism of the encounter highlights the ontological doubleness of any live theatrical event, where by definition real events represent fictional ones. . . . At what point can anyone, including the actors themselves, determine when a pretend caress becomes a real one?[67] (figure 23.9).

The subjective camera viewpoint enhances the sense of the user's identification with one of the performers, and the artists compare the effect to the user being "projected" into a "remote paradise" where they "inhabit" the bodies of the remote performers to engage

Figure 23.9 When does a pretend caress become a real one? The Adam and Eve actors become erotic avatar puppets controlled by users in *Project Paradise* (1998). Photo: Rob Long.

in physical interaction.[68] As David Saltz puts it "the camera strongly implicates me as the subject of my character's actions," while the telerobotic technology "is a conduit that links the participant's subjectivity to the actor's."[69] Saltz's analysis of *Project Paradise* highlights its techno-fetishism and the blurring of lines between fiction and reality. He goes on to present an interesting and persuasive argument in relation to interactive telerobotic art, suggesting that the distinctions between the multiple subjects collapse to produce "a single virtual subject" or a "collaborative subject" that "relies on the contributions of multiple subjects to synthesise a single virtual subject." He also notes the parallels between these forms of interactive works and theatrical performance, where similar collaborative agencies exist between writer, director, designers, and actors. We would add how computers and the Web, both their use and their influence, have vastly extended the collaborative paradigm within society from business to the arts, from social activism to "vote-for-who/what-you-want" reality television.

Paul Sermon's interactive art similarly works as a conversation between two or more visitors separated in real space but telematically brought together to interact on a bed (*Telematic Dreaming*, 1992), on a sofa (*Telematic Vision*, 1993), or in a shower (*A Body of*

Figure 23.10   Remote participants are telematically brought together to interact in Paul Sermon's *Telematic Vision* (1993).

Water, 1999, with Andrea Zapp) (figure 23.10). Sermon's *Peace Talks* (2004) presents an "absurdist" piece of virtual theater where users participate in a simulated peace talks conference. Two identical, yet remote rooms are linked using broadband videoconferencing, and as in *Telematic Dreaming*, the users are "transported" via a monitor into a third telematic space, this time consisting of a room with a table. The two users thereby meet in the third (virtual) "peace talks" room containing a round table set out with UN-style national insignia, papers and microphones. As the remote participants virtually shake hands and improvise a peace talk dialogue together, each user's sense of physical presence is restricted due to the video glasses they wear, and Sermon also uses an optical illusion to make them appear to change scale on the monitor as they move around. Their visual awareness and ability to navigate the room is reliant on the view of the camera, and Sermon explains: "*Peace Talks* serves to ridicule the absurdity of a peace talk charade, whilst simultaneously offering a tongue in cheek, yet very viewable, alternative."[70]

Luc Courchesne's work uses aspects of navigational interactivity, for example, menu options and multiple-choice questions, and combines them with highly conversational modes. In his early interactive videodisc installation *Portrait One* (1990),[71] the user holds a conversation (in one of six languages) with Marie, who appears in close up on screen. A touchpad is used to select textual menu options of possible things to say and, depending on a range of factors (including the user's tact and Marie's mood) she may be frosty and uncooperative, replying with lines such as "Are you staring at me?" or

Figure 23.11 Luc Courchesne's beautiful and highly immersive interactive installation *Landscape One* (1997).

may engage in deep and intimate conversations, including ones about the nature of love in a virtual context. His rich, panoramic four-screen space *Landscape One* (1997) creates a 360-degree public garden, where visitors use voice or touch to select questions and lines of dialogue from imposed sets to communicate with onscreen characters (figure 23.11). The same model is used in *Hall of Shadows* (1996), where the virtual characters (laserdisc video recordings of the actors) are projected onto large reflective panes of glass on the ceiling "making the four characters appear as ghosts within the space shared with visitors."[72]

A conversation with both software and text takes place in Camille Utterback and Romy Archituv's corridor-like installation *Text Rain* (1999), where colored letters fall like drops of rain from the top of a screen that also relays and projects a live black-and-white video image of the visitor. As the falling letter particles come in contact with the outline of the user's body on the video image, they collect on its surface, sometimes creating random word formations, other times forming discernible words and phrases from the poem text the letters come from, Evan Zimroth's *Talk You* (1993). As Bolter and Gromala note, it becomes a kinetic and interactive poem as the letters form and transform like abstracted, Joycean phrases; and the visitor engages in a playful relationship with the technology, at times asserting control, at others unable to collect or hold the descending letters. Pairs of visitors can also hold boards and sheets between them to catch the letters and, by flicking the material upwards, to send them rebounding and scattering into the air. Bolter and Gromala explain how *Text Rain* appeals and is accessible to a broad audience: "not an elite piece of art, but an experience to be appreciated by both construction workers and Ph.D.s in computer science"[73] (figure 23.12).

In *Windows and Mirrors* (2003), Bolter and Gromala analyze installations at the SIGGRAPH 2000 exhibition and argue that many operate as mirrors (as well as windows), either literally offering a mirrorlike reflection through the use of a live camera feed, or in a metaphoric sense, reflecting contemporary society back on itself through layers of cultural and media imagery. Their lengthy analysis of *Text Rain* is used as a centerpiece in their argument that digital design should not attempt to become invisible (in contrast,

Figure 23.12 And a vowel please, Carol. Custom built software controls the falling and bouncing letters in Camille Utterback and Romy Achituv's delightful installation *Text Rain* (1999).

for example, to Donald Norman's argument in *The Invisible Computer* (1998)). They maintain that the goal of pragmatic and "structuralist" computer scientists such as Norman and Jakob Nielsen to make the computer interface transparent is too singular; rather, the aim should be a rhythmic oscillation between the transparent and the reflective. Digital art, they claim, "reminds us that every interface is a mirror as well as a window,"[74] and *TEXT RAIN* is a definitive case in point:

TEXT RAIN is both visible and invisible as a media form. The participants find the interface so easy to use, so natural, that they need no instruction at all. They understand instantly how to project their images on the screen and interact with the falling letters. The space of *TEXT RAIN* is an image of the physical world and at the same time an interface, a space for the manipulation of texts.

Digital art, like other digital applications, often opens a window for us, as we look through the computer screen to see the images or information located "on the other side." But *TEXT RAIN* is also a mirror, reflecting us as we manipulate the letters . . . [and] simultaneously surprises and pleases us by being simultaneously a mirror and a window.[75]

Toni Dove's *Artificial Changelings*

A highly dynamic conversation takes place between the user and Toni Dove's extraordinary interactive movie *Artificial Changelings* (1998), providing one of the most compelling experiences we have encountered on the path to this volume. The key to this magic is not so much the movie itself (excellent though it is) but its interactive structure and freedom, and the opportunity for the user to minutely control it using David Rokeby's *Very Nervous System* software. Users book in for a half-hour individual session in the installation, and use their body movement to interact with and control the movie images and sound of "a romance thriller about shopping" which opens in Paris at the end of the 19th century "and travels to an unnamed future"[76] (figure 23.13).

The installation is an immersive environment with a large curved rear projection screen, and the participant steps into a pool of light in front of the screen and can then move into one of four interactive zones marked out on the floor. Changing your proximity to the screen alters your viewpoint and situation, the sound, and the images on screen—for example, moving closer to the screen results in closer camera angles on the characters or images observed, and the sounds becoming quieter. Once you draw very close to the screen, extreme close-ups and intimate voiceovers suggest that you are "inside" one of the principal character's heads—Arathusa, "a 19th century kleptomaniac with self-destructive tendencies [who] suffers from constraints of Victorian society [and] gets an erotic thrill from stealing" (figure 23.14); and Zileth, "a woman from the future, both real and imagined, [an] encryption hacker searching for enemies, a dreamer and a voyeur obsessed with power"[77] (figure 23.15). Moving into the marked time tunnel floor zone enables the user to traverse the centuries of the narrative, some of which plays as conventional linear movie sequences.

Figure 23.13 An individual user has 30 minutes to navigate through and control Toni Dove's extraordinary interactive "movie" *Artificial Changelings* (1998).

The soundtrack and the behavior of the images react precisely and fluidly to body movements, the whole piece changing speed, color, atmosphere, and feeling as the user crosses the floor zones or makes gestures with her limbs and body. In periods of "dream suspension," body movement such as twists or arm circles give the user absolute control of the visual media, able to play the screen characters' movements forward or in reverse, in direct relation to the speed and nature of the user's movement. As Dove puts it, "the video motion sensing system allows the viewer a theremin-like control over sound and image. . . . Like a video android with a dual personality, the narrative accretes from a kind of "swimming" through the information in the environment[78] (figure 23.16).

One thus literally dances with onscreen characters, and we spent a number of sessions in the installation "scratch-choreographing" the movements of a character in a diaphanous white dress (recalling the figure of Loïe Fuller) running and dancing in a moonlit garden. At the same time that the user's body or arms scratch and play the video images, they also play the music and sonorous soundscapes (which was the original purpose of the *VNS*

Figure 23.14 Arathusa, the "nineteenth-century kleptomaniac with self-destructive tendencies," in *Artificial Changelings*.

Figure 23.15 Zileth, Arathusa's alter-ego, "a woman from the future, both real and imagined," in *Artificial Changelings*.

Figure 23.16 "The video motion sensing system allows the viewer a theremin-like control over sound and image." An image is duplicated numerous times through the user's movements in *Artificial Changelings*.

software before Rokeby also brought visual media under its control). The user's arms and body conduct Peter Scherer's extraordinary audio database so that dense musical chords and sounds ascend or descend or create symphonic effects, while delicate finger movements prompt high melodic scales. The preciseness of the user's control over sound and image feels distinctly cybernetic and genuinely futuristic, and as Dove rightly maintains:

[Your] body is stuck to the movie, a part of it, lost in space and time. This effects [*sic*] the way a viewer moves, and perhaps how we might think about what a body is—its boundaries and edges go soft. . . . This combination of action and physical sensation induces a trance-like state physically connected to the media that contributes to spatialising the narrative experience and disrupting a linear or sequence based notion of plot.[79]

Collaboration

During Nam June Paik's *Exposition of Music—Electronic Television* in 1963, Joseph Beuys made an impromptu participatory impact by attacking a piano with an ax. Though the gesture was wholly in keeping with the "happening" spirit of Paik's exhibition, it transformed what had been up to that point been a participatory interactive space into a collaborative one (even leapfrogging over the interactive category of conversation). Beuys did not just join in (participation), or undertake a dialogue with the artwork (conversation); he did something to alter significantly the artwork/interactive performance space itself (collaboration). Interactive collaboration comes about when the interactor becomes a major author or coauthor of the artwork, experience, performance or narrative. The collaboration may be between a single user and the computer/virtual environment, but more usually occurs when users work together with others to create new work by means of computer technologies or within a virtual environment.

Numerous interactive collaborations have been discussed already in other chapters, and the collaborative spirit in art and performance, particularly on or via the Web in the form of group dramas as well as major projects such as *Oeudis* (1997), is one of digital performance's most pronounced and characteristic features. A sense of creative collaboration is clear from the very title of Company in Space's Web project *home, not alone* (2000), as well as its publicity, which invites us to

ENTER> . . . sit back in the comfort of your own home creating complex movies laden in personalised statements via orchestrated online participation. Watch performers on screen, change the scene, adjust lights and soundtrack, or send a personal message to the actor. Re-create the site at will, but remember . . . you are not alone.
EXIT> and the site remains in continuous dialog with its global audience ensuring the work's history is constantly recreated in real-time, never fixed, permanently integrated.
BEYOND THE WEB> Uniquely, Company in Space reconstitute the site by layering projections of the public's visual, aural and intellectual authorship on urban architectural structures: a new graffiti.[80]

Webbed Feats' *Bytes of Bryant Park* (1997) elicited input from online contributors prior to the event that directly affected the content of performances taking place on six stages around New York's Bryant Park. People accessing the group's website contributed musical, theatrical, creative writing, and choreographic ideas for a partly rehearsed, partly improvised six-hour festival of theater, dance, poetry, and music seen by a park audience of five-thousand, and simultaneously webcast. Performers used and interpreted the myriad stimuli submitted to the site, which included sound effects, soundtrack compositions and rhythm scores, poetry, dance phrases, written and spoken dialogue segments, and set and costume designs. On the Mezzanine stage, four actors and dancers improvised in response to the Web contributions; the Goethe Stage presented a rehearsed interpretation of *Faust* influenced by the Web ideas; and original poetry and creative writing contributions were performed on the Gertrude Stein Stage. On the Promenades beside the park's great lawn, extended dance sequences were created by stitching together submitted choreographic phrases, and by the dancer's free interpretations of descriptive words submitted to the site. On the Dodge Stage, in front of a statue of New Yorker William Earl Dodge, a series of one-minute performances was played, submitted in the form of "soap box editorials."[81]

La Fura Dels Baus' millennium night *Big Opera Mundi* (2000) was an "global live opera" created online by remote artists, musicians, and other participants who sent their inputs progressively in the minute zero of the new year, as it consecutively happened in different world meridians. The company call it a "telepathic event . . . [to] creatively channel the euphoria generated by large events . . . an idea, a hope, a dream, and a utopia for the new millennium."[82] Sita Popat has developed major pan-European dance collaborations for students, who devise separate pieces of choreography and upload them on the Web for discussion and development between the different groups, before they all come together from their various countries to perform the entire piece in real space. For Popat and Satorimedia's *In Your Dreams: Hands-On Dance Project* (2000) three stages of Web-based activity and collaboration formulated the final dance performance. In stage one, remote participants sent in ideas and images around the theme of dreams, and videos of short dance phrases they inspired were uploaded onto the website. In stage two, participants collaborated in videoconferenced rehearsals, watching the Satorimedia performers and offering comments and suggestions; and in stage three participants chose the order of the series of different dance phrases for the final performance.

Douglas Davis's ongoing interactive scriptwriting project *Terrible Beauty* (1997, with Christine Walker) offers its online participants "many roles, as Voyeur, Playwright, as Reader/Critic, as Actor (yes, you can read lines in company with a global cast of volunteers, whom you can already see, hear, and scent.)"[83] The evolving scripts center on the dynamic and changing revelations of the identities of two main characters. Originally called "I.D.", Davis subsequently changed the project's title to reflect his "awe" at "the aesthetic terror slowly emerging and building," renaming it *Terrible Beauty* from a line of a William Butler Yeats poem: "All changed, changed utterly. A terrible beauty is born."[84]

Projects and installations where visitors input material that is then directly stored and incorporated in the artwork can also be regarded as collaborative interaction, although the degree of artistic impact on the piece overall clearly varies from work to work. We would call Stephen Wilson's *Ontario* (1990) a collaborative installation since the visitor input is its primary (rather than secondary or incidental) material. A sound installation in a Netherlands church square, it involves passers-by answering questions about their views on religion, which are recorded, digitized, and stored, and then played back through individual speakers arranged around the square (figure 23.17). The conceptual and emotional content of the opinions are mapped against different criteria that determine the spatial placements of the sound outputs so that, for example, religiously conservative opinions come from one side of the square while liberal or atheistic responses come from another. Other sound elements are added, for example, answers to the question "Why is there evil in the world?" emanating from one speaker are accompanied by the sound of animal yelps from speakers near to it. In Wilson's installation *Father Why?* (1989), different emotions (sadness, anger, longing, forgetfulness) are explored in different areas of a space as a computer senses a visitor's presence and generates music and digitized speech in response.

Figure 23.17 Interactivity as collaboration: in *Ontario* (1990), passersby collaborate with Stephen Wilson's church square audio installation to provide its core content.

Visitors speak a short word or phrase related to each emotion into a microphone, and the phrases are incorporated into the computer's database repertoire. Lingering in one area, such as the "Place of Anger," prompts the computer to explore the emotion with increasing depth and nuance (figure 23.18).

For visitors of both of Wilson installations, those who speak into the microphones and record their inputs are interacting conversationally in the first instance, and collaboratively if (and only if) their words are incorporated and used later as output. However, for those who don't record their voices and prefer to move around and simply listen to the voices of others, the installations are not strictly interactive at all; they are conventional sound installations.

Conclusion: Play

The categories of interaction that we have defined—navigation, participation, conversation and collaboration—are helpful in delineating different forms of interactive art in relation to ascending levels and depths of interactivity, and their openness in accommodating and incorporating the user's own creative inputs. In drawing up this hierarchy, however, we are conscious that it could be argued that one essential element and category is missing—*play*. But rather than being a category unto itself, play pervades and unites all four interactive paradigms we have identified. A sense of play is equally fundamental to the *navigation* of a CD-ROM or interactive movie, *participation* in sensor-active

Figure 23.18 Stephen Wilson's installation *Father Why?* (1989).

environments, *"conversations"* with interactive screen figures, and creative *collaborations* with networked artists or artworks that embrace, remediate, and incorporate user inputs.

Interactive works encourage a playful, childlike fascination for the pleasure of cause and effect, where a simple hand movement or facial grimace causes a domino effect, a ripple through time and space that directly affects and transforms something outside of oneself. Interactivity in digital arts and performance is at its best a marvel of discovery, rekindling childhood feelings of intimate connection to a vast, inexplicable, and beautiful world. As Bolter and Gromala observe, "They ask us to react playfully and to wonder whether it is appropriate to play in an art gallery" as we "see ourselves as participants in the dance of our culture."[85]

We will now move on to the interactive model most obviously associated with ideas of play, and indeed of children—computer and video games. This model, too, is a veritable "dance of our culture," and one that should not be underestimated in its relationship not only to culture, but also to the future of digital art and performance. To date, many of the characters and choreographies in these video games have not been "pretty," but millions of user-practitioners seem as dedicated as Balinese dancers and (where it matters) as physically nimble as prima ballerinas, as they train hour after long hour, fingers callused and bleeding, perfecting this particular art of digit-al dancing.

Videogames

A game is a machine that can get into action only if the players consent to become puppets for a time.
—MARSHALL MCLUHAN, 1964[1]

Academic Legitimization

In recent years, the academic study of computer and video games (which for ease we will shorten to videogames hereafter) has proliferated almost at the level of the rapidly expanding videogames industry itself, with numerous titles emerging to analyze the aesthetic, technological, semiotic, and sociological aspects of gameplay. Steven Poole's *Trigger Happy* (2000) was one of the earliest academic commentaries, and particularly focuses on challenging games demanding fast reflexes, while Henry Jenkins, the person above all who has most consistently flagged the videogame as an art/performance medium, expresses a clear preference for its narrative possibilities. Recent publications have studied the game as a popular cultural phenomenon (Berger 2002), as fictional form (Atkins 2003), and as "cyberdrama," "ludology," and "critical simulation" (Wardrip-Fruin and Harrigan 2004). Wolf and Perron have published the first *Video Game Theory Reader* (2003), which chooses to emphasize storytelling and its interpretation and consequences, as well as ideas around the psychology and "configurative performance" activities of the player, linking gameplay to Allan Kaprow's Happenings.

International journals have also emerged, notably *Game Studies* in 2002, whose second issue includes Kurt Squires's article "Cultural Framing of Computer/Video Games" (2002), which draws together many strands of cognitive science and cultural and educational psychology, and stresses the opportunities for cultural, humanities, and arts theorists to contribute. The online journal *Gamasutra* features announcements of graduate and postgraduate theses on videogames,[2] with topics covering industrial, business, and technical aspects, analysis of gameplay, art and animation, and academic investigations such as how videogames have drawn upon film noir. In just the same way that academic conferences focusing on computing in the arts suddenly blossomed in the 1990s (and now have noticeably declined in frequency), so new organizations and conferences have proliferated to discuss videogames. In 2003 alone, for example, there was a student showcase in San Jose in early March; in late March the First International Conference on Technologies for Interactive Digital Storytelling and Entertainment in Darmstadt, Germany; a Microsoft technical conference in Redwood City, California, in May; an ESRC one in Manchester, England, in September; and, of course, the massive annual SIGGRAPH conference, whose emphasis on computer graphics has always promoted the cause.

MIT was centrally concerned in academic and practical development of the field and in 1999 a conference entitled MIT ("Media in Transition") set out many of the ground rules for the debate by focusing on play aspects of the new media (including but not particularly focusing upon videogames). Janet Sonenberg led what hindsight reveals as a key seminar on "Playing With New Media," where the ambiguity of the term "play" was explored. Eric Zimmerman provided useful distinctions between three aspects that could guide analysis of any specific games: the rules, the implementation of the rules (the play), and "the culture" in which both rules and play were embedded. Tom Kemper drew parallels based on cognitive theory between the relative engagements of sport spectators and videogame players in relation to Zimmerman's three categories, and "attendant notions of interactivity and empowerment." These early distinctions are now resulting in an advanced and complex set of theories that includes a contemporary debate that Gonzalo Frasca has dubbed "The Narratologists versus The Ludologists."[3]

The opposition between them is an ancient one, like the tension between literary analyses of plays as text and commentaries that approach them in relation to their realization in live performance. Ludologists put the emphasis upon the game (its practice, gameplay, visuals, manipulation, the experience of playing it), while narratologists put the emphasis upon its significance, meaning, and the philosophy underlying the progression of events. Both sides of the debate were present at an important one-day public conference in New York in 1999 entitled RE:PLAY,[4] which discussed the past, present, and future of digital games under four headings: Games as Structure, Games as Simulacra, Games as Narrative, and Games as Exchange. The need for specific videogame theories clearly emerged as a key theme for a number of the participants, including Marc LeBlanc:

In an era where art and commerce coexist uneasily at best in *any* medium, what chance do computer games have of creating genuine art? I think it can happen but only if we make the . . . leap, from Industry to Theory. They [videogames] need an analogous "cultural infrastructure," including not only developers, publishers and consumers, but also critics and academics. But that won't happen without a theory of game design.

Chris Crawford continued the theme: "We have a long way to go before we can discuss interactive storytelling with any real familiarity. . . . We must completely purge the concept of narrative from our heads if we are to succeed. . . . We have to think in terms of simulation. . . . We need another layer, a higher level of abstraction." Henry Jenkins drew parallels with the early development of film theory, observing that it was such discussions and debates (rather than the medium itself) that ultimately provided the building blocks for academics to develop theoretical underpinnings that recognized and validated cinema as an art form. He urged a move away from the consideration of videogames in relation to long-established theoretical models, concluding that "we still think of TV and cinema and the book in terms of narrative, when clearly games require us to think about them in terms of games." While acknowledging and broadly agreeing with this principle, in this chapter we will particularly focus on the relationships and links between videogames and theater and performance, and we will trace their convergence both in games design and in manifestations of digital performance.

Videogames as Theater

Videogames—very theatrical—where you control a hero with a stick. You turn the stick right or left and the hero walks to his adventure.
—MILTOS MANETAS[5]

Videogames involve virtual and fantasy worlds which may seem technologically advanced but are largely constructed within the well-known parameters of narrative and theater, simulation, and make-believe. As Janet Murray notes: "games, as the word 'play' reminds us, are intrinsically dramatic, enactments of life situations at varying levels of abstraction."[6] When videogames were first developed, theater terminology was freely adopted by game designers, including "setting," "player," and "character"; and in early parlance the terms "player" and "character" were combined and known by the slightly confusing acronym PC, while other emergent acronyms such as IC (in character) and OOC (out of character) were drawn directly from acting and theater practice. But a key distinguishing feature is that the audience's identification with the character is closer within a videogame than in traditional theater (even though game characters tend to lack theater characters' psychological complexities and depths): the audience is the participant, the participant is the player, the player is the character.

Where Brenda Laurel drew on the fundamental properties of computers to demonstrate their intimate relationships with theater, the same analytic process can be undertaken to draw close correspondences readily between theater and videogames. Both are time-based; both engage in the telling of a repeatable fictional narrative with identifiable characters; the characters develop relationships and, to varying degrees, personalities; both undertake elaborately defined tasks or missions in a single or a series of specific environments; the participants who witness or engage in the time-based activities will be drawn through various responses and emotional states; by the conclusion the characters will have fully achieved, partly achieved, or failed to achieve their particular undertaking; and, finally, main and subsidiary characters will be left either dead or alive. Such parameters are as true of *Hamlet* as they are of *Final Fantasy*.

The French critic Ferdinand Brunetiere (1849–1906) perhaps lived a century too early, for his famous dictum "conflict is the essence of all drama" seems to attain its greatest confirmation in the medium of videogames where dramatic conflict is in abundance, as epitomized in the violence of the shoot-'em-up game. Violent videogames, by far the most popular and high profile of the genre, have also drawn extensively from the same myths, legends, and epics as have classical dramatists from Euripides to Wagner. Wagner's *Der Ring des Nibelungen* remediated the same Germanic myths as Tolkien's *Lord of the Rings*, which has in turn been remediated by countless games reveling in its magical creatures and supernatural characters, its heroics, violence, and morals; and where, in true videogame style, any one monster defeated is immediately replaced with one even more vicious and terrifying. Since the earliest *Dungeons and Dragons* videogames, classical myths have provided games developers with a vast storehouse of plots, heroes, and monsters that repeat the same fabled challenges and victories where the final mishap is averted, good triumphs over evil, the world (be it local or the universe) is saved from calamity and death, and heroes live to go on to the next level and face the next challenge. Neither myths nor violent videogames discuss regional boundaries or compromise solutions: there are only winners and losers, triumphs or abject despair.

But even the worst violent excesses of shoot-'em-up games hardly compare with some of the horrors and desecrations of Greek mythology. Uranus, sky god and first ruler, was castrated by his son Kronos, who was inclined to eat his own children. One he spared, Zeus, had the wise Prometheus punished for giving man the gift of fire, chaining him to a rock with an eagle tearing at his liver, but in true gaming style he escapes, rescued by Hercules. Zeus himself is the perfect videogame action hero: supreme leader, god of justice and mercy, punisher of the wicked, and seducer par excellence (four wives and several mistresses). His son Dionysus, half-mortal and half-god, continues the tradition admirably for a follow-up game or expansion pack. A wild, eccentric, and suffering character, he transgresses animal, human, and gender boundaries and blurs the line between reality and a new state of mind with the mask of theater. God of madness, frenzy and wine, it is Dionysus who presides over the creation of "the mask" as the crossing point from one reality to another—the mask as the threshold of virtual reality. These are the liminal borders between persona and myth, between humanity and the divine, between the finite and the infinite that are rarely reached in contemporary theater—but are by the finest games as our heroes fight against the powers of death, darkness, and evil.

Such battles almost inevitably involve monsters, and Greek monsters were *über*-monsters: from Typheus, a fire-breathing dragon with a hundred heads, and the giants generated from Uranus's blood when he was castrated, to the Hecatoncheires, gigantic beasts with fifty heads and a hundred arms, with which they rained down huge boulders on their foes. Such exaggerated horror is a common mythological norm; and Roman theater tragedy, based on the Greek originals, is even less refined. In Seneca's *Oedipus,* Jocasta rips open her own womb; in *Thyestes*, bodies of children are served at a banquet; in *BloodRayne* (not Roman but GameCube, PS2, and Xbox, re-released March 2003) there is excessive blood, gore, and severed limbs as our heroine battles her way into Nazi death factories and other locales that resemble hell on Earth. Videogames can thus honorably take their places within a long line of classical theatrical plays that have remediated grue-some myths and supernatural horrors.

Theaters of Blood

The dramatic depiction of blood is a significant aspect of violent videogames: a signifier of victory that is sometimes taken to ludicrous extremes. The classic 1996 game *Die Hard with a Vengeance* (part of the *Die Hard Trilogy* for Sony, Sega, and PC) includes a "Blood on/Blood off" option, with "Blood on" resulting in the whole screen appearing to splatter with blood, whereupon inbuilt (virtual) windscreen wipers wash it gorily away. Within performance traditions the emphasis on blood and gore is equally significant and revealing, from its grim reality in the spectacles of Roman gladiatorial battles and (even today) public state executions, to the buckets of stage blood required for Montmartre's infamous Grand Guignol melodramas in the late nineteenth and early twentieth centuries. The very stuff of birth, life, and death, just a spot of it signals Lady Macbeth's guilty con-science in a play that is steeped in it, and blood continues to provide a source of endless theatrical fascination: a shortcut to shock and tragic climax, and arguably also a shortcut to catharsis.

The Grand Guignol[7] opened in 1897 in a suitably spooky abandoned chapel in Montmartre in Paris, and followed on in the tradition of Emile Zola's grimly realistic French naturalism. It attracted and, by report, terrified audiences drawn from every sector of society including European kings and dignities as well as the local Parisienne society. The Guignol opted to portray the daily murders, rapes, and mutilations that featured in the headlines of the time, gratuitous real-life horrors brought to realistic life again onstage, this time as a *"tranche de mort"* (slice of death). The scripts from the period reveal much more dependency upon dialogue than one would expect to find in a contemporary videogame, but many stage directions have a whiff of familiarity about them: "She col-lapses in agony and crawls across the floor, screaming and retching. Henri goes over to her and continues to pour acid on her face."[8]

The choice of real-life stories as a basis for the gore-plots of Grand Guignol is inter-esting in relation to the continuing debates raging around the links between videogame violence and violence in society, and while violent videogame narratives generally the lack the real-world referents of their Parisian predecessors, they have all their props, trappings, and buckets of blood, reinventing Grand Guignol in a modern idiom. Games reviewers and players universally complimented *Grand Theft Auto III: Vice City* (all main formats, 2003) for their graphics and gameplay, but the narrative, which essentially consists of driving and killing people, drew condemnation from outside forces, including a *New York Post* reporter who complained in December 2003 that *Grand Theft Auto III* was "spewing the glorification of mass murder and the celebration of death. . . . Cases surface constantly in which *Grand Theft Auto* has been linked to violence and killing." The debate on the links between real and virtual violence has been particularly fierce given that children have traditionally formed a substantial proportion of gamers, and has led to an age rating system similar to film classifications, although as an essentially home-based activity these are not easily controlled. Japan, unlike Europe and the United States, does not have a ratings system for games, which in the past was not regarded as a problem in a culture known for its lack of violent crime. But Japan has seen a rise in teenage violence over the past few years, sparking controversy and intense media debate over the possible related influence of videogames. As with the parallel and longer-standing debate about film and television violence affecting violence in society, the issues are complex (do games generate real life violence or merely reflect an always-already violent society?) and the point is ultimately unprovable. Clearly, everyone who plays violent videogames does not become a murderer in real life any more than people who play Snakes and Ladders become herpetologists or window-cleaners; and in the absence of conclusive evidence supporting either side, thoughtful commentators tend to reserve judgment.

The Pentagon alone seems to recognize a possible *advantageous* link between VR and RL violence, as demonstrated in their numerous Internet recruitment pop-ups advertising the United States Army on game websites. American games company Sega is also a major defense contractor, and in September 2002 the Army released its own online game, *America's Army: Operations,* a first-person-shooter game available as a free download. It takes the player through a recruitment process, early training, and, controversially, an advanced training section that includes shooting "terrorists" who look suspiciously like Osama bin Laden and Fidel Castro.[9] The game's pre-publicity invites users to "earn the right to call yourself a Soldier, letting the enemies of freedom know that America's Army has arrived," and almost half a million requests for downloads were received in the first week of its release.

But one standard complaint about popular media (and in some cases, theater)—"too much sex and violence"—has a surprising omission in the case of videogames, where there is generally little or no sex.[10] There is an abundance of sex*ism*, and debates about related gender issues have proliferated, but most games avoid any pornographic imagery or depictions of physical sex. This is mainly because videogames originally developed with children as the main market audience, but as the average player age has increased (now estimated by most authorities as mid-twenties) this is a situation that has recently begun to change. In 2002 a Techmo *Dead or Alive* series game featured *Xtreme* (i.e., naked) *Beach Volleyball* (Techmo 2002), and some sex games have been produced by Zenith Publishing that are not so much sexy, or even sexist, as dire. *Sexual Pursuits*, boasts "3000 sexual performance cards" and remediates strip poker with the addition of being able to win "magic spells" for "drunkenness," "striptease," and "favors from opponents." *Sex Party* is a multicouple computer sex game whose rules rather primly announce that the default setting means that couples can only interact with their own partners. The objective of *Panty Raider: From Here to Immaturity* (Simon & Schuster, 2000) is to take clandestine photographs of women in their underwear, which reaped enormous criticism for its concept before it was launched and, from a different group, for the quality of the photographs after it was launched, so neither faction seemed particularly well served. Meanwhile, within nonsexual games, there has been considerable interest from hacker-gamers to discover (against the public wishes of the production companies) the "cheat" code for removing the clothes of the characters so as to play the game with naked avatars (game characters are constructed as wire-frame figures that are then "skinned" and then clothed). It may come as no surprise that chief target for this mischief has been Lara Croft, subsequently nicknamed "Nude Raider," and locatable undraped on the Internet with even rudimentary research skills. Mario the Plumber and Sonic the Hedgehog have attracted less attention for this particular diversion.

Social Theater: *The Sims*

Hey ditch the beardy stuff in favour of a hip new god sim where you get to create your perfect holiday island and cater to the debauched needs of your guests with such amenities as Disco of Doom and the Chalet of Chaos (probably).
—PC GAMES NEWSLETTER, 2002[11]

But the most popular videogame of all time, Will Wright's *The Sims* (2000), is nonviolent and nonsexual, and indeed has nothing to with winning and losing. A "family with problems" simulation that had sold twenty million copies by 2003, *The Sims* finds a suburban family wrestling with the horrors of consumer acquisition and choice, and has well-developed characters with personalities, likes, dislikes, and emotions. It parallels more the concerns of the soap opera and *Big Brother* than a mythical epic or the army target range. It is the kitchen-sink or existential drama of the game world, even if still awaiting the equivalent angst of *Look Back in Anger* (1956). *The Sims* is a drama considered by some reviewers to be fractionally more complicated than life itself.[12] There are few aspects of everyday family life that cannot be simulated in *The Sims*, although sexual intercourse has only just become possible (or rather, new babies can now appear, through a new facility available in an expansion pack)—but only for heterosexual couples that the software recognizes as being officially married.[13] Much the same context existed on the English stage until 1956.

As one of the most popular games worldwide, the *Sims* expansion packs (additional software that allows the characters to undertake a wider range of activities) add both to range and revenue: for example, *The Sims Go On Holiday* (2003) comes with choice of holiday, who goes, what happens, and so on. Several expansion packs emphasize a particular youth-market lifestyle: "Hot Date," "House Party," "Superstar." *The Sims Bustin' Out* (released late 2003, all formats) provided an additional dozen external locations (gym, Club Rubb and party locations), forty new characters, and ten new careers, including Mobster, Athlete, Mad Scientist, and (relatively new as a "career") Fashion Victim. *The Sims Online* has developed the scenario one stage further so that players are online with thousands of other Sims players "creating a dream home, building the trendiest boutique." *The Sims: Unleashed* (Electronic Arts, October 2002) allows members of the family to select pets from an unlikely if not impossible range, the accompanying publicity revealing not only an ironic undertone but also reflecting the desire of games manufacturers to meet a newly perceived audience demand for increased social collaboration within the game: "*The Sims: Unleashed* gives players dozens of new social interactions and expands their neighbourhood. Now the Sims can . . . build their relationships through their adorable animals."

The notion of virtual pets is by no means novel, and the "pet rock" had become an interesting mix of lunacy and performance art in 1975 as these "pets" were taken for walks (and made a millionaire of their inventor, Gary Dahl). *Tamagotchi*, created in Japan in 1997, was an even closer forerunner, a virtual pet that required digital looking after or it would die. Blamed for unnecessary childhood traumas and, among other things, causing traffic accidents, it was banned in schools in several countries and started a debate over the age that young children could cope with the death of a pet (and thereby creating business for bereavement counselors and *tamagotchi* babysitters). Having not quite reached a zenith of absurdity, the *tamagotchi* was followed by the *octogotchi*, which required the owner to keep eight digital pets alive, which in turn was followed by the *Octogotchi Deluxe* (fifteen different pets). There followed Furbies and twenty different versions of Gigas, including species that could be trained to fight friends' pets. A related outcome of this "caring game" has been the production of the computer-chipped baby doll, The Ready-Or-Not TOT, which is issued to American high school teenagers (boys as well as girls; the dolls are male or female and of all races) as part of parenting and sex education classes. Much like the games and simulations they now populate, virtual pets and baby dolls have generally been more popular with females than males, and in the videogame arena this has became part of a process *versus* goal debate, with games such as *The Sims* successfully providing for (or exploiting) the process element.

Women and Videogames

"lots of chores before completing more chores. . . "
—TV REVIEW OF *MARY KING RIDING STAR*.[14]

Girls and women have generally been the second-class citizens of videogames, and in 2000 the Top 100 PlayStation titles only listed two recognizably female names, *Britney* (fortieth—a dance/pop game) and *Veronica* (fifty-eighth—the heroine's task is to rescue her brother Chris, and in the second part of the game Chris takes over). Xbox's Top 100 games only featured one female name, *Buffy the Vampire Slayer* (twenty-eighth, from the popular TV series). In the 1990s, the game industry was more than a little tokenistic when marketing games at girls and women, seeming to assume that beyond Barbie and horses they were a lost cause. Attempts to involve more women gamers were clumsy if not comical: *Mary King Riding Star* (1999) was an attempt to attract younger girls with the ever-popular theme of owning a pony, but the three female presenters on the game review program *Bitz* found that it consisted of "lots of chores before completing more chores," clearly getting the necessary contrast between RL and VR completely wrong. They concluded that "seasoned gamers will want to send *Riding Star* to the glue factory!"[15] The game industry's apparent ineptitude at conceiving effective female games has been evident since the outset: *Pac-Man,* one of the first arcade games (since 1980) and described as "a faceless yellow blob designed to look like a pizza with a slice removed that attempted to gobble up four enemies and 240 dots" was remarketed as *Ms. Pac-Man,* which consisted of a faceless yellow blob designed to look like a pizza with a slice removed, plus lipstick and a perfunctory red bow. James Davies has argued convincingly that one reason for the game industry's inability to gauge and respond to the needs of the female market is by virtue of negative and circular "recursive social and cultural processes with respect to gender" which he calls "gender feedback loops."[16]

Slightly more commercially and critically successful was the release at Christmas 2002 of *Mary-Kate & Ashley: Sweet 16* (GameCube), which features games involving learning to drive, jet-ski holidays, rock-climbing, and buying clothes. But the radical sounding *Macho Women with Guns* (a spoof that first appeared in 1989 and was revived in 2003) was found guilty of a mixed message. The title and narrative genuinely seemed to give women an active role in a shoot-'em-up style game that was complimented for its gun-toting heroines, but other aspects reaped heavy criticism, particularly its "Charisma Factor" feature, which was measured by bra size. Publications were soon appearing such as Cassell and Jenkins's *From Barbie to Mortal Kombat* (2000), which broached the debate about what games might attract girls, the implications of both existing and new games for girls, and how girls might find themselves drawn to new technologies. There are other signs of subtle shifts such as the foundation of womengamers.com in 1999, which has since acted as an effective lobby and creative arena for new ideas.

Brenda Laurel argues that girls' dislike for traditional computer games derives more from the fact that the characters tend to be weak and thus the dramatic experience is "boring," rather than from games' violent or competitive nature. Unlike boys, "girls are typically unmotivated by mastery for its own sake, but demand engaging and relevant experiences from video games. Both boys and girls see video game machines as for boys and computers as gender-neutral."[17] Laurel's VR experience *Placeholder* (1993, with Rachel Strickland) later spawned her successful Purple Moon software company, established in

1996 (and bought by Mattel in 1999) which produced a range of products and merchandise aimed at preteen girls, including the *Rockett's World* game and eight CD-ROMs. Laurel has reflected how the research undertaken through her *Placeholder* and Purple Moon projects provided strong quantitative findings related to how girls and women respond to computer products and experiences. Dance artist Mabel Klies has also reflected on the issue in live performance works such as *Gallery of Memories* (2000), which "avoids empty 'techno-gymnastics' for a more intimate and poetic approach, thus revealing the so often forgotten warmer, deeper and mystical possibilities of the digital imagery through its specific immaterial qualities."[18] The performance uses a VRML environment as a pathway for two dancers to take a journey through dreamlike rooms, and involves the audience in interactive games. But she contrasts masculine-dominated search-and-destroy structures with her own paradigm through which "the quest [is] for emotional and spiritual self/growth and revelation."[19]

Sony/PlayStation have been the leading company to develop games outside the rigid parameters of the male adventure, for example by developing games software that requires participants to dance or compose electronic music using a MIDI interface on the games console. The dance game requires the additional purchase of a PlayStation Dance Mat incorporating touch-sensitive contacts. It is relatively unsophisticated in its demands at the time of writing (though still not easy to do), essentially requiring the gamer to execute sequences of steps that become more difficult as the levels progress. But its very existence indicates an enthusiasm to think of concepts beyond entrenched structures, and it has proved particularly popular with young teenage girls and consistently appears in several of the Top Ten lists. The Football Mat, whereby the player controls a soccer videogame with touch-sensitive floor pads as well as the control console, is a further development of this new principle. But given its complicated foot-to-ball movements one could be forgiven for thinking it might be preferable to go outside and play soccer. *Eyetoy* (2003) was a further interesting development of the genre, a shoot-'em-up game with a distinct difference, since the player sees him/herself on screen battling against the odds via a USB web camera. *EyeToy: Groove* (PlayStation 2003) cleverly combines the interest in both developments—dancing and self on screen—so that the player/dancer can now appear live on the TV monitor. This paradigm has clear parallels with numerous digital dance performance experiments we have discussed in earlier chapters, and the transference to popular game formats represents a significant conceptual breakthrough that can be expected to exert a real influence on the future development of digital games.

Videogames as Art

Lucien King's collection *Game On: The History and Culture of Videogames* (2002), adopts the slightly garish cartoon approach that currently typifies videogame imagery but is, in fact, an exhibition catalogue.[20] As the foreword notes, the first forty years of videogames' existence has been largely ignored by the art world, and the 2002 exhibition was surprisingly the first specifically devoted to videogames at a British art gallery (although others, such as *Serious Games* and *The Art Casino*, had included examples). Lucien King, together with independent games designer Eric Zimmerman, used the catalogue to highlight the absurdity of the art world's detachment from videogames. Both are outspoken about the need to acknowledge games as a significant cultural phenomenon and to repair games' glaring omission from the field of legitimate visual arts. Nonetheless, Zimmerman's contribution "Do Independent Games Exist?" (2002) highlights the "staunchly conservative . . . and completely screwed up" commercial game market dominated by "lookalike, genre–bound drek,"[21] and he describes the games industry as "completely technofetishistic, with the value of games typically being judged on their technical merits. Innovation in games needs to come from sources other than hardware and software technology."[22] It is rare for a national art exhibition catalogue to make such provocative statements, but it is indicative of a growing awareness that the artistic and narrative potentials of videogames are underdeveloped, and that a gauntlet should be thrown down as a challenge to artists as well as games companies.

The response from artists and performance practitioners has been gradual over the last ten years, but is now rapidly increasing. One early game featuring actors and performers, and dubbed the "Weirdest Game Ever Made" by *The Essential Guide to Video Games* had an appropriately theater-related title: *Deus Ex Machina* (Automata 1984). It enlisted such unlikely British luminaries of the time as Frankie Howerd, Jon Pertwee, and Ian Dury, and presented the player with an animated television fantasy including several minigames. The *Essential Guide* now records it as a collector's item, particularly since it includes the late Ian Dury as a giant sperm singing "I'm a fertilizing agent." Another early deviation from the speedy combative videogame norm was *Little Computer People* (Activision, 1985) which tried to insist that within players' consoles (the Commodore 64 in this instance, a machine that realized a number of innovations but was not wholly successful in the market place) lived a very little person who needed some looking after and who, when prompted, could write to you to tell you how he felt. Historically, we can now regard this as influential in the development of both the *tamagotchi* and *The Sims*.

Game Art and Performance

In 1996, Tod Machover combined music, performance art, and games paradigms for innovative sequences in *Brain Opera* (figure 24.1). It included sections where the audience/participants could download software to use as interactive musical games and send their interactions directly to live performers in the space, who would stop playing to facilitate the Internet performers' contributions. This direct interface, playing with patterns and codes either manipulated or in some instances created by external contributors, was also the subject of experimentation for dance companies such as Johannes Birringer's Alien-Nation Co. Their performance installation *Before Night Falls* (1997) is almost as far removed from the norms of videogames as could be imagined—"fantasies/memories of

Figure 24.1 A participant plays a custom designed "rhythm tree" instrument for Tod Machover's game-like performance *Brain Opera* (1996).

specific sexual experiences, bodily orifices, and organic substances/materials linked to a conceptual exploration of deprivation and injury/trauma"[23]—but its sophisticated concept wrestling with space-time dimensions is structured into the mathematical logic of a simple game: hopscotch, which provides a framework for the ordering of complex ideas and movements.

Artists such as Cory Arangel and Olia Lialina modify and customize existing games to imbue them with completely new aesthetic forms and navigational structures, while others adapt games engines for entirely new game forms. Media artist duo Mathias Fuchs and Sylvia Eckermann use and abuse game engines such as Epic Megagames' *UNREAL* engine to create elaborate navigable worlds such as *Expositur (*aka *Unreal Museum*, 2000), which Fuchs describes as "a knowledge space rather than a game." The player's avatar can dance and gesticulate through a Theater History Museum, run and somersault around a Jewish Museum, delve down and then fly through the subconscious labyrinth of the Sigmund Freud Museum, and dive underwater to swim with the fishes at the Museum of Natural History. The game-space is modeled on ancient Greek and Renaissance notions of mnemotechnique used by philosophers and orators to memorize complete speeches:

The orator picked a building and learned every nook and cranny very intensely until he was able to move about the building in his memory. As a preparation for the speech a plethora of items of different complexity and amount of detail could be placed in the memorized rooms, e.g. a scales of justice. While delivering the speech the orator [mentally] wandered from room to room and collected hints while the speech unfolded.[24]

Fuchs notes the average British consumer now spends more time playing videogames than going to the cinema and renting movies, and considers the gaming paradigm to be one of the most important to the future of interactive arts and performance: "Games contain possibilities for knowledge spaces of a delicate nature—if they are thoughtfully conceived, carefully designed and joyfully experienced."[25] Fuchs and Eckermann's *FluID: Arena of Identities* (2003) is a particularly fascinating and performative example of his conception of a knowledge-art-game where on its journey the player's avatar interacts with characters, borrowing aspects of their identities and building up a fluid rather than stable ontology (figures 24.2 and 24.3).

Margarete Jahrmann and Max Moswitzer's *Nibble Engine Toolz* (2002) is a spectacular and dramatic piece of game-art using complex navigation and animal-like forms composed of swirling interlocking loops and spirals of digital code (figure 24.4). Feng Mengbo creates visually stunning game-art by adapting games software engines and inserting full-figure photographic images of himself. In pieces such as *Q4U* (2002) his naked-torso figure is the protagonist (holding a digital camera in one hand and a huge gun in the other) who runs and flies through elaborate Gothic interiors, encountering numerous other clones of himself. Natalie Bookchin's Web-based game *The Intruder* (1999) proceeds through ten

Figure 24.2 The user/character encounters life changing experiences and acquaintances that enable them to establish a fluid identity in Mathias Fuchs and Sylvia Eckermann's *FluID: Arena of Identities* (2003).

Figure 24.3 Some of the dreamlike characters and spaces in Mathias Fuchs and Sylvia Eckermann's *FluID: Arena of Identities* (2003).

Figure 24.4 Margarete Jahrmann and Max Moswitzer's spectacular *Nibble Engine Toolz* (2002).

levels from Pong to war games, like a history of computer games, using Jorge Luis Borge's love story of the same name as inspiration. Bookchin's deeply ironic *Metapet* (2002) resource-management game is based on the premise "that biotech innovation and corporate creativity gave birth to a genetically engineered worker, a new sort of Tamagochi to ensure its productivity for the game's virtual business company whilst meter read-outs keep track of its levels of discipline, health, energy, morale, and visual standards. A class of virtual pet that replaces the all too human worker"[26] (figure 24.5).

In Marc Lafia's online *The Vanndemar MEMEX or Laura Croft Stripped Bare by her Assassins, Even*,[27] the player establishes a code name and undergoes some rudimentary psychological profiling, and is plunged into a particular route and character in a world of espionage, intrigue, and surveillance. For Weibel and Druckrey, it "explores the mythic desires invested in the network as both a space of collective action and human transformation. The *Vanndemar Memex* simultaneously constructs and unravels narratives of self, history, politics, communication and society: it is an engine in which new possibilities are forged."[28]

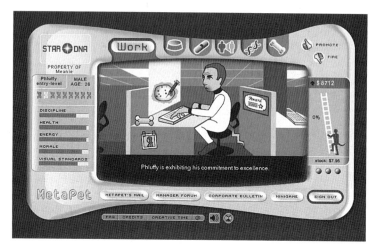

Figure 24.5 Phluffy is one of several genetically engineered worker Tamagochis (complete with tail) that gamers tend and train in Natalie Bookchin's *Metapet* (2002).

Tom Betts's installation *QQQ* is based on the online video game *Quake III* (one of the best known, longest running and most violent of the shoot-'em-up genre) that he located, appropriately, in an abandoned, semiderelict 1960s cinema.[29] Betts filtered and abstracted images from games of *Quake III* to create a frantic procession of image trails that the accompanying program described, with some accuracy, as "the high-speed death-match becoming slow-motion ballet." The images were accompanied by a loud, violent, and over-powering soundtrack that remained constant until a visitor chose to intervene (by select-ing a recycle or pause button), whereupon an eerie silence momentarily fell on the empty, darkened space.

Videogames have also made incursions into stage dramas, including David KS Tse and Yellow Earth Theatre's *Play to Win* (2000) staged at London's Soho Theatre. Videogames become an escapist fantasy world for the bullied schoolchild protagonist, and his fantasies blur into reality as he becomes involved with a Triad gang. The action-packed produc-tion brings together projected game imagery and onstage martial arts performed by gold medalist Tom Wu. In Talking Birds' theater performance *Joy-ridden* (1999), two frustrated and increasingly crazed hitchhikers gesticulate wildly at the passing traffic. High-speed video footage of point-of-view shots from speeding cars (blurred landscapes; road mark-ings) play on screen behind them, then suddenly mix to point-of-view images from different high-velocity videogames.

A number of innovative live performances incorporating games models have already been analyzed in earlier chapters, including ieVR's *A Midsummer Night's Dream* (2000, with the University of Kent), where the fantasy world of the fairy forest was transposed

Figure 24.6 Shakespeare's *A Midsummer Night's Dream* is updated in VR for the videogames age in ieVR's production with the University of Kent (2000).

to become the contemporary fantasy realm of the computer game (figure 24.6). The vastness of the fairy world becomes the vastness of cyberspace and the bickering lovers battle in the midst of violent computer games, while remnants of *Pac-Man* and *Pong* are strewn in a sewer backdrop. A number of important examples of the convergence of theater and games paradigms will be explored in the following chapter on CD-ROMs, while the "performance games" of MUDs, MOOs, and RPGs (role-playing games) have already been discussed in chapter 19.

VR War Games and *Desert Rain*

The first Gulf War (1991) has been described by John A. Barry as the first "technology war," by Carlo Formenti as the first "postmodern war," by Mark Dery as history's first "made-for-TV" war, and, most (in)famously of all, by Jean Baudrillard as a war that "did not take place" (since it was virtual).[30] Television footage, particularly the green phosphor images from cameras mounted at the front of computer-guided "smart bombs," conjured the unreal, sanitized battles of computer games. High technology was deployed not only in the weapons of destruction, but also as a political propaganda weapon that preached high morality, since smart-bombs minimized the so-called collateral damage of civilian casualties. High technology won the headlines and, it was popularly thought, the war. But later the untold story emerged: "the Air Force announced that laser- and radar-guided bombs and missiles made up just 7 percent of all U.S explosives dropped on Iraq and Kuwait. The other 93 percent were conventional 'dumb' bombs, dropped primarily by high-flying B-52s from the Vietnam era."[31]

It was the most obscenely uneven war game in history (Formenti calls it "The War Without Enemies"),[32] a veritable turkey shoot. Just over one hundred American, British, and Allied troops were killed (the majority of British casualties being victims of U.S. "friendly fire") compared to some 100,000 Iraqi civilians and soldiers—most of whom, in an important sense, were civilians themselves, being forced conscripts rather than professional militia loyal to the regime. The war provides the backdrop for Blast Theory and the University of Nottingham Mixed Reality Lab's *Desert Rain* (1999), which, we should stress, offers nothing like the blunt political condemnation of our little outburst of friendly fire. It does, however, constitute what in Gabriella Giannachi's words is "one of the most complex and powerful responses to the first Gulf War to be produced within the sphere of theatrical performance."[33]

One-hundred thousand grains of sand, each representing one Iraqi corpse, are contained in a small box that is secretly put into the coat or jacket pocket of all *Desert Rain* participants. The players/audience members, whose coats and possessions have been taken from them by performers before they entered the main installation, find the sand-filled box sometime (often days or weeks) later, once they have left the VR desert and are back in the real world. The box also contains the text of General Colin Powell's response to a journalist's question about the 100,000 Iraqi dead: "It's really a number I'm not terribly interested in."[34] *Desert Rain* was one the most successful and advanced digital performances of the late 1990s, a collaboration between Blast Theory (led by Matt Adams) and one of Britain's most advanced Virtual Reality computer laboratories, the Mixed Reality Lab led by Professor Steve Benford at Nottingham University, England. Benford describes himself as a "hard scientist,"[35] and the collaboration with Adams, who was determined not to get lost in the technology but to ensure the result raised aesthetic, intellectual, and political questions, spawned a seminal experimental production fusing the technological complexity of hard science skills with a truly original artistic vision.

First performed in a large disused warehouse as part of Now Ninety9 Festival in Nottingham and later toured internationally, *Desert Rain* combines a videogame and performance installation structure, with each participant being required to undertake a mission in a virtual world. Each thirty-minute performance is limited to six players, who are led into a room where their coats, bags, and other hand-held possessions are taken. They each

Figure 24.7 Six players are led into individual gauze cubicles equipped with sprung floorplates to commence the VR war game experience *Desert Rain* (1999, Blast Theory and the University of Nottingham Mixed Reality Lab).

don a blue, hooded jacket uniform. They are each given a picture of a different person (their target) and are led into the main installation space where they are zipped into one of six separate gauze cubicles that are walled on three sides (figure 24.7). In the huge open space of the fourth wall in front of them all, rain is falling hard, in the form of a solid sheet of fine water spray onto which VR environments are projected. The players' task is to work together (they communicate with one another via a hands-free microphone and headphones device) to find their targets within the VR desert landscapes and the mazes of underground bunkers and doors projected in front of them. Amid the rain-screen VR images of numbers, targets, lights, and landscapes, the player's own avatars appear, which the players manipulate and move through the spaces by transferring their weight and rocking in different directions on the sprung floorplates on which they stand. As they navigate to find the flags and pictures representing their targets, two Blast Theory

Figure 24.8   The exit tunnel in Blast Theory and the Mixed Reality Lab's *Desert Rain* (1999).

performers monitor the proceedings "backstage" and provide occasional audio clues, support, and encouragement via the headsets. But if the players collaborative search and find mission is unsuccessful, it ends with the disappointment of any failed computer game: "Game Over."

The players' human targets are all finally to be discovered in a bunker that initially appears empty, and groups that succeed in getting there and finding them within the allotted twenty minutes are rewarded with a true *coup de théâtre* (figure 24.8). The hooded figure of a live performer slowly breaks through the screen of water like some specter of death emerging out of a solid wall, utterly shattering the space between the virtual and the real in a heart-stopping moment of total disorientation. For the players who have been engrossed with increasing anxiety in the VR desert spaces as the clock clicks down, the discovery of their targets is dramatic enough, since it is (brilliantly) unclear whether they will now rescue or murder them. But the thin dividing line between the real and the virtual represented by the VR water-curtain is then suddenly not simply "problematized" but violently, actually, rent asunder (figure 24.9).

The rain-soaked figure approaches the players and, without a word, hands each a swipe-card and leads them through the rain ("a ritual act of purification," suggests Giannachi),[36] over a huge mound of sand at the other side, and into a "motel room." Here they swipe their cards through a wall-mounted device, activating a television to play prerecorded

Figure 24.9 The press and publicity image for *Desert Rain,* which provides a sense of the live figure's emergence out of the VR projections.

video footage of the "real" people who were their targets. They are seen sitting and talking from the same motel room the players are now in, and describe how the Gulf War changed their lives:

The targets were: Glen, a soldier who served in the war; Shona, a soldier who was bedridden at the time of the war and watched it on television; Richard, a peace worker on the Iraqi-Saudi border; Sam, an actor who played a soldier in a television drama about the war; Eamonn, a BBC journalist who was in Baghdad when the air-raids started; and Tony, an actor who was on holiday in Egypt at the time of the conflict.[37]

This final debriefing reveals how these people—like the players themselves, who have each been separate and separated, and have taken a different course toward a different target—hold wholly divergent views on what constituted the "reality" of the Gulf War. Yet all, targets and players alike, have intimately conspired and collaborated in the intricate production of what was and will always remain a war game of sickeningly real and obscenely unreal "virtual" "reality." *Desert Rain* is the most artistically significant and technologically advanced exploration in conjoining videogames and live performance, and we will reserve another of the company's extraordinary explorations in game performance, *Uncle Roy All Around You* (2004), to the concluding chapter.

Conclusion

We began this analysis by noting some close correspondences between theater and videogames, but it is equally obvious that there are also fundamental differences. They are quite different forms, and the medium of transmission of the videogame raises all the usual hackles in the "live" versus "mediatized" debate. Videogames are not live in terms of their technological ontology, but they operate responsively in real time and certainly appear live from the perspective of the player-character, arguably far more so than plays or films, since they demand rapt attention and lightning responses. A more qualitative problem arises in relation to the substance and content of videogames, which in comparison to literary theater could be regarded by academics as simplistic, cartoonish, inconsequential, and essentially plebeian.

But such an analysis puts the focus on subordinate issues and misses the substantive point: that videogames are a most prolific, effective, and developing form of popular theater. With all the attributes (and disadvantages) of "globalization" that they so effectively entertain, videogames, whether console-based or online, embody the most expansive and successful display of involvement in theater-based concerns that the world has ever witnessed. It is as if the *skene* and *orchestra* of the ancient Greek theater suddenly stretches around the world, or the rumbling medieval pageant-wagon is suddenly carrying an extra prop, the Earth, in the spread of a new type of world theater. Its current form might appear somewhat rough and ready, and indeed it is considered by many to be crass, abhorrent, repulsive, and plebeian. But it has appeared, has been adopted in large measure, and is still developing apace. As Paul Rae puts it, taking up Peter Brook's assertion in *The Empty Space* that "A play is play,"[38]

why play with a play, when you can play more(.com) with Microsoft's Xbox; and why bother with an empty space when the Sony PlayStation 2's *Third Place* is arguably the rightful heir to *The Theatre and its Double*? If so, where Artaud's nightmare scenario of the theatre consisted of "an incredible fluttering of men in black suits busy arguing over receipts by the entrance to a white hot box office," the *Third Place* dragoons Stelarc's posthuman cachet into its expansive commodification of play.[39]

We began this chapter by noting the important development of academic studies of videogames, where a whole new research field has emerged. This research relates not only to game studies itself as a distinct area of new media scholarship, but to numerous branches of the humanities where interest in the field has spread—for example, complete issues of academic journals on psychology and sociology are devoted with increasing frequency to the analysis of games and their significant aesthetic, cultural, psychological, and social implications.[40] While there has not been total silence from theater and performance academics, the voices broaching the subject have so far been few and in terms of their impact, they have been relatively quiet. Part of the success of the videogame, and we believe a direct reason for its slow appreciation as a serious medium by theater academics, is that it fundamentally uses a dynamic *visual* rather than verbal/textual narrative. Understandably, theater academics find difficulty in correlating the crude and melodramatic cartoon form of videogames with the great subtleties and depths of the printed classics of drama, and it will take time (perhaps generations, perhaps the time needed for child game-players to become professors of theater) for the field of *game performance theory* to fully develop.

CD-ROMs

CD-ROM is exciting and boring at the same time.
Who wants to put that much effort into a canned art form?
— JOHN REAVES[1]

The Rise and Demise of the Performance CD-ROM

The development of the performance CD-ROM (Compact Disc—Read Only Memory) offers a microcosm of the general development and adoption of digital techniques: how they commenced, developed, became fashionable, were absorbed, were replaced by a more advanced alternative, and then faded into relative obscurity. In the case of the CD-ROM, this whole process was achieved in a few years.

Approximately one hundred years after Edison invented the phonograph (which subsequently went through the stages of cylinder, disc, electric recording, "mono," "stereo," and "long-playing"), a Dutch physicist, Klass Campaan, used a laser lightbeam, first invented in 1958, to record and read *sounds* via light onto a small disc. This became the essential principle of the audio compact disc, developed in the late 1960s by James T. Russell, an avid music listener who was continually frustrated by the wear and tear suffered by vinyl phonograph records. He succeeded in inventing the first digital-to-optical recording and playback system and patented it in 1970. From patent to first digital audio disc prototype took a further seven years before its first demonstration at the Toyko Audio Fair (1977). A further five years of development produced the world's first compact disc system,[2] one that we still currently routinely use but, we are promised, will rapidly decline with the onset of increased music downloading from the Internet onto both domestic PCs and portable hardware systems such as Apple's iPod.

In 1982, compact disc technology was introduced, first in Japan and then the United States, and by 1988 consumers were able to record their own CDs with the introduction of the first CD-recordable discs (CD-Rs). This rapidly gave rise to the era of the amateur CD (and later, the amateur CD-ROM) and the majority of the first performance-related CDs and CD-ROMs were concerts and performance sound tracks. Early adopters and prime movers with multimedia CD-ROM technologies were music aficionados (practitioners, technicians, and collectors) who were already familiar with the audio compact disc principle and were keen to experiment with it as a sound/image recording device. Given all the complexity of international patent laws, and the agreements necessary to market and distribute the new devices, the speed of this development was phenomenal, driven by the overriding belief in the final years of the twentieth century in the new ubiquity of all things digital, and overarching commercial profit motives. Although a range of different systems based on a similar technology competed for adoption, the key companies reached agreement and compromise to adopt Sony/Phillips systems.

CD-ROMs were quickly utilized by the music industry to integrate video tracks into audio CDs (only viewable on a computer), while the computer and videogames industry embraced the technology for their games distribution. Industrial and commercial companies began to use CD-ROMs for marketing and publicity purposes, and specialist educational and so-called edutainment titles proliferated. The British newspaper *The Times* had introduced a weekly supplement entitled *Interface* in September 1995, and featured an article about "The Rom revolution" in December 1995, noting how "sales of CD-ROM are exploding. . . . The number of Rom discs available is doubling every six months and there are now more than 10,000. CD-ROM is truly the new papyrus."[3]

Three Years

Three years in the chronological development of the art and performance-related CD-ROM act as touchstones, or milestones, in its rise and demise: 1994, 1996, and 1999. These were years of key exhibitions and events that afford a snapshot view of the rise and fall of the CD-ROM, and it was significant that ZKM, a hugely influential center for new media art at that time (as well as now), published its first "artintact" collection as a CD-ROM in 1994 (*Artintact* [1]) and published its final one in the collection *Artintact 5* in 1999. It signaled that the zenith of that particular medium had been reached as the subsequent series that took its place, *Digital Arts Edition*, was made available from 1999 both as a CD-ROM and in the new DVD format. Looking beyond the twentieth century, it is also symptomatic that all the *Artintact* CD-ROMs were reissued as a retrospective on DVD in 2002.

Equally significant over the years 1994, 1996, and 1999 were important exhibition events that served to bring together a particular focus on the CD-ROM. 1994 was the first year of a new competition which became an annual event called *New Voices, New Visions*. The competition did not demand that work submitted was presented *on* CD-ROM (though many were), but CD-ROM was the format chosen to record and publish what the organizers felt was the best digital art and performance work submitted in any one year, thereby creating a consecutive archive of new digital art experiments. The email circular that announced the 1994 *New Voices, New Visions in Multimedia* competition described how "the computer is at the heart of a profound shift in the way that humans express themselves" and identified the competition's objective as encouragement of experimental, radical work outside the norms of commercial safety.[4] Over two thousands people from around the world entered, and the winning pieces were shown to a sellout audience at the New York Video Festival and were exhibited for two weeks at Stanford University in Palo Alto, California.[5] Among the prizewinning entries which subsequently featured on the *New Voices, New Visions {1}* CD-ROM was George Legrady's *An Anecdoted Archive from the Cold War* CD-ROM (1994), which cleverly exploited the recording and archiving capabilities of the CD-ROM while making a distinctly individualized and personalized political and artistic statement. Legrady included film clips from the previous twenty years of Communist rule in Eastern Europe, its less than perfect reproduction in QuickTime Movie format yielding an appropriate and evocative archival edge. The following year, the competition announced itself with the tagline, "Do not enter this contest if you want Home Shopping, Encyclopedias and Video Games to define the Information Highway," and the range of work featured in their 1995 CD-ROM ranged from fictional play (*Live Wire* by Stephen Jablonsky) and cartoon (*I Love You* by Laurence Arcadias) to poetry (*Personal Dictionaries* by Gregory Haun) and documentaries on AIDS (*Women at Risk*, by Carolyn Sharins) and the Zapatista movement in central Mexico (*The Revolution Will Be Digitized*, by Tamara Ford, Troy Whitlock and Jef Bekes).

By 1996, the second year we discern as pivotal in the development of performance-related CD-ROMs, there was sufficient art and performance work *on* CD-ROM that a major exhibition, *Burning The Interface*, featured only CD-ROM artworks, opening in Sydney, Australia, and subsequently touring; and a major pan-European *Art and CD-ROM* exhibition took place at the Associació de Cultura Contemporania in Barcelona, Spain. By 1999, CD-ROM art and performance was firmly established in U.S., Australian, and Western European exhibitions and festivals as well as in former Eastern Bloc countries, with examples including the 1999 Media Non Grata Arts Festival at the Estonia Academy of Arts. An elaborate and extensive exhibition, *Contact Zones—The Art of the CD-ROM*, at Cornell University signaled the most complete retrospective of what was fast becoming an art medium that would be regarded as superseded if not entirely defunct a few years later.

In surveying and analyzing performance-based and performance-related CD-ROMs (and in keeping with our strategy in several other chapters) we will divide the field into differentiated categories. In the case of performance CD-ROMs, we discern three broad types: educational, documentary/analytical, and performative.

Educational CD-ROMs

Reference information and educational titles were the mainstays of the CD-ROM when it first emerged in the late 1980s, and continued to be so for over a decade with a range of packages from encyclopedias and school resources to "how to" applications from macramé to golf. Language learning was the CD-ROM's initial forte, with primarily European languages in the 1980s, followed later by Chinese (1992), then the following year by Finnish, Hungarian, Catalan, and Serbo-Croat, followed by Japanese in 1994. That year marked a turning point for the commercial CD-ROM, with an explosion of nonfiction and learning topics from costume jewelry and cookery to management manuals and medical learning applications. The hypermedia CD-ROM appeared ideally suited to educational aims, since it enabled different media to be accessed and brought together (text, diagrams, graphics, animations, photographs, video footage, and so on), while its ease of navigation allowed users to both cross-reference materials and to follow hyperlinks so as to explore particular features in greater depth (and without the pitfalls of the Internet, where surfing can tend to take the user beyond and away from the subject interest).

Christie Carson's rich and detailed scholarly examination of different folio texts and theatrical productions of *King Lear*, published by Cambridge University Press in 2000, provides a notable example in relation to performance. It enables students and scholars—from undergraduates to learned Shakespearean professors—to follow different routes and academic levels of exploration, from the viewing of photographs from important twentieth-century productions and the analysis of particular (hyperlinked) words within the play text, to a profound examination of the developmental metamorphosis of the play's numerous folios. Carson's *King Lear* provides real evidence of the unique educational and academic potentials of the CD-ROM form, in particular by allowing easy and immediate access to different resources (in varied media) to enable detailed and frequently highly illuminating comparisons. Early academic advocates of hypertext and hypermedia had highlighted the significance of this ability to quickly cross-reference texts and other resources, including John Slatin, who argued in 1992 that CD-ROMs constituted a pedagogically progressive new form: "Most of what goes on at a college or university involves large numbers of documents . . . which have to be read, understood, mastered if possible as things-in-themselves; but they also have to be placed in relation to one another and understood *in* their relations; that's what a liberal education is supposed to be for. It's also what hypertext and hypermedia systems are for."[6]

Shakespeare CD-ROMs released by commercial companies similarly brought the use of comparative "texts" to bear on the study, such as Voyager's *Macbeth* (1994), which includes video clips from three different film versions of the play (directed by Roman Polanski, Orson Welles, and Akira Kurasawa). Commercial CD-ROMs examining theater and performance have been dominated by Shakespeare titles, although some more recent (but nonetheless, in their own way, "classic") plays have been explored, such as *The*

Crucible (Penguin, 1995) which includes performed extracts, critical commentaries, historical transcripts from the original Salem trials, and an interview with Arthur Miller.

Other theater CD-ROMs have highlighted interactivity as their key educational aspect, such as the BBC's *Macbeth* (1995) which promises to "dramatically enhance your understanding of the play as you watch, read and listen in an "Interactive Theatre" on your own PC"; and the Open University/BBC's *As You Like It* prototype, which includes a number of interactive exercises. One involves users studying various camera angles foregrounding specific characters within a scene, and then editing the shots in different ways to affect various dramatic effects, emphases, and interpretations:

This approach could not teach users of the CD-ROM to be apprentice editors or directors, but it could give them a very clear personal experience of how meaning can be created and altered within certain absolute parameters. . . . Students /users decide for themselves on several points in the scene which seem "pivotal" or particularly important—moments when the action/mood changes significantly.[7]

Lizbeth Goodman, one of the *As You Like It* producers, has developed other CD-ROMs exploring practical approaches to the performance of Shakespearean drama, as well as projects concerned with transferring theater recordings, particularly feminist drama, to digital media. She argues that the remediation and transposition of theater to computer has very positive implications:

All this work has not taken me away from theatre, but has rather strengthened the case for feminist theatre as an art form which requires the living, breathing atmosphere of live performance, but which can also be captured, in part, and for some good reasons (practical and theoretical) in other media. These other media, I will argue, do not destroy the essence of live theatre, but rather bring it to new audiences, who may in turn be encouraged to attend the theatre.[8]

Something of this principle is brought into a prison context in Geese Theatre and Jubilee Arts' *Lifting the Weight* CD-ROM (1998), where theater paradigms are imaginatively applied to assist male offenders adapt to the outside world upon their release (figure 25.1). In the Bedford Interactive Institute's dance education CD-ROMs such as *The Wild Child* (1999, with Ludus Dance Company), analytical texts and performance recordings combine with overlaid computer graphics to analyze dance movements and sequences dynamically, helping the student to understand and practically apply different techniques and knowledge to their own dance practice. Such CD-ROMs offer creative multimedia approaches to teaching and learning, which, as Bob Cotton and Richard Oliver argue, "represent a return to richer, pre-print modalities of expression, as if we are 'coming to our senses' after the anesthetic of monochrome words. The opportunity it offers to reason, to think, to debate and to learn in more concrete, multi-sensory terms may have a deep

Figure 25.1   An image from Geese Theatre's educational CD-ROM for prison inmates, *Lifting the Weight* (1998). Photo: courtesy of the Northern Echo.

significance . . . a move away from the peculiar abstraction of written or mathematical expression."[9]

Performance Documentation and Analysis CD-ROMs

The most common type of theater, dance, and performance art CD-ROMs are concerned with documentation, be it a single project or performance, or an extensive retrospective of an artist or company's work over a period of years. Examples of the latter approach include a review of Benoît Maubrey and Die Audio Gruppe's experiments with electro-acoustic clothing between 1982–1998, *CD-ROM: photos+videos+texts* (1998);[10] and Orlan's *This Is My Body . . . This Is My Software* (1996). Two leading British theater companies, IOU and Forced Entertainment, have also produced CD-ROM retrospectives that provide a fascinating insight into their creative development and their changing aesthetic styles and approaches over a number of years. While all of the above are professionally produced and distributed, many performance documentation CD-ROMs are homemade by the artists, produced for distribution to friends and contacts, sometimes existing only as single copies for use by the practitioner as a portable disc for presentations, or produced in small numbers as a giveaway to potential venues and funders. While some performance documentation projects use CD-ROM as a purely archival medium, others utilize the form to undertake extensive analysis, such as Ping Cao's *The Loaded Gesture* CD-ROM (1996, with Paul Vanouse), which uses semiotic models derived from de Saussure, Barthes, and Lacan to analyze the aesthetics and diverse meanings of the physical gestures and inflections of Chinese opera.

While many performance documentation CD-ROMs utilize text, most employ video recordings of live performance as the fundamental mode of documentation and communication. These digitized recordings have inevitably led to a return to the liveness debate, and there is wide acknowledgement that most video recordings provide only partial, two-dimensional, and "pale" representations of live theater, dance, and performance art. But, as Marilyn Deegan argues, they nonetheless provide the most concrete and unambiguous documentation form currently available, which enables at least *some* degree of examination of the "primary source," which is not available through textual descriptions:

Writers on other forms of cultural media than text have always had problems "quoting" from the subjects of their analysis, so a great deal of their critical comments include merely summarizing what happens in a scene from a film or play, or describing in words musical motifs. These summaries or descriptions are interpretive acts before the writer even begins to analyse or discuss ideas. For the reader to experience the primary art form, and not someone's description, is vital. . . . One could raise the objection that digitizing is a secondary form of representation which offers a different experience of interaction, at one remove from the original cultural objects, but, while this is true, it is still closer than giving only verbal descriptions and is therefore vastly preferred.[11]

La Compagnie Les Essentiels CD-ROM (2001), by the French theater troupe of the same name, documents two open-air promenade performances with audience participatory elements and large machine constructions. The main menu comprises a graphical head, and passing the cursor across its features prompts video footage, photo galleries, audio files, and weblinks. One of the featured performances, *Je sens donc je suis* (2000), involves performers wheeling around giant facial parts mounted on various contraptions in what is described as "a comico-absurd interactive musical, walkabout and fix." The disembodied body parts, including giant flapping ears and a vast brain, are wheeled around to interact with and sometimes chase the promenade audience. A huge nose sniffs spectators and sneezes, eyeballs loom above the crowd, giant lips laugh, and an eight-foot-long tongue darts out to lick people, before all the elements come into position together as a giant, theatrical version of Mr. Potato–Head. *La Compagnie Les Essentiels* is one of a number of performance CD-ROMs that skillfully conceptualize their multimedia design and graphical interfaces in relation to the specific themes and images of the live performances they examine.

ZKM has been highly influential in developing the CD-ROM as an archiving tool, and in October 1994 it released the first version of the most famous and preeminent performance CD-ROM, *Improvisation Technologies*, which has since been shown at over forty festivals, symposiums, and exhibitions worldwide (figure 25.2). It analyzes the work of Ballett Frankfurt and in particular the choreographic practices of its American director William Forsythe. Instrumental to the development was a ZKM scholarship-holder, Seth Goldstein, who had already worked on a multimedia archive in the United States

Figure 25.2   One of the menu screens for William Forsythe and ZKM's *Improvisation Technologies* (1999). Courtesy of ZKM, Center for Art and Media Karlsruhe.

relating to Robert Wilson's work that had been published in January 1994 as *Robert Wilson—Visionary of Theater*. *Improvisation Technologies* was based on extensive investigations, undertaken by Volker Kuchelmeister, Christian Ziegler, Mohsen Hosseni, and Nick Haffner with the support and participation of William Forsythe, to interrelate previous archival footage and multicamera recordings of new works in order to reveal choreographic connections between the two sources. It is supplemented by extensive interviews with and presentations by Forsythe. During its production the designers discovered both the advantages and limitations of the CD-ROM. On one hand, for recording and analyzing movement it offered a welcome departure from the comparatively laborious and restrictive processes of Laban notation, but on the other, the limitations of the amount of data a single CD-ROM can hold (the essential cause of its later decline in favor of the DVD) led to major sequences being cut from the final CD-ROM.

Improvisation Technologies nonetheless makes extremely varied and powerful use of the CD-ROM form, fusing video with graphics to analyze, dissect, and trace dancer's movements in space (figure 25.3). It features sixty short video lecture-demonstrations by Forsythe, each with accompanying browseable video illustrations of dancers in rehearsal and performance using the specific choreographic element being discussed. It also offers the viewer different camera angles on performance footage; and the combination of all these elements enabled a breadth, depth, and detail to the analysis of dance choreography and performance unrealizable through traditional notation methods. It deservedly created considerable worldwide interest and has subsequently been widely viewed, copied, and built upon by others, although not without some voices of concern being raised,

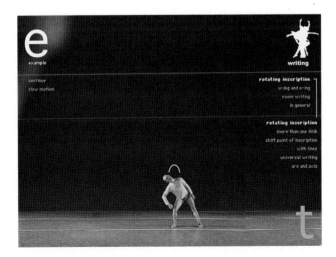

Figure 25.3 A head movement is graphically traced through space in *Improvisation Technologies*. Courtesy of ZKM, Center for Art and Media Karlsruhe.

including Johannes Birringer's. His concerns are not dissimilar to the initial fears expressed by Bill T. Jones during the *Ghostcatching* project we discussed in an earlier chapter, focusing on what might be *lost* to the new medium as well as gained:

It is not clear to me what I could actually learn from the CD-ROM even if I tried to reintegrate its "information" into daily physical and organic practice. . . . The problem . . . lies in the unquestioned or apparently seamless commutation of physical creation and embodied knowledge into computer memory and its graphic user interfaces. The transformation of the dance experience—the training, rehearsal, creative process, performance, and reception—into *information* needs to be fundamentally challenged and examined if we seriously wish to influence the development of new technological systems and their interaction with organic, cultural, and site-specific experience.[12]

A different type of analytical documentation became the first CD-ROM to be published in a refereed performance journal in December 1995, Steve Dixon and The Chameleons Group's *Chameleons 1: Theatrical Experiments in Style, Genre and Multi-Media*.[13] It was authored in *Director* software and documents and analyzes the rehearsal and performance processes employed in the Chameleons Group's theater production *The Dark Perversity of Chameleons* (1994), which combined live performance with five simultaneous video projections. Using performance clips, rehearsal footage, photomontages, and analytical commentaries, the CD-ROM explores the practical working processes and theoretical contexts that frame the group's work. In March 1999, the group's second CD-ROM, *Chameleons 2: Theatre in a Movie Screen*, was published in the journal *TDR: The Drama Review*.[14] It incorporates a complete video recording of the live digital theater performance *Chameleons 2: In Dreamtime* (1996) plus additional rehearsal footage, video environments and critical commentaries (figure 25.4). As well as offering an in-depth analysis of the group's working methods, it attempts to contextualize the work within contemporary performance theory and practice, discussing a range of ideas and issues in a series of commentaries including Artaudian theory, semiotics, surrealism, and psychoanalysis.[15] The CD-ROM also aimed to demonstrate the effectiveness of digital multimedia for archiving, analyzing and presenting practical performance research work, and as Dixon put it in his accompanying *TDR* article:

Hypermedia can simultaneously locate performance research not only in theory, but also *in* performance practice: through the direct juxtaposition of critical discourse with the actual piece of theatre it relates to (presented as digital video). New technologies allow such simultaneity: a marrying of conceptualisation with realisation; of research objectives with research outcomes; of aesthetic experiments with audience reception; and of theory with practice. . . . New multimedia technologies offer a synthesis of written words and moving images, fusing together these traditionally polarised forms. Hypermedia programming offers unique and revolutionary possibilities for documenting, analysing and presenting performance research.[16]

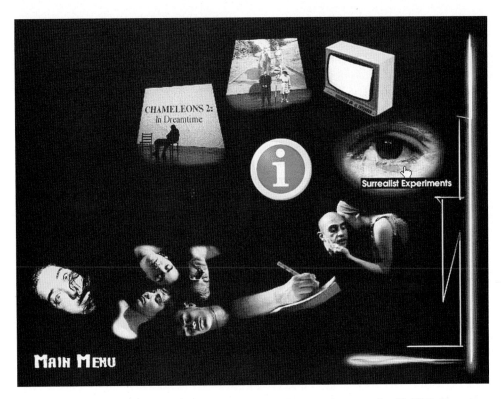

Figure 25.4 The main menu for The Chameleons Group's performance documentation CD-ROM, *Chameleons 2: Theatre in a Movie Screen* (1999), published in the performance studies journal *TDR*.

The UK *Performance Research* journal has published a number of CD-ROMs, including Desperate Optimists' *Stalking Memory* (2000),[17] which uses a split visual frame placing audiovisual performance documentation of a number of the company's productions on one side of the screen, and on the other side texts written about each performance by practitioners such as Tim Etchells and academics including Susan Melrose. The written texts are conceived as their authors' lasting memories of the performances; while accompanying video clips and still photograph slideshows present fragmented sequences and images, sometimes covering the theatrical action from a number of angles. Both the imagery and the texts are thus impressionistic, conceived in relation to memory (incomplete, ruptured). The written texts, being the personal recollections and phenomenological responses of one spectator, generally describe the original performances with genuine simplicity and authenticity—with what one might almost dare venture to call truth.

The parallel of text appearing to the left of screen and video footage or a slideshow to the right is a simple yet brilliantly effective design. The user begins to read the written text while continually glancing to the right to register and absorb the changing images—the individual rhythms of writing and movie footage (and arguably the user's personal biorhythms) dictating an unusual form of interactivity between the two elements. The binary left-right relationship, offering the choice when to look where, when we read, and when we watch images, is a straightforward but fascinating form of interactivity, since a choice of focus exists at every moment, unlike the traditional point and click navigational paradigm of CD-ROMs. The interchange between textual commentary and visual materials is a fluid, dynamic, and poetic exchange like performance itself; taking the viewer into a deep and specific space of memory, recollection, and permanence. Just as performative writing has developed as an important expressive form, the *Stalking Memory* CD-ROM can be said to approach a new kind of reading: performative reading.

Performative CD-ROMs

Early performative CD-ROMs stemmed from disciplines such as the visual and video arts, to which the format offered an alternative and expansive "hypertexted" medium. Bill Seaman, a video maker and self-taught composer, developed works such as *The Exquisite Mechanisms of Shivers* through several transitions from a linear video format in 1991 to an interactive work on videodisc and CD-ROM in 1993; and it appeared as part of ZKM's *artintact* [1] CD-ROM in 1997. It featured thirty-three brief image/sound scenes (from the original video), each accompanied by a sentence of ten words giving a total vocabulary or "poetic menu" of 330 words, with the user able to control and reassemble the three elements (language, image, and sound) as a form of plastic poetry.

ZKM helped to develop a number of CD-ROMs by transposing artists' works from other media, including Luc Courchesne's 1990 laserdisc installation *Portrait One*, which was released as a CD-ROM in 1995 (figure 25.5). It is a delicate, ironic, and seductive interactive piece featuring the head of Marie (actress Paule Ducharme), who asks various questions to which the user can respond using a menu of textual responses so as to develop a conversation. Marie's voice, expression, and conversational topics are reminiscent of the confidential "deep relationship" movies of Bergman or the French New Wave cinema of the 1960s typified by Chabrol, Godard, and Truffaut. Depending upon the user's responses, the conversation either progresses into reminiscence and a depressive "longing for darkness" sequence, or it flounders. The irony comes full circle if the user is lured into admitting some attraction for Marie whereupon they are told to "contact my agent," and the previously animated portrait becomes fixed in stillness. The piece is a forerunner to Stelarc's *Prosthetic Head* (2003), and both pieces establish a personalized conversational interface to build a fictional relationship through dialogue, a paradigm that has been the essence of scripted drama since classical times.

In 1994, a group of visual artists and designers known as ad319[18] collaborated on a CD-ROM entitled *Body, Space, Memory*, which allows the user to navigate around an image of the human body, which acts as a map. It explores the notion that memories are located

Figure 25.5 The original 1990 installation version of Luc Courchesne's *Portrait One*.

in particular locations, and its influence as an ambitious early attempt to use the performing body as a navigational template was followed by many others in subsequent years, not least in documentation CD-ROMs, as we have seen. Reviews following its release acknowledged its significance in raising the status of the CD-ROM to that of a new artform: "*Body, Space, Memory* is an important piece of work. It is ambitious, demanding, touching, and at times, lyrically beautiful. It is also a notable model of collaboration, for which every member of the collective should be commended."[19] But its impact was eclipsed the following year by Laurie Anderson's *Puppet Motel* (1995, with Hsin-Chien Huang), which is one of the few CD-ROMs from this period, or indeed any period, to have achieved collector status and to be selling for several times its initial retail price (four times higher in 2003).

Its popularity then and now in part relates to Anderson's profile as a lauded contemporary musician, and *Puppet Motel* includes over an hour of her compositions, some of which are unavailable elsewhere. It also features "virtual backstage tours" and provides fascinating insights into her notebooks. But its heightened market value relates equally to the real visual originality and digital creativity that Anderson and Huang bring to it. In many respects it is not advanced in its structure, and as with many CD-ROMs of this period it uses a series of room environments (this motel has thirty-three) that the player visits and explores—a paradigm that has remained popular with even the most recent navigational computer applications from videogames to the abiding structural metaphor of online chat rooms. But an essential difference is that the lovingly designed rooms of *Puppet Motel* are not packed with people, conversations, information, or even games, but rather with sounds, stories, hyperreal environments, dreamlike tableaux, and idiosyncratic visual impressions that create distinctive moods and ambiences. Designer Hsin-Chien Huang's previous work *The Dream of Time* (1994) had already achieved awards, and his quasi-surrealistic associative techniques of narrative visualization complemented Anderson's own approaches so that, in her words: "The most amazing thing about working on this project is that it's absolutely the way I think. I don't think in terms of narrative or plot. My mind works through association, and that's how *Puppet Motel* works."[20]

It is significant that the 1995 CD-ROM did not receive the critical acclaim afforded its rerelease following some redesign and the inclusion of additional material in 1998. Perhaps, like any pioneering work, it may have suffered a lack of appreciation because it was "ahead of its time," but equally there were concerns from critics that its content, like its technological form, was brittle and artificial, and therefore alienating. One reviewer called it a "cry in the techno-wilderness . . . information-age melancholy,"[21] while another insisted that by "attempting to conjure a desolate aura within her lonely digital domain, Anderson only adds an unnecessary layer of detachment. Her disc doesn't offer enough rewards to justify the effort of breaking through."[22]

But a few years later, the initial barrenness perceived in Anderson's CD-ROM had arguably been diluted as the form became familiar, and as other technologized visions of alternate environments and realities began to emerge. In 1997, the release of Stelarc's *Metabody: From Cyborg to Symborg* (designed by Gary Zebington) aroused praise from many of the same critics who had damned the similarly eerie atmospherics and high-tech visuals of *Puppet Motel*. *Metabody* remains one of the slickest CD-ROMs ever made, and while much of its content is conventional video and textual documentation of Stelarc's work, the impact of its opening sequence is striking and highly performative, as Barry Smith reflected in a review following its release:

For several moments we both just gawped. . . . Amoeba-type images gorging their way through abstractions of veined tissue accompanied by passing waveforms, humanoid machines, transmutations, a heavy rhythmic heartbeat soundtrack with a lot of bass and "emotional presence." . . . Even the cursor transmuted and pulsated. For long seconds the CD-ROM promised to deliver what the hype had claimed—"how electronic systems can extend performance parameters." Were we on the brink of total cyborg (or is it symborg?) fulfillment? For moments we even felt we were close to understanding the description on the designer's Web site: "But this is not a static or totalising map or model, it is a paradoxical and animated representation of living-in-the-world".[23]

Another CD-ROM that succeeded in bringing a sense of live theatricality to the "canned" artform of CD-ROM around this time was Forced Entertainment and Hugo Glendinning's *Frozen Palaces (Chapter One)*. It was first produced in 1996, but it received its greatest circulation when republished as part of ZKM's *artintact 5* in 1999. *Frozen Palaces* cleverly and quite beautifully employs CD-ROM technology to uncover new depths to the traditional whodunit tale (where the "it"/what? part of the question is as pertinent as the who?) of "high jinks up at the big house," and to this extent it is quintessentially English even though not a word is spoken. Starting from a close-up image of an antique chair, the viewer is able to scan an elegant room in a state of upheaval and to discover two prone young women, apparently asleep, party dresses crumpled, on what appears to be the morning after the night before. There is a deliberate staginess to the impeccably overdressed settings that adds to the drama as the narrative threads gradually unfold but never finally reach a climax or resolution. Discovering links, the user moves into adjoining rooms where decadent or depraved acts seem to have occurred the previous night, and there are indications that a particularly bloody suicide or murder may also have occurred (figure 25.6).

The visual richness and slickness of *Frozen Palaces*, *Puppet Motel*, and *Metabody* reflect an early concern with graphic and photographic sophistication in CD-ROM production by performance artists at this stage of the technology's development. But by 1997 a tangible artistic and cultural backlash was developing against the perceived sheen and artificiality of digital applications, as well as their associations with big business and

Figure 25.6   Tim Etchells/ Hugo Glendinning and Forced Entertainment's intriguing and bloody exploration of the whodunit *Frozen Palaces (Chapter One)* (1996).

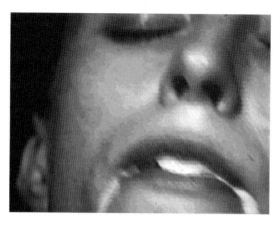

Figure 25.7 A screen shot from half/angel's avowedly "anti-slick" CD-ROM *mouthplace* (1997).

commodification. As a result, many later CD-ROMs such as half/angel's *mouthplace* (1997) specifically sought to undermine such associations, wearing its heart on its sleeve(notes) to declare: "A collaboration between writer Jools Gilson-Ellis and media artist and composer Richard Povall, *mouthplace* rejects the aesthetic of computer-generated slickness and artificial worlds and instead conjures traceries of the feminine body and work with painted text, hand-drawn animation, handwriting, laughter, poetic text, the speaking and singing voice, and rich sonic environments"[24] (figure 25.7).

Anti-slickness became a theme of performer-produced CD-ROMs in the late 1990s, with notable examples including Ruth Gibson and Bruno Martelli's *Windowsninetyeight* (1998) and Forced Entertainment and Hugo Glendinning's *Nightwalks* (1998). *Windowsninetyeight* ironically adopted the title from Microsoft's new PC operating system, released in 1998 with a high saturation advertising campaign, but in contrast to Microsoft's claims of a technological breakthrough in home computing, Gibson and Martelli's "Readme" file claimed: "a completely new kind of soap opera, a *lo-fi* kitchen sink drama in digital image and sound" (our emphasis). It goes on to summarize its artistic intentions and structure concisely:

Windowsninetyeight is a provocative portrait of three women living alone in a highrise. One evening, a mysterious event takes each on a cathartic ride through the deepest fears of the other. The saga chronicles a single 24-hour cycle in the lives of these women. The magical world of their private behaviour, their habits and chores, their dreams and fears, becomes exposed to our scrutiny. As we navigate a passage through their day, three raw and personal domestic existences open up for our viewing pleasure (figure 25.8).

But despite the anti-slick philosophy and nonformulaic structure, the CD-ROM is ingenious and compelling, skillfully drawing together elements and aesthetics from dance,

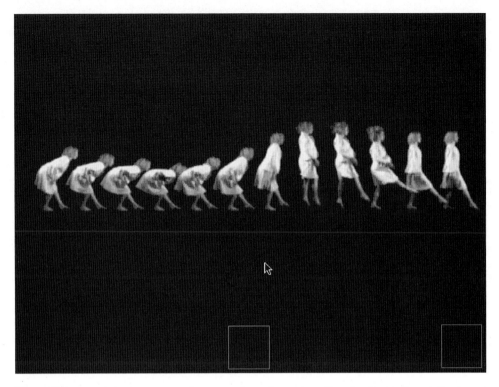

Figure 25.8 One of the three women characters who each experience "a cathartic ride through the deepest fears of the others" in Ruth Gibson and Bruno Martelli's *Windowsninetyeight* (1998).

film, games, animation, and picture storybooks. Narratives from different apartments in a large towerblock are interwoven as the user navigates the building during the course of a day, until the building gradually and atmospherically darkens as day turns to evening and night (figure 25.9). As the artists put it, the spirit of Baudelaire is ignited as the user is gently seduced into the role of a thoughtful Peeping Tom and, as Baudelaire wrote in his prose poem *Windows*,

Whoever looks from outside through an open window will never see as many things as when you look at a closed one. There is no sight with greater depth and mystery and variety, more obscurely suggestive, more brightly revealing . . . [than] behind a window-pane. Inside that black or luminous void, life is being lived, life is being dreamed, life is being suffered.[25]

Nightwalks presents a similarly voyeuristic exploration, but through navigation around "a fragmented city at night" filled with strange, out-of-place characters, and even a pantomime horse: "In this space of interlocking dreams people themselves have the status of

Figure 25.9 The apartment block main menu of Ruth Gibson and Bruno Martelli's *Windowsninetyeight* (1998).

object—strange clues to be found and connected in the otherwise deserted streets. . . . The piece plunges the viewer into a place which is both a distorted portrait of England and a catalogue of forgotten locations for an imaginary film"[26] (figure 25.10). Both the viewers' progress in peering into the windows of the apartment block in *Windowsninetyeight* and the movement through the cityscape of *Nightwalks* is deliberately (and meaningfully) *slow*, in marked contrast to the speed and action of most commercial CD-ROMs and videogames. The two CD-ROMs typify the late-1990s resistance to the speed, sheen, and artificiality of commercial titles, as these practiced performers subvert the norms of the CD-ROM to revisit the "slow motion" performance aesthetics of the 1980s, as discussed in David Gale's classic essay "Against Slowness" (1985).

Conclusion

It is ironic that the CD-ROM established itself as a major new technology for art and performance around 1994, the very year that its technological successor was being developed. In December 1994, Phillips and Sony announced a new high-density disc called MMCD,

Figure 25.10 Sex in the moonlight and the glow of city lights in Tim Etchells/ Hugo Glendinning and Forced Entertainment's "distorted portrait of England," *Nightwalks* (1998).

and Warner and Toshiba quickly followed with the announcement of their double-sided disc, called SD. The impetus of industrial competition for a new system became an immediate driving force for the *next* development even before CD-ROMs had successfully established themselves. In effect, the life-span of the CD-ROM was essentially the time-span it took the different companies to refine the newer format and to reach agreement over how to standardize it and successfully market it at a price where the consumer could be persuaded to abandon the old in favor of the new. As with the CD-ROM, the companies compromised to adopt a single format—with the name "DVD" (Digital Video Disc or, a later improvement, Digital Versatile Disc)—and the halcyon days of the CD-ROM were effectively over almost as soon as the first DVD players were launched in the United States in March 1997.

The one signal failing of the CD-ROM, its inability to store and replay the very large data files needed for full-screen video, was overcome by the high-density DVD which play entire movies, and at even higher resolution than VHS video. The DVD rapidly became the new standard, and the CD-ROM was, at least commercially, revealed to be little more than a bridge technology en route to the DVD. The new format has now almost entirely replaced the old CD-ROM, and is the default format for artists documenting their live performances. But while DVD affords high-quality, full-screen video in contrast to the typically postage-stamp size QuickTime movie footage of CD-ROMs, the new format radically alters the paradigm for performance documentation and analysis. In 1999, Steve Dixon's article "Remediating Theatre in a Digital Proscenium" praised the very limitations of the small, low resolution QuickTime movie files of performance CD-ROMs as their greatest strength, arguing a "paradox of scale" whereby, "like a homeopathic dosage," QuickTime movies remediate live theater more accurately and acceptably than full-screen video recordings. He discusses the advantages of the Brechtian effect and "gritty realism" associated with the tiny, low-resolution footage that produces an evocative and nostalgic effect he compares to nickelodeans and early cinema. He notes how cinema technology rapidly overcame the quaint, flickering effects of early movies to embrace high resolution and thus realism, and how the development of DVD from CD-ROM has marked a parallel path:

However, theatrical archivists and remediators could do well to remember the particular virtues of the smaller window format for theatrical footage, rather than embracing full-screen video as it inexorably becomes the new gold standard. Full-screen digital video is not computational multimedia; it is just television, and television remediates theatre badly, as I have sought to demonstrate.

By contrast, the dual proscenium of small-window digital movie placed within a wider frame . . . becomes a play within a play. The remediated performance footage is ritualised within the wider computer proscenium as a totem, a fetishised object. Though small and flickering, it is nonetheless powerful, evanescent and inherently theatrical.[27]

Jeffrey Shaw, Director of the ZKM-Institute for Visual Media that did so much to promote the art and performance CD-ROM offers another perspective, but with equal aesthetic appreciation and even a nostalgic yearning for this highly distinctive but extremely short-lived medium:

In recent years, the CD-ROM format has been rendered increasingly obsolete by new digital distribution forms such as the Internet and DVD. . . . When taking a fresh look at these works, one should bear in mind that they were created in the period 1994 to 1998 with the assistance of the authoring systems then current and subject to the specific limitations (e.g. speed, resolution, image quality) of the CD-ROM format. . . . But the obsolescence of technological platforms does not compromise the artistic value of the works created within them. Despite the technological time-bound identities of the *artintact* works, therefore, they all embody a depth of conceptual and aesthetic artistry allowing them to enter the timeless realm of universal appreciation.[28]

Conclusion

There's one thing I don't understand about you, lady. How come you're so clever and you made this machine without a fucking off switch?
—DUNCAN GIBBINS AND YALE UDOFF, *EVE OF DESTRUCTION* (1991)[1]

Broken Utopias

The world will be a heaven in the twenty-first century in comparison with what it is now.
—MADAME E. P. BLAVATSKY (1889)[2]

Thirty-four years after the historic *Cybernetic Serendipity* (1968) exhibition at London's Institute of Contemporary Arts (ICA) the institution staged another major computer arts event, *What Do You Want To Do With It?* (2002). The exhibition's title draws on Microsoft's 1990s' slogan "Where do you want to go today?" but is also revealing in its implicit suggestion that while new technologies are now very much here to stay, their application in creative arts is still embryonic. *Cybernetic Serendipity* was an exhibition of an anticipated digital future—a "futurist" exhibition, in one sense—but by 2002 both the landscape and the questions had fundamentally changed. Computers were, and are ubiquitous in Western societies, but following years of experimentation there is still uncertainty about what can be creatively achieved with them. Reviewing the opening, *The Guardian* art critic Sean Dodson compared the two ICA exhibitions:

Looking back at *Cybernetic Serendipity*, a difference strikes you: then, the artists on show were obsessed with the future. But now that the vision of the "future" is commonplace, the show seems obsessed with the past. . . . In 1968, the Guardian said *Cybernetic Serendipity* "lured into Nash House people who would never have dreamed of attending an ICA exhibition before." Now that nearly everyone in the industrialised world has access to computers, will the ICA be able to repeat its success?[3]

The answer was no: the exhibition was reasonably well attended but had little popular impact, unlike the 1968 show which had thousands queuing down The Mall to get in. Things had changed since the '60s, and indeed since the early '90s when exaggerated claims had cast computing and the digital as the foundation of a new way of life that would make the twenty-first century and Shangri-la indistinguishable. Doubt about the accuracy of such prognostication accelerated around the turn of the millennium and particularly after the whimper of the Millennium Bug. The first concrete signs of this shift were in domestic retail markets with a noticeable downturn in sales of computing hardware, followed by the very public difficulties of major dot.com companies that a few years earlier had made millionaires of their developers. The digital bubble, if not exactly bursting overnight, was losing pressure remorselessly and has continued so to do with significant consequences for digital applications across a wide range of associated activities including the arts. The decline in investment, interest and development became endemic. By 2004, headlines such as "Plug is pulled on e-university,"[4] which reported that the British government's "flagship e-university . . . for the 21st century, is to be dismantled after embarrassing performance failures" caused little surprise and merited little media coverage. Launched at the height of the dot-com boom in 2000, the e-university had proved expensive (around $100 million), had underrecruited, had lost its glamour and appeal, and had failed.

The major search engine Google was one of the few business success stories of the Internet boom, and it brought sober historical reminders that most of those who become rich in a gold rush actually sell shovels. But suspicion about dot-com companies was so embedded that when Google announced its intended flotation on the stock market, seasoned financiers differed wildly on estimations of its value and profitability: from $50 billion to virtually zero. Uncertainty and reevaluation was underway in other avenues too. Leading academics such as George Steiner were drawing distinctions between artistic "creativity" and technological "invention," categorizing the former as transcendental and metaphysical (that could last for ever and was "life") and the latter as technological, pragmatic and utilitarian (that was of its time, worldly and would become obsolete and suffer "death").[5] The historical context of computing also began to be explored and compared to other technological "revolutions," no thesis more arresting than the continuing debate about whether or not the first information revolution (telephony) was more influential than computing. Albert Borgman adopted the biblical metaphor of a flood to describe an increasing sense of alarm at an overflow of information, which, instead of irrigating contemporary culture, threatens to ravage and drown it.[6] He suggests that the digitization of culture and reality has another period of expansion ahead of it ("things will get worse before they get better"),[7] but predicts that technological advances will never reach the heights conceived of it. Sophisticated Artificial Intelligence, he contests, is ultimately beyond the reach of computers, and even accurate speech recognition, translation, and deep linguistic analysis are unlikely to be attained. As technologists conceive and build

Figure 26.1 Although installations such as these may once have dazzled our sensibilities, Albert Borgman argues that we have now "anticipated and discounted the greatest marvels of information technology." A child interacts with Margarete Jahrmann and Max Moswitzer's game installation *Nibble Engine Toolz* (2002).

brave new virtual worlds and systems, their use and value will ultimately be considered in the same "distracting and dispensable" light as television: part of a cultural sensibility that balances comfort with boredom. However photorealistic or captivating the new visions of the future may be "the ordinary Joe and Josephine sit on their couch having anticipated and discounted the greatest marvels of information technology"[8] (figure 26.1).

Returns to the Live

The public, academic and commercial crumbling of confidence and optimism in new technologies was quickly reflected in the arts. In September 2003, Britain's foremost contemporary art gallery, the Tate Modern, featured a program of works of "new-wave East Coast video" entitled *Blinky* which claimed "a range of anarchic aesthetic ideas linked by a rejection of digital cool and technical awe."[9] By the following year the wheel turned full circle when the minister of culture called for an *increase* in historical drama productions in order to make the classics more accessible to the young and underprivileged.[10] By 2005, we were attending theater and dance performances by the very pioneers who had led and defined the digital performance movement, but who now seemed to have revised their views on technology's benefits and retreated back to the live. Random Dance Company's previously media-saturated live work was now almost devoid of media projections, and the cyborgic metal arm extensions of their earlier *Nemesis* (2002) had vanished. Elsewhere, digital inputs and outputs had disappeared in the intimate exploration of lost property, left (and lost) luggage, and lost moorings, *Lost and Found* (2005), an avowedly nondigital performance on a canal barge by a company that had also significantly lost part of its name—"Curious" had abandoned its (previously fashionable) ".com" suffix—another sure sign of the times.[11] Troika Ranch's *Surfacing* (2004–2005) contained some hypnotic projections of dancers falling in exquisite slow motion (captured using a specialist high-speed digital camera), but as its program notes explained somewhat apologetically, "For those of you who know Troika Ranch for its use of new media and computer interactivity, you may find *Surfacing* spare in its use of technology. (Even we have come to refer to it as 'Troika Unplugged.') . . . So, we hope you will accept *Surfacing* not in the context of a 'dance and technology' work, but instead in the context of the quite human thesis it presents. *Surfacing* became much less of an exposé of cutting-edge technology, and more a reflection of introspection and quiet solitude"[12] (figure 26.2).

Laurie Anderson's one-woman show *The End of the Moon* (2004–2005) was filled with intimate spoken narratives, fractured language, and absorbing comic anecdotes about her experiences as NASA's first artist-in-residence, and she made music using keyboards and an electronic violin ("actually a hopped up viola designed by Ned Steinberger for maximum range")[13] for which Anderson has designed programs enabling it to generate

Figure 26.2 Troika Ranch directs its focus on the live in *Surfacing* (2004), "less of an exposé of cutting-edge technology, and more a reflection of introspection and quiet solitude." Photo: Richard Termine.

harmonies, chords, and tonal clusters. But the huge projection screens were gone, and apart from the instruments (centre stage) and a wing-backed leather chair (downstage right) the vast Barbican Theatre stage in London was entirely empty, apart from eighty burning candles scattered around the floor. "I find the best way to look at our culture these days is not through a multimedia show, but more directly—with the simpler and sharper tools of words," read her program, which included at the very end of her biographical notes another clear indication of her return to the live and the natural: "Currently she is working on a series of very long walks."[14] The only visual multimedia sequence in *The End of the Moon* was simple and short, when Anderson held up a pen-size video camera to capture first a close-up of her face upside down and then a close shot of her bow as she played the violin, which was relayed onto a comparatively tiny screen (approximately six feet high and three feet wide). "Technically *The End of the Moon* looks pretty simple" she admits, before going on to suggest: "it's actually the most complicated piece I've ever produced. It's just that everything has finally disappeared, turning into software and programs. I hope that eventually it will all fit in my pocket."[15]

Perhaps something of a gorgon was created in the 1990s through the pioneering work of digital performance practitioners, and many might suspect it was maimed or even slain by the turn of the millennium. But, as Anderson intimates, it still lives to tell the tale, albeit in more miniature, low-key forms. Digital developments are now so deeply embedded in the development of performance, as a tool if nothing else, that they have become assimilated and absorbed for perpetuity, as basic as the cog to transport, but no longer blatantly barnstorming the stage as the wheel itself.

Theatrical and Human Uncertainties

... anywhere without a bar with signed photographs of Derek Jacobi.
—JOHN FREEMAN[16]

In 2000, the popular liberal daily newspaper *The Guardian* published an open letter by performance academic John Freeman (a highly appropriate name) demanding the closure of all British theaters: "Turn theatres into snooker halls or massage parlours—do anything but stage plays in them."[17] Initially this does not sound like a resurgence of virtuous Cromwellian morality or the correction of any *fin de siècle* tendencies, although there was a hint of self-righteousness in Freeman's letter and a tendency to embrace the benefits of sackcloth and ashes: "Mainstream drama is outmoded, irrelevant, embarrassing. . . . Mainstream theatre has become a form without function. . . . The play is just the prelude to the eating out, where the acts we see are forgotten by the time we find our cars. . . . We need to kill the theatre off so that new performance can have room to grow."[18] This radical suggestion, prompted by a desire to demolish the old and respond to the promise of the new, inevitably held as part of its rationale the onset of digital technologies that demanded modernisation of the "same old masquerade": "televisions, computers, VCRs and DVDs sit in millions of homes. We . . . make phone calls from aeroplanes. And yet who would think it from our theatre-fare? Who would think, from the theatre, that our world is anything other than an endless loop of dialogue, drawing rooms and denouement?"[19]

Freeman's witty and timely diatribe prompted extensive correspondence stirring all the standard responses and recurrent theater debates: class consciousness and high, low and middling culture; traditions *versus* elitism; entertainment *versus* instruction; subsidy *versus* commercialism; language and dialogue; morality and catharsis; politics, literacy, popularity, innovation. And inevitably the parable of new wine in old bottles: "Mainstream theatre cannot contain the new. . . . New days call for new ways. When everything else in our lives has changed as radically as it has, the idea of theatre as a story interestingly told is redundant."[20]

Mercifully (for some if not for others), Freeman's demands had no direct effect on mainstream commercial theatre whatsoever. Nothing changed in exactly the same way as January 1 of the new millennium seemed strangely like the day after December 31 of the old one: the sun still rose at dawn and set at dusk, observable phenomena and ongoing problems remained unaffected by the arrival of this ostensibly momentous change. Perhaps the only genuine surprise was that the much-promised "Year 2000 Millennium Bug" did not see airplanes tumbling from the sky or elaborate systems of advanced human civilization crashing into chaos. It was generally concluded, with no little sigh of relief, that the danger had been exaggerated and the digital apocalypse avoided.

But not, apparently, for one of the most respected academics in theater and performance studies, Patrice Pavis, who published an essay in 2003 with wholly different concerns from Freeman about the state of new millennium theater. Pavis pleads a passionate humanist case for the live body and for theatrical text in the face of technological spectacle, and digital and robotic performance forms. He begins by presenting an analysis he wrote the day after seeing Robert Lepage's *Zulu Time*, in October 1999: "Every technology, every computer is a foreign body at the heart of theatrical performance. The more complex, sturdy, omnipresent the technology, the more derisory it is to our eyes."[21] As Lepage's stage machinery, robots, and video and digital effects swamp the human beings, he says, the audience searches desperately but in vain to connect with a speaking, living body (figure 26.3). But amid the high-tech tumult, the performer's body is no longer able to "be itself" as it is "pulled in" to the machine and thereafter seems to require techno-sadomasochistic paraphernalia to experience any meaning or pleasure. Lepage has "crossed the limits" to make the human figure "ridiculous," part of a farce, its body engulfed and its voice drowned out. Meanwhile:

So much technology talks so much it forgets what it is talking about, it becomes an end in itself, and exhausts us. A performance conceived, created, understood and appreciated by computer scientists alone. . . . Everything seems organised and planned for the machine, in particular the computer, to the point where the last traces of life and humanity are made to disappear. . . . The body

Figure 26.3 An isolated human dancer in Robert Lepage's *Zulu Time* becomes what Pavis calls "a foreign body" amid "the omnipresent technology." Photo: Reggie Tucker.

and the voice appear displaced in this technological device; they are like a foreign body in steel and plastic, animated by an artificial intelligence.[22]

Pavis's article is not simply another example of conservative criticism resisting or railing against new technology's incursion into theater and performance; and he himself acknowledges the danger of being seen as such and so initially distances himself from his own "excessive," unedited review. His discourse goes further than that, to make clear that the theater and the role and status of the performer within it has changed fundamentally, and perhaps irrevocably. The live human body in digital performance, Pavis suggests, has itself become a foreign body, but the invasive machine is no less foreign, and so "these foreigners [both] blessed with bodies" play out a drama where it is unclear which foreign body will ultimately win out to invade or assimilate the other (figure 26.4). The discourse is not limited to Lepage's performance (which, we would note, is one of the most "machinic" ever staged), but uses it as a metaphor to declare fundamental changes being effected in performance's very ontology, as well as human ontology, through "the computerization of our lives."[23] His analysis of *Zulu Time* ends with a lament, as if he has witnessed the end of theater itself, or at least as it existed in the past: "Speech is over. . . . The parade is over. We have lost the power of speech."[24] Brook's campfires and Grotowski's rituals and chants are also over, he says, their origins so distant that we mock them as "archaic, cut off from the world, 'old hat', like our poor human body."[25]

Without acknowledging or using the word, Pavis places both contemporary performance and the performer into a posthuman frame. Theater's age-old humanism based on words, emotions, live bodies, and intimate, ritualized exchange has been superseded by posthuman theater, and what is more, that succession is now irrevocable: "triumphant . . . technology has got the upper hand on the human for good."[26] While the essay can be seen as yet another example of the reevaluation of technology in the early twenty-first century, it is a rare one within performance studies where interest in digital performance has been generally enthusiastic. At the same time, we suspect many have (secretly) applauded Pavis's honest and brave discourse in the face of the obvious threat of accusations of Luddism and conservatism against him. Pavis's dramatic cries about technology having taking over the theater would have sounded like victory to the futurists who called for that precise outcome almost a century earlier. The futurist's prophecy, like the cries of the last human among the robots in Capek's *R.U.R.*, or the rehearsals for cyborgism of Stelarc and Anthúnez-Roca have, for Pavis at least, come true: "technology has got the upper hand on the human for good."

Futurist Déjà Vu

History does not always repeat itself, and it is to be hoped that twenty-first century digital and performance developments do not exactly echo those of their twentieth-century futurist antecedents, who are now generally held in low esteem because of their

Figure 26.4 An actor is dwarfed by Robert Lepage's giant, mechanistic set in *Zulu Time*. Photo: Reggie Tucker.

associations with fascism, misogyny, and loud, bullish proclamations. In Chapter 3, we argued digital performance's close philosophical and technological associations with futurism, and will conclude our thoughts on their interrelationships here by noting some other uncomfortably close parallels between futurism's evolution and the rise (and rhetoric) of digital technology in the 1990s. Both "movements" were predominantly male-led and emerged following a surge of youthful and aggressive optimism in new technologies, the protagonists dismissing doubters to the new cause as "old-fashioned," out of touch with the times, and "Luddite." Both predicted the future would be new and glorious, and both, in different ways, were wrong: the futurists in their calculations about glorious war, the digitists in failing to foresee a wholesale collapse of financial growth. The promised tomorrow that ostensibly awaited everyone fell badly short and the consequent disappointment inevitably resulted in a severe backlash for the wounds suffered. If the message is wrong it is invariably the messenger who is blamed, perhaps justly if the messenger originated the message as well as the medium by which it was communicated.

The digital conceits of the 1990s already appear an immature celebration of modernity (the twenty-first century, the second millennium) that did not produce anything approaching a glorious Second Coming but rather the mishaps, wars, and fear of very *physical* catastrophes, serving to undermine the joys of the virtual. The technology may still seem extraordinary (although already not to younger generations who accept it as part of their birthright along with television, cars and mobile phones) but "digital" no longer denotes the future or the magical, merely another tool and facility. When the initial fervor about a new technology or a new type of image subsides, once again it becomes the *content* and *meaning* that matters, just as in the 1910s it was the *consequences* of flight, speed, and explosion that brought the daily destruction of the First World War into sharp relief. Both futurism and digital technologies initially presented themselves as *philosophies* of life only for it to be realized a little later that they were merely technical developments that would rapidly become dated and demand further enhancement to avoid becoming cyclically entrenched in their own tropes and limitations.

Political parallels are equally interesting. Mussolini was a futurist only when it suited his political campaign, and he initially gave the active, attractive celebrity Marinetti a position in the party. But in 1921, Mussolini abandoned the futurists as immature following their impossible demands to open the prisons, and once in power in 1923, his prime objectives were to establish "order" and "harmony," neither of which were high on Marinetti's agenda. Politics is necessarily fickle in dealing with the exigencies of the day; and like any known form of motion, no revolution has ever proved perpetual, whether French, communist, futurist, or digital.

Marinetti remained a faithful and active fascist until his death and even signed up at the age of sixty to join Mussolini's campaign in Ethiopia, believing that glorious heroic days were back again. Still later, he joined the disastrous Italian campaign in Russia in 1942. He became secretary to the Fascist Writers Guild and died in one of the last fascist strongholds in 1944. Marinetti was always immature, elitist, intellectually, and politically inconsistent[27] (a left-wing fascist with anarchist tendencies), but he maintained a belief in radical art forms, the transformative power of technology, and the promise of the future. Perhaps the saddest reflection is that Marinetti had complex and powerful ideas for the future role of the artist that were never realized—perhaps until now. In 1921, Marinetti and Cangiullo reviewed the first ten years of futurist performance in *The Theatre of Surprise*. Their reflections were hyperbolic wishful thinking then, but today they read like the words of a critic from 2001 reviewing ten years of digital performance:

If today a young . . . theatre exists with . . . unreal persons in real environments, simultaneity and interpenetration of time and space, it owes itself to our *synthetic theatre*.[28] (figure 26.5).

Figure 26.5 The Builders Association's stylish brand of neo-futurist "synthetic theater," *Alladeen* (2003).

The Challenge to Postmodernism

The culture of time in the late twentieth century has evolved faster than the theoretical reasoning which has accompanied it.

—URSULA HEISE[29]

In chapter 3 we drew close correlations between the philosophical impulses and aesthetic practices of the artistic "movements" of futurism in the 1910s and digital performance in the 1990s. Our identification of digital performance within progressive modernist and avant-garde traditions continued in chapter 21, where we argued that postmodern notions of time provide only partial understandings of the expression and representation of temporality within new media performance practice. Postmodernism's denial of the possibility of anything new consequently denies the possibility of a future, and hence time is theorized as a recurrent present which envelops and is saturated by the past, but never looks toward the future. Jean-François Lyotard characterizes postmodern temporality "as the struggle to take possession of time, the negentropic impulse to conserve and concentrate memory and continuity against change or loss."[30] Frederic Jameson theorizes the postmodern "as an attempt to think the present historically in an age that has forgotten how to think historically in the first place."[31] While modernism was compulsive in its desire for the new and tried to watch its coming into being, "the postmodern looks for breaks, for events rather than new worlds."[32] The moderns were concerned with radical artistic change, whereas postmodernism "knows only too well that the contents are just more images. . . . Postmodernism is what you have when the modernization process is complete."[33]

As Steven Connor puts it, postmodernism has "borrowed from the modern its capacity for breaking with the past, its quality of self-possession, whilst losing all of its forward impulsion."[34] But as we have argued and demonstrated, digital performance is characterized by the very forward impulsions postmodernism lacks: digital performance is an avant-garde that propels itself toward the future; it seeks the "new worlds" that postmodernism eschews. It fiercely resists Jameson's idea that "the modernization process is complete," not least in its utilization of digital developments such as the web, VR, and advanced motion sensing and interactive systems that simply did not exist when the defining treatises of postmodernism emerged in the 1970s and '80s (figure 26.6). In this sense, the "present tense" of both digital performances and their creative artists are marked by excitability and forward-vision, in contrast to the static, backward-looking, "groundhog-day" present of the postmodern experience. We have argued how experimentation with notions of time in digital performance often ignites a sense of the new in creating *extratemporal* representations and experiences. But more than this, the impetus of the digital performance movement can itself be seen as intimately related to the modernist experience and understanding of temporality, as described, for example, by Terry Eagleton:

Figure 26.6 Advanced and minutely responsive interactive installations such as Camille Utterback and Romy Archituv's *Text Rain* (1999) did not exist when postmodern theory emerged in the 1970s and 1980s and challenged the very notion of originality and the new.

If modernism lives its history as peculiarly, insistently present, it also experiences a sense that this present moment is somehow of the future, to which the present is nothing more than an orientation; so that the idea of the Now, of the present as full presence eclipsing the past, is itself intermittently eclipsed by an awareness of the present as deferment, as an empty excited openness to a future which is in one sense already here, in another sense yet to come.[35]

If we return to postmodernism's most canonical work, *Postmodernism: Or, the Cultural Logic of Late Capitalism* (1984), Jameson acknowledges postmodernism's contingency upon the modern, but defines key principles which distinguish them, and draws upon both theory and the arts to characterize postmodernism's separation from the modernist past. Thus, for example, postmodern video art is differentiated from modernist avant-garde film as "surrealism without the unconscious."[36] The concept of "without" is central to Jameson's discourse: an understanding of postmodern culture in relation to an absence or lack of key elements inherent within modernism: History, Spirit, Grand Narratives. But digital performance reignites and reconfigures these very absences, these specific and defining modernist elements and places them center stage. In VR experiences (as we discussed in chapter 15), History is reevaluated and digitally brought to life in Richard Beacham's ancient theater reconstructions, ieVR's restorations of 1920s expressionist theater texts, and Davies, Laurel, and Strickland's immersive journeys into the primordial past. Spirit, rather than an absence, is one of *the* defining features of multimedia and telematic dance-theater where ghostly virtual bodies and digital doubles swirl across stages and virtual spaces (Merce Cunningham, Bill T. Jones, Random Dance Company); human figures transform into shimmering cosmological beings (Igloo, Company in Space); and spiritualized alchemical weddings between the human and the digital are invoked (Troika Ranch). And there can be few "grander" narratives (nor newer ones) than the posthuman rehearsals for man-machine cyborgism of Stelarc and Anthúnez Roca, the transgenic art of Eduardo Kac, or the ultimate futurist spectacle: robots replacing human beings to stage everything from the horrors of war (Survival Research Laboratories) and explicit sex (The Seemen Group, Norman White and Laura Kikauka) to the planet's battle for ecological survival (Amorphic Robot Works, Brett Goldstone) (figure 26.7).

Neither the modern nor the postmodern should be thought of as periods, but rather as aesthetic and sociopolitical positions; as differing types of consciousness and response to culture and society. As Lyotard puts it, "the modern . . . [is] a matter of mood and attitude (or Subject position) rather than a simple indicator of temporality or contemporaneity."[37] The moods, attitudes, and subject positions of digital performance artists predominantly concur not with the postmodern, but the modern; they encompass an acute, overriding awareness of new technologies as instruments of temporal change and future creative forms. Digital performers are the futurists of the turn of the millennium, discontents fiercely resisting postmodernism's hollow cries about the end of history, time, meaning, and the "real." They accept, embrace, and encourage a new "real," every bit as real as it ever was, though naturally different from the past ('twas ever thus) and with technology at its core. They have moved on and forward, seeking to interrogate and artistically express the realities and possibilities of their time, a quite *specific* time, not a conceptual one. They are *modern artists* in every way, quintessentially engaged with precisely the same concern that Baudelaire, more than a century earlier, had memorably and categorically defined. The modern artist is

one who knows how to see and to perpetuate the beauty of his own time. . . . Modernity never stops referring to the present of the one who attempts to define it, on the condition that he knows how to take into account this present, to seize the truth and the necessity of the moment. . . . The value of modernity, if there is one, is awarded to works that cannot belong to other times. (figure 26.8)

The New

In 1975, during the early, heady days of postmodern theory, Michael Kirby wrote in his editorial for *TDR*,

Figure 26.7 Grand Narratives return, and with serious posthuman intent in this image evoking Leonardo da Vinci's Vitruvian Man from David Therrien's *Information Machine* (1994). Photo: Paul Markow.

Experimentation in theatre has not stopped. Some have given up the search for new ideas; some repeat themselves; some copy what has already been done, perhaps while they are claiming originality. But others have moved their work into new areas, continuing to search even when it means rejecting the type or style of performance that has brought them success, acclaim, and popularity. New theatre artists have appeared, presenting original work. The avant-garde of today is not the avant-garde of even a few years ago.[38]

Kirby's reference back to avant-garde performance practices "a few years ago" probably dates back around ten years, to the paradigm-changing performance experiments of the mid- and late 1960s. Looking back as we write in 2005 over an equivalent ten or so years

Figure 26.8 Random Dance Company's *Nemesis* (2002) is a modernist work in Baudelaire's sense of the modernist artist as "one who knows how to see and to perpetuate the beauty of his own time" and who creates art "that cannot belong to other times." Photo: Ravi Deepres.

of significant digital performance practice following its own paradigm-changing experiments in the early/mid-1990s, we must conclude that the same is generally true: "New theatre artists have appeared, presenting original work." Other leading digital commentators give credence to the argument through their understandings of how techniques, processes, bodies, objects, and spaces have not only been transformed but have brought about entirely new ontologies. Peter Weibel, for example, insists that the infinite pliability of the digital form means that "For the first time in history, the image is a dynamic system,"[39] and Margaret Wertheim announces that with networked cyberspace, "We are witnessing here the birth of a new domain, a new space that simply did not exist before."[40] Her sentiments are echoed by numerous digital performance artists, including Yacov Sharir:

I know in my life there is a space and a dancer, and now a new space. An endless space—*cyberspace*—that is brand new. . . . And *it has turned around, upside down almost, what we know about dance.* Cyberspace is zero gravity. There is no gravity in cyberspace. I can make a phrase where the dancer takes off into the air and stays in the air as long as forever with no bending knees, with no sense

Figure 26.9 "Zero gravity has changed the notion of how dancers move in cyberspace." Yacov Sharir, discussing his *Cyber Human Dance Series* (1999).

of gravity, with no sense of groundedness. So the zero gravity has changed the notion of how dancers move in cyberspace. Not physical and human dancers, but cyber-humans and cyber-dancers move differently.[41] (figure 26.9)

Neither can there be any doubt that previously unprecedented interactive motion-sensing, motion-capturing and telematic systems confirm that, in Susan Kozel's words: "The collaboration between dance and technology is a new art form."[42] As Donna Haraway puts it in relation to the cyborg: "new creatures are forming that beg new theories rather than recycle old ones";[43] and the quintessential would-be cyborg Stelarc similarly has no time for postmodern self-containment and retrospection, placing his work as a development of a *modernist* agenda:

I've always felt uneasy about strategies of appropriation and deconstruction. I also think that you don't simply generate discourse by creating a pastiche of archetypical images but rather that you generate alternative aesthetics. I think we still have to critique this kind of post-modern approach. My concern about post-modernist deconstruction and appropriation is that it ultimately becomes so self-referential that it falls into an incestuous discourse and spirals back into itself and doesn't plot any alternate or new strategies and trajectories.[44]

The argument is further sustained if we divert our attention away from the artworks and performances to focus on the ontology of digital technology itself. Despite the popular proclamation that new technologies and the Internet are quintessentially postmodern since they utilize nonlinear, nonhierarchical systems, we suggest an opposite argument, but an equally strong thesis. New digital technologies are *by definition* modern. Computer systems are logical, progressive, essentialist, and rational, pushing technological progress to the fore. The inherent and inextricable relationship between new technologies and modernism extends to the hardware itself, as Julian Stallabras has carefully explored by drawing resemblances between the design of microprocessors and Le Corbusier's drawings of city plans, whereby "everything was done to ensure that traffic moved unimpeded at the highest possible rate. . . . The raw measure of efficiency was speed . . . with no room for (analogue) suburbs."[45] Stallabras goes on to relate Internet exploration to "that old modernist paradigm—discovery" and describes the unifying design of screen interfaces and the visual expression of the Macintosh or Windows systems as being "of a benign technocratic modernism." He argues that computer culture is a living embodiment of the modernist, positivist dream of directed evolution and apparently limitless progress.

Another important factor in our argument is the differing natures, philosophies, and intentions behind postmodern performance and digital performance. Central characteristics that have separated postmodern performance from the modern, such as playfulness, irony and pastiche, are often absent in the more "serious" and frequently "spiritual" terrain of digital performance. We believe this is in part due to the inherent difficulties and complexities associated with conjoining theater and performance with embryonic and gremlin-ridden virtual technologies. The scale and ambition of such a project in the 1990s cast artists as pioneers exploring hostile, uncharted territory (the original meaning of the term *avant-garde*) and led to a highly focused, purposeful, and frequently romantic artistic mindset. The early-twentieth-century modernist concern for progress, and for the creation of meaningful and totalizing images, messages, and metaphors reemerged with renewed vigor in the virtual performance of the late twentieth and early twenty-first centuries. Inevitably, clear traces of the postmodern spirit remained (particularly stylistic eclecticism, appropriation, and remediation), but deconstructive and retrospective tendencies gave way significantly to older, progressive, constructivist ideals, as computer technologies were used as agents of visual unity and conceptual cohesion rather than fragmentation. Where postmodernism broke up and dispersed pieces of the theatrical jigsaw, a fundamental thrust of digital performance was to bring the pieces back together.

But there nonetheless remains a key problem in theorizing digital performance outside of a postmodern philosophical frame, and it provides the reason for the stubborn resistance of critics and commentators to do so. A fundamental and paradoxical "law" of postmodern theory states perversely that even if something is genuinely modern nowadays it simply confirms its own postmodernity by default—by drawing on old modernist modalities. Postmodernism includes, subsumes, neutralizes, and castrates the modern. And, as Ihab Hassan points out, postmodernism suffers from a semantic instability as it contains the word modernism itself—"the enemy within."[46] Thus, postmodern theory can never lose nor be denied, existing in a self-satisfied win-win vacuum, a playful but tyrannical child-king that perpetuates and recrowns itself infinite times.

But we do not accept the inclusion of digital performance within such an undifferentiated and outdated critical terrain, and suggest our evidence of the new in the groundbreaking experiments and technological systems within the field provides not only admissible but also cast-iron evidence to challenge and cast off what the Critical Art Ensemble call "the yoke of catatonia inspired by the postmodern condition."[47] It provides a key to unlock and uncover the self-confirming, self-consuming snake of postmodern theory and bring it out of its state of blind denial of the new. Digital artists and performers around the turn of millennium created something that had not been seen before, something still highly experimental, not fully formed, but nonetheless *new*.

Grand Narratives Return

Following the publication of his "attack" on postmodern literary theory, *After Theory* (2003), Terry Eagleton published an article entitled "Bin Laden sure didn't read any beer mats" (2003), analyzing the different responses he received to his questioning of postmodern trends in cultural theory and his attack on the replacement of theory-as-critique by theory-as-postmodernism. While left-wing academics see his discourse as intellectual betrayal, those on the right rejoice that "the whistle has finally been blown on this orgy of unreason. . . . After a nightmarish interlude in which people gullibly swallowed the notion that there is nothing in the world but language, that Jeffrey Archer is as good as Jane Austen, and that beer mats are as semiotically rich as Balzac, sanity has broken out once more."[48] Eagleton suggests that postmodern theory has become a branch of competitive, late-capitalist commodity production, and its hollow messages about the end of truth, grand narratives and history were dealt a fatal blow on September 11, 2001. "Postmodernism, for all its cosmopolitan flavor, had proved a little parochial," he reflects, "ploughing on with our provincial discourses of vampirism, sadomasochism and body-tatooing while the towers crumble around our heads. . . . Grand narratives might be over in San Diego but not in Saudi Arabia."[49] He argues that the relativism and skepticism of postmodernism are too superficial and brittle to combat fundamentalism, and that cultural theory should once again risk becoming metaphysical: "It should strike out from the well-trodden paths of class, race and gender and look again at all those questions that it has shelved as embarrassingly large: questions of death, love, morality, nature, suffering, foundations, religion, biology and revolution"[50] (figure 26.10).

Cultural theorists may have studiously avoided them, but these "embarrassingly large" modernist questions have been continually posited and intimately explored by recent digital performance artists, as we have seen: death (Dumb Type, Paul Vanouse, Mark Pauline), love (Paulo Henrique, Company in Space, Curious.com), morality (Builders Association, Joel Slayton, Natalie Jeremijenko), nature (Char Davies, Amorphic Robot Works, Brenda Laurel/Rachel Strickland), suffering (Marcel.lí Anthúnez Roca, David

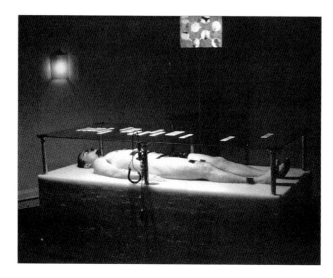

Figure 26.10 Many digital performance works, such as Paul Vanouse's *Items 1-2000* (1996) directly address the "embarrassingly large questions" such as death that Terry Eagleton believes postmodern theory has sidestepped.

Therrien, ieVR), foundations (Blast Theory, Gertrude Stein Repertory Theatre, Stelarc), religion (Bilderwerfer, George Coates Performance Works, Paul Sermon), biology (Eduardo Kac, Critical Art Ensemble, Yacov Sharir/Diane Gromala) and revolution (Guillermo Gómez-Peña, Critical Art Ensemble, Electronic Disturbance Theatre, VNS Matrix).

The first, halting steps in virtual performance harked back to the radical modernist experiments of futurism and the early avant-garde. Rejecting postmodernism's introspection and celebration of the ordinary, the pioneers of digital performance returned to modernist theories of the theater and performance, seeking to complete some unfinished business. There was a realization that Wagner's *Gesamtkunstwerk*, Marinetti's *Synthetic Theatre*, and Artaud's "impossible" visions of an immersive and mesmeric total theater were not, after all, inconceivable. The calls for artistic revolution made by the futurists, the surrealists, and the constructivists of the past palpably rematerialized. They echoed, phantomlike, around the virtual walls of the new cybertheater—and not only were the voices heard, they were also acted upon (figure 26.11).

Art All Around You

Art, technology, and even science seem to me to be three veils for the same face, three metaphors that cover, then dissolve, into a single reality.
—DOUGLAS DAVIS[51]

Figure 26.11 George Coates' theatrical depiction of cyberspace in *Invisible Site: A Virtual Sho* (1991) accords with Antonin Artaud's visions of a mesmeric, immersive theater and with Richard Wagner's notions of the *Gesamtkunstwerk*.

Putting the final touches to the first draft of this book, we participated in *Uncle Roy All Around You* (2004) a "solo experience" created by Blast Theory in collaboration with the Mixed Reality Lab, Nottingham University (figure 26.12). It provided timely food for thought and final reflection, not least in relation to John Cage's idea that the purpose of art is "not to bring order out of chaos nor to suggest improvements in creation, but simply to wake [us] up to the very life we're living."[52] It is fitting to end with an account of our personal experience of *Uncle Roy*, a piece created by a ground-breaking company who have always tested and pushed the boundaries between technology, art, life, and performance, and doubtless will continue to do so. As we have sometimes favored phenomenological perspectives and analyses in the course of this book, we will end by presenting a wholly subjective firsthand account of the author's experience of *Uncle Roy All Around You*:

Enter the Cornerhouse art gallery in Manchester's city center, and be directed to a computer to play an online game. Log on and become an avatar character in the virtual "world," a VR exact-scale reconstruction of Manchester (figure 26.13) locating other people (both online and outside in the real streets), picking up clues and sending messages to help players through their journeys around the streets. Go into a room and check in (like a flight desk) where instructions are given by the friendly flight attendant about how to play the game outside, and she takes all your possessions for

Figure 26.12 Publicity shot for Blast Theory's collaboration with the Mixed Reality Lab, University of Nottingham, *Uncle Roy All Around You* (2004).

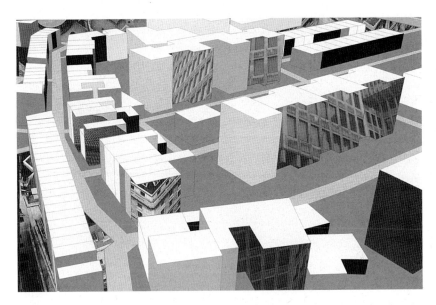

Figure 26.13 Players begin the "game-performance" by navigating around a VR model of Manchester and sending messages to assist other players outside on the (real) Manchester streets on their journeys to find *Uncle Roy.*

safekeeping (bags, items in pockets, money, mobile phone). Go out into the mean streets of the city center with a small portable computer wrapped in clear plastic (it's raining, this is Manchester) showing a zoomable map plan of the streets. Follow clues (targets on the screen, cryptic messages from *Uncle Roy*, text messages from players online trying to help you—or possibly hinder, who's to know?) to go to different points, including road junctions, and some rancid rubbish bins in a deserted backstreet behind a Japanese restaurant.

Each time you get to a destination, you register your route and confirm your position on the computer, then a new clue to where to go next appears (you already know something of how it works as you've been helping others online in the art gallery) (figure 26.14). Get sent to a sinister-looking parking lot and *Uncle Roy* texts you to "act like a criminal, move in and out closely between the cars, brush against them, if you're seen, get out quickly." Wonder if the suspicious NCP attendant is an actor or not (he clearly isn't). Brush along the cars and suddenly a car alarm goes off. Run out of the parking lot, panicking now, messages flashing on the screen. The clock is running down—only forty minutes allocated for the game, I must get to the destination and find *Uncle Roy*. Keep in mind that a friend who played and "failed" told you it ended for her with "Game Over" on the screen and a disgruntled walk back to the gallery to swap the computer for her stuff.

Be determined to win, start to run across roads through the gay village area of Manchester, record voice messages to your online friends who can hear you and they text you back. Hear screeching brakes and a deafening horn as you nearly, *really* get killed by a car, not looking as you scurry across

Conclusion

665

Figure 26.14 At each destination, players confirm their position on the palm computer, and in return receive an instruction or cryptic clue about the next location to go to.

a road, head in the computer. Think things like, "this is too dangerous for arts' sake, *Uncle Roy* is going too far." Suddenly get lost, go off the map and realize time is running out. Go to hidden areas of a canal, where no one's around except a young thug (definitely not an actor) who looks like he's interested in the technology you're clutching. Feel afraid. Remember that at the briefing you were told that if you're mugged, don't resist, just give them the computer straight away. Be relieved as nothing happens, but then see the screen's gone completely dead and last time you looked there was only ten minutes on the clock. Wander around in confusion until a large man approaches, very formally: "Uncle Roy informs me you have a problem." He fixes the computer, "you've been allocated a little more time." Find the next location, another clue and destination to go to, then the computer's down again.

Panic (figure 26.15). Be suddenly angry, then angry at yourself for being angry (this is just a game) then wonder "is this part of the game?" (it isn't). No large man appears, keep sending voice messages hoping there'll be some response, realize you've no mobile phone, no cash—they took it—realize you've nothing in your pockets at all except a card they gave you with a free phone number "in case of problems." Go find a payphone, call, talk to someone who says: "Wait there." Reenter large man who fixes the computer again and disappears. Eight minutes on the clock, ticking down, find the next location, a street, and *Uncle Roy* texts you to enter the double glass doors and go up the lift to the second floor and find one of the women displayed on the screen. Look at

Figure 26.15 "Be determined to 'win', start to run across roads . . . nearly, *really* get killed by a car . . . Suddenly get lost . . . Feel afraid . . . Panic." Just some of the feelings and incidents the author experienced during Blast Theory and the Mixed Reality Lab's *Uncle Roy All Around You*.

screen—it's a photograph, seems like it's from the 1960s, of a crowd of about a hundred women's faces. Five minutes left, see some glass doors (a hotel), up the lift, out, cleaners in the hotel corridor (are they actors?), think, "are any of their faces on this old picture?" Run up and down the long corridor. Realize this isn't the place, check the map plan again, realize the building you want is a little further up the street, take the stairs down, run, sweating—two minutes left—see another pair of glass doors to a building that looks deserted, burst in, take the lift upstairs, get out. There's a door.

Beside it is a blown-up picture of a woman's face from the 1960s, find her in the crowd scene on your screen, drag and drop an icon onto her face and see a screen message to the effect of, "congratulations, you've got here in time and the clock has now stopped. Come in, and go into to the waiting room." Punch the numbers you're given into the door's keypad, and enter a deserted, dusty, large office-floor, empty and no furniture, lots of doors, go into the one marked "Waiting Room." No-one there (always thought *Uncle Roy* would be Godot) but music is playing, and an angle-poise lamp lights a cardboard scale model of the streets you've just traveled. Follow screen instructions to look out of the window, sit down on the cushion on the floor, relax. Look at the spines of a pile of books on the floor beside you—Borges's *Labyrinths*, Moore's *Utopia*, and others of the ilk. Be told by *Uncle Roy* or whoever's writing on your screen that he used to love this room, feel so peaceful there, and how he once let someone go, but he regretted it, knew he shouldn't have. Be told to now go to the office. Find it, go in. No one in there either, there's no one here at all, only you in a vast, long-deserted Victorian office building. Two smart red chairs face each other either side of a table with a telephone, an incongruous installation in the center of the decrepit, empty space. The screen tells you to sit down and complete one of the postcards on the table (with stamp attached) and you do, putting your email address and writing, as prompted, something about someone you have also—in essence—loved and lost. The phone rings and the voice says, "Go out down the fire escape and get into the back seat of the car outside. Bring the postcard."

Go down the stairs, out of the doors and into a deserted back alley to see the *deus ex machina*— a huge, white stretch limousine. Get into the back seat. Once inside, a man (not the large one, another) gets in through the other door, sits down. He says, "Would you trust a stranger?" Feel your heart miss a beat, and wonder what this means (you remember Blast Theory's *Kidnap*), then talk to him as the limo drives slowly through the streets—about trust, about people, about the one *you* loved and lost—he wants details, name, specifics, the whole story. Tell him, feel considerable emotion (figure 26.16). Be told you can post your postcard outside the gallery if you wish and it will be sent on to one of the online players who have expressed an interest in being a friend and

Figure 26.16 "Would you trust a stranger?" The *Deus ex Machina* climax to *Uncle Roy All Around You.*

support to someone else, who will contact you by email and start a friendship. Post it, go and collect your possessions in return for the computer.

Go home, reevaluate yourself, the one you once loved and lost, the nature of memory, time's winged chariot, cities and surveillance, "virtual" realities, the fallibility of computers, the boundaries of bodies and space, the nature of life and its relationship to performance, the meaning of art. Cry like a baby. Realize, again, just how new and unprecedented such work is, and how timeless and humbling is the experience of great art.

Notes

Preface

1. Before 2005, it was known as the Arts and Humanities Research Board.

2. Beuys, interviewed in Filliou, *Teaching and Learning as Performance Arts*, 169, quoted in Ulmer, *Applied Grammatology*, 241.

3. Austin, "Philosophical Papers," 233.

4. *Digital Performance: The Online Magazine for Artists Embracing Technology*, Spring/Summer 2003 <http://www.digitalperformance.org/DigPerfDefined.htm>.

5. Ibid.

Chapter 1

1. Reaves "Theory and Practice: The Gertrude Stein Repertory Theatre," 5.

2. Murray, *Hamlet on the Holodeck: The Future of Narrative in Cyberspace*, 99.

3. Ibid., 15.

4. E-mail sent by Company in Space to the "Dance-Tech" list, 28 August 2001.

5. E-mail sent by Nick Rothwell to the "Dance-Tech" list, 28 August 2001.

6. Puttnam, "Keynote Speech."

7. Stringer, "Navigation: The Missing Ingredient in the Digital Design Process."

8. Norris quoted in Wilson, *Information Arts: Intersections of Art, Science and Technology*, 25.

9. Ibid., 23.

10. Ibid., 26.

11. Russell, *Poets, Prophets, and Revolutionaries: The Literary Avant-Garde from Rimbaud through Post-modernism*, 16, quoted in Rutsky, *High Techne: Art and Technology from the Machine Aesthetic to the Posthuman*, 75.

12. Bürger, *Theory of the Avant-Garde*, 49, quoted in Rutsky, *High Techne: Art and Technology from the Machine Aesthetic to the Posthuman*, 76.

13. Rutsky, *High Techne: Art and Technology from the Machine Aesthetic to the Posthuman*, 81.

14. Huyssen in Rutsky, *High Techne: Art and Technology from the Machine Aesthetic to the Posthuman*, 76.

15. Bürger, *Theory of the Avant-Garde*, 49, in Rutsky, *High Techne: Art and Technology from the Machine Aesthetic to the Posthuman*, 75.

16. Ibid.

17. Russell, *Poets, Prophets, and Revolutionaries*; 16, quoted in Rutsky, *High Techne: Art and Technology from the Machine Aesthetic to the Posthuman*, 75.

18. Rutsky, *High Techne: Art and Technology from the Machine Aesthetic to the Posthuman*, 89.

19. Schwarz, *Media-Art-History*, 8.

20. Shu, *Visual Programming*, 3.

21. The word *theranthrope* derives from *thêra*, wild animals, and *anthropos*, human being. *Theran-thropes* are also known as anthropozoomorphs. See Pradier, "Animals, Angel, Performance," 12.

22. Žižek, "Die Virtualisierung des Herr," 109–110, quoted in (and translated by) Andrea Zapp, "A Fracture in Reality: Networked Narratives as Imaginary Fields of Action," 75.

23. Auslander, "Live from Cyberspace, or, I was sitting at my computer this guy appeared he thought I was a bot." 21.

24. Rayner, "Everywhere and Nowhere: Theatre in Cyberspace," 294, 298.

25. Polli, "Virtual Space and the Construction of Memory," 45.

26. Pavis, "Afterword: Contemporary Dramatic Writings and the New Technologies."

27. Marinetti and Cangiullo quoted in Goldberg, *Performance Art: From Futurism to the Present,* 29.

28. Ryan, "Cyberspace, Virtuality, and the Text," 88.

29. Ibid.

30. Ibid., 8.

31. Ibid., 90.

32. The performance took place on 29 March 2001.

33. Grotowski, *Towards a Poor Theatre*, 19.

34. Ibid.

35. Ibid.

36. Ibid.

37. Ibid., 41.

38. Ibid., 23.

39. Despite Grotowski's significant influence on Barba (who worked with Grotowski and edited *Towards a Poor Theatre*) and Brook, both have employed grand visual spectacle in their work. Barba's outdoor performances make use of lavish costumes and masks. Brook's adaptation of the *Ubu Plays* (1977) employed a custom-built rain machine, and his *The Man Who Mistook* (1994) featured video monitors and projections.

40. Palmer "Technology and the Playwright," 146–147.

41. Brook, *The Empty Space*.

42. Palmer, "Technology and the Playwright, 143.

43. Baudrillard, "Videowelt und Fraktales Subjekt," 123, quoted in Grau, *Virtual Art: From Illusion To Immersion*, 217.

44. Aronson, "Technology and Dramaturgical Development: Five Observations," 188, 193, quoted in Palmer, "Technology and the Playwright," 144.

45. Orton and Pollock, *Avant-gardes and their Partisans, Reviewed*, 230.

46. Rutsky, *High Techne: Art and Technology from the Machine Aesthetic to the Posthuman*, 82.

47. Sontag, "Film and Theatre," 24.

48. Jones, "Monsters of Mediocrity."

Chapter 2

1. Mark Dery, quoted on the back cover sleeve of Packer and Jordon, *Multimedia: From Wagner to Virtual Reality*.

2. Causey, "Screen Test of the Double: the Uncanny Performer in the Space of Technology," 383.

3. Stone, *The War of Desire and Technology at the Close of the Mechanical Age*, 16.

4. Greenfield, *Tomorrow's People: How the 21st Century is Changing the Way We Think and Feel*.

5. Adorno, *Ästhetische Theorie*, 36. (English translation 19), quoted in Grau, *Virtual Art: From Illusion To Immersion*, 7.

6. We would note that this type of direct academic attack on artists' work is rare and was largely a result of the way the brothers presented themselves, which many delegates found vain and pretentious. Having placed themselves so confidently on a pedestal, it was unsurprising that academics aware of the closeness of their ostensibly "original" work to Schlemmer's would wish to "knock them down."

7. Schlemmer, "Man and Art Figure," 29. Quoted in Birringer, *Media and Performance: Along the Border*, 45.

8. Calandra, "George Kaiser's *From Morn to Midnight*: the Nature of Expressionist Performance," 540.

9. Giannachi, *Virtual Theatres: An Introduction*, 1.

10. Birringer, *Media and Performance*, 46.

11. Ibid., 59.

12. Arndt, "Theatre at the Centre of the Core (Technology as a Lever in Theatre Pedagogy)," 66.

13. Norman Klein, *From Vatican to Special Effects*, quoted in Manovich, 2003: 25.

14. Wagner, "The Artwork of the Future," 4.

15. The term "meta-medium" was first coined in relation to the personal computer by Alan Kay in his 1977 essay "Personal Dynamic Media." See Packer and Jordan (eds.), *Multimedia: From Wagner to Virtual Reality*, xvii–xviii.

16. Styan, *Modern Drama in Theory and Practice 2*, 182–183.

17. Schwitters quoted in Grau, *Virtual Art: From Illusion To Immersion*, 145.

18. Meyerhold quoted in Braun, *Meyerhold on Theatre*, 254.

19. Ibid., 257.

20. Unfortunately, most of these were unrealized.

21. Gropius quoted in Burt and Barker, "IOU and the New Vocabulary of Performance Art," 72–73.

22. Schlemmer quoted in Bayer, Ise Gropius, and Walter Gropius, *Bauhaus 1919–1928*, 162.

23. Gropius quoted in ibid., 16.

24. Ibid., 25, original italics.

Chapter 3

1. Breton quoted in Craig, *Dreams and Deconstructions: Alternative Theatre in Britain*, 9.

2. See Berghaus, *Italian Futurist Theatre, 1909–1944*; and Kirby, *Futurist Performance.*

3. Marinetti et al., "The Futurist Cinema," 15.

4. Marinetti, "The Founding and Manifesto of Futurism," 292 and 293.

5. It could be suggested that Kirby's exclusion of the first manifesto be justified on the grounds that it did not specifically address theater. However, it has long been regarded as the movement's quintessential manifesto, and its exclusion in Kirby's otherwise comprehensive study is therefore significant. Interestingly, by contrast, it is the *only* futurist manifesto to be included in Michael Huxley and Noel Witts's collection of fifty essays, interviews, and manifestos by seminal directors, choreographers, and performance artists, *The Twentieth Century Performance Reader* (1996).

6. Marinetti, "The Founding and Manifesto of Futurism," 293.

7. Ibid., 291.

8. For an analysis of Mina Loy's association with futurism, see Schmid, "Mina Loy's Futurist Theatre."

9. Marinetti, "The Founding and Manifesto of Futurism," 293.

10. Kirby, *Futurist Performance*, 5.

11. Goldberg, *Performance Art: From Futurism to the Present*, 11.

12. Marinetti, "The Founding and Manifesto of Futurism," 291.

13. Oliveira, Oxley, Petry and Archer, *Installation Art*, 18.

14. Lista, *Futurism*, 10.

15. Kirby, *Futurist Performance*, 49.

16. Kozintsov, "Eccentrism," 97.

17. Marinetti, "The Variety Theatre," 181.

18. Depero, "Notes on the Theatre," 207–208.

19. Quoted in Kroker, *The Possessed Individual: Technology and the French Postmodern*, 24.

20. Ibid., 23.

21. Ibid., 24.

22. Ibid.

23. Kozintsov, "Eccentrism," 95.

24. In Russia, particularly after the 1917 revolution, futurism became highly influential on directors such as Meyerhold, and spawned companies such as *The Factory of the Eccentric Actor (FEKS)*. Their "Eccentrism" (aka "Eccentric Theater") manifesto was written by Georgy Kozintsov, Georgy Kryzhitsky, Leonid Trauberg, and Sergei Yutkevich and first presented in a public reading and meeting at the Free Comedy Theater in Petersburg on December 5, 1921. The poster advertising the event was headed with the banner announcement "Wear Clown's Pants and Be Saved."

25. Annenkov quoted in Dèak, "The Influence of Italian Futurism in Russia," 91.

26. Ibid.

27. Pavis, "Afterword: Contemporary Dramatic Writings and the New Technologies," 191.

28. Schmid, "Mina Loy's Futurist Theatre."

29. Prampolini, "Futurist Scenography," 206.

30. Bowden, Kaewtrakulpong, and Lewin, "Jeremiah: The Face of Computer Vision," 127.

31. Susan Broadhurst, email to the authors, March 4, 2005. Also see Broadhurst, "Interaction, Reaction and Performance: The Jeremiah Project."

32. Ibid.

33. Montali, "For a New Theatre 'Electric-Vibrating-Luminous,'" 223–224.

34. See Saltz, "Beckett's Cyborgs: Technology and the Beckettian Text."

35. Depero, "Notes on the Theatre," 208.

36. Grau, *Virtual Art: From Illusion To Immersion*, 213.

37. Marinetti, "The Variety Theatre," 181.

38. Such futurist performances were historically significant as early examples of performance art (or "live art"), since they rejected "fourth wall" conventions and involved non-narrative and often task-based actions with performers being "themselves" rather than representing characters. RoseLee Goldberg devotes the entire first chapter of her *Performance Art: from Futurism to the Present* (1979) to a consideration of futurism, and makes clear that futurism constitutes the first clearly defined "movement" of performance art.

39. Henri, *Environments and Happenings*, 13.

40. Mulder and Post, *Book for the Electronic Arts*, 99–100, quoted in Giannachi, *Virtual Theatres: An Introduction*, 21–22.

41. This robot has been in continual stages of design and redevelopment since 1985. See Kac, "The Origin and Development of Robotic Art," 80, and "Towards a Chronology of Robotic Art," 94. Arthur Kroker presents an analysis of the piece in relation to Baudrillard's technological theories in *The Possessed Individual: Technology and the French Postmodern*, 65–66.

42. Marinetti quoted in Kirby, *Futurist Performance*, 27.

43. <http://epidemic.cicv.fr/geogb/art/dtype/histgb.html>.

44. Birringer, "Dance and Interactivity," 31.

45. Pannaggi and Paladini, *Manifesto of Futurist Mechanical Art*.

46. Azari, "Futurist Aerial Theatre," 219.

47. Fillia, "Mechanical Sensuality (Sensualità Meccanica)," 287–288.

48. Marinetti, Settimelli, and Corra, "The Futurist Synthetic Theatre," 197.

49. Edward Braun notes that the "pretentiousness of the Futurist elements" in *The Dawn* was attacked by the critic A. V. Lunacharsky, although he also "considered it a reasonable price to pay for the production's revolutionary fervour." Braun, *Meyerhold on Theatre*, 164.

50. Ibid., 183.

51. See Gordon, "Meyerhold's Biomechanics," 88–89.

52. Braun, *Meyerhold on Theatre*, 183.

53. Meyerhold, "The Actor of the Future and Biomechanics," 197.

54. Ibid., 198.

55. Ibid.

56. Goldberg, *Performance Art: From Futurism to the Present*, 39.

57. Ibid.

58. Eisenstein changed his terminology and the focus of his montage technique over the years "for the even more scientist notion of a montage of shocks or stimuli, conceived on the model of reflexology." See Rutsky, *High Techne: Art and Technology from the Machine Aesthetic to the Posthuman*, 92.

59. Eisenstein quoted in Rutsky, *High Techne: Art and Technology from the Machine Aesthetic to the Posthuman*, 91.

60. Vertov quoted in Wright, *The Long View: An International History of Film*, 56.

61. Manovich, *The Language of New Media*, xv–xxxvi.

62. Ibid., xv.

63. Malevich quoted in Candy and Edmonds, *Explorations in Art and Technology*, 11.

64. Ibid.

65. Ibid., 12.

66. Bolter, *Writing Space: The Computer in the History of Literacy*; Sloane, *Digital Fictions: Storytelling in a Material World*, 44–45; Wooley, *Virtual Worlds: A Journey of Hype and Hyperreality*, 155.

67. Vakuum TV, "Vakuum TV at the VIDEOLOGY."

68. Ibid.

69. See, for example *Emak Bakia* (Leave Me Alone, dir. Man Ray, 1926), *Vormittagsfpuk* (Ghosts in the Morning, dir. Hans Richter, 1928), and *Man with a Movie Camera* (dir. Dziga Vertov, 1929).

70. Foster, *Compulsive Beauty*, 206.

71. Coyne, *Technoromanticism*, 188.

72. Ibid.

73. See Rush, *New Media in Late 20th-Century Art*, 120.

74. Artaud later left the surrealist movement following disagreement with Breton's politicization of surrealism and its alignment with the Communist Party.

75. Schrum, "Introduction" to *Theatre in Cyberspace*.

76. Popovich, "Artaud Unleashed: Cyberspace Meets the Theatre of Cruelty," 233.

77. Metcalf, "Autogeddon"; Plant, "Coming Across the Future."

78. Brecht quoted in Calandra, "George Kaiser's *From Morn to Midnight*: the Nature of Expressionist Performance," 54.

79. See Calandra, "George Kaiser's *From Morn to Midnight*: The Nature of Expressionist Performance," 50.

80. Ibid.

Chapter 4

1. Sartre, in a London *Observer* interview with Kenneth Tynan, quoted in Styan, *Modern Drama in Theory and Practice 2*, 182.

2. See Billington, "Footage and Footlights."

3. Goldberg, *Performance Art: From Futurism to the Present*, 17–18.

4. See Bell, "Dialogic Media Production and Inter-media Exchange,"46; Murray, *Hamlet on the Holodeck: The Future of Narrative in Cyberspace*, 105–106.

5. Builders Association, "Opera."

6. Bowers et al., "Extended Performances: Evaluation and Comparison."

7. Quoted in Dèak, "The Influence of Italian Futurism in Russia," 92.

8. *A Wise Man* was Eisenstein's montage-theater staging of Ostrovsky's *Every Wise Man Stumbles* (written in 1868).

9. Goldberg, *Performance Art*, 46.

10. We discuss the plot of *R.U.R.* and its importance in relation to theoretical perspectives on technology in our chapter on robots. Kiesler's design for *R.U.R.* is examined in detail in Goldberg, *Performance Art: From Futurism to the Present*, 115–116. She inaccurately describes the production as "the first time film and live performance were combined."

11. Kiesler quoted in Goldberg, *Performance Art*, 116.

12. Ibid., 115.

13. Ibid., 116.

14. Sermon, "The Emergence of User- and Performer-Determined Narratives in Telematic Environments," 92.

15. Ibid.

16. Zapp, "A Fracture in Reality: Networked Narratives as Imaginary Fields of Action," 78.

17. Rorrison, "Piscator's Production of 'Hoppla, Wir Leben,' 1927," 35.

18. Cited in ibid., 39.

19. Ibid., 34.

20. Nicholas Hern discusses the controversy surrounding this production. He notes that Ernst Toller, the writer of *Hoppla, Wir Leben!* was one of many famous signatories to a letter to the *Berlin Volksbühne* in defence of Piscator's "radical theatrical innovation." However, as we note later, Toller's opinion of the use of the film screen in theater became far more pessimistic after its use in *Hoppla, Wir Leben!* See Hern, "The Theatre of Ernst Toller," 85.

21. Lumley, *New Trends in 20th Century Drama*, 74.

22. Claudel quoted in ibid., 74.

23. Rorrison, "Piscator's Production of 'Hoppla, Wir Leben', 1927," 38.

24. Toller quoted in Hern, "The Theatre of Ernst Toller," 85.

25. Ibid., 85.

26. Lumley, *New Trends in 20th Century Drama*, 82–83.

27. Ibid., 83.

28. Hern, "The Theatre of Ernst Toller," 85.

29. Goldberg, *Performance Art*.

30. Packard quoted in Unruh, "Dedication" and "The New Theatre of Robert Edmond Jones," vii.

31. Jones, "Theory of Modern Production," 40.

32. Ibid.

33. Delbert Unruh describes *The Dramatic Imagination* as "then a Bible for students of the theatre." Unruh, *Towards a New Theatre: The Lectures of Robert Edmond Jones*, 5.

34. Ibid., 77.

35. Ibid.

36. Ibid.

37. Grotowski, *Towards a Poor Theatre*, 86.

38. Brook, *The Empty Space*.

39. Jones, *Towards a New Theatre*, 72.

40. Ibid., 75.

41. Ibid., 74.

42. Ibid., 75.

43. Ibid., 76.

44. Ibid., 77.

45. Ibid., 73.

46. Svoboda, "Laterna Magika," 142.

47. Burian, *The Scenography of Josef Svoboda*, 77–91. Quoted in Jones, *Towards a New Theatre*, 105–106.

48. From a pamphlet published by the Experimental Studio of the Czechoslovak State Film Industry, Prague. Quoted in Svoboda, "Laterna Magika," 141.

49. Shank, *American Alternative Theatre*, 140.

50. Goldberg, *Performance Art*, 126.

51. Schwarz, *Media-Art-History*, 61.

52. See Rush, *New Media in 20th-Century Art*, 117–118.

53. Paik quoted in ibid., 117.

54. Vostell quoted in ibid.

Chapter 5

1. Duchamp quoted in Sewell, *An Alphabet of Villains*, 7.

2. Ibid., 8.

3. Proctor quoted in Dery, *Escape Velocity: Cyberculture at the End of the Century*, 21.

4. Ibid., 19.

5. Marinetti, "Variety Theater," 179–181.

6. Moore, *The Space Between: Work in Mixed Media, Moving Being 1968–1993*.

7. Ibid.

8. Etchells, *Certain Fragments*, 49.

9. Kirby, "The Uses of Film in the New Theater," 50.

10. Rush, *New Media in Late 20th–Century Art*, 61.

11. Quoted in Goldberg, *Performance Art: From Futurism to the Present*, 133.

12. See Kirby, "The Uses of Film in the New Theater," 53–54.

13. See Grau, *Virtual Art: From Illusion To Immersion*, 164.

14. Banes, *Subversive Expectations: Performance Art and Paratheater in New York 1976–85*, 141.

15. Kirby, "The Uses of Film in the New Theater," 60.

16. Paik, "Cybernated Art," 41.

17. See Hanhardt, *The World of Nam June Paik*, 107–124, for a range of descriptions and wonderful pictures of Paik's magnet manipulations, including two stills of McLuhan's distorted face.

18. Morse, "Video Installation Art: The Body, The Image and the Space-in-between," 161.

19. Packer and Jordon, *Multimedia: From Wagner to Virtual Reality*, 40.

20. Paik quoted in Hanhardt, *The Worlds of Nam June Paik*, 223.

21. Owen Land was formerly known as George Landow.

22. Ponton, "Seen Unsaid."

23. Ponton, "Dies Irae."

24. *Variations on a Theme by Saint-Saëns* (1964).

25. *Concerto for TV Cello* (1971).

26. The poster is reproduced in Hanhardt, *The World of Nam June Paik*, 60.

27. As Michael Archer observes, the piece operates to "show that it is the medium of TV that shapes his work's content, and not the particular subject on screen." Archer, *Art Since 1960* (new edition), 100.

28. We examine *Homage to New York* in more detail in our chapter on robots.

29. Klüver quoted in Obrist, "Turning to Technology: Legendary engineer Billy Klüver on artist-engineer collaborations."

30. See Rush, *New Media in Late 20th–Century Art*, 37.

31. E.A.T. [Experiments in Art and Technology], "9 Evenings: Theater and Engineering," 219.

32. Ibid., 215.

33. Ibid., 221.

34. The Zentrum für Kunst und Mediatechnologies (ZKM) in Karlsruhe, Germany. See <http://www.zkm.de>.

35. Hertz, "The Godfather of Technology and Art: An Interview with Billy Klüver."

36. Klüver quoted in Obrist, "Turning to Technology."

37. Shank's book was later extended, updated, and retitled *Beyond the Boundaries: American Alternative Theater* in 2002, and includes analysis of work from the 1980s and 90s including digital performance practitioners.

38. Grant, "Voicing the Protest: The New Writers," 131.

39. Quoted in Styan, *Modern Drama in Theory and Practice 2*, 181.

40. Ibid.

41. Moore, *The Space Between*.

42. Wilson quoted in Moore, *Moving Being: Two Decades of a Theater of Ideas, 1968–88*, 45.

43. Strindberg quoted in ibid., 27.

44. Ibid., 58.

45. Quoted in ibid., 23.

46. Ibid., 24.

47. The *Cybernetic Serendipity* exhibition ran from August 2 to October 20, 1968. The exact number of participants varies according to different sources, and the figure of 325 is given on page 11 of exhibition curator Jasia Reichardt's book *Cybernetics, Art and Ideas* (1971). In his detailed retrospective study, The Dilemma of Media Art: Cybernetic Serendipity at the ICA London (2002), Rainer Usselmann writes that "the exhibition brought together work from a total of 130 contributors, of whom 43 were composers, artists and poets, and 87 were engineers, doctors, computer scientists and philosophers."

48. Reichardt, *Cybernetics, Art and Ideas*, 11.

49. Masterman, "Computerized Haiku," 181–182.

50. Ibid., 183.

51. Whitelaw, "1968/1998: Rethinking A Systems Aesthetic."

52. Pask, "A Comment, A Case Study and a Plan," 76.

53. Xenakis, "Free Stochastic Music from the Computer," 111.

54. Gabor, "Technological Civilization and Man's Future," 18.

55. Reichardt, *Cybernetics, Art and Ideas*, 11.

56. The 1984 Macintosh computers also featured the first graphical user interface for domestic machines.

57. Usselman, "The Dilemma of Media Art: Cybernetic Serendipity at the ICA London."

58. All press quotes and references are taken from Usselman, "The Dilemma of Media Art: Cybernetic Serendipity at the ICA London."

59. See Whitelaw, "1968/1998: Rethinking A Systems Aesthetic," 51.

60. Brown, "Keynote Speech."

61. The performance is rarely cited, and the only reference we have found is Le Grice's own description in his *Experimental Cinema in the Digital Age*, 301, 304.

62. Wilson, *Information Arts: Intersections of Art, Science and Technology*, 855.

63. Henri, *Environments and Happenings*, 72.

64. King, *Contemporary American Theater*, 265.

65. Bell, "Dialogic Media Production and Inter-media Exchange."

66. Ibid., 52–53.

67. Goldberg suggests that: "Jesurun's video theater was an important indicator of the time; for its high-tech drama was as much an example of the prevailing media mentality as of the new theatricality of performance." Goldberg, *Performance Art: From Futurism to the Present*, 195.

68. See King, *Contemporary American Theater*, 127.

69. Ibid., 126–127.

70. Weems, "Weaving the 'Live' and the Mediated: Marianne Weems in Conversation with Cariad Svich," 51.

71. Ibid.

72. Goldberg, *Laurie Anderson*, 23.

73. See King, *Contemporary American Theater*, 197.

74. Ibid., 198.

75. Ibid., 202.

76. Goldberg, *Laurie Anderson*, 184.

77. King, *Contemporary American Theater*, 198.

78. Goldberg, *Laurie Anderson*, 54.

79. Ibid., 180.

80. Anderson quoted in ibid., 19–20.

81. Banes, *Subversive Expectations*, 160–162.

82. For example, see Duckworth, *Talking Music: Conversations with John Cage, Philip Glass, Laurie Anderson, and Five Generations of American Experimental Composers*.

Chapter 6

1. Tavel, "Gorilla Queen," 201.

2. Louis Daguerre developed the daguerreotype process in 1839, although earlier techniques had been used to create permanent photographs from nature since 1826.

3. Witcombe, "Art History and Technology: A Brief History."

4. Ibid.

5. Benjamin, "The Work of Art in the Age of Mechanical Reproduction," 214.

6. Barthes, *Camera Lucida*, 87.

7. Gibson, *Neuromancer*, 51.

8. Benjamin, "The Work of Art in the Age of Mechanical Reproduction," 214.

9. Benjamin first argued the destruction of the aura through photographic reproducibility in his earlier essay "A Small History of Photography."

10. Benjamin, "The Work of Art in the Age of Mechanical Reproduction," 216.

11. Ibid., 219.

12. Ibid., 218.

13. Ibid.

14. Valéry, *Aesthetics*, 225, quoted in Benjamin, "The Work of Art in the Age of Mechanical Reproduction," 211.

15. Benjamin, "The Work of Art in the Age of Mechanical Reproduction," 216.

16. Ibid., 217.

17. Baudrillard, *Simulacra and Simulation*.

18. Auslander, *Liveness: Performance in a Mediatized Culture*, 50.

19. Etchells, *Certain Fragments*, 32.

20. Sontag, *On Photography*, 164.

21. Barthes, *Camera Lucida*, 87.

22. Ibid., 6.

23. Ibid., 76–77.

24. Ibid., 5.

25. Ibid., 92.

26. Ibid., 9.

27. Ibid., 14.

28. Ibid., 79.

29. Auslander makes no reference to Barthes's ideas in *Camera Lucida*, although he does make a brief, one-sentence reference to his distinctions between drawing and photography in *Image—Music—Text* (1977), applying them to conclude that "whereas drawings, like writing, transforms performance, audio-visual technologies, like photography, record it." Auslander, *Liveness*, 52.

30. Barthes, *Camera Lucida*, 79.

31. Ibid., 81.

32. Ibid., 88.

33. Ibid., 89.

34. Ibid., 88.

35. Ibid.

36. Ibid., 117.

37. Ibid., 87.

38. Derrida, *The Postcard*, 9.

39. Phelan, *Unmarked: The Politics of Performance*, 149.

40. Ibid., 41.

41. Auslander, *Liveness*, 3.

42. Ibid.

43. Ibid., 7.

44. Ibid., 8.

45. Ibid., 38.

46. Ibid.

47. Ibid.

48. Ibid.

49. Ibid., 39.

50. Ibid., 38–39.

51. Pavis, *Theatre at the Crossroads of Culture*, 99.

52. Ibid., 124.

53. Ibid., 134.

54. Auslander, *Liveness*, 41–42.

55. Phelan, "Preface: Arresting Performances of Sexual and Racial Difference: Toward a Theory of Performative Film," 7.

56. Auslander, *Liveness*, 38.

57. Ibid., 43.

58. Ibid., 44.

59. Ibid., 5.

60. Ibid., 45.

61. Ibid.

62. Bell, "Dialogic Media Production and Inter-media Exchange," 43.

63. Causey, "Screen Test of the Double: the Uncanny Performer in the Space of Technology," 383–384.

64. Ibid., 384.

65. Duchamp quoted in Hassan, "Prometheus as Performer: Towards a Posthumanist Culture?" 210.

66. Le Grice, *Experimental Cinema in the Digital Age*, 311.

67. Causey, "Screen Test of the Double: the Uncanny Performer in the Space of Technology," 387.

68. Ibid., 384.

69. Carlson, *Performance: a Critical Introduction*, 137.

70. Sontag, *Where the Stress Falls*, 18–19.

71. Benjamin, "What Is Epic Theatre," 144.

72. Ibid.

73. Lepage quoted in *Canadian Theatre Encyclopaedia*, "Robert Lepage."

74. Moore, *The Space Between: Work in Mixed Media, Moving Being 1968–1993*.

75. Stone, *The War of Desire and Technology at the Close of the Mechanical Age*, 16.

76. For example, see Stanley Carvell cited in Bolter and Grusin, *Remediation*, 234.

77. Carlson, *Performance: a Critical Introduction*, 125–142.

78. Kaye quoted in ibid., 136.

79. Sayre quoted in ibid., 134.

80. Fried quoted in ibid., 125.

81. Ibid., 126.

Chapter 7

1. Popper quoted in Hughes, "What Is Science?".

2. Bolter and Grusin, *Remediation*, 15.

3. Ibid., 15.

4. Ibid.

5. Ibid., 54.

6. Landow, *Hypertext: The Convergence of Contemporary Critical Theory and Technology*, 59.

7. Landow, *Hyper/Text/Theory*, 1.

8. See Soules, "Animating the Language Machine: Computers and Performance."

9. Landow, *Hypertext*, 2.

10. Barrett, *Sociomedia: Multimedia, Hypermedia and the Social Construction of Knowledge*, 8.

11. Gromala, "Pain and Subjectivity in Virtual Reality," 226.

12. Landow, *Hyper/Text/Theory*, 1.

13. Markley, *Virtual Realities and Their Discontents*, 58.

14. Grusin, "What Is an Electronic Author? Theory and the Technological Fallacy," 45.

15. Ibid.

16. See Paulson, "Computers, Minds and Texts: Primary Reflections."

17. Grusin, "What Is an Electronic Author?" 52.

18. Kendrick, "Cyberspace and the Technological Real," 143.

19. Kroker, *The Possessed Individual: Technology and the French Postmodern*, 166.

20. Ibid., 13.

21. Ibid.

22. Baudrillard, *Simulacra and Simulation*, 160.

23. Heidegger, "The Question Concerning Technology," 311.

24. Baudrillard, *Simulacra and Simulation*, 107.

25. Ibid., 56.

26. Ibid., 146.

27. Ibid., 107.

28. Baudrillard, *Paroxysm: Interviews with Philippe Petit*, 23.

29. Baudrillard, "Disneyworld Company."

30. Eco, *Travels in Hyperreality: Essays*, 47–48.

31. Dery, *Escape Velocity: Cyberculture at the End of the Century*, 149.

32. Ibid., 147.

33. Ryan, *Narrative as Virtual Reality*, 40.

34. Ibid.

35. Bey, "Notes for CTHEORY," 154.

36. Kroker, *The Possessed Individual*, 80.

37. Ibid., 81.

38. Nietzsche quoted in Barthes, *Camera Lucida*, 73.

39. Derrida, *Writing and Difference*, 170.

40. Artaud, *The Theatre and its Double*, 109.

41. Ibid., 187.

42. Ibid., 8.

43. Ibid., 184–185.

44. Derrida, *Of Grammatology*, 304.

45. Ibid., 305.

46. We suspect this is because to date Derrida and Baudrillard have simply provided the "best" theories around.

47. Artaud, *The Theatre and Its Double*, 7.

48. Ibid., 19.

49. Warwick, "Cyborg 1.0".

50. Wiener, *The Human Use of Human Beings: Cybernetics and Society*, 69.

51. Wardrip-Fruin and Montfort, *The New Media Reader*, 65.

52. Stelarc, "Remote Gestures / Obsolute [*sic*] Desires," quoted in Dery, *Escape Velocity: Cyberculture at the End of the Century*, 163.

53. Wardrip-Fruin and Montfort, *The New Media Reader*, 65.

54. Hayles, *How We Became Posthuman: Virtual Bodies in Cybernetics, Literature and Informatics*, 85.

55. Ibid., 85–86.

56. Wardrip-Fruin and Montfort, *The New Media Reader*, 65.

57. Wiener, "Men, Machines and the World About," 68.

58. Ibid., 69.

59. Ibid., 71–72.

60. Ibid., 72.

61. Ibid., 72.

62. Dyens, *Metal and Flesh: The Evolution of Man: Technology Takes Over*, 2.

63. Bateson cited in Hayles, *How We Became Posthuman: Virtual Bodies in Cybernetics, Literature and Informatics*, 84.

64. Ibid., 5.

65. Hayles, *How We Became Posthuman*, 293.

66. Halberstam and Livingston, *Posthuman Bodies*; Stone, "Identity in Oshkosh"; and Hayles, "Boundary Disputes: Homeostasis, Reflexivity, and the Foundations of Cybernetics."

67. Brown quoted in Hassan, "Prometheus as Performer: Towards a Posthumanist Culture?" 203.

68. Ibid.

69. Ibid.

70. Ibid., 208.

71. The dramatis personae of Hassam's "University Masque" are Pretext, Mythotext, Text, Heterotext, Context, Metatext, Postext and Paratext.

72. Hassan, "Prometheus as Performer: Towards a Posthumanist Culture?" 207.

73. Ibid., 215.

74. Ibid., 217.

75. Ibid., 6.

76. Ibid., 2–3.

77. Ibid., 25.

78. Poster, "Theorizing Virtual Reality: Baudrillard and Derrida," 42.

79. Causey, "Postorganic Performance: The Appearance of Theater in Virtual Spaces," 198.

80. Blau, *The Eye of Prey*, 164–165.

81. Merleau-Ponty, *The Visible and The Invisible*, 7.

82. Ibid., 7–8.

83. Causey, "Screen Test of the Double: The Uncanny Performer in the Space of Technology," 388.

84. Lacan quoted in ibid., 388.

85. Causey, "Postorganic Performance: The Appearance of Theater in Virtual Spaces."

86. Bharucha, *Theatre and the World*.

Chapter 8

1. Pesce, "True Magic," 223.

2. Ess, *Philosophical Perspectives in Computer-Mediated Communication*, 2.

3. Ehn, "Manifesto for a Digital Bauhaus," 207. Ehn cites a number of writers who have explored the notion of a "third culture," tracing it back to C. P. Snow's 1959 book *The Two Cultures and the Scientific Revolution*. Ehn's examination includes John Brockman's *The Third Culture—Beyond the Scientific Revolution* (1995) and *Wired* magazine editor Kevin Kelly's online article *The Third Culture* (1999) which declares that "the nerds of the third culture are rising."

4. Birkerts, *Readings*, 27.

5. Stone, *The War of Desire and Technology at the Close of the Mechanical Age*, 20.

6. Ibid.

7. Performance theory's fascination with boundary crossing spans the twentieth century, from the avant-garde transgressions of its early decades, through the radical post-'60s politics of feminist, gay, and lesbian performance, to the liminal thresholds of paratheatrics, body art, and shamanism, and the interdisciplinary fence-trampling of postmodernism. In the late 1990s these border discourses blossomed, with some notable books highlighting the concept in their titles: Johannes Birringer's *Media and Performance: Along the Border*, Guillermo Gómez-Peña's *Dangerous Border Crossers: The Artist Talks Back*, and Michael Kobialka's edited collection *Of Borders and Thresholds: Theatre History, Practice, and Theory*. Between just these three works are mapped complex borders of geography, history, media, bodies, pain, sexuality, imagination, identity, and transcendence.

8. Ryan, "Cyberspace, Virtuality, and the Text," 1.

9. Bollier, *The Future of Community and Personal Identity in the Coming Electronic Culture: A Report of the Third Annual Aspen Institute Roundtable on Information Technology,* 35.

10. Saffo, in Brockman, *Digerati: Encounters with the Cyber Elite*, 245.

11. The homestead metaphor was famously evoked by Howard Rheingold in his 1994 book *The Virtual Community: Homesteading in the Age of the Internet.*

12. Cleaver, "The Space of Cyberspace: Body Politics, Frontiers and Enclosures," 239.

13. August, "America Looks to 'John Wayne' to halt Microsoft's stampede," 27.

14. Gómez-Peña, "The Virtual Barrio @ the Other Frontier (or the Chicano Interneta)," 178.

15. Ibid.

16. <http://www.telefonica.es/fat/egomez.html>.

17. <http://creations.morle.com/portfolio/writing/virtuality.html>.

18. Ljubljana Digital Media Lab <http://www.ljudmila.org/>.

19. Statistics from the Japanese Ministry of Economy, Trade and Industry. In *one month* (March 2004) production was £10,242,357,620 GBP ($18,771,906,278 USD), of which £6,129,690,508 GBP ($11,234,325,144 USD) was exported worldwide. <http://www.jeita.or.jp/english/stat/electronic/2004/product/pro_03.htm>.

20. <http:kultur.aec.at/festival/1993/tosa.html>.

21. Rayner, "Everywhere and Nowhere: Theatre in Cyberspace," 299.

22. See, for example, Robinson, *Lost Languages: The Enigma of the World's Undeciphered Scripts.*

23. Pavis, *Languages of the Stage: Essays in the Semiology of the Theatre.*

24. Alter, *A Sociosemiotic Theory of Theatre.*

25. Carlson, *Places of Performance: The Semiotics of Theatre Architecture.*

26. Aston and Savona, *Theatre as Sign System: A Semiotics of Text and Performance.*

27. Fischer-Lichte, *The Semiotics of Theatre*; de Marinis, *The Semiotics of Performance.*

28. Melrose, *A Semiotics of the Dramatic Text (New Directions in Theatre).*

29. Goody, *Representations and Contradictions: Ambivalence Towards Images, Theatre, Fiction, Relics, Sexuality*.

30. Derrida, "The Almost Nothing of the Unpresentable" and "Unsealing ('the old new language')," 87, 116.

31. See, for example, Olson, *Mapping Human History: Discovering Our Past Through Our Genes*; and Pinker, *The Blank Slate: Denying Human Nature in Modern Life*.

32. Haraway, "A Cyborg Manifesto: Science, Technology and Socialist-feminism in the late Twentieth Century," 163.

33. Ibid., 164.

34. See for example, Torvalds and Diamond, *Just For Fun—The Story of an Accidental Revolutionary*; Moody, *Rebel Code: Linux and the Open Source Revolution*; and Wayner, *Free For All*. To give some idea of the extent of the Linux revolution and the subsequent uptake of this free Operating System, in 2001 Amazon (UK) listed approximately 750 books about Linux.

35. Berners-Lee, *Weaving the Web*.

36. See for example, Levy, *Hackers: Heroes of the Computer Revolution*; Dr-K, *A Complete Hacker's Handbook*; Himanen, *The Hacker Ethic and the Spirit of the Information Age*; Thomas, *Hacker Culture*; Verton, *Hacker Diaries: Confessions of Teenage Hackers*. Verton's book highlights how hackers often regard computer systems and the Internet in terms of a challenging game: a three-dimensional crossword puzzle or maze that can be navigated and penetrated by wit and invention. To this end, a growing number of publications consist of real-life tests and challenges for hackers, with solutions provided by security consultants, for example Mike Schiffman's *Hacker's Challenges* (2003). The interplays between freedom and security, between access to information, restriction, and the right to privacy, remain major battlegrounds on the Internet.

37. Cooper, *The Inmates Are Running the Asylum*, 69.

38. Ibid., 95.

39. See Howkins, *CODE: Collaboration and Ownership in the Digital Economy*.

40. Diamond, "Code Zebra: Theorizing Discourse and Play."

41. Wilson, *Information Arts: Intersections of Art, Science and Technology*, 5.

42. Schwarz, *Media-Art-History*, 35.

43. See, for example, Hekell, *The Elements of Friendly Software Design*; Norman, "Foreword;" Norman and Draper, *User Centred Systems Design: New Perspectives on Human-Computer Interaction*; and Laurel, *The Art of Human-Computer Interface Design*, and *Computers as Theater*.

44. Norman, "Foreword," xi.

45. Laurel, *Computers as Theater*, 7.

46. Ibid., 32–33.

47. Ibid., 21.

48. Arndt, "Theatre at the Centre of the Core (Technology as a Lever in Theatre Pedagogy)," 66–67.

49. Saltz, "Beckett's Cyborgs: Technology and the Beckettian Text," 282.

50. Ibid., 284.

51. Dishman, "Performative In(ter)ventions: Designing Future Technologies Through Synergetic Performance," 235.

52. Conquergood, "Of Caravans and Carnivals: Performance Studies in Motion."

53. Dishman, "Performative In(ter)ventions: Designing Future Technologies Through Synergetic Performance," 238.

54. Boal, *Games for Actors and Non-Actors.*

55. Butler, *Gender Trouble: Feminism and the Subversion of Identity*; and *Bodies That Matter.*

56. Dishman, "Performative In(ter)ventions: Designing Future Technologies Through Synergetic Performance," 244.

57. Writer/director James Cameron.

58. Baudelaire quoted in Agacinski, *Time Passing*, 72.

59. Rae, "Presencing."

60. *Wired* 6:03 (March 1998), cover. The article cited is Richard Kadrey's "Carbon Copy."

61. Brooks, "Global Brain."

62. Cohen, "Machine Head."

63. Ananthaswamy, "Mind Over Metal."

64. Mullins, "Quantum Superbrains."

65. Coyne, *Techoromanticism: Digital Narrative, Holism, and the Romance of the Real*, 284–285.

66. Ibid., 9.

67. Ibid., 18–38.

68. Ibid., 40–68.

69. Gelertner's *Mirror Worlds*, quoted in Sawchuk, "Post Panoptic Mirrored Worlds."

70. The Critical Art Ensemble (CAE) is a collective of six artists of different specializations committed to the production of a new genre of art exploring the intersections of critical theory, art and technology. See essay archived at <http://www.ctheory.net/text_file.asp?pick=59>.

71. Kroker and Weinstein, "The Hyper-texted Body, Or Nietzsche Gets A Modem."

72. Kroker and Kroker, "Johnny Mnemonic: The Day Cyberpunk Died."

73. Kroker, "The Image Matrix."

74. Editor's note to "Claves of the Cyber-Market," an interview with the media theorist Geert Lovink by Arnd Wesemann for *Screen Multimedia* (28 June 1995).

75. Paul Virilio, "Speed and Information: Cyberspace Alarm."

76. Strehovec, "The Web as an Instrument of Power and a Realm of Freedom: A Report from Ljubljana, Slovenia."

77. Scott, "The Great Divide in the Global Village."

78. Chesher, "Why the Digital Computer Is Dead."

Chapter 9

1. Paik quoted in Hanardt, *The Worlds of Nam June Paik*, 114.

2. Murray, *Hamlet on the Holodeck: The Future of Narrative in Cyberspace*, 154.

3. Groot, "Streaming Video Killed the CD-ROM: On Modern Dance, Merce Cunningham, William Forsythe, Lara Croft and Olivier Messiaen."

4. At least fifteen of the initial *Tracker* animations can be seen at <http://hotwired.wired.com/kino/95/29/feature/lifeforms.html>.

5. Pierce, "Merce Cunningham's Living Sketchbook." Also see Pierce, "Cunningham at the Computer"; and Copeland, "Cunningham, Collage, and the Computer."

6. Ibid. The Cunningham quotation is attributed to Mazo, "Quantum Leaps."

7. Pierce, "Merce Cunningham's Living Sketchbook."

8. deLahunta, "Virtual Ephemerality: The Art Of Digital Dancing."

9. The project was part of the *Digital Summer '98* Festival in Manchester, England.

10. *Interference* was choreographed electronically by (in order): Merce Cunningham, Greg Baskind, Sophia Lycouris, Rachel Price, Gary Beck, Gary Peploe, Marissa Zanotti, Richie William Hornby, Maurizio Morsiani, Liam Ramsey, John Berry, Noma Siwela, John Berry Snr, Clifford Tucker, Benji Cofie, Laura Scefroust, Kyle Benjamin, Pat Hughes, Andrew Lundon, Jessica, Chelsie Cain, Maria Carney, Peter Kelly, Michele Cucuzzielle, Tracy Foy, Joshua Talent, Anne-Laure Eude, Martin Hyland, Ania Witkowska, John Guilty, Sue Maclennan, Danny Hay, Penny Collinson, Charemaine Seet, Joanne Chow, Rupert Francis, Katerina Moraitis, Susie Crow, Adele Myers, Marah Rosenberg, Josh Stuart/Dr. Elizabeth Bradley, Deitra Lied, Kema T. Ekpei, Yacov Sharir, Christina Paris, Dr. Luke Kahlich, and Merce Cunningham.

11. A surrealist technique, based on an old parlor game, played by several people who write a phrase on a sheet of paper, fold to conceal most of it and pass it on to the next player for a contribution. The name arises from an early-recorded result, "Le cadavre exquis boira le vin nouveau" (The exquisite corpse will drink the young wine). See "Exquisite Links" <http://www.exquisitecorpse.com/definition.html>.

12. E-mail titled "INTERFERENCE calling (again)," sent by Guy Hilton to the Dance and Technology Zone e-mail List, 31 July 1998. <http://www.art.net/~dtz/archive/DanceTech98/0597.html>.

13. Ibid.

14. Ibid.

15. See <http://www.riverbed.com> and <http://www.kaiserworks.com/artworks/artworkscomplete.htm>.

16. *Character Studio* was created by their company UnReal Pictures, published by Discreet of Autodesk, and subsequently part of *3D Max*.

17. Riverbed Artworks: <http://www.kaiserworks.com/ideas/onbipedmain.htm>.

18. See, for example Glidden, "Kinetix Ships Character Studio" for a discussion of the qualities of *Biped*.

19. Reynolds, "Displacing 'Humans': Merce Cunningham's Crowds."

20. Scarry, "In Step with Digital Dance."

21. Ibid.

22. Latham and Atkinson, "Computer Artworks."

23. Riverbed and Bill T. Jones/Arnie Zane Company, "Ghostcatching."

24. Ibid.

25. Ibid.

26. The three press quotes are cited in Keener, "Bill T. Jones and Ghostcatching." The *Time Out* quote is referenced as 15 July 1999 and the *Time* quote as 2 August 1999, but no date is provided for *The Village Voice* review.

27. The name of the company is deliberately obscure reflecting a schoolboy sense of humor frequently encountered in the sciences, relating in this instance to images from a 1974 bicycle catalogue that were used on the website. The company retains an individualistic and new age stance eschewing venture capital and preferring to target aficionados of the creative technology scene.

28. See <http://www.troikaranch.org/>.

29. Ibid.

30. Ibid.

31. Rubidge, e-mail to the authors, 23 August 2004.

32. This event was programmed for the new "The Baltic" [Arts Centre, Newcastle, UK] and also featured at HTBA (Hull Time Based Arts), May 2001. See other ASCII works at <http://www.ljudmila.org/~vuk/>.

33. A description and further information is available at <http://www.barriedale-operahouse.com>.

34. Ibid. For example composers: Ged Barry, Volkmar Klien; designers: Rafal Kosakowski, Kieran McMillan, Kasia Korczak; choreographer: Davide Terlingo; software: Nick Rothwell; technicians: Karsten Tinapp, Haig Avedikian; performer: Samantha Jones.

35. Birringer, "Dance and Interactivity," 21.

36. Quoted in half/angel, from an article in *animated*. <http://socks.ntu.ac.uk/archive/halfangel/index.htm>.

37. *The Irish Times*, November 1999.

38. Bromberg, "Falling to Earth."

39. Ibid.

40. The first being at Madison, Wisconsin, subsequently Toronto and Arizona.

41. Braunarts, "braunarts." See especially <http://www.braunarts.com/past/digidance.html>.

42. In Newcastle, England.

43. Christian Ziegler, one of the designers of the *Improvisation Technologies* CD-Rom for William Forsythe and the Frankfurt Ballet; digital visual and performance artist Guy Hilton; digital sound and video artist Joseph Hyde; software artist and programmer Adrian Ward; and digital media artist Bruno Martelli of Igloo.

44. Roy, "Technological Process."

45. deLahunta, in a letter to the Dance-tech Mail List, 25ᵗʰ March 2002.

46. See <http://www.dance.ohio-state.edu/workshops/ttreport.html>.

47. Henrique, "De agora em Diante/ From Now On."

48. Letter from Jeff McMahon to the *Dance & Technology Zone* Mail List, 8 December 1998.

Chapter 10

1. Novak quoted in Silver, *The Forgotten Amazement . . . Influences on Performance Following Industrialisation*, 12.

2. Plant, *Zeros + Ones: Digital Women + The New Technoculture*, 177.

3. Kroker, *The Possessed Individual: Technology and the French Postmodern,* 32.

4. See Birringer, *Media and Performance: Along the Border* for an excellent discussion of this viewpoint.

5. Socrates quoted in Plant, *Zeros + Ones*, 178.

6. Jameson, *Postmodernism: Or, the Cultural Logic of Late Capitalism*, 186.

7. Socrates quoted in Agacinski, *Time Passing: Modernity and Nostalgia*, 17.

8. Foucault, *Discipline and Punish: The Birth of the Prison*.

9. McLuhan and Watson, *From Cliché to Archetype*, 379, quoted in Bostock, "Cyberwork: The Archetypal Imagination in New Realms of Ensoulment."

10. Stratton, "Not Really Desiring Bodies: The Rise and Rise of Email Affairs," 28.

11. Wilson, "Boundary Violations," 224, quoted in Stratton, "Not Really Desiring Bodies," 29.

12. Stone, "Identity in Oshkosh," 34, quoted in Stratton, "Not Really Desiring Bodies," 28.

13. Stratton, "Not Really Desiring Bodies," 28.

14. Schechner, *Performance Theory*, 57. Grotowski's *Towards a Poor Theatre* also provides an important discussion of this idea.

15. Bolter and Gromala, *Windows and Mirrors*, 157.

16. Ibid., 123.

17. Coleridge quoted in Gelernter, *The Muse in the Machine: Computers and Creative Thought*, 184.

18. Kozel, "Spacemaking: Experiences of a Virtual Body."

19. Ibid.

20. Ibid.

21. Ibid.

22. Ibid.

23. Ibid. Kozel makes reference here to McLuhan's *Understanding Media*, 6–7.

24. Ibid.

25. Bell, *An Introduction to Cybercultures*, 156–157.

26. Waldby, *The Visible Human Project: Informatic Bodies and Posthuman Science*, 6.

27. Ibid., 136.

28. Ibid., 154.

29. Bell, *An Introduction to Cybercultures*, 160.

30. Vanouse, "Items 1–2,000."

31. Ibid.

32. Quotations from the performance are taken from Bleeker, "Death, Digitalization and Dys-appearance."

33. Tyler, "Holoman; Digital Cadaver."

34. Bleeker, "Death, Digitalization and Dys-appearance," 3.

35. Grassi, "Nuclear Body."

36. The animation also incorporates around a hundred supplementary images such as details of body organs, which pulsate intermittently. Some sequences also use a film technique developed by Martin Reinhart, "TX-Transform Effects" which interrelates and transposes the time axis and space axis. Grassi's CD-ROM documenting the project, *Nuclear Body* (2001), includes footage of the animation and the installation performance, as well as photos and text.

37. Samples of internal body sounds were obtained through a variety of medical techniques. Doppler Ultrasound was used to record sounds of the blood flowing in the heart and veins; and EEG (Electroencphalography), EKG (Electrokardiography), and EMG (Electromiography) was employed to record bioelectrical signals sent from the brain, heart, and muscles.

38. Grassi, "Nuclear Body."

39. The Anatomical Theatre, "Subject: Matter."

40. *ACTG* was a collaboration between the Institute for Studies in the Arts (Arizona University), ResCen, and shinkansen.

41. Henrique, "Contract with the Skin."

42. See <http://epidemic.cicv.fr/geogb/art/dtype/prj/orinsgb.html>.

43. Dumb Type quoted in <http://epidemic.cicv.fr/geogb/art/dtype/histgb.html>.

44. Quoted in Asada, "Lovers Installation."

45. Ibid.

46. Rush, *New Media in Late 20th–Century Art*, 153.

47. Asada, "Lovers Installation."

48. Lord, "Web Dances: Lifeblood."

49. *id* is a featured artwork in the *CTHEORY* online journal <http://ctheorymultimedia .cornell.dedu/issue1/menu2.html>.

50. Paul, *Digital Art*, 169.

51. Giannachi, *Virtual Theatres: An Introduction*, 49–50.

52. Auslander, *From Acting to Performance*, 132.

53. Bartosik, "Technogenderbody."

54. Gómez-Peña, *Dangerous Border Crossers: The Artist Talks Back*, 45.

55. Birringer: *Media and Performance*, 16.

56. Ibid., 21, 23, 24.

57. Begusch, "Shells That Matter: The Digital Body as Aesthetic/Political Representation," 30.

58. Sekula, "The Body and the Archive," 343–345.

59. The trilogy was commissioned by London's South Bank Centre.

60. Random Dance, "The Millanarium."

61. McGregor quoted in Smart, "The Technology of the Real: Wayne McGregor's *Nemesis* and the Ecology of Perception," 41.

62. Random Dance Company, "The Trilogy."

63. Smart, "The Technology of the Real," 51–52.

64. Corpos Informáticos Research Group, "Entrasite."

65. Troika Ranch, "In Plane."

66. Kuppers, "Traces."

67. Satorimedia, "TouchDown."

68. Ibid.

69. Schiphorst, "BODYMAPS: ARTIFACTS OF TOUCH: Computer Interactive Proximity and Touch Sensor Driven Audio/Video Installation."

70. Idhe, *Bodies in Technology*, xi.

71. Idid., 7.

72. Mitchell, *Me++: The Cyborg Self and the Networked City*, quoted in Grossman, "A Refresher in Basic Geek," 33.

73. Senft, "Performing the Digital Body—A Ghost Story," 11.

74. Elrich, "Turing, My Love," 202.

75. Lechner, "My Womb, the Mosh Pit," 185.

76. Birringer, *Media and Performance*, 159.

77. The notion of liminality has also been a pervasive theoretical given in performance since anthropological studies of ritual practices and shamanism, as discussed by writers such as Victor Turner, Colin Turnbull, and Richard Schechner, and more recently in Susan Broadhurst's edited study of contemporary performance practice *Liminal Acts: A Critical Overview Of Contemporary Performance And Theory* (2000).

Chapter 11

1. Schneemann quoted in Warr and Jones, *The Artist's Body*, 17.

2. Carlson, *Performance: A Critical Introduction*, 5–6. Carlson notes that performance entails "a consciousness of doubleness, through which the actual execution of an action is placed in mental comparison with a potential, an ideal, or a remembered model of that action. . . . Performance is always performance for someone else . . . even when . . . that audience is the self."

3. Soules, "Animating the Language Machine: Computers and Performance."

4. Artaud, *The Theatre and Its Double*, 5.

5. Ibid., 34.

6. Ibid., 6.

7. Ibid., 35.

8. Ibid., 34.

9. Ibid., 46.

10. Lacan, "The mirror stage as formative of the function of the I," 2.

11. Herzogenrath, "Join the United Mutations: Tod Browning's *Freaks*."

12. Freud, "The Uncanny," 366.

13. Hoffmann, "The Sandman."

14. Freud, "The Uncanny," 368.

15. Ibid., 366.

16. Derrida, "The Double Session," 220.

17. Heidegger, *Being and Time*, 233–234.

18. Heidegger, *Les Concepts Fondamentaux de la Métaphysique: Monde, Finitude, Solitude*, 21, quoted in Agacinski, *Time Passing*, 17.

19. Royle, *The Uncanny*, 23–24.

20. Frazer, *The Golden Bough: A Study in Magic and Religion*, 324.

21. Heine quoted in Royle, *The Uncanny*, 187.

22. Goldberg, *Performance Art: From Futurism to the Present*, 162.

23. Graham quoted in ibid.

24. Rokeby, "Transforming Mirrors : Transforming Mirrors."

25. Lacan, "The mirror stage as formative of the function of the I," 5.

26. It is interesting to recall Marshall McLuhan's reflections on the Narcissus myth, where he notes the name is derived from the Greek word *narcosis* (numbness): "This extension of himself by mirror numbed his perceptions until he became the servomechanism of his own extended or repeated image. The nymph Echo tried to win his love with fragments of his own speech, but in vain. He was numb. He had adapted to his extension of himself and had become a closed system." McLuhan quoted in Rokeby, "Transforming Mirrors : Transforming Mirrors."

27. See Wilson, *Information Arts: Intersections of Art, Science and Technology*, 362, 430.

28. Murray, "Digital Passage: the Rhizomatic Frontiers of the ZKM," 118.

29. Jenniches, Blankert, and Dokter, "Soft Mirror."

30. Coyne, *Techoromanticism Digital Narrative, Holism, and the Romance of the Real*, 221.

31. Lunenfeld, *Snap to Grid: A Users' Guide to Digital Arts, Media and Cultures*, 124.

32. See Bolter, *Writing Space: The Computer in the History of Literacy*; Bolter and Gromala, *Windows and Mirrors*; and Bolter and Grusin, *Remediation*.

33. Baudrillard, *Simulacra and Simulation*, 105.

34. Ibid.

35. Ibid.

36. Ibid., 106–107.

37. Rang, "The Bungled and the Botched: Cyborgs, Rape and Generative Anthropology."

38. Deleuze and Guattari, *A Thousand Plateaus: Capitalism and Schizophrenia*, 3.

39. Holzer, *Encyclopedia of Witchcraft and Demonology*, 240.

40. Ibid.

41. Birringer, "Dance and Interactivity," 31.

42. Marx and Engels quoted in Ehn, "Manifesto for a Digital Bauhaus," 207.

43. Frazer, *The Golden Bough: A Study in Magic and Religion*, 181.

44. Ibid., 668.

45. Kaysler quoted in Calandra, "George Kaiser's *From Morn to Midnight*: the Nature of Expressionist Performance," 48.

46. Rimbaud and Rilke quoted in Stiles, "Parallel Worlds: Representing Consciousness at the Intersection of Art, Dissociation, and Multidimensional Awareness," 52.

47. Sontag, *Where the Stress Falls*, 192.

48. Ibid., 191–192.

49. Ascott, "Seeing Double: Art and the Technology of Transcendence," 66.

50. Igloo, "Viking Shoppers."

51. According to Jeff Cook, Chip Morningstar coined the term *avatar*, from the Sanskrit description of the incarnation of gods in human form, around 1986 as a description for the animated graphical representations of participants in the *Habitat* virtual world. See Cook, "Myths, Robots and Procreation."

52. See Tuomola, "Daisy's Amazing Discoveries: Part 1—The Production."

53. Mistresses of Technology, "I-drunners: re_flesh the body."

54. Wardrip-Fruin and Montfort (eds.), *New Media Reader*, 340.

55. Stern, "Virtual Babyz."

56. See Pinhanez, "Computer Theater"; and "MIT Media Laboratory and the Digital Life Consortium present '*It/I*'."

57. Pinhanez, "SingSong."

58. Saltz, "Tempest 2000."

59. Ibid.

60. Clarke, "CO3. Company in Space—Hellen Sky and John McCormick."

61. A protoype of *Romeo and Juliet in Hades* was presented at the 1998 *Consciousness Reframed: Art and Consciousness in the Post-biological Era Conference*.

62. Ascott, "Seeing Double: Art and the Technology of Transcendence," 82.

63. Ibid., 85.

64. O'Mahony, *Cyborg: The Man-Machine*, 69.

65. Ibid., 68–69.

66. See <http://www.stelarc.va.com.au/prosthetichead/>.

67. "The Prosthetic Head's data-base is a personalized and customized Alice data-base programmed with Artificial Intelligence Mark-Up Language (AIML) interfaced with an IBM text to speech engine and a source code for facial animation. The 3D model was done with 3D Studio Max." Stelarc, email to the authors, 22 April 2004.

68. A limited edition CD, curated by Alessio Cavallard, was released in 2003 as part of the Transfigure Exhibition: *Humanoid: Digital Primate, Prosthetic Head and Ontological Oscillators* [CD]. The

CD consists of six tracks totaling forty-eight minutes entitled "Zombie," "Robot," "Humanoid," "Android," "Schizoid," and "Solipsist." Sometimes presentations feature live musicians: for example, *ScreenPlay Festival*, Broadway Cinemas, Nottingham, England (29 February 2004) with Jan Kapinski (saxophone), Steve Iliffe (keyboards), and Janina Kapinska (viola).

69. It has been publicly demonstrated extensively in Australia, Europe, and North America, and presented as a gallery installation at Transfigure (The Australian Centre for the Moving Image, Melbourne, 2003–4).

70. Stelarc, email to the authors, 22 April 2004.

71. Little, "A Manifesto for Avatars."

72. Lonehead quoted in Little, "A Manifesto for Avatars."

73. Little, "A Manifesto for Avatars."

74. Ibid.

75. Callesen, Kajo and Nilsen, "The Performance Animation Toolbox: Developing tools and methods through artistic research," 75.

76. Causey "Screen Test of the Double: The Uncanny Performer in the Space of Technology," 385–386.

77. Freud, *The Uncanny*, 357.

78. Barthes, *Camera Lucida*, 30–31.

79. Causey, "Screen Test of the Double," 65.

80. Deleuze, *Cinema I: The Movement-Image*, 68.

81. Causey, "Screen Test of the Double," 385–386.

82. Frazer, *The Golden Bough: A Study in Magic and Religion*, 192.

83. Warwick, *March of the Machines: Why the New Race of Robots Will Rule the World*; Dyens, *Metal and Flesh: The Evolution of Man: Technology Takes Over*; Brooks, *Robot: The Future of Flesh and Machines*.

Chapter 12

1. See Wilson, *Information Arts: Intersections of Art, Science and Technology*, 425–445.

2. Clynes and Kline, "Cyborgs and Space," 30.

3. McLuhan, *Understanding Media: The Extensions of Man*.

4. Dyens, *Metal and Flesh: The Evolution of Man: Technology Takes Over*, 8, 32.

5. The word *theranthrope* derives from *thêra*: wild animals and *anthropos*: human being. *Theranthropes* are also known as anthropozoomorphs. See Pradier, "Animals, Angel, Performance," 12.

6. Sontag, *Against Interpretation*.

7. Dyer, "It's Being So Camp as Keeps Us Going."

8. Cleto, "Introduction: Queering the Camp."

9. Sontag, *Against Interpretation*, 275.

10. See Wilson, *Information Arts*, 397.

11. Jones, "Hack: Performance-Based Electronic Art in Canada."

12. De Fontenelle quoted in Laqueur, *Making Sex: Body and Gender From the Greeks to Freud*, 155.

13. Springer, *Electronic Eros: Bodies and Desire in the Postindustrial Age*.

14. Britton, "For Interpretation: Notes against Camp," 141.

15. The Seemen robotic performance group quoted in Wilson, *Information Arts*, 437.

16. Spelletich, "Interview for a Book Called *Transitions*."

17. Kantor, "Executive Machinery Intercourse."

18. Cleto, "Introduction: Queering the Camp," 31.

19. Bergman, "Introduction."

20. Kantor, "Executive Machinery Intercourse."

21. Wiener, *The Human Use of Human Beings: Cybernetics and Society*, 46.

22. Moravec, *Mind Children: The Future of Robot and Human Intelligence*.

23. Moravec, "The Universal Robot," 25.

24. Moravec, *Mind Children*.

25. Dyer, "It's Being So Camp as Keeps Us Going," 111.

26. Dery, *Escape Velocity: Cyberculture at the End of the Century*, 150.

27. Knights, "Tears and Screams: Performances of Pleasure and Pain in the Bolero."

28. Ross, *No Respect: Intellectuals and Popular Culture*, 157.

29. Cleto, "Introduction: Queering the Camp," 29–30.

30. Cited in Britton, "For Interpretation: Notes Against Camp," 141.

31. Ibid., 138.

32. Frisk, "We Are Tin, We Are Titans. We Are Robots."

33. Emerson quoted in Benesch, "Romantic Cyborgs: Technology, Authorship, and the Politics of Reproduction in Nineteenth-Century American Literature."

34. In an essay about his work, Eduardo Kac suggests *A-Positive* "probes the delicate relationship between the human body and emerging new breeds of hybrid machines that incorporate biological elements and . . . metabolic functions. . . . This work proposes that emerging forms of human/ machine interface penetrate the sacred boundaries of the flesh, with profound cultural and philosophical implications. *A-Positive* draws attention to the condition of the human body in the new context in which biology meets computer science and robotics." Kac, "Art at the Biological Frontier," 91–92.

35. O'Mahony, *Cyborg: The Man-Machine*, 81.

36. See <http://robodoc.com/surgery.htm>.

37. O'Mahony, *Cyborg: The Man-Machine*, 100–102.

38. Goldberg, "Introduction: The Unique Phenomenon of a Distance," 7.

39. Kac, "The Origin and Development of Robotic Art," 77.

40. Brooks, *Robot: The Future of Flesh and Machines*.

41. Ibid., 13.

42. Pindar quoted in Cook, "Myths, Robots and Procreation."

43. Von Boehn, *Puppets and Automata*, 8.

44. Needham, *Science and Civilization in China*, vol. 4, part 2.

45. Von Boehn, *Puppets and Automata*, 10.

46. Ibid., 9–10.

47. Sussman, "Performing the Intelligent Machine: Deception and Enchantment in the Life of the Automaton Chess Player," 88.

48. Brooks, *Robot: The Future of Flesh and Machines*, 15.

49. Foucault, *Discipline and Punish: The Birth of the Prison*, 136, quoted in Dery, *Escape Velocity: Cyberculture at the End of the Century*, 141.

50. Max von Boehn asserts that the contest between Napoleon and the automaton chess player did take place, although Mark Sussman casts some doubt on this. Sussman lists a series of reported matches with famous historical figures including Catherine the Great, Benjamin Franklin and Napoleon, but suggests that some stories "are more plausible than others." Von Boehn, *Puppets and Automata*, 9, 13. Sussman, "Performing the Intelligent Machine: Deception and Enchantment in the Life of the Automaton Chess Player," 91.

51. Sussman, "Performing the Intelligent Machine," 93.

52. Benjamin, "Theses on the Philosophy of History," 245.

53. Kasparov quoted in King, *Kasparov v Deeper Blue: The Ultimate Man v Machine Challenge*, 5.

54. Tan quoted in ibid.

55. Ibid.

56. Wiener, *Cybernetics or Control and Communication in the Animal and the Machine*, 39–40.

57. Stark, "Furbys, Audio-Animatronics, Androids, and Robots."

58. Kac, "The Origin and Development of Robotic Art," 78.

59. Tinguely quoted in Klüver, "The Garden Party," 213.

60. Ibid.

61. Klüver, "The Garden Party," 213.

62. Ibid.

63. Hill, "Engineering Multimedia Art."

64. Ibid.

65. Klüver, "The Garden Party," 213.

66. Zivanovic, "Edward Ihnatowicz, including his famous work 'The Senster.'"

67. Whitelaw, "Rethinking Systems Aesthetic."

68. Wilson, *Information Arts*, 443.

69. O'Mahony, *Cyborg: The Man-Machine*, 43.

70. Ibid.

71. Wilson, *Information Arts*, 427.

72. Hershman Leeson, "Tillie the Telerobotic Doll."

73. Penny, "Embodied Cultural Agents."

74. Wilson, *Information Arts*, 427.

75. Penny quoted in ibid., 346.

76. Penny, "Embodied Cultural Agents."

77. McMurtrie, "Interview with Chico McMurtrie."

78. Sayre quoted in Dery, *Escape Velocity*, 135.

79. Spingarn-Koff, "Amorphic Robot Works."

80. McMurtrie, "Interview with the Digital Performance Archive."

81. Ruch, "Artists Statements."

82. See Morse, *Virtualities: Television, Media Art and Cyberculture*; and Cook, "Myths, Robots and Procreation."

83. Cook, "Myths, Robots and Procreation."

84. Brook, *The Empty Space*, 42.

85. For example, Wiener, *Cybernetics*; Rothenberg, *Hand's End: Technology and the Limits of Nature*; Dyson, *Darwin Among the Machines: The Evolution of Global Intelligence*.

86. Kac, "Towards a Chronology of Robotic Art," 92.

87. Cannon quoted in Wilson, *Information Arts*, 398–399. In his essay "Anti-Speed", Cannon relates the speed of contemporary culture to a fear of mortality: "this speeding up of the pace of life, the squeezing of more and more events into a given period of time, is the culture's desperate attempt to live longer." Ibid., 399.

88. Moravec, *Mind Children: The Future of Robot and Human Intelligence*, 107.

89. Dery, *Escape Velocity: Cyberculture at the End of the Century*, 137–138.

90. Kac, "Towards a Chronology of Robotic Art."

91. Freud, "The Uncanny."

92. Rothenberg, *Hand's End: Technology and the Limits of Nature*, 7–8.

93. Marinetti, "The Founding and Manifesto of Futurism," 289.

94. Descartes, *A Discourse on Method*.

95. Haraway, "A Cyborg Manifesto: Science, Technology and Socialist-feminism in the late Twentieth Century," 152.

96. Siggraph, *SIGGRAPH 2000: Electronic Art and Animation Catalog*, 35. Brown quoted in Bolter and Gromala, *Windows and Mirrors*, 157.

97. See Wilson, *Information Arts*, 350–361.

98. Bec quoted in ibid., 347.

99. Rinaldo, "Technology Recapitulates Phylogeny."

100. Bolter and Gromala, *Windows and Mirrors*, 159.

101. Kundera, *The Unbearable Lightness of Being*, 287, quoted in Phillips, "A Dogs Life," 131.

102. Pradier, "Animals, Angels and Performance."

103. Dery, *Escape Velocity*, 118.

104. Pauline quoted in ibid.

105. See Malone, *The Robot Book*.

106. Waldby, "The Instruments of Life: Frankenstein and Cyberculture," 30.

107. O'Mahony, *Cyborg*, 31.

108. Stone, *The War of Desire and Technology at the Close of the Mechanical Age*; Haraway, *Modest_Witness@Second_Millenium, FemaleMan©_Meets_OncoMouse*™; Kember, *Virtual Anxiety: Photography, New Technologies and Subjectivity*.

109. Kember, *Virtual Anxiety*, 134.

110. Ibid., 9.

111. Marinetti quoted in Benjamin, "The Work of Art in the Age of Mechanical Reproduction," 234.

112. Thorpe, "Description of Robot Wars," quoted in Wilson, *Information Arts*, 43.

113. *Robot Wars*, BBC2 Television, UK, March 2002.

114. Dery, *Escape Velocity*, 111.

115. Teleoperation was developed for military operations, and is defined by Howard Rheingold as "the human experience of seeing out of the eyes of a machine, and using natural gestures to manipulate the natural world." Rheingold, *Virtual Reality*, 254. Thus, machines move and are operated at a distance in direct relation to the computer-tracked movements of an operator elsewhere wearing a head-mounted display and datagloves.

116. Pauline quoted in Wilson, *Information Arts*, 432.

117. Kac, "The Origin and Development of Robotic Art," 81.

118. Wilson, *Information Arts*, 434.

119. Dery, *Escape Velocity*, 123.

120. De Landa, "Out of Control: Trialogue," quoted in Wilson, *Information Arts*, 435.

121. Dery, *Escape Velocity*, 128–129.

122. Ibid., 116.

123. McLuhan, *Understanding Media*, 55, quoted in Dery, *Escape Velocity*, 116.

124. McLuhan quoted in Dery, *Escape Velocity*, 121.

125. Pauline quoted in ibid., original italics.

126. Ibid., 131,130.

127. Ibid., 119,112.

128. Ibid., 115.

129. Ibid., 119.

130. Ibid., 126.

131. Pomeroy, "Black Box S-Thetix: Labor, Research, and Survival in the He[Art] of the Beast," 292, 293. Quoted in Dery, *Escape Velocity*, 127.

Chapter 13

1. Descartes, "Meditations on the First Philosophy."

2. The costume was designed by the sculptress Angela Osman. *Cyborg Dreaming* was commissioned by the London Science Museum.

3. Wilson, "Interview with Steve Dixon."

4. See, for example, Hess, "On Low Tech Cyborgs"; Dodds, *Dance on Screen*; Senft, "Performing the Digital Body—A Ghost Story."

5. McLuhan, *Understanding Media: The Extensions of Man*, 236.

6. Haraway, "A Cyborg Manifesto: Science, Technology and Socialist-feminism in the Late Twentieth Century," 150.

7. Ibid., 149.

8. Dixon, "Metal Gender."

9. Warwick, "Interview."

10. De Garis, "Interview."

11. Gibson, *Mona Lisa Overdrive*.

12. Morse, *Virtualities: Television, Media Art and Cyberculture*, 126.

13. Kac, "Time Capsule."

14. Kac, "A-Positive."

15. Technical details of the one hundred electrode array chip are provided on Warwick's website, <http://www.kevinwarwick.org/>.

16. O'Mahony, *Cyborg: The Man-Machine*, 30.

17. Warwick quoted in Ananova, "Microchip hailed as 'end of faked orgasm.'"

18. <http://www.kevinwarwick.org/>.

19. Harvey quoted in Kahney, "Warwick: Cyborg or Media Doll."

20. Warwick, *March of the Machines*, 237. Warwick's reference refers to boxing promoter Don King's evaluation of Lennox Lewis's chances of a rematch with Oliver McCall in 1994.

21. Arthur, "I Cyborg, by Kevin Warwick. Cringe–making world of 'Captain Cyborg.'"

22. Brooks, *Robot: The Future of Flesh and Machines*, 236.

23. Warwick, "Interview."

24. Hawking quoted in Walsh, "Alter our DNA or robots will take over, warns Hawking."

25. Ihde, *Bodies in Technology*.

26. Virilio quoted in Kroker, *The Possessed Individual: Technology and the French Postmodern*.

27. Cook, "Myths, Robots and Procreation."

28. Stelarc, "ParaSite: Event for Invaded and Involuntary Body."

29. Stelarc, "Prosthetics, Robotics and Remote Existence: Postevolutionary Strategies," 594.

30. Stelarc quoted in Ayres, *Obsolete Body/Alternate Strategies—listening to Stelarc*.

31. Stelarc, "ParaSite."

32. Anstey, "We Sing the Body Electric: Imagining the Body in Electronic Art."

33. Restrak quoted in Dery, *Escape Velocity: Cyberculture at the End of the Century*, 164.

34. Birringer, *Media and Performance: Along the Border*, 5, 61.

35. Stelarc, "ParaSite."

36. Stelarc, "Prosthetics, Robotics and Remote Existence," 591.

37. Warr, "Sleeper," 12.

38. Birringer, *Media and Performance*, 63.

39. Stelarc, "Strategies and Trajectories," 76, quoted in Dery, *Escape Velocity: Cyberculture at the End of the Century*, 154.

40. Stelarc, "From Psycho-Body to Cyber-Systems," 572; original italics.

41. Cleto, "Introduction: Queering the Camp," 31.

42. Sontag, "Fascinating Fascism."

43. Deleuze and Guattari, *A Thousand Plateaus: Capitalism and Schizophrenia*, 238, 305.

44. Ibid., 306.

45. Brooks, *Robot: The Future of Flesh and Machines*, 41.

46. See Kac, "Towards a Chronology of Robotic Art."

47. Deleuze and Guattari, *A Thousand Plateaus*.

48. Descartes, *A Discourse on Method*, 45.

49. Aphasia is a condition where cerebral disturbance leads to a loss of speech. In the performance, Roca does not use language and instead makes use of growls, shouts, and screams. Roca's website describes *Afasia* as "a reflection on the unstoppable encroachment of the image as opposed to written language in our culture, and attempts to give an example of the consequences of this situation." See Roca, "Afasia."

50. Marcel.lí Antúnez Roca was one of the founders of the seminal Spanish performance company La Fura Dels Baus, and left the company in 1990.

51. In a later sequence, shot on video, this creature, now played by a human performer with large false ears, is ritually sacrificed by Roca, who slashes its throat. Other theranthropic images include the sea nymph Calypso as a kitsch Barbie doll with a mermaid tail.

52. Dyer, "It's Being So Camp as Keeps Us Going," 110.

53. Ibid., 115.

54. Piggford, "Who's That Girl?" 283–284.

55. Gómez-Peña, *Dangerous Border Crossings: The Artist Talks Back*, 44.

56. Baudrillard quoted in Brockman, *Digerati: Encounters with the Cyber Elite*, 238.

57. Gómez-Peña, *Dangerous Border Crossings*, 174.

58. Cleto, "Introduction: Queering the Camp," 3; original italics.

59. Ibid., 32.

60. Ibid., 25.

61. Sontag, "Notes on Camp," 53.

62. Britton, "For Interpretation: Notes Against Camp," 138.

63. Ibid., 141.

64. Booth, "*Campe-toi!*: On the Origins and Definitions of Camp," 66.

65. Bolter, *Writing Space: The Computer in the History of Literacy*, 13.

66. De Garis, "Interview."

67. Brooks, *Robot: The Future of Flesh and Machines*, ix.

68. Dyson quoted in Lavery, "From Cinespace to Cyberspace: Zionists and Agents, Realists and Gamers in 'The Matrix' and 'eXistenZ,'" 152.

69. Britton, "For Interpretation," 138.

Chapter 14

1. Jones, *Towards a New Theatre: The Lectures of Robert Edmond Jones*, 69.

2. Barrault, *Reflections on the Theatre,* 61.

3. Ibid.

4. Elam, *The Semiotics of Theatre and Drama*.

5. Blossom, "On Filmstage," 70.

6. For a detailed analysis of Ping Chong's prolific work, see Shank, *Beyond the Boundaries: Alternative American Theatre*, 253–263.

7. See Birringer, "Dance and Interactivity," 28.

8. Virmaux, "Artaud and Film," 165.

9. Morse, "Video Installation Art: The Body, The Image and the Space-in-between."; Grosz, "In-Between: The Natural in Architecture and Culture."; Rubidge, "Bodying the Space in Between."

10. Grosz, "In-Between," 90.

11. See Shank, *Beyond the Boundaries*, 264–279, for detailed descriptions and analyses of many of Coates's productions, as well as an exploration of his aesthetic concerns and methodologies. We are indebted to Shank for his research into George Coates Performance Works, which we have drawn from liberally in our own discussion.

12. Shank, *Beyond the Boundaries*, 269.

13. CNET (Coates) "Movers and Shakers: George Coates."

14. Shank, *Beyond the Boundaries*, 278.

15. Illingworth, "George Coates: Toast of the Coast," 45.

16. Coates quoted in Shank, *Beyond the Boundaries*, 279.

17. Ibid., 278.

18. Builders Association, "Jump Cut (Faust)."

19. Weems, "Weaving the 'Live' and the Mediated: Marianne Weems in Conversation with Cariad Svich," 52.

20. *Jump Cut (Faust)* is performed by Jeff Webster, David Pence, Moira Driscoll, and Heaven Phillips.

21. Fisher, "Alladeen."

22. Gardner, "Pure Genies."

23. Anonymous review, <http://www.redhotcurry.com/entertainment/theatre/alladeen.htm>.

24. Clapp, "And for my Next Trick . . ."

25. Gardner, "Pure Genies."

26. Ibid.

27. Weems quoted in Tan, "Globe Trotting with Alladeen & the Global Soul."

28. O'Mahoney, "Aerial Views."

29. Spall quoted in O'Mahoney, "Aerial Views."

30. *A Midsummer Night's Dream* was the first production by a North American director at London's Royal National Theatre.

31. Shuttleworth, "Elsinore."

32. In later productions of *Elsinore*, British actor Peter Darling replaced Lepage.

33. O'Brien, "The Far Side of the Moon: Robert Lepage."

34. Press theatre review quote from *The Times* [UK], cited without the name of the critic or date, in <http://www.albemarle-london.com/rnt-farside.html>.

35. All of these terms have genuinely been applied to Lepage in theatre reviews we have researched, which at this stage (tired, in the dark hours of night), quite frankly, we cannot be bothered to fully reference. Life, sometimes, is too short.

36. Coveney, "Needles and Opium."

37. Gabriel quoted in O'Mahoney, "Aerial Views."

38. Lepage quoted in Gorman, "Elsinore Houses One-Man Wonder."

39. Quoted in <http://www.dublintheatrefestival.com/artist_detail.php?artist_id=95>.

40. Shuttleworth, "Elsinore."

41. Lepage quoted O'Mahoney, "Aerial Views."

42. Rush, *New Media in Late 20th-Century Art*, 71.

43. Anonymous article, <http://epidemic.cicv.fr/geogb/art/lepage/prj/introzulugb.html>.

44. Shuttleworth, "Elsinore."

Chapter 15

1. Huxley, *Brave New World*, 134, quoted in Murray, *Hamlet on the Holodeck: The Future of Narrative in Cyberspace*, 18–19.

2. Ihde, *Bodies in Technology*, 12.

3. Reaney, "Virtual Scenography: The Actor, Audience, Computer Interface," 28.

4. Gromala, "Pain and Subjectivity in Virtual Reality," 223.

5. Grau, *Virtual Art: From Illusion to Immersion,* 4–5.

6. Pimentel and Teixeira, *Virtual Reality: Through the New Looking Glass*, 8.

7. Sandin, "Digital Illusion, Virtual Reality, and Cinema," 14.

8. R. U. Sirius, "R. U. Sirius interviewed by Lynn Hershman Leeson," 55.

9. Rheingold, *Virtual Reality*.

10. Rheingold, "Rheingold's Reality," 34.

11. Ibid.

12. Coates quoted in Pimentel and Teixeira, *Virtual Reality*, 5.

13. Grau, *Virtual Art: From Illusion to Immersion*, 163.

14. Daniel Sandin also highlights the work of D. L. Vickers, who created a different HMD prototype in 1970, which incorporated the major elements of modern VR systems. See Sandin, "Digital Illusion, Virtual Reality, and Cinema," 3.

15. Bolter and Gromala, *Windows and Mirrors*, 126.

16. Paul, *Digital Art*, 125.

17. See Lanier, "The Prodigy," 164.

18. Pimentel and Teixeira, *Virtual Reality*, 7.

19. Ibid., 58.

20. Ibid., 65–67.

21. Ibid., 67.

22. See deLahunta, "Virtual Reality and Performance," 106.

23. See Paul, *Digital Art*, 129.

24. Pimentel and Teixeira, *Virtual Reality*, 75.

25. Rheingold, *Virtual Reality*.

26. Paul, *Digital Art*, 173.

27. Ibid.

28. Sharir, "The Tools."

29. Moser and MacLeod (eds.), *Immersed in Technology: Art and Virtual Environments*, x.

30. Funding was received from the National Department of Communication, Canada, and the Banff Center for the Arts. See "Gromala" at <http://www.lcc.gatech.edu/~gromala/art.htm#virtual>.

31. Laurel, *Computers as Theatre*, 197.

32. Murray, *Hamlet on the Holodeck*, 60.

33. Ryan, *Narrative as Virtual Reality*, 323.

34. The voice filters used when participants "embody" the different characters make "Crow sound raucous and masculine, spider wise and feminine, whereas snake and fish are gender-neutral." Hayles, "Embodied Virtuality: Or How to Put Bodies Back in the Picture," 17.

35. Ryan, *Narrative as Virtual Reality,* 324.

36. Ibid., 324.

37. Ibid., 323.

38. Laurel and Strickland, "Placeholder," 298.

39. Soules, "Animating the Language Machine: Computers and Performance."

40. See, for example Ryan, *Narrative as Virtual Reality*, 322–331; Hayles, "Embodied Virtuality," 15–21; Murray, *Hamlet on the Holodeck*, 60; Soules, "Animating the Language Machine: Computers and Performance." Laurel, Strickland, and Tow's own article about the project, "Placeholder: Landscape and Narrative in Virtual Environments," provides the most detailed technical and conceptual account.

41. Hayles, "Embodied Virtuality," 19–21.

42. Ibid., 21.

43. Grzinic, "Exposure Time, the Aura, and Telerobotics," 216–217.

44. Davies, "Osmose: Notes on Being in Immersive Virtual Space," 65.

45. Ibid., 66.

46. Jones, "Char Davies: VR Through Osmosis."

47. Davies, "Osmose," 69.

48. Ibid., 67.

49. Grau, *Virtual Art: From Illusion to Immersion*, 193.

50. Davies quoted in Wilson, *Information Arts*, 702.

51. Gromala and Sharir, "Dancing with the Virtual Dervish: Virtual Bodies," 282–283.

52. Sharir, "The Tools."

53. Bolter and Gromala, *Windows and Mirrors*, 126.

54. Sharir, "Influence of Technology."

55. Birringer, *Media and Performance,* 124–125.

56. Gromala and Sharir, "Dancing with the Virtual Dervish," 284–285.

57. Booth, "Unmasking the Greek Mysteries: Virtual Reality Revives the Oldest Theatre."

58. Beacham quoted in Bull, "Tech Boost for the Arts."

59. Email to the authors, 3 January 2003.

60. See Dyer, "Virtual_Stages: An Interactive Model of Performance Spaces for Creative Teams, Technicians and Students."

61. See Dyer, "Open Stages."

62. Patel, "Projects by Roma Patel."

63. Ibid.

64. Reaney described the chain of events during an interview with Steve Dixon for the Digital Performance Archive at the University of Kansas, USA, on 28 October 1999.

65. Reaney, "Virtual Reality and the Theatre: Immersion in Virtual Worlds," 183.

66. ieVR, "The Adding Machine: A Virtual Reality Project."

67. Reaney, "Virtual Reality and the Theatre," 185.

68. ieVR, "The Adding Machine."

69. Allen, "The Nature of Spectatorial Distance in VR Theatre," 243.

70. Ibid., 244.

71. The HMDs were "I-glasses" by the Virtual I-O Company.

72. Reaney, "Virtual Reality and the Theatre," 185–186.

73. Gharavi, "i.e. VR: Experiments in New Media and Performance," 260.

74. Reaney, "Press Release for 'Machinal.'"

75. Cage, "Actors Joined by Computer Imagery in U. of Kansas Production," 18.

76. Taken from a voiceover commentary used in videotape documentation of *Brainscore* supplied by the artists to the Digital Performance Archive.

77. Kac, "Darker Than Night."

78. Ibid.

79. Walker, quoted in Pimentel and Teixeira, *Virtual Reality*, 78.

80. Paul, *Digital Art*, 125.

81. deLahunta, "Virtual Reality and Performance," 111–112.

82. Weiser, "The Computer for the 21st Century," 104.

83. Bolter and Gromala, *Windows and Mirrors*, 107.

84. Laurel, Strickland, and Tow, "Placeholder: Landscape and Narrative in Virtual Environments," 181.

85. Ibid., 182.

86. Benedickt quoted in Ryan, "Cyberspace, Virtuality, and the Text," 15.

87. Laurel, Strickland, and Tow, "Placeholder," 183.

88. Lanier, "Jaron Lanier—Interviewed by Lynn Hershman Leeson," 46–49.

Chapter 16

1. Paul, *Digital Art*, 71–72.

2. Novak quoted in Silver, *The Forgotten Amazement . . . Influences on Performance Following Industrialisation*, 23.

3. Novak quoted in Giannachi, *Virtual Theatres: An Introduction*, 99.

4. Ibid., 100.

5. Krueger, "Like a Second Skin," quoted in Wilson, *Information Arts: Intersections of Art, Science and Technology*, 453.

6. Giannachi, *Virtual Theatres: An Introduction*, 100.

7. Silver, *The Forgotten Amazement, Performance Following Industrialisation*. 32.

8. CHOREOTRONICS Inc, "Byte City."

9. Paul, *Digital Art*, 72.

10. Hershman, "Conceiving Ada."

11. Neville and Heliograph Productions, "Ada."

12. Hershman, "Conceiving Ada."

13. *Daily Herald*, 6 February 2003.

14. Deleuze, *Difference and Repetition*, 196.

15. Blumenthal, "Rivermen."

16. Žižek, "Die Virtualisierung des Herr," 109–110, quoted in (and translated by) Andrea Zapp, "A Fracture in Reality: Networked Narratives as Imaginary Fields of Action," 75.

17. Talking Birds, "Smoke, Mirrors & the Art of Escapology."

18. De Certeau, *The Practice of Everyday Life*, 117, quoted in Kaye, *Site-Specific Art: Performance, Place and Documentation*, 4.

19. Kaye, *Site-Specific Art*, 4.

20. Ibid.

21. Ibid., 215.

22. Ibid.

23. Collins, "The Actual and the Imagined," 46.

24. Ibid.

25. Ibid., 50.

26. Ibid.

27. Grau, *Virtual Art: From Illusion to Immersion*, 46.

28. Collins, "The Actual and the Imagined," 51.

29. Ibid.

30. Paul, *Digital Art*, 100.

31. Polli, "Virtual Space and the Construction of Memory," 144.

32. La Fura dels Baus, "Foc Forn."

33. Ceperkovic and Kasprzak, "take take, cake cake."

34. Slayton, "DoWhatDo."

35. Ibid.

36. Slayton, "Conduits."

37. Slayton, "98.6 FM."

38. Slayton, "Panamint Launch at Lucky Jim Wash."

Chapter 17

1. Arns, "Interaction, Participation, Networking: Art and Telecommunication," 336.

2. President George W. Bush, during a televised political speech about the so-called war on terror in 2002.

3. Paik, "Art and Satellite," 42–43.

4. Ibid., 41–42.

5. Quoted in Obrist, "Turning to Technology: Legendary engineer Billy Klüver on artist-engineer collaborations."

6. Rush, *New Media in Late 20th–Century Art*, 63.

7. Collins, "The Actual and the Imagined," 51.

8. See <http://www.gertstein.org/>.

9. Ibid.

10. Reaves, "Theory and Practice, The Gertrude Stein Repertory Theatre."

11. Ibid.

12. Ibid.

13. Bruckner, *"An Epidog*—Mabou Mines."

14. Chalmers, "All the World's a Cyber Stage: The State of Online Theater."

15. See <http://www.gertstein.org/screen/stage-pro.htm>.

16. See <http://www.gertstein.org/details/pro-k12.htm>.

17. Naugle, "Distributed Choreography."

18. Wortzel, "Starboard."

19. Ibid.

20. Hovagimyan, "Art Dirt Im-port."

21. Ellipsis, "Untitled."

22. Peppermint, "Conductor #1: Getting in Touch With Chicken."

23. Kozel, "Ghosts and Astronauts."

24. Durkin, "Shared Identity."

25. See Bolter and Gromala, *Windows and Mirrors*, 96–112.

26. Paul, *Digital Art*, 163.

27. Company in Space, "Escape Velocity."

28. Sutton, "Network Aesthetics: Strategies of Participation within net.art," 27.

29. Motherboard, "M@ggie's Love Bytes."

30. La Fura Dels Baus, "Cabinas."

31. Floating Point Unit, "emergent(c) room."

32. WITS comprised choreographer Lycouris, musicians Sylvia Hallett, Ashleigh Marsh, and Viv Dogan Corringham, and visual artist Gina Southgate.

33. See "Sophia Lycouris" at <http://www.ad406.dial.pipex.com/sophia.htm>.

34. Nyman, *Experimental Music: Cage and Beyond*, 26.

35. Ibid.

36. Raymond, "Some Empty Words with Mr. Cage and Mr. Cunningham," 4–12.

37. Ibid., 6.

38. International Dance and Technology Conference, February 1999, Tempe, Arizona.

39. In a description of the project presented at the Subtle Technologies 03 Symposium, University of Toronto, Canada, 22–25 May 2003: <http://www.subtletechnologies.com/2003/lycourissharir.html>.

Chapter 18

1. Agacinski, *Time Passing*, 10.

2. Kember, *Virtual Anxiety: Photography, New Technologies and Subjectivity*, 55.

3. Davies quoted in Palmer, *Discipline and Liberty: Television and Governance*, 27.

4. Ibid.

5. Ibid., 35.

6. Ibid., 29.

7. Huhtamo, "An Archeology of Networked Art," 40.

8. O'Mahony, *Cyborg: The Man-Machine*, 66.

9. Palmer, *Discipline and Liberty*, 34–35.

10. Michael Rush suggests that Levine's *Slipcover* was the first artwork to relay live video images of gallery visitors: "Never done before, this experience was at once eerie and exhilarating." Rush, *New Media in Late 20th-Century Art*, 121.

11. O'Mahony, *Cyborg*, 66–67; Paul, *Digital Art*, 163–164.

12. See Rush, *New Media in 20th-Century Art*, 72.

13. O'Mahony, *Cyborg*, 67.

14. Sutton, "Network Aesthetics: Strategies of Participation within net.art," 20.

15. See <http://www.critical-art.net/lectures/robot.htm>.

16. See Paul, *Digital Art*, 179–181.

17. Hershman Leeson, "Difference Engine #3."

18. Sutton, "Network Aesthetics: Strategies of Participation within net.art," 25.

19. Jeremijenko quoted in Sutton, "Network Aesthetics: Strategies of Participation within net.art," 26.

20. Ibid.

21. Blast Theory, "Kidnap."

22. W. H. Auden quoted in Geoff Moore, *Moving Being: Two Decades of a Theatre of Ideas, 1968–88*, 18.

23. Diller and Scofidio, "Refresh."

24. Parkbench, "ArTistheater."

25. Their *ArTistheater Performance Archive* contains more than eighty dadaesque, nonnarrative improvisational performance clips. They are assembled within a grid where progressing across and upward from the bottom right hand corner of the screen to the top activates sequences that reflect the evolution of media technology from early black and white pinhole photography to the latest high-tech developments.

26. Collins, "The Actual and the Imagined," 47–48.

27. Waldby, "Circuits of Desire: Internet Erotics and the Problems of Bodily Location."

28. Ibid.

29. Diller and Scofidio, "Refresh."

30. Ibid.

31. Ibid.

32. Ibid.

33. Goldberg, "Introduction: The Unique Phenomenon of a Distance," 13.

34. Hertz, "Telepresence and Digital/Physical Body > Gaining a Perspective."

35. Campanella, "Eden by Wire: Webcameras and the Telepresent Landscape," 27.

36. Ringley, <www.jennicam.org>.

37. Ibid.

38. Ibid.

39. Ibid.

40. Bolter and Grusin, *Remediation: Understanding New Media*, 5–6.

41. Ibid., 204.

42. Ringley, <www.jennicam.org>.

43. Burgin, "Jenni's Room: Exhibitionism and Solitude", 229.

44. <http://www.cybergrrl.com>.

45. Ringley, <www.jennicam.org>.

Chapter 19

1. Zapp, "A Fracture in Reality: Networked Narratives as Imaginary Fields of Action," 62.

2. See Wertheim, *The Pearly Gates of Cyberspace: A History of Space from Dante to the Internet*, 223; Hafner and Lyon, *Where Wizards Stay Up Late: The Origins of the Internet*, 168, 178.

3. Hafner and Lyon, *Where Wizards Stay Up Late*, 242, cited in Wertheim, *The Pearly Gates of Cyberspace*, 223.

4. Wertheim, *The Pearly Gates of Cyberspace*, 223.

5. Ibid., 224.

6. Standage, *The Victorian Internet: The Remarkable Story of the Telegraph and the Nineteenth Century's On-Line Pioneers.*

7. Carey, *Communication as Culture*, 213, quoted in Stratton, "Not Really Desiring Bodies: The Rise and Rise of Email Affairs," 28.

8. Huhtamo, "An Archeology of Networked Art," 42.

9. Ibid.

10. Collins, "The Actual and the Imagined," 55.

11. Wertheim, *The Pearly Gates of Cyberspace*, 221.

12. The Dramatic Exchange <http://www.dramex.org/index.shtml>.

13. See <http://www.virtualdrama.com/vds/research.htm>.

14. Still available (June 2004) at <http://www.virtualdrama.com/vds/research.htm>.

15. Available (as of June 2004) with several additional collections via <http://barryrussell.net/>.

16. *Arts Wire*—Online Communications For The Arts, A Program of the New York Foundation for the Arts, New York, October 12, 1995.

17. These included Argentinian composer Santiago Pereson, Austrian costume designer Ulli Noe, and core members including Jim Terral from British Columbia, Dan Zellner from Chicago, Georg Leyrer from Vienna, and Andrew Garton from Melbourne, Australia.

18. William Gibson, *Neuromancer.*

19. Rheingold, *The Virtual Community: Homesteading in the Age of the Internet*, 27.

20. Willis and Halpin, "When the Personal Becomes Digital: Linda Dement and Barbara Hammer Move Towards a Lesbian Cyberspace," 234.

21. Cheang quoted in Herrup, "Metro Ice Meets Ball and Cheang," 153.

22. Ibid.

23. Zapp, "Introduction," 11.

24. Morse, "Nature Morte: Landscape and Narrative in Virtual Environments," 1996.

25. Zapp, "Introduction," 11.

26. Zapp, "A Fracture in Reality: Networked Narratives as Imaginary Fields of Action," 68–69.

27. Ibid., 79.

28. See Paul, *Digital Art*, 185–189.

29. VNS Matrix, "All New Gen," 38.

30. VNS Matrix, "Cyberfeminist Manifesto for the 21st Century."

31. McLuhan, *Understanding Media: The Extensions of Man*, 55.

32. See, for example, Mark Dery's book *Escape Velocity: Cyberculture at the End of the Century* (1996) for a detailed examination of some of the seamier and sleazier areas of cybersex and pornography.

33. Barber, "VR Sex."

34. Ibid.

35. See Shulgin, "FuckU-FuckMe."

36. See Wilson, *Information Arts: Intersections of Art, Science and Technology*, 403.

37. The Anatomical Theatre, "Mantis."

38. Starbuck, "Honoria in Ciberspazio."

39. Bodies in Flight and spell#7 performance, "Doublehappiness2."

40. Pavis, "Afterword: Contemporary Dramatic Writings and the New Technologies," 192.

41. Gardner, "Stitching."

42. Boon, "Phone Sex Is Cool: Chat-Lines as Superconductors," 163.

43. Gómez-Peña, *Friendly Cannibals*, 45.

44. Ito and Ito, "Joichi and Mizuko Ito—Interviewed by Lynn Hershman Leeson," 80.

45. Stefik, *Internet Dreams: Archetypes, Myths and Metaphors*, xxiii.

46. Franck, "When I enter virtual reality, what body will I leave behind?"

47. Poster, "Postmodern Virtualities," 80.

48. Turkle, *Life on the Screen: Identity in the Age of the Internet*, 20.

49. Ibid., 10.

50. Ibid., 12.

51. Murray, *Hamlet on the Holodeck: The Future of Narrative in Cyberspace*, 86, our italics.

52. Farrar, "Brenda's Loyalty Card Lays her Private Life Secrets Open," 7. Farrar's article discusses the loyalty card research study undertaken by Andrew Smith (University of Nottingham) and Leigh Sparks (Sterling University).

53. Morningstar and Farmer, "Habitat: Reports from an Online Community," 194.

54. Belbin and his researchers from Henley Management College, England, spent nine years studying management teams, particularly focusing on patterns of individuals' behavior and facilitation within the group. Belbin suggests that successful teams require a balance of skills and functional concerns, and he divides individuals into three broad categories, subdivided into nine distinct roles. He defines these as action-oriented roles (Shaper, Implementer, and Completer Finisher), people-oriented roles (Coordinator, Teamworker, and Resource Investigator) and cerebral roles (Plant, Monitor Evaluator, and Specialist). Belbin notes that individuals will often assume more than one of these roles, particularly in small groups.

55. Farmer, "Social Dimensions of Habitat's Citizenry," 205–209.

56. Morningstar and Farmer, "Habitat: Reports from an Online Community," 174.

57. Ibid., 203.

58. Ibid.

59. Murray, *Hamlet on the Holodeck: The Future of Narrative in Cyberspace*, 99.

60. Hilda Ogden was played by Jill Alexander, and the CB trucker was played by the author, Steve Dixon.

61. Turkle, "Rethinking Identity Through Virtual Community," 118.

62. Turkle, *Life on the Screen*, 253.

63. Quoted in Rang, "The Bungled and the Botched: Cyborgs, Rape and Generative Anthropology."

64. Barthes, *The Pleasure of the Text*, 27.

65. Rang, "The Bungled and the Botched."

66. Stone, "Will the Real Body Please Stand Up?: Boundary Stories About Virtual Cultures," 83.

67. Young and Senft, "Hearing the Net: An Interview with Mia Lipner," 111.

68. Poster, "Postmodern Virtualities," 80.

69. Punt, "Casablanca and Men in Black: Consciousness, Remembering and Forgetting," 42.

70. Rajah, "Two Portraits of Chief Tupa Kupa: The Image as an Index of Shifts in Human Consciousness," 57.

71. The concept is explored at length in Jay Bolter and Diane Gromala's book *Windows and Mirrors* (2003).

72. Chalmers, "All the World's a Cyber Stage: The State of Online Theater."

73. Bilderwerfer, "be right back/ The Stolen Identity Project."

74. Ibid.

75. Adamse and Motta, *Online Friendship, Chat-Room Romance and Cybersex*, 208, quoted in Stratton, "Not Really Desiring Bodies: The Rise and Rise of Email Affairs," 37.

76. Reid, ". . . Meanwhile Back in the Bedroom," 6, quoted in Stratton, "Not Really Desiring Bodies: The Rise and Rise of Email Affairs," 37.

77. Stratton, "Not Really Desiring Bodies," 37.

78. Ullman, "Come in CQ: The Body on the Wire," 12, quoted in Stratton, "Not Really Desiring Bodies," 35.

79. Ibid.

80. Ibid.

81. Baudrillard quoted in ibid., 34.

82. Ibid., 35.

83. Senft, "Performing the Digital Body—A Ghost Story," 17.

84. Turkle quoted in Dreyfuss, *On the Internet*, 121.

85. This notion is particularly evident in Turkle's discourses and those of her many followers. However, as Richard Coyne makes clear, "The rationalistic, the romantic, and the postmodern are often entangled or confused in digital narratives of identity. Turkle has no problem conflating the aims of artificial intelligence, romanticism and postmodernism."

86. Kendrick, "Cyberspace and the Technological Real," 152.

87. Renan, "The Net and the Future of Being Fictive," 62–69.

88. Markley, *Virtual Realities and Their Discontents*, 56.

89. Kroker and Kroker, "Code Warriors: Bunkering in and Dumbing Down," 247.

90. Kroker, *The Possessed Individual: Technology and the French Postmodern*, 5.

91. Ibid., 6.

92. Rheingold, "The Citizen," 7.

93. Ibid., 8.

Chapter 20

1. Hassan, "Prometheus as Performer: Towards a Posthumanist Culture?" 210.

2. Murray, *Hamlet on the Holodeck: The Future of Narrative in Cyberspace*, 58.

3. Ibid.

4. Ibid., 134.

5. Moulthrop provides an interesting discussion of the issues around closure in hypertext narratives in his article "Containing Multitudes: The Problem of Closure in Interactive Fiction."

6. Bolter and Gromala define it as a distinct "new type of literary fiction." Bolter and Gromola, *Windows and Mirrors*, 155.

7. Hayles, *Writing Machines*, 62.

8. Sloane, *Digital Fictions: Storytelling in a Material World*, 45.

9. Mathews and Brotchie, *Oulipo Compendium*, 198, quoted in Sloane, *Digital Fictions*, 46.

10. Mathews and Brotchie, *Oulipo Compendium*, 195, quoted in Sloane, *Digital Fictions*, 46.

11. Motte, *Oulipo: A Primer of Potential Literature*, 21, quoted in Sloane, *Digital Fictions*, 45.

12. Bernstein, "Patterns of Hypertext."

13. Sloane, *Digital Fictions*, 104.

14. Kirshenblatt-Gimblett, *Speech Play: Research and Resources for the Study of Linguistic Creativity*.

15. Bolter, *Writing Space: The Computer in the History of Literacy*.

16. Danet, Wachenhauser, Bechar-Israeli, Cividalli, and Rosenbaum-Tamari, "Curtain Time 20:00 GMT: Experiments with Virtual Theater on Internet Relay Chat."

17. Quoted in ibid.

18. Ibid.

19. Ibid.

20. Ibid.

21. Plaintext Players, "The Birth of the Christ Child."

22. Hopkins, "Eight Dialogues."

23. Jenik, "Waitingforgodot.com."

24. Ibid.

25. Ibid.

26. Burk, "ATHEMOO and the Future Present: Shaping Cyberspace into a Theatre Working Place," 110.

27. Schrum, "NetSeduction."

28. Ibid.

29. Ibid.

30. Auslander, "Live from Cyberspace, or, I was sitting at my computer this guy appeared he thought I was a bot," 18.

31. Turing, "Machinery and Computer Intelligence."

32. Hayles, *How We Became Posthuman: Virtual Bodies in Cybernetics, Literature and Informatics*, xi.

33. Quoted in Plant, *Zeros and Ones: Digital Women + The New Technoculture,* 91.

34. Quoted in Murray, *Hamlet on the Holodeck, The Future of Narrative in Cyberspace*, 218.

35. Ibid., 216–217.

36. Leonard, *Bots: The Origin of New Species*, 41, including his citation from *Wired*.

37. See Murray, *Hamlet on the Holodeck*, 218.

38. Quoted in Plant, *Zeros and Ones*, 93.

39. Foner quoted in ibid.

40. Auslander, "Live from Cyberspace, or, I was sitting at my computer this guy appeared he thought I was a bot," 19.

41. The essay's subtitle pastiches a famous Robert Wilson production to both echo and subvert ideas of bots as "hallucinations": "Live from Cyberspace: or, I was sitting at my computer this guy appeared he thought I was a bot." The title of Wilson's production was *I was Sitting on My Patio/ This Guy Appeared I Thought/ I Was Hallucinating* (1977), which comprised a forty-minute monologue composed of fragmentary stories, banalities and stream-of-consciousness. In the first act it was performed solo by Robert Wilson; in the second act the same monologue was repeated identically by Lucinda Childs. The text of the performance was published in 1979 in the *Performing Arts Journal*.

42. Blau, "The Human Nature of the Bot," 134.

43. Phelan, *Mourning Sex: Performing Public Memories*, 3.

44. Auslander, "Live from Cyberspace, or, I was sitting at my computer this guy appeared he thought I was a bot," 21.

45. Blau. "The Human Nature of the Bot," 22–23.

46. Ibid., 24.

47. Paul, *Digital Art*, 147.

48. See Paul, *Digital Art*, 124, 153.

49. See <http://www.vperson.com>.

50. Soules, "Animating the Language Machine: Computers and Performance."

51. Causey, "Postorganic Performance: The Appearance of Theater in Virtual Spaces," 194.

52. Ibid., 195.

53. Ibid., 196–197.

54. Ross quoted in D'Souza, "From online to onstage, kids construct musical for S.J. theater."

55. Stevenson, "MOO Theatre: More Than Just Words?" 141.

56. Schweller, "Staging a Play in a MOO Theater," 147.

57. Rayner, "Everywhere and Nowhere: Theatre in Cyberspace," 280.

58. Ibid., 282.

59. Ibid., 285.

60. Novak, "Liquid Architecture in Cyberspace," 234, quoted in Rayner, "Everywhere and Nowhere: Theatre in Cyberspace," 291.

61. Rayner, "Everywhere and Nowhere," 294, 298.

62. Gómez-Peña, "In Defence of Performance Art," 17.

63. <www.telefonica.es/fat/egomez.html>. Please note that this was an ongoing diary record at the time and various caches have recorded different versions. At various stages the site was updated with additional thoughts (occasionally edits) and inclusion of contributions from friends and email participants.

64. Ibid.

65. Ibid.

66. Ibid.

67. Gómez-Peña, *Dangerous Border Crossings: The Artist Talks Back*, 37.

68. Sifuentes quoted in Giannaci, *Virtual Theatres: An Introduction*, 148.

69. Gómez-Peña, *Dangerous Border Crossings*, 41–43.

70. Ibid., 40.

71. Ibid.

72. Ibid., 41–43.

73. Ibid., 49–50.

74. Ibid., 197.

75. Ibid., 47.

76. The Chameleons Group, "Chameleons 3: Net Congestion."

77. Jenik, "Desktop Theater: Keyboard Catharsis and the Masking of Roundheads," 95.

78. LaFarge and Allen, "The Roman Forum."

79. Morle, "Communitek: Performance in the Electronic Frontier," 10.

80. Publicity announcement for Hooks, *Acting Strategies for the Cyber Age*, Greenwood Press, accessed through <Amazon.co.uk>, July 2004.

81. Chalmers, "All the World's a Cyber Stage: The State of Online Theater."

82. Antohin, "Virtual Theatre Projects."

83. Ibid.

84. See "CBS News," 28 November 2000 <http://www.cbsnews.com/stories/2000/11/28/entertainment/main252718.shtml>.

85. See "BBC Cambridgeshire on stage" (2004) <http://www.bbc.co.uk/cambridgeshire/stage/2004/01/british_dance_edition.shtml>.

Chapter 21

1. Agacinski, *Time Passing*, 3.

2. Ibid., 33.

3. See, for example, Krysztof Pomian's *The Order of Time* (*L'Ordre du Temps*).

4. Osborne, "The Politics of Time."

5. Ibid., 42.

6. Connor, "The Impossibility of the Present: or, from the Contemporary to the Contemporal," 16.

7. Gross, "Temporality and the Modern State," 56, quoted in Connor, "The Impossibility of the Present," 16.

8. Lyotard, *The Postmodern Condition: a Report on Knowledge*, 22, quoted in Connor, "The Impossibility of the Present," 17.

9. Agacinski, *Time Passing*, 46–47.

10. Ibid., 5.

11. Ibid., 15.

12. Nordau, *Degeneration*, 39, quoted in Luckhurst and Marks, "Hurry Up Please, It's Time: Introducing the Contemporary," 2.

13. Baudelaire, *The Painter of Modern Life and Other Essays*, 13, quoted in Luckhurst and Marks, "Hurry Up Please, It's Time," 1.

14. See Harvey, *The Condition of Postmodernity: An Enquiry into the Origins of Social Change*.

15. Baudrillard, "The End of the Millennium, or the Countdown," cited in Connor, "The Impossibility of the Present," 21.

16. Jameson, *Postmodernism: Or, the Cultural Logic of Late Capitalism*, 25.

17. Huyssen, *Twilight Memories: Marking Time in a Culture of Amnesia*, 9, quoted in Luckhurst, "Memory Recovered/Recovered Memory," 83.

18. Simpson, *Technology, Time and the Conversations of Modernity*.

19. Virilio, *The Lost Dimension*, 15, quoted in Luckhurst and Marks, "Hurry Up Please, It's Time," 2.

20. Lyotard, *The Postmodern Condition: A Report on Knowledge*, 81.

21. Foucault, *Dits et Ecrits*, quoted in Manovich, "Spatial Computerisation and Film Language," 72.

22. Levinas, *Le Temps et l'Autre*.

23. The Builders Association, "Jet Lag."

24. In his book *The Third Window*, Paul Virilio describes Krassnoff as "a contemporary heroine who lived in deferred time." Quoted in The Builders Association, "Jet Lag."

25. Builders Association, "Jet Lag."

26. Lepage quoted in Hays, "Theatrical Premonitions."

27. Lepage quoted in Shewey, "Set Your Watch to Now: Robert Lepage's 'Zulu Time.'"

28. Shewey, "Set Your Watch to Now."

29. Ibid.

30. Pavis, "Afterword: Contemporary Dramatic Writings and the New Technologies," 188.

31. Ibid., 189.

32. Lepage "Zulu Time."

33. Ibid.

34. Shewey, "Set Your Watch to Now."

35. Agacinski, *Time Passing*, 8.

36. Causey, "The Aesthetics of Disappearance and the Politics of Visibility in the Performance of Technology" 67.

37. As Theodore Shank points out, Foreman's objective is "a highly conscious condition in which the audience attends to the theatrical moments as they occur in front of them rather than focusing on where these moments might lead or how they reveal character or motivation. His productions keep the audience in a highly attentive state of perception, not allowing them to enter deeply into a fictional world where their attention would be seduced . . . and [they] would perceive less keenly the theatricality of the present moment." Shank, *Beyond the Boundaries: American Alternative Theatre*, 311.

38. La Fura dels Baus, "F@ust version 3.0."

39. Levinas, *Le Temps et l'Autre*, 17, quoted in Docherty, "Now, Here, This," 53.

40. Blossom, "On Filmstage," 69.

41. Ibid., 71–72.

42. Bergson, *Matter and Memory*, quoted in Rush, *New Media in Late 20th-Century Art*, 12.

43. Ibid.

44. Lyotard quoted in Tholen, "In Between: Time, Space and Image in Cross-Media Performance," 56.

45. Benjamin, "The Work of Art in the Age of Mechanical Reproduction," 247.

46. Forced Entertainment, "Spin."

47. The main collaborators were Isabelle Jenniches, Riek Westerhof, Karen Levi, and Radboud Mens.

48. Birringer, "Dance and Interactivity," 33.

49. See, for example, Paul, *Digital Art*, 178.

50. Coates, "Blind Messengers."

51. AlienNation, "Migbot."

52. Rokeby, "Watch."

53. Ibid.

54. Aristotle quoted in Agacinski, *Time Passing*, 40.

55. Ibid., 21.

56. Ibid., 22.

57. Kroker and Kroker, *Hacking the Future: Stories for the Flesh-Eating 90s*, 54.

Chapter 22

1. Kac, "Art at the Biological Frontier," 93.

2. Terdiman, *Present Past: Modernity and the Memory Crisis*, 8.

3. Schechner, "The End of Humanism," 16.

4. Steiner, *In Bluebeard's Castle*, 3–4.

5. Wheeler, "Melancholia, Modernity and Contemporary Grief," 63.

6. Connor, "The Impossibility of the Present: or, from the Contemporary to the Contemporal," 21.

7. Ibid.

8. Baudrillard, *Simulacra and Simulation*, 45.

9. Ibid., 49.

10. Ibid.

11. Jameson, *Postmodernism: Or, the Cultural Logic of Late Capitalism*, 27,71.

12. Huyssen, *Twilight Memories: Marking Time in a Culture of Amnesia*, 7 and 9, quoted in Luckhurst, "Memory Recovered/Recovered Memory," 83.

13. Huyssen, *Twilight Memories: Marking Time in a Culture of Amnesia*, 5, quoted in Luckhurst, "Memory Recovered/Recovered Memory," 82.

14. Luckhurst, "Memory Recovered/Recovered Memory," 83.

15. Nora, "Between Memory and History: Les Lieux de Mémoire," 7, quoted in Luckhurst, "Memory Recovered/Recovered Memory," 83.

16. Luckhurst, "Memory Recovered/Recovered Memory," 83–84.

17. Ibid., 92.

18. During a retrospective entitled *Trisha Brown at 25: Postmodern and Beyond* at the Brooklyn Academy of Music, 1996. See Birringer, "Dance and Media Technologies," 71.

19. Birringer, "Dance and Media Technologies," 71.

20. Terdiman, *Present Past*, 290, quoted in Luckhurst, "Memory Recovered/Recovered Memory," 91.

21. Talking Birds, "Recent Past."

22. Polli, "Virtual Space and the Construction of Memory," 45.

23. Ibid., 47.

24. Proust, *In the Shadow of Young Girls in Flower*, 222.

25. A collaboration for the Cellbytes 2000 festival between the Institute for Studies in the Arts, Arizona State University, and two London-based digital performance organisations, ResCen (Middlesex University) and shinkansen.

26. PPS Danse, "Strata, Memoirs of a Lover."

27. Proust, *The Way by Swanns*, 50.

28. Undrill, "Book Review," 133. Also see Caruth, *Trauma: Explorations in Memory*.

29. Bolter and Gromala, *Windows and Mirrors*, 126.

30. Neumark, "Shock in the Ear."

31. AlienNation, "Before Night Falls."

32. Ulmer, "The Miranda Warnings: An Experiment in Hyperrhetoric," 143.

33. Wing quoted in Tysome, "Dancers Offer Cue to Brain Functions," 9.

34. <http://epidemic.cicv.fr/geogb/art/dtype/histgb.html>.

35. Ibid.

36. Virilio quoted in Kroker, *The Possessed Individual: Technology and the French Postmodern*, 25.

37. Petersen, "The Emergence of Hyper-reality in Performance," 33.

38. Rush, New Media in Late 20th-Century Art, 23.

39. Murray, *Hamlet on the Holodeck: The Future Of Narrative in Cyberspace*, 105.

40. Punt, "Casablanca and Men in Black: Consciousness, Remembering and Forgetting" in Ascott, *Reframing Consciousness*, 42.

41. Curious.com, "Random Acts of Memory."

42. See Ulmer, *Teletheory: Grammatology in the Age of Video*, 134.

43. Hrvatin, "Drive-in Camillo."

44. Wilson, "Memory Map."

45. Proust, *The Way by Swanns*, 49–50.

Chapter 23

1. Duchamp quoted in Rush, *New Media in Late 20th-Century Art*, 15.

2. Benjamin, *Object. Painting*, 17.

3. Goldberg, *Performance Art: From Futurism to the Present*, 13.

4. Carra quoted in ibid., 16.

5. Ibid.

6. Saltz, "The Collaborative Subject: Telerobotic Performance and Identity," 73.

7. Brecht, "The Radio as an Apparatus of Communications."

8. Sutton, "Network Aesthetics: Strategies of Participation within net.art," 26, referring to McLuhan's *Gutenberg Galaxy*.

9. Lippman paraphrased by Stone, *The War of Desire and Technology at the Close of the Mechanical Age*, 10.

10. Penny, "From A to D and Back Again: The Emerging Aesthetics of Interactive Art."

11. Murray, *Hamlet on the Holodeck: The Future of Narrative in Cyberspace*, 126.

12. Morse, "Video Installation Art: The Body, The Image and the Space-in-between," 159.

13. Bolter and Gromala, *Windows and Mirrors*, 147.

14. Lanier, "The Prodigy."

15. Dinkla, "The Art of Narrative—Towards the Floating Work of Art," 38–39, quoted in Zapp, "A Fracture in Reality," 76.

16. Zapp "A Fracture in Reality," 77.

17. Enzenberger quoted in Baudrillard, "Requiem for the Media," 286.

18. Ibid., 280.

19. Ibid., 281.

20. See Morse, *Virtualities: Television, Media Art and Cyberculture*, 10.

21. Wardrip-Fruin and Montfort, *New Media Reader*, 339–340; see also Boal, *Games for Actors and Non-Actors* and *Theatre of the Oppressed*.

22. Wilson, *Information Arts: Intersections of Art, Science and Technology*, 340. Wilson's "quote-in-quote" is taken from the group's website: <www.rtmark.com>.

23. Frasca quoted in Wardrip-Fruin and Montfort, *The New Media Reader*, 340.

24. Boal, *Theatre of the Oppressed*, 156.

25. Ibid.

26. Zapp, "net.drama://myth/mimesis/mind_mapping/," 77.

27. Rokeby, "Transforming Mirrors: Transforming Mirrors."

28. Klüver, "The Garden Party," 213.

29. See, for example, Bolter and Grusin, *Remediation*.

30. Nelson, *TV Drama In Transition: Forms, Values and Cultural Change*, 24.

31. Atchley, "Next Exit."

32. Tuomola and Leskinen, "Daisy's Amazing Discoveries: Part 1—The Production," 85.

33. Brecht quoted in Szperling, "Interactive cinema artists changing the way audiences view and understand film."

34. See, for example, Schwartz, *Media Art History*, 86.

35. Dinkla quoed in ibid., 87.

36. Hershman, "Deep Contact: The First Interactive Sexual Fantasy Videodisk."

37. *Sonata* also includes pictorial inserts with reference to Freud's "Wolfman" case study. Freud's influence on Weinbren is also evident in his earlier *Erkling* (1986), which includes footage relating to Freud's "Story of the Burning Child" from *The Interpretation of Dreams* (1900). See Schwartz, *Media Art History*, 87.

38. Lunenfield, "Myths of Interactive Cinema."

39. Weinbren quoted in Schwartz, *Media Art History*, 87.

40. Dery, *Escape Velocity: Cyberculture at the End of the Century*, 209.

41. Ryan, *Narrative as Virtual Reality*, 271.

42. Yamashita, "Beyond Fear and Exhilaration: Hopes and Dreams for Special Venue Entertainment," 386.

43. Ryan, *Narrative as Virtual Reality*, 271.

44. Ibid., 275.

45. Ibid., 278.

46. Murray, *Hamlet on the Holodeck*, 175.

47. Ryan, *Narrative as Virtual Reality*, 280.

48. Sandin "Digital Illusion, Virtual Reality, and Cinema," 23.

49. Whitby quoted in Lunenfeld, "The Myths of Interactive Cinema," 147.

50. Yamashita, "Beyond Fear and Exhilaration: Hopes and Dreams for Special Venue Entertainment," 386.

51. Sloane, *Digital Fictions: Storytelling in a Material World*, 188.

52. Ibid.

53. Vanouse, "The Consensual Fantasy Engine."

54. Seaman, "Emergent Constructions: Re-embodied Intelligence Within Recombinant Poetic Networks."

55. Quoted in Bolter and Gromala, *Windows and Mirrors*, 132.

56. Domike, Mateas and Vanouse, "Terminal Time."

57. See Bolter and Gromala, *Windows and Mirrors*, 132–137.

58. Pong (1972) was one of the first video games, involving a ball moving across screen and the users moving a "paddle" up and down to "hit" it in order to avoid its going offscreen. It is normally played with two players, like tennis or ping-pong—hence the name (although some maintain the name derives from the "pong" sound the ball makes as it hits the paddle).

59. Sandin, "Digital Illusion, Virtual Reality, and Cinema," 25.

60. Laurel, Strickland, and Tow quoted in Sandin "Digital Illusion, Virtual Reality and Cinema," 182.

61. Schwarz, *Media-Art-History*.

62. Shank, *Beyond the Boundaries: American Alternative Theatre*, 295.

63. Paul, *Digital Art*, 135.

64. Rokeby, "Transforming Mirrors : Transforming Mirrors."

65. Hoberman, "*Faraday's Garden* Description."

66. <www.hoberman.com/perry>.

67. Saltz, "The Collaborative Subject: Telerobotic Performance and Identity," 80, 78.

68. Ibid., 77.

69. Ibid., 78–79.

70. Sermon, "Peace Talks."

71. *Portrait One* was also released in CD-ROM format by ZKM in 1995.

72. Courchesne, "Hall of Shadows."

73. Ibid., 25.

74. Ibid., 26.

75. Ibid.

76. Dove, "*Artificial Changelings*, Overview."

77. Ibid.

78. Ibid.

79. Dove, "Haunting the Movie: Embodied Interface/Sensory Cinema," 110.

80. Company in Space, "home, not alone."

81. See Webbed Feats, "Bytes of Bryant Park."

82. La Fura Dels Baus, "Big Opera Mundi."

83. Davis, "Terrible Beauty."

84. Ibid.

85. Bolter and Gromala, *Windows and Mirrors*, 137–138.

Chapter 24

1. McLuhan, *Understanding Media: The Extensions of Man*, 259.

2. <www.gamasutra.com/education/>.

3. See <http://www.ludology.org>.

4. At Parson School of Design, New York City, 13 November 1999. See <http://www.eyebeam.org/replay/html/basics.html>.

5. From a presentation given by the Greek artist Miltos Manetas at the *RE:PLAY* conference on Digital Gaming: <http://www.eyebeam.org/replay/html/conf.html>.

6. From a presentation given by Janet Murray at the *RE:PLAY* conference: <http://www.eyebeam.org/replay/html/conf.html>.

7. Guignol was a stock character from French puppet theater, an equivalent of Mr. Punch; "Grand" signified that this was adults-only entertainment.

8. Hand and Wilson, *Grand Guignol: The French Theatre of Horror*, 193.

9. The gamer always plays as a member of the Army and always hunts the terrorists, although, interestingly, both sides refer to the other as terrorists.

10. See, for example, Adams, "The Designer's Notebook: Sex in Videogames."

11. Amazon (UK) PC Games newsletter, 19 September 2002.

12. See, for example, Wright, "The Sims in Our Own Image."

13. See Adams, "The Designer's Notebook: Sex in Videogames."

14. Review on *Bitz* TV program, Channel 4, July 1999.

15. Ibid.

16. Davies, "Understanding the social and cultural processes behind the continual male dominance of computer and videogame production and consumption."

17. Laurel, "Technological Humanism."

18. Klies, "Gallery of Memories."

19. Ibid.

20. The exhibition was at the Barbican Gallery, Barbican Centre, London, from 16 May to 15 September 2002.

21. Zimmerman "Do Independent Games Exist?" 122.

22. Ibid., 125.

23. Birringer, "Before Night Falls."

24. Fuchs, "From First Person Shooter to Multi-User Knowledge Spaces."

25. Ibid.

26. Bookchin quoted in Paul, *Digital Art*, 199.

27. <http://www.vanndermar.com>.

28. Weibel and Druckrey, *Net_Condition: Art and Global Media*, 210.

29. The former Odeon Cinema at the Merrion Centre, Leeds, UK. *QQQ* was shown as part of the Lumen Festival Evolution 2002: Process, curated by the Leeds International Film Festival on 10–12 October 2002, commissioned by the Digital Research Unit, the Media Centre, Huddersfield. A further highlight of the Festival, particularly with regard to retro-technology, was a seminar by Billy Klüver.

30. Barry, *Second Front: Censorship and Propaganda in the Gulf War*; Formenti, "La Guerra Senza Nemici" (The War Without Enemies); Dery, *Escape Velocity: Cyberculture at the End of the Century*, 122; Baudrillard, *The Gulf War Did Not Take Place.*

31. MacArthur quoted in Dery, *Escape Velocity: Cyberculture at the End of the Century*, 122.

32. Formenti, "La Guerra Senza Nemici."

33. Giannachi, *Virtual Theatres: An Introduction*, 116.

34. Powell, quoted in the *New York Times*, 23 March 1991.

35. See <http://www.crg.cs.nott.ac.uk/~sdb/>.

36. Giannachi, *Virtual Theatres: An Introduction*, 119.

37. Ibid.

38. Brook, *The Empty Space*, 157.

39. Rae, "Presencing."

40. For example, *Information, Communication & Society* 6, no. 4 (December 2003) was devoted wholly to papers on digital games and society, including essays by Dmitri Williams ("The Video Game Lightning Rod," 523–550); Diane Nutt and Diane Railton ("The Sims: Real Life as Genre," 577–592); Hector Postigo ("From Pong to Planet Quake: Post-Industrial Transitions from Leisure to Work," 593–607); and Alberto Alvisi, Alessandro Narduzzo, and Marco Zamarian ("Playstation and the Power of Unexpected Consequences," 608–627).

Chapter 25

1. Reaves, "Theory and Practice, The Gertrude Stein Repertory Theatre."

2. August 31, 1982. The first CD is recorded as "52nd Street" by Billy Joel. The first fifty titles catered for a range of tastes including classical, popular, and rock releases, and by 1990 CDs had reached worldwide sales of a billion.

3. Fox, "The Rom Revolution."

4. See *FineArt Forum* 7, no. 11 (15 November 1993) <http://www.cdes.qut.edu.au/fineart_online/Backissues/Vol_7/faf711.html>.

5. Information from an email circular by Terry Winograd announcing the 1995 competition, 4 April 1995.

6. Slatin, "Hypertext and the Teaching of Writing," 127.

7. Goodman, Coe and Williams, "The Multimedia Bard: Plugged and Unplugged," 30–31.

8. Goodman, "Representing Gender/ Representing Self: A Reflection on Role Playing in Performance Theory and Practice," 200–201.

9. Cotton and Oliver, *Understanding Hypermedia*, 88.

10. It was produced by the company as part of a booklet, *Die Audio Gruppe 1982–1998*.

11. Deegan, "Electronic Publishing," 412.

12. Birringer, *Media and Performance*, 98.

13. It was included as a free insert with a contextualizing article in volume 12 of *Studies in Theatre Production* (December 1995).

14. *TDR: The Drama Review* 43, no. 1 (Spring 1999).

15. See Smith, "Changing Shades: Review of *Metabody* and *Chameleons 2*."

16. Dixon, "Digits, Discourse and Documentation: Performance Research and Hypermedia," 171.

17. The *Stalking Memory* CD-ROM was published in volume 5, no. 3 (Winter 2000) of *Performance Research*.

18. ad319 involved Nan Goggin, Joseph Squire, Kathleen Chmelewski, and, later, Robb Springfield.

19. Ure and Russ "Web Art 101."

20. <http://www.ffward.com/03pul.html>.

21. Rosenberg, "Laurie Anderson's Heartbreak 'Motel.'"

22. "Barren Magic," Ian Christe, *HotWired* (4 Dec 1995), <http://hotwired.wired.com/cdroms/95/49/index1a.html>.

23. Smith "Changing Shades: Review of *Metabody* and *Chameleons 2*."

24. Sleeve notes to *Mouthplace* CD-ROM, Jools Gilson-Ellis and Richard Povall (Frog Peak Music, 1997).

25. Cited as "(extract from 'Windows' Baudelaire)".

26. Text from the "Readme" file of the *Nightwalks* CD-ROM.

27. Dixon, "Remediating Theatre in a Digital Proscenium," 142.

28. Shaw, "Introduction: *artintact*—Past Present," 31–32, in booklet included in the CD-Rom set *The Complete artintact* (Karlsruhe: ZKM and Katje Cantz).

Chapter 26

1. Gibbins and Udoff, Screenplay for *Eve of Destruction*, directed by Duncan Gibbins (1991).

2. The final words of Madame E. P. Blavatsky's *The Key to Theosophy*. Quoted in Kandinski, *Concerning the Spiritual in Art*, 14.

3. Dodson, "Institute of Computer Art."

4. Baty, "Plug is pulled on e-university."

5. Steiner, *Grammars of Creation*.

6. Borgman, *Holding on to Reality: The Nature of Information at the Turn of the Millennium*, 213.

7. Ibid.

8. Ibid., 215.

9. See "A Constructed World at the Tirana Biennale opening 13th September 2003" at <http://www.tiranabiennale.org/>. *Blinky* ran at the Auditorium, Tate Modern, 14–21 September 2003, and featured works by A Constructed World, Cory Arcangel, Paper Rad, and Seth Price, curated by Foxy Productions (Michael Gillespie and John Thomson).

10. Tessa Jowell, "Government and the Value of Culture."

11. Helen Paris of Curious has explained that this was primarily because a commercial company owned the domain name "curious.com" (Interview with Steve Dixon, 17 July 2005). But we feel it is likely that an equal impetus may have been provided by the fact that the previously fashionable ".com" suffix had lost is mystique.

12. Program notes for Troika Ranch's *Surfacing*, Chancellor Hall, Chelmsford, 12 May 2005.

13. Program notes for Laurie Anderson's *The End of the Moon* as part of the BITE: 05 season at the Barbican Theatre, London, May 2005.

14. Ibid.

15. Ibid.

16. Freeman, "I accuse."

17. Ibid.

18. Ibid.

19. Ibid.

20. Ibid.

21. Pavis, "Afterword: Contemporary Dramatic Writings and the New Technologies," 188.

22. Ibid., 189.

23. Ibid., 190.

24. Ibid.

25. Ibid.

26. Ibid., 188.

27. See Gramsci <http://www.marxists.org/archive/gramsci/>.

28. Marinetti and Cangiullo quoted in Goldberg, *Performance Art: From Futurism to the Present*, 29.

29. Heise, *Chronoschisms: Time, Narrative and Postmodernism*, 31.

30. Connor, "The Impossibility of the Present: or, from the Contemporary to the Contemporal," 21.

31. Jameson, *Postmodernism: Or, the Cultural Logic of Late Capitalism*, ix.

32. Ibid.

33. Ibid.

34. Connor, "The Impossibility of the Present: or, from the Contemporary to the Contemporal," 21.

35. Eagleton, "Capitalism, Modernism and Postmodernism," 39, quoted in Connor, "The Impossibility of the Present: or, from the Contemporary to the Contemporal," 21.

36. Jameson, *Postmodernism: Or, the Cultural Logic of Late Capitalism*, 67.

37. Osborne, "The Politics of Time," 51.

38. Kirby, "New Performance & Manifestos: An Introduction," 3.

39. Weibel quoted in Rush, *New Media in Late 20th-Century Art*, 168.

40. Wertheim, *The Pearly Gates of Cyberspace: A History of Space from Dante to the Internet*, 21.

41. Sharir, "Virtually Dancing."

42. Kozel, "Spacemaking: Experiences of a Virtual Body."

43. Haraway, "A Cyborg Manifesto: Science, Technology and Socialist-feminism in the Late Twentieth Century."

44. Stelarc in Ayres, *Obsolete Body/Alternate Strategies—Listening to Stelarc*, 2–3.

45. Stallabras, "The Ideal City and the Virtual Hive: Modernism and the Emergent Order in Computer Culture," 109.

46. Hassan, *The Postmodern Turn: Essays in Postmodern Theory and Culture*.

47. Critical Art Ensemble quoted in Wardrip-Fruin and Monfort, *The New Media Reader*, 783.

48. Eagleton, "Bin Laden sure didn't read any beer mats."

49. Ibid.

50. Ibid.

51. Davis quoted in Hassan, "Prometheus as Performer: Towards a Posthumanist Culture?" 210.

52. Cage quoted in King, *Contemporary American Theatre*, 264.

Bibliography

Adams, Ernest. 2000. "The Designer's Notebook: Sex in Videogames." <http://www.gamasutra.com>.

Adamse, M., and S. Motta. 1996. *Online Friendship, Chat-Room Romance and Cybersex*. Deerfield Beach, Fla.: Health Communications Inc.

Adorno, Theodor W. 1973. *Ästhetische Theorie*. Frankfurt am Main: Suhrkamp.

Agacinski, Sylviane. 2003. *Time Passing*. Trans. Jody Gladding, New York: Columbia University Press.

AlienNation Co. 1998. "Migbot." Database entry, Digital Performance Archive. <http://art.ntu.ac.uk/dpa>.

———. 1997. "Before Night Falls." Database entry, Digital Performance Archive. <http://art.ntu.ac.uk/dpa>.

Allen, David-Michael. 1999. "The Nature of Spectatorial Distance in VR Theatre." In *Theatre in Cyberspace*, edited by Stephen A. Schrum. New York: Peter Lang.

Alter, Jean. 1990. *A Sociosemiotic Theory of Theatre*. Philadelphia: University of Pennsylvania Press.

Ananova. 2000. "Microchip hailed as end of faked orgasm." <http://www.ananova.com/news/story/sm_76805.html>.

Ananthaswamy, Anil. 2002. "Mind Over Metal." *New Scientist* 2331 (23 February 2002): 26–29.

Anatomical Theatre. 2000. "Subject: Matter." Database entry, Digital Performance Archive. <http://art.ntu.ac.uk/dpa>.

———. 1997. "Mantis." Database entry, Digital Performance Archive. <http://art.ntu.ac.uk/dpa>.

Anders, Peter. 2001. "Antropic Cyberspace: Defining Electronic Space from First Principles." *Leonardo*, 34, no. 5:409–416.

Anstey, Josephine. 1998. "We Sing the Body Electric: Imagining the Body in Electronic Art." <http://www.evl.uic.edu/anstey/AECevents/bodypaper.html>.

Antohin, Anatoly. 2000. "Virtual Theatre Projects." <http://filmplus.org/vtheatre/faq.html>.

Archer, Michael. 2002 [1997]. *Art Since 1960.* London: Thames and Hudson.

Arndt, Michael J. 1999. "Theatre at the Centre of the Core (Technology as a Lever in Theatre Pedagogy)." In *Theatre in Cyberspace*, edited by Stephen A. Schrum, 65–84. New York: Peter Lang.

Arns, Inke. 2004. "Interaction, Participation, Networking: Art and Telecommunication." In *Media Art Net: Survey of Media Art*, edited by Rudolf Frieling and Dieter Daniels, translated by Tom Morrison, 333–349. Vienna and New York: Springer-Verlag.

Aronson, Arnold. 1999. "Technology and Dramaturgical Development: Five Observations." *Theatre Research International* 24, no. 2:188–197.

Artaud, Antonin. 1974 [1938]. *The Theatre and Its Double.* In *Collected Works Vol. 4.* London: Calder.

Arthur, Charles. 2002. "I Cyborg, by Kevin Warwick. Cringe-making world of 'Captain Cyborg.'" *The Independent*, 13 August 2002.

Asada, Akira. 1997. "Lovers Installation." Translated by Seiji Mizuta Lippit. <http://epidemic.cicv.fr/geogb/art/dtype/prj/loversgb.html>.

Ascott, Roy. 1999. "Seeing Double: Art and the Technology of Transcendence." In *Reframing Consciousness: Art, Mind and Technology*, edited by Roy Ascott, 66–71. Exeter: Intellect.

———. 1990. "Is There Love in the Telematic Embrace?" *Art Journal* 49, no. 3:241–247.

Aston, Elaine, and George Savona. 1991. *Theatre as Sign System: A Semiotics of Text and Performance.* London: Routledge.

Atchley, Dana. 2000. "Next Exit." Database entry, Digital Performance Archive. <http://art.ntu.ac.uk/dpa>.

Atkins, Barry. 2003. *More Than a Game: The Computer Game as Fictional Form.* Manchester: Manchester University Press.

August, Oliver. 1996. "America Looks to 'John Wayne' to Halt Microsoft's Stampede." *The Times*, 31 December 1996.

Auslander, Phillip. 2002. "Live from Cyberspace, or, I was sitting at my computer this guy appeared he thought I was a bot." *Performing Arts Journal* 70:16–21.

———. 1999. *Liveness: Performance in a Mediatized Culture.* London: Routledge.

———. 1997. *From Acting to Performance.* London: Routledge.

Ayres, Robert. 1998. *Obsolete Body/Alternate Strategies—Listening to Stelarc.* Live Art Letters 3 (February). Nottingham: Live Art Letters/Live Art Archive.

Azari (Fedele). 1975 [1919]. "Futurist Aerial Theatre." In Michael Kirby, *Futurist Performance*, 218–221. New York: PAJ Publications.

Banes, Sally. 1998. *Subversive Expectations: Performance Art and Paratheater in New York 1976–85*. Ann Arbor: University of Michigan Press.

Barber, Trudy. 1993. "VR Sex." Database entry, Digital Performance Archive. <http://art.ntu.ac.uk/dpa>.

Barrault, Jean-Louis. 1951 [1947]. *Reflections on the Theatre*. Translated by Barbara Wall. London: Theatre Book Club.

Barrett, Edward (ed.). 1988. *Text, ConText, and HyperText: Writing for the Computer*. Cambridge, Mass.: MIT Press.

———. 1992. *Sociomedia: Multimedia, Hypermedia and the Social Construction of Knowledge*. Cambridge, Mass.: MIT Press.

Barry, John A. 1992. *Second Front: Censorship and Propaganda in the Gulf War*. New York: Hill and Wang.

Barthes, Roland. 2000 [1980]. *Camera Lucida*. Translated by Richard Howard. London: Vintage.

———. 1987. *Image–Music–Text*. Translated by Stephen Heath. New York: Hill and Wang.

Bartosik, Kimberly. 2000. "Technogenderbody." *Body, Space and Technology* 1, no. 2. <http://www.brunel.ac.uk/depts/pfa/bstjournal/1nol2/journal1no2.htm>.

Baty, Phil. 2004. "Plug is pulled on e-university." *The Times Higher Education Supplement*, 30 April 2004.

Baudelaire, Charles. 1964. *The Painter of Modern Life and Other Essays*. Translated and edited by Jonathan Mayne. New York: Da Capo.

Baudrillard, Jean. 2003. "Requiem for the Media." In *The New Media Reader*, edited by Noah Wardrip-Fruin and Nick Montfort, 278–288. Cambridge, Mass.: MIT Press.

———. 1998. *Paroxysm: Interviews with Philippe Petit*. Translated by Chris Turner. London: Verso.

———. 1997. "The End of the Millenium, or the Countdown." Lecture delivered at the Institute of Contemporary Arts, London, 8 May 1997.

———. 1996. "Disneyworld Company". *CTHEORY*, 3/27/1996 <http://www.ctheory.net/text_file.asp?pick=158>.

———. 1995. *The Gulf War Did Not Take Place*. Translated by Paul Patton. Sydney: Power Publications.

———. 1994. *Simulacra and Simulation*. Translated by Sheila Faria Glaser. Ann Arbor: University of Michigan Press.

———. 1989. "Videowelt und Fraktales Subjekt." In *Philosophien der Neuen Technologie: Ars Electronica*, edited by Jean Baudrillard and Hannes Böhringer, Vilem Flusser, et al., 113–131. Berlin: Merve.

Bauman, Zygmunt. 1997. *Postmodernity and Its Discontents*. London: Polity Press.

Bayer, Herbert, Ise Gropius, and Walter Gropius (eds.). 1959. *Bauhaus 1919–1928*. Boston: Charles T. Branford.

Begusch, Harald. 1999. "Shells That Matter: The Digital Body as Aesthetic/Political Representation." *Performance Research* 4, no. 2:30–32.

Belbin, R. Meredith. 1993. *Team Roles at Work*. London: Butterworth/Heinemann.

Bell, David. 2001. *An Introduction to Cybercultures*. London and New York: Routledge.

Bell, Phaedre. 2000. "Dialogic Media Production and Inter-media Exchange." *Journal of Dramatic Theory and Criticism* (Spring 2000):41–55.

Benesch, Klaus. 1997. "Romantic Cyborgs: Technology, Authorship, and the Politics of Reproduction in Nineteenth-Century American Literature." *Node9* 1 (January 1997). <http://node9.phil3.uni-freiburg.de/1997/benesch2.html>.

Benjamin, Andrew. 1994. *Object.Painting*. London: Academy Editions.

Benjamin, Walter. 1999 [1936]. "The Work of Art in the Age of Mechanical Reproduction." In *Illuminations*, translated by Harry Zorn, 211–245. London: Pimlico.

———. 1999 [1950]. "Theses on the Philosophy of History". In *Illuminations*, translated by Harry Zorn, 245–255. London: Pimlico.

———. 1999 [1939]. "What is Epic Theatre." In *Illuminations*, translated by Harry Zorn, 144–151. London: Pimlico.

———. 1979 [1931]. "A Small History of Photography." In *One Way Street*, translated by Edmund Jephcott and Kingsley Shorter, 240–257. London: NLB.

Berger, Arthur Asa. 2002. *Video Games: A Popular Culture Phenomenon*. London: Transaction.

Berghaus, Günter. 1998. *Italian Futurist Theatre, 1909–1944*. Oxford: Oxford University Press.

Bergman, David. 1993. "Introduction." In *Camp Grounds: Style and Homosexuality*, edited by David Bergman. Amherst: University of Massachusetts Press.

Berners-Lee, Tim. 2000. *Weaving the Web*. New York and London: Texere.

Bernstein, Mark. 1999. "Patterns of Hypertext." <http://www.eastgate.com/patterns/prints.html>.

Bey, Hakim. 1997. "Notes for CTHEORY". In *Digital Delirium*, edited by Arthur and Marilouise Kroker, 152–155. New York: St. Martin's.

Bharucha, Rustom. 1990. *Theatre and the World*. South Asia Books.

Bilderwerfer. 2000. "be right back/ The Stolen Identity Project." Database entry, Digital Performance Archive. <http://art.ntu.ac.uk/dpa>.

Billington, Michael. 1996. "Footage and Footlights." *The Guardian*, 23 November 1996.

Birkerts, Sven. 1999. *Readings*. Saint Paul, Minn.: Graywolf Press.

Birringer, Johannes. 2002. "Dance and Media Technologies." *Performing Arts Journal* 70:84–93.

———. 2002. "Dance and Interactivity." *Gramma: Journal of Theory and Criticism* 10:19–40.

———. 1998. *Media and Performance: Along the Border*. Baltimore: Johns Hopkins University Press.

————. 1997. "Before Night Falls." Database entry, Digital Performance Archive. <http://art.ntu.ac.uk/dpa>.

Blast Theory. 1998. "Kidnap." Database entry, Digital Performance Archive. <http://art.ntu.ac.uk/dpa>.

Blau, Herbert. 2002. "The Human Nature of the Bot." *Performing Arts Journal* 70:22–24.

————. 1987. *The Eye of Prey: Subversions of the Postmodern*. Bloomington: Indiana University Press.

Bleeker, Maaike. 1999. "Death, Digitization and Dys-appearance." *Performance Research* 4, no. 2:1–7.

Blossom, Roberts. 1966. "On Filmstage." *TDR: Tulane Drama Review* 2, no. 1:68–73.

Blumenthal, Bud. 1999. "Rivermen." Database entry, Digital Performance Archive. <http://art.ntu.ac.uk/dpa>.

Boal, Augusto. 1992. *Games for Actors and Non-Actors*. Translated by Adrian Jackson. New York: Routledge.

————. 1985 [1974]. *Theatre of the Oppressed*. Translated by Charles McBride and Maria-Odilia Leal McBride. New York: Theatre Communications.

Bodies in Flight and spell#7 performance. 2000. "Doublehappiness2." Database entry, Digital Performance Archive. <http://art.ntu.ac.uk/dpa>.

Bollier, David. 1995. *The Future of Community and Personal Identity in the Coming Electronic Culture: A Report of the Third Annual Aspen Institute Roundtable on Information Technology*. Aspen Colo.: Aspen Institute.

Bolter, Jay. 1990. *Writing Space: The Computer in the History of Literacy*. Hillsdale, N.J.: Lawrence Erlbaum.

Bolter, Jay, and Diane Gromala. 2003. *Windows and Mirrors*. Cambridge, Mass.: MIT Press.

Bolter, Jay, and Richard Grusin. 1999. *Remediation*. Cambridge, Mass.: MIT Press.

Boon, Marcus. 1996. "Phone Sex Is Cool: Chat-Lines as Superconductors." *Women & Performance: A journal of feminist theory* 9, no. 1:161–178.

Borsook, Paulina. 2000. *Cyberselfish: A Critical Romp Through the Terribly Libertarian Culture of High Tech*. New York: Public Affairs.

Booth, J. 1998. "Unmasking the Greek mysteries: Virtual reality revives the oldest theatre." *The Times*, 25 November 1998.

Booth, Mark. 1999. "*Campe-toi!*: On the Origins and Definitions of Camp." In *Camp: Queer Aesthetics and the Performing Subject: A Reader*, edited by Fabio Cleto, 66–79. Edinburgh: Edinburgh University Press.

Borgman, Albert. 1999. *Holding On to Reality: The Nature of Information at the Turn of the Millennium*. Chicago: University of Chicago Press.

Bostock, Cliff. 1999. "Cyberwork: The Archetypal Imagination in New Realms of Ensoulment." <http://soulworks.net/writings/essays/site_05.html>.

Bowden, Richard, Pakorn Kaewtrakulpong, and Martin Lewin. 2002. "Jeremiah: The Face of Computer Vision." *Smart Graphics: 2nd International Symposium on Smart Graphics*, 124–28. Hawthorn, N.Y.: ACM International Conference Proceedings Series.

Bowers, John, and Sally Jane Norman, Heike Staff, Detlev Schwabe, Lawrence Wallen, Monika Fleischmann, and Yngve Sundblad. 1998. "Extended Performances: Evaluation and Comparison." <http://cid.nada.kth.se/pdf/cid_80.pdf.>.

Braun, Edward (ed.). 1969. *Meyerhold on Theatre*. London: Methuen.

Braunarts. 2004. "braunarts." <http://www.braunarts.com/>.

Brecht, Bertolt. 1964. "The Radio as an Apparatus of Communications." In *Brecht on Theatre*, edited and translated by John Willet. New York: Hill and Wang.

Britton, Andrew. 1999. "For Interpretation: Notes Against Camp." In *Camp: Queer Aesthetics and the Performing Subject: A Reader*, edited by Fabio Cleto, 136–142. Edinburgh: Edinburgh University Press.

Broadhurst, Susan. 2004. "Interaction, Reaction and Performance: The Jeremiah Project." *TDR: The Drama Review* 48, no. 4 (December):47–57.

———. 2000. *Liminal Acts: A Critical Overview Of Contemporary Performance and Theory*. London: Cassel Academic.

Brockman, John. 1996. *Digerati: Encounters with the Cyber Elite*. London: Orion Business Books.

———. 1995. *The Third Culture: Beyond the Scientific Revolution*. New York: Simon and Schuster.

Bromberg, Ellen. 1998. "Falling to Earth." Database entry, Digital Performance Archive. <http://art.ntu.ac.uk/dpa>.

Brook, Peter. 1968. *The Empty Space*. London: MacGibbon & Kee Ltd.

Brooks, Michael. 2000. "Global Brain." *New Scientist*, 24 June 2000, 22–27.

Brooks, Rodney A. 2002. *Robot: The Future of Flesh and Machines*. London: Penguin.

Brown, Paul. 1998. Keynote speech at the opening of *FOLDBACK*, presented by the Australian Network for Art and Technology (ANAT), Telstra Adelaide Festival of the Arts, 8 March 1998. <http://www.anat.org.au/archived/foldback/fb_intro.htm>.

Bruckner, J. D. R. 1996. "*An Epidog*—Mabou Mines." *New York Times*, 30 January 1996. <http://www.inch.com/~kteneyck/epidog.html>.

The Builders Association. 1999. "Jet Lag." Database entry, Digital Performance Archive. <http://art.ntu.ac.uk/dpa>.

———. 1997. "Jump Cut (Faust)." Database entry, Digital Performance Archive. <http://art.ntu.ac.uk/dpa>.

———. 2000. "Opera." Database entry, Digital Performance Archive. <http://art.ntu.ac.uk/dpa>.

Bull, Martyn. 2005. "Tech Boost for the Arts." *The Times Higher Education Supplement*, 3 June 2005.

Bürger, Peter. 1984. *Theory of the Avant-Garde*. Translated by Michael Shaw. Minneapolis: University of Minnesota Press.

Burgin, Victor. 2002. "Jenni"s Room: Exhibitionism and Solitude." In *CTRL {SPACE}: Rhetorics of Surveillance from Bentham to Big Brother*, edited by Thomas Y. Levin, Ursula Frohne, and Peter Weibel, 228–235. Karlsruhe: ZKM Centre for Art and Media, and Cambridge, Mass.: MIT Press.

Burk, Juli. 1999. "ATHEMOO and the Future Present: Shaping Cyberspace into a Theatre Working Place." In *Theatre in Cyberspace*, edited by Stephen A. Schrum, 109–134. New York: Peter Lang.

Burian, Jarka. 1971. *The Scenography of Josef Svoboda*. Middletown, Conn.: Wesleyan University Press.

Burnham, Jack. 1968. "Systems Esthetics." *Artforum* 7, no. 1 (September 1968).

———. 1969. "Real Time Systems." *Artforum* 8, no. 1 (September 1969).

Burt, Susan, and Clive Barker. 1980. "IOU and the New Vocabulary of Performance Art." *Theatre Quarterly* 10, no. 37 (Spring):70–94.

Butler, Judith.1993. *Bodies That Matter*. New York: Routledge.

———. 1990. *Gender Trouble: Feminism and the Subversion of Identity*. New York: Routledge.

Cage, Mary Crystal. 1995. "Actors Joined by Computer Imagery in U. of Kansas Production." *Chronicle of Higher Education*, 30 June 1995.

Calandra, Denis. 1976. "George Kaiser's *From Morn to Midnight*: The Nature of Expressionist Performance." *Theatre Quarterly* 6, no. 21:45–54.

Callesen, Jorgen, Marika Kajo, and Karine Nilsen. 2004. "The Performance Animation Toolbox: Developing Tools and Methods Through Artistic Research." In *New Visions in Performance: The Impact of Digital Technologies*, edited by Gavin Carver and Colin Beardon, 69–92. Lisse, The Netherlands: Swets and Zeitlinger.

Campanella, Thomas J. 2001. "Eden by Wire: Webcameras and the Telepresent Landscape." In *The Robot in the Garden: Telerobotics and Telepistemology in the Age of the Internet*, edited by Ken Goldberg, 22–46. Cambridge, Mass.: MIT Press.

Canadian Theatre Encyclopaedia. 2003. "Robert Lepage." <http://www.canadiantheatre.com/dict.pl>.

Candy, Linda, and Ernest Edmonds (eds.). 2002. *Explorations in Art and Technology*. London: Springer.

Capek, Karel. 1923. *R.U.R. (Rossum's Universal Robots)*. Translated by Paul Selver. Garden City, N.Y.: Doubleday.

Carey John. 1988. *Communication as Culture*. Boston: Unwin Hyman.

Carlson, Marvin. 1996. *Performance: A Critical Introduction*. London and New York: Routledge.

———. 1993. *Places of Performance: The Semiotics of Theatre Architecture*. Ithaca, N.Y.: Cornell University Press.

Caruth, Cathy (ed.). 1995. *Trauma: Explorations in Memory*. Baltimore: Johns Hopkins University Press.

Cassell, Justine, and Henry Jenkins (eds.). 1998. *From Barbie to Mortal Combat: Gender and Computer Games*. Cambridge, Mass.: MIT Press.

Causey, Matthew. 2002. "The Aesthetics of Disappearance and the Politics of Visibility in the Performance of Technology." *Gramma* 10:59–72.

————. 1999. "Screen Test of the Double: The Uncanny Performer in the Space of Technology." *Theatre Journal* 51, no. 4 (December 1999):383–394.

————. 1999. "Postorganic Performance: The Appearance of Theater in Virtual Spaces." In *Cyberspace Textuality: Computer Technology and Literary Theory*, edited by Marie-Laure Ryan, 182–201. Bloomington: Indiana University Press.

Ceperkovic, Slavika, and Michelle Kasprzak. 2000. "take take, cake cake." Database entry, Digital Performance Archive. <http://art.ntu.ac.uk/dpa>.

Chalmers, Jessica. 1998. "All the World's a Cyber Stage: The State of Online Theater." <http://www.villagevoice.com/arts/9849/chalmers.shtml>.

Chameleons Group. 2000. "Chameleons 3: Net Congestion." Database entry, Digital Performance Archive. <http://art.ntu.ac.uk/dpa>.

Chesher, Chris. 2002. "Why the Digital Computer is Dead." *CTHEORY*, 4 April 2002. <http://www.ctheory.net/text_file.asp?pick=334>.

Choreotronics. 1997. *Byte City*. Database entry, Digital Performance Archive. <http://art.ntu.ac.uk/dpa>.

Clapp, Susanna. 2003. "And for my Next Trick . . ." *The Observer*, 27 July 2003.

Clarke, Julie. 2001. "CO3. Company in Space—Hellen Sky and John McCormick." *Body, Space and Technology* 2, no. 3. <http://www.brunel.ac.uk/depts/pfa/bstjournal/2no1/journal2no1.htm>.

Cleaver, Harry. 1996. "The Space of Cyberspace: Body Politics, Frontiers and Enclosures." *Women & Performance: A Journal of Feminist Theory* 9, no. 1:239–248.

Cleto, Fabio. 1999. "Introduction: Queering the Camp." In *Camp: Queer Aesthetics and the Performing Subject: A Reader*, edited by Fabio Cleto, 1–42. Edinburgh: Edinburgh University Press.

Clynes, Manfred, and Nathan Kline. 1995 [1960]. "Cyborgs and Space." In *The Cyborg Handbook*, edited by Chris Hables Gray, 29–34. New York and London: Routledge.

CNET. 1998. "Movers and Shakers: George Coates." <http://www.cnet.com/Content/Voices/Movers/coates.html>.

Coates, George. 2000. "Blind Messengers." Database entry, Digital Performance Archive. <http://art.ntu.ac.uk/dpa>.

Cohen, David. 2001. "Machine Head." *New Scientist,* 24 February 2001, 26–29.

Collins, Susan. 2004. "The Actual and the Imagined." In *Networked Narrative Environments as Imaginary Spaces of Being*, edited by Andrea Zapp, 45–61. Manchester: MIRIAD/FACT.

Company in Space. 2000*a*. "Escape Velocity." Database entry, Digital Performance Archive. <http://art.ntu.ac.uk/dpa>.

———. 2000*b*. "home, not alone." Database entry, Digital Performance Archive. <http://art.ntu.ac.uk/dpa>.

Conquergood, Dwight. 1995. "Of Caravans and Carnivals: Performance Studies in Motion." *TDR: The Drama Review* 39, no. 4:137–141.

Cook, Jeffrey J. 1997. *Myths, Robots and Procreation.* <http://murlin.va.com.au/metabody/text/mythrobopro.htm>.

Cooper, Alan. 1999. *The Inmates Are Running the Asylum.* Indianapolis: Sams-Macmillan Computer Publishing.

Corpos Informáticos Research Group. 1999. "Entrasite." Database entry, Digital Performance Archive. <http://art.ntu.ac.uk/dpa>.

Connor, Steven. 1999. "The Impossibility of the Present: Or, from the Contemporary to the Contemporal." In *Literature and the Contemporary: Fictions and Theories of the Present*, edited by Roger Luckhurst and Peter Marks, 15–35, Harlow, Essex: Pearson/Longman.

Copeland, R. 1999. "Cunningham, Collage, and the Computer." *Performing Arts Journal* 21, no. 63:42–54.

Cotton, Bob, and Richard Oliver. 1992. *Understanding Hypermedia.* London: Phaidon Press.

Couchet, Edmond. 1994. "Between the Real and the Virtual." *Annual InterCommunication '94*, Tokyo: ICC.

Courchesne, Luc. 1996. "Hall of Shadows." Database entry, Digital Performance Archive. <http://art.ntu.ac.uk/dpa>.

Coveney, Michael. 1992. "Needles and Opium." *The Observer*, 3 May 1992.

Coyne, Richard. 1999. *Technoromanticism: Digital Narrative, Holism, and the Romance of the Real.* Cambridge, Mass.: MIT Press.

Craig, Sandy (ed.). 1980. *Dreams and Deconstructions: Alternative Theatre in Britain.* Ambergate, Derbyshire: Amber Lane Press.

Curious.com. 1998. "Random Acts of Memory." Database entry, Digital Performance Archive. <http://art.ntu.ac.uk/dpa>.

Danet, Brenda, Tsameret Wachenhauser, Haya Bechar-Israeli, Amos Cividalli, and Yehudit Rosenbaum-Tamari. 1995. "Curtain Time 20:00 GMT: Experiments with Virtual Theater on Internet Relay Chat." <http://jcmc.indiana.edu/vol1/issue2/contents.html>.

Davies, Char. 1998. "Osmose: Notes on Being in Immersive Virtual Space." *Digital Creativity* 9, no. 2:65–74.

Davies, James. 2002. "Understanding the social and cultural processes behind the continual male dominance of computer and videogame production and consumption." Graduate dissertation, Middlesex University, May 2002.

Davis, Douglas. 1999. "Terrible Beauty." Database entry, Digital Performance Archive. <http://art.ntu.ac.uk/dpa>.

Dèak, Frantisek. 1975. "The Influence of Italian Futurism in Russia." *TDR: The Drama Review* 19, no. 4 (December):88–94.

de Certeau, Michel. 1984. *The Practice of Everyday Life*. Berkeley: University of California Press.

Deegan, Marilyn. 1996. "Electronic Publishing." In *New Technologies for the Humanities*, edited by Christine Mullins, Stephanie Kenna, Marilyn Deegan, and Seamus Ross. East Grinstead, UK: Bowker.

de Garis, Hugo. 2001. Interview in *Battle of the Robots: The Hunt for AI*. Television documentary, Oxford Film and Television/ Channel 4, 13 October 2001.

deLahunta, Scott. 2002. "Virtual Reality and Performance." *Performing Arts Journal* 70:105–114.

———. 2000. "Virtual Ephemerality: The Art Of Digital Dancing." *maska: Journal for performing arts*. <http://www.ljudmila.org/maska/eng/dancing.htm>.

de Landa, Manuel. 1995. "Out of Control: Trialogue." *Wired* Magazine, <http://www.srl.org/interviews/out.of.control.html>.

Deleuze, Gilles. 1994. *Difference and Repetition*. Translated by Paul Patton. New York: Columbia University Press.

———. 1986. *Cinema I: The Movement-Image*. Translated by Hugh Tomlinson and Barbara Habberjam. Minneapolis: University of Minnesota Press.

Deleuze, Gilles, and Felix Guattari. 1988 [1980]. *A Thousand Plateaus: Capitalism and Schizophrenia*. Translated by Brian Massumi. London: Athlone Press.

de Marinis, Marco. 1993. *The Semiotics of Performance*. Translated by Aine O'Healy. Bloomington and Indianopolis: Indiana University Press.

Denzin, Norman. 1991. *Images of Postmodern Society*. London: Sage.

Depero, Fortunato. 1971 [1916]. "Notes on the Theatre." In Michael Kirby, *Futurist Performance*, 207–210. New York: PAJ Publications.

Derrida, Jacques. 1995. "The Almost Nothing of the Unpresentable" and "Unsealing ("the old new language")." In *Points . . . : Interviews 1974–1994*. Stanford, Calif.: Stanford University Press.

———. 1987 [1980]. *The Postcard*. Translated by Alan Bass. Chicago: University of Chicago Press.

———. 1981 [1970]. "The Double Session." In *Dissemination*. Translated by Barbara Johnson. Chicago: University of Chicago Press.

———. 1976 [1967]. *Of Grammatology*. Baltimore: Johns Hopkins University Press.

———. 1978. *Writing and Difference*. London: Routledge and Kegan Paul.

Dery, Mark. 1996. *Escape Velocity: Cyberculture at the End of the Century*. New York: Grove Press.

Descartes, René. 1975 [1637]. *A Discourse on Method*. London: Dent.

———. 1907 [1641]. "Meditations on the First Philosophy." In *The Method, Meditations, and Selections from the Principles*. 14th ed. Translated by John Veitch. Edinburgh and London: William Blackwood and Sons.

Diamond, Sara. 2001. "Code Zebra: Theorizing Discourse and Play." <http://culturalpolicy. uchicago.edu/conf2001/papers/diamond.html>.

Dibbell, Julian. 1999. *My Tiny Life: Crime and Passion in a Virtual World*. London: Fourth Estate.

————. 1994. "A Rape in Cyberspace; Or How an Evil Clown, a Haitian trickster Spirit, Two Wizards, and a Cast of Dozens Turned a Database into a Society." *Flame Wars: The Discourse of Cyberculture*, edited by Mark Dery, 237–262. Durham, N.C.: Duke University Press.

Diller, Elizabeth, and Ricardo Scofidio. 1999. "Refresh." Database entry, Digital Performance Archive. <http://art.ntu.ac.uk/dpa>.

Dinkla, Söke. "The Art of Narrative—Towards the *Floating Work of Art*." In *New Screen Media: Cinema/Art/Narrative*, edited by Martin Rieser and Andrea Zapp, 27–41. London: British Film Institute.

Dishman, Eric. 2002. "Performative In(ter)ventions: Designing Future Technologies Through Synergetic Performance." In *Teaching Performance Studies*, edited by Nathan Stucky and Cynthia Wimmer, 235–246. Carbondale: Southern Illinois University Press.

Dixon, Joan Broadhurst, and Eric J. Cassidy (eds.). 1998. *Virtual Futures: Cyberotics, Technology and Post-Human Pragmatism*. London and New York: Routledge.

Dixon, Steve. 2003*a*. "Absent Fiends: Internet Theatre, Posthuman Bodies and the Interactive Void." *Performance Arts International*, 'Presence' online issue. <http://www.mdx.ac.uk/www/epai/ presencesite/index.html>.

————. 2003*b*. "Metal Gender." *CTHEORY* 26, nos. 1–2. <http://www.ctheory.net/text_file. asp?pick=3842004>.

————. 1999*a*. "Digits, Discourse and Documentation: Performance Research and Hypermedia." *TDR: The Drama Review* 43, no. 1:152–175.

————. 1999*b*. "Remediating Theatre in a Digital Proscenium." *Digital Creativity* 10, no. 3:135–142.

Docherty, Thomas. 1999. "Now, Here, This." In *Literature and the Contemporary: Fictions and Theories of the Present*, edited by Roger Luckhurst and Peter Marks, 50–62, Harlow, Essex: Pearson/Longman.

Dodds, Sherril. 2001. *Dance on Screen*. Basingstoke: Palgrave.

Dodson, Sean. 2002. "Institute of Computer Art." *The Guardian*, 24 October 2002.

Dodsworth, Clark (ed.). 1998. *Digital Illusion*. New York: ACM Press.

Domike, Steffi, Michael Mateas, and Paul Vanouse. 1999. "Terminal Time." Database entry, Digital Performance Archive. <http://art.ntu.ac.uk/dpa>.

Dove, Toni. 2004. "Haunting the Movie: Embodied Interface/Sensory Cinema." In *New Visions in Performance: The Impact of New Technologies*, edited by Gavin Carver and Colin Beardon, 107–120. Lisse, The Netherlands: Swets and Zietlinger.

————. 2001. "Artificial Changelings Overview." <http://www.tonidove.com/af_overview_hold.html>.

Dr-K. 2000. *A Complete Hacker's Handbook*. London: Carlton Books.

Dreyfus, Hubert. 2001. *On the Internet*. London: Routledge.

D'Souza, Karen. 2000. "From online to onstage, kids construct musical for S.J. theater." *San Jose Mercury News*, 21 May 2000.

Duckworth, William. 1995. *Talking Music: Conversations with John Cage, Philip Glass, Laurie Anderson, and Five Generations of American Experimental Composers*. New York: Schirmer Books.

Durkin, Scott C. 2000. "Shared Identity." Database entry, Digital Performance Archive. <http://art.ntu.ac.uk/dpa>.

Dyens, Ollivier. 2001. *Metal and Flesh: The Evolution of Man: Technology Takes Over*. Cambridge, Mass.: MIT Press.

Dyer, Chris. 2000. "Open Stages." <http://www.openstages.com/>.

————. 1999. "Virtual_Stages: An Interactive Model of Performance Spaces for Creative Teams, Technicians and Students." *Digital Creativity* 10, no. 3:143–152.

Dyer, Richard. 1999. "It's Being So Camp as Keeps Us Going." In *Camp: Queer Aesthetics and the Performing Subject: A Reader*, edited by Fabio Cleto. Edinburgh: Edinburgh University Press.

Dyson, Frances. 1996. "When Is the Ear Pierced? The Clashes of Sound, Technology, and Cyberculture." In *Immersed in Technology: Art and Virtual Environments,* edited by Mary Anne Moser with Douglas MacLeod, 73–101. Cambridge, Mass.: MIT Press.

Dyson, George B. 1998. *Darwin Among the Machines: The Evolution of Global Intelligence*. New York: Helix Books.

E.A.T. (Experiments in Art and Technology). 2003. "9 Evenings: Theatre and Engineering." Event Program, October 1966, in *The New Media Reader*, edited by Noah Wardrip-Fruin and Nick Montfort, 214–215. Cambridge, Mass.: MIT Press.

Eagleton, Terry. 2003*a*. *After Theory*. London: Penguin/Allen Lane.

————. 2003*b*. "Bin Laden sure didn't read any beer mats." *Times Higher Education Supplement*, 3 October 2003.

————. 1986. "Capitalism, Modernism and Postmodernism." In *Against the Grain: Selected Essays, 1975–1985*. London: Verso.

Eco, Umberto. 1986. *Travels in Hyperreality: Essays*. Translated by William Weaver. San Diego: Harcourt Brace Javonovich.

Ehn, Pelle. 1998. "Manifesto for a Digital Bauhaus." *Digital Creativity* 9, no. 4:207–217.

Elam, Keir. 1980. *The Semiotics of Theatre and Drama*. London: Routledge.

Ellipsis. 1997. "Untitled." Database entry, Digital Performance Archive. <http://art.ntu.ac.uk/dpa>.

Elrich, Matthew. 1996. "Turing, My Love." *Women & Performance: A Journal of Feminist Theory* 9, no. 1:187–204.

Ess, Charles (ed.). 1996. *Philosophical Perspectives in Computer-Mediated Communication.* Albany: State University of New York Press.

Etchells, Tim. 1999. *Certain Fragments.* London and New York: Routledge.

Farmer, F. Randall. 2001 [1992]. "Social Dimensions of Habitat's Citizenry." In *True Names and Vernor Vinge and the Opening of the Cyberspace Frontier*, edited by James Frenkel, 205–212. New York: Tor.

Farrar, Steve. 2004. "Brenda's Loyalty Card Lays her Private Life Secrets Open." *Times Higher Education Supplement*, 2 April 2004.

Fillia. 1971 [1927]. "Mechanical Sensuality" (Sensualità Meccanica). In Michael Kirby, *Futurist Performance*, 286–288. New York: PAJ Publications.

Filliou, Robert. 1970. *Teaching and Learning as Performance Arts.* Cologne and New York: Verlag Gebr Koenig.

Fischer-Lichte, Erika. 1992. *The Semiotics of Theatre.* Translated by Jeremy Gaines and Doris L. Jones. Bloomington and Indianapolis: Indiana University Press.

Fisher, Philip. 2003. "Alladeen." <http://www.britishtheatreguide.info/reviews/alladeen-rev.htm>.

Floating Point Unit. 1997. "emergent(c) room." Database entry, Digital Performance Archive. <http://art.ntu.ac.uk/dpa>.

Forced Entertainment. 1999. "Spin." Database entry, Digital Performance Archive. <http://art.ntu.ac.uk/dpa>.

Formenti, Carlo. 1991. "La Guerra Senza Nemici" (The War Without Enemies). In *Guerra Virtuale e Guerra Reale: Riflessioni sul Conflicto del Golfo* (The Virtual and the Real War: Reflections on the Gulf War), edited by Tiziana Villani and Pierre Dalla Vigna. Milan: A.C. Mimeesis.

Fornäs, Johan. 1998. "Digital Borderlands: Identity and Interactivity in Culture, Media and Communications." *Nordicom Review* 19, no. 1:27–38.

Foster, Hal. 2000. *Compulsive Beauty.* Cambridge, Mass.: MIT Press.

Foucault, Michel. 1997. *Dits et Ecrits.* New York: New Press.

———. 1979. *Discipline and Punish: The Birth of the Prison.* New York: Vintage.

Fox, Barry. 1995. "The Rom Revolution." *The Times: Interface*, 6 December 1995.

Franck, Karen A. 1995. "When I enter virtual reality, what body do I leave behind?" In *Architectural Design Profile No. 118: Architects in Cyberspace I*, 20–23. London: Academy Edition.

Frazer, James. 1925 [1922]. *The Golden Bough: A Study in Magic and Religion.* London: Macmillan.

Freeman, John. 2000. "I accuse." *The Guardian*, 4 October, p.14.

Freud, Sigmund. 1985 [1919]. "The Uncanny." In *Pelican Freud Library*, vol. 14, translated by James Strachey, 339–376. Harmondsworth: Penguin.

———. 1961 [1930]. *Civilization and Its Discontents*. Translated by James Strachey. New York: Norton.

Fried, Michael. 1968. "Art and Objecthood." In *Minimal Art: A Critical Anthology*, edited by Gregory Battock, 116–147. New York: Dutton.

Frisk, Brian. 2002. *We are Tin, We are Titans. We Are Robots.* <http://www.wearerobots.com>.

Fuchs, Mathias. 2001. "From First Person Shooter to Multi-User Knowledge Spaces." <http://www.cosignconference.org/cosign2001/papers/Fuchs.pdf>.

Fukuyama, Francis. 1992. *The End of History and the Last Man*. Harmondsworth: Penguin.

Gabor, Dennis. 1971. "Technological Civilization and Man's Future." In *Cybernetics, Art and Ideas*, edited by Jasia Reichardt, 18–24. London: Studio Vista.

Gale, David. 1985. "Against Slowness." *Performance Magazine*, 33 (February/March 1985):22–26.

Gardner, Lyn. 2003. "Pure Genies." <http://www.guardian.co.uk/arts/critic/feature/0,1169,999209,00.html>.

———. 2002. "Stitching". *The Guardian*, 5 August 2002.

Gelernter, David. 1994. *The Muse in the Machine: Computers and Creative Thought*. London: Fourth Estate.

———. 1991. *Mirror Worlds*. New York: Oxford University Press.

Gharavi, Lance. 1999. "i.e. VR: Experiments in New Media and Performance." In *Theatre in Cyberspace*, edited by Stephen A. Schrum, 249–272. New York: Peter Lang.

Giannachi, Gabriella. 2004. *Virtual Theatres: An Introduction*. London: Routledge.

Gibson, William. 1988. *Mona Lisa Overdrive*. Toronto and New York: Bantam Books.

———. 1984. *Neuromancer*. New York: Ace.

Glidden, Rob. 1996. "Kinetix Ships Character Studio." *The WAVE Report on Digital Media* 603 (19 July 1996) <http://www.wave-report.com/>.

Goffman, Erving. 1959. *The Presentation of Self in Everyday Life*. Garden City, N.Y.: Doubleday.

Goldberg, Ken (ed.). 2001. *The Robot in the Garden: Telerobotics and Telepistemoogy in the Age of the Internet*. Cambridge, Massachusetts: MIT Press.

Goldberg, RoseLee. 2000. *Laurie Anderson*. London: Thames and Hudson.

———. 1998. *Performance: Live Art since the 60s*. London: Thames and Hudson.

———. 1979. *Performance Art: From Futurism to the Present*. London and New York: Thames and Hudson.

Gómez-Peña, Guillermo. 2002. "In Defence of Performance Art." Lecture delivered at the Bluecoat Art Gallery, Liverpool, 18 September 2002.

———. 2000. *Dangerous Border Crossings: The Artist Talks Back*. London: Routledge.

———. 1996a. *Friendly Cannibals*. San Francisco: Artspace Books.

————. 1996*b*. "The Virtual Barrio @ the Other Frontier (or the Chicano Interneta)." In *Clicking In: Hot Links To A Digital Culture,* edited by Lynn Hershman Leeson, 173–179. Seattle: Bay Press.

Goodman, Lizbeth. 1997. "Representing Gender/Representing Self: A Reflection on Role Playing in Performance Theory and Practice." In *Drama on Drama*, edited by Nichole Boireau. London: Macmillan.

Goodman, Lizbeth, Tony Coe, and Huw Williams. 1998. "The Multimedia Bard: Plugged and Unplugged." *New Theatre Quarterly,* February 1998, 20–42.

Goodman, N. 1992 [1976]. "Art and Authenticity." In *Languages of Art*, edited by B. Swann. Indianapolis: Hackett Publishing.

Goody, Jack. 1997. *Representations and Contradictions: Ambivalance Towards Images, Theatre, Fiction, Relics, Sexuality*. London: Blackwell.

Gordon Craig, Edward. 1983 [1908]. "The Actor and the Ubermarionette." In *Craig on Theatre,* edited by J. Michael Walton. London: Methuen.

Gordon, Mel. 1995. "Meyerhold's Biomechanics." In *Acting Reconsidered*, edited by Phillip B. Zarrilli, 85–107. London: Routledge.

Gorman, Brian. 1997. "Elsinore Houses One-Man Wonder." *Ottawa Sun*, 10 September 1997.

Grant, Steve. 1980. "Voicing the Protest: The New Writers." In *Dreams and Deconstructions: Alternative Theatre in Britain*, edited by Sandy Craig, 116–144. Ambergate, Derbyshire: Amber Lane Press.

Grassi, Davide. 1999. "Nuclear Body." Database entry, Digital Performance Archive. <http://art.ntu.ac.uk/dpa>.

Grau, Oliver. 2003. *Virtual Art: From Illusion To Immersion*. Cambridge, Mass.: MIT Press.

Gray, Chris Hables (ed.). 1995. *The Cyborg Handbook*. New York and London: Routledge.

Greenfield, Susan. 2003. *Tomorrow's People: How the 21st Century is Changing the Way We Think and Feel*. London: Allen Lane/Penguin Press.

Gromala, Diane. 2002. "Gromala." <http://www.lcc.gatech.edu/~gromala/art.htm#virtual>.

————. 1996. "Pain and Subjectivity in Virtual Reality." In *Clicking In: Hot Links to a Digital Culture,* edited by Lynn Hershman Leeson, 222–237. Seattle: Bay Press.

Gromala, Diane, and Yacov Sharir. 1996. "Dancing with the Virtual Dervish: Virtual Bodies." In *Immersed in Technology,* edited by Mary Anne Moser with Douglas MaCleod, 281–286. Cambridge, Mass.: MIT Press.

Groot, Paul. 1999. "Streaming Video Killed the CD-ROM: On Modern Dance, Merce Cunningham, William Forsythe, Lara Croft and Olivier Messiaen." <http://www.mediamatic.net/article-200.5740.html>.

Grossman, Wendy M. 2004. "A Refresher in Basic Geek." *Times Higher Education Supplement*, 6 February 2004.

Gross, David. 1985. "Temporality and the Modern State." *Theory and Society* 14:53–82.

Grosz, Elizabeth. 2001. "In-Between: The Natural in Architecture and Culture." In *Architecture from the Outside: Essays on Virtual and Real Space*. Cambridge, Mass.: MIT Press.

Grotowski, Jerzy. 1968. *Towards a Poor Theatre*. Edited by Eugenio Barba. London: Methuen.

Grusin, Richard. 1996. "What Is an Electronic Author? Theory and the Technological Fallacy." In *Virtual Realities and Their Discontents*, edited by Robert Markley, 39–54. Baltimore: Johns Hopkins University Press.

Grzinic, Marina. 2001. "Exposure Time, the Aura, and Telerobotics." In *The Robot in the Garden: Telerobotics and Telepistemology in the Age of the Internet*, edited by Ken Goldberg, 214–225. Cambridge, Mass.: MIT Press.

Hafner, Katie, and Matthew Lyon. 1996. *Where Wizards Stay Up Late: The Origins of the Internet*. New York: Simon and Schuster.

Halbertsam, Judith, and Ira Livingston (eds.). 1995. *Posthuman Bodies*. Bloomington: Indiana University Press.

Hall, Doug, and Sally Jo Fifer (eds.). 1990. *Illuminating Video: An Essential Guide to Video Art*. New York: Aperture Foundation.

Hanardt, John G. 2000. *The Worlds of Nam June Paik*. New York: Guggenheim Museum Publications.

Hand, Richard J., and Michael Wilson. 2002. *Grand Guignol: The French Theatre of Horror*. Exeter: University of Exeter Press.

Haraway, Donna. 1997. *Modest_Witness@Second_Millenium, FemaleMan©_Meets_OncoMouse™*. London: Routledge.

————. 1991. "The Actors are Cyborg, Nature is Coyote, and the Geography Is Elsewhere: Postscript to Cyborgs at Large." In *Technoculture*, edited by C. Penley and A. Ross, 25–26. Minneapolis: University of Minnesota Press.

————. 1991 [1985]. "A Cyborg Manifesto: Science, Technology and Socialist-feminism in the late Twentieth Century." In Donna Haraway, *Simians, Cyborgs and Women: The Reinvention of Nature*, 149–181. London: Free Association Books.

Harries, Dan (ed.). 2002. *The New Media Book*. London: BFI.

Harris, Stuart. 1995. "Virtual Reality Drama." In *Cyberlife!*, 497–520. Indianapolis: Sams.

————. 1994. "Much ado about IRC." *Online Access* 9:28–32.

Harvey, David. 1989. *The Condition of Postmodernity: An Enquiry into the Origins of Social Change*. Oxford: Blackwell.

Hassan, Ihab. 1987. *The Postmodern Turn: Essays in Postmodern Theory and Culture*. Columbus: Ohio State University Press.

————. 1977. "Prometheus as Performer: Towards a Posthumanist Culture?" In *Performance in Postmodern Culture*, edited by Michael Benamou and Charles Caramello. Madison, Wis.: Coda Press.

Hays, Matthew. 2002. "Theatrical Premonitions: Robert Lepage's eerily prophetic 9/11 parable *Zulu Time* arrives in Montreal." <http://www.montrealmirror.com/ARCHIVES/2002/061302/theatre.html>.

Hayles, N. Katherine. 2002. *Writing Machines*. Cambridge, Mass.: MIT Press.

————. 1999. *How We Became Posthuman: Virtual Bodies in Cybernetics, Literature and Informatics*. Chicago: University of Chicago Press.

————. 1996*a*. "Boundary Disputes: Homeostasis, Reflexivity, and the Foundations of Cybernetics." In *Virtual Realities and Their Discontents*, edited by Robert Markley, 11–37. Baltimore: Johns Hopkins University Press.

————. 1996*b*. "Embodied Virtuality: Or How to Put Bodies Back in the Picture." In *Immersed in Technology: Art and Virtual Environments*, edited by Mary Anne Moser with Douglas McLeod, 297–298. Cambridge, Mass.: MIT Press.

Heckell, Paul. 1982. *The Elements of Friendly Software Design*. New York: Warner.

Heidegger, Martin. 1992 [1929]. *Les Concepts Fondamentaux de la Métaphysique: Monde, Finitude, Solitude*. Translated by Daniel Panis. Paris: Gallimard.

————. 1977 [1954]. *The Question Concerning Technology and Other Essays*. Translated by William Lovitt. New York: Harper and Row.

————. 1962. *Being and Time*. Translated by John Macquarrie and Edward Robinson. Oxford: Blackwell.

Heim, Michael. 1991. "The Erotic Ontology of Cyberspace." In *Cyberspace: First Steps*, edited by Michael Benedikt, 59–80. Cambridge, Mass.: MIT Press.

Heise, Ursula. 1997. *Chronoschisms: Time, Narrative and Postmodernism*. Cambridge: Cambridge University Press.

Henri, Adrian. 1974. *Environments and Happenings*. London: Thames and Hudson.

Henrique, Paulo. 2000. "Contract with the Skin." Database entry, Digital Performance Archive. <http://art.ntu.ac.uk/dpa>.

————. 1998. "De agora em Diante/From Now On." Database entry, Digital Performance Archive. <http://art.ntu.ac.uk/dpa>.

Hern, Nicholas. 1972. "The Theatre of Ernst Toller." *Theatre Quarterly* 2, no. 5 (January–March): 72–92.

Herrup, Mocha Jean. 1996. "Metro Ice Meets Ball and Cheang." *Women & Performance: A Journal of Feminist Theory* 9, no. 1:150–159.

Hershman Leeson, Lynn. 2000. "Difference Engine #3." Database entry, Digital Performance Archive. <http://art.ntu.ac.uk/dpa>.

————. 1999. "Deep Contact: The First Interactive Sexual Fantasy Videodisk." Database entry, Digital Performance Archive. <http://art.ntu.ac.uk/dpa>.

————. 1996. "Tillie the Telerobotic Doll." Database entry, Digital Performance Archive. <http://art.ntu.ac.uk/dpa>.

————. 1994. "Conceiving Ada." Database entry, Digital Performance Archive. <http://art.ntu.ac.uk/dpa>.

Hertz, Garnet. 1996. "Telepresence and Digital/Physical Body > Gaining a Perspective." <http://www.conceptlab.com/interface/theories/reality/index.html>.

————. 1995. "The Godfather of Technology and Art: An Interview with Billy Klüver." <http://www.conceptlab.com/interviews/kluver.html>.

Herzogenrath, Bernd. 2002. "Join the United Mutations: Tod Browning's *Freaks*." *Post Script* 21, no. 3 (Summer 2002):8–13.

Hess, David J. 1995. "On Low Tech Cyborgs." In *The Cyborg Handbook*, edited by Chris Hables Gray, 371–378. New York and London: Routledge.

Hill, Logan. 2000. "Engineering Multimedia Art," *Wired*. <http://www.wired.com/news/print/0,1294,34840,00.html>.

Himanen, Pekka. 2001. *The Hacker Ethic and the Spirit of the Information Age*. London: Secker and Warburg.

Hoberman, Perry. 1999. "*Faraday's Garden* Description." <http://www.portola.com/PEOPLE/PERRY/perry.html>.

Hoffmann, E. T. A. 1982. "The Sandman." In *Tales of Hoffman*, translated by R. J. Hollingdale, 85–126. London: Penguin.

Holzer, Hans. 1974. *Encyclopedia of Witchcraft and Demonology*. London: Octopus Books.

Hopkins, John. 1999. "Eight Dialogues." Database entry, Digital Performance Archive. <http://art.ntu.ac.uk/dpa>.

Hovagimyan, G. H. 1997. "Art Dirt Im-Port" Database entry, Digital Performance Archive. <http://art.ntu.ac.uk/dpa>.

Howkins, John (ed.). 2002. *CODE: Collaboration and Ownership in the Digital Economy*. London: The Arts Council of England and Academia Eurpaea.

Hrvatin, Emil. 2000. "Drive-in Camillo." Database entry, Digital Performance Archive. <http://art.ntu.ac.uk/dpa>.

Hughes, Joan. 1999. "What Is Science?" <http://www.mdx.ac.uk/www/study/Science.htm>.

Huhtamo, Erkki. 2004. "An Archeology of Networked Art." In *Networked Narrative Environments as Imaginary Spaces of Being*, edited by Andrea Zapp, 32–44. Manchester: MIRIAD/FACT.

Huxley, Michael, and Noel Witts (eds.). 1996. *The Twentieth Century Performance Reader*. London and New York: Routledge.

Huxley, Aldous. 1953 [1932]. *Brave New World*. New York: Bantam.

Huyssen, Andreas. 1995. *Twilight Memories: Marking Time in a Culture of Amnesia*. London: Routledge.

Igloo. 2000. "Viking Shoppers." Database entry, Digital Performance Archive. <http://art.ntu.ac. uk/dpa>.

ieVR (The Institute for the Exploration of Virtual Realities). 1995. "The Adding Machine: A Virtual Reality Project." Database entry, Digital Performance Archive. <http://art.ntu.ac.uk/dpa>; expanded version at: <http://kuhttp.cc.ukans.edu/~mreaney/reaney/>.

Ihde, Don. 2002. *Bodies in Technology, Electronic Meditations*, Vol. 5. Minneapolis: University of Minnesota Press.

————. 1990. *Technology and the Lifeworld: From Garden to Earth*. Bloomington: Indiana University Press.

Illingworth, Monteith M. 1995. "George Coates: Toast of the Coast." *CyberStage* 1, no. 2 (Spring).

Ito, Joichi, and Mizuko Ito. 1996. "Joichi and Mizuko Ito—Interviewed by Lynn Hershman Leeson." In *Clicking In: Hot Links To A Digital Culture,* edited by Lynn Hershman Leeson, 78–104. Seattle: Bay Press.

Jameson, Frederic. 1991 [1984]. *Postmodernism: Or, the Cultural Logic of Late Capitalism*. London: Verso.

Jay, Martin. 2001. "The Speed of Light and the Virtualization of Reality." In *The Robot in the Garden: Telerobotics and Telepistemology in the Age of the Internet*, edited by Ken Goldberg, 144–163. Cambridge, Mass.: MIT Press.

Jenik, Adriane. 2001. "Desktop Theater: Keyboard Catharsis and the Masking of Roundheads." *TDR: The Drama Review* 45, no. 3:95–112.

————. 2000. "Waitingforgodot.com." Database entry, Digital Performance Archive. <http://art.ntu.ac.uk/dpa>.

Jenniches, Isabelle, Beppie Blankert, and Caroline Dokter. 1998. "Soft Mirror." Database entry, Digital Performance Archive. <http://art.ntu.ac.uk/dpa>.

Jonas, Joan. 1997. "Untitled." In *Illuminating Video,* edited by Doug Hall and Sally Jo Fifer, 366–374. New York: Aperture/BAVC.

Jones, Mark. 2001. "Hack: Performance–Based Electronic Art in Canada." Lecture delivered at the University of Salford, 16 January 2001.

————. 1999. "Monsters of Mediocrity." <http://www.cyberstage.org/archive/cstage31/ editorial.html>.

————. 1995*a*. "Stelarc: Still Hanging Around." *CyberStage* 1, no. 2 (Spring).

————. 1995*b*. "Char Davies: VR Through Osmosis." In *Cyberstage* 2, no. 1 (Fall):24–28.

Jones, Robert Edmond. 1992. *Towards a New Theatre: The Lectures of Robert Edmond Jones*. Transcribed and edited by Delbert Unruh. New York: Limelight Editions.

————. 1941. *The Dramatic Imagination*. New York: Theatre Arts Books.

————. 1929. "Theory of Modern Production." In *Encyclopaedia Britannica*, 14th ed.

Jowell, Tessa. 2004. "Government and the Value of Culture." <http://www.culture.gov.uk/default.htm>.

Kac, Eduardo. 2001*a*. "The Origin and Development of Robotic Art." *Convergence: The Journal of Research into New Media Technologies* 7, no. 4 (Spring):76–86.

———. 2001*b*. "Towards a Chronology of Robotic Art." *Convergence: The Journal of Research into New Media Technologies* 7, no. 4 (Spring): 87–111.

———. 2000*a*. "Time Capsule." Database entry, Digital Performance Archive. <http://art.ntu.ac.uk/dpa>.

———. 2000*b*. "Darker Than Night." Database entry, Digital Performance Archive. <http://art.ntu.ac.uk/dpa>.

———. 1999. "Art at the Biological Frontier". In *Reframing Consciousness: Art, Mind and Technology*, edited by Roy Ascott, 90–94. Exeter: Intellect.

———. 1998. "A-Positive." Database entry, Digital Performance Archive. <http://art.ntu.ac.uk/dpa>.

Kahney, Leander. 2000. "Warwick: Cyborg or Media Doll." *Wired*. <http://www.wired.com/news/print/0,1294,38467,00.html>.

Kaiser, Paul. 2000. "Ghostcatching." Database entry, Digital Performance Archive. <http://art.ntu.ac.uk/dpa>.

Kantor, Istvan. 2002. *Executive Machinery Intercourse*. Database entry, Digital Performance Archive. <http://art.ntu.ac.uk/dpa>.

Kaplan, E. Anne (ed.). 1988. *Postmodernism and Its Discontents*. New York: Verso Books.

Kaye, Nick. 2000. *Site-Specific Art: Performance, Place and Documentation*. London: Routledge.

Keener, Christine A. 1999. "Bill T. Jones and Ghostcatching." <http://www.news.harvard.edu/net_news2000/05.31/ghostcatching.5.31.html>.

Kelly, Kevin. 1999. "The Third Culture." <http://www.edge.org/3rd_culture/kelly/>.

Kember, Sarah. 1998. *Virtual Anxiety: Photography, New Technologies and Subjectivity*. Manchester: Manchester University Press.

Kendrick, Michelle. 1996. "Cyberspace and the Technological Real." In *Virtual Realities and Their Discontents*, edited by Robert Markley, 143–160. Baltimore: Johns Hopkins University Press.

King, Bruce (ed.). 1991. *Contemporary American Theatre*. London: Macmillan.

King, Daniel. 1997. *Kasparov v Deeper Blue: The Ultimate Man v Machine Challenge*. London: B. T. Batsford.

King, Lucien (ed.). 2002. *Game On: The History and Culture of Videogames*. London: Laurence King.

Kirby, Michael. 1987. *A Formalist Theatre*. Philadelphia: University of Pennsylvania Press.

———. 1975. "New Performance & Manifestos: An Introduction." *TDR: The Drama Review* 19, no. 4:3.

————. 1971. *Futurist Performance*. New York: PAJ Publications.

————. 1966. "The Uses of Film in the New Theatre." *TDR: Tulane Drama Review* 11, no. 1: 49–61.

Kirshenblatt-Gimblett, Barbara (ed.). 1976. *Speech Play: Research and Resources for the Study of Linguistic Creativity*. Philadelphia: University of Pennsylvania Press.

Klies, Mabel. 2000. "Gallery of Memories." Database entry, Digital Performance Archive. <http://art.ntu.ac.uk/dpa>.

Klüver, Billy. 2003 [1961]. "The Garden Party." In *The New Media Reader*, edited by Noah Wardrip-Fruin and Nick Montfort, 213. Cambridge, Mass.: MIT Press.

Knights, Vanessa. 2003. "Tears and Screams: Performances of Pleasure and Pain in the Bolero." Paper delivered at the 12th Biennial Conference of the International Association for the Study of Popular Music, July 2003. McGill University, Montreal.

Kobliakla, Michael. 1999. "Introduction of Borders and Thresholds." In *Of Borders and Thresholds*, edited by Michael Kobliakla, 1–26. Minneapolis: University of Minnesota Press.

Kozel, Susan. 1998. "Ghosts and Astronauts." Database entry, Digital Performance Archive. <http://art.ntu.ac.uk/dpa>.

————. 1994. "Spacemaking: Experiences of a Virtual Body." <http://art.net/~dtz/kozel.html>.

Kozintsov, Georgy. 1975 [1921]. "Eccentrism." *TDR: The Drama Review* 19, no. 4: 95–98.

Kroker, Arthur. 2002. "The Image Matrix." *CTHEORY*, 20 March 2002. <http://mail.sarai.net/pipermail/reader-list/2002-March/007366.html>.

————. 1992. *The Possessed Individual: Technology and the French Postmodern*. New York: St. Martin's.

Kroker, Arthur, and Marilouise Kroker. 1999. "Road Stories for the Flesh Eating Future." Database entry, Digital Performance Archive. <http://art.ntu.ac.uk/dpa>.

————. 1996a. "Code Warriors: Bunkering In and Dumbing Down." In *Clicking In: Hot Links To A Digital Culture,* edited by Lynn Hershman Leeson, 247–257. Seattle: Bay Press.

————. 1996b. *Hacking the Future: Stories for the Flesh-Eating 90s*. New York: St. Martin's Press.

————. 1995. "Johnny Mnemonic: The Day Cyberpunk Died." *CTHEORY*, 14 June 1995. <http://www.ctheory.net/text_file.asp?pick=150>.

Kroker, Arthur, and Michael Weinstein. 1994. "The Hyper-texted Body, Or Nietzsche Gets A Modem." *CTHEORY*, 24 November 1994. <http://www.ctheory.net/text_file.asp?pick=144>.

Krueger, Ted. 1996. "Like a second skin, living machines." *Architectural Design* 66, nos. 9–10: 29–32.

Kundera, Milan. 1985. *The Unbearable Lightness of Being.* London: Faber.

Kuppers, Petra. 1999. "Traces." Database entry, Digital Performance Archive. <http://art.ntu.ac.uk/dpa>.

Kurzweil, Ray. 2000. *The Age of Spiritual Machines*. London: Penguin Books.

Lacan, Jacques. 1977. "The mirror stage as formative of the function of the I." In *Ecrits: A Selection*, translated by A. Sheridan, 1–7. New York: Norton.

LaFarge, Antoinette, and Robert Allen. 2000. "The Roman Forum." Database entry, Digital Performance Archive. <http://art.ntu.ac.uk/dpa>.

La Fura Dels Baus. 2000. "Big Opera Mundi." Database entry, Digital Performance Archive. <http://art.ntu.ac.uk/dpa>.

———. 1999. "Foc Forn." Database entry, Digital Performance Archive. <http://art.ntu.ac.uk/dpa>.

———. 1998. "F@ust version 3.0." Database entry, Digital Performance Archive. <http://art.ntu. ac.uk/dpa>.

———. 2001. "Cabinas." Database entry, Digital Performance Archive. <http://art.ntu.ac. uk/dpa>.

Landow, George P. 1994. *Hyper/Text/Theory*. Baltimore: Johns Hopkins University Press.

———. 1992. *Hypertext: The Convergence of Contemporary Critical Theory and Technology*. Baltimore: Johns Hopkins University Press.

Lanier, Jaron. 1996. "The Prodigy." In *Digerati*, edited by John Brockman, 163–174. London: Orion Business Books.

———. 1996. "Jaron Lanier—Interviewed by Lynn Hershman Leeson." In *Clicking In: Hot Links To A Digital Culture*, edited by Lynn Hershman Leeson, 43–53. Seattle: Bay Press.

Laqueur, Thomas. 1990. *Making Sex: Body and Gender From the Greeks to Freud*. Cambridge, Mass.: Harvard University Press.

Latham, William, and Mark Atkinson. 2004. "Computer Artworks." <http://www.artworks. co.uk/>.

Laurel, Brenda. 1998. "Technological Humanism and Values-Driven Design." Keynote address at *CHI-98*, April 1998. <http://www.tauzero.com/Brenda_Laurel/Severed_Heads/Technological_ Humanism.html>.

———. 1991. *Computers as Theater*. Reading, Mass.: Addison-Wesley.

———. 1990. *The Art of Human-Computer Interface Design*. Reading, Mass.: Addison-Wesley.

Laurel, Brenda, and Rachel Strickland. 1996. "Placeholder." In *Immersed in Technology: Art and Virtual Environments*, edited by Mary Anne Moser with Douglas McLeod, 297–298. Cambridge, Mass.: MIT Press.

Laurel, Brenda, Rachel Strickland, and Rob Tow. 1988. "Placeholder: Landscape and Narrative in Virtual Environments." In *Digital Illusion*, edited by Clark Dodsworth, 181–208. New York: ACM Press.

Lavery, David. 2001. "From Cinespace to Cyberspace: Zionists and Agents, Realists and Gamers in 'The Matrix' and 'eXistenZ.'" *Journal of Popular Film and Television* 28 (Winter): 150–158.

Lechner, Sharon. 1996. "My Womb, the Mosh Pit." *Women & Performance: A Journal of Feminist Theory* 9, no. 1: 179–186.

Leeson, Lynn. (ed.). 1996. *Clicking In: Hot Links to a Digital Culture.* Seattle: Bay Press.

Le Grice, Malcolm. 2001. *Experimental Cinema in the Digital Age.* London: British Film Institute.

Leonard, Andrew. 1997. *Bots: The Origin of New Species.* San Francisco: HardWired.

Lepage, Robert. 2001. "Zulu Time." <http://www.exmachina.qc.ca>.

Levinas, Emmanuel. 1991. *Le Temps et l'Autre.* Paris: Quadrige/PUF.

Levy, Steven. 2001 [1984]. *Hackers, Heroes of the Computer Revolution.* London: Penguin Books.

Lista, Giovanni. 2001. *Futurism.* Paris: Finest SA/Éditions Pierre Terrail.

Little, Gregory. 1998. "A Manifesto for Avatars." <http://art.bgsu.edu/~glittle/ava_text_1.html>.

Lord, Richard. 1997. "Web Dances: Lifeblood." Database entry, Digital Performance Archive. <http://art.ntu.ac.uk/dpa>.

Loring, Dawn Davis. 2001. "Exhibitionism." *Austin Chronicle*, 4 May 2001.

Luckhurst, Roger. 1999. "Memory Recovered/Recovered Memory." In *Literature and the Contemporary: Fictions and Theories of the Present*, edited by Roger Luckhurst and Peter Marks, 80–93. Harlow, Essex: Pearson/Longman.

Luckhurst, Roger, and Peter Marks. 1999. "Hurry Up Please, It's Time: Introducing the Contemporary." In *Literature and the Contemporary: Fictions and Theories of the Present*, edited by Roger Luckhurst and Peter Marks, 1–12. Harlow, Essex: Pearson/Longman.

Lumley, Frederick. 1972. *New Trends in 20th Century Drama.* 4th ed. London: Barrie and Jenkins.

Lunenfeld, Peter. 2002. "The Myths of Interactive Cinema." In *The New Media Book*, edited by Dan Harries, 144–154. London: BFI.

———. 2000. *Snap to Grid: A Users' Guide to Digital Arts, Media and Cultures.* Cambridge, Mass.: MIT Press.

———, (ed.). 2000. *The Digital Dialectic.* Cambridge, Mass.: MIT Press.

Lyotard, Jean-François. 1984. *The Postmodern Condition: a Report on Knowledge.* Translated by Brian Massumi and Geoff Bennington. Manchester: Manchester University Press.

Malone, Robert. 1978. *The Robot Book.* New York: Jove Publications.

Manovich, Lev. 2002. "Spatial Computerisation and Film Language." In *New Screen Media: Cinema/Art/Narrative*, edited by Martin Rieser and Andrea Zapp, 64–76. London: British Film Institute.

———. 2001. *The Language of New Media.* Cambridge, Mass.: MIT Press.

———. 1999. "Avant-Garde as Software." <http://manovich.net/docs/avantgarde_as_software.doc>.

Marinetti, Filippo Tommaso. 1996 [1909]. "The Founding and Manifesto of Futurism." Translated by R. W. Flint. In *The Twentieth Century Performance Reader*, edited by Michael Huxley and Noel Witts, 289–293. London and New York: Routledge.

———. 1971 [1913]. "The Variety Theatre." In Michael Kirby, *Futurist Performance*, 179–186. New York: PAJ Publications.

Marinetti, Filippo Tommaso, Emilio Settimelli, and Bruno Corra. 1971 [1915]. "The Futurist Synthetic Theatre." In Michael Kirby, *Futurist Performance*, 196–202. New York: PAJ Publications.

Marinetti, Filippo Tommaso, Bruno Corra, Emilio Settimelli, Arnaldo Ginna, Giacomo Balla, and Remo Chiti. 2001 [1916]. "The Futurist Cinema." Translated by R. W. Flint. In *Multimedia: From Wagner to Virtual Reality*, edited by Randall Packer and Ken Jordan, 10–15. London: Norton.

Markley, Robert (ed.). 1996. *Virtual Realities and Their Discontents.* Baltimore: Johns Hopkins University Press.

Marranca, Bonnie. 1979. "The Self As Text: Uses of Autobiography in the Theatre." *Performing Arts Journal* 4, nos. 1 and 2: 85–105.

Masterman, Margaret. 1971. "Computerized Haiku." In *Cybernetics, Art and Ideas*, edited by Jasia Reichardt, 175–183. London: Studio Vista.

Mathews, Harry, and Alastair Brotchie (eds.). 1998. *Oulipo Compendium*. London: Atlas Press.

Maudlin, Michael. 1994. "Chatter-Bots, TinyMUDs, and the Turing Test". Paper presented at the Twelfth National Conference on Artificial Intelligence, Menlo Park, California. <http://fuzine.mt.cs.cmu.edu/mlm/aaai94.html>.

Mazlish, Bruce. 2002 [1993]. "The man-machine and artificial intelligence." <http://www.stanford.edu/group/SHR/4-2/text/mazlish.html>.

McLuhan, Marshall. 1964. *Understanding Media: The Extensions of Man.* London: Routledge and Kegan Paul.

McLuhan, Marshall, and Wilfred Watson. 1995. "From Cliché to Archetype." In Marshall McLuhan, *Essential McLuhan*, edited by Erick McLuhan and Frank Zingrone. New York: Harper Collins.

McMurtrie, Chico. 2001. "Interview with Chico McMurtrie." <http://www.timesup.org/rearview/McMurtrie.html>.

———. 2000. "Interview with the Digital Performance Archive." Nottingham, 26 October 2000.

Melrose, Susan. 1993. *A Semiotics of the Dramatic Text (New Directions in Theatre).* London: Palgrave.

Merleau-Ponty, Maurice. 1968. *The Visible and the Invisible.* Evanston, Ill.: Northwestern University Press.

Metcalf, Stephen. 1998. "Autogeddon." In *Virtual Futures*, edited by Joan Broadhurst Dixon and Eric J. Cassidy, 111–115. London and New York: Routledge.

Meyerhold, Vsevolod. 1969. *Meyerhold on Theatre,* edited and translated by Edward Braun. London: Methuen.

Mistresses of Technology. 2000. "I-drunners: re_flesh the body." Database entry, Digital Performance Archive. <http://art.ntu.ac.uk/dpa>.

Mitchell, William J. 2003. *Me++: The Cyborg Self and the Networked City.* Cambridge, Mass.: MIT Press.

————. 1999. *E-Topia.* Cambridge, Mass.: MIT Press.

————. 1995. *Being Digital.* Sydney: Hodder and Stoughton.

Montalti, Mauro. 1971 [1920]. "For a New Theatre 'Electric-Vibrating-Luminous.'" In Michael Kirby, *Futurist Performance*, 222–224. New York: PAJ Publications.

Moody, Glyn. 2002 [2001]. *Rebel Code: Linux and the Open Source Revolution.* London: Penguin Books.

Moore, Geoff. 1993. "The Space Between: Work in Mixed Media, Moving Being 1968–1993." In program notes for "The Darwin Project: Part 3," St. David's Hall, Cardiff, 22 and 23 September, 1993.

————. 1989. *Moving Being: Two Decades of a Theatre of Ideas, 1968–88.* Cardiff: Moving Being Ltd.

Moravec, Hans. 1991. "The Universal Robot." In *Out of Control: Ars Electronica 1991*, edited by Gottfried Hattinger and Peter Weibel, 13–28. Linz: Landesverlag.

————. 1988. *Mind Children: The Future of Robot and Human Intelligence.* Cambridge, Mass.: Harvard University Press.

Morle, Phil. 1995. "Communitek: Performance in the Electronic Frontier." *CyberStage* 1, no. 2 (Spring).

Morningstar, Chip, and F. Randall Farmer. 2001 [1992]. "Habitat: Reports from an Online Community." In *True Names and Vernor Vinge and the opening of the cyberspace frontier*, edited by James Frenkel, 171–220. New York: Tor.

Morse, Margaret. 1998. *Virtualities: Television, Media Art and Cyberculture.* Bloomington and Indianapolis: Indiana University Press.

————. 1997 [1989]. "Video Installation Art: The Body, The Image and the Space-in-between." In *Illuminating Video,* edited by Doug Hall and Sally Jo Fifer, 153–167. New York: Aperture/BAVC.

————. 1996. "Nature Morte: Landscape and Narrative in Virtual Environments." In *Immersed in Technology: Art and Virtual Environments*, edited by Mary Anne Moser and Douglas MacLeod, 195–232. Cambridge, Mass.: MIT Press.

Moser, Mary Anne, and Douglas McLeod (eds.). 1996. *Immersed in Technology: Art and Virtual Environments.* Cambridge, Mass.: MIT Press.

Motherboard. 1999. "M@ggie's Love Bytes." Database entry, Digital Performance Archive. <http://art.ntu.ac.uk/dpa>.

Motte, Warren. 1986. *Oulipo: A Primer of Potential Literature.* Lincoln: University of Nebraska Press.

Moulthrop, Stuart. 1988. "Containing Multitudes: The Problem of Closure in Interactive Fiction." *Association for Computing and Humanities Newsletter* 10: 1–7.

Mulder, A., and M. Post. 2000. *Book for the Electronic Arts*. Rotterdam: De Balie.

Mullins, Justin. 2002. "Quantum Superbrains." *New Scientist,* 8 June 2002, 24–29.

Mulvey, Laura. 1975. "Visual Pleasure and Narrative Cinema." In Laura Mulvey, *Visual and Other Pleasures*. Basingstoke: Macmillan.

Murray, Janet. 1997. *Hamlet on the Holodeck: The Future of Narrative in Cyberspace*. New York: Free Press.

Murray, Timothy. 2002. "Digital Passage: the Rhizomatic Frontiers of the ZKM." *Performing Arts International* 70: 115–119.

Naugle, Lisa. 2002. "Distributed Choreography." *Performing Arts Journal* 71: 56–61.

———. 2000. "Boundaries." Database entry, Digital Performance Archive. <http://art.ntu.ac.uk/dpa>.

Neumark, Norie. 1999. "Shock in the Ear." Database entry, Digital Performance Archive. <http://art.ntu.ac.uk/dpa>.

Nelson, Robin. 1997. *TV Drama in Transition: Forms, Values and Cultural Change*. London: Macmillan.

Neville, Sarah, and Heliograph Productions. 1999. "Ada." Database entry, Digital Performance Archive. <http://art.ntu.ac.uk/dpa>.

Nora, Pierre. 1989 [1984]. *Between Memory and History: Les Lieux de Mémoire*. Paris: Galliard.

Nordau, Max. 1993 [1895]. *Degeneration*. Lincoln: University of Nebraska Press.

Norman, Donald A. 1991. "Foreword." In *Computers as Theater*, by Brenda Laurel. Reading, Mass.: Addison-Wesley.

Norman, Donald A, and Draper, S. (eds.). 1986. *User Centred Systems Design: New Perspectives on Human-Computer Interaction*. Hillsdale, N.J.: Lawrence Erlbaum.

Novak, Marcos. 1994. "Liquid Architecture in Cyberspace." In *Cyberspace: First Steps*, edited by Michael Benedikt, 225–254. Cambridge, Mass.: MIT Press.

Needham, Joseph. 1975. *Science and Civilization in China*, vol. 4, part 2. Cambridge: Cambridge University Press.

Nichols, Bill. 1988. "The Work of Culture in the Age of Cybernetic Systems." *Screen* 29, no. 1: 22–46.

Nyman, Michael. 1974. *Experimental Music: Cage and Beyond*. New York: Schirmer Books.

O'Brien, Harvey. 2003. "The Far Side of the Moon: Robert Lepage." <http://www.culturevulture.net/Theater6/FarSide.htm>.

Obrist, Hans Ulrich. 1998. "Turning to Technology: Legendary engineer Billy Klüver on artist-engineer collaborations." <http://www.artnode.se/artorbit/issue3/i_kluver/i_kluver.html>.

Oliveira, Nicholas, Nicola Oxley, Michael Petry, and Michael Archer. 1994. *Installation Art*. London: Thames and Hudson.

Olson, Steve. 2002. *Mapping Human History: Discovering Our Past Through Our Genes*. Boston: Houghton Mifflin.

O'Mahoney, John. 2001. "Aerial Views." *The Guardian*, 23 June 2001.

O'Mahony, Marie. 2002. *Cyborg: The Man-Machine*. London: Thames and Hudson.

Orton, Fred, and Griselda Pollock. 1996. *Avant-gardes and their Partisans, Reviewed*. Manchester: Manchester University Press.

Osborne, Peter. 1999. "The Politics of Time." In *Literature and the Contemporary: Fictions and Theories of the Present*, edited by Roger Luckhurst and Peter Marks, 36–49. Harlow, Essex: Pearson/Longman.

Packer, Randall, and Ken Jordan (eds.). 2001. *Multimedia: From Wagner to Virtual Reality*. London: Norton.

Paik, Nam June. 2001*a* [1984]. "Art and Satellite." In *Multimedia: From Wagner to Virtual Reality*, edited by Randall Packer and Ken Jordan, 41–43. New York and London: Norton.

———. 2001*b* [1966]. "Cybernated Art." In *Multimedia: From Wagner to Virtual Reality*, edited by Randall Packer and Ken Jordan, 39–41. New York and London: Norton.

Palmer, Gareth. 2003. *Discipline and Liberty: Television and Governance*. Manchester: Manchester University Press.

Palmer, Richard H. 2002. "Technology and the Playwright." *Gramma* 10: 143–156.

Pannaggi, Ivo, and Vinici Paladini. 2003 [1922]. "Manifesto of Futurist Mechanical Art." <www.futurism.org.uk>.

Parkbench. 1994. "ArTistheater." Database entry, Digital Performance Archive. <http://art.ntu.ac.uk/dpa>.

Pask, Gordon. 1971. "A Comment, a Case Study and a Plan." In *Cybernetics, Art and Ideas*, edited by Jasia Reichardt, 76–99. London: Studio Vista.

Patel, Roma. 1999. "Projects by Roma Patel." Database entry, Digital Performance Archive. <http://art.ntu.ac.uk/dpa>.

Paul, Christiane. 2003. *Digital Art*. London: Thames and Hudson.

Paulson, William. 1989. "Computers, Minds and Texts: Primary Reflections." *New Literary History* (Winter 1989): 291–303.

Pavis, Patrice. 2003. "Afterword: Contemporary Dramatic Writings and the New Technologies." In *Trans-global Readings: Crossing Theatrical Boundaries*, edited by Cariad Svich, 187–202. Manchester: Manchester University Press.

———. 1992. *Theatre at the Crossroads of Culture*. London: Routledge.

———. 1987. *Languages of the Stage: Essays in the Semiology of the Theatre*. New York: PAJ Publications.

Pesce, Mark. 2001. "True Magic." In *True Names and Vernor Vinge and the Opening of the Cyberspace Frontier*, edited by James Frenkel, 221–238. New York: Tor.

Penny, Simon. 2001. "Embodied Cultural Agents." <http://www-art.cfa.cmu.edu/www-penny/index.html>.

———. 1996. "From A to D and back again: The emerging aesthetics of Interactive Art." <http://www-art.cfa.cmu.edu/Penny/texts/AtoD.html>.

Peppermint, Cary. 1999. "Conductor #1: Getting in Touch With Chicken." Database entry, Digital Performance Archive. <http://art.ntu.ac.uk/dpa>.

Perron, Bernard, and Mark J. P. Wolf (eds.). 2003. *The Video Game Theory Reader*. London and New York: Routledge.

Petersen, Kjell Yngve. 2004. "The Emergence of Hyper-reality in Performance." In *New Visions in Performance: The Impact of Digital Technologies*, edited by Gavin Carver and Colin Beardon, 31–40. Lisse, The Netherlands: Swets and Zeitlinger.

Phelan, Peggy. 1993a. "Preface: Arresting Performances of Sexual and Racial Difference: Toward a Theory of Performative Film." *Women & Performance: A Journal of Feminist Theory* 6, no. 2: 5–10.

———. 1993b. *Unmarked: The Politics of Performance*. London, New York: Routledge.

Phillips, Andrea. 2000. "A Dog's Life." *Performance Research* 5, no. 2: 125–130.

Pierce, Anne. 1995. "Merce Cunningham's Living Sketchbook." *Hotwired.* <http://hotwired.wired.com/kino/95/29/feature/>.

———. 1991. "Cunningham at the Computer." *Dance/USA Journal* (Summer 1991): 14–15.

Piggford, George. 1999. "'Who's That Girl?' Annie Lennox, Woolf's *Orlando*, and Female Camp Androgyny." In *Camp: Queer Aesthetics and the Performing Subject: A Reader*, edited by Fabio Cleto, 283–299. Edinburgh: Edinburgh University Press.

Pimentel, Ken, and Kevin Teixeira. 1995. *Virtual Reality: Through the New Looking Glass*. New York: McGraw-Hill.

Pinhanez, Claudio. 1999. "SingSong." Database entry, Digital Performance Archive. <http://art.ntu.ac.uk/dpa>.

———. 1997a. "Computer Theater." <http://web.media.mit.edu/~pinhanez/isea/isea.html>.

———. 1997b. "MIT Media Laboratory and the Digital Life Consortium present '*It / I*'." <http://www.media.mit.edu/~iti/>.

Pinker, Steven. 2002. *The Blank Slate: Denying Human Nature in Modern Life*. London: Allen Lane/Penguin.

Plaintext Players. 1999. "The Birth of the Christ Child." Database entry, Digital Performance Archive. <http://art.ntu.ac.uk/dpa>.

Plant, Sadie. 1998a. "Coming Across the Future." In *Virtual Futures*, edited by Joan Broadhurst Dixon and Eric J. Cassidy, 30–44. London and New York: Routledge.

———. 1998b. *Zeros and Ones: Digital Women + The New Technoculture*, London: Fourth Estate.

Polli, Andrea. 1999. "Virtual Space and the Construction of Memory." In *Reframing Consciousness: Art, Mind and Technology*, edited by Roy Ascott, 42–47. Exeter: Intellect.

Pomeroy, Jim. 1991. "Black Box S-Thetix: Labor, Research, and Survival in the He[Art] of the Beast." In *Technoculture*, edited by Constance Penley and Andrew Ross, 283–288. Minneapolis: University of Minnesota Press.

Pomian, Krysztof. 1984. *L'Ordre du Temps*. Paris: Gallimard.

Ponton, Anita. 1998*a*. "Dies Irae." Database entry, Digital Performance Archive. <http://art.ntu.ac.uk/dpa>.

———. 1998*b*. "Seen. Unsaid." Database entry, Digital Performance Archive. <http://art.ntu.ac.uk/dpa>.

Popovich, George. 1999. "Artaud Unleashed: Cyberspace Meets the Theatre of Cruelty." In *Theatre in Cyberspace: Issues of Teaching, Acting and Directing*, edited by Stephen A. Schrum, 221–238. New York: Peter Lang.

Poster, Mark. 1999. "Theorizing Virtual Reality: Baudrillard and Derrida." In *Cyberspace Textuality: Computer Technology and Literary Theory*, edited by Marie-Laure Ryan, 42–60. Bloomington: Indiana University Press.

———. 1995. "Postmodern Virtualities." In *Cyberspace, Cyberbodies, Cyberpunk: Cultures of Technological Embodiment*, edited by Mike Featherstone and Roger Burrows, 79–95. London: Sage.

PPS Danse. 2000. "Strata, Memoirs of a Lover." Database entry, Digital Performance Archive. <http://art.ntu.ac.uk/dpa>.

Pradier, Jean-Marie. 2000. "Animals, Angel and Performance." *Performance Research*, 5, no. 2:11–22.

Prampolini, Enrico. 1971 [1915]. "Futurist Scenography." In Michael Kirby, *Futurist Performance*, 203–206. New York: PAJ Publications.

Proust, Marcel. 2002 [1913]. *In Search of Lost Time, Volume 1: The Way by Swanns*. London: Penguin.

———. 2002 [1919]. *In Search of Lost Time, Volume 2: In the Shadow of Young Girls in Flower*. London: Penguin.

Punt, Michael. 1999. "Casablanca and Men in Black: Consciousness, Remembering and Forgetting." In *Reframing Consciousness*, edited by Roy Ascott, 38–42. Exeter: Intellect Books.

Puttnam, Lord David. 1999. "Keynote Speech." Paper delivered at the CADE 99 (Computers in Art and Design Education) Conference, 7 April 1999. Middlesborough, University of Teeside.

Rae, Paul. 2003. "Presencing." *Performance Arts International*, <http://www.mdx.ac.uk/www/epai/presencesite/html/rae00.html>.

Rajah, Niranjan. 1999. "Two Portraits of Chief Tupa Kupa: The Image as an Index of Shifts in Human Consciousness." In *Reframing Consciousness*, edited by Roy Ascott. Exeter: Intellect Books.

Random Dance Company. 2000. "The Trilogy." Database entry, Digital Performance Archive. <http://art.ntu.ac.uk/dpa>.

———. 1998. "The Millanarium." Database entry, Digital Performance Archive. <http://art.ntu.ac.uk/dpa>.

Rang, Lloyd W. 1998. "The Bungled and the Botched: Cyborgs, Rape and Generative Anthropology." <http://fragment.nl/archive/2001/09/05/new_links_added/index.php>.

Raymond, Silvy Panet. 1980. "Some Empty Words with Mr. Cage and Mr. Cunningham." *Performance* 7:4–12.

Rayner, Alice. 1999. "Everywhere and Nowhere: Theatre in Cyberspace." In *Of Borders and Thresholds: Theatre History, Practice and Theory*, edited by Michael Kobialka, 278–302. Minneapolis: University of Minnesota Press.

Reaney, Mark. 1999*a*. "Press Release for 'Machinal.'" Email Press Release sent to the vw-theater list, 26 August 1999.

———. 1999*b*. "Virtual Reality and the Theatre: Immersion in Virtual Worlds." *Digital Creativity* 10, no. 3:183–188.

———. 1996. "Virtual Scenography: The Actor, Audience, Computer Interface." *Theatre Design and Technology* 32, no. 1:36–43.

———. 1992. "The Theatre of Virtual Reality: Designing Scenery in an Imaginary World." *Theatre Design and Technology* 29, no. 2:29–32.

Reaves, John. 1995. "Theory and Practice: The Gertrude Stein Repertory Theatre." *CyberStage* 1, no. 3 (Summer).

Reichardt, Jasia (ed.). 1971. *Cybernetics, Art and Ideas*. London: Studio Vista.

Reid, Susan. 1996. ". . . Meanwhile Back in the Bedroom." *Weekend Australian*, 17–18 February 1996.

Renan, Sheldan. 1996. "The Net and the Future of Being Fictive." In *Clicking In: Hot Links To A Digital Culture,* edited by Lynn Hershman Leeson, 61–72. Seattle: Bay Press.

Reynolds, Dee. 2000. "Displacing 'Humans': Merce Cunningham's Crowds." <http://www.brunel.ac.uk/depts/pfa/bstjournal/1no1/DEEreynolds.htm>.

Rheingold, Howard. 1994*a*. "Rheingold's Reality." *CyberStage* 1, no. 1.

———. 1994*b*. *The Virtual Community: Homesteading in the Age of the Internet*. San Francisco: Harper Perennial.

———. 1991. *Virtual Reality.* London: Secker and Warburg.

Rinaldo, Ken. 1998. "Technology Recapitulates Phylogeny." <http://mitpress.mit.edu/e-journals/LEA/ARTICLES/alife1.html>.

Riverbed and Bill T. Jones/Arnie Zane Company. 1999. "Ghostcatching." Database entry, Digital Performance Archive. <http://art.ntu.ac.uk/dpa>.

Robinson, Andrew. 2002. *Lost Languages: The Enigma of the World's Undeciphered Scripts.* New York: McGraw-Hill.

Roca, Marcel-Lí Antúnez. 1998. "Afasia." <http://www.marcel-li.com/>.

Rokeby, David. 1999. "Transforming Mirrors: Transforming Mirrors." <http://www.interlog.com/~drokeby/mirrorsmirrors.html>.

————. 1998. "Watch." Database entry, Digital Performance Archive. <http://art.ntu.ac.uk/dpa>.

Rorrison, Hugh. 1980. "Piscator's Production of 'Hoppla, Wir Leben', 1927." *Theatre Quarterly* 10, no. 37 (Spring):30–41.

Rosenberg, Scott. 1995. "Laurie Anderson's Heartbreak 'Motel.'" <www.wordyard.com/dmz/digicult/anderson-motel-5-10-95.html>.

Ross, Andrew. 1989. *No Respect: Intellectuals and Popular Culture.* London: Routledge.

Rothenberg, David. 1995. *Hand's End: Technology and the Limits of Nature.* Berkeley and Los Angeles: University of California Press.

Roy, Sanjoy. 2002. "Technological Process." *Dance Theatre Journal* 17, no. 4 (January).

Royle, Nicholas. 2003. *The Uncanny.* New York: Routledge.

Rubidge, Sarah. 2001. "Bodying the Space in Between." Proceedings of Consciousness Reframed III, Centre for Advanced Enquiry into Interactive Arts, University of Wales, Newport.

Ruch, Mark. 2001. "Artists Statements." <http://cronos.net/~bk/amorphic/info/html>.

Rush, Michael. 1999. *New Media in Late 20th-Century Art.* London: Thames and Hudson.

R. U. Sirius. 1996. "R. U. Sirius interviewed by Lynn Hershman Leeson." In *Clicking In: Hot Links To A Digital Culture,* edited by Lynn Hershman Leeson, 54–60. Seattle, WA: Bay Press.

Ruskin, John. 1862. "Unto This Last." <http://www.lancs.ac.uk/postgrad/debooj/untothislast.txt>.

Russell, Charles. 1985. *Poets, Prophets, and Revolutionaries: The Literary Avant-Garde from Rimbaud through Postmodernism.* Oxford: Oxford University Press.

Rutsky, R. L. 1999. *High Techne: Art and Technology from the Machine Aesthetic to the Posthuman.* Minneapolis: University of Minnesota Press.

Ryan, Marie-Laure. 2001. *Narrative as Virtual Reality.* Baltimore: Johns Hopkins University Press.

————. 1999. "Cyberspace, Virtuality, and the Text." In *Cyberspace Textuality: Computer Technology and Literary Theory*, edited by Marie-Laure Ryan, 78–107. Bloomington: Indiana University Press.

Sadler, Michael T. H. 1977. "Introduction." In *Concerning the Spiritual in Art* by Wassily Kandinsky, translated by Michael Sadler, xii. New York: Dover Publications.

Said, Edward W. 1995 [1978]. *Orientalism: Western Conceptions of the Orient.* London: Penguin.

Saltz, David Z. 2001. "The Collaborative Subject: Telerobotic Performance and Identity." *Performance Research* 6, no. 3 (Winter):70–83.

————. 2000. "Tempest 2000." Database entry, Digital Performance Archive. <http://art.ntu.ac.uk/dpa>.

————. 1999. "Beckett's Cyborgs: Technology and the Beckettian Text." In *Theatre in Cyberspace*, edited by Stephen A. Schrum, 273–290. New York: Peter Lang.

Sandin, Daniel J. 1998. "Digital Illusion, Virtual Reality, and Cinema." In *Digital Illusion*, edited by Clark Dodsworth, 3–26. New York: ACM Press.

Satorimedia. 2000. "TouchDown." Database entry, Digital Performance Archive. <http://art.ntu.ac.uk/dpa>.

Sawchuk, Kimberly Anne. 1993. "Post Panoptic Mirrored Worlds." *CTHEORY*. <http://www.ctheory.net/text_file.asp?pick=230>.

Scarry, Siobhan. 1999. "In Step with Digital Dance." *Wired News*, 26 April. <http://www.wired.com/news/culture/0,1284,19312,00.html>.

Schechner, Richard. 2000. "Post-Poststructuralism." *TDR: The Drama Review* 44, no. 3 (Fall): 4–7.

————. 1979. "The End of Humanism." *Performing Arts Journal* 4, nos. 1–2:4–7.

————. 1977. *Performance Theory*. New York and London: Routledge.

Schiffman, Mike. 2003. *Hacker's Challenges*. Emeryville, Calif.: Osborne McGraw-Hill.

Schiphorst, Thecla. 1998. "BODYMAPS: ARTIFACTS OF TOUCH: Computer Interactive Proximity and Touch Sensor Driven Audio/Video Installation." <http://www.art.net/~dtz/schipo1.html>.

Schlemmer, Oskar. 1961. "Man and Art Figure." In *The Theater of the Bauhaus*, edited by Walter Gropius, 17–49. Middletown, Conn.: Wesleyan University Press.

Schmid, Julie. 2002. "Mina Loy's Futurist Theatre." <http://muse.jhu/journals/performing_arts_journal/v018/18.1schmid.html.>.

Schrum, Steve. 1996. "NetSeduction." Database entry, Digital Performance Archive. <http://art.ntu.ac.uk/dpa>.

————. 1998. "NetSeduction." <http://www2.hn.psu.edu/Faculty/Sschrum/RMTCo/NetSeduction.html>.

————, (ed.) 1999. *Theatre in Cyberspace*. New York: Peter Lang.

Schwarz, Hans-Peter. 1997. *Media-Art-History*. Munich: Prestel-Verlag.

Scott, Bruce R. 2001. "The Great Divide in the Global Village." *Foreign Affairs* 80, no. 1 (January–February):160–177.

Seaman, Bill. 2002. "Emergent Constructions: Re-embodied Intelligence Within Recombinant Poetic Networks." In *Digital Creativity: A Reader*, edited by Colin Beardon and Lone Malborg, 137–144. Lisse, Netherlands: Swets and Zeitlinger.

Sekula, Allan. 1989. "The Body and the Archive." In *The Conquest of Meaning: Critical Histories of Photography*, edited by Richard Bolton, 343–389. Cambridge, Mass.: MIT Press.

Sermon, Paul. 2004a. "The Emergence of User- and Performer-Determined Narratives in Telematic Environments." In *Networked Narrative Environments as Imaginary Spaces of Being*, edited by Andrea Zapp, 82–98. Manchester: MIRIAD/FACT.

————. 2004b. "Peace Talks." <www.artdes.salford.ac.uk/news/articles/bitparts.html>.

Senft, Teresa M. 1996. "Performing the Digital Body—A Ghost Story." *Women & Performance: A Journal of Feminist Theory* 9, no. 1:9–34.

Sewell, Brian. 1995. *An Alphabet of Villains*. London: Bloomsbury.

Shank, Theodore. 2002. *Beyond the Boundaries: American Alternative Theatre*. Ann Arbor: University of Michigan Press.

———. 1982. *American Alternative Theatre*. Ann Arbor: University of Michigan Press.

Shannon, Claude. 1950 [1949]. "Programming a Computer for Playing Chess." *Philosophical Magazine* Ser. 7, vol. 41, no. 314 (March):256–275.

Sharir, Yacov. 1999. "The Tools." <http://www.arts.state.tx.us/studios/Sharir/tools.htm>.

———. 1997. "Influence of Technology." <http://www.arts.state.tx.us/studios/sharir/techno.htm>.

Shewey, Don. 2001. "Set Your Watch to Now: Robert Lepage's 'Zulu Time.'" <http://www.donshewey.com/theater_reviews/zulu_time.html>.

Shu, Nan C. 1992. *Visual Programming*. New York: Van Nostrand Reinhold.

Shulgin, Alexej. 2001. "FuckU-FuckMe." In *Net_Condition: Art and Global Media*, edited by Peter Weibel and Timothy Druckrey, 112–113. Cambridge, Mass.: MIT Press.

Shuttleworth, Ian. 1996. "Elsinore." *Financial Times* <http://www.cix.co.uk/~shutters/reviews/96094.htm>.

SIGGRAPH. 2000. *SIGGRAPH 2000: Electronic Art and Animation Catalog*. New York: Association for Computing Machinery.

Silver, Stephan. 1999. "The Forgotten Amazement . . . Influences on Performance Following Industrialisation." MA thesis. London: Central Saint Martin's College of Art and Design.

Simpson, Lorenzo. 1995. *Technology, Time and the Conversations of Modernity*. London: Routledge.

Singh, Simon. 2000. *The Code Book: The Science of Secrecy from Ancient Egypt to Quantum Cryptography*. London: Fourth Estate.

Slatin, John M. 1992. "Hypertext and the Teaching of Writing." In *Sociomedia: Multimedia, Hypermedia and the Social Construction of Knowledge,* edited by Edward Barrett. Cambridge, Mass.: MIT Press.

Slayton, Joel, and the CADRE Institute. 1999. "Panamint Launch at Lucky Jim Wash." Database entry, Digital Performance Archive. <http://art.ntu.ac.uk/dpa>.

———. 1994. "Conduits." Database entry, Digital Performance Archive. <http://art.ntu.ac.uk/dpa>.

———. 1993. "Do What Do." Database entry, Digital Performance Archive. <http://art.ntu.ac.uk/dpa>.

———. 1992. "98.6 FM." Database entry, Digital Performance Archive. <http://art.ntu.ac.uk/dpa>.

Sloane, Sarah. 2000. *Digital Fictions: Storytelling in a Material World*. Stamford, Conn.: Ablex.

Smart, Jackie. 2004. "The Technology of the Real: Wayne McGregor's *Nemesis* and the Ecology of Perception." In *New Visions in Performance: The Impact of New Technologies*, edited by Gavin Carver and Colin Beardon, 41–54. Lisse, Netherlands: Swets and Zietlinger.

Smith, Barry. 1998. "Changing Shades: Review of *Metabody* and *Chameleons 2*." <http://info.ox. ac.uk/ctitext/publish/comtxt/ct16-17/smith.html>.

Snow, C. P. 1959. *The Two Cultures and the Scientific Revolution*. Cambridge: Cambridge University Press.

Sontag, Susan. 2002. *Where the Stress Falls*. London: Jonathan Cape.

———. 1999. "Notes on Camp." In *Camp: Queer Aesthetics and the Performing Subject: A Reader*, edited by Fabio Cleto, 53–65. Edinburgh: Edinburgh University Press.

———. 1994. *Against Interpretation*. London: Vintage.

———. 1980. "Fascinating Fascism." In Susan Sontag, *Under the Sign of Saturn*, 73–105. New York: Farrar, Straus & Giroux.

———. 1979. *On Photography*. London: Penguin.

———. 1966. "Film and Theatre." *TDR: Tulane Drama Review* 11, no. 1:24–37.

Soules, Marshall. 2000. "Animating the Language Machine: Computers and Performance". <http://www.mala.bc.ca/~soules/animate.htm>.

Spelletich, Kal. 2001. "Interview for a Book Called *Transitions*." <http://www.laughingsquid. com/seemen/>.

Spingarn-Koff, Jason. 1997. "Amorphic Robot Works." <http://www.rhizome.org/object. rhiz?932>.

Springer, Claudia. 1996. *Electronic Eros: Bodies and Desire in the Postindustrial Age*. Austin: University of Texas Press.

Squires, Kurt. 2002. "Cultural Framing of Computer/Video Games." <http://www.gamestudies. org>.

Stallabras, Julian. 1999. "The Ideal City and the Virtual Hive: Modernism and the Emergent Order in Computer Culture." In *Technocities*, edited by John Downey, 108–120. London: Sage.

Standage, Tom. 1998. *The Victorian Internet: The Remarkable Story of the Telegraph and the Nineteenth Century's On-Line Pioneers*. New York: Walker and Company.

Starbuck, Madelyn. 1996. "Honoria in Ciberspazio." Database entry, Digital Performance Archive. <http://art.ntu.ac.uk/dpa>.

Stark, M. 2003. "Furbys, Audio-Animatronics, Androids, and Robots." <http://www.cs.umd.edu/ ~mstark/furby/Essays/robots.html>.

Stefik, Mark (ed.). 1996. *Internet Dreams: Archetypes, Myths, and Metaphors*. Cambridge, Mass.: MIT Press.

Steiner, George. 2002. *Grammars of Creation*. London: Faber and Faber.

—————. 1971. *In Bluebeard's Castle*. New Haven: Yale University Press.

Stelarc. 2000. "From Psycho-Body to Cyber-Systems." In *The Cybercultures Reader,* edited by David Bell and Barbara M. Kennedy, 560–576. London: Routledge.

—————. 1999. "ParaSite: Event for Invaded and Involuntary Body." <http://www.stelarc.va.com.au/parasite/index.htm>.

—————. 1993. "Remote Gestures / Obsolute [sic] Desires." Lecture delivered at the Kitchen Center for Video, Music, Dance, Performance, Film and Literature, New York, 9 March 1993.

—————. 1991. "Prosthetics, Robotics and Remote Existence: Postevolutionary Strategies." *Leonardo* 24, no. 5:389–400.

—————. 1984. "Strategies and Trajectories." In *Obsolete Body / Suspensions / Stelarc*, edited by James D. Paffrath with Stelarc. Davis, Calif.: JP Publications.

Stern, Andrew. 1999. "Virtual Babyz." Database entry, Digital Performance Archive. <http://art.ntu.ac.uk/dpa>.

Stiles, Kristine. 1999. "Parallel Worlds: Representing Consciousness at the Intersection of Art, Dissociation, and Multidimensional Awareness." In *Reframing Conciousness*, edited by Roy Ascott, 52–56. Exeter: Intellect Books.

Stone, Allucquere Rosanne (Sandy). 1996. *The War of Desire and Technology at the Close of the Mechanical Age*. Cambridge, Mass.: MIT Press.

—————. 1995. "Identity in Oshkosh." In *Posthuman Bodies*, edited by J. Halberstam and I. Livingstone, 23–27. Bloomington: Indiana University Press.

—————. 1992. "Will the Real Body Please Stand Up?: Boundary Stories About Virtual Cultures." In *Cyberspace: First Steps*, edited by Michael Benedikt, 82–85. Cambridge, Mass.: MIT Press.

Stratton, Jon. 1997. "Not Really Desiring Bodies: The Rise and Rise of Email Affairs." *Media International Australia* 84 (May):28–38.

Strehovec, Janez. 1997. "The Web as an Instrument of Power and a Realm of Freedom: A Report from Ljubljana, Slovenia." *CTHEORY*, 26 June 1997. <http://www.ctheory.net/text_file.asp?pick=92>.

Stringer, Roy. 1999. "Navigation: The Missing Ingredient in the Digital Design Process." Paper delivered at the CADE 99 (Computers in Art and Design Education) Conference, 8 April 1999, Middlesborough, University of Teeside.

Styan, J. L. 1981. *Modern Drama in Theory and Practice 2*. Cambridge: Cambridge University Press.

Sussman, Mark. 1999. "Performing the Intelligent Machine: Deception and Enchantment in the Life of the Automaton Chess Player". *TDR: The Drama Review* 43, no. 3:81–96.

Sutton, Gloria. 2004. "Network Aesthetics: Strategies of Participation within net.art." In *Networked Narrative Environments as Imaginary Spaces of Being*, edited by Andrea Zapp, 16–31. Manchester: MIRIAD/FACT.

Svoboda, Josef. 1966. "Laterna Magika." *TDR: Tulane Drama Review* 11, no. 1:141–149.

Szperling, Margi. 2001. "Interactive cinema artists changing the way audiences view and understand film." <http://www.moviemaker.com/issues/44/cinevation.htm>.

Talking Birds. 1998*a*. "Recent Past." Database entry, Digital Performance Archive. <http://art.ntu.ac.uk/dpa>.

———. 1998*b*. "Smoke, Mirrors & the Art of Escapology." Database entry, Digital Performance Archive. <http://art.ntu.ac.uk/dpa>.

Tan, Felix. 2003. "Globe Trotting with Alladeen & the Global Soul." <http://www.rsi.com.sg/english/artsarena/view/20030703132558/1/.html>.

Tavel, Ronald. 1972 [1966]. "Gorilla Queen." In *The Off Off Broadway Book*, edited by Albert Poland and Bruce Mailman, 199–230. Indianapolis & New York: Bobbs-Merrill.

Terdiman, Richard. 1993. *Present Past: Modernity and the Memory Crisis*. Ithaca, N.Y.: Cornell University Press.

Terry, Brett. 1999. "The Work of Art in the Age of Digital Historiography." In *Reframing Consciousness: Art, Mind and Technology*, edited by Roy Ascott, 145–150. Exeter: Intellect.

Tholen, Georg Christoph. 2001. "In Between: Time, Space and Image in Cross-Media Performance." *Performance Research* 6, no. 3 (Winter):52–60.

Thomas, Douglas. 2002. *Hacker Culture*. Minneapolis: University of Minnesota Press.

Thorpe, Marc. 1994. "Description of Robot Wars." <http://www.robotwars.com/rwi/>.

Tofts, Darren, Annemarie Johnson, and Alessio Cavallero (eds.). 2002. *Prefiguring Cyberculture: An Intellectual History*. Cambridge, Mass.: MIT Press.

Torvalds, Linus, and David Diamond. 2001. *Just For Fun: The Story of an Accidental Revolutionary*. New York and London: Texere.

Troika Ranch. 1994. "In Plane." Database entry, Digital Performance Archive. <http://art.ntu.ac.uk/dpa>.

Tuomola, Mika, and Heikki Leskinen. 1998. "Daisy's Amazing Discoveries: Part 1—The Production." *Digital Creativity* 9, no. 2:75–90.

Turing, Alan. 1950. "Machinery and Computer Inteligence." *Mind* 59, no. 236:433–460.

Turkle, Sherry. 1997. *Life on the Screen: Identity in the Age of the Internet*. London: Phoenix.

———. 1996. "Rethinking Identity Through Virtual Community." In *Clicking In: Hot Links To A Digital Culture*, edited by Lynn Hershman Leeson, 116–122. Seattle: Bay Press.

Tyler, Mike. 1997. "Holoman; Digital Cadaver." Database entry, Digital Performance Archive. <http://art.ntu.ac.uk/dpa>.

Tysome, Tony. 2004. "Dancers Offer Cue to Brain Functions." *Times Higher Education Supplement*, 6 February 2004.

Ullman, Ellen. 1996. "Come in CQ: The Body on the Wire." In *Wired Women: Gender and New Realities in Cyberspace*, edited by L. Cherney and E. R. Weise, 3–23. Seattle: Seal Press.

Ulmer, Gregory. 1994*a*. *Teletheory: Grammatology in the Age of Video*. New York and London: Routledge.

————. 1994*b*. "The Miranda Warnings: An Experiment in Hyperrhetoric." In *Hyper/Text/Theoy*, edited by George P. Landow, 345–378. Baltimore: Johns Hopkins University Press.

————. 1985. *Applied Grammatology: Post(e)-Pedagogy from Jacques Derrida to Joseph Beuys*. Baltimore: Johns Hopkins University Press.

Undrill, Guy. 2000. "Book Review." *Performance Research* 5, no. 3 (Winter):133–135.

Unruh, Delbert. 1992. "Dedication" and "The New Theatre of Robert Edmond Jones." In *Towards a New Theatre: The Lectures of Robert Edmond Jones*, by Robert Edmond Jones, transcribed and edited by Delbert Unruh. New York: Limelight Editions.

Ure, Jim, and Biff Russ. 1995. "Web Art 101." *HotWired*, April 1995.

Usselmann, Rainer. 2002. "The Dilemma of Media Art: Cybernetic Serendipity at the ICA London." <http://mitpress2.mit.edu/e-journals/LEA/LEA2002/LEA/BKISSUES/lea_9-6new.html#journal>.

Vakuum TV. 1997. "Vakuum TV at the VIDEOLOGY." Database entry, Digital Performance Archive. <http://art.ntu.ac.uk/dpa>.

Valéry, Paul. 1964. *Aesthetics*. Translated by Ralph Manheim. New York: Pantheon Books.

Vanouse, Paul. 1999. "Items 1–2,000." Database entry, Digital Performance Archive. <http://art.ntu.ac.uk/dpa>.

————. 1996. The Consensual Fantasy Engine." Database entry, Digital Performance Archive. <http://art.ntu.ac.uk/dpa>.

Verton, Dan. 2002. *Hacker Diaries: Confessions of Teenage Hackers*. Portland, Ore.: Osborne McGraw-Hill.

Vinge, Vernor. 2001. "True Names." in *True Names by Vernor Vinge and the Opening of the Cyberspace Frontier*, edited by James Frenkel, 239–330. New York: Tor.

Virilio, Paul. 1995. "Speed and Information: Cyberspace Alarm." *CTHEORY*, 27 August 1995. <http://www.ctheory.net/text_file.asp?pick=72>.

————. 1991. *The Lost Dimension*. Translated by Daniel Moshenburg. New York: Semiotext(e).

————. 1979. *Vitesse et Politique*. Paris: Galilée.

Virmaux, Alain. 1966. "Artaud and Film." *TDR: Tulane Drama Review* 11:1.

VNS Matrix. 1999. *Cyberfeminist Manifesto for the 21st Century*. <http://sysx.org/vns>.

————. 1998. "All New Gen." In *Virtual Futures: Cyberotics, Technology and Post-Human Pragmatism*, edited by Joan Broadhurst Dixon and Eric J. Cassidy, 37–44. London and New York: Routledge.

Von Boehn, Max. 1972 [1929]. *Puppets and Automata*. Translated by Josephine Nicoll, New York: Dover Publications.

Wagner, Richard. 2001 [1849]. "The Artwork of the Future." In *Multimedia: From Wagner to Virtual Reality*, edited by Randall Packer and Ken Jordan, 3–9. London: Norton.

Waldby, Catherine. 2002. "The Instruments of Life: Frankenstein and Cyberculture." In *Prefiguring Cyberculture: An Intellectual History*, edited by Darren Tofts, Annemarie Jonson and Alessio Cavallaro, 28–37. Cambridge, Mass.: MIT Press.

———. 2000. *The Visible Human Project: Informatic Bodies and Posthuman Science*. London: Routledge.

———. 1997. "Circuits of Desire: Internet Erotics and the Problems of Bodily Location." <http://kali.murdoch.edu.au/~cntinuum/VID/Circuits3.html>.

Walsh, Nick Paton. 2001. "Alter our DNA or robots will take over, warns Hawking." *The Observer*, 2 September 2001.

Wardrip-Fruin, Noah, and Nick Montfort (eds.). 2003. *The New Media Reader*. Cambridge, Mass.: MIT Press.

Wardrip-Fruin, Noah, and Pat Harrigan. 2004. *First Person: New Media as Story, Performance, and Game*. Cambridge, Mass.: MIT Press.

Warr, Tracey. 1996. "Sleeper." *Performance Research* 1, no. 2 (Summer):1–19.

Warr, Tracey and Amelia Jones. 2000. *The Artist's Body*. London: Phaidon Press.

Warwick, Kevin. 2001. "Interview." In *The Android Prophecy*, television documentary, Channel 4, 21 September 2001.

———. 2000. "Cyborg 1.0." *Wired* magazine, <http://www.wired.com/wired/archive/8.02/warwick_pr.html>.

———. 1997. *March of the Machines: Why the New Race of Robots Will Rule the World*. London: Century Books.

Wayner, Peter. 2001. *Free For All*. New York: HarperCollins.

Webbed Feats. 1999. "Bytes of Bryant Park." Database entry, Digital Performance Archive. <http://art.ntu.ac.uk/dpa>.

Weems, Marianne. 2003. "Weaving the 'Live' and the Mediated: Marianne Weems in Conversation with Cariad Svich." In *Trans-global Readings: Crossing Theatrical Boundaries*, edited by Cariad Svich, 50–55. Manchester: Manchester University Press.

Weissberg, Jed. 1996. "The Art of Puppetry in the Age of Digital Manipulation." *Puppetry International* 2:39–40.

Weibel, Peter, and Timothy Druckrey (eds.). 2001. *Net_Condition: Art and Global Media*. Cambridge, Mass.: MIT Press.

Wertheim, Margaret. 1999. *The Pearly Gates of Cyberspace: A History of Space from Dante to the Internet*. London: Virago.

Wesemann, Arnd. 1997. "Mirror Games with New Media: The Story of Dance has Always Been the Story of Technology." *International Ballet Tanz Aktuell* 8/9.

Wheeler, Wendy. 1999. "Melancholia, Modernity and Contemporary Grief." In *Literature and the Contemporary: Fictions and Theories of the Present*, edited by Roger Luckhurst and Peter Marks, 63–79. Harlow, Essex: Pearson/Longman.

Wright, K. 2000. "The Sims in Our Own Image." <http://www.womengamers.com/articles/thesims.html>.

White, Michéle. 2001. "Visual Pleasure in Textual Places." In *Virtual Gender: Technology, Consumption and Identity*, edited by Alison Adam and Eileen Green, 124–150. London: Routledge.

Wiener, Norbert. 2003 [1954]. "Men, Machines and the World About." In *The New Media Reader*, edited by Noah Wardrip-Fruin and Nick Montfort, 67–72. Cambridge, Mass.: MIT Press.

———. 1961 [1948]. *Cybernetics or Control and Communication in the Animal and the Machine*. 2nd ed. New York and London: MIT Press and John Wiley & Sons.

———. 1954. *The Human Use of Human Beings: Cybernetics and Society*. 2nd ed. New York: Doubleday Anchor.

———. 1947. "A Scientist Rebels." *Atlantic Monthly*, January 1947.

Willis, Holly, and Mikki Halpin. 1996. "When the Personal Becomes Digital: Linda Dement and Barbara Hammer Move Towards a Lesbian Cyberspace." *Women & Performance: A Journal of Feminist Theory* 9, no. 1:233–238.

Wilson, Julie. 2000. "Interview with Steve Dixon." Digital Performance Archive, 30 December 2000.

Wilson, Peter Lamborn. 1996. "Boundary Violations." In *Technoscience and Cyberculture*, edited by S. Aronowitz et al. New York: Routledge.

Wilson, Stephen. 2002. *Information Arts: Intersections of Art, Science and Technology*. Cambridge, Mass.: MIT Press.

———. 1999. "The Telepresent." Database entry, Digital Performance Archive. <http://art.ntu.ac.uk/dpa>.

———. 1994. "Memory Map." Database entry, Digital Performance Archive. <http://art.ntu.ac.uk/dpa>.

Witcombe, Christopher L. C. E. 2003. *Art History and Technology: A Brief History*. <http://witcombe.sbc.edu/arth-technology/arth-technology3.html>.

Whitelaw, Mitchell. 1998. "1968/1998: Rethinking A Systems Aesthetic." <http://www.anat.org.au/archived/deepimmersion/diss/mwhitelaw.html>.

Wolf, Mark J. P., and Bernard Perron (eds.). 2003. *Video Game Theory Reader*. London: Routledge.

Woolley, Benjamin. 1993. *Virtual Worlds: A Journey of Hype and Hyperreality*. London: Penguin.

Wortzel, Adrienne. 1997. "Starboard." Database entry, Digital Performance Archive. <http://art.ntu.ac.uk/dpa>.

Wright, Basil. 1976. *The Long View: An International History of Film*. St Albans, Herts.: Paladin.

Xenakis, Iannis. 1971. "Free Stochastic Music from the Computer." In *Cybernetics, Art and Ideas*, edited by Jasia Reichardt, 124–142. London: Studio Vista.

Yamashita, Allen. 1998. "Beyond Fear and Exhilaration: Hopes and Dreams for Special Venue Entertainment." In *Digital Illusion*, edited by Clark Dodsworth, 381–389. New York: ACM Press.

Young, Cathy, and Teresa Senft. 1996. "Hearing the Net: An Interview with Mia Lipner." *Women & Performance: A Journal of Feminist Theory* 9, no. 1:111–123.

Zapp, Andrea. 2002. "net.drama://myth/mimesis/mind_mapping." In *New Screen Media: Cinema/Art/Narrative*, edited by Martin Rieser and Andrea Zapp, 77–89. London: British Film Institute.

————, ed. 2004. *Networked Narrative Environments as Imaginary Spaces of Being*. Manchester: MIRIAD/FACT.

Zimmerman, Eric. 2002. "Do Independent Games Exist?" In *Game On: The History and Culture of Videogames*, edited by Lucien King, 120–130. London: Laurence King.

Zivanovic, Aleksandar. 2002. "Edward Ihnatowicz, including his famous work 'The Senster.'" <http://members.lycos.co.uk/zivanovic/senster/>.

Žižek, Slavoj. 2004. "Iraq War, Chips and Chocolate Laxatives." *Times Higher Education Supplement*, 30 January 2004.

————. 1996. "Die Virtualisierung des Herr." In *Wunschmaschine Welterfindung: Eine Geschichte der Technikvisionen seit dem 18. Jahrhundert*, edited by Brigitte Felderer. Vienna/New York: Springer Verlag.

Index

Antimedia theory 140–141, 540, 561, 615

Antitheater perspective, 11, 122, 144–146, 165

Antohin, Anatoly, 511

Anytime Interaction software, 263

Apollo space mission, 11, 457

Appalachian State University, 381

Appel, Jackie, 473

Appia, Adolphe, 54

Arangel, Cory, 611

Arcadias, Laurence, 625

Architecture Machine Group, MIT, 103

Archituv, Romy
Text Rain, 589–591, 655

Argonne Remote Manipulator (ARM), 366

Aristotle, 28, 141, 171, 537, 562

Arizona State University
Institute of Studies in the Arts, 204–205, 427

Armstrong, Keith
 # 14, 415, 416
Hacking a Private Space, 399–400
transit_lounge, 583

Arndt, Michael J., 172

Arns, Inke, 419

Aronson, Arnold, 28

ARPANET, 18, 457–458

ART + COM, 466

Art and Virtual Environments Project, 368

Artaud, Antonin, 48, 70, 81, 131, 144–146, 256, 266, 342–343, 662
Theater and Its Double, 13, 241–242, 268

Artemis, Moroni and the *.* group, 320

Arthur, Charles, 310–311

Artificial character software, 404–405

Artificial Intelligence (AI), 167, 278, 279, 283, 309, 317, 491, 644–645
the Turing Test, 491–493

Artificial Intelligence Lab, MIT, 167, 311

Artificial life (A-life) technologies, 295

Arts and Humanities Research Council, UK, ix

Art-science collaborations, 10–11, 96–99, 101–102, 169–170

Arts Wire Current journal, 461

Art theft, 477

ASCII, 199, 255–256

ASCII Art Ensemble, 199

Ascott, Roy, 238, 254

Asimo robot, 286

Aston, Elaine, 165

Atchley, Dana
Next Exit, 566

ATHEMOO, 490

Athey, Ron, 213

Atkins, Barry, 599

ATR Media Integration and Communications Laboratories, Japan, 262

Auden, W. H., 443

Audience participation, 20, 559, 571–572, 581–584

Audience-performer relationship, 509, 562–563

Audio motion tracking, 201–203

Audioroom
0+E, 432

August, Oliver, 160

Auslander, Phillip, 19
Liveness, 11, 117, 120, 123–126
"Live from Cyberspace," 493–494

Australian Centre for the Moving Image, 374

Autobiography, 19

Automata, 281–285

Avant-garde modernism, 5, 8, 23, 28, 47, 68.
See also Futurism
cabaret performances, 68, 74
cult of the machine, 9, 53–54, 60–63, 71
multimedia theater, 10, 73, 75, 78, 82–83
theater scenography, 9, 16, 54, 58, 78
visions of mechanized theatre, 53–54

Avatar, 259–265, 391–392, 472, 587

Azari (Fedele), 63

B, Franko, 213

Babuscio, Jack, 278

Birmingham Behavioural Sciences Centre, UK, 546–547

Birringer, Johannes, 39, 206, 233, 240, 317, 318, 378, 541, 632. *See also* AlienNation Co.

BIT. *See* Bureau of Inverse Technology (BIT)

Blair, David
WAXWEB, 570–571

Blake, William, 341–343

Blanket, Beppie, 246

Blast Theory, 2, 10, 13, 662
10 Backwards, 246–247, 248, 552–555
Desert Rain, 21, 75, 109, 615–620
Kidnap, 441, 668
Uncle Roy All Around You, 23, 663–669

Blau, Herbert, 153, 494

Blavatsky, Madame E. P., 643

Bleeker, Maaike, 223

Blinky exhibition, 645

Blossom, Roberts, 93, 336, 525
Filmstage, 89–90

Blue Blouse Group, 74

Blumenthal, Bud, 17
Les Entrailles de Narcisse, 51
Rivermen, 408–410

Boal, Augusto, 175–176, 562

Bocciono, Umberto, 51

Bodies in Flight
Doublehappiness2, 468

Body. *See* Embodiment

Bodycoder system, 303–304

Bohn, Christian
Liquid Views, 245–246, 248

Bollier, David, 159

Bolter, Jay, 11, 67, 135–137, 331–332, 393, 450, 483, 486, 560, 578
Windows and Mirrors, 136, 215–216, 365, 376, 378, 393, 560, 580, 590–591, 598
Remediation, 135–137
Writing Space, 137, 486

Bond, Edward, 475

Bonde, Niels, 439

Bookchin, Natalie, 611–613
Metapet, 614
The Intruder, 611, 613

Boon, Marcus, 469–470

Booth, Mark, 331

Borgman, Albert, 644–645

Borsook, Paulina, 176

Boundary crossing, 159, 688n.7

Bowden, Richard, 55

Bowen, Laurence Llewelyn, 327

Bragaglia, Anton Guilo and Arturo, 50–51

Brain-machine implants, 298, 307–309

Brassard, Marie, 355

Breathing interface vests, *373*

Brecht, Bertolt, 70–71, 129, 145, 560, 568
Brechtian media use, 345, 347–348, 562

Brenneis, Lisa, 489–490

Brenton, Howard, 475

British Broadcasting Corporation (BBC), 22, 511, 560
As You Like It CD-ROM, 627
Thunder Road, 568

British Dance Edition, 511

Britton, Andrew, 275, 278, 331, 332

Broadhurst, Susan
Blue Bloodshot Flowers, 55–56

Broadwell, Peter, 246

Brockman, John, 157

Bromberg, Ellen
Falling to Earth, 204–205

Bromwich, Mark, 303

Brook, Peter, 27, 81, 88, 291, 650

Brooks, Frederick, 210, 219, 365–366

Brooks, Rodney A., 270, 282, 311, 332
Ghengis robot, 287
My Real Baby, 319

Brotchie, Alastair, 485

Brown, Paul, 103

Brown, Richard, 295

Brown, Tony
Two Machines for Feeling, 52–53

Brown, Trishia. *See* Trishia Brown Dance Company

Choreography
dance simulation software, 12, 183–184, 197–198, 206–209
digital, 185–187, 200
scratch-choreography, 592
CHOREOTRONICS Inc.
Byte City, 398
Chronometric time, 532–537
Chronophotography, 50, 527
Cinematrix system, 580
Cividalli, Amos. *See* Danet, Brenda
Clapp, Susannah, 350
Clark, Jonny, 397. *See also* Schiller, Gretchen, *trajets*
Claudel, Paul
Livre de Christophe Colomb, 77–78
Cleaver, Harry, 160
Cleto, Fabio, 273, 275, 319, 331
Cloning, 296
Clynes, Manfred, 272
Coates, George. 1, 364. *See also* George Coates Performance Works
Code
computer code, 101, 166–171, 199
historical code use, 164–166
Code Zebra software, 170
Cohen, Bruno
Camera Virtuoso, 582
Cohen, Milton, 85
Coleman, Anna Mosby, 477
Coleridge, Samuel Taylor, 216
Collaboration. 8, 20, 594–597. *See also* Networked performance
collaborative virtual environments, 261–262
Collaborative level of interaction, 20, 433–434
Collectivism, 8
Collins, David, xi
Collins, Susan, 17, 444–445, 459
In Conversation, 411–414
Company in Space, 1, 5, 427–429, 656, 661
Cybernetic Organism 3, 260–261
Escape Velocity, 247–248

home, not alone, 595
Incarnate, 56–57, 254–255, 428–429
Computational editing, 67
Computer Aided Design (CAD) software, 382–384, 396
Computer code, 101, 166–171, 199
Computer games, 19–20. *See also* Videogames
Computer-mediated communication, 478–480. *See also* Digital media software and systems
Computer memory, 544–545, 547–550, 551
Computer Resource Group, University of Nottingham
Avatar Farm, 261–262
Computer technology, 5, *10*, 393, 511, 517
as theater, 11–12, 163, 170–176, 370
Conceptualism, 27
Confessions online, 499–502
Coniglio, Mark, 197–199. *See also* Troika Ranch
Connor, Steven, 540, 654
Consciousness, 140–141, 406. *See also* Memory; Narrative; Time
mind-body relation, 218–219
Constructivism, 64–67
Conversation level of interaction, 20, 563–565, 584–591
Cook, Jeff, 282, 291
Cooney, Ray, 469
Cooper, Alan, 169
Cooper, Tommy, 131
Copyright restrictions, 167–170, 183
Cora, Bruno, 50, 58
Corachan, Paco, 324
Corcoran, Marlena, 488
Corley, Eric, 168
Corpos Informáticos Research Group, 13, 234–236
Hungry@Corpos, 236
Corringham, Viv Dogan, 434

Disembodiment, 211, 317, 478, 488
the body as obsolete, 316–319
of cyberspace, 214–216
Dishman, Eric, 175–176
Disney, Walt, 141
audio-animatronic figures, 284
Dixon, Steve, 251–252. *See also* Chameleons
Group
"Absent Fiends," 508
and Chameleons Group, 504, 506
"Remediating Theatre in a Digital
Proscenium," 641–642
Dodge, Martin, 466
Dodson, Sean, 643
Dokter, Caroline, 246
Dolly (cloned sheep), 550
Domike, Steffi
Terminal Time, 20, 579–580, *581*
doo cot
Frankenstein, 224
Doppelgänger, 13, *14*, 224, 242, 244, 251. *See
also* Digital double
Dove, Toni, 1, 20
Artificial Changelings, 330, 591–594
Archaeology of a Mother Tongue, *121*, 366, 368,
369, 548, *549*
Dramatic Exchange, The, 460
Druckrey, Timothy, 613
Dualism. *See* Cartesian mind-body divide
Duchamp, Marcel, 70, 85, 87, 127, 559
Ducharme, Paule, 634
Duckworth, William, 109
Dumb Type, 13, 60, 524, 661
Lovers, 228–230
Memorandum, 547, *548*
OR, 226–227
pH, 60–61
S/N, 227–228
Dungeons and Dragons videogame, 602
d'Urbano, Alba, 246
Durkin, Scott T.
Shared Identity, 425–426
Dury, Ian, 609

DVD technology, 640–641
Dyens, Ollivier, 149, 270, 272
Dyer, Chris, 383, 384
Dyer, Richard, 273, 278, 325, 326
Dyson, George B., 332
Dystopian views of technology, 4, 177–181,
329–330, 481, 540, 553–554
technological nihilism, 140–143
Dziga Vertov Performance Group, 66–67

Eagleton, Terry, 654–655, 661
E.A.T. *See* Experiments in Arts and
Technology
Eckermann, Sylvia, 21. *See also* Fuchs, Mathias
Eco, Umberto
Travels in Hyperreality, 141
Edelman, Gerald and Guilio Tononi, 406
Edmonds, Ernest, 67
Ehn, Pelle, 39, 157
Eisenstein, Sergei, 66–67, 74, 76
El Mexterminator (character), 328–329
Elam, Keir, 164–165, 336
Electric-Vibrating-Luminous Theatre, 57
Electronic Dance Theatre
Cyborg Dreaming, 303, 304
Electronic Disturbance Theatre, 8, 562, 662
Ellipsis group, 424
Elrich, Matthew, 239
Elsenaar, Arthur, 266–267
Email relationships, 214
Embodiment
the digital body, 215, 234–238, 406–410,
648–649
hyperembodiment, 266
involuntary bodies, *151*, 313–314
the living body, 16, 22, 212, 224 (*see also*
Liveness)
mechanical embodiment, 13–14, *307*, *309*,
310, 314, *315*, 317–318, 321
media as extensions of the body, 93–94, 147,
152–153, 214, 219, 305
the telematic body, 216–220, 235–238,
429

the virtual body, 13, 211–212, 230–233, 239–240, 376–378, 478–479
Emin, Tracey
My Bed, 451
Emotion recognition, 163
English language dominance, 11, 161–163
Enzenberger, Hans Magnus, 561
Ephemerality, 490, 517
Eshkar, Shelley. *See* Riverbed Company
Ess, Charles, 157
Etchells Tim, 89, 118, 633. *See also* Forced Entertainment
eToys war, 562
e-university, 644
Ex Machina Company. *See* Lepage, Robert
Experiments in Art and Technology (E.A.T.), 97–98
Export, Valie,
Tapp und Tast kino, 585
Expressionism, 70–71
External memory, 307
Extratemporality, 522–525, 654–655
EyeCon software, 12, 201–203
Eye-tracking systems, 66–67, 382–383, 396

Factory of the Eccentric Actor (FEKS), 74
Fake hologram, 109–110
"Fakeness" of digital images, 23–24
Fakeshop
Capsule Hotel, 426, 427
Lifescience-Fakeshop, 426
Farabough, Laura, 104
Farmer, Randall F.,
Habitat, 472–473
Fatal Beauty (online soap opera), 566
Faver, Cheryl, 421. *See also* Gertrude Stein Repertory Theatre
Feingold, Ken, 271
FEKS. *See* Factory of the Eccentric Actor
Feminist cybernetics, 298, 466–467. *See also* Haraway, Donna
Fenley, Melissa, 111

Fiction, interactive, 485, 485–486, 577–578
Fillia,
Sensualità Meccanica (Mechanical Sensuality), 63
Fillion, Carl, 355
Film, 126
film-theater synthesis, 10, 77–82
film versus theater, 130–131
Fischer-Lichte, Erika, 165
Fleishman, Monika
Liquid Views, 245–246, 248
Floating Point Unit
emergent(c) room, 432
Fluxus group, 18, 88
Foner, Leonard, 493
Forced Entertainment, 629
Frozen Palaces, 22, 637
Nightwalks, 639–640, 641
Spin, 531
Force-field simulation software, 393, 397
Ford, Tamara, 625
Foreman, Richard, 523–524. *See also* Ontological-Hysteric Theatre
Formenti, Carlo, 615, 616
Forreger, Nikolai, 65, 290
Forsythe, William, 1, 22, 200–201, 208
Improvisation Technologies, 30, 32, 158, 163, 630–632
Foster, Hal, 69
Foucault, Michel, 150, 214, 222, 282, 475
on the panopticon, 437, 438, 446
on time, 517–518
4D Art
Anima, 241, 250–251
Fox, Barrett, 264–265
Franck, K. A., 470
Franke, Herbert W., 100
Frankenstein, 280, 293, 298, 300, 318. *See also* Monsters
Frasca, Gonzalo, 562
Frazer, Sir James, 244, 253, 269–270
Freeman, John, 647–648
"Free software" movement, 168

Mabou Mines, 422

Machover, Tod
  Brain Opera, 582, 609, *610*

MacDonald, Alistair. *See* Rubidge, Sarah;
  Sensuous Geographies

Mackenzie, Michael, 121
  Archaeology of a Mother Tongue, *121*, 366, 368,
  369, 548, 549

MacLeod, Douglas, 368

Macromedia Director software, 174, 267, 398,
  632

Madonna webcast, 511

"Magic mirror," 77–78

Magic Theater performances, 581

Magritte, Rene, 120

Malevich, Kazimir, 67

Malraux, André, 28

Manetas, Miltos, 601

Mannequin, 13, 259–263, 266–267,
  268–269. *See also* Avatar

Mann, Steve, 439–440

Manovich, Lev, 5–6
  "Avant Garde as Software," 9
  The Language of New Media, 67

Marber, Patrick
  Closer, 469

Marcelo, Karen, 264–265

Marinetti, Filippo Tommaso, 652–654,
  662
  futurist manifestos, 22–23, 48–50, 58, 60,
  61, 63, 560
  Roi Bombance, 559–560
  "The Pleasure of Being Booed," 560

Markley, Robert, 138, 143–144

Marranca, Bonnie
  "The Self As Text," 539

Martelli, Bruno, 166, 199, 206. *See also*
  Igloo
  Windowsninetyeight, 166, 230, 565, 638–639,
  640

Martín, Fernando, 408, *409*

Marx, Karl, 243, 253

Mary-Kate & Ashley videogame, 607

Masaki Fujihata
  Global Interior Project, 163

Massachusetts Institute of Technology (MIT)
  Architecture Machine Group, 103
  Artificial Intelligence Lab, 167, 311
  Digital Life Consortium, 259
  Interactive Cinema Project, 262–263, 570
  Media in Transition Conference, 600
  Media Laboratory, 259, 460

MASSIVE, 261–262

Masterman, Margaret
  Computerized Haiku, 101

Mateus, Michael
  Terminal Time, 579–580, *581*

Mathews, Harry
  Oulipo Compendium, 485

Mathews, Max, 195

Matos, Jean-Marc, 320

Maubray, Benoit, 109, 629

Maudlin, Michael, 491
  Julia, 492–494
  Sylvie, 495

Max/MSP software, 183, 195, 403

May, Rowan, 432

Mayhew, Mike, 503, 507

Mazlish, Bruce, 281–282

McCay, Winsor
  Gertie the Dinosaur, 73–74, 250

McGregor, Wayne, 206, 233–234. *See also*
  Random Dance Company
  Cyborg, 41

McLuhan, Marshall, 560, 599
  the global village, 150, 158, 465
  media as extensions of the body, 93–94, 147,
  152–153, 214, 219, 272, 305
  media as numbing or disembodying, 214,
  300, 698n.26

McMurtrie, Chico, 288–291. *See also*
  Amorphic Robot Works
  The Trees are Walking, 292–293
  Skeletal Reflections, 268

Mechanical reproductions, 116–118, 129

Mechanized theater, 53–54

Index

Textual bodies, 478–480

Theater. *See also* Cybertheater; Digital theater;
  Live performance; Multimedia performance
  computers as, 11–12, 163, 170–176, 370
  3D reconstructions of ancient theaters,
    378–384, 656–657
  integrating media technologies, 123–125
  on-line (*see* Cybertheater)
  performances inspired by videogames,
    614–615
  semiotics of, 164–165, 336
  as virtual reality, 363–365

Theater design software applications, 382–384

Theater of Dionysus 3, 379

Theater of Pompey, *380, 381*

Theater of the absurd, 70

Theater scenography, 9, 16, 54, 58, 78

Theater versus cinema debate, 28–29

Theranthropes, 14, 272, 320

Therrien, David, 662
  Bodydrum, 62
  Information Machine, 657
  Machines for a New Inquisition, 61–62

Thorpe, Mark, 299

Three-dimensional space, 335, 339, 364. *See*
  also Virtual 3D scenography
  navigable environments, 398
  3D virtual models, 16, 54, 384–389, 543
  reconstructions of ancient theaters, 378–384

Time, 19, 64, 537–538, 553–555
  chronometric time, 532–537
  destabilization of, 68–69
  ephemerality, 490, 517
  extratemporality, 516, 522–525, 654–655
  lacking universal definition, 515–516
  postmodernism and, 516–518
  presentness, 123, 529
  standing still, 525–531
  technology speeding up, 515, 547, 703n.87
  temporal synchronicity, 519

Time-based installation, 449–450

Tinguely, Jean
  Homage to New York, 96, 284–285

Todd, Steven, 192

Tofts, Darren, 40

Toller, Ernst
  Hoppla, Wir Leben, 78–80

Torentsson, Johan, 267

Torvalds, Linus, 168

Toshio Iwai
  Another Time, Another Space, 535–536

trans/forms
  remote collaborative performance, 433–434

Tow, Rob, 393–394, 580

trAce (interactive writing), 485

Transgenic art, 297–298, 308, 656

Transmute Collective
  transit_lounge, 583

Traumatic memory, 545–547

Treadwell, Sophie
  Machinal, 71, 387–388

Trishia Brown Dance Company, 89, 111, 208
  Homemade, 541–542

Troika Ranch, 1, 196–197, 304, 656
  Bank/ Perspective 1, 197–198
  Electronic Disturbance, 423–424
  Future of Memory, 128
  In Place, 236–237
  Isadora software, 12, 197–198, 404
  16 {R}evolutions, 198
  Surfacing, 646
  The Chemical Wedding of Christian Rosenkrantz,
    256–259
  Yearbody for Solo Dancer and Internet,
    532–533

Trojan coffee-pot webcam, 452–453

Trubshaw, Roy, 470

Trychin, Sam, 264–265

Tse, David KS
  Play to Win, 614

Tudor, David, 97

Tuomola, Mika, 259
  Daisy's Amazing Discoveries, 567

Turing, Alan, 149
  "Machinery and Computer Intelligence, 18,
    491–492

Turing Test, 491–493

Turkle, Sherry
Life on the Screen, 471, 474, 479–480

TX-Transform Effects film technique, 695n.36

Tyler, Mike
Holoman, 222–223

Tzara, Tristan, 67

Ullman, Ellen, 478

Ulmer, Gregory, 138, 546

Ultrasound, 239

Uninvited Guests, 17
Film, 525–531
Guest House, 17, 400–401

University of Kent
A Midsummer Night's Dream, 109, 614–615

University of Nottingham
Computer Resource Group, 261–262
Mixed Reality Lab, 21, 75, 615–620, 663–669

UNREAL game engine system, 611

Unruh, Delbert, 80

URL (Uniform Resource Locator), 463

User interface, 560, 563, 591

Usselman, Reiner, 102

Utopian views of technology, 5, 101, 153, 246, 256–260, 480–481, 652–653

Utterback, Camille and Romy Arthituv
Text Rain, 589–591, 655

VakuumNet, 68

Vakuum TV, 68, 69

Valéry, Paul, 117

Vampires, 298

Vanderbeek, Stan, 87, 96

Vanguard art (early 20th century). *See* Avant-garde modernism

Vanouse, Paul, 20, 629, 661
Items 1-2000, 211, 222, 223, 662
Terminal Time, 579–580, 581
The Consensual Fantasy Engine, 579

Verdicchio, Maria. *See* Rubidge, Sarah, *Sensuous Geographies*

Verspucci, Generico, 534–535

Vertov, Dziga
Man With A Movie Camera, 66–67

Very Nervous System (VNS) software, 427, 545, 591, 592, 594

Vesna, Victoria, 230

Victoria, Theodosius, 103

Videogame engine systems, 611

Videogames, 20–21, 599–601, 620–621
academic studies of, 588–601, 620–621
artful performance games, 608–615
computer enhanced, 553
depiction of women in, 604–608
interactive properties of, 565
online videogames, 611–613
as theater, 601–603
war games, 604, 615–620

Video scratching techniques, 416

Video tracking system, 267

Vihjálmsonn, Hannes, 259

Vinge, Vernor, 472

Violence, 21, 218, 296–298
robot wars, 299–302
in videogames, 602–605
virtual rape, 474–476
war games, 604, 615–620

Virilio, Paul, 53, 179–180, 302, 312, 517, 547

Virmaux, Alain, 93

Virtual body, 13, 211–212, 230–233, 239–240, 376–378, 478

Virtual characters, 55–60, 494–495

Virtual drama sites, 460–461

Virtual Drama Society, 460

Virtual gender
changing gender, 479–480
extreme stereotypes, 504
feedback loops, 607

Virtual hoaxes, 475–478

Virtual nature, 375–376

Virtual pets, 606